H U M A N

S E X U A L I T Y :

C O N T E M P O R A R Y

P E R S P E C T I V E S

About the Author

George Zgourides, Psy.D., received his doctorate in clinical psychology from Pacific University in 1989. Dr. Zgourides is a licensed psychologist (Arizona, Texas), a full-time faculty member at the University of Portland (Oregon), an ordained minister, and a resident chaplain in a men's dormitory at the campus where he teaches. His clinical and academic interests include human sexuality, anxiety disorders, and cognitive therapies. In addition to a number of journal articles, Dr. Zgourides is the author of the self-help book *Don't Let Them Psych You Out!* (1993, Loompanics Unlimited) and coauthor of the professional book *Anxiety Disorders: A Rational-Emotive Perspective* (1991, Pergamon Press/Allyn and Bacon). The recipient of various awards and honors including the 1993 Outstanding Faculty Member of the Year and Outstanding Advisor of the Year awards at the University of Portland, he is also an avid composer of liturgical and classical music, and an enthusiastic Scottish bagpiper.

HUMAN SEXUALITY: CONTEMPORARY PERSPECTIVES

George Zgourides
The University of Portland

HarperCollins*CollegePublishers*

Acquisitions Editor: Bonnie Roesch / Jill Leckta
Director of Development: Bonnie Roesch
Project Editorial Manager: Thomas R. Farrell
Design Manager: Mary McDonnell
Cover and Text Design: Mary McDonnell
Cover Photo: Keith Tishken
Chapter Opening Photos: Keith Tishken
Art Rendering: Rosemarie D'Alba
Photo Researcher: Mira Schachne
Electronic Production Manager: Angel Gonzalez, Jr.
Desktop Administrator: LaToya Wigfall
Manufacturing Manager: Alexandra Odulak
Electronic Page Makeup: RR Donnelley Barbados
Printer and Binder: RR Donnelley & Sons Company
Cover Printer: Coral Graphic Services, Inc.

For permission to use copyrighted material, grateful acknowledgment is made to the copyright holders on page 431, which is hereby made part of this copyright page.

Human Sexuality: Contemporary Perspectives

Library of Congress Cataloging-in-Publication Data
Zgourides, George D.
    Human sexuality : contemporary perspectives / George Zgourides.
       p.   cm.
    Includes bibliographical references and index.
    ISBN 0-06-500884-7
    1. Sex.   I. Title.
HQ21.Z46   1995
306.7—dc20

                                        94-15537
                                        CIP

96 97 98   9 8 7 6 5 4 3 2

To the memory of my grandmother Tacia Peet Zgourides (1908–1993),
who more than anyone else wanted me to complete this book.

CONTENTS IN BRIEF

CONTENTS IN DETAIL

IX
Contents in Detail

CHAPTER 13

CONTRACEPTION AND ABORTION   263

CHAPTER 18

SEXUALITY AND THE LAW 375

PREFACE

When I first began teaching human sexuality, I searched for a textbook that my students would find accessible, informative, practical, and enjoyable. While there were many texts to choose from, all of which covered the appropriate topics, I found many too long and overly detailed. Some were filled with needless asides or excessive citations. Others pushed the "warm" and "experiential" approach to learning to such an extreme that I was distracted from the main points of the subject. And a few tried to impose values, their authors forgetting that above all a textbook should be neutral in its presentation of information, not a forum for a specific position or political agenda. For these reasons, I decided to write *Human Sexuality: Contemporary Perspectives.*

I've purposely kept the book concise, the writing direct and free of sexism and bias. I've avoided superfluous detail and trendy social commentary. And in the interest of encouraging students' critical and independent thinking, I've approached controversial topics from a balanced point of view, presenting both sides equally and fairly. In short, *Human Sexuality: Contemporary Perspectives* is a straightforward, balanced textbook, written with students' needs in mind. I sincerely hope that it will play a valuable part in their overall education.

ORGANIZATION AND THEMES

I've written and organized the text from an interdisciplinary perspective, considering the biological, psychological, and sociological factors of various aspects of human sexuality. Cultural differences and influences are also carefully addressed. I've chosen to present the material holistically; students will explore gender issues, the full spectrum of sexual orientation, and the diversity of loving relationships before beginning the material on sexual behaviors and pleasuring. Sexual behavior chapters are grouped together and include coverage of sexuality and the challenged individual and sexuality throughout the life span. This is compatible with the concept of discussing sexual behaviors across the full range of human experience. The variety of sexual interactions, both personal and societal, are covered in the remaining chapters of the text, including up-to-date coverage of sexually transmitted diseases. The text concludes with a thoughtful chapter on sexual laws, morals, and ethics.

While each chapter is self-contained, and the text can easily be adapted to any introductory human sexuality course, the 18 chapters of *Human Sexuality: Contemporary Perspectives* are logically organized to reflect these interdisciplinary and inclusive themes.

SPECIAL FEATURES

I've used a number of special features throughout *Human Sexuality: Contemporary Perspectives:*

- *Concise Presentation* The breadth of topics covered in the text will match most course syllabi. I've made every effort, however, to keep the material to a manageable level, giving the students enough information to fully understand major concepts without overwhelming them with details that can't be covered and discussed in a one-semester course.

- *Decision-Making Skills* Throughout the text, students are encouraged to think critically about their own sexuality as well as societal issues. The inclusion of *Personal Assessments, Personal Reflections, Questions for Thought,* and *Activities* help guide students toward making meaningful decisions about their attitudes, beliefs, and responsibilities concerning human sexuality.

- **Personal Assessments** Each chapter begins with a brief assessment allowing students the opportunity to evaluate their knowledge and attitudes before reading the material. After reading the chapter, students should look back at the answers they gave the first time and see how many of their answers may have changed as a result of their study and new understandings.
- **For Personal Reflection** Appearing throughout the text, these scenarios and questions are designed to assist students' incorporating chapter material into their everyday life. Students may wish to keep track of their responses to these questions in a journal.
- **Perspective Boxes** Every chapter includes at least one boxed *Perspective,* which presents an issue, concern, historical fact, or cross-cultural phenomenon of particular interest. Most *Perspective* features end with one or more *Questions for Thought* for the reader to consider.
- **On a Personal Note** I've drawn upon my clinical experiences as a licensed psychologist and university chaplain to bring the book to life with numerous case examples. These quotations from assorted clients, students, and people I've known over the years add a personal dimension to the text.
- **Illustrations** The line drawings and photographs within this book have been carefully developed to enhance the textual material. Line drawings are clear and informative. I've selected photographs that represent the wide diversity of human life and lifestyles. Students will find the full-color illustrations appealing, understandable, and helpful in amplifying the subject matter.

LEARNING AIDS

In addition to the special features noted above, I've incorporated several pedagogical devices throughout in an effort to enhance students' learning experiences:

- **Chapter Objectives** Each chapter begins with a detailed chapter outline and a list of *Learning Objectives* that help students anticipate the chapter's content.
- **Marginal Glossary** Throughout the text, I've highlighted and defined key terms in the margins on the page where they are first introduced. This quick reference aid eases students' study of new material learned in the chapter.
- **Key Points** Each chapter ends with a numbered list that summarizes the major concepts and information introduced in the chapter. These *Key Points* are page-referenced for added study value for students.
- **Activities and Questions** Following the *Key Points,* each chapter offers students a selection of activities that will help them put the information learned in the chapter to practical use or give them an opportunity to expand upon what they already know about the topic. The questions encourage students to evaluate their understanding of the material just covered.
- **Recommended Readings** Each chapter offers students a list of readings to further enhance their study. All listings have been briefly annotated to help direct students to what interests them most.

ANCILLARIES

A complete set of supplementary materials are available to support the use of **Human Sexuality: Contemporary Perspectives** by both students and instructors:

- **Instructor's Manual**
- **Acetate Transparencies**
- **Testbank**
- **Testmaster**
- **Quizmaster**
- **Student Workbook**
- **Videos**

ACKNOWLEDGMENT

When I signed on to write this book, I had no idea what a monumental task developing, writing, and producing a textbook would be. I therefore wish to thank all of the people at HarperCollins who helped me along the way. I'm especially indebted to Bonnie Roesch and Glyn Davies, who gave me the chance to prove myself as a textbook author, and to Emily Ross and Marshall Sanderford, whose eyes for detail and excellent ideas helped me to write the best book possible. I also wish to thank Tom Farrell, Angel Gonzalez, Kathi Kuntz, Mary McDonnell, Mira Schachne, Andria Ventura, Bob Nirkind, Barbara Conover, and Meryl Muskin for helping to make *Human Sexuality: Contemporary Perspectives* a reality.

I would be neglectful if I did not mention some of the other people who contributed to this book. I'm particularly grateful to Gail Taggart Bolte, Christie Slaton, Traci Boyd, Don Jenni, Rebecca Slaton, Cynthia Earle, Anna Eveson, Allison Aluli, Josh Holowatz, Jennie Grey, Peggy Colgan, Keith Hendrix, Rayne Funk, Josh Simison, Matt Elerding, George Stephanopoulos, Lisa Griffis, Dr. Martin Monto, Dr. Robert Duff, Dr. James Baillie, Dr. Thomas Loughran, The Rev. Richard Berg, C.S.C., The Rev. James King, C.S.C., Gayle Alderman (especially for the coffee and "crumb cake"!), the residents of Christie Hall (for their never-ending supply of information), and the rest of the staff, administration, and faculty of the University of Portland. I also wish to thank my family and friends for their help, encouragement, and inexhaustible patience.

Finally, writing a good textbook is not possible without the insights and suggestions of faculty teaching this course across the country. I'm grateful to the following reviewers for their valuable comments, ideas, and suggestions:

Kwablah Attigobe
City College of San Francisco

Charles Baffi
Virginia Polytechnic Institute

Judith Baker
Texas Woman's University

Kenneth Becker
University of Wisconsin at LaCrosse

Robert Brown
Georgia State University

Teresa Jean Byrne
Kent State University

Jeffrey Cornelius
New Mexico State University

Beverly Drinnin
Des Moines Area Community College

Philip Elias Duryea
University of New Mexico

Randy Fischer
University of Central Florida

Elizabeth Guillette
University of Florida

Gillian Harrison
The Sage Colleges

Joeph Hudak
Eastern Ohio University

Bill Keever
Western Illinois University

John Leach
Western Illinois University

Marcia McCoy
(no affiliation)

Sandra O. Mollenauer
San Diego State University

Elaine Osbourne
Humboldt State University

Peggy Skinner
South Plains College

Margaret Smith
Oregon State University

Sherman Sowby
California State University at Fresno

Jeffrey Stern
University of Michigan

Patricia M. Vidmar
University of Illinois

Charles Weichert
San Antonio College

Nancy White
Youngstown State University

Deborah McDonald Winters
New Mexico State University

Michael Young
University of Arkansas

I hope that this book will play a meaningful role in developing your students' understanding of human sexuality. I welcome and invite your perceptions about this textbook. Suggestions and comments can be sent to me in care of HarperCollins, or directly to my university address.

GEORGE ZGOURIDES, PSY.D.
Department of Psychology
The University of Portland
5000 North Willamette Boulevard
Portland, Oregon 97203-5798

TO THE STUDENT

Welcome to the fascinating field of **sexology**—the scientific study of human sexuality. By choosing to take a sex education course and reading *Human Sexuality: Contemporary Perspectives,* you've accepted the challenge to learn about the many aspects of sexuality, examine your personal values, and make informed sexual decisions. I sincerely hope that the information presented in the upcoming chapters will help you in this process.

You may be wondering why I wrote *Human Sexuality: Contemporary Perspectives.* Over the years as both a student and a professor, I've found that the vast majority of college textbooks are too long and too detailed. Instructors cannot realistically expect their students to read and comprehend several 800-page texts in one quarter or semester. Furthermore, most sexuality texts approach their subject matter in one or more of the following ways: (1) a "warm and fuzzy" experiential approach, (2) a biased political approach, and/or (3) a needlessly complicated approach. I disagree with all three. Instead, I believe that it is important for students to have a text that is manageable, practical, and friendly, but also neutral in its presentation of material.

Sexology is a dynamic field of study, with new research and information appearing daily. I use a number of learning devices throughout *Human Sexuality: Contemporary Perspectives* to assist you in mastering the enormous amount of material that you'll encounter:

- I open each chapter with a detailed outline and a list of *Learning Objectives*. Read these first for a general idea of the chapter's content and structure.
- Following the outline and objectives, each chapter includes a *Personal Assessment*. Use this to test your prior knowledge of the subject matter and to examine your position on potentially controversial topics.
- *For Personal Reflection* sections appear throughout the text. These include scenarios and questions designed to help you apply what you've learned to your daily life. You may wish to keep track of your responses to the questions in a journal.
- *On a Personal Note* quotations from clients, students, and other people I've known over the years also appear throughout the text. These add a personal dimension to *Human Sexuality: Contemporary Perspective.*
- I include at least one boxed *Perspective* feature in each chapter. These present expanded discussions of particularly interesting issues, concerns, historical facts, or cross-cultural phenomena. Most end with one or more *Questions for Thought*. You may want to keep track of your responses to these questions in a journal as well.
- Throughout the text, new terms appear in **boldface** type and are defined in the text, as well as in the marginal and end-of-text glossaries.
- I end each chapter with a list of *Key Points* that summarize the main topics of the chapter, a set of *Activities and Questions*, and a list of *Recommended Readings*. Use these effective tools to reinforce the material that you've just reviewed, and to follow up with further research on subjects of personal interest.
- Citations of original sources of information appear throughout the text. I use the format "(Zgourides, 1993)" for example, to refer to a 1993 publication by the author Zgourides. By looking up "Zgourides" in the References at the end of the text and noting which of his works was published in 1993, you can find the exact bibliographic listing for that particular source of information.

Individual study habits vary considerably, but here are a few additional ideas to help you get the most of *Human Sexuality: Contemporary Perspectives:*

- First and foremost, adopt an *active* approach to learning. All of the pedagogical devices and suggestions in the world will be of little value unless you decide to put them to use.
- Quickly skim each chapter before reading it. Pay close attention to chapter headings and the captions that appear under photos and figures.
- Read and *reread* Chapter 1, several times if necessary. This first chapter is the foundation of the entire book, so make sure that you have a solid understanding of its contents before proceeding.
- Use the **Student Study Guide** that accompanies this text. In it you'll find outlines, objectives, individual and group discussion questions, activities, and sample test questions to enhance your learning.
- Take the *Practice Tests* found in your **Student Study Guide.** These professionally written test questions will help you review material and study for examinations.

Ultimately, the decision to learn is yours. Only *you* can decide to attend class meetings, take adequate and effective notes, and participate in discussions. Only *you* can decide to read this textbook and think about how the material relates to your life. *Only you can decide to make it all happen.*

Again, welcome to sexology!

GEORGE ZGOURIDES

A Visual Guide To:

Human Sexuality
Contemporary Perspectives

George Zgourides
University of Portland

ISBN 0-06-500884-7

This accessible, practical, and timely text provides an unbiased, holistic, and balanced survey of different perspectives on human sexuality. *Human Sexuality: Contemporary Perspectives* approaches controversial topics in an equal and fair manner, discussing sexual orientations and gender issues before moving logically on to discussions of sexual behavior across various life-styles. The text is designed through a sound biopsychosocial framework to help students access and comprehend all material, even under the constraints of a full course load. Emphasizing decision-making skills, students are provided with the information they need to examine their personal values and to make informed, effective sexual decisions now and for the rest of their lives. Numerous pedagogical devices, personal reflection questions and activities, and actual examples are integrated throughout to facilitate students' complete understanding of the material.

CONTENTS IN BRIEF

LOGICAL ORGANIZATION OF MATERIAL

In order to provide students with the most natural, holistic, and unbiased presentation of human sexuality, the text first explores gender issues, the full spectrum of sexual orientation, and the diversity of relationships before examining sexual behaviors across various life-styles.

THE ORGASM PHASE

During the *orgasm phase* ("climax" or "coming"), the buildup of sexual tension is released. Orgasm for both sexes involves numerous muscular contractions, (always in the genitals but often in other parts of the body, such as the abdomen and limbs), warm feelings of intense erotic pleasure, and an inward shift of concentration. In the female, rhythmic contractions occur in the orgasmic platform, and the uterus and rectal sphincter contract. Breast size and the sexual flush reach their peak. Some women even report "ejaculating" a semenlike fluid. In the male, orgasm is usually accompanied by ejaculation, which consists of *emission* and *expulsion*. During emission, the accessory sexual glands contract, and seminal fluid is released into the urethra. During expulsion, penile and urethral contractions move the semen along the urethra and propel it out of the body through the meatus. For most people, orgasm itself lasts for only a few moments. Increasingly, evidence suggests that some individuals are able to extend their orgasms by practicing various pelvic muscle and other exercises (Brauer & Brauer, 1990).

What does an orgasm feel like? Do men and women have different experiences of orgasm? These questions are difficult to answer. The subjective descriptions of orgasm for both men and women appear to be virtually identical, so much so that even expert judges have had trouble identifying the gender of the author of a particular description (Vance & Wagner, 1976).

For Personal Reflection

Do you think having orgasms during sexual activity is a sure sign of intimacy between partners? Why or why not?

THE RESOLUTION PHASE

In both sexes, the genitals and rest of the body gradually return to an unaroused state during the *resolution phase*. Muscles relax, heart rate and respiration return to normal, and the genitals return to their usual shape and size. Feelings of satisfaction and relaxation are common.

The resolution phase can differ for men and women. First, the majority of men enter a *refractory period* immediately following ejaculation, meaning that a certain period of time must pass (from minutes to hours to days, depending on the person) before sexual arousal and orgasm are once again possible. In contrast, women usually do not enter a refractory period, and in some cases may have **multiple orgasms**, or more than one orgasm during any single episode of sexual activity. Female resolution is usually slower and less drastic than its male counterpart. Some men can also have two or more orgasms before losing their erection (Dunn & Trost, 1989; Robbins & Jensen, 1978). According to one student:

MULTIPLE ORGASMS
Experiencing more than one orgasm during any single episode of sexual activity.

On a Personal Note (Sid, age 21)

I was very surprised the first time it happened. I was extremely turned on and masturbating, when I started to have an orgasm. It felt wonderful, but then subsided. There was no ejaculation. So I kept going, and a few seconds later came another orgasm—this time even more intense and with ejaculation. (Author's files)

"FOR PERSONAL REFLECTION" SCENARIOS AND QUESTIONS

Appearing throughout the text, these thought-provoking scenarios and questions help students incorporate chapter material into real life. Students are further encouraged to keep track of their responses in a journal.

The belief that there is a dramatic reduction in the frequency of sexual activity following middle adulthood is unfounded. Actually, the best predictor of future sexual behavior is past and present sexual behavior: the more sexually active a person was and is in her or his earlier years, the more active she or he will probably be in later years (Bretschneider & McCoy, 1988). This is particularly true of activities like touching, caressing, and stimulating oneself and the partner, although not necessarily so of intercourse. There seems, then, to be at least some truth to the old saying, "Use it or lose it" (Cross, 1993)! Barring unrealistic expectations about sexuality and the elderly, a major problem older adults face when it comes to sexual activity is not lack of sexual interest or capability, but absence of a suitable partner (Turner & Adams, 1988). This is a special problem for women, who, having a longer life expectancy than men, find themselves with few or no choices for potential partners. Also, our society generally favors older men marrying younger women, but not the reverse, leaving older women with only one option—celibacy.

Aging rarely means that youthful activities must end, just that they must be approached and enjoyed differently. This is true of tennis (where skill and placement of the ball often replaces sprinting and power), of exercise (where walking briskly might replace jogging), and of sexual activity (where patience and caring often replace sweaty passion). In none of these cases do (or should) the changes that accompany aging in any way detract from the enjoyment of the activity.

This still leaves us with society's negative attitudes about sexuality in the later years. To help put an end to these attitudes, sex researcher Edward Brecher (1984), quoting a 67-year-old consultant, recommended the following: "The common view that the aging and aged are nonsexual, I believe, can only be corrected by a dramatic and courageous process—the *coming-out-of-the-closet* of sexually active older women and men, so that people can see for themselves what the later years are really like" (pp. 20–21).

For Personal Reflection

Identify some of the attitudes you have concerning sexuality and the elderly. Where do you think your attitudes come from? What are some of the things you can do to help society see that older adults, like all people, are sexual beings?

SEX EDUCATION AND THE LIFE CYCLE

Sex education is just for preteens and teens, right? By now (having read most of this book) you should know the answer to this question. No, it's not just for teens and preteens: *Sex education is for everyone—young and old alike.* The most important message of *Human Sexuality: Contemporary Perspectives* is that sex education—at home or elsewhere—is the primary vehicle through which correct sexual information is disseminated to people of all ages. Correct information about sexuality is the foundation upon which people can challenge unrealistic expectations and stereotypes; make good, effective sexual decisions; and overcome and prevent various sexual diseases and problems. Although I described many of the benefits of sex education in Chapter 1, a few more points are in order along these lines.

First, *sex education is a lifelong process that should begin in childhood and continue through the life cycle*. No one can honestly boast of knowing everything about human sexuality, regardless of their age or occupation. A single lifetime is not long enough to grasp the many aspects of human sexuality. Every interaction, every word spoken, every page read carries with it the potential for a new experience and new learning. Therein lies the beauty of human sexuality.

PERSPECTIVE BOXES WITH "QUESTIONS FOR THOUGHT"

Each chapter includes at least one boxed *Perspective,* which presents an expanded discussion of a particularly interesting issue, concern, historical fact, or cross-cultural phenomenon. Each ends with one or more *Questions for Thought.*

Klassen, A. D., Williams, C. J., & Levitt, E. E. (1989). *Sex and morality in the U.S.* Middletown, CT: Wesleyan University Press. The Kinsey Institute's national survey of sexual morality.

Masters, W. H., & Johnson, V. E. (1966). *Human sexual response.* Boston: Little, Brown. Masters and Johnson's classic account of their mid-1960s observational studies of human sexual response.

PERSPECTIVE

Generation Sex: The Details/Mademoiselle Report

Details and *Mademoiselle* magazines each asked 9000 subscribers (all single, between ages 18 and 30) 92 questions about their sex lives. Following are 7 of the more interesting findings from this recent magazine survey:

- 44 percent of men and 36 percent of women respondents have had sex outside their main relationship.
- 96 percent of men and 74 percent of women respondents who have cheated say "feeling horny" is enough reason.
- 35 percent of men and 7 percent of women respondents say they masturbate on average three times a week. In contrast, 18 percent of men and 36 percent of women say they masturbate "a few times a month."
- 60 percent of men and 16 percent of women respondents say it is "all right" to have sex on the first date.
- 43 percent of men and 29 percent of women respondents say they act out their sexual fantasies at least some of the time.
- 56 percent of men and 48 percent of women respondents say they have had sex at least once because of having "too much to drink."
- 25 percent of men and 69 percent of women respondents say they have faked an orgasm during sex at least once.

Questions for Thought

What kinds of information do magazine surveys provide about readers' sex lives? What do they not provide? What do they provide about sexuality and the general public? Would you ever consider participating in a magazine sex survey? Why or why not?

Source: C. Rubenstein, (1993). Generation sex: The Details/Mademoiselle report, *Details,* June, 82–89.

PERSPECTIVE

How to Do a Breast Self-Examination

Your aim in performing monthly *breast self-examinations* (BSEs) is to discover cancerous lumps or growths while they are still small and localized. A cancer that hasn't spread to another area of the body is much easier to treat. Almost 90 percent of breast cancers detected in the early stages of development are discovered by women doing BSEs. Regularly performing BSEs helps you to become more familiar with your breast anatomy and detect abnormalities more easily.

The best time to perform a BSE is about one week following your period. If periods are irregular, then self-examine on a monthly schedule. The best time to self-examine is during or immediately following a warm shower or bath. There are three stages to a typical BSE: in the shower, lying down, and in front of a mirror.

In the Shower

While in the shower, soap up your left hand and run it along the right breast from the collarbone to the nipple. Notice if there have been any changes since your last exam. Repeat this procedure with the right hand and left breast.

Lying Down

Next, lie down on a bed, placing a pillow beneath your right shoulder, and your right hand behind your head. Using the palm of your left hand, examine the right breast by slowly moving it in circular fashion around the whole breast. With the fingers of your left hand, repeat this circular motion, beginning at the nipple and moving out until you've examined the entire breast. To check for discharge from the nipple, gently squeeze the nipple. To check for a lump beneath the nipple, gently press the nipple into the breast. Repeat this procedure with the right hand and left breast.

In Front of a Mirror

Finally, stand in front of a mirror with your arms at your sides, and compare the breasts. Note any differences in color, size, shape, and position, as well as changes since your last exam. Gently squeeze your waist with your hands, again noting any differences or changes. With hands behind your head, rotate your torso and note any differences or changes.

You may notice that your breasts are normally lumpy. (For example, there are firm ridges of tissue in the lower areas of the breasts.) Finding a distinct lump is no reason to panic. Some 80 to 90 percent of breast lumps are benign. Still, bring to the immediate attention of your health-care practitioner any lump, growth, thickening, discoloration, or discharge.

As an example of this, consider how stereotypes and rigid gender roles interfere with sexuality. In many cases, people define personal masculinity and femininity through their sexual behaviors. With men taught to be aggressive and superior and women passive and yielding, no wonder the penis becomes a symbol of power and dominance, and the vagina one of dependence and submission. Conforming to such restrictive, age-old sexual stereotypes leaves little room for creativity or self-expression in the bedroom.

Gender stereotypes and rigid gender roles loom large in creating sexual dysfunctions. Men who battle anxieties related to sexual performance often develop an arousal, erectile, or orgasm dysfunction, as do women who struggle to find sexual fulfillment within a gender role of passivity and compliance (Kaplan 1974; Masters & Johnson, 1970). Why is this? Perhaps it is because men and women who carry rigid gender assumptions become so wrapped up in their irrational expectations about the way sex and lovers are *supposed* to be that they fail to "let go" and give themselves over to the erotic pleasures of lovemaking.

On a Personal Note (Paula, age 32)

I've always believed that as a woman my sole sexual function is to just lie there and let my husband have his way in bed. I never felt like I should or could take a more active role, you know, tend to my own needs. Women aren't supposed to do that, right? That's what I was always taught—the wife is there for the husband. After a couple of months of therapy, though, it finally occurred to me that my attitudes about sexuality probably have something to do with my never having had an orgasm. It's so hard to fight these old tapes in my head! (Author's files)

Where do gender stereotypes come from? The weight of scientific evidence points to the fact that people, especially children, learn gender stereotypes (Basow, 1992; Signorielli, 1990). But from where and whom? That is, what influences teach and reinforce gender stereotypes in our children? As with gender roles, socializing agents—parents, peers, teachers, the media, and religious leaders—pass along gender stereotypes from one generation to the next.

How can we free individuals from gender "typecasting" so that they can lead more fulfilling lives? One method is to challenge gender roles and stereotypes just as we challenge other unrealistic, irrational expectations. This has been a social theme in the United States for a long time, culminating in *feminism*, the *women's liberation movement*, the *men's movement*, and the concept of *androgyny*.

For Personal Reflection

1. What are some of the traditional concepts of "male" and "female" that you hold? Where did these come from? How have traditional gender stereotypes both positively and negatively affected your life?
2. To what extent do you believe our society is challenging traditional gender roles and stereotypes? What evidence do you have to support your position?
3. What are your feelings on the changing roles of women and men in our society?

"ON A PERSONAL NOTE" CASE EXAMPLES

Inspired by George Zgourides's clinical experiences as a licensed psychologist, numerous case examples from assorted clients, students, and other individuals help personalize the material.

By week 7, the already formed respiratory and digestive organs (lungs, kidneys, liver, pancreas, and intestines) begin limited functioning. Even though the fetus's gender is not clearly visible at this point, the gonads have already begun to develop.

By week 8, the fetus weighs 1/30 of an ounce and is 1¼ inches in length. At this time outlines of the fetus's facial features (lips, tongue, eyes, ears, and nose) are visible. Its head is proportionally larger than the rest of its body due to rapid development of the brain. Arms, hands, legs, feet, and toes are readily apparent by the tenth week. And within another two weeks, the fetus weighs approximately 1 ounce, is 3 to 4 inches in length, and has discernible sex organs.

Most of the mother's physical and emotional experiences during the first trimester are the result of hormonal changes. High levels of estrogen cause stomach irritation, including nausea and vomiting. High levels of progesterone produce drowsiness and fatigue, relax the rectal muscles, and prompt irregular bowel movements and constipation. These hormones also alter the body's water balance, so water retention and swelling are likely. Other physical changes during this trimester include increased breast sensitivity, increased vaginal discharge and a frequent need to urinate and defecate as the uterus expands and presses against the bladder and rectum. As one friend explained:

On a Personal Note (Toni, age 23)

I've been really amazed at how many unusual changes I've noticed since discovering I'm pregnant. The worst is swelling in my feet. I'm usually on my feet quite a bit during the day, but now my shoes feel so tight sometimes that I have to walk around the house barefoot. I also need to go to the bathroom about every hour, especially at night—not terribly convenient when you're trying to get some sleep. (Author's files)

By weeks 10 to 12, the fetus looks like a miniature human.

roles and stereotypes is the concept of *androgyny*, or the blending of masculine and feminine attributes within an individual.

GROUP EXERCISES

Appearing at the end of every chapter are collaborative questions and activities that are designed to encourage decision-making skills, independent thinking, and class discussion.

ACTIVITIES AND QUESTIONS

1. Survey a number of students outside your class concerning what personality traits and characteristics they associate with "male" and "female." Generally speaking, what characteristics do the women in your survey associate with "male," and men with "female"? What about women with "female," and men with "male"? What did you learn?
2. As children, should boys be encouraged to play with dolls, to play house, and so forth? Should girls be encouraged to play with toy guns, to play football, and so forth? Why or why not? As a parent, would you encourage your children to participate in gender-specific play, gender-neutral play, or both? Explain.
3. What are some of the gender assumptions that you've identified in your own life? How have these affected your relationships? If they have ever caused conflicts for you and a partner, how willing were you to work at changing your gender assumptions? Did you expect your partner to change her or his assumptions, too?
4. Watch one to two hours of prime-time television shows each day for one week. How many of these shows portray traditional American gender roles? Nontraditional roles? Androgynous lifestyles? How do you feel about your findings?
5. Imagine for a moment that our government decided to conduct the "Great American Social Experiment" and passed laws requiring all citizens to become androgynous. What do you think would happen to our society? What are some of the positive and negative changes that you might observe? If the "experiment" failed, do you think people would return to life as usual, or would there be some lasting changes? If the latter, what kinds of changes?

RECOMMENDED READINGS

Cook, E. (1985). *Psychological androgyny*. Elmsford, NY: Pergamon Press. A review of the professional literature on androgyny and androgynous lifestyles.

Feminist Review (Eds.). (1987). *Sexuality: A reader*. London: Virago Press. A lively set of contributions from feminist writers on such topics as sexual politics, sexual differences, women and psychoanalysis, lesbianism, pornography, and sexual violence.

Hyde, J. S. (1991). *Half the human experience: The psychology of women* (4th ed.) Lexington, MA: D. C. Heath. Explores and summarizes contemporary theories and works on the psychology of women.

Matthews, G. (1987). *"Just a housewife": The rise and fall of domesticity in America*. New York: Oxford University Press. Surveys the history of housewifery in the United States from colonial times to today.

Mead, M. (1963). *Sex and temperament in three primitive societies*. New York: Morrow. A fascinating sociocultural study of the Arapesh, Mundugumor, and Tchambuli peoples, including the ways in which their gender/sex roles differ from those of Western cultures.

Rubin, L. B. (1990). *Erotic wars: What happened to the sexual revolution?* New York: Farrar, Straus, & Giroux. A fascinating look at how the "sexual revolution" of the 1960s has affected today's assumptions about gender.

ACTIVITIES AND QUESTIONS

1. In this class exercise, generate a list of excuses that people commonly use for not practicing safer sex. Write these on one side of a blackboard. On the other side, create a list of "Pro-Safer Sex" responses to challenge these excuses. For example, you might confront the excuse, "I'll lose my erection if I have to put on a condom" with, "You'll stay hard the way I'll put the condom on you." After creating the two lists, break into pairs to role-play both parts and practice responding to a partner who pressures you against safer sex.
2. For two weeks, make note of all magazine features, newspaper articles, and television programs dealing with STDs. Return to class and describe the various ways these diseases are presented by the media.
3. What are the pros and cons associated with mandatory HIV testing? Should such testing be done? If so, on whom? Everyone? Health-care workers? Restaurant employees? Prison inmates? Why or why not? What effect might mandatory testing have on those individuals found to be HIV-positive?
4. Identify some of the myths and stereotypes about HIV—who contracts it and how, how you can tell if your partner is HIV-positive, and so on. Where do you think these stereotypes come from? What role do the popular media play in perpetuating myths about HIV and AIDS? What about family, friends, the government, religious institutions, special interest groups, and other organizations? What can you do to help eliminate these myths and stereotypes?
5. Visit an AIDS counseling center, agency, or crisis hotline. Interview a staff member about available services and programs, such as diagnostic testing, medical treatment, emotional support/counseling, financial resources for the poor, and community outreach and educational programs. Report your findings in class. Be sure to pick up some written materials to show your classmates.
6. Given their typical failure rate of 12 percent for preventing conception (and unknown failure rate for preventing the transmission of STDs), do you think condoms should be distributed at public colleges and universities? High schools? Junior high schools? With or without instructions? For free? Explain your position.

RECOMMENDED READINGS

Ankerberg, J., & Weldon, J. (1993). *The myth of safe sex: The tragic consequences of violating God's plan*. Chicago: Moody Press. The authors of this thoroughly documented Christian book promote abstinence and take a strong stand against relying on condoms for "safe sex."

Bayer, R. (1989). *Private acts, social consequences*. New York: Free Press. A volume dealing with individuals' rights and public health policies in the age of HIV and AIDS.

Centers for Disease Control. *The Morbidity and Mortality Weekly Report*. A weekly publication of the CDC that frequently contains updated information on all aspects of HIV and AIDS.

Davis, M., & Scott, R. S (1988). *Lovers, doctors, and the law*. New York: Harper & Row. Presents the legal implications of "harming" another, intentionally or not, by transmitting an STD. The authors discuss the importance of sharing sexual histories

THE FALLOPIAN TUBES

**FALLOPIAN TUBES
(FAL-LO-PE-AN)**
*Pair of tubes connecting the ovaries
and the uterus.*

The **fallopian tubes** are the pair of tubes that move the released ovum into the uterus. Each tube is about 4 inches long, is located next to an ovary, and opens into the uterus. In a typical adult female, a mature egg bursts forth from the ovary near the fallopian tube once every 28 days or so. The waving and swaying of *fimbriae* (finger-shaped projections at the entrance of the fallopian tubes) move the released ovum into the fallopian tube. Muscular contractions of the fallopian tubes, as well as movement of *cilia* (small hairlike structures) within the tubes, move the ovum toward the uterine cavity. The ovum travels about 1 inch per 24 hours. Sperm in the fallopian tube can fertilize the ovum, usually in the outer quarter of the tube, the part closest to the ovary.

THE UTERUS

UTERUS (YOO-TE-RUS)
*Female reproductive organ that
receives and nurtures the zygote.*

The **uterus** is the female reproductive organ responsible for receiving and nurturing the fertilized egg, or *zygote*. The fertilized egg attaches itself to the uterine wall, where it remains throughout the period of *gestation*, or the duration of the pregnancy.

In its nonpregnant state, the uterus is "pear-shaped." It is about 3 inches long, tapered at one end, about 2 inches wide at the other end, and lies superior to the bladder (Figures 4.3 and 4.4). During pregnancy the size and shape of the uterus change dramatically.

Three layers of tissue make up the uterine walls (Figure 4.5). The *endometrium* is the innermost layer of the uterus, a portion of which sheds during *menstruation*. The next layer of uterine tissue is the *myometrium*, or muscle tissue that contracts during orgasm, menstruation, and childbirth. The *perimetrium* is the outer layer of tissue that maintains the shape and position of the uterus in the pelvic cavity.

The narrow, outer portion of the uterus that opens into the vagina is the **cervix**, the passageway for sperm, menstrual fluid, and birth. The opening of the cervix, or *os*, contains mucus that normally prevents bacteria from entering into the uterus. The cervix is the site of the *Pap smear* test, which is used to check for cervical cancer.

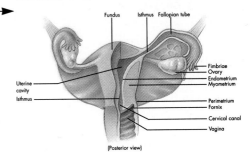

Location of the ovaries, fallopian tubes, uterus, and vagina. Source: C. E. Rischer & T. A. Easton (1992), Focus on human biology (New York: HarperCollins). Reprinted by permission.

FULL-COLOR LINE DRAWINGS AND PHOTOGRAPHS

Carefully developed to enhance textual material, these illustrious drawings and photographs bring the subject matter to life. Line drawings are clear and informative, and photographs represent the wide diversity of life-styles.

FIGURE 9.13 *Face-to-face, both partners standing.*

Face-to-Face, Standing Positions In this variation of face-to-face intercourse, both partners stand (Figure 9.13). The woman may lean back in this position, or she may wrap her legs around the man's waist, requiring him to hold her up while they both thrust. This position allows a couple to have intercourse in alternative settings, such as in a compact shower; however, intromission can be difficult.

Rear-Entry Positions In this second basic category of intercourse positions, the partners do not face one another. Instead, the man inserts his penis in the woman's vagina from behind her. In one variation ("doggy style"), the woman gets on her knees and hands, her buttocks facing her partner, and the man kneels and enters her from the rear. He is also free to fondle her clitoris, buttocks, inner thighs, and breasts (Figure 9.14). This position is highly stimulating for the man, as his sensitive frenulum rubs against his partner's anterior vaginal wall and pubic bone. It may or may not be as stimulating for the woman.

In another variation ("spooning"), the couple lie on their sides, the woman's backside facing the man. Again, intromission occurs from behind, and the man is free to hold and caress his partner (Figure 9.15). This tends to be a relaxing position for both parties, and especially recommended for partners who must monitor and minimize their levels of physical exertion.

These items should also be reexamined a number of days after the initial treatment to confirm the elimination of all of the parasites.

On a Personal Note (Joel, 38)

When I was in college, I remember getting crabs from a woman I met at a party. The horrible itching started some hours later. I'll never forget trying not to scratch in class the next day.

OTHER SEXUALLY TRANSMITTED INFECTIONS

In addition to the STDs discussed thus far, are other genital infections can be sexually transmitted. Two of the most common are *trichomonas* and *monilia*.

TRICHOMONAS

Trichomonas vaginalis is a single-celled organism that lives in the vagina, causing *trichomonas*, or "trich." Although the organism can be transmitted by sexual intercourse, it can be contracted following extended exposure to moisture. Women who take oral contraceptives may be more prone to trichomonas due to heightened levels of progesterone, which increases the alkalinity in the vagina, creating a more hospitable environment for the trichomonas organism. Typical symptoms in the female include a vulva-irritating, odorous, white or yellowish vaginal discharge. The male with trichomonas is usually asymptomatic. Since the infection can be passed back and forth between partners, both should be treated should the organism be confirmed in the female partner. The prescription medication *metronidazole* (brand name, *Flagyl*) is the only effective systemic drug used to treat trichomonas.

MONILIA

Some women suffer from *monilia* (or *candidiasis*), a vaginal yeast infection caused by *Candida albicans*. Like "trich," yeast infections grow well in alkaline environments and therefore proliferate under similar circumstances. Symptoms of monilia in women include vaginal itching, irritation, and discharge; in men, penile itching, redness, and a burning sensation. For women with diagnosed yeast infections, *clotrimazole* (brand name, *Lotrimin*) and *miconazole* (brand name, *Monistat*) can be helpful.

PREVENTING SEXUALLY TRANSMITTED DISEASES

Education is the single most important weapon in fighting STDs. Teaching individuals and groups about safer sex practices and communication is vital halting the pandemic of STDs (Keeling, 1993; Willis, 1993).

To this end, individuals should be aware of a number of precautions and **prophylactic,** or preventive, measures. The following guidelines for individuals choosing to be sexually active are from the brochure *What Are Sexually Transmitted Diseases?*, published by the American College Health Association (1989):

1. Form a monogamous relationship in which you and your partner make an agreement to be faithful sexually and stick to it. Avoid sexual intimacy until you and [your partner have] been tested for pre-existing STDs.

UNIQUE COVERAGE OF SAFER SEX EDUCATION

Continuing its balanced, unbiased, and frank coverage, the text examines a number of vital and often neglected issues.

Weitzman, S., Kuter, I., & Pizer, H. F. (1986). *Confronting breast cancer*. New York: Vintage Books. Contains useful information about detecting and treating breast cancer.

Willmuth, M. E. (1987). Sexuality after spinal cord injury: A critical review. *Clinical Psychology Review*, 7, 389–412. A journal article review of some of the many aspects of sexuality that are affected by a spinal cord injury.

PERSPECTIVE

Sexual Rights of the Developmentally Challenged

In this day of increased sensitivity to special needs, we must be careful not to downplay or forget *sexual rights* of others. This is especially true of developmentally challenged individuals, whose sexual rights appear below.

1. The right to receive training in social-sexual behavior that will open more doors for social contact with people in the community.
2. The right to all the knowledge about sexuality they can comprehend.
3. The right to enjoy love and be loved by the opposite sex, including sexual fulfillment.
4. The right to the opportunity to express sexual impulses in the same forms that are socially acceptable for others.
5. The right to marry.
6. The right to have a voice in whether or not they should have children.
7. The right for supportive services which involve those rights as they are needed and feasible. [p. 247]

Source: W. Kempton, (1977), The mentally retarded person. In H. L. Gochros & J. S. Gochros (Eds.), *The sexually oppressed* (New York: Association Press) (pp. 239–256).

STRONG COVERAGE OF CHALLENGED INDIVIDUALS

Zgourides provides needed information about an often neglected audience. Chapter 10, "Sexuality, Health and the Challenged Individual," is entirely devoted to this issue.

C H A P T E R 1

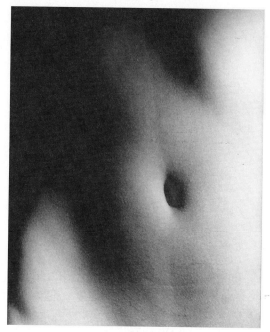

SEXUALITY AND THE BIOPSYCHOSOCIAL PERSPECTIVE

O B J E C T I V E S

AFTER READING THIS CHAPTER YOU SHOULD BE
ABLE TO . . .

1. DEFINE *SEXOLOGY*.
2. IDENTIFY SOME OF THE REASONS WHY PEOPLE
   STUDY HUMAN SEXUALITY.
3. DEFINE THE *BIOPSYCHOSOCIAL PERSPECTIVE*.
4. LIST AND DESCRIBE VARIOUS BIOLOGICAL,
   PSYCHOLOGICAL, AND SOCIAL PERSPECTIVES
   OF HUMAN SEXUALITY, AS WELL AS EXPLAIN
   HOW THEY RELATE TO ITS STUDY.
5. IDENTIFY YOUR REASONS FOR TAKING A
   COURSE IN HUMAN SEXUALITY, INCLUDING
   YOUR EXPECTATIONS OF THE COURSE AND
   INSTRUCTOR.

PERSONAL ASSESSMENT

TEST YOUR GENERAL KNOWLEDGE OF A FEW SELECT ASPECTS OF HUMAN SEXUALITY BY ANSWERING THE FOLLOWING STATEMENTS *true* OR *false*.

_____ 1. Males are incapable of having erections and reaching orgasm prior to puberty.

_____ 2. Women generally prefer vaginal orgasms to clitoral ones.

_____ 3. Only women are capable of having multiple orgasms.

_____ 4. Women can't become pregnant while breast-feeding.

_____ 5. Condoms are about 98 percent effective in preventing pregnancy and/or transmission of sexual diseases.

_____ 6. The most common sexual problem for males is the inability to attain or sustain erections.

_____ 7. The most common sexual problem for women is pain during intercourse.

_____ 8. Both men and women lose interest in intercourse by age 65.

_____ 9. Researchers have determined that homosexuals can alter their sexual orientation with relative ease, but only if they're motivated to do so.

_____ 10. Most child molesters are strangers to their victims prior to the abuse.

ANSWERS

The above statements are common sexual myths. Therefore, the correct answers are all *false.*

---

*S*exual pleasure, widely used and not abused, may prove the stimulus and liberator of our finest and most exalted activities.

Havelock Ellis

It was Michael's first day at the university. Besides feeling a little overwhelmed, he was concerned about obtaining the right signatures from the right advisors, dealing with the financial aid office, locating the right buildings, and finding his classrooms. During orientation week, Michael had also found registering for classes to be a nightmare. Long lines. Short tempers. And he couldn't get into all the classes he wanted, at least not at convenient times. Michael certainly didn't relish the thought of being in class at 8:00 every weekday morning.

Michael had signed up for some of the usual courses: Math, History, Art Appreciation, English, and Human Sexuality. These classes sounded interesting, but the idea of also taking Human Sexuality really appealed to him: "Taking a sex class is going to be a breeze! I'm already an expert. I probably won't even have to open the book. I can look for dates. X-rated videos. Sexy stories. Way to go, Mike! At least I'll have one 'easy A' this semester!"

If you're like Michael, your initial expectation of a course in human sexuality might be to watch sex education films, listen to people talk about their sex lives, and follow the instructor's discussion of sexual activities you've already experienced. You may see the class as a way of meeting potential sexual partners or maintaining a good grade point average. If you already think of yourself as a sexual expert, you may even consider this course a less than valuable way to spend your time.

You'll soon realize, however, that studying human sexuality involves much more than just reading stimulating sexual case studies and watching videos. You'll encounter a great deal of new material. You'll spend time rethinking your values and attitudes about sexuality. The differing viewpoints of your classmates will at times challenge your beliefs about what is acceptable. You'll come to view human sexuality for what it is—a beautiful and integral, but complex, part of life.

WHAT IS HUMAN SEXUALITY?

Most people have an intuitive understanding of what the phrase *human sexuality* means. To many, sexuality is merely the pursuit of sexual pleasure, either alone or with a partner. To others, it is a biological function, a matter of gender and reproduction. And to others, it is intimacy, a means of expressing love. If you ask ten people their definition of sexuality, you'll probably receive at least ten different answers.

All civilizations have developed some means of conceptualizing sexuality and describing sexual behaviors, although these are not always consistent with Western terminology and descriptions. The English term *sexual* derives from the Latin terms *sexualis* and *sexus*, each referring to a person's reproductive anatomy—that is, whether a person is male or female. By the nineteenth century, the term *sexuality* also included behaviors involving the sex organs for the purpose of bearing children. In the last hundred years or so, *sexuality, or sex,* has come to refer not only to *procreational* activities (bearing children), but also to *recreational* (masturbation) and *relational* ones (love and intimacy).

As sexual terminology can be confusing, throughout *Human Sexuality: Contemporary Perspectives* I'll use the term *sex* to refer to sexual behaviors ("having sex") and biological makeup ("The baby's sex is female"), except when it's clear from the context of a passage that *sex* is a shortened version of the more formal terms *sexual* and *sexuality* ("sex

Sexuality is an important part of life for all people.

education," "sex research," and "sex therapy"). I'll also use *gender* to refer to both an individual's anatomical sex and the psychological aspects of being female or male; *gender identity*, to an individual's personal sense of being female or male; *gender role*, to outward expression of one's gender identity within a social or cultural context; and *sexual orientation*, to an individual's relative sexual attraction to members of the same and/or other sex. I'll use *sexual identity* to refer to all of these together.

With the advent of sophisticated research methods, our understanding of sexuality has grown considerably in recent decades. Many professionals now consider human sexuality to be an area of serious scientific study and inquiry (Reiss, 1993; Tiefer, 1994). And given the availability of much new information, it is apparent that the scientific discipline of human sexuality, or *sexology*, is *holistic*, embodying many different perspectives. A holistic approach to sexuality accounts for the various biological, psychological, and social influences that interact and shape an individual's experience of sexuality. I'll have more to say about these interacting influences later in this chapter.

Everyone is sexual from birth until death. Even though some choose to remain *celibate* (abstinent from sexual relations), they are still sexual beings. Furthermore, humans are dynamic and constantly changing. The more life experiences you have, the more your attitudes about sexuality change. *Your* views of human sexuality have probably changed dramatically in the last five years, and perhaps even in the last year.

Although each person's experience of sexuality is unique, there are many common patterns and trends in human beings' collective experience of sexuality. The ability to interpret and understand these patterns and trends gives you a more in-depth understanding of others' sexuality, as well as your own. Many people forget that human sexuality is a global phenomenon and not something that is of exclusive interest to Americans.

Sexology, then, is a discipline of scientific inquiry that recognizes humans of all cultures as sexual beings "in process," and identifies the interacting biological, psychological, and social aspects that influence this process. A comprehensive overview of the field of sexuality includes discussions of sexual research, gender identity and roles, sexual anatomy and physiology, sexual arousal and response, sexual orientation, loving relationships and communication, sexual behavior, sexuality and disability, sexuality throughout the life span, conception, pregnancy, birth, contraception, abortion, sexually transmitted diseases, sexual dysfunctions and therapies, sexual variations, commercialism, harassment and victimization, and legal and ethical standards. The following chapters will present these and many other sexuality topics.

SEXOLOGY
Scientific discipline devoted to the study of human sexuality.

WHY STUDY HUMAN SEXUALITY?

Sex is natural, isn't it? Won't everything be okay if you just let nature take its course? Didn't the world exist long before anyone decided to study sex? Why not just leave things the way they've always been? *Why study human sexuality?*

Unfortunately, those who avoid thinking critically about important aspects of life, including their sexuality, are more apt to make poor decisions when confronted with confusing situations. *Learning to make rational, effective decisions about sexuality is a primary goal of studying human sexuality.* To quote Susan Walen (1985), "Sex is perfectly natural, but rarely naturally perfect" (p. 131). Yes, we can all benefit from learning more about this important topic. Below are ten of the many reasons why people study human sexuality.

TO OBTAIN KNOWLEDGE

Knowledge is power. If you have correct information about a topic, you're in a much stronger position to make healthy, effective life decisions. You can take more complete charge of your life and circumstances, and make choices that improve the quality of life for yourself and others.

TO GAIN PERSONAL INSIGHT

Because your beliefs affect your behavior and vice versa, personal insight allows you to make more informed decisions about your behavior. Gaining insight into yourself and the reasons why you believe or do something is the first step to gaining insights into others. When you know and accept yourself, you'll find it easier to know and accept others, including the sexual decisions they might make.

TO BECOME MORE AT EASE WITH ONE'S OWN SEXUALITY

Knowledge of and respect for others' sexuality helps you become more comfortable with your own. Many people are unsure of themselves sexually, their discomfort resulting from misinformation and misconceptions about sexuality. This is one reason why sex education is so important. As one student commented:

On a Personal Note (Sarah, age 34)

Several years ago, I read about women who have multiple orgasms. For some reason, I got the impression that having multiple orgasms was a sign of being a "real woman." My impression was reinforced by some other stuff I saw on TV. Anyway, I started worrying about not measuring up. I've never had more than one orgasm at a time. Sometimes I'm lucky if I get that. I don't want to give the impression that my husband and I don't have a good sex life. We do. But the multiple orgasm thing really bothered me. I finally saw a sex counselor who assured me that having multiple orgasms has nothing to do with my worth as a person or woman. It seems that some women have them, but a lot of others don't. (Author's files)

TO DEVELOP SEXUAL SELF-ACCEPTANCE

Developing sexual self-acceptance is one benefit of becoming more at ease with your own sexuality. People often confuse the terms *self-concept*, *self-esteem*, and *self-acceptance*. *Self-concept* refers to the views and opinions you hold about yourself, whether positive or negative. *Self-esteem* involves feelings of self-worth, but carries a connotation of "measuring up" to internal or external criteria (Ellis & Harper, 1975). *Self-acceptance* refers to the degree to which you accept yourself as you are, regardless of others' opinions or your behavior (or "performances," to use cognitive psychology lingo).

Albert Ellis (1988) and other experts argue that self-acceptance is preferable to self-esteem. Self-esteem involves rating yourself based on your performances, which can lead to feelings of sexual inadequacy when you have a "poor" performance. In contrast, self-acceptance means taking yourself the way you are, regardless of your faults or weaknesses. Your sexual abilities, whatever they may be, won't affect the way that you view yourself.

TO MAXIMIZE COMMUNICATION AND INTIMACY

Many people find talking about sexual matters embarrassing, a pattern that usually begins in childhood. Communication skills, once learned and put into practice, can help you improve your relationship with your sexual partner. Talking about your experience of sexuality is essential for communicating likes and dislikes, desires and fears, and for becoming more sexually secure. When communication is open, intimacy is present and increases. Being able to share yourself fully with another is one of life's greatest pleasures. According to one client:

Talking about sexual matters maximizes intimacy between partners.

On a Personal Note (John, age 66)

As I've gotten older, I've slowed down some in the bedroom. I just don't become as excited or hard and fast as I used to. I guess that's natural. Well, for a long time, I've worried what my wife thinks. I mean, does she still think I'm masculine? Does she still love me? And worrying makes getting it up even more difficult. Finally, I figured we needed to talk about it. To make a long story short, we did, and what a difference! She was so understanding and willing to help me out in any way possible. I've decided it's better to use my energy talking about my feelings instead of trying to hide them. (Author's files)

Communication can also do much to reduce or eliminate common relationship conflicts. Although couples often complain in therapy about money and sexual problems, much of the time the real problem has to do with ineffective patterns of communication (Tannen, 1990). People usually find it easier to work through their problems when they are able to communicate with one another.

TO MAXIMIZE SEXUAL PLEASURE

For most people sexual activity is very pleasurable. Increasing your knowledge of human sexual stimulation and response can further enhance this pleasure. For example, knowing how to stimulate your partner's particularly sensitive areas can make the difference in whether you both have a mildly pleasing sexual experience or an ecstatic, exhilarating one. And as mentioned above, communication plays a major role in this process. When you freely express your likes and desires, inhibitions tend to disappear. You and your partner are then better able to ask for whatever pleases you the most.

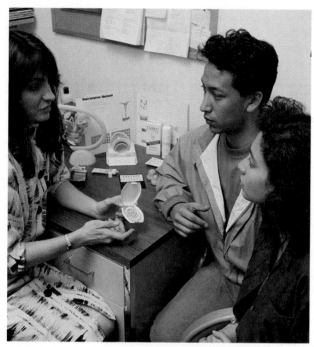

Learning about sexually transmitted diseases and "safer sex" practices is an important step in becoming a sexually responsible individual.

TO MANAGE FERTILITY

Studying human sexuality gives you practical, factual information about managing fertility. With such information, you can either improve or reduce your chances of conceiving. Few of us can afford not to have this valuable information.

TO AVOID SEXUAL DYSFUNCTIONS

At some point almost everyone experiences difficulty in sexual functioning. Most of these episodes are temporary. But if the difficulty becomes chronic, a *sexual dysfunction* may develop. When accurate information is available, sexual dysfunctions can often be avoided or eliminated in the early stages of development. For example, a man who has a single episode of *impotence* (the inability to attain an erection) may become so fearful of being forever impotent that he loses his erection whenever he has intercourse. If this pattern continues, he may develop *male erectile disorder*. Likewise, a woman who focuses too hard on becoming sexually aroused during sexplay may distract herself to such a degree that arousal is difficult or impossible. If this pattern continues, she may develop *female sexual arousal disorder*. In both cases, a vicious cycle forms as a result of *self-fulfilling prophecy*, in which the person's fears and expectations actually come to pass.

TO AVOID SEXUALLY TRANSMITTED DISEASES

In the 1990s the study of human sexuality must include sexually transmitted diseases (STDs), many of which have become epidemic. STDs can be fatal, can negatively affect a couple's ability to have healthy children, or can be downright painful nuisances. Therefore, before having sex with a partner, you must consider the risks of contracting STDs. In the "heat of the moment," many individuals, particularly young people, forget about STDs. "It'll never happen to me. I'm not at risk. I'm not an intravenous drug user." Or, "I hate using condoms. Anyway, it's no big deal these days if I catch gonorrhea. I'll just get a shot of penicillin." Feelings of invincibility often characterize young minds. Remember that the more prevalent STDs become, the greater the risk is of contracting one if appropriate precautions aren't taken.

TO BRING ABOUT POSITIVE SOCIAL CHANGES

By working to improve yourself and your relationships, you're working to improve society. Any positive and healthy changes that you make for yourself will influence your interactions with others. With information and insight, you can work to prevent further transmission of STDs; you can help others more fully understand people of different races, creeds, and cultures; and you can teach others to respect different beliefs, values, rights, and sexual choices. You can also take social and political responsibility to be informed when controversy arises around sexual issues, such as the use of fetal tissue in medical research, the RU-486 "abortion pill," and efforts to lift the military ban on gays.

For Personal Reflection

At this point, you may want to consider how studying human sexuality will be a valuable experience. I present these questions as thought-provokers to increase your awareness of both "where you've been" and "where you're going" sexually. Many students find it helpful to keep a journal of their answers to the various "Personal Reflection" questions posed throughout this text—a practice that I highly recommend.

1. *Is it easy for you to talk openly about sexuality with friends? Instructors? Family? Why or why not?*
2. *Where or from whom did you learn about sexuality? What influences have had the greatest impact on shaping your values and attitudes about sexuality? Do you feel that what you've learned is accurate or inaccurate?*
3. *Why do you want to take a human sexuality course?*

PERSPECTIVE

AIDS Knowledge Among College Freshmen Students

Do college freshmen need sex education about AIDS? Fielstein et al. (1992) administered a 40-item measure of AIDS knowledge to 175 entering college freshmen. Students averaged 90 percent correct responses on this measure, yet there were some significant gaps in AIDS knowledge discovered on particular items. The percentages of correct responses for each item appear in Tables 1.1 and 1.2.

Questions for Thought

Based on your interpretation of these data, to what extent do you think freshmen college students need more education about AIDS? In what areas? Only 89 percent of students correctly answered that "anal intercourse increases risk." What is your reaction to this finding?

Source: Tables from E. M. Fielstein, L. L. Fielstein, & M. G. Hazlewood (1992), AIDS knowledge among college freshmen students: Need for education? *Journal of Sex Education and Therapy, 18,* 45–54. Reprinted by permission of the Guilford Press.

TABLE 1.2 **Percentages Correct on Each Item of AIDS Knowledge Test: General Knowledge Test**

Items	Percentage Correct
1. Identify the disease name (recognize acronym AIDS)	99
2. Recognize immune system breakdown	95
3. Sexual transmission	99
4. Distinguish AIDS from other sexually transmitted diseases	98
5. Deteriorating course	99
6. Early detection does not enable cure of disease	95
7. Causes death in nearly 100% of cases	92
8. There is no cure for AIDS	96
9. Any sex, race or ethnic group is vulnerable	99
10. AIDS not solely a homosexual disease	96
11. Large urban areas have largest number of AIDS cases	93
12. AIDS discovered within the last 10 years	77
13. Distinguish implausible theories of AIDS origin	97
14. Screening test of antibodies, not disease itself	71
15. Negative result does not mean immunity to AIDS	99
16. Positive results without symptoms is possible	90
17. Positive results does not indicate AIDS	38
18. Severe flu-like symptoms are early signs of AIDS	93
19. Seven year or more incubation period after infection	95
20. After infection symptoms do not appear within days	95

TABLE 1.2 **Percentages Correct on Each Item of AIDS Knowledge Test: Transmission and Prevention**

Items	Percentage Correct
21. No risk through casual contact	94
22. Not spread by public toilets, telephones, drinking fountains	95
23. Not spread through sneezing or coughing	90
24. Not spread through shared drinking cups or utensils	85
25. Not spread through handshaking, bumping together	98
26. Hugging, touching, and massaging are not high risk	81
27. Direct oral or anal contact increases risk	94
28. Anal intercourse increases risk	89
29. Heterosexual and homosexual transmission are possible	97
30. Certain heterosexual behaviors increase risk	91
31. Semen ejaculated during intercourse is a mode of transmission	96
32. Sexual contact with multiple partners increases risk	95
33. Not all homosexual behavior is high risk for AIDS	87
34. Donating blood is not a risk factor	82
35. Until recent safeguards, donor blood spread AIDS	95
36. Sharing needles during drug use increases risk	98
37. AIDS may be spread through blood or blood products	95
38. Avoiding certain behaviors may prevent spread	95
39. Safe sex practices may reduce the risk	95
40. Proper use of condoms may reduce the risk of AIDS	97

WHAT IS THE BIOPSYCHOSOCIAL PERSPECTIVE?

**BIOPSYCHOSOCIAL
PERSPECTIVE**

*View that attributes complex sexual
phenomena or events to interacting
biological, psychological, and social
causes.*

The definition of sexology given earlier referred to the interrelationship of biological, psychological, and social perspectives. These three interacting perspectives form the essence of the **biopsychosocial perspective** of human sexuality, which attributes complex sexual phenomena or events to multiple causes (Figure 1.1). In contrast to the biopsychosocial perspective is the *reductionist perspective*, which "reduces" complex sexual phenomena or events to a single cause.

Let's consider an example of applying the biopsychosocial model to human sexuality. Some women find it difficult or impossible to have orgasms during intercourse. This type of sexual problem may be the result of any of a number of causes: *injunctions*, or messages received during childhood—for example, that sex is sinful and not for women's enjoyment; fears of pregnancy; poor communication with the partner about needs and desires; poor control of her pelvic muscles; and inadequate physical stimulation, to name but a few. As a real-life example of how interacting biological, psychological, and social processes can cause a chronic sexual problem, Sally was raised to believe that "nice" women do not enjoy sex or have orgasms. Because she experiences distress about not having orgasms during intercourse with her husband (psychological), she concentrates too much on her sexual performance, which distracts her from fully immersing herself in sexual activity (psychological). In time, her nervous system becomes so aroused that orgasm is difficult or impossible (biological). Berating herself about not having orgasms (psychological), she makes excessive demands of her husband and inadvertently creates a hostile sexual environment that only adds to her problems (social).

The remainder of this chapter discusses each of the three major perspectives of the biopsychosocial model of human sexuality, as well as various perspectives subsumed within each category.

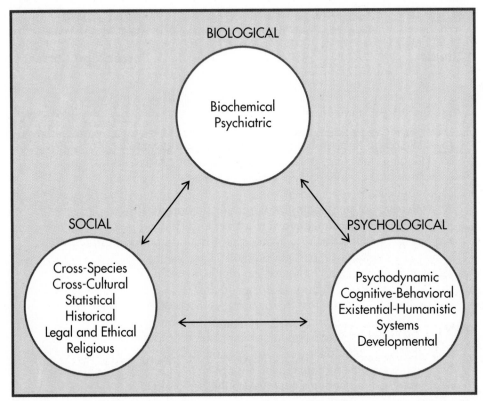

FIGURE 1.1 *The interrelationship of biological, psychological, and social perspectives, according to the biopsychosocial perspective.*

BIOLOGICAL PERSPECTIVES IN HUMAN SEXUALITY

The **biological perspectives** are primarily concerned with the effects of biological and physical processes on an individual's sexual functioning. Topics of sexuality reflecting this category include female and male sexual anatomy and physiology, sexual arousal and response, conception, pregnancy, birth, contraception, abortion, STDs, and the effects of disabilities and illnesses on sexuality. Again, psychological and social factors influence each of these areas, too. For example, although an induced abortion involves medically removing the fetus from the womb, the procedure is inseparable from numerous complex attitudinal, social, legal, ethical, and moral considerations. The biological perspectives include the *biochemical* and *psychiatric perspectives*.

BIOLOGICAL PERSPECTIVES
Views concerned with the effects of biological and physical processes on sexuality.

THE BIOCHEMICAL PERSPECTIVE

At the heart of the **biochemical perspective** lies the belief that all aspects of human functioning—sexual and otherwise—reflect biological and chemical processes. According to this model, sexual disorders are the result of physical disease, structural problems, or chemical imbalances. Biological therapists, such as certain physicians, treat sexual problems by attempting to correct or reverse impaired biological processes. For example, biological therapies for impotence include drug therapy and penile prosthesis implantation.

BIOCHEMICAL PERSPECTIVE
View that sexual functioning reflects biological and chemical processes.

Two popular subcategories of the biochemical perspective are the *neural* and *genetic* perspectives. According to the *neural perspective*, all aspects of human functioning—behavior, thoughts, and emotions—have a basis in nervous system activity. Although neural processes are fairly well understood, the functioning of the nervous system as a whole in controlling behavior is not.

Proponents of the *genetic perspective* believe that all or most aspects of human functioning are genetically determined prior to birth. Nearly all cells of the body have 23 pairs of *chromosomes*, the structures that contain genetic material. Within each pair, one chromosome is received from the father and the other from the mother. Chromosomes contain *genes*, the "blueprint" information about the structure and functioning of the body, including sexual functioning.

THE PSYCHIATRIC PERSPECTIVE

The **psychiatric perspective** has its basis in the biochemical perspective and one or more of the psychological perspectives, described below. For example, for a psychiatrist using the Freudian model, sexual disorders are the result of both biochemical imbalances and repressed desires or conflicts. Treatment, then, might include both drug therapy to correct chemical imbalances and psychoanalysis to help lift the patient's repression. Although today's psychiatrists generally consider biological, psychoanalytic, and psychosocial *etiologies* (causes) to be of equal importance, traditional psychiatry has relied heavily on classical Freudian theory. People often confuse the psychiatric perspective with one or more of the psychological perspectives. These differ primarily in the psychiatric perspective's focus on both biological and mental processes.

PSYCHIATRIC PERSPECTIVE
View that both biological and psychological processes are responsible for sexual functioning.

PSYCHOLOGICAL PERSPECTIVES IN HUMAN SEXUALITY

Those who favor **psychological perspectives** of human sexuality examine how thoughts, attitudes, emotions, and behaviors, accumulated from a lifetime of experiences, affect sexual attitudes and functioning. These perspectives are concerned with attitudes about

PSYCHOLOGICAL PERSPECTIVES
Views concerned with the effects of thoughts, attitudes, emotions, and behaviors on sexuality.

sexuality ("I believe premarital sex is morally wrong"), openness about discussing feelings ("My partner might reject me if I tell him I get turned on by oral sex"), different forms of sexual behavior, how unusual sexual desires and sexual dysfunctions develop, and methods of influencing these areas, among others. The psychological perspectives include the *psychodynamic, cognitive-behavioral, existential-humanistic, systems,* and *developmental perspectives*.

THE PSYCHODYNAMIC PERSPECTIVE

PSYCHODYNAMIC PERSPECTIVE

View that an individual's unconscious motivations determine her or his patterns of interacting in the world.

Based on Freudian theory, the **psychodynamic perspective** is the view that an individual's unconscious motivations and desires determine how he or she interacts in the world. This perspective is similar to the traditional psychiatric perspective, but differs in its focus on psychological rather than biological influences. For example, traditional psychiatric treatment of *vaginismus* (painful spasms of the outer portion of the vagina that make penile penetration difficult or impossible) would typically include drug therapy, whereas psychodynamic treatment would not. Both approaches, however, can reflect common methods of Freudian interpretation. A Freudian psychiatrist and a psychodynamic therapist might consider a woman with vaginismus to have deep-seated conflicts about her "unacceptable" sexual desires, which lead to a "symptom" that prevents the woman from acting out her fantasies.

THE COGNITIVE-BEHAVIORAL PERSPECTIVE

Behaviorists are primarily concerned with the roles that behavior and learning play in an individual's overall functioning. They base their position on *learning theory*, a psychological theory holding that permanent (or relatively permanent) changes in behavior occur as a result of experience. Strict behaviorists like B. F. Skinner have asserted that cognitive, or thinking, activity is relatively unimportant when studying behavior. Yet in recent decades, researchers like David Barlow (1986) have challenged this view, leading to what

A person's thoughts play a major role in sexual arousal and response.

some behavioral scientists have labeled the "cognitive revolution"—widespread acknowl-edgment of the role that cognitive processes play in affecting behavior and emotions.

Central to *cognitive theory* is the idea that thought processes significantly affect daily living. Or as the ancient Greek philosopher Epictetus noted, "People are not disturbed by things but by their view of things." Put simply, the individual's *perception* of events is of critical importance, not necessarily the events themselves.

Many experts believe that the learning perspective is incomplete if the role of cogni-tion is ignored. This position has given rise to the **cognitive-behavioral perspective,** which incorporates both learning and cognitive theories. One example of a comprehen-sive model of cognitive-behaviorism is Albert Ellis's (1962) *rational-emotive therapy* (RET), a type of therapy for eliminating irrational beliefs. Besides proving useful for deal-ing with issues of everyday living, RET has been successfully applied to numerous clinical problems, including sexual dysfunctions (Bernard & DiGiuseppe, 1989) and anxiety dis-orders (Warren & Zgourides, 1991).

COGNITIVE-BEHAVIORAL PERSPECTIVE
View that learning, behavior, and thinking processes each play a role in determining how an individual interacts in the world.

THE EXISTENTIAL-HUMANISTIC PERSPECTIVE

The **existential-humanistic perspective** stresses the importance of immediate experience, self-acceptance, and self-actualization. Being aware of feelings is an important aspect of this perspective. Sexually speaking, focusing too much on the past or future detracts from the present experience of sexual pleasure, a frequent cause of sexual problems. In contrast, being self-accepting and at ease with sexuality can do much to promote self-fulfillment through a loving relationship.

EXISTENTIAL-HUMANISTIC PERSPECTIVE
View that stresses the importance of immediate experience, self-acceptance, and self-actualization.

THE SYSTEMS PERSPECTIVE

"No man is an island": Here John Donne reminds us that the great majority of people exist as members of one or more social groups or systems. The **systems perspective** is con-cerned with how different social systems interact and influence individuals, couples, and families. The most common social systems are family, school, work, community, and reli-gious systems.

People may receive conflicting or unhealthy messages about sexuality from their par-ents, school, and/or religion. Knowing which system gave what message is both enlight-ening and helpful for challenging these messages. Furthermore, identifying and analyzing how particular social systems interact is basic to understanding sexual behavior. Consider a child who acts out sexually at school, exposing himself to classmates. He may be doing this in response to problems at home, such as trouble getting along with siblings or being a victim of sexual abuse.

SYSTEMS PERSPECTIVE
View concerned with how different social systems interact and influence individuals, couples, and families.

THE DEVELOPMENTAL PERSPECTIVE

Sexuality is a dynamic process, even though many of our sexual patterns form early in childhood. From birth until death, people are sexual beings. They continue to learn, change, and grow. The **developmental perspective** deals with various changes, including sexual, that occur throughout the life span. Developmental specialists confront such ques-tions as these: Are children sexual? How does puberty affect an individual's view of the world? What are the unique sexual needs of older adults?

DEVELOPMENTAL PERSPECTIVE
View concerned with how changes occur throughout the life span.

SOCIAL PERSPECTIVES IN HUMAN SEXUALITY

What is typical for a particular group of people is only one aspect of the **social perspec-tives,** which are concerned with social and cultural influences and values. Topics of human sexuality within this category of perspectives include gender identity and roles,

SOCIAL PERSPECTIVES
Views concerned with the effects of society and culture on sexuality.

We are sexual beings from birth until death.

sexuality throughout the life span, sexual orientation, sexual commercialism, sexual victimization, law and ethics, and religion. Of course, biology and psychology are strong influences in many of these areas. At least one current explanation for sexual orientation, for example, acknowledges the presence of both social and biological antecedents (Money, 1988). The social perspectives include the *cross-species, cross-cultural, statistical, historical, legal and ethical,* and *religious perspectives.*

CROSS-SPECIES PERSPECTIVE
View that similarities and differences exist across species.

THE CROSS-SPECIES PERSPECTIVE

Obviously, humans beings are members of the animal kingdom. The **cross-species perspective** considers the similarities in and differences between human behavior and that of

Understanding the sexual behavior of animals can increase understanding of our own sexuality.

other animals. Such a comparison of sexual behavior across species can provide valuable insights into the nature of human sexuality. For example, masturbation occurs in various species of mammals besides humans, as does homosexual behavior (Carpenter, 1942; Erwin & Maple, 1976; Ford & Beach, 1951).

THE CROSS-CULTURAL PERSPECTIVE

The study of human sexuality must address cultural differences and issues. Research studies and social investigations have determined that sexual beliefs, practices, and values can differ considerably from culture to culture (Suggs & Miracle, 1993). That which is acceptable to one group may not be to another. Hence, the term *cross-cultural relativity* refers to the comparative nature of customs and standards of behavior within a community or system. Remaining alert to cultural differences increases opportunities to challenge *sex-role stereotypes*, or beliefs within a society as to how members of each sex should appear and act. The **cross-cultural perspective,** then, takes into account the many variations that exist across cultures.

CROSS-CULTURAL PERSPECTIVE
View that variations in customs, norms, and standards exist across cultures.

THE STATISTICAL PERSPECTIVE

The **statistical perspective** is based on the frequency of occurrence of an attitude or practice within a society. Although extremes occur within any group, statistical measurement is concerned with the characteristics of the largest number of members—in other words, the "average" members' characteristics. For example, research suggests that male masturbation is very common. Michael et al. (1994) found that about 60 percent of surveyed males ages 18 to 59 reported having masturbated in the past year.

STATISTICAL PERSPECTIVE
View that group norms are defined by the frequency of occurrence of an attitude or behavior within a society.

THE HISTORICAL PERSPECTIVE

The **historical perspective** deals with sexual topics and issues from the point of view of historical attitudes, values, practices, and contexts. Making sense of the many complex issues associated with human sexuality is easier when we examine the roles that such issues have played in history. For instance, many of today's social attitudes concerning homosexuality reflect Jewish mores and standards, first elucidated around 1400 B.C. (Ryrie, 1978).

HISTORICAL PERSPECTIVE
View that variations in customs, norms, and standards exist across time and influence the future.

Sexuality often has different meanings for people of different backgrounds and cultures.

THE LEGAL AND ETHICAL PERSPECTIVE

LEGAL AND ETHICAL PERSPECTIVE
View that legal and ethical standards affect an individual's choice of behavior.

The **legal and ethical perspective,** as the name implies, concerns the effects of legal and ethical standards on individuals. Members of society elect officials who pass *laws* permitting or forbidding certain types of conduct. Laws allow society as a whole to regulate the behavior of its members.

Ethics are self-regulatory guidelines. Individuals use ethics to guide their daily life decisions. They also use ethics to define their professional organizations and the expected conduct of their members. Many such organizations, including the American Psychological Association and the American Association of Sex Educators, Counselors, and Therapists, have developed *ethical codes* that guide practitioners as they self-regulate behavior, with the intention of not harming others by assuring proper use of skills and techniques.

THE RELIGIOUS PERSPECTIVE

RELIGIOUS PERSPECTIVE
View that religious doctrine and scriptures affect an individual's choice of behavior.

The **religious perspective** deals with the effects that religious doctrines, scriptures, and spirituality have on individuals and society. For people raised in a religious environment, the teachings, morals, and values set forth by organized religion can play a powerful role for life, be it healthy, harmful, or neutral. Nowhere is this more the case than with sexuality.

Religion can play a significant role in shaping people's attitudes about sexuality.

A specific subcategory of the religious perspective is the *supernatural perspective*, which holds that supernatural forces (for example, God, angels, demons, and/or animal spirits) can influence human thinking and behavior. Supernatural forces work in two ways: either internally (the Holy Spirit versus demonic possession) or externally (angelic intervention versus demonic influence). Accordingly, an unusual sexual practice might be viewed as symptomatic of demonic activity rather than unconscious conflicts, faulty learning, and the like. Treatments for unsanctioned behavior or attitudes range from praying to "good forces" for help to exorcising evil spirits. Still endorsed by many groups today, the supernatural perspective was most prevalent from the days of antiquity until the eighteenth century.

For Personal Reflection

To what extent is the religious perspective an important part of your personal view of human sexuality?

KEY POINTS

1. The term *sexual* originally referred to person's being male or female. In the last hundred years or so, *sexuality*, or *sex*, has come to refer to *procreational*, *recreational*, and *relational* activities.

2. *Sexology* is a discipline of scientific inquiry that recognizes humans of all cultures as sexual beings "in process," and identifies the interacting biological, psychological, and social components that influence this process.

3. Reasons for studying human sexuality vary. Some of the more common reasons include to obtain knowledge, gain personal insight, become more at ease with one's own sexuality, develop sexual self-acceptance, maximize communication and intimacy, maximize sexual pleasure, manage fertility, avoid sexual dysfunctions, avoid sexually transmitted diseases, and bring about positive social changes.

4. Taking a human sexuality class is one form of *sexual education*, a primary goal of which is *learning to make rational, effective decisions about sexuality*.

5. The field of human sexuality is *holistic* and embodies numerous diverse perspectives. Interacting biological, psychological, and social perspectives form the essence of the *biopsychosocial perspective* of human sexuality.

6. The *biological perspectives*, which include the *biochemical* and *psychiatric perspectives*, are primarily concerned with the effects of biological and physical processes on sexual functioning.

7. The *psychological perspectives*, which include the *psychodynamic*, *cognitive-behavioral*, *existential-humanistic*, *systems*, and *developmental perspectives*, are primarily concerned with the roles that thoughts, attitudes, emotions, and behaviors play in sexual functioning.

8. The *social perspectives*, which include the *cross-species*, *cross-cultural*, *statistical*, *historical*, *legal and ethical*, and *religious perspectives*, are primarily concerned with the effects of social and cultural forces on sexual functioning.

ACTIVITIES AND QUESTIONS

1. With a discussion partner, take turns talking about your expectations for studying human sexuality. How do you think your expectations might change during your course of study? What do you hope to gain by taking this course? Regroup as a class and discuss these same topics.

2. Write down some of the messages about sexuality that you received during childhood and adolescence. What patterns, if any, are apparent? In a small-group format, compare your findings.

3. As a class, discuss the pros and cons of sexual education. Should sex education be taught in public school? At what grade? What are the roles of family and religion in the sex education process? What are some of the important elements of a good sex education program? What are some elements to avoid? How can an instructor help or hinder personal reflection and group discussion about sexuality?

4. What are some of the benefits of remaining alert to cultural issues when studying human sexuality? Interview someone from a culture other than yours on her or his attitudes about human sexuality. What is considered normal and abnormal for that culture? Are people in that culture free to talk openly about sexuality? Are people in that culture sensitive to the mores and standards of *other* cultures?

5. How can restricting certain sexual behaviors be helpful or harmful to a society?

RECOMMENDED READINGS

Calderone, M. S., & Johnson, E. W. (1989). *The family book about sexuality* (rev. ed.). New York: Harper & Row. A readable overview of human sexuality, with sections on sexually transmitted diseases and sexual education.

Gregersen, E. (1983). *Sexual practices: The story of human sexuality*. New York: Franklin Watts. Detailed information on human sexuality, collected from various cultures.

Kiefer, D.(1993). *Sexual life in ancient Rome*. New York: Dorset Press. Describes the sexual practices of the Romans, including the role that power played in the people's "appetite for sadism."

Licht, H. (1993). *Sexual life in ancient Greece*. New York: Dorset Press. Describes the sexual practices of the Greeks, including the influence of sexuality on human creativity and artistic expression.

Masters, W. H., Johnson, V. E., & Kolodny, R. C. (1994). *Heterosexuality*. New York: Harper Collins. Advertised as the "up-to-date, comprehensive book of male-female love, pleasure, health and well-being by the world's foremost team of sexual researchers-therapists."

Suggs, D. N., & Miracle, A. W. (Eds.). (1993). *Culture and human sexuality*. Pacific Grove, CA: Brooks/Cole. An up-to-date and informative collection of readings that describe sexual attitudes and practices from different parts of the world.

Tannahill, R. (1980). *Sex in history*. New York: Scarborough House/Stein and Day. A classic volume on the history of sexuality from prehistoric times to the present.

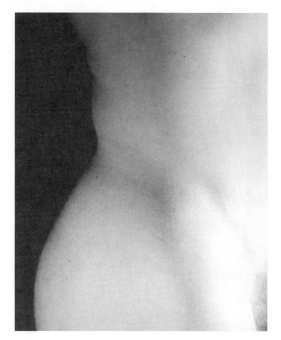

C H A P T E R   2

S E X U A L   R E S E A R C H

O B J E C T I V E S

AFTER READING THIS CHAPTER YOU SHOULD BE
ABLE TO . . .

1. DESCRIBE THE MOST COMMON RESEARCH
   METHODS USED TO STUDY HUMAN SEXUALITY.
2. DISCUSS THE ADVANTAGES AND DISADVANTAGES
   OF EACH METHOD OF SEX RESEARCH.
3. IDENTIFY SOME OF THE LEADING SEX
   RESEARCHERS, AS WELL AS THEIR
   CONTRIBUTIONS TO THE FIELD OF SEXOLOGY.
4. EXPLAIN THE DIFFERENCES BETWEEN THE SEX
   RESEARCH OF SCIENTISTS AND THAT OF POPULAR
   MAGAZINES.
5. DISCUSS HOW SEX RESEARCH CAN BENEFIT
   BOTH INDIVIDUALS AND SOCIETY.

P E R S O N A L   A S S E S S M E N T

WHAT ARE YOUR THOUGHTS AND FEELINGS ON SEX RESEARCH? TO EXPLORE THIS, READ THE FOLLOWING STATEMENTS AND RESPOND USING THE RATING SCALE: 3 = I *completely agree* WITH THE STATEMENT; 2 = I *mostly agree* WITH THE STATEMENT; 1 = I *mostly disagree* WITH THE STATEMENT; 0 = I *completely disagree* WITH THE STATEMENT. REMEMBER, THERE ARE NO RIGHT OR WRONG ANSWERS HERE; IT'S YOUR OPINION THAT COUNTS.

_____ 1. Sex researchers are probably "peeping toms" at heart.

_____ 2. Sex researchers should mainly focus their studies on young people.

_____ 3. I feel comfortable talking to others about my sex life.

_____ 4. I'd be willing to participate in a sexual survey.

_____ 5. If anonymity were assured, my answers to a sexual survey would be 100 percent true.

_____ 6. As part of a sex research project, I'd be willing to be videotaped in a laboratory setting while talking about my sex life.

_____ 7. As part of a sex research project, I'd be willing to be videotaped in a laboratory setting while engaging in sexual activity.

_____ 8. Some sexual topics are so personal that they shouldn't be researched.

_____ 9. Sex research published in popular magazines is just as important as research published in scientific journals and books.

_____ 10. Sexologists should be allowed to conduct basically any kind of research they want, as long as the research is done to increase knowledge and advance the field of sexology.

Truth in science can be defined as the working hypothesis best suited to open the way to the next better one.

Konrad Lorenz

At one time you may have seen an announcement somewhere—perhaps at your college or in the newspaper—calling for volunteers for a sex research project. You may have heard about sex research from a teacher or friend. Or you may have read about the latest sex survey in a magazine. If you're like most people, you probably want to know more about these studies. How do investigators study sexuality? What methods do they use? How do they know if people are being honest when they fill out questionnaires? Do some researchers actually monitor people while they masturbate or have sex? Intriguing questions, indeed.

WHAT IS SEX RESEARCH?

People are curious about anything that has to do with sexuality. Just consider the popularity of magazines, movies, television shows, commercials, and books that include it. Sex sells! At least that is what the advertising industry would have us believe. Nor is interest in sexuality new. People have always wanted to know more about the sexual practices, feelings, and attitudes of others.

Interest in gathering information about sexuality prompted researchers earlier in this century to devise methods of studying sexuality in a systematic, organized fashion. **Sexual research** is the scientific means of gathering information about various aspects of sexuality for the purpose of acquiring knowledge that is applicable to both individuals and

SEXUAL RESEARCH
Scientific means of gathering information and drawing conclusions about sexuality.

groups. The earliest methods of studying sexuality involved reviewing case histories of patients and interviewing large numbers of people. More recent methods include observing volunteers' sexual responses in a laboratory and conducting experiments. Sexology has made advances in recent decades as sex researchers have used more sophisticated techniques and as the general public has become more open to the idea of sex research (Reiss, 1993; Tiefer, 1994; Udry, 1993).

For Personal Reflection
Why do you think sex research was for the most part neglected until this century?

SEXOLOGY AS SCIENCE

The definition of sexology presented in Chapter 1 made use of the phrase *scientific discipline*. What is science? And how is the study of sexuality scientific?

Many students (and even some instructors) do not think of social sciences, like sociology and psychology, as true sciences, like physics and chemistry. While there are inherent differences between the "soft" and "hard" sciences, the same basic principles of inquiry apply. The term *science* comes from the Latin *scire*, meaning "to know." For many centuries, *science* referred to nearly every discipline of inquiry. Only in the last couple of hundred years or so has the term come to refer to specific research methods and values. Today, a particular area of study is a *scientific discipline* if its researchers use the **scientific method**—a systematic approach to investigating questions and problems through accurate and objective *observation*, *direct experimentation*, *collection and analysis of data*, and *replication* of these procedures. In other words, scientists emphasize the importance of gathering information carefully, remaining unbiased when evaluating information, observing phenomena, conducting experiments, and accurately recording procedures and results. They are also concerned with having their findings confirmed by other scientists.

Is sex research scientific? *Absolutely*. By definition, *sexology* is the scientific study of sexuality. But *why* is sexology a science? Because *sexologists* (professional sex researchers, educators, and therapists) rely on the scientific method. Like other scientists, sex researchers stress accurate and unbiased collection and analysis of data, systematic observation, experimentation, and skepticism about their findings. In short, whether or not a particular discipline is a science has more to do with the methods used than with the particular subject area studied.

SCIENTIFIC METHOD
Systematic approach to research involving specific methods and values.

BASIC CONCEPTS IN SEX RESEARCH

Before discussing methods of sex research, a review of some basic research concepts is in order. Investigators often begin a research study after deriving ideas for their study from a specific *theory*, or an integrated set of statements for explaining various phenomena. Because a theory is too general or vague to test in a study, they generate a *hypothesis*, or a specific testable prediction from the theory, and test this instead of the theory. The results of the study either *disprove* or do *not disprove* the hypothesis. If disproved, the investigators cannot make predictions and must question the accuracy of the theory. If not disproved, they can then make predictions based on the hypothesis.

A primary goal of sex research is to discover the sexual differences, trends, and patterns of members of a *population*, or a group that is the object of study. *Subjects* are the members of a population who participate in a study. Investigators hope that the characteristics of their *sample* of the population are representative of the characteristics of the entire population. If so, they can *generalize*, or apply, their results to the population. The most representative sample is generally a *random sample*, in which each member of a population has an equal chance of being selected as a subject.

A researcher who uses a test or questionnaire in a study is concerned with the test's *reliability*, or its ability to provide consistent results when administered on different occasions. He or she is also interested in the test's *validity*, or its ability to measure what it purports to measure.

In *qualitative research* information collected from subjects may take the form of verbal descriptions of particular events, such as what an orgasm feels like, or direct observations of events, such as sexual behavior among primates. In *quantitative research* information collected from subjects (for example, a subject's marital status) may take the form of or be converted into numbers (single = 1; married = 2). Although verbal descriptions and observations can be useful in and of themselves, many scientists prefer information collected in the form of numbers to facilitate analysis of data.

To analyze data, investigators use *statistics*, or mathematical procedures for describing and drawing inferences from the data. There are two types of statistics: *descriptive*, used for describing data ("72 percent of women in this study reported having sexual fantasies during intercourse"), and *inferential*, used for making predictions about a larger population based on significant differences found between individuals or groups ("Men exposed to violent pornography are more likely to see violence against women as being acceptable than those men who are not"). Researchers use both types of statistics to draw general conclusions about their sample and population.

EVALUATING SEX RESEARCH

How do you know if the sex research you're reading is quality research? How would you know if it's based on sound scientific methods? How do you decide if the conclusions drawn from the data are true or applicable to you or anyone else? These are questions you should ask yourself whenever you come across a piece of sex research.

Sources of sex research—scholarly journals and books, national magazine surveys, and "television tabloids"—vary considerably in the quality of information published. So you're wise not to accept at face value everything that you read or hear about sex research. The ability to evaluate research and its findings is of critical importance when studying human sexuality (or any other topic, for that matter). Although much accurate information is available, so is a great deal of inaccurate information. Poorly conducted or designed research tends to fuel society's misconceptions about sexuality, if not cause downright panic.

Professional journals and periodicals are perhaps the most important sources of scientific information about sexuality. Because professional researchers and clinicians contribute the majority of material to these journals, and because peers review their material, the research published tends to be of very high quality. Some of the leading sexuality journals are *Annual Review of Sex Research, Archives of Sexual Behavior, Family Life Educator, Family Planning Perspectives, Journal of Homosexuality, Journal of Marriage and the Family, Journal of Psychology & Human Sexuality, Journal of Sex & Marital Therapy, Journal of Sex Education and Therapy, Journal of Sex Research, Medical Aspects of Human Sexuality,* and *Planned Parenthood Review.* Popular magazines and television generally are not accurate sources of scientific information about sexuality, because studies reported in these media tend to be sensationalistic and poorly constructed.

You should think about several general issues when deciding if a piece of research is valid. Asking the following questions can help you in this process:

1. Are the researchers qualified to conduct sexual studies? What are their credentials? Are they associated with a clinic, academic institution, or laboratory?

How do you know if the sex research you read about is scientifically sound?

2. What research method is used? What are the advantages and disadvantages of this method? Do the researchers acknowledge the limitations associated with their particular methods?
3. Are the questionnaires or tests used both reliable and valid?
4. Do the researchers make generalizations about a larger population? If so, how representative of the population is their sample?
5. Is the sample sexually biased, consisting of more men than women, or vice versa? Is the sample biased in any other way? Does it include minorities? Is the sample exclusively urban or rural?
6. If the research is an experiment, is there a *control group* not exposed to the experimental conditions to compare with the experimental group?
7. Do the researchers use the most appropriate statistical test(s) to analyze data, or do they simply comment on what appear to be patterns?
8. Are the conclusions drawn from the data presented in such a way as to acknowledge other possibilities?
9. Are there any published studies that support or contradict the researchers' methods or findings?

As any seasoned researcher will tell you, this list of questions is by no means exhaustive. Colleges and universities offer entire courses of study in statistics and research methodology, the contents of which are beyond the scope of this book. Nevertheless, reading through and thinking about these questions should give you a general sense of the kinds of issues to consider as you evaluate various research studies.

METHODS OF SEX RESEARCH

Researchers use many different methods to study sexuality. Six of the most popular of these are *case study, survey, observational, cross-cultural, correlational,* and *experimental* research methods.

CASE STUDY RESEARCH

CASE STUDY RESEARCH
In-depth study of an individual or small group.

In **case study research,** investigators conduct a focused study of an individual, or in some cases a small group of individuals. The individual typically has a rare condition or has responded favorably to a new treatment. Hence, a case study is usually clinical in nature. The researchers (often a physician, psychologist, social worker, counselor, or educator) may or may not use self-report measures and questionnaires to obtain quantifiable data on the client. Like experimental research, a case study can involve weeks, months, or even years of contact between the investigator and subject.

A typical case report follows a four-part format:

1. *Presenting problem*—the condition or problem that brings the client into treatment, including assessment of the problem.
2. *Case history*—a brief social history that is pertinent to the client's condition.
3. *Treatment*—a description of the treatment process, including procedures and details of each session.
4. *Results of treatment*—a description of treatment effects, if any.

Case studies are valuable in that they provide useful information about individuals, rare conditions, and new therapies. For example, much information about sexual abuse, rape, and sexual disorders has emerged in this way. On the negative side, case studies tend to focus on pathology and their results generally apply only to individuals with similar conditions instead of the general public. Moreover, the high probability of interviewer bias affecting clients' reactions to treatment limits the generalizability of this method of research.

Let's now turn to two of the best-known early researchers to employ the case study method to investigate sexuality: Kraft-Ebing and Freud.

Kraft-Ebing Richard von Kraft-Ebing (1840–1902) was a Victorian physician who worked mostly with sexually disordered patients. He based his writings about sexuality on about two hundred case studies. Kraft-Ebing supported popular Victorian views about sexuality. In his *Psychopathia Sexualis* (1886/1978), he claimed that sexual activity for anything other than reproductive purposes was deviant. Focusing on the bizarre sexual behaviors of his patients, Kraft-Ebing helped to perpetuate Victorian myths of sexuality as equivalent to "disease" and therefore something to fear.

Freud Like Kraft-Ebing, Sigmund Freud (1856–1939) based his writings about sexuality on his clinical work with sexually disordered patients, although most of these initially came to Freud complaining of assorted nonsexual problems. Freud trained as a neuropathologist at the University of Vienna, but he later decided to devote his energy to studying conscious and unconscious mental processes. As a result, Freud developed a comprehensive theory of human behavior known as *psychoanalytic theory*.

In short, Freud believed humans are sexual beings from birth until death, and that most mental disorders are due to unconscious sexual conflicts arising during sensitive developmental periods. For example, Freudian theory might hold that a 6-year-old boy who is punished for handling his genitals could develop conflicts about genital play and later become impotent. One of Freud's most famous books on sexuality is *Three Essays on the Theory of Sexuality* (1905).

More Recent Case Studies Kraft-Ebing and Freud were not the only professionals to use case study method. Today's researchers frequently publish reports of novel treatments of clients with unusual conditions. Most leading sexology journals publish such case studies. For instance, a 1990 issue of the *Journal of Psychology & Human Sexuality* carried two accounts of *paraphilias* (unusual sexual desires and behaviors) in females, and

Sigmund Freud.

a 1992 issue of this same journal carried one on *transvestism* (cross-dressing). Many sexuality books also contain one or more case reports to illustrate innovative approaches to treatment. *Principles and Practice of Sex Therapy*, edited by Sandra Leiblum and Raymond Rosen (1989), is a compilation of chapters and case reports on various sexual disorders and their treatment, written by sexuality experts.

SURVEY RESEARCH

One method of obtaining information about a topic of interest is to ask people about their experiences. **Survey research,** the most frequently used method to research sexuality, involves just that—interviewing or administering written surveys to large numbers of people. Researchers analyze the data obtained from surveys to determine the presence of trends, similarities, and differences. They then draw conclusions about the patterns of the population under investigation.

Conducting survey research has both advantages and disadvantages. Advantages include obtaining information from a large number of subjects, flexibility in timing interviews (for example, conducting personal interviews when it is convenient for the subject) and techniques used (telephone follow-ups), and their relative inexpensiveness. "Mail-in" surveys have the special advantage of assuring anonymity and thus inclining subjects to respond honestly.

Disadvantages include *distortion, interviewer bias,* and *volunteer bias. Distortion* occurs when a subject, for whatever reason, does not respond to questions truthfully. *Interviewer bias* involves an interviewer's expectations or insignificant gestures, like smiling or frowning, inadvertently swaying a subject's responses one way or the other. *Volunteer bias* occurs when a sample of volunteers is not representative of the general population. People who are willing to talk about sexual matters may respond differently on surveys than those who

SURVEY RESEARCH
Use of questionnaires, self-report measures, or interviews with large numbers of people.

are not. Interestingly, there is little or no empirical support for the notion that repeated questionnaire completion will affect sexual behaviors (Halpern et al., 1994).

Several factors can affect the outcome of any type of research, survey or otherwise. One involves finding a sample that is representative of the population being studied. Another involves controlling for extraneous variables, such as room temperature or noise level, that might affect the results of the research. Still another is *experimenter bias,* in which the researcher's expectations about what should or should not happen in the study affect the results.

Ellis   A key figure in early sex research was Henry Havelock Ellis (1859–1939), one of the first investigators to use sexual surveys. A British psychologist, Ellis worked to increase society's understanding and acceptance of sexuality by acquiring information from "well-balanced" rather than disturbed individuals. Many of his beliefs about sexuality—that masturbation is a normal practice for both sexes and does not cause insanity, that children need sex education at an early age, that sexual behavior varies across cultures—were "ahead of their time," contradicting the generally accepted beliefs of his day. Ellis's most famous writings on sexuality are a series of volumes entitled *Studies in the Psychology of Sex* (1896–1928/1936) and *Psychology of Sex: A Manual for Students* (1933).

Kinsey   Certainly the most famous wide-scale sexual surveys are those of Alfred Kinsey (1894–1956), a biologist with a background in evolutionary processes. When asked in 1937 to teach a course in human sexuality at Indiana University, Kinsey was unable to locate a sufficient amount of reliable information on the topic. During the next 16 years, Kinsey and his associates collected data themselves, interviewing and obtaining sexual histories on 5,300 American men and 5,940 American women of different ages and backgrounds. His research culminated in the publication of *Sexual Behavior in the Human Male* (1948) and *Sexual Behavior in the Human Female* (1953), two books that were widely publicized in both scientific journals and the popular media. Until the mid-1960s, Kinsey's research was the only sexual information of its type available to social scientists.

Kinsey set out to dispel myths about sexuality. With special interest in Americans' sexual "outlets," Kinsey amassed data on such topics as masturbation, extramarital relationships, and homosexuality. Naturally, some of his findings were (and still are) controversial. For example, respondents reported having more extramarital relationships than researchers had previously suspected. The same was found true of respondent's homosexual experiences.

Alfred Kinsey.

Although generally regarded as the largest and most comprehensive sexual survey to date, Kinsey's research exemplifies some of the problems inherent in survey research. He based his reports on information from volunteers, who may or may not have had ulterior motives for participating in the studies (volunteer bias). The surveys recorded what subjects *said* they did, not necessarily what they actually did (distortion). And Kinsey's subjects were mostly educated, urban, and white (nonrepresentative sample). Although most sexologists still respect Kinsey's work as the first large-scale survey of Americans' sexual attitudes and behavior, noting how remarkable it was that he was able to conduct such research when he did, others claim much of his research is unscientific and therefore the source of some of today's sexual misinformation (Reisman & Eichel, 1990).

Hunt In the early 1970s, the Playboy Foundation commissioned the Research Guild, an independent research organization, to conduct a large-scale survey of American's sexual practices. Journalist Morton Hunt wrote up his findings in a series of *Playboy* magazine articles. The foundation was interested in updating Kinsey's findings, this time including in the study those groups of people that Kinsey had not surveyed, as well as comparing Kinsey's and Hunt's results to see if there had been any changes in sexual patterns since the 1940s and 1950s. In fact, Hunt found that certain sexual practices, such as premarital intercourse, were more commonplace than in Kinsey's day. He also found fewer differences in gender roles. Hunt's findings later appeared in the book *Sexual Behavior in the 1970s* (Hunt, 1974).

Hunt's sample, gathered by random selection from telephone listings across America, consisted of 982 males and 1,044 females. Only about 20 percent of those originally contacted were willing to participate in the study, which consisted of small group discussions followed by self-administered questionnaires. Hunt also conducted a number of follow-up interviews. His sample supposedly represented the nation's population in terms of sex, age, race, level of education, occupation, and rural versus urban background. The self-report questionnaires contained 1,000 to 1,200 items covering such topics as sexual practices, experiences, and attitudes.

Critics have questioned Hunt's report for several reasons. Because only 20 percent of potential subjects agreed to participate in his study, there was an 80 percent refusal rate, increasing the likelihood that volunteer bias influenced his results. Moreover, Hunt's sample was drawn from telephone listings, so people with unlisted phone numbers or no telephone at all were excluded from the study.

Hite Shere Hite published the results of her survey of female sexuality in *The Hite Report* (1976). She mailed an essay-style questionnaire to 100,000 individuals and women's organizations between 1972 and 1976, many of whom had responded to Hite's advertisements in such magazines as *Bride's*, *Ms.*, *The Village Voice*, and *Mademoiselle*. Hite received 3,019 completed questionnaires from women who expressed their views and feelings about a variety of sexual topics, from orgasm to masturbation to same-sex affairs. Hite also surveyed about 7,000 men for *The Hite Report on Male Sexuality* (1981), and 4,500 women for *Women and Love: A Cultural Revolution in Progress* (1987).

Are Hite's reports representative of the sexual attitudes of American women and men in general? Clearly not. In fact, critics have repeatedly questioned her research methods and conclusions because of self-selected biased samples, low questionnaire return rate, and anecdotal evidence in the form of essays, rather than statistical analysis of data.

Magazine Surveys In the last 20 years or so, a number of popular magazines have conducted large-scale surveys of readers' sexual behaviors and attitudes. Some of the more famous are *Psychology Today* (Athanasiou et al., 1970; Rubenstein, 1983), *Redbook* (Levin & Levin, 1975; Tavris & Sadd, 1977), *Ladies' Home Journal* (Schultz, 1980), *McCall's*

PERSPECTIVE

Sex in America: A Definitive Survey

Highly respected researchers Robert Michael, John Gagnon, and Edward Laumann designed and administered a scientific survey to a random sample of 3,432 Americans, ages 18-59. Following are just a few of the interesting findings from this groundbreaking survey:

- Men reported having sex on average 7 times per month; women, 6 times per month.
- Seventy-five percent of men reported always having an orgasm during sex, compared with 29 percent of women.
- Sixty percent of men and 40 percent of women reported having masturbated during the past year.
- Forty-one percent of men and 16 percent of women reported having purchased erotic materials during the past year.
- Twenty-four percent of husbands reported having had at least one affair, compared with 15 percent of wives.
- Twenty-two percent of women reported having been forced to engage in sexual activity, compared with 2 percent of men.
- Altough 2.8 percent of men and 1.4 percent of women identified themselves as bisexual or homosexual, about 9 percent of men and 4 percent of women reported having had at least one same-sex experience.

Questions for Thought

What kinds of information do surveys such as this one provide about American's sex lives? What do they not provide? Would you ever consider participating in a sex survey? Why or why not?

(Gittelson, 1980), *Cosmopolitan* (Bowe, 1992; Wolfe, 1981), *Consumer Reports* (Brecher et al., 1984), *New Woman* (Schwartz & Jackson, 1989), and *Details/Mademoiselle* (Rubenstein, 1993; Radakovich, 1994). Data from these surveys can sometimes be "eye-opening," given their often enormous number of respondents. Yet very little, if any, of their information is necessarily applicable to the general public.

OBSERVATIONAL RESEARCH

Distortion is one serious limitation of sexual surveys. Subjects may not give completely honest accounts of their sexual experiences and responses. They may feel embarrassed, fail to remember an event, or not take the survey seriously. Beginning in the 1960s, a number of researchers decided that one way around this problem was to monitor subjects' sexual responses directly, usually in a laboratory. This method of research is **observational research.**

OBSERVATIONAL RESEARCH
Monitoring subjects visually and/or physiologically.

Masters and Johnson Probably the best-known research team to employ observational methods is William Masters and Virginia Johnson. The goal of their observational research into human sexuality was to focus "quite literally upon what men and

Maxine © Marian Henley. *Reprinted by permission of the artist*

women do in response to effective sexual stimulation, and why they do it, rather than on what people say they do or even think their sexual reactions and experiences might be" (1966, p. 20).

Masters and Johnson's observational research involved having 312 male and 382 female subjects engage in a variety of sexual activities while connected to various types of equipment designed to measure physiological responses. For example, some female subjects masturbated using a camera-equipped artificial penis. Masters and Johnson observed and analyzed approximately 10,000 sexual episodes over a period of 12 years, leading to publication of their famous book *Human Sexual Response* (1966). Their book on treating sexual problems, *Human Sexual Inadequacy* (1970) followed shortly thereafter.

William Masters and Virginia Johnson.

More recently, Masters and Johnson (1979) used observational research to study the sexual responses of 94 homosexual males and 82 homosexual females. They were interested in discovering if any differences exist between homosexual and heterosexual responses. None were noted, except that homosexuals tended to be more knowledgeable about techniques for stimulating their partners.

Like survey research, observational research has limitations, especially volunteer bias. Volunteers may not be representative of the population as a whole. Individuals who agree to be monitored during sexual activity may function differently than those who do not. Subjects may also function differently in a laboratory setting than they do at home.

For Personal Reflection

Consider this scenario: Your favorite instructor tells you she recently secured a grant from a major sexuality foundation to study masturbation, with the eventual goal of producing a series of videotapes on the subject. The instructor asks you to participate in the project and to masturbate while being videotaped. She guarantees your anonymity; no one will watch you. The camera will already be on before you start, and set so that your face won't be taped. You'll turn in your tape anonymously to the instructor, so that she doesn't know who is masturbating on any particular tape. She also says that the project has been approved by your university's institutional review board, and that you'll be given an informed consent release to sign. Your instructor tells you that she is in a fix and really needs volunteers, especially students she can count on, like you.

Would you agree to participate in this project? If so, under what conditions? What issues or concerns would influence your decision? Would you feel comfortable asking to see a copy of your instructor's grant? Why or why not?

CROSS-CULTURAL RESEARCH

CROSS-CULTURAL RESEARCH
Studying the varaiations that exist across cultures.

PARTICIPANT OBSERVATION RESEARCH
Studying subjects from within their community or social system.

Being sensitive to others' customs, attitudes, and practices requires knowledge of their cultures and societies. This is why some sex researchers conduct **cross-cultural research,** or research designed to reveal the variations existing among different groups of people. Most cross-cultural research involves survey, direct observation, and *participant observation* methods of research. The latter of these—**participant observation**—involves an "observer" actually becoming a member of his or her subjects' community. An advantage of participant observeration research is the opportunity it provides to see what really happens sexually in a community, and then consider that information within the existing social, political, economic, and religious systems.

One society that has been the subject of cross-cultural research is Mangaia, a small South Pacific, Polynesian island. The sexual practices of the Mangaians differ significantly from those of North Americans. In general, Mangaians believe that frequent sexual contact is beneficial and necessary for good health. Sexual training begins early. Mangaian families typically live in one-room huts, where children watch their parents engage in sexual activity. Parents encourage their children to masturbate. Adolescents improve their sexual skills by practicing with one another, in the hope of eventually attracting a suitable marriage partner. Adult males emphasize bringing their female partners to orgasm, which in Mangaian society appears to be almost universal for both sexes (Marshall, 1971).

All societies have concepts of what defines acceptable sexual behavior within the family and society. Cross-cultural research shows us that what is sexually "normal" or acceptable for one culture may be "abnormal" or unacceptable for another. In other words, Western standards do not necessarily apply to other cultures and societies.

Cross-cultural research helps us better understand the variations existing among different groups of people.

CORRELATIONAL RESEARCH

Is an increase in experience with oral sex associated with an increase in viewing sex as a pleasurable activity? To determine if such a relationship exists, investigators might conduct **correlational research.** A *correlation* is a relationship between two *variables* (or "factors"), which can be events, behaviors, characteristics, or attitudes. The goal of correlational research is to determine if a relationship exists between two variables, and the degree of that relationship. Investigators can use case study method, surveys, interviews, observational research, and participant research to determine if correlations exist.

Correlations are either positive or negative. In a positive correlation, the values of the variables increase or decrease together. In a negative correlation, one value increases while the other decreases. In the case of experience with oral sex and pleasure, Whitley (1989) found a positive correlation for women. That is, the more oral sex experiences the women in his study reported, the more likely they were to think of sex as a pleasurable experience.

Students often confuse correlation with causation. Correlational data do not imply *cause-and-effect* relationships; they do not tell you if one variable causes or has an effect on the other, only that both variables are related in some way. When there is a correlation, changes in the value of one variable reflect changes in the value of the other. To study the effects that one variable has on the other, a researcher must conduct an experiment.

CORRELATIONAL RESEARCH
Identifying the nature of the relationship between two variables.

EXPERIMENTAL RESEARCH

The goal of **experimental research** is to test the effect that the *independent variable*, the variable that the experimenters manipulate, has on the *dependent variable*, the variable that the experimenters observe. More simply, experimental research is concerned with cause-and-effect relationships, or *why* something happens. Only when experimenters carefully control for *extraneous variables* that might interfere with the experiment can they make valid conclusions about the effects of specific variables on other variables.

EXPERIMENTAL RESEARCH
Identifying cause-and-effect relationships.

An example of an area of sex research amenable to experimentation is drug-testing. Within the last several years, investigators have become increasingly interested in testing drugs that might prolong the lives of individuals with HIV (human immunodeficiency virus) infection and AIDS (acquired immunodeficiency syndrome). Much experimental research on the drug *zidovudine* (previously called AZT, or *azidothymidine*) has, in fact, shown that zidovudine slows the progression of AIDS (Goodpasture, 1991; Lundgren et al., 1994; Vella et al., 1992).

Researchers often conduct drug trials on animals to test for effects of drugs proposed for humans. As an example, let's say a researcher gives an experimental AIDS drug to one group of monkeys infected with simian AIDS ("Group A"), but not another group of monkeys ("Group B"), who then serve as a control group. After several drug trials, the researcher wants to see if one group of monkeys lives longer than the other. If Group A lives longer than Group B, the researcher cautiously concludes that the new drug might have an effect on prolonging the lives of monkeys with AIDS. If neither group, or Group B, lives longer, the researcher questions the effectiveness of the experimental drug. Of course, as with all good science, this researcher and others must replicate this study and confirm their results many times before drawing more absolute conclusions.

ETHICS OF SEX RESEARCH

For some, the phrase *sex research* conjures up images of outlandish experiments in which unscrupulous scientists expose unsuspecting subjects to obscene materials, ask them personal questions, or make them undress and have sex with the lab assistants. But are such images true? Are sex researchers really unscrupulous "peeping toms"? Is sex research dangerous? Is it realistic to think of sex research as "fringe" research? The answer to these questions is *no*. Sex researchers, like other scientists, comply with the ethical guidelines set forth by their professional organizations.

You'll recall from Chapter 1 that *ethics* are self-regulatory guidelines that individuals and groups use to make decisions and define their professional organizations and the expected conduct of their members. By implementing an ethical code, such organizations *maintain the integrity of the profession* and *protect the welfare of clients and subjects*. In addition, ethical codes give professionals direction when it comes to dealing with confusing situations. A case in point would be a researcher's decision regarding if and when to intentionally deceive subjects.

Although many professions and organizations, like the American Psychological Association, have ethical principles, the need for such guidelines in sex research is obvious. Given the sensitive nature of sexuality, researchers must take special care to protect their subjects from any harm that might result from participating in a study. For instance, researchers who require extensive interviewing about subjects' sexual histories should screen their subjects beforehand to ensure that such interviewing will not be upsetting. They should also inform subjects about their expected roles in the study, and the potential risks of participating. Subjects should understand that they can decline to participate or withdraw from the study at any time. Agreeing to participate in a study based on having this kind of information is *informed consent*. Once the study is completed, researchers should provide their subjects with complete details about the study. Providing such details at the conclusion of an experiment is *debriefing*. The great majority of today's sex researchers abide by their respective organizations' ethical principles.

The use of research *deception*, or concealing the purpose and procedures of a study from participants, is especially objectionable to many researchers. Some even believe the intentional use of deception is never justified (Baumrind, 1985). To these researchers, deception reduces the general public's acceptance of and support for research. Yet to other researchers, deception is necessary when prior knowledge of a study would sway subjects' responses and invalidate the results. If subjects learn that the purpose of a study is to measure attitudes of sexual discrimination, they may go to great lengths to avoid appearing prejudiced.

Investigators' primary duty is protecting subjects' welfare. However, even the most ethical and cautious investigators might not be able to anticipate every risk associated with participating in a study. For the most part, by carefully screening subjects, providing subjects with as much information as possible prior to the study, informing subjects of their rights, avoiding deception whenever possible, and debriefing following the study, investigators can do much to minimize the risks of harm to their subjects.

For Personal Reflection

Think about how you'd feel if you'd participated in a sexual experiment only to learn later that you'd been deceived as part of the study. Would your feelings be different if you learned of this deception from the researcher during debriefing, rather than from a lab assistant weeks or months later? What would you say to the researcher in either scenario?

KEY POINTS

1. *Sex research* is a scientific means of gathering information about sexuality. Sexology is a scientific discipline because its researchers use the *scientific method*. Scientists systematically investigate questions and problems through accurate and objective observation, direct experimentation, collection and analysis of data, and replication of these procedures.

2. To conduct sex research, sexologists must generate a testable *hypothesis* from a *theory* about sexuality. They then choose the research method most appropriate for studying the particular topic.

3. It is important to evaluate research findings based on such information as researchers' credentials, techniques used, quality of the sample, and use of statistical analysis.

4. Researchers employ any of a number of methods to study sexuality. In *case study research*, investigators conduct a focused study of an individual, or in some cases a small group of individuals. *Survey research* involves interviewing or administering written surveys to large numbers of people. In *observational research*, investigators visually and/or physiologically monitor subjects' responses in a laboratory setting. Investigators conduct *cross-cultural research* to discover the variations that exist among different groups of people. In *participant observation research*, investigators observe subjects by becoming members of the subjects' community. Investigators use *correlational research* to determine if a relationship exists between two variables. The goal of *experimental research* is to identify cause-and-effect relationships.

5. The need for *ethics* in sex research is obvious. Given the sensitive nature of sexuality, researchers must take special care to protect their subjects from any harm that might result from participating in a study.

ACTIVITIES AND QUESTIONS

1. Divide into small groups and consider the following scenario. As part of a research project, a graduate student visits a men's prison, interviews 20 men, and discovers that a few of these prisoners engage in homosexual activity. The student concludes that almost all the rest of the inmates engage in homosexual activity and are

therefore homosexuals. He then reasons that most criminals must be homosexuals and that most homosexuals are criminals. What is wrong with this student's interpretation of the results of his surveys?

2. Write down the pros and cons of choosing to become a sex researcher. Would you ever consider sex research as a career? Why or why not?

3. As a class, discuss how each of the major sex research studies described in this chapter has influenced the field of sexology. Whose research, in your opinion, has provided the most valuable information about sexuality?

4. How would you go about studying students' attitudes on abortion at your school?

5. Most texts and articles on the ethics of sex research address researchers' responsibilities to subjects and the profession. But what about subjects? Do they have ethical responsibilities, too? Are subjects ethically obliged to answer questions to the best of their abilities? Is it acceptable for subjects to agree to participate in a study, not out of interest in advancing knowledge, but for money or class credit?

RECOMMENDED READINGS

Brecher, E. M. (1979). *The sex researchers*. San Francisco, CA: Specific Press. Readable and interesting accounts of the history of sex research.

Byrne, D., & Kelley, K. (Eds.). (1986). *Alternative approaches to the study of sexual behavior*. Hillsdale, NJ: Lawrence Erlbaum. A review of the various techniques used in modern sex research.

Klassen, A. D., Williams, C. J., & Levitt, E. E. (1989). *Sex and morality in the U.S.* Middletown, CT: Wesleyan University Press. The Kinsey Institute's national survey of sexual morality.

Masters, W. H., & Johnson, V. E. (1966). *Human sexual response*. Boston: Little, Brown. Masters and Johnson's classic account of their mid-1960s observational studies of human sexual response.

Michael, R. T., Gagnon, J. H., Laumann, E. O., & Kolata, G. (1994). *Sex in America: A definitive survey*. Boston: Little, Brown. A survey of American's sexual attitudes and behaviors, heralded by its authors as a "book about sex in America, a true story about sex, based on scientifically accurate survey data."

•**S**EXUALITY AND GENDER

•GENDER IDENTITY

•GENDER ROLES

•GENDER STEREOTYPES

•ANDROGYNY

C H A P T E R   3

GENDER IDENTITY, ROLES, AND STEREOTYPES

O   B   J   E   C   T   I   V   E   S

AFTER READING THIS CHAPTER YOU SHOULD BE
ABLE TO . . .

1. DEFINE AND DISTINGUISH AMONG *SEXUAL ASSIGN-
   MENT, GENDER, GENDER IDENTITY, GENDER ROLE, SEX
   ROLE, SEXUAL ORIENTATION,* AND *SEXUAL IDENTITY.*
2. IDENTIFY THE BIOPSYCHOSOCIAL SOURCES OF
   GENDER IDENTITY AND GENDER ROLES.
3. DESCRIBE THE PROCEDURES INVOLVED IN SEX-
   REASSIGNMENT ("SEX-CHANGE") SURGERY.
4. DESCRIBE THE INFLUENCE THAT GENDER ROLES
   AND STEREOTYPES HAVE ON OUR SOCIETY.
5. DISCUSS THE PROS AND CONS OF ANDROGYNY
   AS A LIFESTYLE.

*B*oys will be boys—and even that wouldn't matter if we could only prevent girls from being girls.

Anthony Hope

Boys are unruly and aggressive. Girls are nurturing and caring. Boys are independent. Girls are dependent. Boys are analytical. Girls are suggestible. Boys have self-confidence. Girls have low self-esteem. The tenacity with which these gender assignments have remained with us is worthy of study in and of itself. In a social environment where equal rights for the sexes is the ideal but double standards the norm, where the feminist movement fights for women's rights, and where sexual harassment is a daily issue for many women and men, it seems ironic that the major manufacturers of disposable diapers continue to market pretty pink ones for girls and baby blue ones for boys. And that's just the beginning. In day care centers, workers give blocks and trucks to boys and dolls to girls. In grade schools, teachers encourage boys to be athletic and girls to be ladylike. In many high schools, advisors suggest that young men take body shop classes and young women take home economics. But who says boys shouldn't sew and girls shouldn't wrestle? Why all this fuss about instilling "traditional" gender roles in our children? Can't we allow children to explore and develop their talents according to their own interests and wants?

The answer to these questions for a lot of people is simple: Males and females of every age are *supposed* to play out their respective *culturally defined* masculine and feminine roles. But there is fallacy in such a statement. Believing that one *must* live out a *predetermined* gender role is one of those irrational rules in life that most people follow, but few really understand. Just because our society defines what behaviors, perceptions, and emotions are "masculine" and "feminine" does not mean these roles are necessarily desirable. Of course, the situation has begun to change with respect to challenging traditional gender roles (Crispell, 1992; Kipnis & Herron, 1993).

"Some women to see you, Anne."

Drawing by Handelsman; © 1978 The New Yorker Magazine, Inc.

Life frequently deviates from fairy tales. The consequences of culturally determined gender assignment and gender roles are real—economically, socially, physically, and psychologically. Because of this, in the following pages we'll closely examine what we know about gender, allowing us to arrive at understandings that are congruent with objective reality and ultimately benefit ourselves, our children, and our society.

SEXUALITY AND GENDER √

In this chapter, you've already encountered the terms *gender* and *gender roles*. So before proceeding, let's back up and define these and some of the other commonly confused terms having to do with gender and related issues. First, the term **sexual assignment,** or **sex** (the latter not to be confused with the popular term for sexual activity, especially intercourse), refers to an individual's biological makeup—her or his genetic, hormonal, and reproductive identity as a female or male. **Gender** refers to both an individual's anatomical sex and the social and cultural aspects of being female or male. An individual's personal sense of being female or male is her or his **gender identity.** Outward expression of her or his gender identity within a social context and according to cultural expectations is a **gender role.** Either sex can enact a gender role (for example, being a homemaker), but not a **sex role,** which is anatomically limited to one sex or the

SEXUAL ASSIGNMENT
An individual's biological makeup as male or female.

GENDER
An individual's anatomical and psychological makeup as male or female.

GENDER IDENTITY
An individual's personal sense of being male or female.

GENDER ROLE
Outward expression of an individual's gender according to cultural expectations.

SEX ROLE
A gender role that is anatomically limited to one sex or the other.

SEXUAL ORIENTATION

An individual's sexual, emotional, romantic, and affectionate attraction to members of the same, opposite, or both sexes.

SEXUAL IDENTITY

An individual's sexual assignment, gender, gender identity, gender role, sex role, and sexual orientation.

other (bearing children). An individual's **sexual orientation** refers to her or his relative sexual attraction to members of the same sex (homosexual), other sex (heterosexual), or both sexes (bisexual). All of these—sexual assignment, gender, gender identity, gender role, sex role, and sexual orientation—form an individual's **sexual identity.**

GENDER IDENTITY

As noted above, *gender identity* refers to an individual's personal, subjective sense of maleness or femaleness—that is, one's internal assertion that "I am female," or "I am male." Where does such identity come from? Are we born with it? Do we learn it? Or both?

While there remains a great deal of uncertainty concerning exactly how gender identity forms, there is virtual unanimity on at least one point—gender identity develops very early in life and is most likely irreversible by age 4. If you don't believe this, try calling a 3- or 4-year-old girl a boy, or boy a girl, and see what happens!

Clearly, there are biological, psychological, and social aspects to the formation of gender identity. Genetics, prenatal and postnatal hormones, differences in the brain and the reproductive organs, and unique socialization patterns all play a role in shaping a person's gender identity. Naturally, these various realities make a strong case for a biopsychosocial model of gender.

In an attempt to sort through the various influences on gender, we first turn our attention to the biological mechanisms believed to bring about gender identity, as well as conditions that arise from abnormalities in these mechanisms.

BIOLOGICAL INFLUENCES ON GENDER IDENTITY

SEXUAL DIFFERENTIATION (DIF-E-REN-SHE-A-SHUN)

Processes that determine sexual assignment.

Without a doubt, males and females differ biologically, both before and after birth. In fact, **sexual differentiation,** or the biological processes by which males become males and females become females, begins early in gestation. The differences brought about by these biological processes ultimately interact with social-learning influences after birth to establish a person's gender identity. Thus, not until postpartum do authorities speak of gender,

Early learning plays a major role in the development of gender identity—the personal sense of being male or female.

gender identity, and gender roles. Male-female differences, whether they be biological or psychological, are termed **sexual differences.**

Chromosomal and Gonadal Differences Determination of an embryo's chromosomal sex is genetic and occurs at conception. In particular, it is a matter of *chromosomes*—the biological structures containing genes or biological "blueprints." The ovum always carries an X chromosome. The sperm carries either a Y or X chromosome. A male baby (XY) is the product of the fusion of an ovum with a sperm carrying a Y chromosome; a female baby (XX), the product of the fusion of an ovum with a sperm carrying an X chromosome. The Y chromosome, which is smaller than its X counterpart, carries little more than the instructions for producing a male, while the X chromosomes provide valuable genetic material essential to life and health, possibly giving the female a "backup" in the event of a defect on one or the other X chromosome.

Male internal and external reproductive organs develop in the presence of the Y chromosome. Consequently, in the absence of the Y chromosome (but normally in the presence of two Xs), female organs develop. It appears that one gene on the tiny Y chromosome—the *testis determining factor* (TDF)—triggers male development (Tortora, 1992); TDF initiates development of the undifferentiated *gonads* (the male and female sexual glands) into testes. Without TDF, the gonads develop into ovaries.

Other than differences in chromosomal makeup, a human embryo has no apparent distinguishing sexual characteristics through the first 6 weeks of prenatal development. At this early stage, the gonads appear able to develop into either testes or ovaries. Not until approximately 7 to 8 weeks after conception do a number of mechanisms activate the eventual development of the fetus's reproductive structures. If a Y chromosome is present, the *medulla* (inner part) of the gonad rapidly develops into a mature testis, usually within several days. If this chromosome is absent, the *cortex* (outer part) of the gonad gradually develops into a mature ovary, usually about 12 weeks after conception.

Hormonal and Sex Structure Differences Once the gonads develop into either testes or ovaries, further determination of biological sex becomes a function of the *endocrine system*, or the ductless glands that secrete hormones directly into the bloodstream, such as the pituitary, thyroid, and adrenal glands. The adrenals secrete low levels of sexual hormones, but the hormones that most powerfully and directly affect gender are those produced by the gonads—in particular, the *estrogens* and *progesterone* of the ovaries, and *testosterone* of the testes. The estrogens influence development of the female reproductive structures and secondary sexual characteristics, while also helping to regulate the menstrual cycle. Progesterone stimulates development of the uterine lining in preparation for pregnancy. Testosterone influences development of the male reproductive structures and secondary sexual characteristics, while also affecting libido.

A large body of research testifies to the contribution of gonadal sexual hormones to the differentiation of the internal and external sexual structures. As mentioned above, before week 6, the embryo appears neither male nor female. Around weeks 7 and 8, the undifferentiated gonads develop into either testes or ovaries. If the fetal gonads develop into testes, they will soon secrete testosterone, which in turn stimulates continued development of male internal and external structures. Should the male fetus not secrete enough testosterone, female reproductive organs develop, regardless of the Y chromosome. From this we can conclude that development of the female structures in the fetus is *not* dependent on a specific female hormone, but instead on the presence or absence of testosterone.

Two different groups of fetal tissue, which are present in both males and females, give rise to the internal sex structures. In the female, the *Müllerian ducts* become the fallopian tubes, uterus, cervix, and perhaps part of the vagina. In the male, the *Wolffian ducts* become the epididymis, vas deferens, and seminal vesicles. The presence or absence of testosterone and *Müllerian inhibiting hormone* determine which duct develops into internal

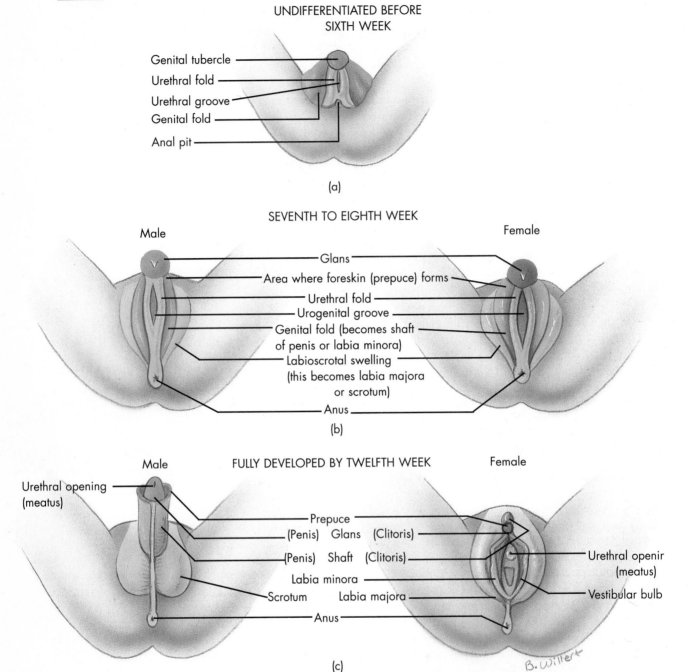

UNDIFFERENTIATED BEFORE
SIXTH WEEK

Genital tubercle
Urethral fold
Urethral groove
Genital fold
Anal pit

(a)

SEVENTH TO EIGHTH WEEK

Male   Female

Glans
Area where foreskin (prepuce) forms
Urethral fold
Urogenital groove
Genital fold (becomes shaft
of penis or labia minora)
Labioscrotal swelling
(this becomes labia majora
or scrotum)
Anus

(b)

FULLY DEVELOPED BY TWELFTH WEEK

Male   Female

Urethral opening
(meatus)

Prepuce
(Penis)   Glans   (Clitoris)
(Penis)   Shaft   (Clitoris)   Urethral openir
(meatus)
Labia minora
Scrotum   Labia majora   Vestibular bulb
Anus

B. Willert

(c)

FIGURE 3.1 *Prenatal development and sexual differentiation of the external genitals. Source: C. E. Rischer & T. A. Easton (1992), Focus on human biology. (New York: HarperCollins). Reprinted by permission.*

sexual structures and which one diminishes, given the fetus's sex. Under normal circumstances, the sex structures fully differentiate by week 12 (Figure 3.1).

Because the various male and female sexual structures arise out of the same embryonic tissues, each female structure has a *homologous* (corresponding) male structure, and vice versa. These structures appear in Table 3.1.

Brain Differences   Prenatal sexual differentiation also occurs in the brain. Indeed, researchers have identified important sexual differences within the brains of females and

TABLE 3.1   **Homologous Sexual Structures**

Female	Male
Clitoral glans	Penile glans
Clitoral shaft	Penile shaft
Clitoral hood	Foreskin
Labia majora	Scrotum
Labia minora	Underside of the penile shaft
Ovaries	Testes
Bartholin's glands	Cowper's glands
Skene's gland	Prostate gland

Source: Adapted from G. J Tortora & S. R. Grabowski (1993), *Principles of anatomy and physiology* (7th ed.) (New York: HarperCollins).

males. These normally involve two major areas: (1) the *cerebral hemispheres* (the left and right sides of the brain), and (2) the *hypothalamus* (a brain structure governing motivation and emotional responses). Although most research into sexual differences in the brain has employed animal studies, the same differences probably exist within the brains of all mammals, including humans (Mix et al., 1992).

Sexual differences exist in the cerebral hemispheres of males and females (Gooren, 1991; Reinisch et al., 1991). While an overview of the two cerebral hemispheres leaves the impression that they are mirror images of each other, each hemisphere is specialized in function. In humans the right hemisphere tends to be specialized for *spatial functions* (the ability to detect relationships between different-sized and -shaped objects); the left hemisphere, for *verbal functions* (the ability to comprehend and use language). Although these differences are quite small, males generally demonstrate increased spatial abilities, and females increased verbal abilities (Kelly, 1985; Linn & Hyde, 1989). One explanation for these sexual differences in cerebral functioning has to do with the presence of testosterone leading to greater development of the right hemisphere in the male fetus, with the lack of testosterone not having this effect in the female (Geschwind & Behan, 1982).

Differences in the hypothalamus also seem to be associated with levels of testosterone in the bloodstream, in much the same way that the presence or absence of testosterone affects other aspects of prenatal differentiation (Gooren, 1991; Kelly, 1985). Among its many vital functions, the hypothalamus plays a role in controlling the production and secretion of sexual hormones by regulating the pituitary gland, which stimulates the other endocrine glands into secreting their respective hormones.

Generally speaking, the effects of prenatal sexual differentiation on the hypothalamus are not readily visible until puberty. At that time, the male-differentiated hypothalamus directs the pituitary to prompt *constant* release of sexual hormones. The female-differentiated hypothalamus directs the pituitary gland to prompt *periodic* release of sexual hormones. Consequently, females—but not males—experience cyclic fertility in the form of the menstrual cycle.

ABNORMAL PATTERNS OF SEXUAL DIFFERENTIATION

Up to this point, we've considered the mechanisms involved in, and the effects of, normal sexual differentiation. Most of the time everything works out according to design. Occasionally, however, one of the mechanisms malfunctions. If the sex organs fail to differentiate, the baby may be born with a combination of the organs of both sexes, such as a vaginal orifice just beneath the penis—a condition known as *hermaphroditism*. In the body of the *true hermaphrodite*, a very rare occurrence in humans, both testicular and ovarian tissues are present. There may be two testes and two ovaries, or one of each of these gonads. In the *pseudohermaphrodite*, a slightly more common occurrence (about 1 in 1,000 births), the individual's sex organs are also ambiguous but the gonadal tissue is consistent with his or her chromosomal makeup.

Three syndromes that result from problems with sexual differentiation at the chromosomal level are *Turner's syndrome*, *Klinefelter's syndrome*, and *XYY syndrome*.

Turner's Syndrome Turner's syndrome refers to the condition in which a fetus has a single X chromosome. Children with Turner's syndrome develop female external genitals, and usually consider themselves female. However, their internal sexual structures never develop. At puberty their breasts fail to develop, and menstruation does not occur. Adult women with this condition are sterile. About 1 in 2,500 female births is OX (Rischer & Easton, 1992).

Klinefelter's Syndrome Children with Klinefelter's syndrome have an XXY chromosomal makeup, and are therefore anatomically male (due to the presence of the Y chromosome). Although these individuals appear normal as children, as adolescents they have undeveloped testes, undersized genitals, breast growth, feminine muscular structure, unusual height, and high voice; they are also sterile and sometimes mentally retarded. About 1 in 400 male births is XXY (Rischer & Easton, 1992).

XYY Syndrome XYY syndrome refers to the condition in which a fetus has an XYY chromosomal makeup. Males with the extra Y chromosome often have lower than average intelligence and above-average height. The research is unclear concerning these individuals' tendencies toward excessive aggression and violence. About 1 in 1,000 male births is XYY (Rischer & Easton, 1992).

PSYCHOLOGICAL AND SOCIAL INFLUENCES ON GENDER IDENTITY

While most individuals' gender identity is ultimately based on their sexual makeup and appearance, this does not imply that psychological and social processes are absent or without influence. To the contrary, social learning, including how children are raised and react to the rules and roles society and culture create for that gender, certainly plays a significant part in the eventual formation of gender identity (Hyde, 1991). In short, if a child is told he is a male and raised as a male, the child believes he is male; if told she is a female and raised as a female, the child believes she is female.

From day one, the majority of parents treat their children according to the appearance of their sex organs (Sidorowicz & Lunney, 1980). It begins in the delivery room with "It's a girl!" or "It's a boy!" Next come pink or blue baby clothes and furniture, followed by a multitude of statements from family, friends, and strangers, such as "What a sweet little girl!" or "What a strong little boy!" Parents even handle their little boys more aggressively than their little girls. And it does not take long for these sorts of sex-biased behaviors to begin influencing gender identity. Within a very short time—less than two years according to some experts—children develop a clear understanding that they are either male or female, usually followed by a strong desire to adopt sex-appropriate behaviors and mannerisms. Biology lays the foundation for gender identity, but it is ultimately children's interactions with the social environment that construct gender identity.

Of course, gender identity formation, like anything else, is not always perfectly straightforward and free of mishap. Some individuals experience great difficulty reconciling and merging the biological, psychological, and social components of their gender. They experience **gender dysphoria**—emotional pain and confusion over their gender identity. In particular, some of these individuals believe they were born into the wrong-sex body, that their "true" gender is inconsistent with their sexual appearance.

GENDER DYSPHORIA (DIS-FO-RE-A)

Distress and confusion over one's gender identity.

Without question, *transsexualism (gender identity disorder)*—the subjective sense that an individual possesses the body of the other sex—is the most extreme form of gender misidentification. The phenomenon differs from *homosexuality, bisexuality,* or *transvestism.* The homosexual individual is attracted to members of his or her own sex, while the bisexual is attracted to members of both sexes. The transvestite receives sexual gratification from dressing in the clothes of the other sex (American Psychiatric Association, 1994).

A transsexual individual is a biologically appearing male or female who, as mentioned above, believes that he or she should have been born a member of the other sex. Unlike heterosexuals and homosexuals, who are usually proud of and receive pleasure from their genitals, transsexuals typically hate their sex organs, many refusing to handle or look at them. That they have the "wrong" genitals is to them a mistake of nature. For this reason, transsexuals usually desire to rid themselves of their assigned sexual characteristics and to acquire those of the other sex by means of *sex-reassignment surgery.*

Scientists have yet to discover a definite cause for the phenomenon. Several popular theories include improper brain differentiation due to prenatal exposure to other-sex hormones, postnatal hormonal imbalances, early identification with the other-sex parent, and assorted early learning experiences (Bockting & Coleman, 1992; Gooren, 1991). Because no direct evidence supports any single explanation, transsexualism most likely results from multiple causes.

We know that transsexuals suffer tremendous psychological conflicts (Cohen-Kettenis & Gooren, 1992). While their bodies proclaim them to be one sex, their psyches argue the opposite. Sexual desires are cast aside. Emotional pain is suffered in silence. The result is often confusion, fear, depression, and self-loathing.

Tennis champion Renee Richards, having competed both as a man and as a woman, is certainly one of the most famous transsexuals.

When these conflicts are powerful enough, the transsexual might undergo therapy leading to *sex-reassignment surgery* ("sex-change surgery"). In order to qualify for such a procedure, the transsexual must first go through a number of different steps to assess whether he or she is an appropriate candidate. The first involves thorough psychiatric or psychological counseling and evaluation to ensure that the individual contemplating a sex-change operation is, in fact, a transsexual. If the evaluation confirms this, the individual undergoes hormone therapy. The male-to-female transsexual (by far the most common type) receives estrogen to bring about feminization, including enlarged breasts, fatty deposits on the hips, diminished prostate secretions, and less frequent erections. The female-to-male transsexual receives testosterone to bring about masculinization, including facial hair, deepened voice, increased muscle mass, and enlarged clitoris. The next step involves the individual cross-dressing and living as a member of his or her new sex for a year or two. This critical aspect of the procedure allows the individual to experience and adjust to the realities of being the other gender.

Surgery is the final step in the long process of sexual reassignment. The male-to-female change is fairly straightforward. The physician first removes the transsexual's penis and testes (leaving intact the nerves that supply the penis), then constructs an artificial vagina lined with penile skin so as to have sensory nerve endings and the ability to respond to sexual stimulation.

The female-to-male operation is somewhat more complicated and not always as successful as the male-to-female procedure. The physician surgically removes the breasts, ovaries, and uterus; closes the patient's labia to form a scrotum; and constructs a penis from abdominal skin and fat. Because the new penis does not have the capacity to become erect, many patients prefer to use a penile *prosthesis* for erections and sexual intercourse. Silicon spheres may be used to create artificial testicles.

For Personal Reflection

1. *What do you think it would be like to live as a transsexual? As a transsexual, would you consider sex-reassignment surgery? Why or why not?*
2. *How would you react if someone you were dating told you that he or she had had a sex-change operation a few years earlier?*

GENDER ROLES

Few aspects of human sexuality stir the emotions as much as *gender roles*. What is feminine? What is masculine? Should the majority's standards concerning femaleness and maleness be imposed on all members of a society? Gender roles affect nearly all aspects of life, forming a nexus between our gender identity and sexual attitudes and expressions. Gender roles are both *personal* and *cultural*, determining how we as females and males dress, speak, and interact within the parameters of our society.

Learning plays a primary role in shaping and forming our gender roles, beginning with appearances. We all have *gender schemas* (Bem, 1984)—or deeply entrenched cognitive frameworks regarding what constitutes masculinity or femininity. As with most things, we make quick judgments concerning these qualities in others, often based on such trivial things as dress, hairstyle, and vocal cues. Added to what we perceive are those things we *expect* to perceive. Thus, in our encounters with others we weigh a person's actual appearance and manner against what we believe his or her appearance and manner *should be*— again, based on our assumptions about maleness and femaleness. While gender roles are taught and reinforced throughout the life cycle by numerous *socializing agents*—parents,

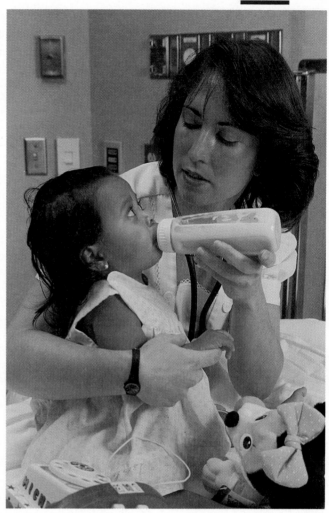

Our gender roles stem from the assumptions and expectations we have about what is feminine and masculine in our society.

teachers, peers, movies, television, music, books, and religion—parents undoubtedly have the greatest effect, especially on very young children.

How do children acquire gender roles? Learning is the principle vehicle. Research indicates that parents (and other adults) describe and treat male and female infants differently. They seem to do this, at least in part, because they—themselves recipients of gender roles and expectations—*perceive* the infants as being different (Sidorowicz & Lunney, 1980). From the first "What a sweet little girl!" or "What a big, brave boy!" parents reinforce sex-typed behaviors. Traditionally, fathers tend to show boys how to build and fix things, while mothers teach their girls how to keep house, cook, and sew. And so it goes through childhood and adolescence. In this way, children receive parental approval by *conforming* to gender expectations and adopting culturally accepted, conventional roles— all of this being continually reinforced by other socializing agents, such as television. The learning of gender roles always occurs within a social and cultural context, the values of the parents and society passing down to the children of each successive generation.

The gender roles adopted during childhood generally carry over into adulthood. In the home, people have certain presumptions regarding decision-making, work and financial responsibilities, and childrearing practices. Likewise, in the work place, people have presumptions regarding the division of labor, power, and organizational structures. This is not to say that gender roles, *per se,* are good or bad. They merely exist; they are realities in the

"That wasn't very nurturing of you."

Drawing by Mankoff; © 1984 The New Yorker Magazine, Inc.

lives of most everyone. The question of their value really depends on the individuals and groups involved. For some, "traditional" gender roles provide security—a constant reminder of the way things have been, are, and will be. For others, they are a source of limits and frustration—a constant reminder of the way things have been, are, but need not be.

GENDER STEREOTYPES

GENDER STEREOTYPES

Generalizations about the gender attributes, differences, and roles of others.

A discussion of gender roles would be incomplete without some mention of **gender stereotypes,** or simplistic generalizations about the gender attributes, differences, and roles of particular groups or individuals. Stereotypes can be positive ("This group of people is bright") or negative ("That group is shiftless and lazy"). They rarely make a good basis for forming opinions about others.

What's the difference between a gender role and a gender stereotype? Actually, the two are related. We all live according to the gender roles we learned as children—assumptions about what is expected and normal in terms of maleness and femaleness. However, when we automatically apply our gender assumptions to others, *regardless of evidence to the contrary,* we are engaging in gender stereotyping.

Many people recognize the dangers of gender stereotyping, yet continue to make gender assumptions about others. Traditionally, the female stereotypic role is to marry and have children—home and hearth. Moreover, a woman should put her family's needs before her own; be sympathetic, caring, loving, and compassionate; and find time to be beautiful and sexy. The male stereotypic role is to be the financial provider. A man should

PERSPECTIVE

Gender Roles and the Yąnomamö

Eminent anthropologist Napoleon A. Chagnon observed some interesting gender role differences in the division of labor among the Yąnomaö of South America, as described in his book *Yąnomaö: The Fierce People* (1977):

> Yąnomamö society is decidedly masculine.... Female children assume duties and responsibilities in the household long before their brothers are obliged to partici- pate in useful domestic tasks. For the most part, little girls are obliged to tend their younger brothers and sisters, although they are also expected to help their mothers in other chores such as cooking, hauling water, and collecting firewood. By the time girls have reached puberty they have already realized that their world is decided- ly less attractive than that of their brothers....
>
> Marriage does not enhance the status of the girl, for her duties as wife require her to assume difficult and laborious tasks too menial to be executed by the men. For the most part these include incessant demands for firewood and drinking water, particularly the former. Women spend several hours each day scouring the neigh- borhood for suitable wood. There is usually an abundant supply in the garden with- in a year of clearing the land, but this disappears rapidly. Thereafter, the women must forage further afield to collect the daily supply of firewood, sometimes travel- ing several miles each day to obtain it. It is a lucky woman who owns an axe, for collecting wood is a tedious job without a steel tool....
>
> Women must respond quickly to the demands of their husbands. In fact, they must respond without waiting for a command. It is interesting to watch the behav- ior of women when their husbands return from a hunting trip or a visit. The men march slowly across the village and retire silently to their hammocks. The woman, no matter what she is doing, hurries home and quietly but rapidly prepares a meal for the husband. Should the wife be slow to do this, the husband is within his right to beat her. (pp. 81–82)

Questions for Thought

How do you think male-dominated societies like that of the Yąnomamö begin? How are they sustained? Are there any parallels between the male-female gender role differences of the Yąnomamö described above and those of our society?

Source: N. A. Chagnon (1977). *Yąnomamö: The fierce people* (2nd ed.) (New York: Holt, Rinehart, and Winston).

On a Personal Note (Shawn, age 43)

As a guy, I'm always on the defensive for being a florist. You wouldn't believe the kind of flack I've had to put up with over the years. I come from a real traditional European fam- ily, where men do men things—like fish and drink—and women do women things—like cook and wash clothes all day. It's pretty disgusting sometimes. Anyway, I began working in floral design during college, and still haven't heard the end of it from my relatives. And although I'm not married, I'm not gay either. I'm sure you can imagine the conversation around the TV on holidays when all the relatives and I are watching football, which by the way, I despise. (Author's files)

be assertive, independent, competitive, and career-focused; hold his emotions in check; and always initiate sexual activity. And he must *never* appear feminine in any respect. Added to this is the demand for him to be successful, aggressive, tough, and always in control.

Are gender stereotypes ever associated with negative consequences for individuals and society? *Yes.* They can stifle creativity and individual expression. They can hinder personal growth. They can prevent people from "finding themselves." In short, gender stereotypes can negatively affect almost every area of life.

As an example of this, consider how stereotypes and rigid gender roles interfere with sexuality. In many cases, people define personal masculinity and femininity through their sexual behaviors. With men taught to be aggressive and superior and women passive and yielding, no wonder the penis becomes a symbol of power and dominance, and the vagina one of dependence and submission. Conforming to such restrictive, age-old sexual stereotypes leaves little room for creativity or self-expression in the bedroom.

Gender stereotypes and rigid gender roles loom large in creating sexual dysfunctions. Men who battle anxieties related to sexual performance often develop an arousal, erectile, or orgasm dysfunction, as do women who struggle to find sexual fulfillment within a gender role of passivity and compliance (Kaplan 1974; Masters & Johnson, 1970). Why is this? Perhaps it is because men and women who carry rigid gender assumptions become so wrapped up in their irrational expectations about the way sex and lovers are *supposed* to be that they fail to "let go" and give themselves over to the erotic pleasures of lovemaking.

On a Personal Note (Paula, age 32)

I've always believed that as a woman my sole sexual function is to just lie there and let my husband have his way in bed. I never felt like I should or could take a more active role, you know, tend to my own needs. Women aren't supposed to do that, right? That's what I was always taught—the wife is there for the husband. After a couple of months of therapy, though, it finally occurred to me that my attitudes about sexuality probably have something to do with my never having had an orgasm. It's so hard to fight these old tapes in my head! (Author's files).

Maxine © *Marian Henley. Reprinted by permission of the artist.*

Where do gender stereotypes come from? The weight of scientific evidence points to the fact that people, especially children, learn gender stereotypes (Basow, 1992; Signorielli, 1990). But from where and whom? That is, what influences teach and reinforce gender stereotypes in our children? As with gender roles, the same socializing agents—parents, peers, teachers, the media, and religious leaders—pass along gender stereotypes from one generation to the next.

How can we free individuals from gender "typecasting" so that they can lead more fulfilling lives? One method is to challenge gender roles and stereotypes just as we challenge other expectations. This has been a social theme in the United States for a long time, culminating in *feminism*, the *women's liberation movement*, the *men's movement*, and the concept of *androgyny*.

For Personal Reflection

1. *What are some of the traditional concepts of "male" and "female" that you hold? Where did these come from? How have traditional gender stereotypes both positively and negatively affected your life?*
2. *To what extent do you believe our society is challenging traditional gender roles and stereotypes? What evidence do you have to support your position?*
3. *What are your feelings on the changing roles of women and men in our society?*

Gender stereotypes come from a variety of sources, including parents, teachers, peers, religious leaders, and the media.

 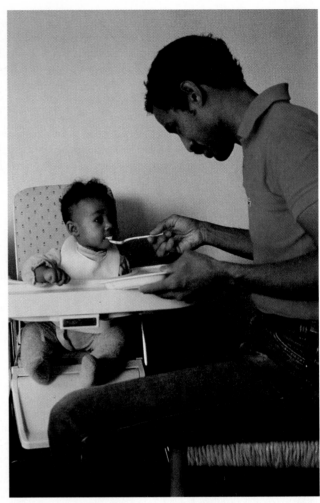

Many Americans are now challenging the traditional gender roles and stereotypes of previous generations.

✓ ANDROGYNY

**ANDROGYNY
(AN-DRAH-GI-NE)**

Blending of feminine and masculine attributes within an individual.

Many people in our society consider masculinity and femininity to be gender opposites, masculine attributes being the sole domain of males, and feminine attributes the sole domain of females. Men are described as strong, active, tough, directive, and physical; women, as weak, compliant, pretty, delicate, and gentle. These kinds of attitudes and gender role stereotypes directly affect work, play, education, and worship—often to the detriment of individuals and society at large.

One approach to challenging traditional gender roles and stereotypes is the concept of **androgyny** (from the Greek *andros,* meaning "man," and *gyne,* meaning "woman")—the blending of masculine and feminine attributes within an individual. The androgynous person, or *androgyne,* does not neatly fit into a female or male gender role; she or he can comfortably express both feminine and masculine sides of the self. Given this, it would not be unusual or inappropriate to find an androgynous father serving as the nurturing parent while the mother pursues a career.

Although androgyny might seem a radical departure from traditional norms and a potential source of individual and social chaos, psychologist Sandra Bem and others have demonstrated that androgynous men and women are less conforming, more flexible, more nurturing, and emotionally healthier than their gender-typed counterparts (Bem, 1974, 1984; Bem et al., 1976). In fact, androgynes tend to evidence heightened achieve-

PERSPECTIVE

The Women's Movement and Sexuality

Emerging as a powerful sociopolitical force beginning in the 1960s, the *feminist movement*, or *women's liberation movement*, has fought hard for the rights of women and minorities, by challenging and redefining traditional, stereotypic gender roles. The following excerpt from a 1987 feminist reader should give you an idea of the movement's position on women, gender, and sexuality.

> We believe that there are two major problems which we must confront if we are both to widen our understanding and assert our right to an active and pleasurable sexuality of our own. The first problem is one that has always been with us—although its meaning and effects may have changed to some extent by the past ten years: that is the very extent and power of what might be called the "masculinization" of human sexuality. A major concern of feminists over the past decade has been to make *visible* the extent to which sexuality has been defined by men and is experienced by women as coercive and objectifying. (It is perhaps one of the most extreme forms of alienation when not even one's sexuality is one's own.). . .
>
> The second major problem also arises out of advances that have been made rather than any failures of the movement. To acknowledge that we needed to develop both a theoretical understanding of sexuality, and a personal sexual life which supported and sustained us and simultaneously expressed the political objective of feminism, did not just make it happen—it quickly became apparent that the spontaneous will which led thousands of women with no political experience to organize and speak out with some success could not easily be harnessed to change sexual desire; to practice nonmonogamy or to live collectively did not automatically abolish jealousy and romantic longings. At that time, there was no theoretical work which could explain the construction of "femininity." The very theories that purported to explain sexuality, that is theories based on psychoanalysis, seemed the most insulting attempts to legitimate male power. We had all experienced the use of concepts such as "penis envy" and "castration" to explain and justify assertions that women are inferior. To be beaten around the head with a phallic symbol was supposed to bring us to a chastened acceptance of our inferior genital equipment—the ultimate reality principle. Many of us had grown up with the specter of the woman who refused to "accept her femininity." At one level the women's movement was a collective refusal to accept the feminine role. (pp. 1–3)

Question for Thought

In your opinion, has the feminist movement successfully made "visible the extent to which sexuality has been defined by men and is experienced by women as coercive and objectifying"? Explain.

Source: Feminist Review (Eds.) (1987), *Sexuality: A reader* (London: Virago Press).

ment motivation, self-esteem, and social skills (Bem & Lenney, 1976; Flaherty & Dusek, 1980).

Interestingly, androgyny may also have implications for sexual activity. The assumption is that androgynous individuals are more flexible in their approach to life, and therefore more willing to experiment with and incorporate different sexual behaviors into their lovemaking (Garcia, 1982). Androgynes feel just as comfortable making sexual advances as receiving them. They also enjoy different methods of sexual expression and various sexual positions. Not all studies or researchers, however, support this idea of differences in

PERSPECTIVE

Chaucer and Feminism

Some readers are surprised to learn of English poet Geoffrey Chaucer's seemingly profeminist stand in his "Envoy to the Clerk's Tale"—a rather unusual perspective for the Middle Ages:

Strong-minded women, stand at your defence,
Since you are strong as camel and don't ail,
Suffer no man to do you offence;
And slender women in a contest frail,
Be savage as a tiger there in Ind;
Clatter like mill, say I, to beat the male.

Source: B. I. Murstein, (1974), *Love, sex, and marriage through the ages* (New York: Springer).

sexual satisfaction between androgynous and gender-typed individuals, nor do they proclaim androgyny to be a problem-free lifestyle (Gilder, 1986). Thus, we as a society must accept androgyny for what it really is—one *alternative* to challenging typecast gender roles. Androgyny is not a panacea for all people in all situations.

In the final analysis, the most appropriate gender role for an individual is the one that she or he finds the most comfortable and rewarding. It is the role that permits the greatest degree of self-actualization and fulfillment. It is the role that allows the person to become who she or he chooses to be. This freedom to be oneself, then, is what true gender liberation is all about.

KEY POINTS

1. *Sexual assignment* refers to an individual's biological makeup—her or his genetic, hormonal, and reproductive identity as a male or female. *Gender* refers to both an individual's anatomical sex and the social and cultural aspects of being female or male. An individual's personal sense of being female or male is her or his *gender identity*. Outward expression of gender identity within a social context and according to cultural expectations is a *gender role*. A *sex role* is a gender role that is anatomically limited to one sex or the other. An individual's *sexual orientation* refers to her or his relative sexual attraction to members of the same and/or other sex. Sexual assignment, gender, gender identity, gender role, sex role, and sexual orientation form an individual's *sexual identity*.
2. *Sexual differentiation* refers to the biological processes by which males become males and females become females. There are biological, psychological, and social components to the formation of gender identity. Genetics, prenatal and postnatal hormones, differences in the brain and the reproductive organs, and unique socialization patterns all play a role in shaping a person's gender identity.
3. Abnormal patterns of sexual differentiation include *hermaphroditism, Turner's syndrome, Klinefelter's syndrome,* and *XYY syndrome.*
4. Some individuals experience *gender dysphoria,* or emotional pain and confusion over their gender identity. *Transsexuals* are individuals who believe they were born into the wrong-sex body and who usually desire sex-change surgery.
5. *Gender stereotypes* are simplistic generalizations about the gender attributes, differences, and roles of particular groups or individuals. Stereotypes can be positive or negative, but are often associated with negative consequences for individuals and

society. One recent approach to challenging traditional gender roles and stereo-types is the concept of *androgyny*, or the blending of masculine and feminine attributes within an individual.

ACTIVITIES AND QUESTIONS

1. Survey a number of students outside your class concerning what personality traits and characteristics they associate with "male" and "female." Generally speaking, what characteristics do the women in your survey associate with "male," and men with "female"? What about women with "female," and men with "male"? What did you learn?

2. As children, should boys be encouraged to play with dolls, to play house, and so forth? Should girls be encouraged to play with toy guns, to play football, and so forth? Why or why not? As a parent, would you encourage your children to participate in gender-specific play, gender-neutral play, or both? Explain.

3. What are some of the gender assumptions that you've identified in your own life? How have these affected your relationships? If they have ever caused conflicts for you and a partner, how willing were you to work at changing your gender assumptions? Did you expect your partner to change her or his assumptions, too?

4. Watch one to two hours of prime-time television shows each day for one week. How many of these shows portray traditional American gender roles? Nontraditional roles? Androgynous lifestyles? How do you feel about your findings?

5. Imagine for a moment that our government decided to conduct the "Great American Social Experiment" and passed laws requiring all citizens to become androgynous. What do you think would happen to our society? What are some of the positive and negative changes that you might observe? If the "experiment" failed, do you think people would return to life as usual, or would there be some lasting changes? If the latter, what kinds of changes?

RECOMMENDED READINGS

Hyde, J. S. (1991). *Half the human experience: The psychology of women* (4th ed.) Lexington, MA: D. C. Heath. Explores and summarizes contemporary theories and works on the psychology of women.

Matthews, G. (1987). *"Just a housewife": The rise and fall of domesticity in America.* New York: Oxford University Press. Surveys the history of housewifery in the United States from colonial times to today.

Mead, M. (1963). *Sex and temperament in three primitive societies.* New York: Morrow. A fascinating sociocultural study of the Arapesh, Mundugumor, and Tchambuli peoples, including the ways in which their gender/sex roles differ from those of Western cultures.

Rubin, L. B. (1990). *Erotic wars: What happened to the sexual revolution?* New York: Farrar, Straus, & Giroux. A fascinating look at how the "sexual revolution" of the 1960s has affected today's assumptions about gender.

C H A P T E R 4

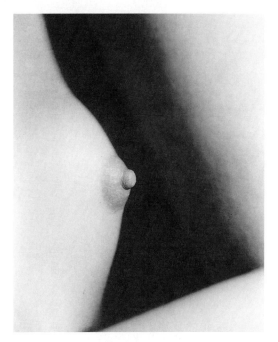

FEMALE SEXUAL ANATOMY AND PHYSIOLOGY

O B J E C T I V E S

AFTER READING THIS CHAPTER YOU SHOULD BE ABLE TO . . .

1. IDENTIFY AND EXPLAIN THE APPEARANCE AND FUNCTION OF THE FEMALE EXTERNAL AND INTERNAL SEX STRUCTURES AND BREASTS.

2. DISCUSS THE ROLES THAT GLANDS AND HORMONES PLAY IN FEMALE SEXUALITY AND REPRODUCTION.

3. EXPLAIN THE PROCESSES OF OVULATION AND MENSTRUATION.

4. DESCRIBE SOME OF THE COMMON PROBLEMS ASSOCIATED WITH THE MENSTRUAL CYCLE.

5. EXPLAIN WHY EVERY WOMAN SHOULD SCHEDULE REGULAR GYNECOLOGICAL EXAMINATIONS AND PERFORM MONTHLY BREAST SELF-EXAMINATIONS.

PERSONAL ASSESSMENT

TEST YOUR GENERAL KNOWLEDGE OF FEMALE SEXUAL ANATOMY AND PHYSIOLOGY BY ANSWERING THE FOLLOWING STATEMENTS *true* OR *false*.

_____ 1. The term *vagina* refers collectively to the external female genitals.

_____ 2. A hymen that is no longer intact is a sure sign that a woman isn't a virgin.

_____ 3. The inner two-thirds of the vagina are the most sensitive and responsive to sexual stimulation

_____ 4. Only males produce male sexual hormones.

_____ 5. The average menstrual cycle lasts 28 days.

_____ 6. All the eggs (or ova) that a woman will ever release are present in her ovaries prior to her birth.

_____ 7. The female breasts continuously produce milk from the onset of puberty through menopause, although the breasts release milk only after pregnancy.

_____ 8. The larger a woman's breasts are, the more milk she produces and releases.

_____ 9. The causes of premenstrual syndrome (PMS) are mostly psychological.

_____ 10. A woman should begin having regular gynecological exams as soon as she reaches puberty or begins having sexual intercourse, whichever occurs first.

1. F; 2. F; 3. F; 4. F; 5. T; 6. T; 7. F; 8. F; 9. F; 10. F

ANSWERS

*H*er pure and eloquent blood
Spoke in her cheeks, and so distinctly wrought,
That one might almost say, her body thought.

John Donne

In our society, people talk a lot about sexuality. Have you ever wondered, then, why so many use words like "my you-know-what," "privates," and "the parts below" to refer to their genitals? Maybe it's because most children learn at an early age to avoid touching or talking about "down there." Children quickly pick up on their parents' fears about sexual matters, and may even carry these negative feelings into their own adulthood.

So should *you* want to learn more about the sex organs, yours and those of the other sex? *Of course.* How can you become truly at ease with your own sexuality or be fully sexual with a loved one if you don't know how your own body works? Remember, it isn't enough to rely on "nature" and hope that everything works out okay. Although you may feel that there are more important things out there to think about, one of the best actions you can take to improve the quality of your sex life is to learn more about your sexual self.

Even after the "sexual revolution" of the 1960s and 1970s, most people remain ignorant about the sex organs. Almost everyone knows what a vagina or a penis is. Yet they may know very little about the clitoris or how to stimulate it. They may not know that the most sensitive part of the penis is its glans, or where this structure lies. Sadly enough, *the average person doesn't have an adequate understanding of the genitals of either sex,* which can lead to sexual fears, problems, inhibition, and dissatisfaction. My purpose in writing this chapter is to provide you with basic information about *anatomy* (structure) and *physiology* (function) of the female sexual organs, as well as the opportunity to think about a variety of related issues and concerns.

DIRECTIONAL TERMS AND ANATOMICAL POSITIONS

Any discussion of anatomy and physiology must begin with a brief discussion of *directional terms*, which are precise words anatomists use to describe *anatomical positions, or* the locations of various structures within the body. Terms like *above, below, front,* and *back* are confusing when referring to anatomical positions that are relative to the viewer. Anatomists also use directional terms to avoid wordy descriptions. For instance, the term *anterior* is specific and concise, and is therefore preferable to the vague and wordy *in front of*. Table 4.1 lists some of the more common directional terms.

THE EXTERNAL SEXUAL STRUCTURES

The external female genitals ("genitalia"), or **vulva,** consist of several structures. These are the *mons veneris, labia majora, labia minora, vestibule,* and *clitoris* (Figure 4.1).

VULVA (VUL-VA)
External genitals of the female.

THE MONS VENERIS

The **mons veneris** (the Latin for "mound of Venus") is an area of fatty tissue and padding between the pubic bone and skin. In the adult female, pubic hair covers this structure. The mons veneris is very sensitive to stimulation because of the many nerve endings present in the area.

MONS VENERIS (MONZ VEN-ER-IS)
Hair-covered fat pad over the pubic bone.

THE LABIA MAJORA

The **labia majora** (meaning "larger lips") are the outer folds of the vulva. These folds lie close together, but when spread open expose other sexual structures. Of the same tissue as the male scrotum, the labia majora extend from the mons veneris to the *perineum,* the area between the vulva and anus. Pubic hair covers the outer portions of the labia majora, but not the inner portions. Numerous nerve endings make this area sensitive in the same way that the male scrotum is sensitive.

LABIA MAJORA (LA-BE-A MA-JO-RA)
Outer folds or "lips" of the vulva.

THE LABIA MINORA

The inner folds of the vulva are the **labia minora** (meaning "smaller lips"). Located underneath the labia majora, these hairless folds begin as the *clitoral hood* and connect with the labia majora near the perineum. Nerve endings and blood vessels richly supply the labia minora, making them very sensitive to stimulation. The labia minora also protect the urethral and vaginal *orifices,* or openings, discussed below.

LABIA MINORA (LA-BE-A MIN-OR-A)
Inner folds or "lips" of the vulva.

TABLE 4.1 **Some Common Directional Terms**

Term	Definition
Superior	Toward the head or upper part of a structure
Inferior	Away from the head
Anterior	Nearer to or at the front of the body
Posterior	Nearer to or at the back of the body
Intermediate	Between two structures
Superficial	Toward or on the surface of the body
Deep	Away from the surface of the body

Source: Adapted from G. J. Tortora & S. R. Grabowski (1993), *Principles of anatomy and physiology* (7th ed.) (New York: HarperCollins).

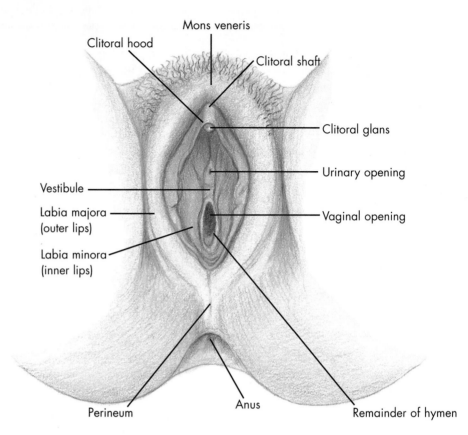

FIGURE 4.1 *The external genitals of the female.*

THE VESTIBULE

The **vestibule** is the area between the labia minora from which the *urethra* and *vagina* open. Located between the clitoris and vaginal orifice is the **urethral orifice,** or opening of the *urethra,* the tube that carries urine from the bladder to the outside of the body.

Between the urethral opening and the perineum is the **vaginal orifice,** or opening of the vagina. At birth, a fold of mucous membrane, the **hymen,** covers a woman's vaginal orifice, at least partially (Figure 4.2). A hymen that partially covers the vaginal orifice generally does not interfere with menstrual flow; however, an *imperforate hymen* (one that fully covers the vaginal orifice) does. In most women, the hymen eventually tears on its own during strenuous exercise, douching, masturbation, or sexual intercourse. A physician's incision may be required to open a particularly thick or imperforate hymen.

Two small glands, one lying on each side of the lower part of the vagina, also open into the vestibule. During sexual arousal, these **Bartholin's glands** secrete small amounts of fluid just before orgasm. The function of this secretion is unknown.

THE CLITORIS

The **clitoris** is an organ of erectile tissue, homologous (corresponding) to the male glans penis. It lies between the urethral opening and the area where the labia minora meet to form the **prepuce,** or **clitoral hood.** The clitoral shaft and its roots, or *crura* (small tips; singular, *crus*), extend into the woman's body and attach to the pubic bone. The clitoris's sole purpose is to sense sexual pleasure. The structure is highly sensitive, containing as many nerve endings as the penis but in a much smaller space. The clitoral erectile tissue engorges with blood and becomes erect in response to sexual stimulation. Prior to orgasm,

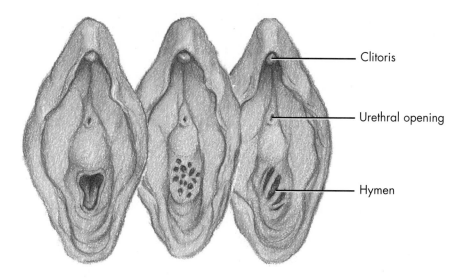

Clitoris

Urethral opening

Hymen

FIGURE 4.2 *Variations of the hymen.*

the clitoris becomes extremely sensitive to touch and retracts under its clitoral hood. Directly touching the clitoris at this time can be painful for the woman.

A woman should keep her external genitals clean by washing regularly, especially the labia minora and clitoral areas. Otherwise, *smegma*, a cheesy matter formed of bacteria and glandular secretions from the vagina and vestibule, can accumulate in these areas. Sexual arousal and activity can be painful should smegma accumulate under the clitoral hood and become hard and lumpy.

THE PERINEUM

Lying between the vaginal orifice and the anus is a smooth, sensitive area of skin known as the **perineum.** Because of the concentration of nerve endings in the perineum, many women find rubbing this area to be both pleasurable and sexually stimulating.

PERINEUM (PER-I-NE-UM)
Sensitive area of skin between the vaginal orifice and anus.

For Personal Reflection

"Are my genitals normal?" This is an often-asked question. Many women and men are sensitive about the appearance of their genitals. They're concerned that their genitals are in some way abnormal looking. One woman may worry about having dark and thick pubic hair, another about having light and sparse hair. One man may worry that his penis is not as long as it should be, another that it is too long. Too many people worry needlessly about what their genitals are supposed to look like.

If you ever worry about not having perfectly shaped genitals (whatever that means), keep in mind that "normality" is relative. Genitals vary a great deal in size, shape, and color from person to person. Knowing that there are plenty of ordinary variations can help you better appreciate the beauty of the sexual body.

How sensitive are you about looking at or talking about the genitals?

PERSPECTIVE

Freud and Genital Symbolism

Students usually find that the writings and theories of Sigmund Freud make fascinating, and sometimes amusing, reading. Freud used *dream analysis* to uncover repressed sexual wishes, because he believed that most dreams include images symbolic of hidden sexual desires. Below is an excerpt from one of Freud's lectures on symbolic representations of the female genitals.

The female genitals are symbolically represented by all such objects as share their characteristic of enclosing a hollow space which can take something into itself: by *pits, cavities* and *hollows,* for instance by *vessels* and *bottles,* by *receptacles, boxes, trunks, cases, chests, pockets,* and so on. Some symbols have more connection with the uterus than with the female genitals: thus, *cupboards, stoves* and, more especially, *rooms.* Here room-symbolism touches on house-symbolism. *Doors* and *gates,* again, are symbols of the genital orifice. Materials, too, are symbols for women: *wood, paper* and objects made of them, like *tables* and *books.* Among animals, *snails* and *mussels* at least are undeniably female symbols; among parts of the body, the *mouth* (as a substitute for the genital orifice); among buildings, *churches* and *chapels.* Not every symbol, as you will observe, is equally intelligible.

The breasts must be reckoned with the genitals, and these, like the larger hemisphere of the female body, are represented by *apples, peaches,* and *fruit* in general. The pubic hair of both sexes is depicted in dreams as *wood* and *bushes . . .*

Another symbol of the female genitals which deserves mention is a *jewel-case. Jewel* and *treasure* are used in dreams as well as in waking life to describe someone who is loved. *Sweets* frequently represent sexual enjoyment. Satisfaction obtained from a person's own genitals is indicated by all kinds of *playing,* including *piano-playing.* Symbolic representations *par excellence* of masturbation are *gliding* or *sliding* and *pulling off a branch.* The *falling out of a tooth* or the *pulling out of a tooth* is a particularly notable dream symbol. Its first meaning is undoubtedly castration as a punishment for masturbating. We come across special representations of sexual intercourse less often than might be expected from what has been said so far. Rhythmical activities such as *dancing, riding* and *climbing* must be mentioned here, as well as violent experiences such as *being run over;* so, too, certain *manual crafts,* and, of course, *threatening with weapons.* (pp. 156–157)

Questions for Thought

Many people enjoy analyzing dreams. Imagine that a friend asks you to interpret her or his recurrent dream of playing a piano while traveling on a ship. How might Freud have interpreted such a dream? How would you interpret it?

Source: S. Freud (1966), Symbolism in dreams. In J. Strachey (Ed.), *Introductory lectures on psychoanalysis* (New York: Norton). (Original work published 1917)

THE INTERNAL SEXUAL STRUCTURES

The internal female sex structures consist of the *ovaries, fallopian tubes, uterus,* and *vagina* (Figure 4.3).

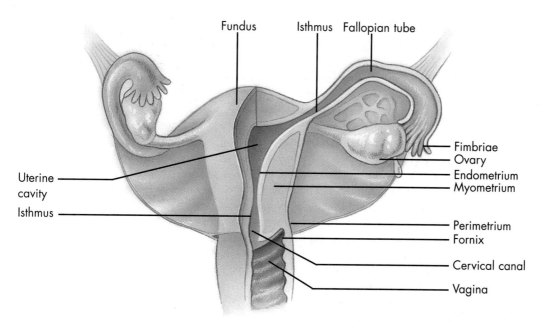

Fundus   Isthmus   Fallopian tube

Uterine cavity

Isthmus

Fimbriae
Ovary
Endometrium
Myometrium

Perimetrium
Fornix

Cervical canal

Vagina

FIGURE 4.3 *Location of the ovaries, fallopian tubes, uterus, and vagina. Source: C. E. Rischer & T. A. Easton (1992),* Focus on human biology *(New York: HarperCollins). Reprinted by permission.*

THE OVARIES

The paired **ovaries** are the female reproductive structures responsible for producing and releasing *ova* (eggs; singular *ovum*) and secreting sexual hormones. Ligaments hold each ovary in place on either side of the uterus. The ovaries are homologous to the male *testes*.

Prior to birth a female's ovaries already carry all the ova she will release throughout her life, and many more—a total of about 400,000. Thin sacs, or **follicles,** contain the unreleased, immature ova. During the process of **oogenesis,** the ova mature within the follicles. At the onset of each menstrual cycle, a number of follicles begin to mature. Only one follicle, now called the **Graafian follicle,** usually matures to the point for **ovulation** to occur, when an egg is released from the follicle and ovary. Following ovulation, the empty follicle becomes the **corpus luteum.** This yellow mass releases the hormone *progesterone,* which prepares the woman's uterus for pregnancy. During her lifetime a woman releases about 500 or fewer eggs (an average of one per month during the years that she ovulates); the rest degenerate and dissolve. Ovulation begins at *puberty* (the start of sexual maturation) and concludes at *menopause* (the end of reproductive capability).

THE FALLOPIAN TUBES

The **fallopian tubes** are the pair of tubes that move the released ovum into the uterus. Each tube is about 4 inches long, is located next to an ovary, and opens into the uterus. In a typical adult female, a mature egg bursts forth from the ovary near the fallopian tube once every 28 days or so. The waving and swaying of *fimbriae* (finger-shaped projections at the entrance of the fallopian tubes) move the released ovum into the fallopian tube. Muscular contractions of the fallopian tubes, as well as movement of *cilia* (small hairlike structures) within the tubes, move the ovum toward the uterine cavity. The ovum travels about 1 inch per 24 hours. Sperm in the fallopian tube can fertilize the ovum, usually in the outer quarter of the tube (the part closest to the ovary).

OVARIES (O-VAR-EZ)
Female reproductive organs that produce and release ova.

FOLLICLES (FOL-I-KULZ)
Thin sacs containing unreleased ova.

OOGENESIS (O-O-JEN-E-SIS)
Maturation of the ovum.

GRAAFIAN FOLLICLE (GRAF-E-AN)
Follicle that releases the matured ovum.

OVULATION (O-VYOO-LA-SHUN)
Monthly process whereby ova are released from the ovaries.

CORPUS LUTEUM (KOR-PUS LYOO-TE-UM)
Hormone-secreting, empty Graafian follicle.

FALLOPIAN TUBES (FAL-LO-PE-AN)
Pair of tubes connecting the ovaries and the uterus.

THE UTERUS

UTERUS (YOO-TE-RUS)

Female reproductive organ that receives and nurtures the zygote.

The **uterus** is the female reproductive organ responsible for receiving and nurturing the fertilized egg, or *zygote*. The fertilized egg attaches itself to the uterine wall, where it remains throughout the period of *gestation*, or the duration of the pregnancy.

In its nonpregnant state, the uterus is "pear-shaped." It is about 3 inches long, tapered at one end, about 2 inches wide at the other end, and lies superior to the bladder (Figures 4.3 and 4.4). During pregnancy the size and shape of the uterus change dramatically.

Three layers of tissue make up the uterine walls (Figure 4.5). The *endometrium* is the innermost layer of the uterus, a portion of which sheds during *menstruation*. The next layer of uterine tissue is the *myometrium*, or muscle tissue that contracts during orgasm, menstruation, and childbirth. The *perimetrium* is the outer layer of tissue that maintains the shape and position of the uterus in the pelvic cavity.

CERVIX (SER-VIKS)

Neck of the uterus that opens into the vagina.

The narrow, outer portion of the uterus that opens into the vagina is the **cervix,** the passageway for sperm, menstrual fluid, and birth. The opening of the cervix, or *os*, contains mucus that normally prevents bacteria from entering into the uterus. The cervix is the site of the *Pap smear* test, which is used to check for cervical cancer.

THE VAGINA

VAGINA (VA-JI-NA)

Female reproductive structure connecting uterus and vaginal orifice.

The **vagina** is the muscular, tubular canal that connects the uterus and the vaginal orifice. The vagina lies inferior to the bladder and superior to the rectum. Its walls form folds and stretch easily. The vagina's elastic quality permits comfortable accommodation of the erect penis during coitus, and passage of the child during birth.

Vasocongestion (blood flow into the vagina) increases during sexual arousal. The lining of the vaginal walls in turn "sweat," secreting a lubricating fluid. The great majority of sensory nerves are present in the outer third of the vagina closest to the vaginal opening.

The G *spot*, or *Grafenberg spot*, came to the attention of the popular media in the early 1980s (Ladas et al., 1982). The G spot is reportedly a highly sensitive area within the

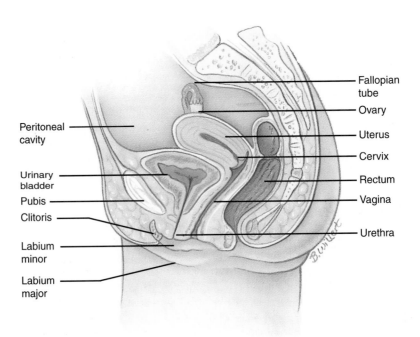

FIGURE 4.4 *Side view of the female reproductive system. Source: C. E. Rischer & T. A. Easton (1992),* Focus on human biology *(New York: HarperCollins). Reprinted by permission.*

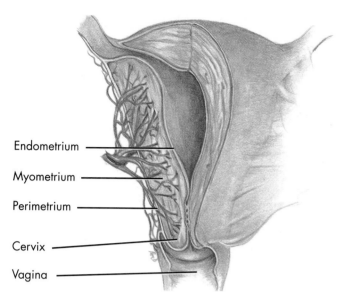

Endometrium

Myometrium

Perimetrium

Cervix

Vagina

FIGURE 4.5 *The vagina, cervix, and three tissue layers of the uterus.*

anterior wall of the vagina that increases sexual arousal when touched or pressed (Zaviacic & Whipple, 1993; Figure 4.6). Following stimulation of the G spot, some women report experiencing "female ejaculation," the release of ejaculatory-like fluid out of the urethra.

Does the G spot really exist? Many women say *yes*, but many others say *no*. Some pathologists conducting postmortem autopsies have identified prostatic-like tissue in the general area of the G spot , although these and other findings remain controversial (Heath, 1984). Results of biochemical analyses of "female ejaculate" are also inconclusive. While some researchers maintain that female ejaculate is merely urine, others claim it contains components different from urine (Zaviacic et al., 1988).

Where is the G spot? According to Ladas et al. (1982):

> The Grafenberg Spot lies directly behind the pubic bone within the front wall of the vagina. It is usually located about halfway between the back of the pubic bone and the front of the cervix, along the course of the urethra (the tube through which you urinate) and near the neck of the bladder, where it connects with the urethra. The size and exact location vary. (Imagine a small clock inside the vagina with 12 o'clock pointing towards the navel. The majority of women will find the G spot located in the area between 11 and 1 o'clock.) Unlike the clitoris, which protrudes from the surrounding tissue, it lies deep within the vaginal wall, and a firm pressure is often needed to contact the G spot in its unstimulated state. (p. 33)

SEXUAL GLANDS AND HORMONES

Besides the genitals, a number of glands and hormones are vital to female sexual and reproductive functioning. A **gland** is an organ that secretes one or more substances, usually *hormones*. A **hormone** is a chemical that stimulates cellular activity elsewhere in the body. Hormones stimulate cells by attaching to specific receptor sites that activate chemical processes within the cells. *Endocrine* glands release hormones directly into the bloodstream, while *exocrine* glands release hormones into the body via ducts. Endocrine glands are responsible for secreting female sexual hormones.

GLAND

Organ that secretes one or more substances.

HORMONE

Secretion affecting cellular processes elsewhere in the body.

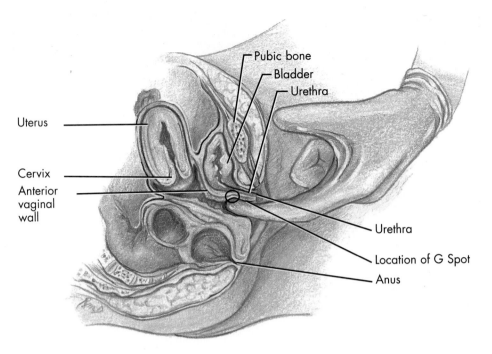

Uterus

Cervix

Anterior
vaginal
wall

Pubic bone
Bladder
Urethra

Urethra

Location of G Spot

Anus

FIGURE 4.6 *Location of the G spot.*

THE HYPOTHALAMUS

A center of female sexual hormone control lies in the brain structure known as the *hypothalamus*. In the female, the hypothalamus acts on the *pituitary gland*, which in turn acts on the *ovaries*. The female ovaries (and the male testes) are *gonads*, or sexual glands. The pituitary gland and the gonads are endocrine glands.

THE PITUITARY GLAND, GONADOTROPIN-RELEASING HORMONE, FOLLICLE-STIMULATING HORMONE, AND LUTEINIZING HORMONE

In the female, the hypothalamus releases *gonadotropin-releasing hormone* (GnRH), which stimulates the *pituitary gland* to release two *gonadotropins* (gonad-affecting hormones): *follicle-stimulating hormone* (FSH) and *luteinizing hormone* (LH). FSH stimulates maturation of ovarian follicles, and LH stimulates ovulation (Figure 4.7).

THE OVARIES, ESTROGENS, AND PROGESTERONE

The hormones FSH and LH from the pituitary stimulate the ovaries to produce *estrogens* and *progesterone*. The *estrogens* (or "estrogen") are female sexual hormones responsible for the development and maintenance of the female reproductive organs and *secondary sexual characteristics* (which distinguish females from males), such as breasts and fatty deposits on the hips. *Progesterone* is the female hormone responsible for preparing the endometrium of the uterus to receive the fertilized egg. Feedback about the levels of these hormones in the bloodstream regulates the amount of LH and FSH that the pituitary releases. The corpus luteum within the ovary is the primary source of progesterone.

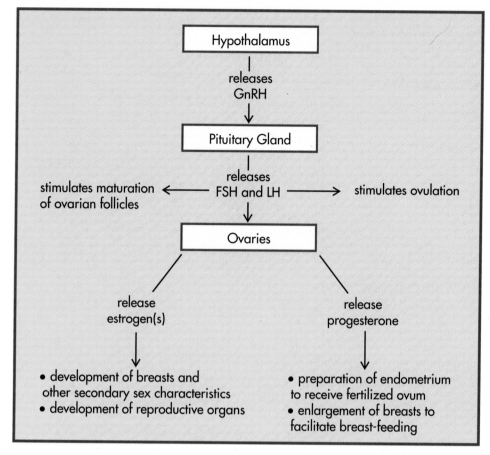

FIGURE 4.7 *Glands, hormones, and female reproductive functioning.*

THE ADRENAL GLANDS, OVARIES, AND ANDROGENS

The *adrenal glands* (a pair of endocrine glands, each situated above one kidney) and the ovaries secrete small amounts of *androgens,* or male sexual hormones, in the female. Androgens affect bone structure, the amount of skeletal muscle present, the amount and pattern of body hair, and female sexual drive.

HUMAN CHORIONIC GONADOTROPIN

Detection of *human chorionic gonadotropin* (HCG) in the urine forms the basis of most pregnancy tests. This hormone is produced by the *placenta,* the structure that develops during pregnancy to pass nutrients and waste between mother and fetus, so HCG is present only during pregnancy. The primary purpose of HCG is to maintain the corpus luteum, which halts the menstrual cycle during pregnancy.

HORMONES AND THE MENSTRUAL CYCLE

The **menstrual cycle** refers to a woman's monthly reproductive cycle. A woman's first menstrual cycle, or *menarche,* usually occurs between ages 12 and 13, although the cycle can begin as early as age 9 or as late as age 17. The menstrual cycle ceases permanently at *menopause* ("the change of life"), usually between ages 45 and 60.

MENSTRUAL CYCLE (MEN-STROO-AL)
Woman's 28-day reproductive cycle.

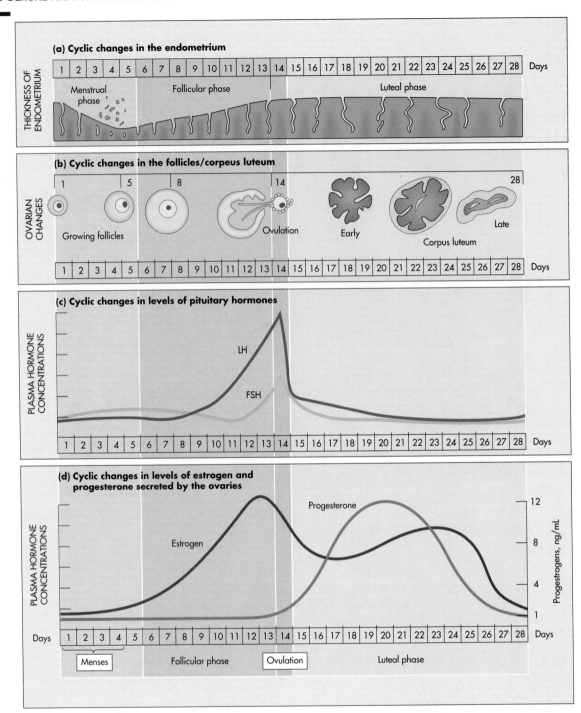

FIGURE 4.8 *The menstrual cycle of the human female. Source: C. E. Rischer & T. A. Easton (1992), Focus on human biology (New York: HarperCollins). Reprinted by permission.*

The menstrual cycle is under hormonal control and typically lasts 28 days, although normal cycles can last anywhere from 21 to 40 days. The cycle consists of three phases: *menstrual, proliferative,* and *secretory.* Another name for the menstrual and proliferative phases is the *follicular phase,* and for the secretory phase, the *luteal phase* (Figure 4.8).

The first day of monthly menstrual bleeding, or **menstruation,** marks the beginning of the *menstrual phase* of a new cycle. Menstruation ("period" or "menses") may last several days. The menstrual discharge, which consists of blood, other secretions, and tissue debris

MENSTRUATION (MEN-STROO-A-SHUN)

Monthly menstrual bleeding.

from the uterus, occurs following drastic reductions in the levels of estrogen and progesterone. During the whole menses a woman may lose an average of 2 to 3 ounces (4 to 6 tablespoons) of uterine tissue and blood. The heaviest menstrual flow is generally during the first few days of the new cycle.

During the next phase, the *proliferative phase*, FSH released from the pituitary gland causes the ovary to stimulate maturation of 10 to 20 egg follicles. Estrogen released from these follicles causes the endometrium to thicken and the hypothalamus to secrete GnRH. The GnRH stimulates secretion of FSH and LH from the pituitary. One of the follicles, the Graafian follicle, matures by about day 14 of the cycle, and in time the other follicles degenerate. A surge in LH on about day 14 forces the Graafian follicle to discharge the ovum, which then moves into the fallopian tube.

During the *secretory phase* and after ovulation, the remains of the Graafian follicle become the corpus luteum, which produces estrogen and progesterone. These hormones inhibit the release of GnRH, which prevents additional follicles from maturing at this time in the cycle. If a sperm does not fertilize the egg, the corpus luteum begins to degenerate on about day 24 of the cycle. As a result, the levels of estrogen and progesterone drop considerably, the endometrium sheds, and menstrual flow begins on about day 28. The cycle repeats itself when the lowered levels of estrogen and progesterone once again signal the hypothalamus to secrete GnRH.

For Personal Reflection

Many women and men find it hard to talk about sexual matters with their children. How would you go about telling your 10-year-old daughter or son about menstruation and the menstrual cycle?

PROBLEMS AND THE MENSTRUAL CYCLE

At some time, many women will experience pain, discomfort, or other problems associated with their monthly cycle. The most common **menstrual problems** are *amenorrhea, dysmenorrhea, endometriosis,* and *premenstrual syndrome. Toxic shock syndrome* is a serious condition caused by the overuse or misuse of tampons, especially superabsorbant types.

MENSTRUAL PROBLEMS
Pain, discomfort, or other problems associated with a woman's monthly cycle.

Amenorrhea The absence of menstruation is termed *amenorrhea*. There are three types of amenorrhea: *primary*, in which the woman has never menstruated; *secondary*, in the which the woman "skips" one or more periods; and *normal*, in which the woman experiences the expected cessation of periods during pregnancy and breast-feeding. Primary amenorrhea is most often due to endocrine disorders of the hypothalamus and pituitary gland, or genetic abnormalities of the uterus and ovaries. Secondary amenorrhea, which most women experience at one time or another, can be due to malnutrition, eating disorders, extreme emotional states, rigorous exercise, hormonal deficiencies, or disease. Many cases of secondary amenorrhea have to do with an exceptionally low percentage of body fat. Treatment involves identifying and correcting the underlying cause of the condition, and may include hormone therapy.

Dysmenorrhea and Endometriosis Painful or difficult menstruation is termed *dysmenorrhea*. Typical symptoms are severe menstrual cramps, headache, nausea, constipation or diarrhea, and urinary urgency. *Primary dysmenorrhea* is painful menstruation associated with higher than normal levels of *prostaglandins*, or substances that cause uterine contractions. This form of dysmenorrhea is often treated with medications that inhibit production of prostaglandins, like ibuprofen. *Secondary dysmenorrhea* is painful menstruation associated with some form of pelvic pathology.

One frequent cause of secondary dysmenorrhea is *endometriosis,* or growth of endometrial tissue outside the uterus, such as in the ovaries, in the fallopian tubes, or on the abdominal walls. About four to ten million American women experience this painful condition (Clark & Carroll, 1986). Like endometrial tissue inside the uterus, this "out-of-place" tissue develops and shreds with each menstrual cycle. This can cause extreme pain during ovulation, menstruation, and sexual activity. Endometriosis can also lead to miscarriages and infertility. Treatment of this condition generally requires hormone therapy or removal of the tissue through surgery.

Premenstrual Syndrome   Women with *premenstrual syndrome* (PMS) experience a number of physical, behavioral, and emotional symptoms just prior to (and sometimes during) menstruation. Symptoms of PMS can range in intensity from mildly annoying to incapacitating (Table 4.2). In severe cases, PMS drastically limits a woman's ability to work and carry on with daily activities for up to two weeks of the month. Estimates are that 75 percent of women experience at least some recurring PMS symptoms, although only a relatively small number of these women—perhaps less than 10 percent—experience PMS to the degree that it significantly disrupts usual daily functioning (Brody, 1989a; Hurt et al., 1992).

The exact causes of PMS are unknown, although experts suspect that hormonal deficiencies, blood sugar disorders, fluid retention, and/or psychological factors may play a part. Individual treatments vary, but often involve attempts to alleviate uncomfortable symptoms (Freeman et al., 1992). Depending on her condition, a woman might be instructed to make dietary or lifestyle changes, get more exercise, or take medications. Severe cases of PMS may require a combination of hormone therapy, counseling, group support, and education.

TABLE 4.2 Symptoms of Premenstrual Syndrome

Physical Symptoms	Psychological Symptoms (emotional and behavioral)
Fluid retention and weight gain	Mood swings (for example, suddenly feeling sad, tearful, irritable, or angry)
Breast swelling and tenderness	Persistent irritability or anger
Abdominal distention	Depression (feeling hopeless) or anxiety (feeling "keyed up")
Backache and joint pain	Problems concentrating
Constipation	Poor coordination
Skin eruptions	Excessive need for or inability to sleep
Changes in appetite, such as cravings for salty or sweet foods, overeating, or undereating	Fatigue and lack of energy
	Diminished interest in usual activities (school, hobbies)

Most women with PMS experience at least two or three of these symptoms. Rarely would a woman experience all of them during any one episode of PMS.

Sources: American Psychiatric Association. (1994). *Diagnostic and statistical manual of mental disorders* (4th ed.). Washington, DC: Author

Tortora, G. J., & S. R. Grabowski. (1993). *Principles of anatomy and physiology* (7th ed.). New York: HarperCollins.

Toxic Shock Syndrome Caused by toxins from the bacterium *staphylococcus aureus, toxic shock syndrome* (TSS) is a disease primarily affecting women who use super-absorbant tampons or misuse "barrier method" contraceptives (for example, leaving a diaphragm or cervical cap in the vagina for prolonged periods of time). These situations create a suitable environment for staphylococci to proliferate and spread into the uterus and fallopian tubes. The released toxins then enter the bloodstream and quickly over-power the body's defenses. Symptoms of TSS include low blood pressure, headache, high fever, sore throat, abdominal pain, vomiting, diarrhea, rash, vaginal irritation, fatigue, fainting, and impaired liver and kidney function. Severe cases of TSS can be fatal. To avoid TSS, women are generally advised to use regular tampons and to change them at least every 4 to 8 hours during menstruation. Interestingly, not all cases of TSS occur among menstruating women; TSS can also strike men and children.

SEXUAL ACTIVITY AND THE MENSTRUAL CYCLE

What about sexual activity during menstruation? There are no health-related reasons for avoiding intercourse at this time, with the possible exception of certain menstrual prob-lems, like excessive bleeding or dysmenorrhea. In some cases, sexual intercourse can alle-viate the discomfort of menstrual cramps if the woman has an orgasm, probably by relax-ing pelvic organs and muscles. A candid discussion before menstruation begins can elim-inate possible misunderstanding, hurt feelings, or embarrassment.

For Personal Reflection

Would you have sexual intercourse with your partner during menstruation? Why or why not?

THE BREASTS

Why include a discussion of the breasts in a chapter on female sexual anatomy and phys-iology? The breasts play a significant role in female sexuality and nursing infants, even though they are not female reproductive organs *per se*. That is, they are *secondary* sexual structures, not *primary* ones (which directly involve reproduction).

At the center of the breast is the **nipple,** through which milk passes to the nursing infant (Figure 4.9). The darker **areola** surrounds the nipple, and often contains small *seba-ceous* (oil) glands that help lubricate the nipple during breast-feeding. Sebaceous glands appear as little bumps on the areola. A woman may also notice hair growth around her areolas, which is normally due to age-related hormonal changes. The nipple may become erect when exposed to cold or tactile stimulation, like rubbing against certain kinds of clothing.

In the adult female, *mammary glands* produce milk, which travels to the nipple by way of numerous milk ducts. These glands produce milk in response to hormonal changes fol-lowing childbirth. Nipple secretions can occur anytime, however.

Breast size varies considerably from one woman to another, depending on the amount of fatty tissue present around the mammary glands. Although larger breasts may have a certain visual appeal to some individuals, there is little or no functional differ-ence between larger and smaller breasts. Breast size has nothing to do with sexual drive, for example, and little if anything to do with the amount of milk that the woman produces.

The amount and size of a woman's glandular tissue can also vary at different times in her life. The mammary glands are particularly sensitive to hormonal changes, such as

NIPPLE
Center structure of the breast through which milk passes.

AREOLA (A-RE-O-LA)
Area immediately surrounding the nipple.

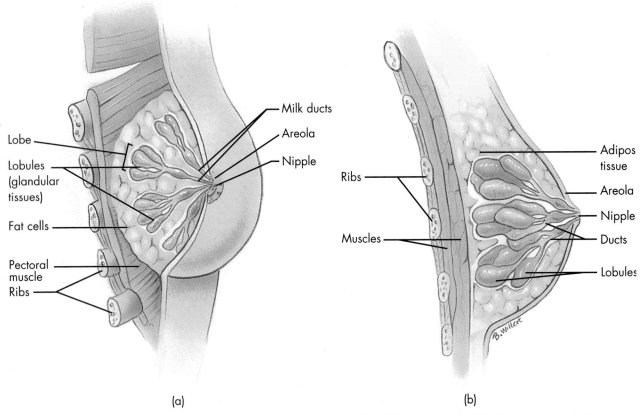

FIGURE 4.9 *Front and side views of the female breast. Source: C. E. Rischer & T. A. Easton (1992). Focus on human biology (New York: HarperCollins). Reprinted by permission.*

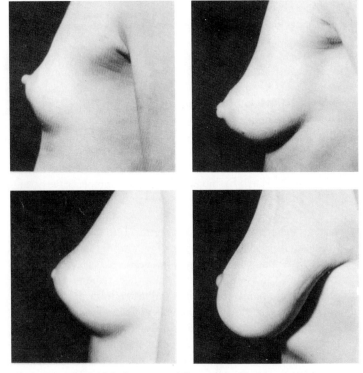

The size and shape of the breasts can differ considerably from woman to woman.

those occurring during the menstrual cycle or pregnancy, or while a woman is taking oral contraceptives. A woman's breasts may enlarge to nearly twice their normal size during pregnancy.

On a Personal Note (Maria, age 20)

I've had really big breasts ever since sixth grade. I hit puberty pretty early, and I developed very fast. My problem, and nobody seems to believe me, is having oversized breasts. It's a drag when I go jogging. It's even painful sometimes. And I'm super fed up with guys at college constantly undressing me with their eyes. Their comments get irritating, too. People think I'm sex-crazed or something just because I've got a large bust. (Author's files)

LACTATION AND BREAST-FEEDING

Production of breast milk is termed **lactation.** The mammary glands produce milk from substances circulating in the woman's blood. During pregnancy, glandular changes create the conditions necessary for lactation. The *placenta* (the structure through which nutrients and waste pass between mother and fetus), produces increased levels of both progesterone and estrogen, which cause milk glands and milk ducts, respectively, to develop. The pituitary hormone *prolactin* stimulates milk production, although higher than normal levels of progesterone and estrogen block its action. The levels of these hormones drop following discharge of the placenta from the uterus after birth. For the first few days after birth, instead of milk, the breasts release *colostrum*, a milklike fluid that is rich in infection-fighting antibodies. Shortly thereafter, the hypothalamus receives nerve signals from the nipple as the baby sucks, and directs the pituitary gland to secrete *oxytocin*, the hormone that causes the milk glands to contract and release milk. When the baby is weaned and milk is no longer released on a regular basis, the hypothalamus directs the pituitary to cease secretion of prolactin.

LACTATION (LAK-TA-SHUN)
Production of milk by the mammary glands.

FERTILITY DURING BREAST-FEEDING

In most cases, breast-feeding temporarily inhibits ovulation due to increased levels of prolactin, which inhibit secretion of LH. The frequency and intensity of breast-feeding tends to keep prolactin levels high. But as these levels drop off with fewer episodes of breast-feeding, the woman once again becomes fertile (Labbock, 1989). Although resumed menstrual periods signal the return of fertility, ovulation can begin during lactation and before menstrual bleeding resumes. So, a word of caution: A woman who is still breast-feeding and does not want to become pregnant should use a nonhormonal form of contraception during sexual intercourse.

GYNECOLOGICAL EXAMINATIONS

Potentially serious conditions are generally easier to treat earlier than later. This is why a woman should schedule routine **gynecological examinations**—medical exams pertaining to women's reproductive disorders. Exams should begin about age 18 or when the woman becomes sexually active, whichever comes first. Yearly exams are the most common, although the woman's age, medical history, and use of contraception will determine the frequency of her appointments. Some women avoid having a gynecological exam out of embarrassment or fear of pain, yet this exam is a crucial first step in identifying potential

GYNECOLOGICAL EXAMINATIONS (GI-NE-KO-LO-JI-CUL)
Medical exams pertaining to women's reproductive disorders.

problems and diseases. A typical gynecological exam consists of a *general medical history and exam, pelvic exam,* and *Pap smear test*. Some women also undergo a *mammogram*.

THE GENERAL MEDICAL HISTORY AND EXAM

Providing the *gynecologist* (a physician whose speciality is treating female reproductive dis-orders) or other health-care practitioner with a thorough medical and social history is an important part of any gynecological exam. The physician gains a clearer picture of the patient's overall state of health from details about previous or current diseases, conditions, or problems; family medical history; medications; and sexual history. Many women also make use of this time with the gynecologist to talk over their sexual concerns, such as the advantages and disadvantages of specific contraceptives.

The general medical exam involves all the usual procedures: listening to the heart and lungs with a stethoscope; checking pulse, blood pressure, and weight; testing blood and urine; and in some cases testing for sexually transmitted diseases. The gynecologist considers any abnormalities in light of the patient's medical history, and may order further tests.

THE PELVIC EXAM

A prominent feature of gynecological exams is the *pelvic exam,* which consists of four parts. These are (1) visual inspection of the external genitals, (2) visual inspection of as many of the internal structures as possible, (3) a *bimanual* examination of internal struc-tures, and in some cases (4) a *rectovaginal* examination.

The patient lies on her back on an examination table, with her legs spread open and feet resting in table "stirrups." The physician or health-care practitioner, wearing latex gloves, first inspects the external genitals for sores, irritation, swelling, and signs of infec-tion. Next, she or he uses a *speculum* (a plastic or steel device) to spread open the vaginal walls to inspect both the vagina and cervix. After removing the speculum, the physician

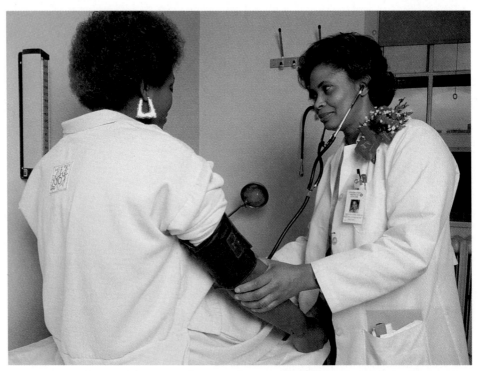

Many women make use of their time with a gynecologist to ask questions about different aspects of sexuality.

performs a *bimanual* exam by inserting two gloved fingers into the vagina and *palpating* (pressing against) various portions of the lower abdomen. She or he then notes any tenderness or irregularities in the size and shape of the various pelvic organs. In some cases, the physician also performs a *rectovaginal exam*. Here, she or he places one finger in the rectum and another in the vagina, and then checks the patient's pelvic organs, rectum, and anus for abnormalities.

THE PAP SMEAR

Perhaps the most important part of a gynecological exam is the *Pap smear*, a test designed to detect the presence of abnormal cells associated with inflammation, infection, benign or premalignant growths, and/or cancer. This potentially life-saving test effectively detects early cancer of the cervix, although not 100 percent of the time (Ruffin & Van Noord, 1991). Once the physician spreads open the vaginal walls with the speculum and collects some cells by swabbing the cervix with a small spatula, she or he prepares a slide and examines it under a microscope. Abnormal cells, if present, are visibly distinct from normal cells.

MAMMOGRAPHY

Mammography is a specialized X-ray test that can detect tiny lumps in the breasts before they are noticeable by manual examination. The American Cancer Society, as well as most physicians and nurses, recommend that women have a baseline mammogram before age 40, yearly or biyearly mammograms during the 40s, and yearly ones during the 50s and

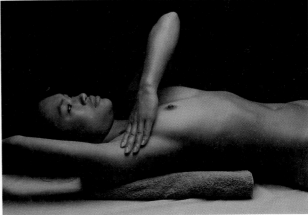

Breast self-examinations (BSEs) are usually performed in the shower, lying down, and in front of a mirror.

PERSPECTIVE

How to Do a Breast Self-Examination

Your aim in performing monthly *breast self-examinations* (BSEs) is to discover cancerous lumps or growths while they are still small and localized. A cancer that hasn't spread to another area of the body is much easier to treat. Almost 90 percent of breast cancers detected in the early stages of development are discovered by women doing BSEs. Regularly performing BSEs helps you to become more familiar with your breast anatomy and detect abnormalities more easily.

The best time to perform a BSE is about one week following your period. If periods are irregular, then self-examine on a monthly schedule. The best time to self-examine is during or immediately following a warm shower or bath. There are three stages to a typical BSE: in the shower, lying down, and in front of a mirror.

In the Shower

While in the shower, soap up your left hand and run it along the right breast from the collarbone to the nipple. Notice if there have been any changes since your last exam. Repeat this procedure with the right hand and left breast.

Lying Down

Next, lie down on a bed, placing a pillow beneath your right shoulder, and your right hand behind your head. Using the palm of your left hand, examine the right breast by slowly moving it in circular fashion around the whole breast. With the fingers of your left hand, repeat this circular motion, beginning at the nipple and moving out until you've examined the entire breast. To check for discharge from the nipple, gently squeeze the nipple. To check for a lump beneath the nipple, gently press the nipple into the breast. Repeat this procedure with the right hand and left breast.

In Front of a Mirror

Finally, stand in front of a mirror with your arms at your sides, and compare the breasts. Note any differences in color, size, shape, and position, as well as changes since your last exam. Gently squeeze your waist with your hands, again noting any differences or changes. With hands behind your head, rotate your torso and note any differences or changes.

You may notice that your breasts are normally lumpy. (For example, there are firm ridges of tissue in the lower areas of the breasts.) Finding a distinct lump is no reason to panic. Some 80 to 90 percent of breast lumps are benign. Still, bring to the immediate attention of your health-care practitioner any lump, growth, thickening, discoloration, or discharge.

beyond. Although not error-free, mammography can be a very effective diagnostic tool. Yet the test is controversial. Some professionals believe that too many mammograms may actually increase a woman's risks of developing cancer. A combination of periodic mammograms, physician examinations, and monthly breast self-examinations appears to be the safest, most reliable way to detect breast tumors.

KEY POINTS

1. Anatomists use precise *directional terms* to describe *anatomical positions*, or the locations of various structures within the body.

2. The external female genitals, or *vulva*, consist of the *mons veneris*, *labia majora*, *labia minora*, *vestibule*, and *clitoris*. The *mons veneris* is a mound of fatty padding between the pubic bone and skin. The *labia majora* are the outer folds of the vulva; the *labia minora* are the inner folds. The labia minora begin as the *clitoral hood* and connect with the labia majora near the perineum. The *vestibule* is the area between the labia minora from which the urethra and vagina open. The two small *Bartholin's glands* also open into the vestibule. The *clitoris* is an organ of erectile tissue, homologous to the male glans penis. Lying between the vaginal orifice and the anus is a smooth, sensitive area of skin known as the *perineum*.

3. The internal female sex structures consist of the *ovaries*, *fallopian tubes*, *uterus*, and *vagina*. The paired *ovaries* are the female reproductive organs responsible for secreting sexual hormones and producing and releasing eggs, or *ova*. Release of ova from the ovaries is termed *ovulation*, which begins at *puberty* and ends at *menopause*. The *fallopian tubes* are a pair of tubes that move the released ovum into the uterus. The *uterus* is the reproductive organ responsible for receiving and nurturing the fertilized egg. The narrow, outer portion of the uterus that opens into the vagina is the *cervix*. The *vagina* is the muscular, tubular canal that connects the uterus and the vaginal orifice.

4. A number of glands and hormones are vital to female sexual and reproductive functioning. The hypothalamus releases *gonadotropin-releasing hormone*, which stimulates the *pituitary gland* to release *follicle-stimulating hormone* (stimulating maturation of the ovarian follicles) and *luteinizing hormone* (stimulating ovulation). These pituitary gland secretions also stimulate the ovaries to secrete *estrogen* (responsible for development of secondary sexual characteristics and the reproductive organs) and *progesterone* (responsible for preparation of the woman's body for pregnancy). The *corpus luteum* (formed from the empty *Graafian follicle*) is the primary source of progesterone.

5. A woman's 28-day reproductive cycle, or *menstrual cycle*, is hormonally controlled and consists of three phases: *menstrual*, *proliferative*, and *secretory*. *Menstruation* refers to the monthly discharge of blood and uterine tissue from the vagina.

6. Many women experience pain, discomfort, or other problems associated with their monthly cycles. The most common menstrual problems are *amenorrhea* (absence of menstruation), *dysmenorrhea* (painful menstruation), *endometriosis* (painful growths of uterine tissue outside the uterus), and *premenstrual syndrome* or *PMS* (physical, behavioral, and emotional discomfort prior to menstruation). *Toxic shock syndrome* (release of toxins into the bloodstream) is a serious condition caused mainly by the overuse or misuse of tampons, especially superabsorbant types.

7. The *breasts* are secondary reproductive structures that produce and release milk to the nursing infant. The *mammary glands* produce milk that travels to the *nipple* by way of numerous *milk ducts*. Production of breast milk is termed *lactation*. The pituitary gland secretes *prolactin* (which stimulates milk production) and *oxytocin* (which causes the milk glands to contract and release milk).

8. Every woman should schedule routine *gynecological examinations*. A typical gynecological exam consists of a *general medical history and exam*, *pelvic exam*, *Pap smear test*, and in some cases a *mammogram*. She should also perform monthly *breast self-examinations*.

ACTIVITIES AND QUESTIONS

1. Divide into two same-sex groups. List common slang terms for female sexual organs and structures. Each group can also discuss why people develop and use slang to talk about sexuality. Now regroup as a class. On a chalkboard, create two lists: "words men use" and "words women use." How do the words in these two lists differ? How are they the same? Whose list is longer?
2. How has American society fostered myths and misinformation about women's sexuality? What can you do to help eliminate these myths?
3. Consider the statement "bigger is always better." Do you think this is an exclusively American perspective? How do the media help perpetuate this idea? How does "bigger is always better" affect individuals and groups?
4. Locate and bring to class representations of female sexual anatomy as portrayed in different media (paintings, photos, or anatomy textbooks) and other cultures. How do your representations differ from each other?

RECOMMENDED READINGS

Boston Women's Health Book Collective (1992). *The new our bodies, ourselves*. New York: Simon & Schuster. A source of information on female reproductive anatomy, physiology, and sexuality. Covers reproduction and sexuality, contraception, health care, and heterosexual and lesbian relationships. Also includes sections on detecting and treating female cancers.

Harrison, M. (1985). *Self-help for premenstrual syndrome*. New York: Random House. A guide to self-treating PMS.

Ladas, A. K., Whipple, B., & Perry, J. D. (1982). *The G spot and other recent discoveries about human sexuality*. New York: Dell. One of the books that started people talking about the Grafenberg spot. The authors make a rather convincing argument for the existence of the G spot.

Stewart, F., Guest, F., Stewart, G., & Hatcher, R. (1987). *Understanding your body*. New York: Bantam Books. Addresses common gynecological concerns, such as fertility and infections.

•THE EXTERNAL SEXUAL STRUCTURES

•THE INTERNAL SEXUAL STRUCTURES

•SEXUAL GLANDS AND HORMONES

•MEDICAL EXAMINATIONS

C H A P T E R   5

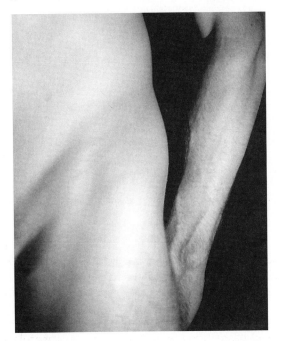

MALE SEXUAL ANATOMY AND PHYSIOLOGY

O B J E C T I V E S

AFTER READING THIS CHAPTER YOU SHOULD BE
ABLE TO . . .

1. IDENTIFY AND EXPLAIN THE APPEARANCE AND
   FUNCTION OF THE MALE EXTERNAL AND
   INTERNAL SEX STRUCTURES.
2. DISCUSS THE ROLES THAT GLANDS AND
   HORMONES PLAY IN MALE SEXUALITY AND
   REPRODUCTION.
3. EXPLAIN THE PROCESSES OF HORMONE AND
   SPERM PRODUCTION.
4. DESCRIBE SOME OF THE COMMON PROBLEMS
   ASSOCIATED WITH THE MALE REPRODUCTIVE
   SYSTEM.
5. EXPLAIN WHY EVERY MAN SHOULD SCHEDULE
   REGULAR MEDICAL EXAMINATIONS, AND
   SELF-EXAMINE HIS TESTICLES MONTHLY.

PERSONAL ASSESSMENT

TEST YOUR GENERAL KNOWLEDGE OF MALE SEXUAL ANATOMY AND PHYSIOLOGY BY ANSWERING THE FOLLOWING STATEMENTS *true* or *false*.

_____ 1. The term *penis* collectively refers to the male external genitals.
_____ 2. The most sensitive part of the penis is its base.
_____ 3. The pubic bone extends partially inside the penis when erect.
_____ 4. The larger a man's penis, the more intense are his orgasms.
_____ 5. The size of a man's erect penis is the most important factor in determining whether a woman has an orgasm during sexual intercourse.
_____ 6. Sperm compose about 80 percent of the total volume of semen.
_____ 7. Because the testes lie in the scrotum outside the body cavity, they maintain a temperature about 3.1°C (5.6°F) above that of the rest of the body.
_____ 8. The hormone testosterone stimulates descent of the testes just prior to birth.
_____ 9. A woman can become pregnant even if the man withdraws his penis from the vagina before he ejaculates.
_____ 10. A sperm count below 20 million per milliliter means the man is probably infertile.

© ANSWERS 1. F; 2. F; 3. F; 4. F; 5. F; 6. F; 7. F; 8. T; 9. T; 10. T

A man possesses nothing certainly save a brief loan of his own body: and yet the body of man is capable of much curious pleasure.

James Branch Cabell

We now turn our attention to male sexual anatomy and physiology—a topic that many mistakenly assume needs little explanation. As in the last chapter, my purpose is to provide you with basic information about the design and workings of the male sexual organs, as well as the opportunity to think about related issues and concerns.

THE EXTERNAL SEXUAL STRUCTURES

The external male genitals ("genitalia") consist of two major structures. These are the *penis* and *scrotum* (Figure 5.1).

THE PENIS

The **penis** is the male organ of urination and sexual response. Its purpose is to pass urine and semen through the urethra and out of the body. Protruding from the lower abdominal wall, the penis consists of a *glans, shaft,* and *root.* **Erection** is the process whereby the organ lengthens and becomes rigid. **Ejaculation** is the process whereby semen discharges from the penis. Ejaculation normally occurs when the penis is erect, urination when the penis is **flaccid,** or not erect.

The size and shape of the penis differ little from man to man.. The average length of a flaccid penis is between 3 and 4 inches, the average length of an erect penis between 5

PENIS (PE-nis)
Male organ of urination and sexual response.

ERECTION (E-REK-SHUN)
Process in which the penis engorges with blood, lengthens, and stiffens.

EJACULATION (E-JAK-YOO-LA-SHUN)
Process in which semen is expelled from the penis.

FLACCID (FLAK-SID)
Nonerect state of the penis.

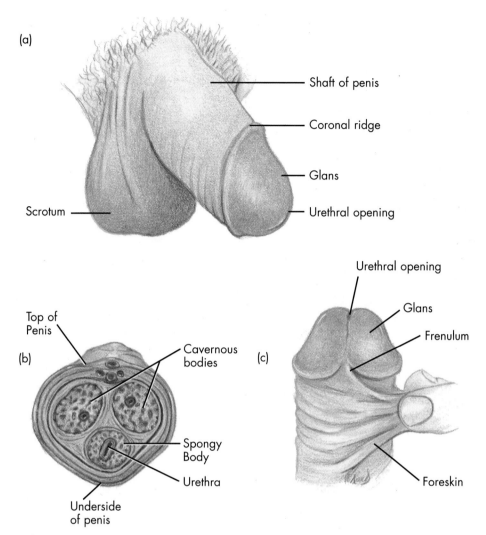

FIGURE 5.1 *The external genitals of the male: (a) side view, (b) cross-section of the penis, and (c) under-side of the penis. Source: W. H. Masters, V. E. Johnson, & R. C. Kolodny (1992), Human Sexuality (4th ed.) (New York: HarperCollins).Reprinted by permission of HarperCollins Publishers, Inc.*

and 7 inches (Reinisch, 1990). Many men and women place great erotic importance on penis length. This "bigger is always better" attitude has caused needless emotional distress for men. The size of an erect penis is relatively unimportant—physically or psychologically—when it comes to stimulating a woman's genitals during intercourse (Baldwin, 1993). Nor does the size of a man's penis have anything to do with his sexual drive or the intensity of his orgasms.

The Outer Structures of the Penis The outer structures of the penis include the *glans, shaft,* and *root.* The **glans,** or **head,** is the soft, sensitive area at the end of the penis from which the urethra opens. The urethral orifice (*meatus*) is at the center of the tip of the glans. The portion of skin closest to the glans is the **foreskin,** or **prepuce.** In an uncircumcised male, the foreskin is a thin sheath of skin that almost completely covers the glans. In a circumcised male, the foreskin has been removed, exposing the glans.

Although the entire penis is sensitive to touch, the glans is its most innervated and sensitive region, and is homologous to the female clitoris. Two areas of the glans are particularly sensitive to touch: the **coronal ridge,** or **corona,** which lies where the glans and shaft join, and the **frenulum,** which lies on the underside of the coronal ridge (Figure 5.1).

GLANS (GLANZ)
Head of the penis.

FORESKIN OR PREPUCE (PRE-PYOOS)
Thin sheath of skin covering the glans.

CORONAL RIDGE OR CORONA (KO-RO-NAL; KO-RO-NA)
Sensitive area where the glans joins the shaft of the penis.

FRENULUM (FREN-YOO-LUM)
Sensitive area lying on the underside of the corona.

SHAFT

Body of the penis.

ROOT

Base of the penis.

The **shaft,** or body, of the penis is its largest region. It is made up of three cylinders of erectile tissue that engorge with blood during erection. Loose skin covers the shaft to allow the penis to enlarge.

The **root,** or base, of the penis connects the shaft and the inferior surface of the abdomen. Beyond the root the inner erectile cylinders of the penis taper to form *crura* (small tips; singular, *crus*) that attach to the pubic bone.

CIRCUMCISION (SER-KUM-SIZH-UN)

Surgical removal of the penile foreskin.

Circumcision. At birth the foreskin is intact and covers most of the glans region of the penis. **Circumcision** is the surgical removal of this sheath of skin (Figure 5.2).

Why circumcise? The reasons people give for the practice vary. Throughout the centuries and in assorted cultures, religious rituals and/or rites of passage have included circumcision. And the practice continues in this form today in many parts of the world. For example, the Jewish and Muslim religions require circumcision of infant males.

In many Western countries, circumcision of newborns has become a routine procedure. Today about 60 percent of males in the United States are circumcised—some for religious reasons, although most for hygienic ones (Wilkes & Blum, 1990). Many health-care professionals believe that circumcision protects against infection and even cancer of the penis by making it easier for a man to keep his genitals clean and free of *smegma,* particularly the areas around and underneath the foreskin. They also believe that circumcision may prevent transmission of bacteria to the partner's vagina, reducing her risk of cervical or uterine cancer.

One condition generally necessitates circumcision. Some males suffer from *phimosis,* in which the foreskin is so tight that erection is very painful. Circumcision generally eliminates the problem.

With the exception of phimosis, are there valid medical/health reasons for circumcision? According to the American Academy of Pediatrics, the practice has potential medical benefits as well as risks (Schoen et al., 1989). But according to a growing anticircumcision movement the risks far outweigh the benefits (Boyd, 1990). Circumcision has risks of its own, including the potential for accidental mutilation of the penis during the procedure, infection, and eventual desensitization to sexual stimulation. Opponents of the practice claim that circumcision for religious or aesthetic reasons is one thing, but another matter for supposed medical reasons. The proceedure is likely to remain controversial for some time (Snyder, 1991).

For Personal Reflection

Imagine for a moment that you're the proud parent of baby boy. Your physician approaches you and asks if you want the newborn to be circumcised. How would you answer and why?

CAVERNOUS BODIES (KA-VER-NUS)

Two columns of erectile tissue in the penis.

SPONGY BODY

Smaller column of erectile tissue, the tip of which forms the glans penis.

VASCULAR SPACES (VAS-KYOO-LAR)

Small cavities within erectile tissue that fill with blood.

The Inner Structures of the Penis The glans and shaft of the penis consist of three columns, or cylinders, of erectile tissue. The two larger cylinders are the **cavernous bodies.** The smaller cylinder through which the urethra passes is the **spongy body.** The cavernous and spongy bodies extend the length of the penile shaft, and the tip of the spongy body forms the glans penis. All three cylinders contain **vascular spaces**—small cavities, much like those of a sponge, that fill with blood and cause the penis to stiffen. The spongy body is the most prominent of the cylinders when the penis is erect.

During sexual arousal impulses from the nervous system increase blood flow into the cavernous and spongy bodies by signaling blood vessels in the penis to dilate. As the penis engorges, the veins that move blood back out of the penis constrict, causing more blood to remain within the cavernous bodies than leave. This results in erection of the penis.

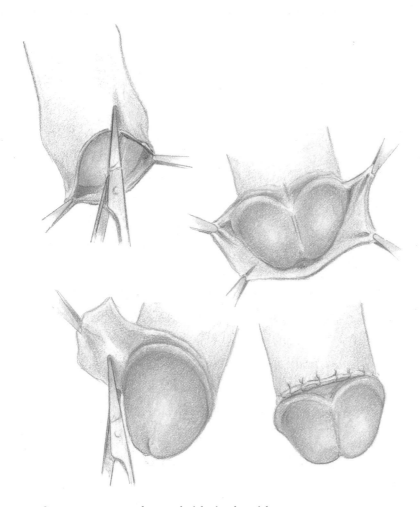

FIGURE 5.2 *Circumcision—surgical removal of the foreskin of the penis.*

As the nerve impulses diminish, normal blood flow in and out of the penis resumes, and it returns to its flaccid state. Contrary to popular myth, erection does not involve any sort of penile *bone*, even though one popular word for an erection is "boner."

Erection is not an all-or-nothing phenomenon. The penis may be flaccid, partially erect, or fully erect (Figure 5.3). The *degree* of erection varies according to the amount of sexual arousal and stimulation present, as well as any number of other factors such as general health, age, medications, alcohol intake, diabetes, cardiovascular disease, anxiety, and depression. Men can experience different degrees of erection during any one episode of masturbation, oral sex, or intercourse. However, a man's erection typically becomes hardest and longest just before ejaculation.

The *angle* and *curvature* of a full erection also differ from man to man—anywhere from pointing straight up toward the man's face, to straight out from the body, to either the left or the right (Figure 5.4). This angle normally changes over the course of his life.

On a Personal Note (Jake, age 37)

For a long time I've been sensitive about my hard-ons. You see, my penis sticks straight up when hard, I mean almost at a 90° angle. I've watched a few pornos, looked at a few magazines, but I've never seen a hard-on that looks quite like mine. Most guys stick straight out, but not me. My wife doesn't seem to mind, though, but I'd still rather be more like other guys. (Author's files)

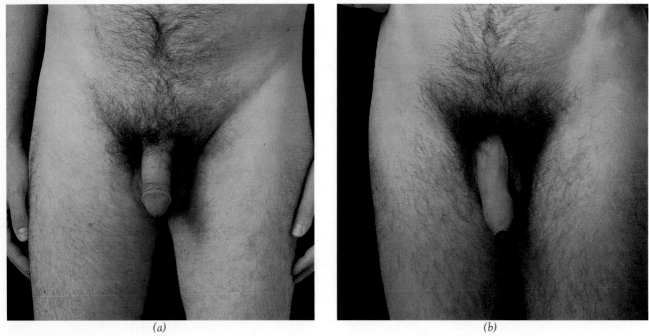

(a)   *(b)*

The appearance of the male genitals can vary from one man to the next. Because the foreskin has been removed, the entire glans is visble on a circumcised penis (a). Photo (b) shows an uncircumcised penis.

Erection is not a purely biological event, but involves psychological and social factors as well (Figure 5.5). In general terms, when a sexual stimulus in the environment triggers erotic thoughts and perceptions, the brain and nervous system signal the penis to become erect. Stroking and manipulating the penis further stimulates nerve centers in the spinal cord, which sustains the erection and increases erotic sensations and thoughts. The man's behavior may also affect the sexual stimulus, further increasing stroking and erotic thoughts. As long as the sexual stimulus is present, the cycle continues. When the sexual stimulus is absent, or when fear or other inhibiting factors are present, the cycle is interrupted and the man's body returns to an unaroused state.

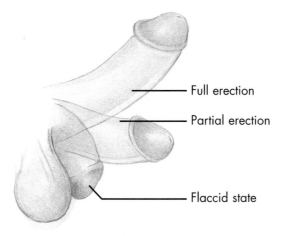

— Full erection

— Partial erection

— Flaccid state

FIGURE 5.3 *Fully erect, partially erect, and flaccid penis.*

THE SCROTUM

Beneath the penis is a loose sac of skin called the **scrotum.** Within the scrotum are the two male gonads—the *testicles*. Two **spermatic cords** hold the testes in place. Each spermatic cord contains nerves, veins and arteries, tissue, and a duct for carrying sperm from each testicle.

THE PERINEUM

The *perineum* is a smooth area of skin lying between the scrotum and the anus. This area contains many nerve endings, so it is particularly sensitive to touch. Rubbing the perineum and/or anus is erotic for many men.

THE INTERNAL SEXUAL STRUCTURES

The internal male sex structures consist of the *testes, vas deferens, seminal vesicles, prostate gland,* and *Cowper's glands* (Figures 5.6 and 5.7).

THE TESTES

The **testicles,** or **testes** (singular, *testis*), are the male gonads that produce sperm and the hormone *testosterone*. In the adult male, each testis is oval shaped and measures about 1 inch in diameter and 2 inches in length. Within each testis are lobes containing the *seminiferous tubules* and *interstitial cells of Leydig* (discussed below).

Until the seventh month of fetal development, the testes remain in the abdominal cavity. During about the second half of the seventh month, they descend into the scrotum. *Cryptorchidism* is the condition in which the testes fail to descend. This occurs in about 30 percent of premature infants and 3 percent of full-term infants. In many cases the testes spontaneously descend during the first year following birth. Otherwise, physicians use injections of human chorionic gonadotropin (HCG) or surgery to correct this condition.

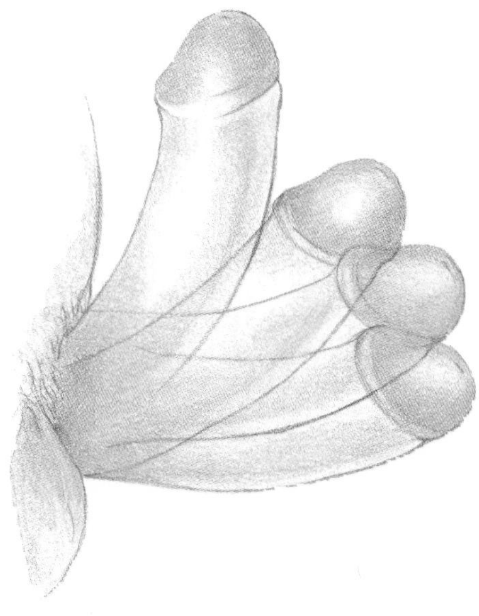

SCROTUM (SKRO-TUM)
Sac behind the penis containing two testes.

SPERMATIC CORDS (SPER-MAT-IK)
Supporting structures that contain nerves, blood vessels, tissue, and a sperm-carrying duct.

TESTICLES OR TESTES (TES-TI-KULZ; TES-TEZ)
Male gonads that produce sperm and testosterone.

FIGURE 5.4 *The angle of a full erection can differ from one man to the next.*

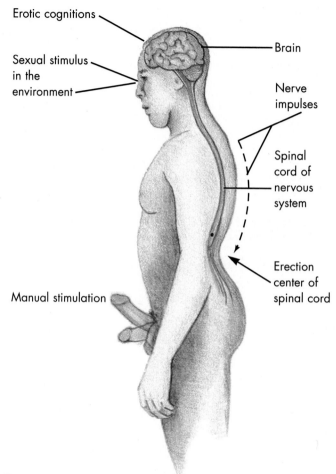

Erotic cognitions

Sexual stimulus
in the
environment

Brain

Nerve
impulses

Spinal
cord of
nervous
system

Erection
center of
spinal cord

Manual stimulation

FIGURE 5.5 *Erection occurs in response to a combination of biological, psychological, and social factors.*

SPERM OR SPERMATOZOA
(SPER-MA-TO-ZO-A)
Male sexual cells.

SPERMATOGENESIS
(SPER-MA-TO-JEN-E-SIS)
Production of sperm.

SEMINIFEROUS TUBULES
(SEM-I-NI-FER-US
TOO-BYOOLZ)
Structures that produce sperm.

SENSORY IMPAIRMENT
*Inability to adequately process sensory
information.*

SERTOLI CELLS
(SER-TO-LE)
*Provide secretions that nourish the
developing sperm.*

CREMASTER MUSCLES
(KRE-MA-STER)
*Scrotal muscles that raise and lower the
testes within the scrotum.*

EPIDIDYMIS
(EP-I-DID-I-MIS)
*Coiled structure in which sperm mature
and are stored.*

Sperm and Testosterone Production Sperm, or **spermatozoa,** are male sex
cells. A mature sperm consists of a *head*, *midpiece*, and *tail*. Within the head are genetic
materials and an *acrosome*, which releases an enzyme to help the sperm penetrate the
woman's ovum. Within the midpiece are *mitochondria*, which produce the energy the tail
needs to propel the sperm to the ovum (Figure 5.8).

Spermatogenesis—the production of sperm—occurs in the seminiferous tubules of the
testes. About 1,000 of these coiled tubules exist within each testis. **Sertoli cells** within the
seminiferous tubules provide secretions that nourish the developing sperm. A healthy
male produces approximately 300 million sperm each day (Tortora & Grabowski, 1993).
Spermatogenesis begins at puberty and continues until death, although the process tends
to taper off with advancing age.

Spermatogenesis requires a constant environment of about 3°C (5.5°F) *below* normal
body temperature (Tortora & Grabowski, 1993). The temperature inside the scrotum
remains constant as the scrotal **cremaster muscles** contract and relax. As the external
temperature rises and the testes warm, the cremaster muscles relax, and the testes move
away from the body (cooling them). Likewise, as the external temperature drops, the cremaster muscles contract, and the testes move closer to the body (warming them).

Sperm move from the seminiferous tubules into the **epididymis,** a coiled structure lying
along the posterior surface of each testis (Figure 5.9). Sperm fully mature and are stored
for up to six weeks within the epididymis. After that, if not ejaculated they disintegrate
and are absorbed by the body.

PERSPECTIVE

Phallic Worship in Ancient Times

Worship of the penis, or *phallus* (from the Greek *phallos,* meaning "penis"), was a prominent feature of many ancient world religions. Representations of the male genitals often symbolized fertility. For example, the ancient Greeks believed symbols of the penis to have special powers of fertility, protection, and immortality. A great deal of Greek phallic worship centered around Diony-sus, the god of wine, and Priapus, the son of the goddess of love, Aphrodite. The Greeks generally depicted Priapus as a smiling man with an enormous penis, often erect. Phallic emblems were prevalent throughout ancient Greek society and included phallic-shaped monuments, giant phallic representations used in the Dionysian festivals, and phallic jewelry.

Phallic worship was also a prominent feature of ancient Roman religious practices. The Roman Bacchanalian festivals borrowed many elements of phallic worship from the Greek Dionysian festivals. As in Greece, Roman phallic emblems represented fertility, and fertility festivals assured healthy offspring and harvests for the coming year. Statues, monuments, erotic art, and amulets worn around the neck were commonplace.

People today in different parts of the world still practice phallic worship. Phallic Shiva cults thrive in some parts of India, and many of the religions of Africa, China, and Japan incorporate phallic symbols in their worship.

Question for Thought

Why do you think worship of the male genitals has played such a prominent role in history?

Sources: B. E. Akerley, (1989), *The X-rated Bible* (Austin, TX: American Atheist Press).
G. Parrinder, (1980), *Sex in the world's religions* (New York: Oxford).

Interstitial cells of Leydig, which lie between the seminiferous tubules, are responsible for producing and secreting testosterone. Testosterone easily passes into the bloodstream given these cells' close proximity to testicular blood vessels.

INTERSTITIAL CELLS OF LEYDIG (LI-DIG)
Cells that produce testosterone.

THE VAS DEFERENS

Sperm stored in the epididymis eventually move into the **vas deferens,** or **seminal duct**—a small tube inside the spermatic cord that carries sperm to the urethra. At the base of the bladder, the vas deferens joins the duct of the *seminal vesicle* and becomes the **ejaculatory duct.** The two ejaculatory ducts open into the urethra within the *prostate gland.* During erection, sphincters close off the entrance to the bladder, which prevents sperm from entering the bladder and urine from entering the urethra during ejaculation.

VAS DEFERENS OR SEMINAL DUCT (VAZ DEH-FER-ENZ)
Sperm-carrying tube joining the testis and the urethra.

EJACULATORY DUCT
Sperm-carrying tube joining the vas deferens and the urethra.

THE ACCESSORY SEXUAL GLANDS

The *seminal vesicles* and *prostate gland* secrete fluids that, along with sperm, make up **semen,** or **seminal fluid**—a thick, sticky fluid with a milky appearance. The fluid from these glands serves to nourish the sperm, activate the sperm's *motility* (ability to move about freely), and neutralize the acid environments of the male urethra and female vagina (acidic environments kill sperm). The average volume of semen ejaculated is between 2.5 and 5 milliliters (0.5 to 1 teaspoon). Sperm make up about 1 percent of the total vol-

SEMEN OR SEMINAL FLUID (SE-MEN; SEM-I-NAL)
Collective term for sperm and various fluids ejaculated from the penis.

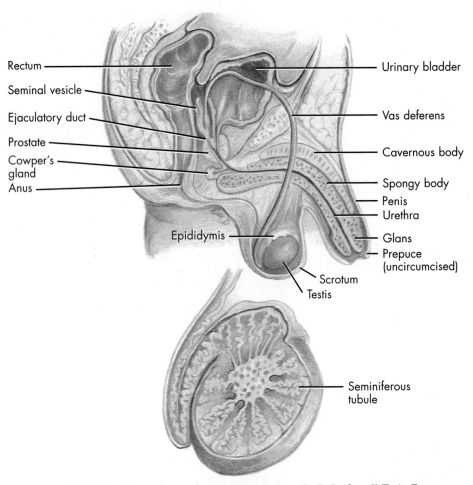

Rectum

Seminal vesicle

Ejaculatory duct

Prostate

Cowper's gland

Anus

Urinary bladder

Vas deferens

Cavernous body

Spongy body

Penis

Urethra

Glans

Prepuce (uncircumcised)

Epididymis

Scrotum

Testis

Seminiferous tubule

FIGURE 5.6 *Side view of the male reproductive system. Source: C. E. Rischer, & T. A. Easton, (1992), Focus on human biology (New York: HarperCollins). Reprinted by permission.*

ume of semen, the average number of sperm ejaculated being between 50 million and 100 million per milliliter. Thus, one ejaculation may contain as many as 500 million sperm (Tortora & Grabowski, 1993). For a man to be considered *fertile* (able to fertilize a woman's ovum), his semen must contain at least 20 million sperm per milliliter.

The Seminal Vesicles The paired **seminal vesicles** are saclike structures that lie posterior to and at the base of the bladder. They secrete an acid-neutralizing fluid rich in fructose that fuels the sperm as they move. This secretion accounts for about 60 percent of the total volume of semen.

The Prostate Gland Once in the ejaculatory duct, sperm and fluid from the seminal vesicles mix with fluid secreted from the **prostate gland**—a single, donut-shaped organ about the size of a chestnut lying directly inferior to the bladder. Prostatic fluid, which makes up about 30 percent of semen, also increases the sperm's motility while neutralizing acids in the urethra and vagina.

The prostate gland is small in a child, but enlarges to its full size during adolescence. It may begin to grow again after age 50, and in some cases can squeeze the urethra to the point that passing urine becomes difficult or impossible. One treatment for enlarged prostate is *prostatectomy,* a procedure in which a surgeon removes all or part of the prostate gland. Another treatment, especially for less severe cases of prostatic enlargement, is *transurethral resection,* a procedure in which a surgeon removes portions of prostatic tissue via the urethra.

SEMINAL VESICLES (VES-I-KULZ)

Accessory sexual glands that secrete an acid-neutralizing fluid that provides nourishment for sperm.

PROSTATE GLAND (PROS-TAT)

Accessory sexual gland that secretes an acid-neutralizing fluid that improves sperm motility.

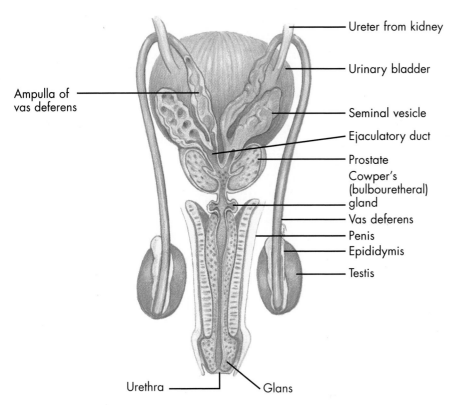

Ureter from kidney

Urinary bladder

Ampulla of
vas deferens

Seminal vesicle

Ejaculatory duct

Prostate

Cowper's
(bulbouretheral)
gland

Vas deferens

Penis

Epididymis

Testis

Urethra

Glans

FIGURE 5.7 *Posterior view of the male reproductive system.*

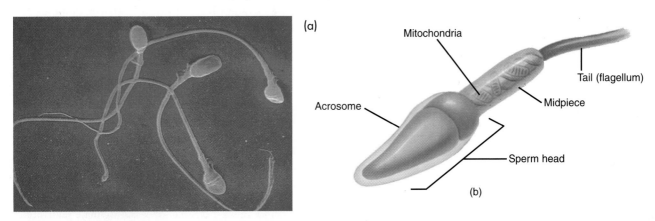

(a)

Mitochondria

Tail (flagellum)

Midpiece

Acrosome

Sperm head

(b)

FIGURE 5.8 *The human sperm: (a) magnified × 4500, and (b) side view. Source: C. E. Rischer, & T. A. Easton, (1992), Focus on human biology (New York: HarperCollins). Reprinted by permission.*

Infection and inflammation of the prostate can also cause it to enlarge and interfere with urination. Symptoms of *prostatitis* include frequent but difficult urination, an urgent need to urinate that is not relieved, pain in the genital area, diminished sexual drive and impotence, discharge from the penis, and fever. Antibiotic medications are usually the treatment of choice for prostatitis.

Cancer of the prostate claims the lives of over 32,000 men in the United States each year (Tortora & Grabowski, 1993). In fact, prostate cancer is the second leading cause of death from cancer among men, especially those over age 65. Benign and malignant tumors of the prostate, rectum, and colon are detectable by *rectal examination* (described below). The American Cancer Society recommends that all men over age 40 have a yearly rectal exam.

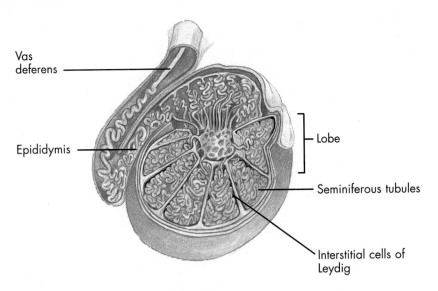

Vas deferens

Epididymis

Lobe

Seminiferous tubules

Interstitial cells of Leydig

FIGURE 5.9 *Sectional view of a testis.*

The Cowper's Glands   Just inferior and anterior to the prostate, on either side of the urethra, are the paired **Cowper's glands.** Prior to ejaculation these pea-size accessory sexual glands secrete a small amount of fluid that neutralizes any urine still present within the urethra. Fluid from the Cowper's glands sometimes appears in the form of a couple of clear, sticky droplets at the tip of the penis just prior to ejaculation. The drops are not semen, although Cowper's fluid can contain live sperm. For this reason, withdrawing the penis from the vagina before ejaculation ("coitus interruptus") is not an effective method of birth control.

SEXUAL GLANDS AND HORMONES

As is the case with females, various glands and hormones are important to male sexual and reproductive functioning. You'll recall from Chapter 4 that a *gland* is usually a hormone-secreting organ, and a *hormone* is a powerful chemical that stimulates cellular activity elsewhere in the body. A gland that secretes its hormone directly into the bloodstream is called an *endocrine* gland. Endocrine glands are responsible for secreting male sexual hormones.

THE HYPOTHALAMUS

The brain's *hypothalamus* controls hormonal aspects of male reproductive and sexual functioning, as well as other functions. The hypothalamus acts on the *pituitary gland*.

THE PITUITARY GLAND, GONADOTROPIN-RELEASING HORMONE, FOLLICLE-STIMULATING HORMONE, AND INTERSTITIAL CELL-STIMULATING HORMONE

In the male, the hypothalamus releases *gonadotropin-releasing hormone* (GnRH), which stimulates the *pituitary gland* to release two *gonadotropins* (gonad-affecting hormones):

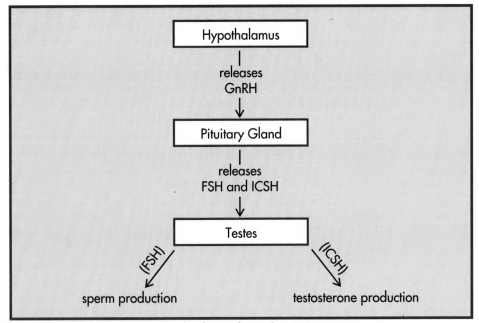

FIGURE 5.10 *Glands, hormones, and male reproductive functioning.*

follicle-stimulating hormone (FSH) and *interstitial cell-stimulating hormone* (ICSH). FSH causes the testes to produce sperm cells; ICSH is chemically identical to female *luteinizing hormone* and causes *interstitial cells of Leydig* (which lie in tissue between the seminiferous tubules of the testes) to produce testosterone. The levels of FSH and ICSH remain relatively constant in adult males (Figure 5.10).

THE TESTES, TESTOSTERONE, AND SPERM PRODUCTION

The hormones FSH and ICSH from the pituitary gland stimulate the testes to produce testosterone and sperm. *Testosterone* is the male sexual hormone responsible for final maturation of spermatozoa, maturation of the sex structures, and development of secondary sexual characteristics, such as facial hair and lowered vocal pitch. It also plays a significant role in stimulating male sexual drive and general body growth, including bone and muscular development. The production of this hormone begins at puberty (between ages 11 to 13, on average) and continues for the rest of a man's life. Feedback regarding the level of testosterone in the bloodstream serves to regulate the amount of ICSH released by the pituitary. Males produce a far greater amount of testosterone than do females— about 7 milligrams per day versus 0.5 milligrams for females.

FSH initiates spermatogenesis, which occurs in the seminiferous tubules of the testes. ICSH and testosterone assist sperm production by stimulating *Sertoli cells* of the tubules to produce secretions that nourish developing sperm. Sertoli cells also control the rate of spermatogenesis by releasing the hormone *inhibin*, which inhibits the amount of FSH released by the pituitary.

MEDICAL EXAMINATIONS

All men, like women, should schedule routine medical examinations. While women may see a *gynecologist* (a physician who specializes in women's medicine), men may see a primary care physician or a *urologist* (a physician who specializes in disorders of the urinary and reproductive systems). A urologist assesses and treats such problems as urinary incontinence and retention, painful urination or ejaculation, biologically based sexual dysfunctions, and infertility, to name a few (Kursh & Resnick, 1987).

Taking a medical history and performing a general examination are typical. The comprehensive medical history includes asking questions about previous or current diseases and conditions, family medical history, medications, and sexual history. The general medical exam includes inspecting as many external and internal body structures as possible; listening to the heart and lungs with a stethoscope; checking pulse, blood pressure, and weight; testing blood and urine; and in some cases testing for sexually transmitted diseases.

As part of a routine medical exam, the physician closely examines the man's genitals for abnormalities. Wearing latex gloves, the physician handles and inspects the penis, scrotum, and anal area. He or she checks the urethral opening for discharge, feels the testes for lumps or growths, and examines the anus and perineum for unusual sores, discharge, or swelling.

Perhaps the most important part of a man's medical exam is the *rectal examination* of his prostate gland. After asking the patient to bend over or lie with knees drawn toward his chest, the physician inserts a well-lubricated, gloved finger into the patient's rectum. He or she feels the prostate through the rectal wall, noting its condition (Figure 5.11). A "rock hard" or overly tender prostate could indicate trouble, such as prostatic cancer. The rectal examination is also helpful for identifying problems of the anus and rectum, such as hemorrhoids, polyps, and tumors.

Rectal examination of the prostate might also include a *prostatic massage*. Here, the physician strokes the prostate during the rectal exam to release prostatic fluid into the urethra. He or she then collects this fluid on a slide and later examines it under a microscope. Pus found in the sample indicates infection. The physician may also use prostatic massage to relieve pelvic congestion.

If the physician suspects the presence of a tumor, he or she may obtain a sample of prostatic tissue by inserting a needle directly into the gland via the rectum, using *transrectal ultrasonography*, a procedure for detecting tumors by bouncing sound waves off the prostate, or test for levels of *prostate-specific antigen* (PSA) in the blood.

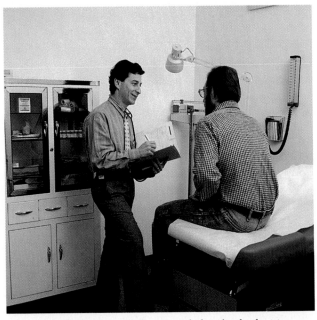

Many men talk about sexual concerns with their family physician.

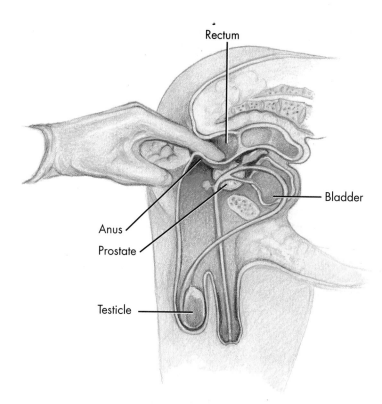

FIGURE 5.11 *Insertion of a gloved finger into the anus during rectal examination of the prostate.*

Many men object to having a rectal exam, often out of embarrassment, fear of pain, or homosexual associations. Even so, this exam is a crucial first step in identifying potentially serious disorders of the prostate, rectum, and colon. A few moments of embarrassment is a small price to pay for what could turn out to be a life-saving test.

PERSPECTIVE

How to Do a Testicular Self-Examination

In addition to routine medical examinations, every man should become familiar with his testicles and scrotum, and regularly examine them for abnormalities. Unusual changes in one or both testes sometimes signal testicular cancer.

The best time to perform a *testicular self-examination* (TSE) is right after a hot shower or bath, when the scrotum relaxes and the testes hang lower away from the body. While seated or lying down, gently roll each testicle between your thumb and fingers. Check for abnormalities such as lumps or growths (which may be hard, soft, painful, or painless), swelling or pain in the scrotum or groin, or enlarged lymph nodes. Finally, check for tenderness or swelling in one or both breasts. You should bring any unusual features to the immediate attention of your health-care practitioner. Although testicular cancer tends to be rarer than other cancers, it can be deadly, so you should get into the habit of doing TSEs. Early detection of a malignant tumor may someday save your life.

Every man should regularly perform testicular self-examinations (TSEs) to become more familiar with his genitals.

KEY POINTS

1. The external male genitals consist of the *penis* and *scrotum*. The *penis* is the male organ of urination and sexual intercourse. Its outer structures are the *glans, shaft,* and *root.* Its inner structures are three cylinders of erectile tissue: two *cavernous bodies* and one *spongy body.* When the vascular spaces of all three engorge with blood, the penis becomes erect. Beneath the penis is a loose sac of skin called the *scrotum,* which contains the two male gonads, the *testes.* The *perineum* is a smooth, highly sensitive area of skin lying between the scrotum and the anus.

2. The internal male sex structures consist of the *testes, vas deferens, seminal vesicles, prostate gland,* and *Cowper's gland.* The *testes* are the male gonads that produce sperm and testosterone. Within each testis are lobes consisting of the *seminiferous tubules* and *interstitial cells of Leydig.* Sperm fully mature and are stored for up to six weeks in the *epididymis.* The *vas deferens* is a small tube inside the spermatic cord that carries sperm to the urethra. At the base of the bladder, the vas deferens joins the duct of the *seminal vesicle* and becomes the *ejaculatory duct.* The two ejaculatory ducts open into the urethra within the *prostate gland.*

3. *Semen* consists of sperm and the secretions of the accessory sexual glands. Fluid from the *seminal vesicles* nourishes the sperm. Fluid from the *prostate gland* activates sperm motility and neutralizes the acidic environments of the urethra and vagina. Fluid from the *Cowper's glands* neutralizes any urine still present in the urethra.

4. Various glands and hormones are important to male sexual and reproductive functioning. The *hypothalamus* releases *gonadotropin-releasing hormone,* which stimulates the *pituitary gland* to release *follicle-stimulating hormone* (stimulating the testes to produce sperm cells) and *interstitial cell-stimulating hormone* (stimulating the *interstitial cells of Leydig* of the testes to produce testosterone).

5. *Testosterone* is the male sexual hormone responsible for final maturation of spermatozoa, maturation of the sex structures, and development of secondary sexual characteristics. It also plays a significant role in stimulating male sexual drive and general body growth.

6. Every man should schedule routine medical examinations with either a primary care physician or a *urologist*. A *rectal examination* to assess the condition of the prostate is an important part of a man's medical exam. He should also perform monthly *testicular self-examinations*.

ACTIVITIES AND QUESTIONS

1. Divide into two same-sex groups. List common slang terms for male sexual organs and structures. Each group can also discuss the reasons why people develop and use slang to talk about sexuality. Now regroup as a class. On a chalkboard, create two lists: "words men use" and "words women use." How do the words in these two lists differ? How are they the same? Whose list is longer?

2. In small groups identify some of the sources of male sexual myths. How long do you think male sexual myths have been around? Why do they continue? What can be done to eliminate them?

3. In what ways are the genitals of both sexes similar and different?

4. Locate and bring to class representations of male sexual anatomy as portrayed in different media (paintings, photos, or anatomy textbooks) and other cultures. How do your representations differ from each other?

RECOMMENDED READINGS

Baldwin, D. (1993). *Understanding male sexual health: A handbook for adult males, partners, and parents*. New York: Hippocrene Books. A readable and comprehensive self-help guide to male health problems and hygiene.

Boyd, B. R. (1990). *Circumcision: What it does*. San Francisco: Taterhill Press. Describes the practice of and rationale for circumcision from an anticircumcision point of view. The appendix "The Victims Speak" contains numerous comments from circumcised men. Makes for lively reading.

Zilbergeld, B. (1992). *The new male sexuality: The truth about men, sex, and pleasure*. New York: Bantam Books. Another book on male sexuality by this noted author. Among other things, he suggests ways to deal with disorders of sexual arousal and desire.

C H A P T E R   6

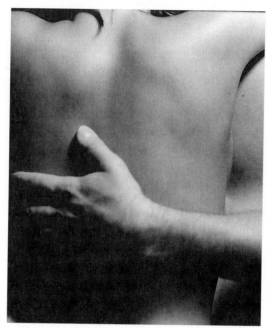

SEXUAL AROUSAL AND RESPONSE

O B J E C T I V E S

AFTER READING THIS CHAPTER YOU SHOULD BE
ABLE TO . . .

1. DEFINE *SEXUAL AROUSAL* AND *SEXUAL RESPONSE*.

2. IDENTIFY SOME OF THE MANY BIOLOGICAL,
   PSYCHOLOGICAL, AND SOCIAL SOURCES OF
   SEXUAL AROUSAL.

3. DESCRIBE MASTERS AND JOHNSON'S
   FOUR-PHASE MODEL OF SEXUAL RESPONSE.

4. DESCRIBE KAPLAN'S, ZILBERGELD AND
   ELLISON'S, AND WALEN AND ROTH'S MODELS OF
   SEXUAL RESPONSE.

5. IDENTIFY MALE/FEMALE DIFFERENCES IN SEXUAL
   AROUSAL AND RESPONSE.

PERSONAL ASSESSMENT

TEST YOUR GENERAL KNOWLEDGE OF HUMAN SEXUAL AROUSAL AND RESPONSE BY ANSWERING THE FOLLOWING STATEMENTS *true* OR *false*.

_____ 1. Little or no variation exists among members of the same sex in terms of sexual arousal and response.

_____ 2. Men find auditory stimuli more arousing; women find visual stimuli more arousing.

_____ 3. Men and women don't normally have sexual fantasies during masturbation or sexual intercourse.

_____ 4. During the plateau phase, a woman's labia minora swell and deepen in color.

_____ 5. A man's testes must elevate at least partially before he can have an orgasm.

_____ 6. All women experience multiple orgasms; men never do.

_____ 7. Significant differences exist between men's and women's written descriptions of what it feels like to have an orgasm.

_____ 8. The length of the refractory period varies from man to man.

_____ 9. Women and men undergo the same basic sexual response cycle regardless of the type of sexual activity.

_____ 10. The brain is the most important sexual organ of the human body.

ANSWERS
1. F, 2. F, 3. F, 4. T, 5. T, 6. F, 7. F, 8. T, 9. T, 10. T

The sexual drive is nothing but the motor memory of previously experienced pleasure.

Wilhelm Reich

The topics of sexual arousal and response frequently elicit people's interest and enthusiasm. Virtually everybody at one time or another has experienced a sexual "turn-on"—a phenomenon that most people find pleasurable. And many students (as well as people in general) want to know more. They ask about increasing their sexual appeal, adding romance to lovemaking, becoming more intimate with a loved one, learning how the body responds to sexual stimulation, and enhancing sexual responsiveness. They may also ask about sexual attractants, sexual fantasies, erotic films and magazines, and aphrodisiacs. People enjoy and value sexuality, and naturally want to increase the quality of their sexual experiences.

SEXUAL AROUSAL

DRIVE

State of tension that motivates the individual to reduce a need.

Like eating when hungry and drinking when thirsty, sexual behaviors are responses to a **drive,** or a state of tension (brought on by deprivation) that motivates the individual to reduce the tension. Drives like hunger and thirst assure the survival of the organism, while sex assists in the survival of the species.

In humans, both internal and external stimuli strongly influence primary drives. For example, an external stimulus (for instance, an erotic photo) arouses a motive or drive (a sexual urge), which in turn prompts goal-directed behavior (sexual relations). **Sexual**

SEXUAL AROUSAL

Excitation of a person's libido.

arousal is the excitation of an individual's sexual drive, or *libido.*

Obviously, human beings become sexually aroused. But why and in response to what? To answer these questions, let's consider various biological, psychological, and social sources of sexual arousal.

BIOLOGICAL SOURCES OF SEXUAL AROUSAL

Biological processes, including nervous system and brain activity, hormones, physical stimulation of the senses, and a number of drugs, strongly influence human sexual arousal. In this respect, human sexual arousal *resembles* that of other species. But because human and animal processes are not identical, some intriguing questions arise. What is it about human biology that makes human sexuality unique in the animal kingdom? What effect does biology have on a person's interest in and desire for sexual activity? Is biology solely responsible for human sexual responsiveness, or are there other factors involved as well?

The Nervous System and Brain Nervous system and brain activity provide the basis of human sexual desire and arousal. The center of the brain's influence on sexual drive, arousal, and response seems to be the *limbic system*, a set of structures that play a role in memory, learning, and emotional reactions, including sexual behavior (Rischer & Easton, 1992). Although many of the neural aspects of sexuality remain a mystery, physiologists believe that signals sent to and from specific "sexual centers" in the spinal cord and brain control sexual functioning. Perceptions, memories, erotic associations, and tactile stimulation of the genitals prompt the brain to send nerve impulses to an "erection center" in the lower portion of the spinal cord, which in turn sends impulses to the muscles that regulate clitoral and penile erection. For instance, neural impulses cause the muscles surrounding the penile arteries to relax, which allows increased blood flow into the penile shaft. As the penile veins are compressed, blood flow out of the penis lessens and erection occurs (Tortora & Grabowski, 1993). A similar neural process underlies ejaculation. Nerve impulses from the "ejaculation center" of the spinal cord cause various muscles of the reproductive organs to contract, which initiates both the *emission* and *expulsion* stages of ejaculation, described later in this chapter.

For Personal Reflection

With the limited amount of information presented thus far, how do you respond to the statement, "The brain is the most important sexual organ of the human body"?

Hormones You will recall from the last two chapters that *hormones*, or chemical activators, powerfully influence human sexual drive and arousal. Endocrine glands secrete these substances directly into the bloodstream.

Testosterone appears to affect the sexual drives of both men and women (Bancroft, 1990; Masters et al., 1993), while estrogen may or may not (Myers et al., 1990). Males produce a far greater amount of testosterone than do females, about 7 milligrams per day for males versus 0.5 milligrams for females. Generally, lower levels of testosterone are associated with decreased interest in sexual activity; higher levels with active interest. Men with lower than normal levels of testosterone typically have difficulty attaining and keeping erections adequate for sexual activity. When such men undergo *hormone replacement therapy*, in which a physician administers testosterone to appropriate levels, normal sexual arousal and activity often resume (Carey et al., 1988). However, hormone levels do not necessarily affect sexual drive, as some individuals with low testosterone levels have powerful libidos and maintain active sex lives. For instance, some *eunuchs* (castrated males, whose testicles have been removed or destroyed) continue to have erections and engage in sexual activity (Leshner, 1978). And drugs that reduce the amount of circulating testosterone reduce libido in some individuals but not all (Masters et al., 1994). The conclusion here is that although hormones are important in sexual desire and arousal, so are other biological and psychosocial processes.

Physical Stimulation of the Senses   All information about the outside world comes to us via *sensory receptors*. These specialized cells within certain organs of the body—the *sensory organs* (for example, the eyes and ears)—pick up information from the environment in the form of physical energy (light and sound waves) and convert this energy into neural impulses that the nervous system and brain can understand. In fact, the brain is incapable of reacting directly to physical energy of the environment. It instead processes sensory information from the nervous system and senses, and then directs various systems of the body to react accordingly.

First and foremost, the skin is the largest sensory organ, embodying a number of specific types of receptors that are sensitive to pressure, warmth, cold, and pain. **Erogenous zones** are areas of the skin that are richly endowed with such receptors. *Primary erogenous zones* are especially endowed with nerve endings, are sensitive to touch, and generally evoke erotic pleasure. The most common primary erogenous zones are the mouth, ears, neck, breasts, sides, palms of the hands, genitals, perineum, anus, buttocks, inner thighs, and soles of the feet. *Secondary erogenous zones*, which can be virtually any part of the body, evoke erotic pleasure as a result of prior learning. For example, a woman's shoulder may become a secondary erogenous zone after her partner repeatedly kisses her there.

One specific form of touch, *kissing*, has erotic value for members of many different societies. Although members of certain groups tend to kiss to express affection or offer greetings (for example, people of Greece and Italy), members of other groups do not (people of traditional Asian cultures). In America and other Western societies, kissing is often an erotic activity, and as such involves the use of multiple sensory organs—kissing each other's lips, nibbling on the partner's earlobe, using the tongue to probe the partner's mouth, and kissing the partner's genitals.

EROGENOUS ZONES (E-ROJ-e-nus)
Erotically sensitive areas of the body.

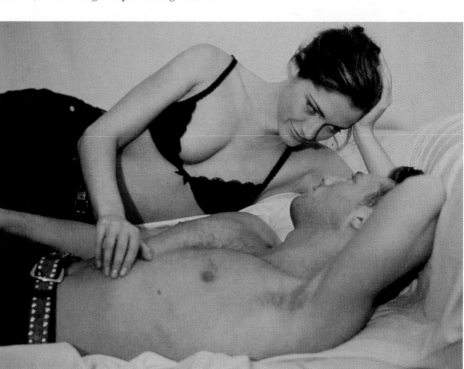

Stimulating erogenous zones is one way to enhance erotic pleasure.

For Personal Reflection

1. *How important do you think nonsexual touch is in a relationship?*
2. *How would you go about telling your partner that you would like to be touched or held more often?*

Research suggests that certain naturally occurring odorous chemicals, termed *pheromones*, exert a powerful influence on the sexual behavior of insects and animals, and possibly human beings (Cobb & Jallon, 1990; Durden-Smith, 1980; Hassett, 1978). Many female animals presumably attract mates by secreting *copulins,* or odorous vaginal substances that seem to act as a sex attractant on males of that particular species (Michael et al., 1974). But what about human beings? Can smelling copulins excite a couple into a lovemaking frenzy? Maybe, but probably not. Humans, like other primates and numerous other animals, seem to secrete pheromones—copulins in females and *exaltolide* in males (Hassett, 1978; Lake, 1991). Some couples, but not all, report finding these secretions sexually stimulating (Morris & Udry, 1978). (Interestingly, our society's enormous perfume industry has relied on the assumption that men and women will find artificial, pheromone-like fragrances arousing.) Research on pheromones often yields conflicting results, suggesting that we still have a great deal to learn about the link between smell and human sexual attraction.

Many people become sexually excited while watching or listening to erotic materials, including erotic films, books, magazines, tapes, and "1-900" phone sex services. Research suggests that arousal from erotic materials can enhance overt sexual behavior (Mosher & MacIan, 1994).

Many women and men turn on by listening to music, reading poetry out loud, or talking about sexuality with a partner. Others turn on by vocalizing ("moaning") or listening to a partner vocalize during sexual activity. Concerning such *erolalia*, Robert Chartham (1971) wrote in his *The Sensuous Couple:*

> I cannot imagine a session of lovemaking in which neither partner speaks or makes any kind of appreciative sound. . . . There are a number of us, and I am one of them, who are automatically "noisy lovers." We just can't help ourselves, try as we may to stifle our appreciative words or noises when a particularly sensitive spot is given a particularly effective caress. When we are in the throes of coming we are at our most noisy, and it was when one of my partners once protested that the neighbors in all the rest of the apartments would hear me if I didn't control myself, that I discovered, I think, why we do it, which, in turn, decided me to recommend erolalia to those who do not naturally use the technique. (pp. 145–146)

Aphrodisiacs and Anaphrodisiacs Everyone has heard about them—**aphrodisiacs** (named after the Greek goddess of love, *Aphrodite*), those seemingly magical drugs or foods that supposedly provide a user with an insatiable sexual appetite. These purportedly love-enhancing substances have been a source of great fascination throughout recorded history. From eating phallic-or testicular-shaped foods like bananas or oysters, to ingesting pulverized rhinoceros horn for increased sexual prowess and potency, humankind has actively sought the ultimate sexual aid.

Probably the most famous alleged aphrodisiac, *Spanish fly* or *cantharidin,* is in reality poisonous. As David Reuben (1969) explained in his classic *Everything You Always Wanted to Know About Sex But Were Afraid to Ask:*

> Spanish fly, strangely enough, is simply a Spanish fly. Almost. Actually it is made from small, shiny iridescent beetles found in Southern France and Spain. The bodies of these insects are dried and pulverized, then treated chemically to extract a

APHRODISIAC (AF-RO-DIZ-I-AK)
Chemical sexual stimulant.

PERSPECTIVE

One Touch Is Worth a Thousand Words

Is good sexual touching also sensual? The answer is an emphatic *yes!*, at least according to Sherry Cohen in her article *The Power of Touch* (1987):

> A sensual touch is one that gratifies the senses—all the senses. It is voluptuous. It is slow, searching, and attentive to reactions. It gives and receives. It is enjoyed as much by the giver as the receiver. Although sensual touch is related to sexual touch, it doesn't necessarily lead to sex. Sensual touch is glorious in itself. Wise lovers know that sex does not necessarily mean intercourse but rather sharing the exquisite delight of exploring one another's bodies. A sensitive toucher can evoke wonders. With sensual fingers, a partner's touch can instantly cool head and eyes that are burning with fever. With sensual touch, he or she can instantly gentle your damaged psyche and send it to a calming sleep. And then, when the time is ripe, he or she knows how to transform the sensual touch into the sexual.
>
> Fingers and hands that have practiced the craftsmanship of sensuality can touch your libido, make it surge with desire and burn brighter than you ever imagined possible. The same language of sensual touch that nourishes the infant comes into adult fruition during erotic play. (p. 40)

And what of male and female differences in touching? According to Cohen:

> Generally, young girls are more likely to be touched than boys are—although that is slowly changing as people become aware of how such actions perpetuate the notion of woman as nurturer. In the meantime, while extra touching may make women warm and affectionate, it also makes them tend to take what they get and not be assertive in the getting. Many women learn to let themselves accept sexual touching rather than initiate it. They are believed to be more passive sexually, and thus they train themselves to be so. They worry that men will find them pushy, unfeminine, or grabby if they are sexually aggressive in touching. Boys, on the other hand, learn to be the touching aggressors. When they are men, they often have little patience for lying back and receiving touches in foreplay. Lie back and just enjoy? Is that really manly?
>
> Although this attitude seems old-fashioned, it still persists in spite of many studies and books to the contrary. Our generation is supposed to be one of sexual sophistication, yet insidious double standards continue. (pp. 41–42)

Questions for Thought

How comfortable are you with touching others and/or being touched? Does touch always have a sexual overtone? Do you believe it's "unfeminine" for a woman to initiate sexual touching with her partner? Is it "unmanly" for a man to receive and enjoy being touched by his partner? Why do you think traditional stereotypic Western views about touch persist?

Source: S. S. Cohen (1987), The power of touch, *New Woman*, April, 40–42.

drug called "cantharidin." Then, supposedly, the real fun begins. All one has to do, according to the stories, is slip a few drops into your girl friend's drink. No matter how cold she has been to you in the past, she will be transformed instantly into an insatiable sex maniac begging you to quench her pelvic fires.

Remember the story about the fellow who slipped some Spanish fly to his date, drove out to the lover's lane, and awaited the results? The young lady became

Can the smell of perfume sexually excite human beings?

Watching explicit films is a turn-on for some people and a turn-off for others.

worked up, exhausted her boy friend's resources after four times at bat, and proceeded to have intercourse with the gear-shift lever and most of the knobs on the dashboard. Nice story.

Here's a more likely version: Ten minutes after drinking the "love potion" the girl collapses in convulsions—she goes to the hospital, and Casanova goes to the clink. If she lives (fifty-fifty chance), he gets off lightly. If she dies, it's murder second. . . .

Spanish fly is a truly great aphrodisiac—for farm animals. (pp. 89–90)

Two drugs that *might* have sexuality-enhancing effects in humans are *caffeine* and *bupropion hydrochloride*. Preliminary results of research indicate that these compounds may improve sexual functioning and increase potency (Crenshaw et al., 1987; Diokno et al., 1990). Other substances that supposedly increase sexual desire and prowess include marijuana, cocaine, psychedelics, amphetamines ("uppers"), amyl nitrate ("poppers"), *yohimbine hydrochloride*, and assorted foods. Many of these are dangerous (psychedelics), are habit-forming (cocaine), or can have serious side effects (yohimbine). Concerning the latter, some individuals have reported extreme panic following administration of this compound (Barlow, 1988). Yohimbine appears to have an aphrodisiac effect on rats, and there is some evidence that the drug might increase sexual desire and performance for some people (Buffum, 1985; Rosen, 1991). To date, scientists have not proved the existence of a drug or food that is a *true* aphrodisiac. Any reported positive effects from moderate use of certain substances may actually be due to anticipated effects; that is, users' perceptions may be the enhancer rather than the substances themselves.

ANAPHRODISIAC (AN-AF-RO-DIZ-I-AK)
Chemical sexual inhibitor.

A number of drugs, termed **anaphrodisiacs,** do appear to interfere with sexual functioning. The most common of these are alcohol, tranquilizers, narcotics, nicotine, antihypertensives, antidepressants, and antipsychotics. The most famous anaphrodisiac, *potassium nitrate* ("saltpeter"), actually does nothing directly to reduce libido.

Some confusion exists about whether alcohol increases sexual prowess. Although many people attest to alcohol's aphrodisiac properties, the drug is technically a nervous system depressant, not a stimulant. Perhaps one reason so many people believe alcohol helps them sexually is that, in small to moderate amounts, it lowers their sexual inhibitions (Crowe & George, 1989). Increasing levels of intoxication, though, disrupt sexual functioning.

For Personal Reflection

If you read about a new prescription drug that was reported to increase libido, would you ask your physician to let you try it? Why or why not?

PSYCHOLOGICAL SOURCES OF SEXUAL AROUSAL

Although people pay a great deal of attention to the biological processes that underlie sexual arousal, psychological processes also shape a person's sexuality. As Masters and Johnson (1966) noted, women and men respond consistently to "effective sexual stimulation" (p. 20), whether that stimulation is physiological or psychological—an essentially biopsychosocial position. The ways in which our thoughts, perceptions, evaluations, and feelings affect our biology accounts for the great variability in human sexual behavior across individuals, cultures, and societies.

COGNITIVE LABELS
An individual's interpretations and evaluations of events.

Psychologically speaking, people's **cognitive labels,** or their interpretations and evaluations of internal and external events, heavily determine what, if, or when a stimulus is sexually arousing. Given variations in life experiences, social environment, upbringing, and attitudes, two individuals might interpret the same sexual stimulus differently. In part, researchers use cognitive theory to explain why some people might refer to certain behaviors as "lovemaking" or "romance," while others might refer to them as "sex." Moreover, *sexual scripts*—cognitive labels that guide sexual interpretations, decision-making, and behavior (Simon & Gagnon, 1986)—help individuals, for example, to distinguish between the stroking received during a therapeutic massage and that of a sexual partner.

The nature of people's thoughts largely determine how they will respond sexually. In general, guilt-free and accepting kinds of thoughts enhance sexual experiences. However, too many people have *sexual blocks*, or irrational, unrealistic expectations that disrupt sexual communication and functioning. Susan Walen (1985) described several typical sexual blocks that people might have:

- I can't take control.
- I couldn't ask for that!
- As long as he's happy, I'm happy.
- It's not nice to do that.
- What *would* he think?
- That doesn't look very ladylike.
- Lord, I've just been lying here like a piece of lox.
- I must sound like a rutting hog.
- I just know I'm not making as much noise as I should.
- I bet I'm not doing this right.
- I wonder if I'm as good as her last lover. (p. 135)

Do any of these sound familiar? Don't feel alone. These kinds of cognitive and sexual blocks are extremely common, tending to interfere with what a person finds sexually acceptable, and therefore sexually arousing. If a person is preoccupied with "It's not nice to do that!" he or she might be so distracted during sexual activity as to miss out on all but the very basics. Yes, thinking processes and sexual arousal/expression go hand in hand.

One final point along these lines has to do with *prior learning* (O'Donahue & Plaud, 1994). Most of us are conditioned to experiencing certain stimuli as erotic. To one person the genitals are beautiful, to another they are ugly. One person desires caressing, another sexual talk. Much of what a person finds sexually arousing has to do with the "mental programming" formed from *injunctions* (early messages) received during childhood from parents, relatives, teachers, neighbors, authority figures, and society. This can be beneficial if the individual's social environment has fostered healthy attitudes about sexuality, unconditional acceptance, and love. But what about those who receive other messages? Negative messages from childhood (or any other time) influence us by reinforcing old negative behavioral patterns. Consider a woman who is taught as a child that sexual desire and activity are "dirty." She may grow up to feel guilty about her sexual feelings. She may have trouble "turning on" and "letting go" during sex, never experience orgasms, become repulsed at the sight of her partner, and suffer from anxiety and depression. In short, her negative thoughts and experiences may interfere with her ability to become sexually aroused and responsive. They may cause her to find sexual activity unappealing, boring, and even disgusting.

Sexual Fantasies   As far as we know, human beings are unique in their ability to form self-generated sexual images, or **sexual fantasies.** Although people report a variety of fantasy themes, such as being wealthy and powerful, sexual themes are some of the most common (Masters et al., 1994; Reinisch, 1990). The frequency and intensity with which people fantasize varies considerably from person to person.

SEXUAL FANTASIES
Self-generated sexual images.

Some individuals express concerns about sexual fantasizing, believing that embarrassing fantasies might somehow become a reality. Fortunately, fantasizing about and actually engaging in a particular sexual behavior are very different (Gold et al., 1991). As an example, a person who fantasizes about having a sexual encounter with multiple partners might never actually wish to engage in such behavior. As one student described:

On a Personal Note (Will, age 20)

I've been troubled for a long time about some of my masturbation fantasies, well, actually one in particular. I often fantasize about having sex with two or three women. I know I would never really do that, but it's such an irresistible daydream. I guess I keep telling myself that if I masturbate about it, I'll eventually do it. (Author's files)

Having an attractive partner can be a source of intense sexual arousal, yet standards of attractiveness vary considerably across cultures.

What are some of the most common sexual fantasies? And do the sexual fantasies of men differ from those of women? These are fascinating questions, the answers to which might surprise you. In general, men's fantasies tend to be visually oriented and sexually active, while women's tend to be more romantic and passive. In a survey of 263 undergraduate students, researchers Arndt et al. (1985) found that females' sexual fantasies generally involved romance, mood, and setting, while males' fantasies generally involved attraction to specific body parts, sexual activity, and appearing sexually desirable to women.

For Personal Reflection

1. *Think about your most intimate sexual fantasy. How inclined would you be to share this fantasy with your partner? Why or why not? Under what conditions might you be willing to share your fantasy with a friend, relative, teacher, or professional?*
2. *What would you do if your partner asked you to act out a sexual fantasy that made you feel uncomfortable?*

Sharing sexual fantasies with your partner can improve your sexual relationship.

Drawing by Shirvanian; © 1979 The New Yorker Magazine, Inc.

SOCIAL SOURCES OF SEXUAL AROUSAL

A view of the city on Saturday night. Soft music. Rain hitting lightly against the window. Being with someone you love. For a lot of people these and similar images conjure up feelings of love and romance. The right mood and setting for lovemaking are critical, yet also a matter of individual taste and preference. That's the beauty of it; there aren't any rules. You can be creative or traditional, daring or reserved—the choice is up to you and your partner.

Many people would agree that having a loving, available, attractive partner in the right setting makes for quality lovemaking. But partner attractiveness is relative, and standards of attractiveness vary across cultures. The right setting is also relative. What is an erotic setting for one partner, like having sex with all the lights on, might be a turn-off for the other. Furthermore, what a person perceives as erotic may differ considerably from occasion to occasion. For example, a nude body may be rather unremarkable during a physical exam, but in the bedroom it may carry an entirely different set of erotic meanings. The difference here lies with the cognitive labels that people attach to sexual events and partners.

For Personal Reflection

What social and interpersonal stimuli sexually excite you? Which ones turn you off? Which past experiences have shaped your attitudes about sexual responsiveness and expression? How did they affect you?

SEXUAL RESPONSE: MASTERS AND JOHNSON'S FOUR-PHASE MODEL

SEXUAL RESPONSE

The body's reaction to sexual stimulation.

Probably the most widely known model of human **sexual response,** or the body's reaction to sexual stimulation, is that of William Masters and Virginia Johnson (1966), the pioneers of *observational research* in sexology. Over a period of 12 years, these researchers studied human sexual response by observing, monitoring, and filming 312 male and 382 female volunteers who engaged in over 10,000 separate sexual acts. Masters and Johnson found that both women and men pass through four phases of sexual arousal and response: the *excitement phase, plateau phase, orgasm phase,* and *resolution phase* (Figures 6.1, 6.2, 6.3, 6.4, and 6.5).

THE EXCITEMENT PHASE

Most of the information presented in this chapter regarding sexual anticipation and arousal involves this first phase of sexual response, the *excitement phase.* Here, both sexes experience *myotonia* (generally increased muscle tension); *pelvic vasocongestion* (increased

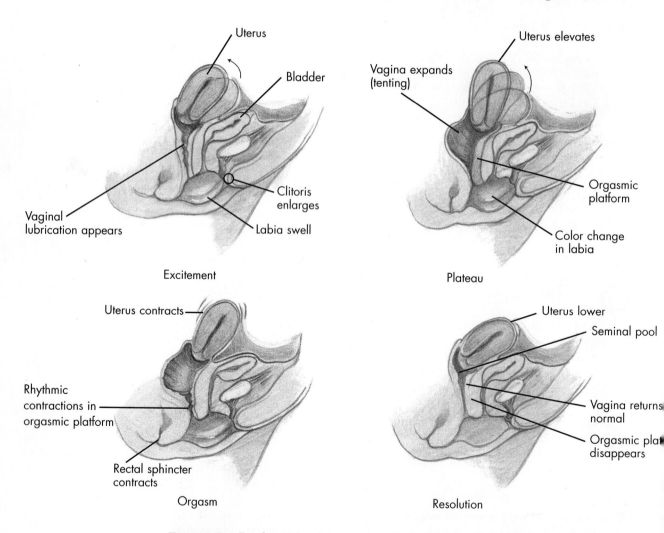

FIGURE 6.1 *Female sexual response. Source: W. H. Masters, V. E. Johnson, & R. C. Kolodny, (1992).* Human sexuality *(4th ed.). New York: HarperCollins. Reprinted by permission of HarperCollins Publishers, Inc.*

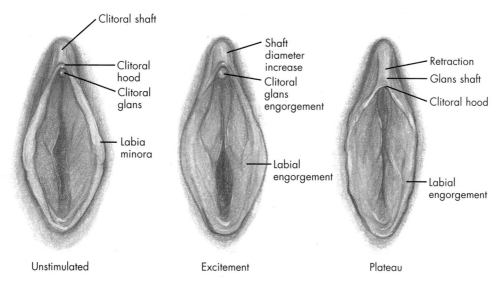

Unstimulated

Excitement

Plateau

FIGURE 6.2 *The clitoris and labia and female sexual response. Source: W. H. Masters, V. E. Johnson, & R. C. Kolodny (1992). Human sexuality (4th ed.). New York: HarperCollins. Reprinted by permission of HarperCollins Publishers, Inc.*

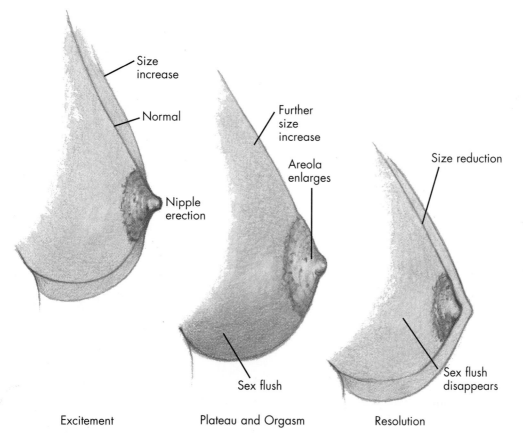

Excitement

Plateau and Orgasm

Resolution

FIGURE 6.3 *Breast changes and female sexual response. Source: W. H. Masters, V. E. Johnson, & R. C. Kolodny (1992). Human sexuality (4th ed.). New York: HarperCollins. Reprinted by permission of HarperCollins Publishers, Inc.*

blood flow into the genitals and surrounding areas); increased respiration, heart rate, and blood pressure; and the beginnings of a *sexual flush* (red blotches on the skin). In the female, the clitoris enlarges, the labia swell, drops of lubrication appear in the vagina, the breasts increase in size, and the nipples of the breasts become erect. In the male, the penis becomes erect and the testes begin elevating closer to the abdominal wall. Men may also experience erection of their breast nipples at this time. This phase of sexual response normally lasts anywhere from a few minutes to hours, depending on the situation, level of arousal, and individual differences.

THE PLATEAU PHASE

During the *plateau phase*, the individual experiences intense sexual excitement and pleasure. Myotonia and vasocongestion increase, causing numerous changes in both sexes. In the female, the labia continue to swell and deepen in color, the clitoris retracts under its clitoral hood, the inner portion of the vagina expands ("tenting"), the uterus elevates, the breasts continue to increase in size, the areolas of the breasts expand, and the sexual flush continues to develop. The outer third of the vagina also narrows, forming the *orgasmic platform*. In the male, the penis continues to engorge and deepen in color, the scrotum thickens, the testes increase in size while fully elevating, and the prostate enlarges. Before reaching the orgasm phase, the two pea-sized Cowper's glands release a few drops of urine-neutralizing fluid into the urethra. Toward the end of the plateau phase, the feeling that orgasm is inevitable sweeps over both sexes. Like the excitement phase, the duration of the plateau phase varies across individuals and situations.

THE ORGASM PHASE

During the *orgasm phase* ("climax" or "coming"), the buildup of sexual tension is released. Orgasm for both sexes involves numerous muscular contractions (always in the genitals but often in other parts of the body, such as the abdomen and limbs), warm feelings of intense erotic pleasure, and an inward shift of concentration. In the female, rhythmic contractions occur in the orgasmic platform, and the uterus and rectal sphincter contract. Breast size and the sexual flush reach their peak. Some women even report "ejaculating" a semenlike fluid. In the male, orgasm is usually accompanied by ejaculation, which consists of *emission* and *expulsion*. During emission, the accessory sexual glands contract, and seminal fluid is released into the urethra. During expulsion, penile and urethral contractions move the semen along the urethra and propel it out of the body through the meatus. For most people, orgasm itself lasts for only a few moments. Yet evidence suggests that some individuals are able to extend their orgasms by practicing various pelvic muscle exercises (Brauer & Brauer, 1990).

What does an orgasm feel like? Do men and women have different experiences of orgasm? These questions are difficult to answer. The subjective descriptions of orgasm for both men and women appear to be virtually identical, so much so that even expert judges have had trouble identifying the gender of the author of a particular description (Vance & Wagner, 1976).

For Personal Reflection

Do you think having orgasms during sexual activity is a sure sign of intimacy between partners? Why or why not?

THE RESOLUTION PHASE

In both sexes, the genitals and rest of the body gradually return to an unaroused state during the *resolution phase*. Muscles relax, heart rate and respiration return to normal, and the genitals return to their usual shape and size. Feelings of satisfaction and relaxation are common.

The resolution phase can differ for men and women. First, the majority of men enter a *refractory period* immediately following ejaculation, meaning that a certain period of time must pass (from minutes to hours to days, depending on the person) before sexual arousal and orgasm are once again possible. In contrast, women usually do not enter a refractory period, and in some cases may have **multiple orgasms,** or more than one orgasm during any single episode of sexual activity. Female resolution is usually slower and less drastic than its male counterpart. Some men can also have two or more orgasms before losing their erection (Masters et al., 1994).

MULTIPLE ORGASMS

Experiencing more than one orgasm during any single episode of sexual activity.

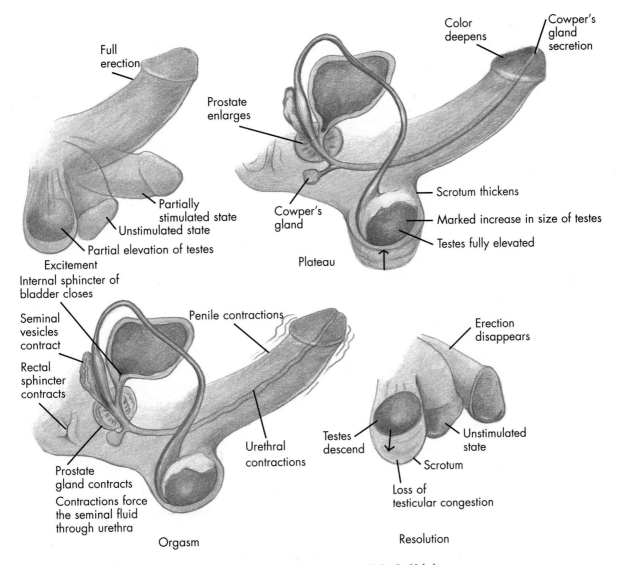

FIGURE 6.4 *Male sexual response.Source: W. H. Masters, V. E. Johnson, & R. C. Kolodny (1992). Human sexuality (4th ed.). New York: HarperCollins. Reprinted by permission of HarperCollins Publishers, Inc.*

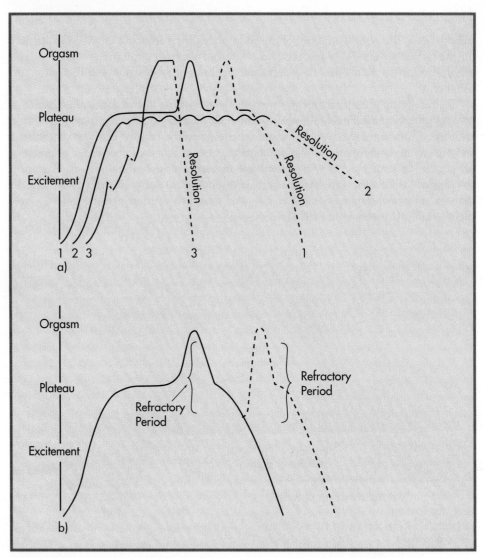

FIGURE 6.5 *The sexual response cycle. (a) Three representative variations of female sexual response. Pattern 1 shows multiple orgasm, pattern 2 shows arousal that reaches the plateau level without going on to orgasm (note that resolution occurs very slowly), and pattern 3 shows several brief drops during the excitement phase followed by an even more rapid resolution phase. (b) The most typical pattern of male sexual response. The dotted line shows one possible variation: a second orgasm and ejaculation occurring after the refractory period is over. Numerous other variations are possible, including patterns that would match patterns 2 and 3 of the female response cycle. Source: W. H. Masters, V. E. Johnson, & R. C. Kolodny, (1992). Human sexuality (4th ed.). New York: HarperCollins. Reprinted by permission of HarperCollins Publishers, Inc.*

SEXUAL RESPONSE: THREE OTHER MODELS

Although the four-phase sexual response model of Masters and Johnson is probably the most famous, it is not the only one. The professional literature cites three other models: those of Helen Singer Kaplan (1979), Bernie Zilbergeld and Carol Ellison (1980), and Susan Walen and David Roth (1987). All of the models are attempts to describe the same phenomena. Each has its own advantages and disadvantages, depending on its use.

KAPLAN'S THREE-PHASE MODEL

Kaplan (1979) proposed a sexual response model consisting of three distinct phases: (1) *sexual desire*, (2) *excitement*, and (3) *orgasm*. Kaplan's model evolved from a "biphasic" one (1974) that first included only excitement and orgasmic phases (physiological), but later came to include a desire phase (psychological). It is this desire phase that separates Kaplan's model from that of Masters and Johnson. Kaplan has successfully applied her "triphasic" model to helping individuals and couples overcome sexual dysfunctions, such as sexual desire disorders.

ZILBERGELD AND ELLISON'S FIVE-PHASE MODEL

Zilbergeld and Ellison's (1980) five-phase model of sexual response originally developed out of these therapists' concern that Masters and Johnson's model emphasized physiology at the expense of cognitions, emotions, and subjective experiences. Zilbergeld and Ellison's phases of sexual response are (1) *interest*, (2) *arousal*, (3) *physiological readiness*, (4) *orgasm*, and (5) *satisfaction*. Like Kaplan's model, this one easily accommodates treatment of sexual dysfunctions involving one or more phases of response.

WALEN AND ROTH'S COGNITIVE-BEHAVIORAL MODEL

Another model that acknowledges the role of cognitions in sexual response is that of Walen and Roth (1987). These psychologists have noted that *sexual behavior* follows *positive evaluation* of the *perception of sexual arousal*, which follows *positive evaluation* of the *perception of a sexual stimulus*. In addition, *positive evaluation* of the *perception of sexual behavior* is necessary for arousal and sexual behavior to continue. In other words, regardless of what is happening physiologically, a person's thoughts and evaluations of events are of great importance.

KEY POINTS

1. Like eating when hungry and drinking when thirsty, sexual behaviors are responses to a *drive*, or a state of tension (brought on by deprivation) that motivates the individual to reduce the tension. *Sexual arousal* is the excitation of an individual's sexual drive, or *libido*.
2. The three general sources of sexual arousal are biological, psychological, and social. Biological sources include the nervous system and brain, hormones, physical stimulation of the senses, and perhaps certain drugs. Psychological sources include cognitive processes and sexual fantasies. Social sources include setting and the attractiveness and availability of a partner.
3. Researchers believe that brain structures within the *limbic system* play an important role in sexual processes. The hormone *testosterone* has a major effect on the sex drives of both men and women. The *sensory organs*, including specialized *sensory receptor cells*, are another biological source of sexual arousal. The most common forms of sensory stimulation include touch, smell, hearing, and vision.
4. Thoughts, perceptions, evaluations, and feelings shape an individual's sexuality. Interpretations are called *cognitive labels*, which develop into *sexual scripts* that guide sexual decision-making and behavior. *Sexual blocks* are irrational, unrealistic expectations that disrupt sexual communication and functioning. Also, human beings are unique in their ability to form self-generated sexual images, or *sexual fantasies*.

5. The most widely known model of human sexual response is that of Masters and Johnson, the pioneers of *observational research*. Masters and Johnson found that both women and men pass through four phases of sexual arousal and response: the *excitement*, *plateau*, *orgasm*, and *resolution* phases. There are both similarities and differences in the sexual response cycles of men and women.

6. The professional literature cites three other sexual response models: Kaplan's (1979) three-phase model, Zilbergeld and Ellison's (1980) five-phase model, and Walen and Roth's (1987) cognitive-behavioral model.

ACTIVITIES AND QUESTIONS

1. Form several small groups. Discuss what you believe every individual should know about his or her partner's sexual fantasies and patterns of arousal and response. What might it be better for someone *not* to know? Are there elements of fantasy and arousal that partners might not want to share? Why?

2. In this exercise, each member of the class writes his or her gender and an anonymous, brief description of what it feels like to have an orgasm, regardless of how or when it occurred. Those who don't wish to write about an orgasm or have never experienced one can write "pass" on their paper. Someone collects and then reads the responses aloud. Class members try to identify the gender of the author of each description.

3. Create a panel to discuss the benefits and limitations associated with studying sexual response by means of direct observation. Under what circumstances might such research methods be necessary? Why? When would direct observation be inadvisable? Why?

4. As a class, compare and contrast female and male sexual arousal and response. For example, are women or men more interested in foreplay? Do women or men become more sexually aroused? What effect have the media had on our society's assumptions about female and male sexuality?

RECOMMENDED READINGS

Brauer, A. P., & Brauer, D. J. (1990). *The ESO ecstasy program: Better, safer sexual intimacy and extended orgasmic response*. New York: Warner Books. A fully illustrated guide to experiencing "extended sexual orgasm" from a "safer sex" perspective. The authors provide many simple, erotic exercises for couples.

Brecher, R., & Brecher, E. (1966). *An analysis of human sexual response*. Boston: Little, Brown. A thoughtful, readable review of Masters and Johnson's classic text.

Rosen, R. C., & Beck, J. G. (1988). *Patterns of sexual arousal: Psychophysiological processes and clinical applications*. New York: Guilford. A comprehensive review of the physiological processes involved in sexual arousal.

Schwartz, B. (1992). *The one hour orgasm*. Houston, TX: Breakthru Publishing. Although its title is a bit misleading, this book contains some helpful information on enhancing sexual arousal and response.

C H A P T E R 7

SEXUAL ORIENTATION AND HOMOSEXUALITY

O B J E C T I V E S

AFTER READING THIS CHAPTER YOU SHOULD BE ABLE TO . . .

1. DEFINE THE TERMS *SEXUAL ORIENTATION*, *HETEROSEXUAL*, *HOMOSEXUAL*, AND *BISEXUAL*.
2. IDENTIFY THE MOST GENERALLY ACCEPTED BIOLOGICAL, PSYCHOLOGICAL, SOCIAL, AND INTERACTIONAL THEORIES OF HOW HOMOSEXUALITY DEVELOPS.
3. DISCUSS THE IMPLICATIONS OF ATTEMPTING TO "REORIENT" HOMOSEXUAL OR BISEXUAL PERSONS.
4. DISCUSS THE IMPLICATIONS OF "COMING OUT" FOR HOMOSEXUAL AND BISEXUAL PERSONS, ALSO SPEAKING TO THE PROS AND CONS OF AN "OUT-OF-THE-CLOSET" HOMOSEXUAL LIFESTYLE.
5. IDENTIFY SOME OF THE CAUSES AND CONSEQUENCES OF HOMOPHOBIA IN AMERICAN SOCIETY.

P E R S O N A L   A S S E S S M E N T

TEST YOUR GENERAL KNOWLEDGE OF SEXUAL ORIENTATION AND HOMOSEXUALITY BY ANSWERING THE FOLLOWING STATEMENTS *true* OR *false*.

_____ 1. Noted sex researcher Alfred Kinsey suggested in the late 1940s and early 1950s that sexual orientation exists along a continuum.

_____ 2. Homosexuality is no longer considered a "mental disorder" by the American Psychiatric Association.

_____ 3. Homosexual experimentation among adolescent peers is a certain indication that these individuals are homosexuals.

_____ 4. Internal conflicts over homosexual inclinations are at the heart of most emotional problems and mental disorders.

_____ 5. Researchers are certain that homosexuality is directly caused by social factors only.

_____ 6. Bisexuals face problems "coming out" similar to those of homosexuals.

_____ 7. With most forms of therapy, a person can easily change his or her sexual orientation.

_____ 8. Transvestites and transsexuals are really homosexuals.

_____ 9. If a man and woman are married, neither can possibly be bisexual or homosexual.

_____ 10. Many consider that the Gay Rights Movement came into full swing with the Stonewall Rebellion of 1969.

ANSWERS: 1. T, 2. T, 3. F, 4. F, 5. F, 6. T, 7. F, 8. F, 9. F, 10. T

Can you be funny and give a political message? Yes . . . I'm still very clear that I'm a lesbian, but I'm not talking about my softball team all the time.
Kate Clinton

She was very friendly, interested, talkative, and open. I felt like I was a friend whom she was inviting in to share part of her life. I liked her paintings, her roommate's photographs of the Bay Area, and the warm togetherness of their home. She and her roommate were obviously very much in love. Like most people who have a good, stable, five-year relationship, they seemed comfortable together, sort of part of one another, able to joke, obviously fulfilled in their relationship. They work together, have the same times off from work, do most of their leisure activities together. She is helping her roommate learn to paint, while her roommate is teaching her about photography. They sent me home with a plateful of cookies, a good symbolic gesture of the kind of welcome and warmth I felt in their home. (Bell & Weinberg, 1978, p. 220)

So wrote a sex researcher after visiting a lesbian couple's home to interview them about lesbian and gay lifestyles. Words like *friendly, interested, talkative, open, comfortable together,* and *fulfilled,* however, might surprise some readers who hold certain stereotypes about gays and lesbians. Yet these are exactly the words that the researcher used to describe this lesbian couple.

No doubt, *sexual orientation*—especially when we talk about homosexuality and bisexuality—is a hotly debated topic today. The Gay Rights Movement. Gay liberation. Gay pride. The National Gay and Lesbian Task Force. Lesbian bars and clubs. "Coming out"

Homosexuality and bisexuality are controversial topics in contemporary America.

or "passing." Gay "equal rights" legislation. The military ban on gays and lesbians. Gay parents. Publications like *The Ladder, The Advocate, New York Native, Out, Outweek,* and even the *Journal of Homosexuality.* All of these aspects of gay lifestyles—and many more—are controversial in the eyes of many Americans. For this reason, I devote an entire chapter to exploring such complex issues as the causes of sexual orientation and the impact of being homosexual or bisexual on individuals and society.

WHAT IS SEXUAL ORIENTATION?

SEXUAL ORIENTATION

An individual's sexual, emotional, romantic, and affectionate attraction to members of the same, other, or both sexes.

HETEROSEXUALITY

Sexual attraction to people of the other sex.

HOMOSEXUALITY

Sexual attraction to people of the same sex.

BISEXUALITY OR AMBISEXUALITY

Sexual attraction to people of both sexes.

Sexual orientation refers to a person's emotional, romantic, affectionate, and sexual attraction to members of the same sex, the other sex, or both. A person who is attracted to members of the other sex is **heterosexual** (from the Greek *heteros*, meaning "different"). Many people use the term *straight* to refer to a male or female heterosexual. A person who is attracted to members of the same sex is **homosexual** (from the Greek *homos*, meaning "same"). Many also use the term *gay* to refer to a male homosexual, and *lesbian* to refer to a female homosexual. Homosexuals are not to be confused with *transvestites* (individuals who cross-dress for purposes of sexual satisfaction) or *transsexuals* (individuals who believe they were born into the wrong-sex body). A person who is attracted to members of both sexes is **bisexual** (from the Latin and Middle English *bi*, meaning "two") or **ambisexual** (from the Latin *ambi*, meaning "both"). In the broadest sense, *sexual orientation* refers to *any* form of sexual, emotional, romantic, and affectionate attraction. Hence, there are many sexual orientations, not just three. In the narrowest, most often used sense, the term refers only to attraction to adults of the same and/or other sex.

We hear a great deal these days about *sexual preference*, or one's object of sexual desire. More and more sexologists and other professionals, however, are opting for the term *sexual orientation* over *sexual preference*, the latter suggesting that sexual attraction is always a matter of choice. As noted sexologist John Money (1987) put it:

> *Sexual preference* is a moral and political term. Conceptually it implies voluntary choice, that is, that one chooses, or prefers, to be homosexual instead of heterosexual or bisexual, and vice versa. Politically, sexual preference is a dangerous term, for it implies that if homosexuals choose their preference, then they can be legally forced, under threat of punishment, to choose to be heterosexual.
>
> The concept of voluntary choice is as much in error here as in its application to handedness or to a native language. You do not choose your native language, even though you are born without it. (p. 385)

In the 1940s and 1950s, Alfred Kinsey and his associates suggested that sexual orientation exists along a continuum. Prior to Kinsey's research into the sexual habits of Americans, professionals (as well as much of the general public) generally believed that individuals were for the most part either heterosexual or homosexual. As part of his research, Kinsey surmised that the categories of sexual orientation are not so clear-cut as once believed. On Kinsey's 0- to 6-point scale to measure sexual orientation (0 meaning exclusive heterosexuality, 6 meaning exclusive homosexuality; Figure 7.1), many people reported having had at least minimal attraction to members of the same sex, although the majority did not act on their desires. In other words, except for the few heterosexuals *and* homosexuals who reported having exclusive sexual interests one way or the other, Kinsey found that many people are to some degree bisexuals, although most limit their sexual activity to members of one sex only.

As is the case with most social science research, Kinsey's conclusions about people's inherent bisexuality have been challenged. For instance, Carson & Butcher (1992) wrote:

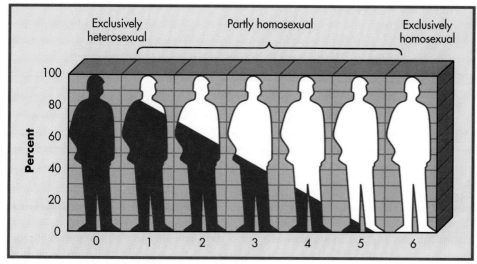

FIGURE 7.1 *Kinsey's continuum of sexual orientation.*
Source: J. R. Gerow (1992), Psychology: An introduction (3rd ed.) (New York: HarperCollins). *Reprinted by permission.*

It is our view therefore that Kinsey and colleagues' figures do not confirm the universality of bisexuality as some sort of fundamental libidinal gender neutrality. What they do suggest, as is now well known from research on prison populations and the like, is that many men denied sexual access to women can and do "make the best of it" by having sexual relations with other men. (p. 375)

It is important to remember that heterosexuality is as much a matter of sexual orientation as homosexuality, bisexuality, or any other attraction. Although people who claim that it is possible to alter one's sexual orientation are often heterosexuals referring to homosexuals, such an assertion (be it right or wrong) would need to be equally applied to people of all sexual orientations. And as we'll see in a later section, altering sexual orientation via therapy appears to be extremely difficult, if not impossible (Welch, 1990).

It is also necessary to distinguish between sexual *orientation* (or *attraction*) and sexual *behavior* (or *expression*). A person may or may not choose to act on his or her sexual orientation through behaviors (Money, 1987). In other words, he or she can have a homosexual orientation, but choose not to be sexually expressive with a partner. Of course, this same principle applies to heterosexuals and bisexuals. As one man described:

On a Personal Note (Jay, age 51)

I'm a gay priest, but I must say that I don't buy into the "I was born gay, so it's okay" argument. I know my opinion is probably the unpopular one, but I believe same-sex romantic relationships are morally wrong. I absolutely respect others' opinions and rights to make their own decisions about the matter, and I don't believe in discriminating against anyone. But I want to clarify the point about choice. You see, I have a very strong attraction to men, but I choose to be celibate and not act on my inclinations for moral reasons. I also know a lot of straight priests who do the same thing, that is, not act on their sexual impulses. So I definitely believe it's possible to separate *attraction* from *action*. (Author's files)

And as one woman described:

On a Personal Note (Sally, age 29)

To me this whole choice thing is irrelevant. I've always been gay—I'm sure I was born that way—and I'm not about to live like a nun. I don't have a choice about how I'm wired together, so I don't hesitate to find my sexual self in relationships with other women. (Author's files)

HOW COMMON IS HOMOSEXUAL BEHAVIOR?

At one time or another, homosexual thoughts have probably crossed the minds of most everyone. How prevalent is homosexual behavior in the general population? And how many Americans are exclusively homosexuals?

Given that sexual orientation exists along a continuum, that finding representative samples to survey is difficult, and that many people are hesitant to answer sexual surveys fully or honestly, obtaining exact percentages is difficult. Kinsey and colleagues (1948, 1953) found that about 37 percent of men and 13 percent of women surveyed reported having had at least one homosexual experience. In another study, Fay et al. (1989) found that roughly 20 percent of 1,227 men surveyed reported having had at least one homo-

PERSPECTIVE

Misconceptions and Stereotypes About Sexual Orientation

Assorted researchers, clinicians, academics, and other professionals have identified what they believe to be myths about sexual orientation—misconceptions and stereotypes that our society must challenge in order to overcome homophobia and eliminate prejudice and antigay violence. Following is a list of 12 of these myths:

- Myth 1.   Sexual orientation, especially homosexuality and bisexuality, is entirely a choice.
- Myth 2.   Sexual orientation, especially homosexuality and bisexuality, is easily changed.
- Myth 3.   It is always easy to identify homosexuals and bisexuals by the way they dress, walk, talk, and so on.
- Myth 4.   Homosexuals and bisexuals are more likely to molest children than heterosexuals.
- Myth 5.   Homosexuals and bisexuals never marry or have children.
- Myth 6.   People who never marry are probably homosexual or bisexual.
- Myth 7.   Children raised by homosexuals and bisexuals will automatically become homosexuals or bisexuals themselves.
- Myth 8.   Having a homosexual or bisexual orientation negatively affects one's ability to work, function in the military, socialize, and contribute to society.
- Myth 9.   The only thing homosexuals and bisexuals think about is sex.
- Myth 10. All homosexuals enjoy perverted sex.
- Myth 11. All homosexuals and bisexuals are out to recruit heterosexuals into changing their sexual orientation.
- Myth 12. All homosexuals have AIDS.

sexual encounter, and 3 percent had such homosexual contacts either "occasionally" or "fairly often." In this same study, 8 percent of married men also reported having had homosexual contacts either "occasionally" or "fairly often." Current estimates are that up to 4 percent of men and 1 to 2 percent of women in the United States are exclusively homosexual (Michael et al., 1994; Reinisch, 1990). These data indicate that the popular figure of 10 percent of the population being homosexual is an overestimate. Of course, estimates of homosexuality in certain settings like prisons, where there is *situational homosexuality* (homosexual behavior brought on by the absence of other-sex partners), are going to be higher than national averages.

Survey research suggests that a substantial percentage of the population of the United States has had at least one same-sex experience. For instance, Janus and Janus (1993) found that out of 1,335 men and 1,384 women surveyed, 22 percent of men and 17 percent of women reported having had homosexual experiences. Of these 294 men and 235 women, 5 percent of men and 6 percent of women reported having had homosexual experiences "once"; 56 percent of men and 67 percent of women, "occasionally"; 13 percent of men and 6 percent of women, "frequently"; and 26 percent of men and 21 percent of women, "ongoing." These data indicate that the largest number of men and women who have had homosexual experiences report doing so "occasionally." How many of these individuals actually label themselves as homosexual or bisexual is unknown.

Information on bisexuality is less available than that on homosexuality because many people think of bisexuality as a subcategory of homosexuality. Another difficulty in obtaining good information on bisexuality is that many people who have same-sex encounters do not necessarily think of themselves as bisexual. An example of this is the inmate who has sex with other men only while in prison, but who considers himself heterosexual. Still another difficulty is that many gays who are married and raise children as a social "cover" think of themselves as gay, not bisexual.

People sometimes think of bisexuality as "the best of both worlds," yet many bisexuals disagree with this view. They often feel isolated and alienated from both heterosexuals and homosexuals. Bisexual support groups and communities exist, but they are few compared with homosexual groups. No doubt, as people become more comfortable "coming out" this population will become increasingly visible in the future.

For Personal Reflection

How would you react if a close same-sex friend confided in you that he or she is gay, lesbian, or bisexual? How would you react if a close other-sex friend told you the same?

THEORIES OF HOMOSEXUALITY

The exact causes of homosexuality, like those of heterosexuality and sexual orientation in general, continue to elude researchers (Herek, 1991). However, a number of theories attempt to explain why people fall at the upper end of Kinsey's continuum. These theories fall into *biological, psychological, social,* and *interactional* categories.

BIOLOGICAL THEORIES

Attempts to identify specific, exact biological causes of homosexuality have to date yielded inconclusive results. Traditional physiological theories include too little testosterone in males, too much testosterone in females, prenatal hormonal imbalances, prenatal biological errors due to maternal stress, and genetic influences, among others (Bailey & Pillard, 1991; Burr, 1993; Ellis & Ames, 1987; Money, 1987, 1988; Turner, 1994).

PERSPECTIVE

Homosexuality in Ancient Greece

Historical records tell us that same-sex love was an acceptable part of the ancient Greek lifestyle. But what exactly was the nature of Grecian homosexuality? According to Bernard Murstein (1974), in his book, *Love, Sex, and Marriage Through the Ages:*

> In ancient Greece the maladjustive implications of homosexuality for men were largely absent. The incidence of homosexuality was proportionally larger than that which exists in our society, although even among the very wealthy it was never more than a minor phenomenon. Psychologically, it was not characterized by the inability to respond to the opposite sex. Most homosexuals were bisexual.... Such individuals generally fulfilled their biological duties and married, however reluctantly, in order to raise offspring for the continuity of the state.
>
> From the social point of view, the situation among Americans and Athenians differs greatly. The American male has the opportunity to marry a woman, who despite discrimination against her, is frequently his equal in education, intelligence, and emotional maturity. The Athenian man had to marry a cloistered girl, often much younger than himself, less experienced in the ways of life, and probably foisted on him by his father. What could he have in common with such a creature? The only individuals with the money and freedom of movement, as well as education, to attract adolescent Greek youths were wealthy older Greek men. Homosexuality, in short, was in no small measure a direct consequence of the vilification of the Grecian wife.
>
> In the homosexual relationship, the youths played the passive role. The typical age range was from 12 to 20; the older male was usually somewhat below 40. Many relationships ceased when the youth grew a beard....
>
> It is important to note that the homosexual relationship implied something much more than a carnal experience. The word "pederasty" stems from the Greek *paiderasteia,* meaning "love of boys." Today, the term signifies simple sexual inversion. To the Greeks, however, the term referred to both bodily pleasures and a kind of pure, passionate love. The lover was to embody a fusion of the two loves, teach and inspire his beloved to become the most worthy of men.
>
> The ideal of masculinity... was typified by the teacher whose sexual longing for procreation was transformed into the education of beautiful adolescent boys. It was considered natural that an educated masculine man would want to create a copy of himself in his student, whereas a baser person would simply procreate with a woman in the ordinary biological manner. (pp. 56–57)

And according to Christine Downing (1989), in her book *Myths and Mysteries of Same-Sex Love:*

> *The* model of socially validated homosexuality was *paiderastia*... the love of an older man for a youth. (By older man here we mostly mean men in the twenties, while the youths were adolescents.) The context was the *gymnasium,* where the youths went to exercise (and display) their physical gifts, and the older men went to watch, appreciate, and select. The arena was an upper-class one; paiderastia was essentially an aspect of the *paideia,* the training for citizenship of aristocratic youths. (That same-sex love tended to be mocked in comedy, an art form that attracted the masses, may indicate it played a less focal role in their lives.) (p. 137)

Sources: C. Downing (1989), *Myths and mysteries of same-sex love* (New York: Continuum).

B. I. Murstein (1974), *Love, sex, and marriage through the ages* (New York: Springer).

Three recent studies may lend some support to the biological theory of homosexuality, although their results must be viewed as preliminary only. First, Bailey and Pillard (1991) found homosexuality to occur in identical twins (52 percent) more often than in fraternal twins (22 percent) and adoptive brothers (11 percent), suggesting the important role of heredity and genetics in shaping sexual orientation. Second, LeVay (1991) found that a certain area (the third interstitial nucleus) of the anterior hypothalamus was significantly smaller in autopsied homosexual men than in their heterosexual counterparts. (You'll recall that the hypothalamus regulates human sexual behavior by controlling secretion of various sexual hormones.) Third, Hamer et al. (Pool, 1993) in a genetic analysis of 40 pairs of homosexual brothers discovered a link between a small segment of DNA on the X chromosome and some instances of male homosexuality.

Findings from studies such as those presented here must be interpreted with caution. First, the samples were not representative, as all of the subjects were males. (This is nothing new. The vast majority of research into and discussions about homosexuality involve males rather than females.) Second, the findings imply *correlational* associations of variables, but not necessarily *causal* ones. For example, does the abnormally small area in the hypothalamus cause homosexuality, vice versa, or not at all? Or does whatever causes the abnormally small area in the hypothalamus also cause homosexuality? A great deal more research is needed before solid conclusions can be drawn about the effects of various biological factors on the development of sexual orientation.

On a Personal Note (Alex, age 34)

I've been attracted to males ever since I can remember. Back as a kid, maybe in first or second grade, I remember one incident where some of the boys were talking in the school restroom. They were saying how much they wanted to see what girls looked like naked because they said you could always look at yourself naked if you wanted to see boy parts. I remember thinking to myself at the time that I'd be happy just to see boys naked. I knew even then that I could never say anything to my friends about the matter. (Author's files)

PSYCHOLOGICAL AND SOCIAL THEORIES

Early childhood seems to be the critical period in which sexual orientation forms, suggesting that learning plays a role in the development of homosexuality. Freudians have traditionally held that homosexuality is rooted in early childhood developmental conflicts, particularly during the *Oedipal stage*. Freudians believe that homosexuality may develop in response to a passive father and an overly affectionate and dominant mother, troubled family relationships, and/or loss of one or both parents (Bieber et al., 1962; Wolff, 1971). These notions cannot explain why homosexuality develops in individuals who do not come from such family backgrounds.

More recently, researchers have proposed that numerous social-learning factors are responsible for homosexuality, perhaps even more so than biological factors. It may be that homosexuality develops when a child's or teenager's sexual drive emerges during a period of primarily same-sex friendships (Storms, 1981). Or it may have something to do with early *cross-gender behaviors* (engaging in behaviors stereotypical of the other sex) (Zuger, 1988, 1989). Like the biological theories of sexual orientation, these and a multitude of other psychological and social theories suggest correlational associations, but not causal ones.

For Personal Reflection

What would you do if you discovered your 10-year-old son and his same-sex, same-age friend were engaging in same-sex play? What about your 10-year-old daughter and her same-sex, same-age friend? What about your 15-year-old son or daughter?

INTERACTIONAL THEORIES

It would seem that neither biological factors nor specific childhood events are solely responsible for the development of homosexuality. The **interactional theory** of homosexuality states that sexual orientation develops in response to a complex interaction of biological, psychological, and social factors. The relative weight of these various factors in determining sexual orientation in a particular individual remains to be determined (Small, 1993).

Perhaps the most widely accepted interactional theory is that of John Money, who explained the development of sexual orientation as a "two-step" process. According to Money (1987), prenatal hormones first act on the embryo and fetus's brain, creating a biological predisposition for a particular sexual orientation. After birth and during early childhood, social-learning factors in the environment act on the child, inhibiting or facilitating the predisposition. The sexual orientation that eventually results is then reinforced by conditioning through orgasm, making "reorientation" more difficult as time passes.

HOMOSEXUAL ADJUSTMENT

The first perspectives on homosexuality were theological. From ancient Jewish condemnations of homosexual practices to Thomas Aquinas's references to "unnatural lusts," Judeo-Christian societies have traditionally considered homosexual practices sinful. Beginning in the late nineteenth and early twentieth centuries, the mental health community, strongly influenced by Freud in particular, began viewing homosexuality as a psychiatric or mental disorder. For example, Bieber et al. (1962) wrote, "We consider homosexuality to be a pathological, biosocial, psychosexual adaptation to persuasive fears surrounding the expression of heterosexual impulses. In our view, every homosexual is, in reality, a 'latent' heterosexual" (p. 220).

However, in keeping with growing evidence to the contrary and increasingly open attitudes about sexuality in the United States, the American Psychiatric Association voted in 1973 to remove homosexuality as a diagnostic category from its *Diagnostic and Statistical Manual of Mental Disorders*. In the DSM-III (1980), the only reference to homosexuality was that of *Ego-Dystonic Homosexuality*, a diagnosis given to a person who is uncomfortable with his or her homosexual orientation. The APA removed even this category from the DSM-III-R (1987) and DSM-IV (1994) and replaced it with *Sexual Disorder Not Otherwise Specified*, a general classification for sexual disorders that do not fit the usual criteria. In 1975 the American Psychological Association endorsed the American Psychiatric Association's landmark decision to remove homosexuality from its list of mental disorders.

The decision to view or not view homosexuality as a mental disorder or abnormality has implications for whether treatment of some sort is warranted or even appropriate. Can sexual orientation be changed? Should homosexuality be treated? Should mental health professionals help homosexuals become heterosexuals? These are difficult questions.

Logically speaking, if on the one hand homosexuality is not a disorder, what is there to treat? Researchers suggest that homosexuals are hardy and as psychologically adjusted as anyone else. They experience similar physical and mental health as do their heterosexual counterparts, regardless of their sexual orientation or preference (Herek, 1991; Marcus, 1993). From this perspective, homosexuals enter into therapy to deal with *secondary* issues related to their sexual orientation, such as anxiety associated with coming out to family, harassment at work, or discrimination in housing—but not to treat their orientation as if it were a mental disorder. If, on the other hand, homosexuality is a disorder, are there effective conversion therapies available? Most experts claim *no*. At this time there do not appear to exist any reputable biological or psychological therapies that effectively and universally facilitate conversion of sexual orientation, although not all agree with this position (Welch, 1990). As Herek (1991) noted:

Research suggests that same-sex couples are as emotionally and physically adjusted as other couples.

The assertion that homosexuality is a choice that can be changed is erroneous for the vast majority of lesbians and gay men. Although the origins of sexual orientation are not well understood, neither heterosexuality nor homosexuality appear to represent a conscious choice for most people. Attempts to change sexual orientation that have been documented sufficiently to permit critical evaluation appear to have been largely unsuccessful. (p. 152)

Sexologists generally agree that there is no reason, at least in terms of mental health, to attempt to reorient a homosexual client. But the matter is not so simple. What about clients who want to change their sexual orientation? Are therapists obliged to offer such services, if a viable therapy were available? Davison (1978) argued that offering homosexual clients reorientation therapies is inappropriate, because these might encourage social prejudices against these individuals. In contrast, Sturgis and Adams (1978) argued that offering treatment to those who request it is appropriate, regardless of the clinician's view on the issue of homosexuality as an abnormality. To refuse clients who request reorientation therapy would be a violation of their basic "right to treatment." Of course, the therapist would be obliged to inform the client about the relative effectiveness of such therapy.

A number of practitioners, religious groups, and clients claim success with sexual reorientation therapy. Unfortunately, most of these reports are anecdotal and/or not scientifically verifiable. This is not to say that altering sexual orientation is impossible; there just is not enough scientific evidence to make an accurate judgment about its possibility. Such questions as "Can sexual orientation be changed?" and "Should homosexuality be treated?" will probably be with us for quite some time.

On a Personal Note (Sam, age 31)

It wasn't until my senior year in high school that I noticed I had any sexual attraction to women. Until then I had been exclusively attracted to guys. Well, given my background, I could never accept being gay, so I went to a psychologist to work on "changing" my sexual orientation. Actually, I've been pretty pleased with our progress. Over a period of 13 years, I've gone from having no sexual interest in women to having had a number of heterosexual relationships. I must admit, though, that we were never able to completely eliminate the gay side of myself. It's still there, nagging at me sometimes. But I'm able to deal with it. I guess what we did in therapy was add to my sexual repertoire to the point that I can comfortably function as a straight male. (Author's files)

HOMOSEXUAL LIFESTYLES

Homosexuals come from a wide range of backgrounds and lifestyles. In fact, there is no such thing as *the homosexual lifestyle*, just as there is no such thing as *the heterosexual lifestyle*. It is possible to make a few observations, however. Three important aspects of many homosexual lifestyles are *coming out, relationships and children,* and *sexual behaviors*.

COMING OUT

How open are homosexual men and women about their sexual attractions? Evidence indicates that perhaps as few as 10 percent of the homosexuals in the United States have actually *come out of the closet* (made known) to family and friends about their being gay or lesbian (Gordon & Snyder, 1989). The rest who "stay in the closet" are *passing* ("passing" themselves off as heterosexual). On the topic of coming out, one lesbian was quoted as saying:

On a Personal Note

I hate being in the closet. It's so boring having people ask if I have a boyfriend. I feel like putting the most horrified look possible on my face, and as if I'm deeply insulted exclaim, "I beg your pardon? I certainly hope not!" If I were sure of a job and safe living conditions, everyone would be fully informed that I'm gay. I am seriously contemplating getting a T-shirt with "Support Gay Liberation" on it. (Jay & Young, 1979, p. 75)

And as one client noted:

On a Personal Note (Harry, age 23)

I've come out to most of my friends, but I'm still trying to gather up the courage to tell my folks. It's going to be really hard, and I know they won't take it well, but until I do it, I feel like I'm living a lie. Most of my friends have really been supportive. (Author's files)

Why don't more people come out? Consider for a moment all that is potentially at stake by announcing one's homosexuality to the world. Family rejection. Job termination. Eviction. Social stigma. Antigay violence. For those who want to come out, support groups are available. Also, National Coming Out Day, which is celebrated every October 11, is a visible campaign to help individuals tell their families and friends about their sexual orientation (Marcus, 1993).

RELATIONSHIPS AND CHILDREN

Research indicates that between 40 and 60 percent of gays and lesbians are involved in some type of committed relationship (Peplau & Cochran, 1990). Homosexual couples are sometimes together for as many years as comparable heterosexual couples. Like heterosexuals, they may or may not find satisfaction in such relationships.

PERSPECTIVE

Homosexuality: The Normal Versus Abnormal Controversy

The issue of homosexuality being "normal/natural" or "abnormal/unnatural" is likely to prompt discussion for some time. Experts continue to try to convince one another of the merits of their particular viewpoints. On the "normal" side of the argument, we have philosopher Burton Leiser's (1989) paper, "Is Homosexuality Unnatural?," which in part stated:

> Studies of animal behavior and anthropological reports indicate that such nonreproductive sex acts as masturbation, homosexual intercourse, and mutual fondling of genital organs are widespread, both among human beings and among lower animals. Under suitable circumstances, many animals reverse their sex roles, males assuming the posture of females and presenting themselves to others for intercourse, and females mounting other females and going through all the actions of a male engaged in intercourse. Many peoples all around the world have sanctioned and even ritualized homosexual relations. It would seem that an excessive readiness to insist that human sex organs are designed only for reproductive purposes and therefore ought to be used only for such purposes must be based on a very narrow conception that is conditioned by our society's particular history and taboos.
>
> ...[T]he proposition that any use of an organ that is contrary to its principal purpose or function is unnatural assumes that organs *have* a principal purpose or function, but this may be denied on the ground that the purpose or function of a given organ may vary according to the needs or desires of its owner. It may be denied on the ground that a given organ may have more than one principal purpose or function, and any attempt to call one use or another the only natural one seems to be arbitrary, if not question-begging. Also, the proposition suggests that what is unnatural is evil or depraved. (pp. 171–172)

In response to this type of position, we have philosopher Michael Levin's (1993) paper, "Why Homosexuality Is Abnormal," a brief portion of which stated:

> This paper defends the view that homosexuality is abnormal and hence undesirable—not because it is immoral or sinful, or because it weakens society or hampers evolutionary development, but for a purely mechanical reason. It is a misuse of bodily parts. Clear empirical sense attaches to the idea of *the use* of such bodily parts as genitals, the idea that they are *for* something, and consequently to the idea of their misuse. I argue on grounds of natural selection that misuse of bodily parts can with high probability be connected to unhappiness. I regard these matters as prolegomena to such policy issues as the rights of homosexuals, the rights of those desiring not to associate with homosexuals, and legislation concerning homosexuality, issues which I shall not discuss here....
>
> Despite the publicity currently enjoyed by the claim that one's "sexual preference" is nobody's business but one's own, the intuition that there is something unnatural about homosexuality remains vital. The erect penis fits the vagina, and fits it better than any other natural orifice; penis and vagina seem made for each other. This intuition ultimately derives from, or is another way of capturing, the idea that the penis is not *for* inserting into the anus of another man—that so using the penis is not the way it is *supposed,* even *intended,* to be used.... Furthermore, when we understand the sense in which homosexual acts involve a misuse of genitalia, we will see why such misuse is bad and not to be encouraged. (p. 119)

Sources: B. M. Leiser (1989), Is homosexuality unnatural? In J. Rachels (Ed.), *The right thing to do: Basic readings in moral philosophy* (New York: Random House).

M. Levin (1993), Why homosexuality is abnormal. In S. J. Gold (Ed.), *Moral controversies: Race, class, and gender in applied ethics* (Belmont, CA: Wadsworth Publishing Company).

Many gays and lesbians prefer to socialize at gay bars and clubs.

What are homosexual relationships like? Homosexuals and bisexuals, like heterosexuals, live together, alone, with family or friends, and have housemates. They also come from all walks of life, economic levels, and backgrounds. It is difficult to make generalizations about homosexual or bisexual relationships—romantic, social, working, or otherwise—just as it is difficult to make generalizations about heterosexual ones. Nevertheless, in their pre-AIDS study of nearly 1,000 gays and lesbians, Bell and Weinberg (1978) found that over 70 percent fell into one of the following five relationship categories:

1. *Close-coupled* relationships, which resemble monogamous heterosexual marriages.
2. *Open-coupled* relationships, which involve one-on-one relationships, but where both partners have a number of sex partners.
3. *Functional* homosexuals, who are "single," have many sex partners, and have few or no sexual problems or regrets about being homosexual.
4. *Dysfunctional* homosexuals, who are "single," have many sex partners, but also have sexual problems and regrets about being homosexual.
5. *Asexual* homosexuals, who are "single," have few or no sex partners, and also have sexual problems, low levels of sexual interest, and regrets about being homosexual.

As is apparent from these categories, many of which are also applicable to heterosexuals, homosexual relationships are diverse.

But aren't some homosexuals promiscuous? *Yes*, just as some heterosexuals and bisexuals are. Before HIV and AIDS, research indicated that gays as a group were more likely than heterosexuals to be promiscuous. Bell and Weinberg (1978) found that 47 percent of the white gay males surveyed had had 100 to 999 partners during their lifetime, and that 28 percent of white gay males had had 1,000 or more. These figures—as well as those for heterosexuals and bisexuals—have fallen dramatically as AIDS has become an increasingly serious public health threat.

Sexual activity outside the primary relationship remains common for gays. Blumstein and Schwartz (1990) found that 79 percent of the gay males who had lived with a partner between two and ten years reported at least one instance of nonmonogamy within the previous year. Eleven percent of heterosexual males in a committed relationship reported engaging in sexual activity outside of the primary relationship.

Homosexual couples may decide to raise children. Researchers suggest that children raised by homosexual couples do not differ from children raised by heterosexual couples

The "AIDS quilt" and frequent gay and lesbian demonstrations seeking more funding for AIDS research are continual reminders of the reality of AIDS.

on important measures of general life adjustment, gender identity, gender role, and intelligence. They also suggest that children raised by homosexuals are no more likely to become homosexuals themselves than are children raised by heterosexuals (Klein, 1992; Marcus, 1993).

SEXUAL BEHAVIORS

Homosexuals, heterosexuals, and bisexuals all progress through the same stages of sexual arousal and response. That is, gays and lesbians respond to sexual stimuli and engage in the same types of sexual behaviors as do heterosexuals and bisexuals. Research also suggests that homosexuals as a group tend to evidence no more difficulties in sexual functioning than do heterosexuals (Masters & Johnson, 1979).

Contrary to popular opinions, not all gay couples engage in anal sex nor do all lesbian couples use "dildo" type sex toys (Blumenfeld & Raymond, 1993; Marcus, 1993). As one woman described:

On a Personal Note (Colleen, age 42)

People get the idea that all of us lesbians and gays enjoy bizarre, perverted sexual practices or something. Which couldn't be less true! My partner and I hug, kiss, massage each other—the usual kind of stuff. We don't tie each other up, beat each other up, or go to all-night orgies. (Author's files)

How often do homosexual couples engage in sex? As with heterosexuals, there are no absolutes in terms of the frequency of sexual activity (Marcus, 1993). The national average of two to three times a week is probably as applicable for homosexual and bisexual couples as it is for heterosexual couples. Research shows that both male and female couples, just like male-female couples, report having sex less often the longer they have been together (Blumstein & Schwartz, 1990).

Many same-sex couples choose to raise children.

HOMOPHOBIA

HOMOPHOBIA

*Both irrational fear of being perceived
as homosexual and contempt for gays
and lesbians.*

"Out-of-the-closet" gays and lesbians are often forced to deal with the verbal, physical, and sexual assaults of *homophobic* individuals. **Homophobia** refers not only to an irrational fear of being perceived as homosexual, but also to a persistent contempt for and hatred of gays and lesbians (Friedman, 1989; Van de Ven, 1994). In one report, for example, 81 percent of lesbians and 92 percent of gays reported having been verbally abused at some time because of their sexual orientation (Herek, 1989). Those who are more traditional in their sex role behaviors tend to give higher negative scores on measures of attitudes toward homosexuals (Whitley, 1987). On the topic of homophobia, Jay Friedman (1989) wrote:

> I believe that homophobia, which I define as more than a fear or hatred of homosexuals and homosexuality but a fear of being perceived as gay, is perhaps the *greatest* pressure boys face while growing up. It sparks male hatred of women and fear of closeness to other people.
>
> Homophobia begins in early elementary school when "girl," "sissy," "queer," "virgin," "and "fag" are the worst putdowns a boy can hear. Many boys, at that time, also begin to enjoy the "skirt" game—dropping their pens on the floor as an excuse to look up a girl's skirt at her "underwear." Meanwhile, music, television, and advertisements teach them that women are objects for men's sexual pleasure. Then homophobia begins to play itself out in locker-room talk where "the guys" boast of "scoring." To be "cool," and to avoid being called "gay," boys forcibly push for

intercourse with girls. Recent studies indicate that the average age of first intercourse for inner-city boys is 12. Even masturbation is affected by homophobia and
misogyny. In the hallways, and in sexuality education classes, boys often say, "only
fags masturbate," or "why masturbate, you can always find an ugly girl willing to
have sex." Homophobia thus encourages boys to label people based on stereotypes;
to compete with and distance themselves from other boys; and to objectify, and
even rape, girls. (pp. 8–9)

Homophobia leads some individuals to *gay bash,* or verbally abuse and/or brutally beat
up homosexuals and heterosexuals mistaken for homosexuals (Herek & Berrill, 1992).
Why would anybody engage in such *antigay violence?* Some speculate that people's linking
homosexuality with AIDS plays a part. Others speculate that negative attitudes about
AIDS only serve as an excuse for antigay sentiments that were already present (Berrill,
1990). Whatever the cause, antigay violence seems to be on the rise in the United States.
Nearly 25 percent of gays and lesbians report having been victims of physical violence on
account of their sexual orientation (Herek, 1989).

Many instances of homophobia probably stem from our society's condemnation of
homosexual acts, particularly anal intercourse. Westerners have met the topic of anal
sex—perhaps more than any other sexual activity (including masturbation)—with
disapproval, condemnation, and reactions of disgust and repulsion. Yet this is not the
case in other parts of the world (Suggs & Miracle, 1993). For example, 49 of 76 societies
(64 percent) other than ours approved of some form of homosexual activity for at least
some individuals (Ford & Beach, 1951). Male and female Mangaians of the South
Pacific engage in anal intercourse during times of menstruation (Marshall & Suggs,
1971). Boys and men of the Siwan of Africa practice it, as do the boys and men of the
Kiraki of New Guinea during their initiation rites (Morin, 1986). Also, many heterosexual couples in the United States engage in anal sex (Janus & Janus, 1993; Michael et
al., 1994).

So why does our culture give such negative press to homosexuality? Like so many
aspects of sexuality, many of our culturally determined views are rooted in Judeo-Christian
mores and values. In the Old Testament scriptures (for example, Malachi 2:1–3), feces
carried a very negative connotation—one that no doubt became associated with homosexuality, anal sexual practices, and pagan idolatry (Prager, 1993). Given the severity of
many interpretations of Biblical passages that refer to and condemn homosexual practices,
it is no wonder that our society so strongly disapproves of homosexuality. As sex
researcher Alfred Kinsey explained in his *Sexual Behavior in the Human Female* (Kinsey et
al., 1953):

The general condemnation of homosexuality in our particular culture apparently
traces to a series of historical circumstances which had little to do with the protection of the individual or the preservation of the social organization of the day. In
Hittite, Chaldean, and early Jewish codes there were no over-all condemnations of
such activity, although there were penalties for homosexual activities between persons of particular social status or blood relationships, or homosexual relationships
under other particular circumstances, especially when force was involved. The
more general condemnation of all homosexual relationships (especially male) originated in Jewish history in about the seventh century, B.C., upon the return from
the Babylonian exile. . . . Many of the Talmudic condemnations were based on the
fact that such activities represented the way of the Canaanite, the way of the
Chaldean, the way of the pagan, and they were originally condemned as a form of
idolatry rather than a sexual crime. Throughout the middle ages homosexuality
was associated with heresy. The reform in the custom (the mores) soon, however,
became a matter of morals, and finally a question for action under criminal law.
(pp. 481–482)

To this, Klein (1992) added:

American advertising contributes, too. Because so many ads rely on getting people to question their sexual adequacy (so they can sell products pitched to relieve this anxiety), they plant a troubling question into people's unconscious: Am I man enough? Woman enough? This makes homosexuality frightening because it undermines people's confidence in their heterosexuality. . . .

When a straight person's sense of sexual identity is this fragile, homosexuality can trigger deep emotional turmoil. It's easy to blame gay people for it. Besides, although everyone knows and sees gay individuals all the time, most people don't know it. This makes it easy to see gays as "them" rather than "us," as things rather than people. And that makes hatred easy. (p. 232)

HOMOSEXUAL POLITICAL ACTIVISM

Gays and lesbians, especially in the last 20 years, have actively sought to end what they perceive as prejudice and discrimination against them based on their sexual orientation. They have worked at all levels of society to change laws, fight job discrimination and harassment, eliminate homophobia and gay bashing, lobby for AIDS funding, and educate the public about homosexuality and homosexuals. Although many gays and lesbians believe they have come a long way toward achieving their goals, others believe they still have much work to do before achieving true "gay liberation."

The *gay rights movement*, as it is popularly known today, came into full swing with the 1969 Stonewall riot. The New York police had a long history of targeting patrons of gay bars for harassment and arrests. In June 1969 they raided the Stonewall Inn, a gay bar in New York's Greenwich Village. When the patrons of the bar resisted, a riot followed that lasted into the next day. The incident prompted the formation of numerous gay rights groups and the organization of marches, demonstrations, and yearly commemorative parades and activities, including Gay Pride Week (Blumenfeld & Raymond, 1993).

Many people incorrectly assume that the gay rights movement began with the Stonewall riot, when in fact more than 40 gay and lesbian organizations were already in place at that time (Marcus, 1993). Two of the more visible groups in the 1950s and 1960s were the Mattachine Society and the Daughters of Bilitis. After the Stonewall riot, gays and lesbians organized into such political groups and service agencies as Act Up, the Gay Liberation Front, Gay Activists Alliance, Gay and Lesbian Advocates and Defenders, Lesbian Rights Project, National Gay and Lesbian Task Force, National Gay Rights Advocates, and Queer Nation, to name only a few (Blumenfeld & Raymond, 1993).

On the topic of gay and lesbian political activism, Warren Blumenfeld and Diane Raymond (1993) concluded:

Being politically active requires that one be able to undertake certain sorts of risks, for the political arena is first and foremost a public one. For many gay and lesbian people who lack job protections, rights to child custody, or are not "out" to their families, it is simply not possible to engage in political activism. Further, political activity should not be construed in an overly narrow way, that any open affirmation of homosexuality in a predominantly heterosexual society is a political act. Finally, the fact that there are so many openly lesbian and gay organizations, political groups, and service agencies testifies to the success of these political struggles. Indeed, the sense of identity and community which has grown out of this movement, though taken for granted today by some, is a radical change from the early days prior to the homophile movement where gay people felt alone, isolated, and starved for culture.

Though gay and lesbian people may disagree about political strategies for liberation, there is nonetheless a gay and lesbian identity, or, as sociologists refer to it, a "consciousness of kind." (p. 316)

Gays and lesbians—and even some parents—often participate in "Gay Rights" and "Gay Pride" marches and demonstrations.

As I mentioned at the beginning of this chapter, sexual orientation—especially homo-sexuality and bisexuality—is a hotly debated, even volatile, topic today. Yet every struggle has a positive side to it, regardless of one's opinion. The "homosexual issue" in America affords us the opportunity to think critically about ourselves and our neighbors. It helps us learn to work with people with whom we might disagree. It prompts us to examine our tra-ditional views and decide whether or not they are valid. Homosexuality has been with us for a very long time. It's only right that we now give the issue our attention.

KEY POINTS

1. *Sexual orientation* refers to a person's emotional, romantic, affectionate, and sexual attraction to members of the same sex, the other sex, or both. A person who is attracted to members of the other sex is *heterosexual*, or *straight*. A person who is attracted to members of the same sex is *homosexual*, or *gay* (male) or *lesbian* (female). A person who is attracted to members of both sexes is *bisexual*, or *ambi-sexual*. The term *sexual orientation* is preferable to *sexual preference*, the latter sug-gesting that sexual attraction is always a matter of choice.

2. In the 1940s and 1950s, Alfred Kinsey and his associates suggested that sexual ori-entation exists along a continuum. It is also necessary to distinguish between sexu-al *orientation* and sexual *behavior*. A person may or may not choose to act on his or her sexual orientation. Estimates are that up to 4 percent of men and 1 to 2 percent of women in the United States are exclusively homosexual.

3. No one knows for sure what causes homosexuality. Attempts to identify specific biological, psychological, and social causes of homosexuality have to date yielded inconclusive results. In all likelihood, homosexuality results from a complex inter-action of biological, psychological, and social factors. This position is known as the *interactional theory* of homosexuality.

4. The mental health community, strongly influenced by Freud in particular, has tra-ditionally viewed homosexuality as a mental disorder. However, in keeping with growing evidence to the contrary and increasingly open attitudes about sexuality in

President Bill Clinton's efforts to lift the military ban on gays and lesbians have stimulated a great deal of discussion on both sides of the issue.

the United States, the American Psychiatric Association voted in 1973 to remove homosexuality as a diagnostic category from its DSM-III. Many sexuality experts argue that there is no reason, at least in terms of mental health, to attempt to "reorient" a homosexual client.

5. Research indicates that between 40 and 60 percent of gays and lesbians are involved in some type of committed relationship, and that homosexuals, like heterosexuals, find satisfaction in such relationships. Sexual activity outside the primary relationship remains common for gays.

6. Some homosexual couples decide to raise children. Children raised by homosexual couples do not seem to differ from children raised by heterosexual couples on important measures of general life adjustment, gender identity, gender role, and intelligence. Children raised by homosexuals do not seem more likely to become homosexuals than children raised by heterosexuals.

7. Homosexuals, heterosexuals, and bisexuals all progress through the same stages of sexual arousal and response. Gays and lesbians respond to sexual stimuli and engage in the same types of sexual behaviors as do their heterosexual and bisexual counterparts.

8. "Out-of-the-closet" gays and lesbians are often forced to deal with the verbal, physical, and sexual assaults of homophobic individuals. *Homophobia* refers not only to an irrational fear of being perceived as homosexual, but also to a persistent contempt for and hatred of gays and lesbians. Homophobia leads some individuals

to *gay bash*, or verbally abuse and/or brutally beat up homosexuals and heterosexuals mistaken for homosexuals.

9. Gays and lesbians have worked at all levels of society to change laws, fight job discrimination and harassment, eliminate homophobia and gay bashing, lobby for AIDS funding, and educate the public about homosexuality and homosexuals. The *gay rights movement* came into full swing with the 1969 Stonewall riot. Following Stonewall, gays and lesbians organized into numerous groups, such as the National Gay and Lesbian Task Force.

ACTIVITIES AND QUESTIONS

1. As a class, discuss some of the many problems associated with defining heterosexuality, homosexuality, and bisexuality. Note the pros and cons of conceptualizing sexual orientation as existing along a continuum.

2. Make a list of the behaviors that you believe most Americans associate with gay and lesbian sexuality. How do these behaviors differ from what you now know about homosexual relations after having read this chapter?

3. What are some of the typical problems homosexuals and bisexuals face when "coming out" to their friends and family? Can you think of any methods that a homosexual individual might use to minimize the stress associated with telling others about his or her sexual orientation?

4. Attend a campus or local gay rights meeting, rally, lecture, or debate. Afterwards, discuss your observations with friends or classmates of both sexes and various sexual orientations. What did you learn from the experience?

5. To study the causes of sexual orientation, should sexuality researchers be permitted to try intentionally to produce homosexuality in young children by manipulating assorted biological and/or environmental factors? Why or why not? What are some of the potential ethical problems associated with such research?

6. What are some of the pros and cons of legislating "equal rights" for gays and lesbians? What about legislating "special rights"?

RECOMMENDED READINGS

Blumenfeld, W. J., & Raymond, D. (1993). *Looking at gay and lesbian life*. Boston: Beacon Press. A comprehensive resource on virtually every aspect of homosexual lifestyles, from gender roles to politics to religion.

Boswell, J. (1994). *Same-sex unions in premodern Europe*. New York: Villard Books. Examines the author's discovery of premodern Catholic and Orthodox liturgies, apparently for same-sex unions.

Clunis, D. M., & Green, G. D. (1988). *Lesbian couples*. Seattle, WA: Seal Press. Offers insights into the lesbian lifestyle from a developmental relationship perspective.

Downing, C. (1989). *Myths and mysteries of same-sex love*. New York: Continuum. Examines Freud's and Jung's theories of homosexuality ("Psychology's Myths"), as well as the ancient Greek mythological perspectives ("Mythology's Mysteries").

Marcus, E. (1993). *Is it a choice? Answers to 300 of the most frequently asked questions about gays and lesbians*. New York: HarperCollins. A readable, informative guide to homosexuality written in a question/answer format.

Opposing Viewpoints Pamphlets. (1993). *Can homosexuals change their sexual orientation? Should society encourage increased acceptance of homosexuality? Should society legally sanction gay relationships?* San Diego, CA: Greenhaven Press. Three excellent pamphlets presenting both sides of the homosexual issue.

Wolf, J. G. (1989). *Gay priests*. New York: Harper & Row. Examines the social issue of gay clergy in the Roman Catholic Church, including personal reflections by four gay priests.

•LOVE

•COMMUNICATION

C H A P T E R   8

LOVING RELATIONSHIPS

O B J E C T I V E S

AFTER READING THIS CHAPTER YOU SHOULD BE
ABLE TO . . .

1. DESCRIBE THE PROMINENT THEORIES OF LOVE.

2. DISTINGUISH AMONG THE VARIETIES OF LOVE
   ACCORDING TO STERNBERG, IDENTIFYING THE
   PRINCIPAL CHARACTERISTICS OF EACH.

3. DESCRIBE SOME OF THE COMMON MYTHS
   PEOPLE HOLD ABOUT LOVE, ATTRACTION,
   INTIMACY, AND SEXUAL RELATIONSHIPS.

4. EXPLAIN THE ROLES OF VERBAL AND NONVERBAL
   COMMUNICATION IN LOVING RELATIONSHIPS.

5. DETAIL WAYS OF IMPROVING COMMUNICATION
   AND RESOLVING CONFLICTS WITH YOUR PARTNER.

PERSONAL ASSESSMENT

TEST YOUR GENERAL KNOWLEDGE OF LOVING RELATIONSHIPS BY ANSWERING THE FOL-LOWING STATEMENTS *true* OR *false*.

_____ 1. Only one ideal lover is out there for each person.

_____ 2. Loving relationships must be sexual to be rewarding.

_____ 3. If you no longer feel passion for someone, it means you don't love him or her.

_____ 4. When "true" love strikes, you'll know it—it'll be totally positive and never fade.

_____ 5. "True" love lasts forever and conquers all problems.

_____ 6. Physical attractiveness is the most important factor to consider when screening for prospective dates.

_____ 7. It's impossible for individuals who are sexually attracted to each other to be friends and not lovers.

_____ 8. Men tend to develop stronger interpersonal bonds with other men than women do with other women.

_____ 9. During a conflict with a partner, it's essential to get your point across first, and then carefully listen to your partner.

_____ 10. If a couple is really in love, they don't need to worry about communicating wants, needs, and concerns to each other—everything will be understood and work out fine.

The above statements are actually common myths about love, sex, attraction, intimacy, and interpersonal communication. Therefore, the correct answers are all *false*.

ANSWERS

*L*ove is a human emotion that wisdom will never conquer.

Percy White

Have you ever tried to define love? It isn't easy, is it? Don't feel alone, though. Artists, philosophers, theologians, and assorted other scholars have wrestled with this question for centuries. And probably more literature has been devoted to the subject of love than to any other. Take, for example, this famous poem by Elizabeth Barrett Browning (1806–1861):

How do I love thee? Let me count the ways.
I love thee to the depth and breadth and height
My soul can reach, when feeling out of sight
For the ends of Being and ideal Grace.
I love thee to the level of everyday's
Most quiet need, by sun and candle-light.
I love thee freely, as men strive for Right;
I love thee purely, as they turn from Praise.
I love thee with the passion put to use
In my old griefs, and with my childhood's faith.
I love thee with a love I seemed to lose
With my lost saints—I love thee with the breath,
Smiles, tears, of all my life!—and, if God choose,
I shall but love thee better after death.

What then is love? Everybody seems to want it. A lot of people talk about it. Many experience it. And our pop culture certainly has something to say about love. It makes the world go round. Money can't buy it. It's a many splendored thing. It even means never having to say you're sorry. But do these witty sayings really give us a clear picture of what love is all about? *Hardly!* They can have just the opposite effect, in many cases hindering our ability to see life as it really is. We need something more than popular clichés and myths to understand what we mean by love.

To this end, I devote the following pages to a discussion of love. I'll examine the theories and varieties of love, debunk common myths, and explain several theories on why relationships begin and end. I'll also teach you some of the basics of effective interpersonal communication, in particular, how to improve communication and resolve conflicts.

LOVE

One of the inherent problems in defining love is that there are so many kinds of love. Consider a parent's love for a child, love between friends, or romantic love for one's mate—all similar as loving relationships, but different in many ways. Given this, the ancient Greeks used several different words to distinguish among the varieties of love: *agape,* for altruistic and unselfish love; *eros,* for erotic or romantic love; *philia,* for friendship love; *pragma,* for logical love; and *storge,* for affectionate love. For the Greeks, a single term was not enough. It's no wonder, then, that English-speaking people find it so difficult to explain love. We try to use one word to describe this complex and many-sided experience.

As you'll see later in this chapter, researchers have proposed various theories to explain the origins and nature of love. Suffice it to say for the moment that **love** is characterized by intense feelings of joy within a relationship, especially in the presence of a loved object, such as one's spouse (Gray, 1993; Livermore, 1993). But that's not all. Love is also action, desire, involvement, trust—the list goes on and on. In all forms, however, love consists of one or more of three primary components: *intimacy* (closeness), *passion* (arousal), and *decision/commitment* (obligation and continuity). The varieties of love involve varying mixtures of these components (Sternberg, 1986, 1988).

LOVE
Intense feelings of joy within a relationship.

MYTHS ABOUT LOVE

We've all heard them. We know others who believe them, and we probably even believe a few ourselves—myths about love. First love is always wild love. True love lasts forever. One special person is waiting for me. Real passion never dies. Lovers never argue. True love means living happily ever after. Thanks to the mass media, messages like these seem to be everywhere.

To speak of love requires listing at least a few of our society's myths. Albert Ellis in his classic text *Sex Without Guilt* (1966) presented some of the more common of these:

1. Love is mysterious and no one knows what it is.
2. There is such a thing as "real" or "true" love.
3. It is difficult to tell when one is in love.
4. Love and marriage always go together.
5. One can truly love only one person at a time.
6. When one loves, one has no sexual desires for individuals whom one does not love.
7. One loves one's beloved steadily or all the time. (pp. 153–157)

Many people believe these and similar myths, often to the detriment of their love lives and relationships. For example, the young woman who believes there really is such a thing

Many types of love exist between people—parent-child love, friendship, and romantic love—to name just a few.

as "true" love might turn down assorted dates while waiting for "Prince Charming" to knock at her door. In real life, though, the prince never shows up, and she misses out on opportunities to meet and date numerous young men who, although fallible and imperfect, have the potential to be loving life-long partners. Her love life suffers because she chooses to keep irrational expectations concerning what romance is *supposed* to be like—no doubt a result of believing popular myths and stereotypes about love.

For Personal Reflection
What are some other common myths about love you've held or known others to hold?

THEORIES OF LOVE

Before the 1970s there were few scientific studies into the nature of romantic love. Much to the objection of critics like Senator William Proxmire (who in 1977 gave two psychologists—Ellen Berscheid and Elaine Hatfield—his "Golden Fleece Award" for "wasting" federal funding on researching romantic love), psychologists and sociologists now pursue and research the topic. The hope of such researchers, in addition to learning more about one of the most important areas of human functioning, is to find ways of preventing the emotional unhappiness present in so many relationships.

Regardless of Senator Proxmire's "Golden Fleece Award," what did researchers Berscheid and Hatfield discover about romantic love? Basically, they found a useful distinction between **passionate love** and **companionate love** (Hatfield & Rapson, 1993). The former is intense, obsessive, and lovesick—which is why people often use expressions like "puppy love," "love-crazed," and "having a crush" when talking about passionate love. The latter is less intense and more warm, affectionate, intimate, attached, and committed. Berscheid and Hatfield discovered that a person experiences and associates physiological/emotional arousal with another person before falling in love. That is, when a person labels their physiological/emotional arousal as romantic love, he or she in turn develops feelings of love toward the other person. These researchers' findings may explain, at least in part, why individuals who share an emotionally intense experience (pleasant or unpleasant) are also likely to fall in love.

An early theory of love that captured the attention of the professional community was Ira Reiss's **wheel of love** (Reiss, 1960). According to Reiss, love increases as rapport, self-revelation, and mutual dependency develop, and as both partners' personal needs are met. Love decreases as rapport and dependency lessen, communication breaks down, and needs are not met.

Other experts have suggested that people learn to love. The ability to love and develop loving partnerships is strongly affected by individuals' backgrounds and past experiences. People who have had loving, affectionate, attachments as children are more likely to experience the same in friendships and relationships as adults (Hatfield & Rapson, 1993). Even the way in which men and women are raised and socialized determines how they will view love and approach loving relationships (Tannen, 1990). While socialization is helpful in terms of instilling in children healthy values and attitudes, it also tends to perpetuate stereotypes about the sexes and love.

For Personal Reflection
What are some of the influences in your life that have helped you learn to love others?

PASSIONATE LOVE
Intense, obsessive love.

COMPANIONATE LOVE
Warm, affectionate, and committed love.

WHEEL OF LOVE
Theory that love increases as rapport, self-revelation, and mutual dependency develop and personal needs are met.

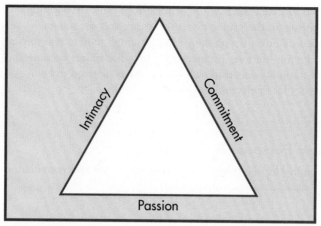

FIGURE 8.1 *Sternberg's triangle of love. Love has three interacting components: passion, intimacy, and decision/commitment.*
Source: R.J. Sternberg (1986). A triangular theory of love,
Psychological Review, 93, 119-135. *Copyright 1986 by the American Psychological Association. Reprinted by permission.*

TRIANGULAR THEORY OF LOVE

Theory that the basic components of love are passion, commitment, and intimacy.

PASSION

Feelings of arousal, especially sexual.

DECISION/COMMITMENT

Decision to maintain a loving relationship.

INTIMACY

Sense of closeness, warmth, and self-disclosure within a loving relationship.

In more recent years, sexologists have paid considerable attention to Robert Sternberg's (1986, 1988) **triangular theory of love** (Figure 8.1).

As mentioned above, Sternberg proposed that love consists of three components: *passion, decision/commitment,* and *intimacy*. **Passion** refers to the intense feelings of physiological arousal and excitement (especially sexual feelings) present in a loving relationship, while **decision/commitment** refers to the decision to love and maintain the relationship. **Intimacy** refers to the closeness and sense of warmth in a loving relationship, including the desire to self-disclose and help the partner. People express intimacy in three ways: (1) *physical intimacy*, which involves giving and receiving affection including sexual activity; (2) *psychological intimacy*, which involves sharing one's thoughts and feelings; and (3) *social intimacy*, which involves having mutual friends and enjoying the same kinds of recreation. The many varieties of love, described below, consist of varying degrees of these components. For instance, romantic love often involves passion and intimacy, but not commitment.

For Personal Reflection

What does intimacy mean to you? How do you express intimacy in your life? Is sex without intimacy possible? What about the reverse?

VARIETIES OF LOVE

Sternberg (1986, 1988) suggested that the three components of love—passion, intimacy, and decision/commitment—combine in different ways to create varieties of love. These are *non-love, friendship, infatuation, empty love, romantic love, fatuous love, companionate love,* and *consummate love* (Figure 8.2).

Nonlove The first variety of love is actually no love at all. *Nonlove* involves neither passion, intimacy, nor commitment. Many of our relationships, like those with casual acquaintances, are of a nonloving nature.

Intimate partners feel free to share their thoughts, feelings, hopes, and dreams with one another.

Variety of Love	Intimacy	Passion	Commitment
1. Nonlove	○	○	○
2. Friendship	●	○	○
3. Infatuation	○	●	○
4. Empty love	○	○	●
5. Romantic love	●	●	○
6. Fatuous love	○	●	●
7. Companionate love	●	○	●
8. Consummate love	●	●	●

FIGURE 8.2 *Sternberg's varieties of love and their respective patterns of passion, intimacy, and decision/commitment.*
Source: R.J. Sternberg (1986). A triangular theory of love, Psychological Review, *93, 119-135. Copyright 1986 by the American Psychological Association. Reprinted by permission.*

Friendship The first form of love that most people encounter outside their families, *friendship* or *liking,* is characterized by intimacy, but neither passion nor commitment. In other words, closeness and warmth are present without feelings of passionate arousal and permanence. Friends normally enjoy each other's company, share interests, and come from similar backgrounds. With time, friends can grow closer and find their friendship evolving into something deeper. As one student explained:

On a Personal Note (Stuart, age 26)

I knew Paula for about four years before I got sexually interested in her. We even dated some on and off over the years, but without any sexual feelings on my part. We've always been able to talk just about anything, and we've even had a few quarrels. Sort of like a married couple, but more like really good friends. Now, we're in love and engaged to be married in about six months—isn't this backwards from the way it's supposed go? (Author's files)

Infatuation This variety of love involves only passion. The infatuated person is intensely emotional, longs for the other person, constantly thinks about the person, and places her or him on a pedestal. Tenderness, highs, lows, anxiety, stress, and sexual desire can all be present. Also known as "puppy love" or "love at first sight," infatuation is usually shallow love, and can end just as suddenly as it begins. Couples can move from infatuation to more committed types of love.

Empty Love Sternberg referred to committed love lacking passion and intimacy as *empty love*. This is the type of love seen in a decades-old marriage that has become stagnant, lacking movement and growth. The couple may have been passionate and intimate in the past, but these feelings have long since died. All that remains for the couple is their commitment to stay together. Although in our society empty love is often the end result of a romantic relationship, in other societies, such as those in which arranged marriages are commonplace, this variety of love can be the starting point of a long-term relationship.

Romantic Love *Romantic love* has passion and intimacy, but no commitment. It is similar to infatuation, except the couple are physically and emotionally intimate. A summer affair while vacationing in a foreign country is a good example of this type of love. It is intense and exciting, but it is over as soon as the partners go their separate ways at the end of the summer.

Fatuous Love A whirlwind, Hollywood-style courtship is an example of what Sternberg labeled *fatuous love*, meaning "foolish" love. Two people meet. A week later they're engaged. A month later they're married. This variety of love has passion and commitment, but no intimacy. Fatuous love relationships rarely work out.

Companionate Love *Companionate love* includes both intimacy and commitment, but lacks passion. A permanent partnership in which passion has faded is a typical example of this variety of love. Another form of companionate love is a special, long-term friendship.

Consummate Love Love that involves all three components—passion, intimacy, and commitment—is *consummate love*, meaning "complete" love. This variety of love is devoted, unselfish, and most often associated with romantic partnerships. When people talk of their search for ideal love, they are usually referring to consummate love. Unfortunately, developing consummate love, as Sternberg noted, is similar to losing weight: Getting started is easy; sticking to it is a lot harder.

BEGINNINGS AND ENDINGS: THE COURSE OF ROMANTIC LOVE

Most couples will tell you that romantic love changes over time. The typical romantic relationship begins with heated passion, only to cool off in a relatively short period. Other important aspects of love can develop and take over as time passes. Sternberg (1986,

"Ezra, I'm not inviting you to my birthday party, because our relationship is no longer satisfying to my needs."

Drawing by Koren; © 1976 The New Yorker Magazine, Inc.

1988) specifically noted that although passion peaks early and declines in intensity, intimacy and commitment continue to build gradually throughout a relationship.

So much for what happens after a relationship begins. Why do people fall in love in the first place? Why do they fall out of love? Is there anything a couple can do to make their partnership last? To answer these and other questions, let's take a look at what some of the professional literature has to say about the usual course of love.

Why Romantic Relationships Begin It can happen anywhere and anytime. Sharing glances across a room at a crowded party. Smiling at someone in the library. Sitting next to and talking with someone you like in class. The opportunities for love seem endless.

Explaining *why* people "fall in love" is no easier than defining love. Not only do researchers find it difficult, but most lovers cannot even figure it out. Yet, when asked why they love someone, people manage to come up with some sort of answer, however trite ("She's pretty" or "He's understanding"). As author Francisco José Moreno (1977) noted:

There are essentially two ways of explaining why we have the special feelings we call love. The first one is by asserting that those whom we claim to love are objectively deserving of special consideration: "If you knew her as well as I do, you would realize how wonderful she really is." The problem with this type of explanation is that the special qualities we see in those we say we love are seldom, and never to the same degree, seen by anyone else not equally in love with the person in question. So sooner or later we resort to the other type of explanation: "I love her because I love her." We abandon the pretension that our loved ones are really special or we try to make ourselves believe that others are unable to see their true qualities, and we explain how, regardless of whether or not they are endowed with special qualities, and regardless of whether or not other people can detect these qualities, they are special to us by the mere fact that we feel deeply about them. This second explanation, which is the more common one and which is always put forward when the first is challenged, is of course no explanation at all. "I love her because I love her" only means that I am unable or unwilling to explain my feelings toward her. This kind of explanation also assumes that other people experience similar feelings too and that they are able to understand the explanation by comparing it with the way they feel toward people who are special to them. (pp. 36–37)

Research has provided us with some interesting insights into why people fall in love. It makes sense that a principal player in this process is **interpersonal attraction,** or the sense of attraction experienced between two people. The exact processes whereby two people become attracted and fall in love are not entirely understood, but do seem to involve both *personal characteristics* and *interaction factors.*

Most people have some sense of what they are looking for in a potential romantic partner or mate. That is, they have preconceived ideas concerning the qualities or traits that their "ideal" lover ought to possess. Desirable attributes can range anywhere from having a good sense of humor to being wealthy to having a good tan—it really is a matter of individuals' preferences. Of course, our preferences stem at least in part from society telling us with whom we *should* fall in love.

Remember that the definition of a desirable trait varies a great deal across people, cultures, and time. Americans of today generally value the physical attribute of thinness, especially for women. But for people of sixteenth-century France, large, buxom women represented the standard for beauty and desirability. Even today, many non-Western societies view larger women as more attractive than smaller ones.

So what do Americans as a whole value when it comes to personal characteristics? Again, it's an individual choice, although some general patterns are discernible. Table 8.1 summarizes the characteristics ordinarily sought in a mate, as rated by males and females (Buss, 1985).

Notice that there are gender differences when it comes to desirable traits for romantic attachments, although these are fewer than one might first expect (Livermore, 1993). Men rated physical attractiveness higher than did women, while women gave more weight to earning capacity than did men. Both men and women ranked other traits (kindness, understanding, and intelligence) higher than physical and monetary attributes, at least for forming permanent relationships. For purely sexual relationships, though, physical attractiveness does appear to be the most desirable characteristic for both sexes (Hatfield & Rapson, 1993).

INTERPERSONAL ATTRACTION

Feelings of attraction that develop between two people.

TABLE 8.1 The Ideal Partner: Desirable Characteristics

Rank	Characteristics Preferred by Males	Characteristics Preferred by Females
1	Kindness and understanding	Kindness and understanding
2	Intelligence	Intelligence
3	Physical attractiveness	Exciting personality
4	Exciting personality	Good health
5	Good health	Adaptability
6	Adaptability	Physical attractiveness
7	Creativity	Creativity
8	Desire for children	Good earning capacity
9	College graduate	College graduate
10	Good heredity	Desire for children
11	Good earning capacity	Good heredity
12	Good housekeeper	Good housekeeper
13	Religious orientation	Religious orientation

Source: D. M. Buss (1985). Human mate selection. *American Scientist, 73,* 47–51. Reprinted by permission.

Most people know what traits they expect an ideal lover to possess.

For Personal Reflection

1. *What is it about a prospective partner that you find attractive?*
2. *How would you go about letting someone know that you find her or him attractive?*

A number of factors important to the start of a relationship have little to do with one partner or the other. They instead revolve around what happens between the couple, or the way in which they interact with one another. The most common of these **interaction factors** are *proximity, familiarity, similarity, equity,* and *self-disclosure*.

INTERACTION FACTORS

Factors existing between two people that influence their relationship, such as proximity and familiarity.

Proximity, or being in the same place at the same time, is certainly one of the most important interaction factors. Just think how difficult it would be for two people to become attracted and fall in love if they never met in the first place. The term encompasses all forms of spatial closeness, whether a seating assignment, a place of residence, or the office. Of course, living or interacting in close proximity does not assure that attraction will take place, but it certainly helps. Living on the same floor in a dorm, for example, increases the likelihood of social interactions, but does not determine whether they will be positive.

Related to proximity is *familiarity,* which refers to the frequency of contact between people, as well as their getting to know one another. Both proximity and familiarity are necessary for attraction to occur, but do not guarantee it. Just because two people work in the same office does not mean they will necessarily become anything other than casual acquaintances.

Another important factor in interpersonal attraction is *similarity,* or the degree to which two people share similar physical, emotional, attitudinal, and social characteristics. Proverbial wisdom gives us seemingly contradictory messages concerning similarity:

The physical distance between people, or their proximity, has much to do with whether attraction and intimacy will develop.

"Opposites attract" and "Birds of a feather flock together." Which is correct? Social scientists have certainly found more support for the latter; in fact, couples tend to be *demographically* similar in terms of age, education, intelligence, social class, race, religion, and physical health (Hatfield & Rapson, 1993). They also tend to be similar with respect to attitudes, temperament, personality, and physical attractiveness (Feingold, 1990).

Why is similarity so appealing? One possible explanation is that similarity between persons can be affirming and reassuring in terms of self-concept and their view of others and the world (Byrne et al., 1986). It may be that "similars" find *consensual validation,* or mutual support, for their attitudes and behaviors. Another explanation has to do with searching for the "ideal" partner (Brehm & Kassin, 1990). Specifically, when waiting or

We tend to be attracted to those who have similar looks, attitudes, interests, and backgrounds.

looking for that special someone, people seem to be drawn to those with the characteristics they admire the most—their own! Some individuals are attracted to both "similars" and "opposites," perhaps in some way hoping to confirm their own positive characteristics while also making up for personal deficiencies (Smeaton et al., 1989).

Equity also plays heavily into the process of interpersonal attraction. An equitable relationship is one in which neither partner dominates—both partners benefit according to their contributions to the relationship. People in equitable relationships believe the benefits of being in the relationship outweigh the costs involved (Hatfield & Rapson, 1993).

One final factor, *self-disclosure*, or sharing personal and intimate information, is the basis of mutual trust found in all intimate relationships. According to **social penetration theory**, attraction and self-disclosure increase as a relationship develops (Altman & Taylor, 1973). In particular, people upon first meeting share mostly superficial information about themselves. With time, however, they gradually divulge more and more, presumably as their attraction and ease with one another increase. The more self-disclosure present early in a relationship, the greater its quality and likelihood of lasting.

So far we've examined some of the factors that determine why people become attracted to each other. Now let's consider the other side of the coin—why some romantic relationships end while others last.

SOCIAL PENETRATION THEORY

Theory that self-disclosure increases as a relationship develops.

Why Romantic Relationships End   Currently, about 50 percent of all marriages in United States end in divorce, the median duration of these marriages being about seven years (*Statistical Abstract of the United States*, 1992). And of those that do last (this long or longer), marital bliss is not always a prominent feature. Why do so many partnerships and marriages dissolve, and is there anything partners can do to help their relationship work?

When discussing breakups and divorce, bear in mind that every relationship is different. There are as many reasons for dissolved relationships as there are relationships. In some cases, the partners change and simply grow apart. In other cases, the partners are totally incompatible, and were that way from the very beginning of their relationship. Long-term partnerships rarely end because of difficulties with just one of the partners; conflicts, problems, and growing out of love inevitably involve both parties (Dym & Glenn, 1993).

As I mentioned previously, the course of love changes over time. For most couples, this means passion fades, while intimacy and commitment build. Does this mean that those wonderful feelings of passion are doomed, that they must inevitably fade? The answer seems to be *yes* in many cases. But never fear! It does not have to be that way, nor do these changes necessarily spell the end of the relationship. To the contrary, many couples find effective ways of rekindling their flames of passion, increasing emotional intimacy, improving their ability to communicate, and growing together throughout a life-long relationship. The understanding and predictability that develop between two people over time can be remarkable.

For many, the end of passion signals the end of their relationship. Some individuals become so enamored with feelings of passion that they fail to approach their loving relationships with realistic expectations. This is especially true for those whose partnership was based on infatuation or formed on the assumption that true love will take care of any problems that might arise. So when their fires of passion are quenched or the going gets rough, these partners feel that it is time to move on to a new campfire. As one client explained:

On a Personal Note (Barry, age 42)

I was so in love with Laura. I thought there'd never be anyone else for me. But after a few years of marriage, the excitement of being in love began to fade. I mean, sex was so good in the beginning. But, let's face it, after you've done it with the same person umpteen times, the novelty wears off. At least I resisted my initial urges to have an affair or separate. I still love her, and there's more to our relationship now than just sex. But I can really see how a husband or wife can get sexually bored and want to look for it someplace else. (Author's files)

Cathy *copyright 1994 Cathy Guisewite. Reprinted with permission of Universal Press Syndicate. All rights reserved.*

Relationships also tend to dissolve when a couple commits prematurely, such as eloping after knowing each other and dating for only two months. In the case of fatuous love, the partners do not have adequate time to get to know one another. And when the thrill and excitement of it all subside, a great many of these people find they do not care for or even like their partner.

Interpersonal disagreements often increase as individuals become better acquainted and intimate with each other. Individuals who do not know how to communicate their needs, wants, and concerns with their partner, or know how to resolve conflicts, are more likely than not to join the ranks of the divorced and separated. Even though most couples quarrel and argue, few seem to know how to resolve conflicts effectively.

On the topic of disagreements, quarrels, conflicts, and separation, a very serious problem confronting some couples is violence, abuse, and rape within relationships. I'll have more to say about the tragedy of violence in relationships in Chapter 18.

As a concluding thought on ending relationships, there comes to mind another well-known poem, this one by Michael Drayton (1563–1631):

> Since there's no help, come let us kiss and part;
> Nay have I done, you get no more of me;
> And I am glad, yea, glad with all my heart,
> That thus so cleanly I myself can free;
> Shake hands for ever, cancel all our vows,
> And when we meet at any time again,
> Be it not seen in either of our brows
> That we one jot of former love retain.
> Now at the last gasp of love's latest breath,
> When his pulse failing, passion speechless lies,
> When faith is kneeling by his bed of death,
> And innocence is closing up his eyes,
> Now if thou would'st, when all have given him over,
> From death to life thou might'st him yet recover.

The end of passion does not necessarily spell the end of a relationship.

Why Romantic Relationships Last What is it that determines whether a loving relationship will continue or end? Long-term relationships appear to have several factors in common, including both partners verbally and physically expressing love, admiration, and appreciation; regarding the relationship as an important, long-term commitment; considering each other as best friends; and offering emotional support (Livermore, 1993).

In the remaining sections of this chapter, we'll continue our discussion of what makes love last, examining what is perhaps the most critical factor in determining both the quality and staying power of a relationship—*communication*.

COMMUNICATION

Essential to preserving a quality relationship is *effective communication* between partners. Beyond the mere transmission of information, communication is the means of establishing and nurturing intimacy within a relationship. Communication helps partners better understand and relate to each other. It helps them feel warm, close, and connected. It creates an atmosphere of mutual cooperation in which active problem-solving can take place. The ability to communicate effectively and realistically is the foundation of a healthy and satisfying partnership (Wolf, 1994).

Talking about sexuality is particularly difficult for many people. "What if I get embarrassed?" "What words should I use?" "What if I hurt my partner's feelings?" Many people

"Look, will you forget about them? They're in the past. The important thing is what I feel now—about you!"

simply do not like to talk about the more intimate aspects of their lives, such as their sexuality. As a result, sex is one of the significant trouble spots in loving relationships. Interestingly, sexual problems are often an indicator of what is happening in other areas of the relationship—problems in the bedroom reflecting problems outside the bedroom, and vice versa. It never fails that relationship trouble starts when talking stops, which is all the more reason for a couple to learn, practice, and master good communication skills. The following suggestions should help you improve your general ability to communicate with your romantic partner.

Verbally

1. Be as clear and direct as possible when talking with your partner. Don't "beat around the bush," whine, belittle, or manipulate your partner to get what you want.
2. Avoid accusatory *you* statements. Instead use *I* statements.

   Betty: You make me so angry!

         versus

   Betty: I let myself get angry sometimes.

   Or

   Jim: You forgot to put the cap back on the toothpaste!
   Betty: You left hair in the sink after you shaved!

         versus

   Jim: I appreciate it when the cap is left on the toothpaste.
   Betty: I'll remember to put the cap back on. By the way, I appreciate a clean sink.
   Jim: So do I. I'll be sure to clean up the sink the next time I shave.

3. Avoid *allness* words like "always" and "never."

   Betty: You always leave the back door open! You never listen to me.
   Jim: You always nag me!

         versus

   Betty: I dislike the back door being left open.
   Jim: I'll work on it.

4. Avoid *closed* ("Yes/No") questions, which can cause the other person to feel that he or she is being grilled. Instead use *open* questions.

   Betty: Did you leave the toilet seat up again?

         versus

   Betty: What can I do to help you remember to leave the toilet seat down?

5. Take turns talking *and* listening, giving *and* receiving feedback. Make sure that you're accurately hearing what your partner is saying. Ask questions if you don't understand something.
6. Remember to keep your conversations focused. Stay on the same topic until you're both ready to move on to something else.
7. Make sure the tone of your voice and the rate of your speech reflect interest in what your partner is saying.

Nonverbally

1. Maintain good eye contact with your partner.
2. Use attentive body language. Remain at a comfortable distance, refrain from crossing legs and arms, and lean slightly forward if sitting.
3. Use *encouraging gestures*, such as head nods and openhanded gestures, to encourage your partner to continue talking.

PERSPECTIVE

Men Who Can't Love

In their bestseller *Men Who Can't Love* (1987), Steven Carter and Julia Sokol described what appears to be a growing phenomenon in our society—men who are afraid to commit to marriage and other long-term relationships. Although specifically written for female "victims" of commitment-phobic males, the material in *Men Who Can't Love* certainly applies to male "victims" of commitment-phobic females. Here's how the authors conceptualized this phenomenon:

> HERE'S THE PROBLEM: Many men have an exaggerated fear of commitment. If you are a contemporary woman, there is a very good chance that you are going to be involved with at least one man, possibly more, who chooses to walk away from love. It may be the man who doesn't call after a particularly good date; it may be the ardent pursuer who woos you only to leave after the first night of sex; it may be the trusted boyfriend and lover who sabotages the relationship just as it heads for marriage, or it may be the man who waits until after marriage to respond to the enormity of his commitment by ignoring your emotional needs and becoming unfaithful or abusive. However, whenever it happens, chances are you are dealing with a man who has an abnormal response to the notion of commitment. To *him* something about *you* spells out wife, mother, togetherness—*forever*—and it terrifies him. That's why he leaves you.... All he knows is the relationship is "too close for comfort." Something about it, and therefore you, makes him anxious.
>
> If his fear is strong enough, this man will ultimately sabotage, destroy, or run away from any solid, good relationship. He wants love, but he is terrified—genuinely phobic—about commitment and will run away from any woman who represents "happily ever after." In other words, if his fear is too great, the commitment-phobic will not be able to love, no matter how much he wants to.
>
> But that's not how it seems in the beginning. At the beginning of the relationship, when you look at him you see a man who seems to need and want love. His blatant pursuit and touching displays of vulnerability convince you that it is "safe" for you to respond in kind. But as soon as you do, as soon as you are willing to give love a chance, as soon as it's time for the relationship to move forward, something changes. Suddenly the man begins running away, either figuratively, by withdrawing and provoking arguments, or literally, by disappearing and never calling again. Either way, you are left with disappointed dreams and destroyed self-esteem. What happened, what went wrong, and why is this scenario so familiar to so many women? (pp. 3–4)

Questions for Thought

Have you ever been involved in a "commitment-phobic" relationship? Have you ever experienced commitment phobia yourself? If so, with whom and under what circumstances?

Source: S. Carter & J. Sokol (1987), *Men who can't love.* (New York: Berkley Books).

*Honest communication is fundamental to creating and maintaining a
quality loving relationship.*

"I love you, and I want you to be my bird."

One of our society's popular myths is that genuine love means never quarreling or disagreeing. Anyone who has been involved in an ongoing relationship can testify to the fallacy of this one. When two people are involved, disagreements are bound to come up, some of which will turn into arguments. Although never pleasant, *occasional* arguments are healthy for a relationship, because they help both partners clear the air and work together to resolve conflicts. Practicing effective communication can help minimize the hurt from what can be one of the greatest challenges in any relationship. Here are ten suggestions for couples who want to learn more effective strategies for dealing with their conflicts (Zgourides, 1993):

1. As a couple, identify the problems in your relationship and agree to work them out together by practicing effective communication.
2. Take active responsibility for finding a solution. Avoiding issues and conflicts only makes things worse in the long run.
3. Reevaluate your expectations for the relationship. Expecting too much or too little from your partner or yourself can be a major source of conflict for both parties.
4. Determine what it is you want out of the relationship, but also respect your partner's freedom to determine what he or she wants out of the relationship.
5. Practice tolerance. Nobody's perfect, so why get upset when you or your partner make mistakes? Remember the two rules of life—*Rule #1*: Don't sweat the small stuff; *Rule #2*: It's all small stuff!
6. Remind yourself that, although it's easier to focus on the negative things people do, it's more helpful to build on the positive. In other words, keep a realistic perspective about it all.
7. Don't get into the "blaming" game. Accept responsibility for your own actions, and try giving your partner the benefit of the doubt.

Everyone appreciates a good listener.

What are these partners saying to each other with their bodies?

8. Don't give in to the idea that working through problems is "easier said than done." After generating alternatives and deciding on a solution, see it through! This is frequently the hardest part for couples to do.
9. Don't hesitate to seek the services of a professional therapist to help you overcome relationship obstacles.
10. Hang in there as long as both of you think there's a possibility of the relationship working. However, there's no point to staying with a sinking ship. There may come a time when both partners should go their separate ways. (pp. 132–133)

KEY POINTS

1. *Love* is characterized by intense feelings of joy within a relationship, especially in the presence of a loved object. Many experts distinguish between *passionate love*, or sexual love, and *companionate love*, or committed and affectionate love. Two popular models for explaining love are Reiss's *wheel theory of love* and Sternberg's *triangular theory of love*.
2. According to Sternberg, love consists of *passion* (arousal), *intimacy* (closeness), and *decision/commitment* (obligation and continuity). These three components combine in different ways to create the varieties of love, including *nonlove* (absence of all three components); *friendship* (intimacy only); *infatuation* (passion only); *empty love* (commitment only); *romantic love* (passion and intimacy); *fatuous love* (passion and commitment); *companionate love* (intimacy and commitment); and *consummate love* (passion, intimacy, and commitment).
3. The exact processes whereby two people fall in love are not entirely understood, but do seem to involve both *personal characteristics* and *interaction factors*. Personal characteristics commonly sought in a mate include kindness, understanding, intel-

Conflicts arise within all relationships.

Constructive quarreling can help a relationship grow. In contrast, destructive quarreling only causes long-term dissatisfaction and unhappiness.

ligence, and physical attractiveness. Typical interaction factors affecting interpersonal attraction include *proximity, familiarity, similarity, equity,* and *self-disclosure.*

4. Relationships that dissolve often do so for reasons such as the couple having made a premature commitment and/or lacking effective communication skills. Relationships that last do so for reasons such as the partners verbally and physically expressing their love, admiration, and appreciation; regarding the relationship as an important, long-term commitment; considering each other as best friends; and offering emotional support.

5. Essential to preserving a quality relationship is *effective communication* between partners. Beyond the mere transmission of information, communication is the means of establishing and nurturing intimacy within a relationship. The ability to communicate effectively and realistically is the foundation of a healthy and satisfying partnership.

ACTIVITIES AND QUESTIONS

1. Pair off with a discussion partner. Take turns sharing the qualities you believe make someone lovable. How can a person increase her or his lovableness?

2. Write down some of the messages you received as a child concerning loving yourself and others. Have these injunctions helped or hindered your ability to love? Who are some of the people in your life who have helped shape your attitudes about love?

3. Outside of class, ask women and men how they would answer the question, "Is it possible to have good sex without being in love with the other person?" Record their responses, noting any differences between the sexes. Bring the results of your survey to class.

4. What are the pros and cons of adopting a "love conquers all" attitude when beginning a loving relationship?

RECOMMENDED READINGS

Carter, S., & Sokol, J. (1987). *Men who can't love.* New York: Berkley Books. This "pop" psychology book addresses "commitment-phobic" men who find it difficult or impossible to maintain intimate relationships.

Fromm, E. (1956). *The art of loving.* New York: Harper & Row. Social psychologist Erich Fromm's famous volume on human loving and relationships.

Hatfield, E., & Rapson, R. (1993). *Love, sex, and intimacy: Their psychology, biology, and history.* New York: HarperCollins. A comprehensive, user-friendly volume on the nature of love and relationships.

Tannen, D. (1990). *You just don't understand: Women and men in conversation.* New York: Ballantine. A fascinating look into gender differences in communication.

Zgourides, G. (1993). *Don't let them psych you out!* Port Townsend, WA: Loompanics Unlimited. A "pop" psychology, cognitive-behavioral approach to dealing with problems in relationships, be they romantic, familial, social, working, or business. (In order to obtain permission to reprint sections of this book, the editorial director at Loompanies asked me to provide the following ISBN: 1-55950-097-2 and address: P.O. Box 1197, Port Townsend, WA 98368.)

C H A P T E R   9

SEXUAL BEHAVIOR AND PLEASURING

O B J E C T I V E S

AFTER READING THIS CHAPTER YOU SHOULD BE ABLE TO . . .

1. EXPLAIN THE OVERALL ROLE OF SEXPLAY IN SEXUAL PLEASURING.

2. DESCRIBE HOW AND WHY MALES AND FEMALES MASTURBATE.

3. DISTINGUISH AMONG FELLATIO, CUNNILINGUS, AND "SIXTY-NINING."

4. LIST AND DESCRIBE THE MOST COMMON INTERCOURSE POSITIONS, INCLUDING SOME OF THE POTENTIAL ADVANTAGES AND DISADVANTAGES OF EACH.

5. EXPLAIN THE IMPORTANCE OF AFTERPLAY.

PERSONAL ASSESSMENT

TEST YOUR GENERAL KNOWLEDGE OF SEXUAL BEHAVIOR AND PLEASURING BY ANSWER-
ING THE FOLLOWING STATEMENTS *true* OR *false*.

_____ 1. Sexplay activities like kissing often continue once intercourse has begun.
_____ 2. Both sexes masturbate, although the practice is more common among males than females.
_____ 3. A great deal of evidence supports the notion that masturbation is physically and emotionally harmful, explaining why so many individuals experience guilt and shame over the practice.
_____ 4. Many couples incorporate masturbation into their lovemaking. Some partners enjoy watching each other masturbate, while others enjoy manually stimulating their partner's genitals.
_____ 5. Oral sex is a popular form of sexplay in the United States, with more couples than not having experienced oral-genital activity at least once.
_____ 6. The least popular sexual position for Western couples is the male-on-top ("missionary") position, which usually implies male sexual superiority.
_____ 7. Married couples in their 20s and 30s report having sexual intercourse two to three times per week, on average.
_____ 8. Oral-anal contact between partners is termed *anilingus*.
_____ 9. Only homosexual males engage in anal intercourse.
_____ 10. *Afterplay* (sexplay after intercourse) is a natural transition between sexual intercourse and the activities of daily life.

ANSWERS
1. T, 2. T, 3. F, 4. T, 5. T, 6. F, 7. T, 8. T, 9. F, 10. T

*S*ex is the great amateur art.

David Cort

This chapter's topic—sexual behavior and pleasuring—is one of the most popular in any human sexuality class. (A good number of students first turn to the sexual pleasuring chapter when looking through a new sexuality textbook. How about you?) In the following pages, you'll find information about *sexplay*, *masturbation*, *oral sex*, *sexual intercourse*, *anal sex*, and *afterplay*, including how, when, and why people engage in these activities. Please bear in mind, however, that not everyone engages in all of these behaviors. It's up to individuals and couples to decide what is comfortable and right for them.

SEXPLAY

"Wham. Bam. Thank-you, Ma'am!" Doesn't sound very loving or exciting, does it? But this is the way some people think about sexual activity. You're always supposed to be ready for it, take up anybody's offer, perform like a machine, have that all-important orgasm, and then move onto someone else.

Some people forget the importance of helping their partner become adequately aroused in order to give and receive the most out of their sexual experiences. At one level, sexual activity is impossible, difficult, or at best unexciting if both partners are not physically prepared. At another level, sexual activity is meaningless or at best uninteresting if the partners are not emotionally prepared.

Sexplay is sexual pleasuring that precedes, continues during, and follows sexual intercourse. Typical sexplay activities involve using the mouth, hands, genitals, and/or sex toys to stimulate one's partner and self. I prefer the term *sexplay* to *foreplay*, because the latter suggests that certain activities serve only as a prelude to sexual intercourse, and cease as soon as intercourse begins. Sexplay activities are complete in and of themselves and do not necessarily have to lead to intercourse.

TOUCHING AS SEXPLAY

Touching, or *tactile stimulation*, is an exceptionally powerful source of sexual arousal. The body's most erotically sensitive areas, or *erogenous zones*, are the mouth, ears, neck, breasts, sides of the torso, hands, genitals, buttocks, inner thighs, and feet—although virtually any part of the body can be an erogenous zone. Lovers commonly stimulate these areas with their mouth, hands, genitals, and/or a variety of sex toys.

Using the Mouth   The mouth is one of the most sensitive areas of the human body, hence the popularity of activities like kissing. Many people kiss to express affection or offer greetings. In Western societies, "deep" kissing ("French" or "open-mouth" kissing),

SEXPLAY
Nonintercourse sexual activities.

Touch can be a very powerful source of sexual arousal.

Kissing as a sign of affection and sexual attraction is a very popular activity for many Americans.

involves exploring the partner's mouth with one's tongue, and is generally reserved for sexually oriented relationships.

Couples can use their mouths in other ways to sexually entice and excite one another. Licking various parts of the body (for instance, the side of the neck), gentle biting on the earlobes, and sucking on the breasts are all common. Some couples also kiss each other's genitals, which in many cases serves as a transition to other sexual activities, such as oral sex or intercourse.

Using the Hands Caressing and fondling are the two most common sexplay activities involving the hands. Light scratching and pinching are also exciting for many. Partners may hold each other, explore their bodies with their fingers and hands, give body massages, and/or fondle each other's breasts, buttocks, and genitals. While stimulating the erogenous zones with the hands can be particularly pleasurable, many people prefer to "build suspense" by waiting to fondle the genitals.

Using the Breasts and Genitals Many people overlook the fact that they can use their breasts and genitals to caress their partner. For example, a woman might gently rub her breast over her partner's erogenous zones, and a male might use his penis to stroke various parts of his partner's body.

Using Sex Toys Sometimes termed *sexual aids*, sex toys appear to be more popular than ever. Below is a small sample of the many toys and aids sold by one national mail-order catalog:

- Latex phalluses for vaginal or anal insertion
- Harnesses to hold these phalluses in place
- Anal probes, ticklers, and plugs
- G spot trigger wands
- Penile "pleasure sheaths" that when slipped over the penis supposedly give the feel of a body orifice. Some of these include a hand-held pump to enhance masturbation.

- "Chinese anal love beads" for inserting into a partner's rectum during sex and pulling out when she or he orgasms.
- Erotic lingerie
- Various oils and lotions
- Sensual massage and erotic videos
- Assorted phallus-shaped and nonphallus-shaped *vibrators* (electric vibrating devices used for massage)

Regarding the latter, at least one West Coast mail order company carries and sells a wide selection of vibrators, which come in a variety of shapes and sizes, and are either plug-in or battery-operated. Both women and men report intense sexual pleasure from using such devices (Reinisch, 1990).

LOOKING AND LISTENING AS SEXPLAY

Although touching of one sort or another is the most common form of sexplay, people also enjoy and respond to *visual* (sight) and *auditory* (sound) types of stimulation. A great many people find the sight of a sexy body (or pictures of such) and/or the sounds of passion sexually arousing. Many couples "get in the mood" by undressing in front of each other, being undressed by the partner, and/or looking at erotic photos. Some take photos or make home videos of themselves dancing, stripping, or having sex, while others enjoy "talking dirty" to each other to prepare for sex. Still others are aroused by listening to music, reading erotic poetry, or hearing a partner "moan" in the throes of sexual passion.

MASTURBATION

Masturbation (*autoeroticism*) involves manually self-stimulating the genitals for the purpose of sexual excitement and gratification. Both males and females masturbate, generally to orgasm. A number of masturbatory techniques are possible for each of the sexes.

MASTURBATION (MAS-TUR-BA-SHUN)
Genital self-stimulation for the purpose of sexual gratification.

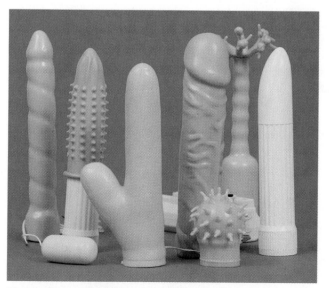

Electric vibrators come in a variety of shapes and sizes, and are available from various stores and mail order companies.

FIGURE 9.1 *Male masturbation.*

MALE MASTURBATION TECHNIQUES

Males typically masturbate by grasping the erect penis with one or both hands, and stimulating the glans and shaft with up-and-down stroking movements (Figure 9.1). Here, the hand (which is usually lubricated) can be turned thumb-down or thumb-up, or a "ring" can be made with the thumb and forefinger. Other men roll the penis between their hands, and still others rub the penis against the abdomen with the palm of the hand or against a pillow. In all cases, the rapidity of movement and the degree of pressure used can vary considerably, although it is common for men to increase the speed and intensity of their stroking as orgasm approaches. Many men also enjoy caressing other erogenous zones, such as their inner thighs, while masturbating.

FEMALE MASTURBATION TECHNIQUES

Females typically masturbate by rubbing the clitoral shaft, G spot, and nearby structures with one or both hands (Figure 9.2). In one variation, the woman lubricates her major and minor labia, clitoris, vestibule, and vaginal opening. She then uses any of a number of rubbing, tugging, or stroking movements to bring herself to orgasm. In another variation, the woman may move fingers or penile-shaped objects ("dildos") in and out of her vagina. Or, she may direct a stream of water over her genitals, rub up against a pillow, or stimulate her clitoral area with an electric vibrator. As with men, the degree of pressure and speed of movements can vary considerably. Many women also enjoy caressing other erogenous zones, such as their breasts, while masturbating.

INCIDENCE OF MASTURBATION

Masturbation seems to be a universal sexual behavior, crossing all age groups and cultures. From infants touching their genitals to the elderly engaging in self-pleasuring, people from all walks of life masturbate. Kinsey and colleagues (1948, 1953) found that nearly all the males surveyed (92 percent)—and most of the females as well (62 percent)—had masturbated at least once, with many of them masturbating frequently. Other studies, too,

FIGURE 9.2 *Female masturbation.*

have found that a significant portion of the population has had some experience with autoeroticism (Blumstein & Schwartz, 1983; Hite, 1976, 1981; Hunt, 1974; Janus & Janus, 1993; Michael et al., 1994; Petersen et al., 1983; Reinisch, 1990; Rubenstein, 1993; Sorensen, 1973; Wolfe, 1981).

How many college students masturbate, and how often do they do it? In their survey of 593 college men and 584 college women, Atwood and Gagnon (1987) found that approximately 80 percent of men and 32 percent of women masturbated during college. Of those males who reported masturbating, 18.9 percent did so twice per week; 20.7 percent, once per week; and 19.7 percent, less than once per month. Of those females who reported masturbating, 6.5 percent did so twice per week; 7 percent, once per week; and 54 percent, less than once per month. Data from the Atwood and Gagnon survey appear in Table 9.1.

Why do people masturbate? It would seem that they do so for a variety of reasons, one of which is enjoying the erotic sensations of this particular activity. This explains why many adults continue to masturbate even when a sexual partner is available. Some couples masturbate instead of having intercourse as a form of birth control. Others use masturbation as a way of learning what it is that they find sexually gratifying. Some men masturbate to learn ejaculatory control; some women to learn to be orgasmic (Dodson, 1987; Hurlbert & Whittaker, 1991; McCarthy, 1989).

TABLE 9.1 **The Frequency of Masturbation During College by Gender**

Frequency	Males	Females
Daily	3.1%	0%
Twice per week	18.9%	6.5%
Once per week	20.7%	7.0%
Once every two weeks	19.7%	10.3%
Once per month	17.8%	21.6%
Less than once per month	19.7%	54.6%
N =	477	185

Source: J. D. Atwood & J. Gagnon (1987), Masturbatory behavior in college youth, *Journal of Sex Education and Therapy, 13,* 35–42. Reprinted by permission of the Guilford Press.

For Personal Reflection

Your 9-year-old child first heard the word masturbation today on the school playground, and she or he asks you what this means. How would you explain?

ORAL-GENITAL SEX*

ORAL-GENITAL SEX OR ORAL SEX

Sexual activity involving the mouth, lips, and tongue of one partner and the genitals of another.

Because the mouth and the genitals are primary erogenous zones, many people enjoy oral-genital stimulation. **Oral-genital sex,** or **oral sex,** which can be a part of sexplay or a sexual act in and of itself, involves contact between one partner's mouth, lips, and tongue and the other partner's genitals. Both heterosexual and homosexual couples may practice oral-genital sex.

FELLATIO

FELLATIO (FEL-LA-SHE-O)

Performing oral sex on the male genitals.

Oral contact with the male genitals, especially the penis, is termed **fellatio** (Figure 9.3). During fellatio (from the Latin *fellare,* meaning "to suck"), all or a portion of the penis is taken into the partner's mouth and sucked and stimulated with the tongue and lips. Some men enjoy fellatio that mimics the moist and gentle sensations of the vagina, while others enjoy the vigorous sucking, blowing, and licking that only the mouth can provide. Some men delight in watching the partner perform fellatio, as well as having the partner fondle and lick the testicles, caress the perineum and inner thighs, and alternate sucking and manually stroking the shaft of the penis.

Whether or not the man ejaculates in his partner's mouth is a matter for the couple to decide beforehand. Some people object to both the taste of semen and the thought of swallowing it. Contrary to popular myth, however, semen is not fattening or harmful when swallowed, although some find that it stings a little in the mouth and throat, and choose to spit it out.

*Oral sex, like any other sexual activity involving partners and the exchange of body fluids, carries with it the risk of transmission of HIV and other sexually transmitted diseases. See Chapter 14 for information on safer sex practices.

PERSPECTIVE

Life-Threatening Masturbation

An article entitled "Life-Threatening Autoerotic Behavior: A Challenge for Sex Educators and Therapists," which described two potentially deadly masturbatory practices, appeared in a 1989 issue of the *Journal of Sex Education & Therapy.* Author Edward L. Saunders noted:

> While youths are now assured by most parents and counselors that masturbation is not sinful or harmful, there is reason to believe, based on reviews of the medical and psychiatric literature, that certain masturbatory activities are, in fact, harmful and even life-threatening. The primary life-threatening behavior is typically referred to as "autoerotic asphyxia." Fatal asphyxia is accomplished by hanging or other oxygen-depriving activities. In addition, there are reports of fatalities from electrocution during masturbation. (p. 83)

What is the rationale for engaging in life-threatening masturbatory behaviors? No one knows for sure. Some researchers point to the promise of erotic ecstasy resulting from diminished oxygen and increased levels of carbon dioxide in the blood, while others believe an element of sexual risk-taking is responsible. Whatever the causes, at least several hundred males die each year from life-threatening masturbation (Saunders, 1989). Two studies of autoerotic deaths reported victims' ages ranging from 14 to 75 (Burgess et al., 1983; Walsh et al., 1977).

Sources: A. W. Burgess, P. E. Dietz, & R. R. Hazelwood (1983), Study design and characteristics. In R. R. Hazelwood, P. E. Dietz, & A. W. Burgess (Eds.), *Autoerotic fatalities* (Lexington, MA: Lexington Books).

E. L. Saunders, (1989), Life-threatening autoerotic behavior: A challenge for sex educators and therapists, *Journal of Sex Education and Therapy, 15,* 82–91.

F. M. Walsh, C. J. Stahl, H. T. Unger, O. C. Lilienstern, & R. G. Stephens (1977), Autoerotic asphyxial deaths: A medicolegal analysis of forty-three cases. In C. H. Wecht (Ed.), *Legal medicine annual: 1977* (New York: Appleton-Century-Crofts).

FIGURE 9.3 *Female performing fellatio.*

Interestingly, a few men can perform fellatio on themselves, termed *auto-fellatio* ("blowing your own horn"). This maneuver typically involves the man lying on his back, throwing his legs over his shoulders, and inserting his penis into his mouth. Fewer than 3 out of every 1,000 males are capable of sucking their own penises (The Diagram Group, 1976).

CUNNILINGUS

CUNNILINGUS (KUN-I-LIN-GUS)

Performing oral sex on the female genitals.

Cunnilingus (meaning "one who licks the vulva ") refers to oral contact with and stimulation of the female genitals (Figure 9.4). Specifically, the partner licks, kisses, and sucks the woman's clitoris, labia minora, and/or vestibule. Some women report exceptionally good feelings when their partner's moist, soft tongue comes in contact with the clitoris, although other women find the clitoris too sensitive for tonguing. During cunnilingus the partner may also place a finger in the vagina, move the tongue in and out of the vaginal opening, and use hands to caress the woman's mons pubis, perineum, and inner thighs. Some women prefer lighter, gentler tonguing; others more rapid and vigorous movements.

One women from the *Cosmopolitan* survey (Wolfe, 1981) described enjoying oral sex with her boyfriend as follows:

On a Personal Note ("a 22-year-old from West Virginia")

Oral sex is gorgeous! I love putting my boyfriend's penis in between my lips and pulling and pulling at it with my mouth and making it grow bigger and bigger and imagining how it's going to feel when he puts it inside me. And I love his going down on me and flicking his tongue back and forth on my clitoris, and then taking it between his lips and making it all moist and ready. How did people ever get excited before there was oral sex? (p. 102)

As with swallowing semen during fellatio, some partners object to the taste of vaginal secretions during cunnilingus. Covering the clitoris and surrounding areas with a latex dental dam or other membranous material is one solution to this problem.

FIGURE 9.4 *Male performing cunnilingus.*

"SIXTY-NINING"

Some couples perform oral sex on one another at the same time. The partners face each other, lie head to toe, and simultaneously stimulate each other's genitals—called **sixty-nining,** presumably because the positioning of the partners' bodies resemble the number "69" (Figure 9.5).

Many couples enjoy sixty-nining because they believe it allows both partners to be fully involved in oral pleasuring. Others find the position too acrobatic or have difficulty simultaneously giving and receiving oral-genital pleasure.

SIXTY-NINING
Simultaneous oral sex.

INCIDENCE OF ORAL SEX

According to various surveys, oral sex appears to be a popular sexual pastime for many (but not all) Americans. In an early 1970s *Playboy* survey, about 90 percent of married couples under age 25 reported having had at least some experience with oral sex (Hunt, 1974). In a mid-1970s *Redbook* survey of over 100,000 women, 91 percent of respondents reported having both given and received oral sex with their partners (Levin & Levin, 1975). And in an early 1980s *Playboy* survey, more than 90 percent of husbands and between 72 and 81 percent of wives reported performing oral sex on their spouses (Petersen et al., 1983). More recently, in a *Details/Mademoiselle* survey of 9,000 sub-scribers, 54 and 57 percent of men reported giving and receiving oral sex, respectively, at least half the time; and likewise for 44 and 42 percent of women, respectively (Rubenstein, 1993). Of course, readers of *Playboy*, *Redbook*, and *Details/Mademoiselle* may be more sexually liberal than others in the United States. The respondents of all of the above-mentioned studies are also *self-selected* and therefore not necessarily representative of the general public. Nevertheless, studies such as these can have merit even though their sampling is not representative, providing us with insights into the sexual practices of at least certain groups of people.

Finally, some people and governments consider oral sex to be unnatural, immoral, and therefore illegal. In fact, the majority of states have laws prohibiting *sodomy*, a term loosely describing anything from heterosexual or homosexual anal intercourse to oral sex and bestiality. Although oral sex is illegal in some states, the courts rarely enforce these laws today.

FIGURE 9.5 *"Sixty-nining."*

GENITAL-GENITAL SEX*

SEXUAL INTERCOURSE
Genital-genital sex.

The most widely accepted and practiced form of sexual activity in our society is genital-genital sex, or **sexual intercourse.** *Coitus* (from the Latin *coire,* meaning "to copulate") is sexual intercourse involving insertion of a man's penis into a woman's vagina. Mutual cooperation between partners facilitates *intromission* (insertion) of the penis into the vagina. Some couples also use artificial lubrication to prevent pain and irritation of the vagina and/or penis. One or both of the partners may move their hips; thrusting may be shallow or deep, fast or slow, gentle or forceful; partners may change movements or positions, starting and stopping several times; and they may continue sexplay—all perhaps during a single act of intercourse. As with other aspects of a relationship, couples should communicate their likes and dislikes to one another so that sexual activity can be freeing and pleasurable for both parties.

In the next few sections, I'll describe the most common intercourse positions, as well as identify some of the advantages and disadvantages of each. You should also note that the following positions are not exclusive to heterosexual couples; homosexual partners utilize many of the same basic intercourse positions as do heterosexuals.

SEXUAL INTERCOURSE POSITIONS

Sexual partners have available a variety of intercourse positions to experiment with and enjoy. In fact, Jessica Stewart's (1990) *Complete Manual of Sexual Positions* contains over 200 photographs of different intercourse positions, and even this is not an exhaustive listing. An arm moved here, a leg positioned there, hands and lips doing this or that—the possibilities are limited only by one's imagination and physical agility. Intercourse positions, however, generally fall into two basic categories: (1) *face-to-face* and (2) *rear entry,* each of which divide into a virtually infinite number of variations.

Face-to-Face, Male-on-Top Positions Perhaps the most common heterosexual coital position is the face-to-face, male-on-top "missionary position." (Natives who observed foreign missionaries having sex in this manner supposedly coined this phrase.) Here, the woman lies on her back, facing the man, who lies on top of her (Figure 9.6). The woman typically spreads her legs to allow easy penetration of her vagina by his penis. Also, when the woman's legs are open, the man is able to rest his thighs and legs on the bed or floor, reducing the amount of his weight pressed against her body. A heavy man on top of a slight woman can be uncomfortable for the woman, although the weight of a partner can also be a turn-on.

The male-on-top position has several advantages, one being full frontal body contact. In this position, both partners are facing so they can talk and kiss, and their arms and hands are free to hold, caress, and fondle. The man can enhance his experience by positioning himself lower on the woman and rubbing his sensitive frenulum just inside her vaginal orifice (against the muscles of the outer portion of the vagina). The male-on-top position is also one of the most effective for the purposes of conception, especially if the woman raises her legs and pelvis following ejaculation so his semen can more easily move into her uterus.

The male-on-top position also has some disadvantages. First, the man may experience some strain because of the weight placed on his knees and elbows as he supports himself over the woman. Second, depending on the man's positioning above the woman, she may or may not experience maximal clitoral stimulation. Manual stimulation of the woman's clitoris can be difficult, especially if both partners' torsos press closely together and/or the man is using his hands to support himself. The woman, though, can stimulate her own

*Genital-genital sex carries with it the risk of pregnancy and transmission of sexually transmitted diseases. See Chapters 13 and 14 for information on contraception and safer sex practices.

FIGURE 9.6 *Face-to-face, male-on-top coital position.*

clitoris in this position. Finally, the male-on-top position is not terribly effective for men who have difficulty controlling or delaying their ejaculation, given the intense penile stimulation associated with this position.

Many variations of the male-on-top position are possible. The man may lie atop her with her legs raised over his shoulders (Figure 9.7), or he may kneel while she lies facing him on the edge of a bed, chair, or couch (Figure 9.8). This face-to-face "kneeling" position can be especially enjoyable for both partners, reducing the amount of his weight on her and better allowing both partners to thrust. Because he is not supporting himself with his elbows, his hands are free to stimulate her clitoris and breasts.

Face-to-Face, Female-on-Top Positions In this variation of face-to-face intercourse, the man lies on his back, facing the woman, who lies above him. If he keeps his legs closed, she usually spreads hers around the outside of his (Figure 9.9).

FIGURE 9.7 *Face-to-face, male-on-top, female raising legs over male's shoulders.*

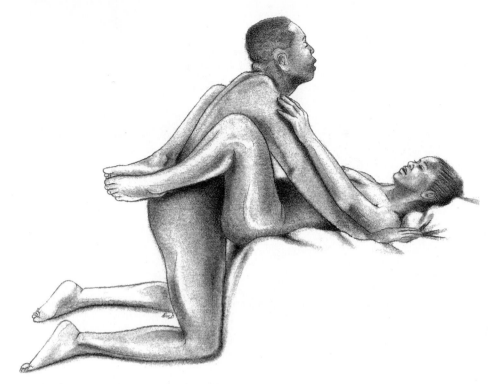

FIGURE 9.8 *Face-to-face, male-on-top, male kneeling.*

FIGURE 9.9 *Face-to-face, female-on-top coital position.*

If the man spreads his legs open, she may keep hers closed, her vagina then providing an exceptionally tight grip around his penis. As with the man in the male-on-top position, the woman rests her knees/thighs and hands/elbows on the bed or couch, and proceeds to move her hips in ways that pleasure both herself and her partner. In the female-on-top position, the woman can sit astride the man, or both partners can sit (Figures 9.10 and 9.11).

The female-on-top position has a number of advantages for both sexes. This position affords the woman maximum movement, control, and stimulation, as she is able to regulate the angle, speed, and depth of thrusting. She also need not feel "pinned in" under the weight of a partner when she is on top. For the man, the female-on-top position frees his hands to fondle the woman's breasts and clitoris. He may also find this position especially relaxing when the woman takes a very active role in their lovemaking.

FIGURE 9.10 *Face-to-face, female-on-top, female sitting astride male.*

FIGURE 9.11 *Face-to-face, female-on-top, both partners sitting.*

The female-on-top position also has some disadvantages. It is not particularly effective if the couple is having difficulty conceiving, because the semen can flow out of the vagina following ejaculation. This position is also less stimulating for the man—one reason why sex therapists often recommend this position for males who ejaculate prematurely and wish to learn ejaculatory control. Further, the female-on-top "sitting" position may not be possible if the man has a particularly high angle of erection. One note of caution, too, concerning the female-on-top position: Whenever a woman is atop a man with his erect penis inside her, she must be particularly careful to control her movements, not bending too far backward lest she accidentally rupture his penis.

Face-to-Face, Side-by-Side Positions Here, the partners lie on their sides, facing each other, and intertwine their legs and arms (Figure 9.12). Many variations of this are possible. The woman may lift one leg over the man's hip, leaving the other leg under him while he puts one leg between hers and leaves the other outstretched. Or she may place one leg between his legs and lift the other over his hip, while he positions one leg between hers and supports her body with the other.

The various side-by-side positions allow maximal freedom of movement. Neither partner is weighed down, there is no strain on the knees or arms, the hands are free to caress and fondle, and the couple face so they can kiss and talk. Side-by-side positions are also more comfortable for the woman during pregnancy. Side-by-side intromission can be difficult, and some people report that these positions are not as stimulating as others.

Face-to-Face, Standing Positions In this variation of face-to-face intercourse, both partners stand (Figure 9.13). The woman may lean back in this position, or she may wrap her legs around the man's waist, requiring him to hold her up while they both thrust. This position allows a couple to have intercourse in alternative settings, such as in a compact shower. Like side-by-side positions, intromission while standing can be difficult.

Rear-Entry Positions In this second basic category of intercourse positions, the partners do not face one another. Instead, the man inserts his penis in the woman's vagina from behind her. In one variation ("doggy style"), the woman gets on her knees and hands, her buttocks facing her partner, and the man kneels and enters her from the rear

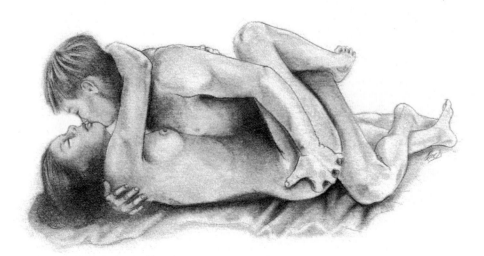

FIGURE 9.12 *Face-to-face, side-by-side coital position.*

FIGURE 9.13 *Face-to-face, both partners standing.*

(Figure 9.14). He is also free to fondle her clitoris, buttocks, inner thighs, and breasts. This position can be highly stimulating for the man, as his sensitive frenulum rubs against his partner's anterior vaginal wall and pubic bone. It may or may not be as stimulating for the woman.

In another variation ("spooning"), the couple lie on their sides, the woman's backside facing the man. Again, intromission occurs from behind, and the man is free to hold and caress his partner (Figure 9.15). This tends to be a relaxing position for both parties, and is especially recommended for partners who must monitor and minimize their levels of physical exertion.

In still another variation, the woman lies flat on her stomach, and the man spreads her legs and buttocks in order to enter her (Figure 9.16). Once inside, the woman may leave her legs open, or she may close them, positioning his legs around hers to tighten the vaginal muscles surrounding his penis. This variation, while stimulating for the man, affords the woman only minimal opportunities to move, perhaps even causing her to feel pinned down or trapped.

The rear-entry positions facilitate conception. As penetration is deeper when the woman raises her hips, the semen has a shorter distance to travel to the cervix than with other positions. Rear entry can also provide a novel change for the couple. However, some women may find rear entry painful, depending on the man's angle of insertion. Others object to the position because of its resemblance to animal copulation.

Given all of this information on the basic intercourse positions and some of their popular variations, a very natural question follows: "Which position is the *best?*" The answer,

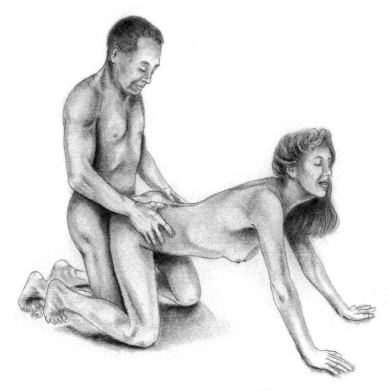

FIGURE 9.14 *Rear-entry, "doggy style" coital position.*

FIGURE 9.15 *Rear-entry, "spooning."*

as you've probably suspected, is there isn't a *best* position. It's all a matter of choice and preference. Many couples enjoy experimenting to find what works best for them, taking into account such factors as weight, height, degree of stimulation, potential pain, and the desire to conceive. They may also enjoy trying different positions at different times.

INCIDENCE OF SEXUAL INTERCOURSE

Many people want to know what is "normal" regarding incidence, frequency, and timing of intercourse (Adler, 1993). "How many people do it?" "How often do they do it?" "Do

FIGURE 9.16 *Rear-entry, female lying on stomach.*

my partner and I do it too much?" "How long should it last?" There are no rules in terms of how, when, where, or how often people *should* have sexual intercourse.

Research indicates that for over 80 percent of men and nearly 70 percent of women, intercourse is the preferred way to achieve orgasm (Janus & Janus, 1993). Further, the *median frequency* (middle score breaking a distribution in half) of sexual intercourse for married couples in their 20s and 30s in the United States is about two to three times per week. (Remember, figures like "three times a week" are only averages, and by no means indicative of what is "normal." Also, age and the number of years together can affect these "averages.") Of those who had been together for less than two years, Blumstein and Schwartz (1990) found that 45 percent of married couples, 61 percent of heterosexual cohabiting (unwed) couples, 67 percent of male couples, and 33 percent of female couples reported having intercourse three times a week or more. Of those who had been together between two and ten years, only 27 percent of married couples, 38 percent of cohabiting couples, 32 percent of male couples, and 7 percent of female couples reported the same.

How long does intercourse usually last? It all depends on the couple, although 10 to 20 minutes is one average. Some partners enjoy "quickies," climaxing very soon, often less than a minute or two after intromission. Others practice *coitus reservatus*, "extending" sexual activity for an hour or more by starting and stopping, alternating between sexplay and intercourse, and practicing ejaculatory control. Several books are available for individuals who want to learn to "last longer" and extend their orgasms, such as Alan and Donna Brauer's (1990) *The ESO Ecstasy Program: Better, Safer Sexual Intimacy and Extended Orgasmic Response.*

Research suggests that for both sexes, manual stimulation of the genitals is frequently more *physically* satisfying than stimulation through sexual intercourse (Masters & Johnson, 1966). Why, then, do so many men and women prefer intercourse? Generally speaking, intercourse is unique in that it requires equal participation and mutual cooperation between partners, probably more so than any other type of sexual activity. Both partners give and receive, providing the basis for the emotional expression, communication, and intimacy that is shared before, during, and after sexual intercourse. As one woman interviewee so aptly observed of her husband, as quoted in Philip Blumstein & Pepper Schwartz's (1983) *American Couples:*

On a Personal Note ("Mitzi," age 41)

Intercourse is great. We tend to both come that way, fully, totally, a good way to end our lovely task. . . . I love intercourse because it's the time we communicate the best. We communicate best because it doesn't require my husband to talk. Most American males raised in the fifties—and every decade before—are not allowed to emote—which is communication—talking. American males are effectively verbally castrated. I hope my sons will be part of a generation of males who can express feelings. Intercourse is the emitting of emotion, and I think males only allow themselves to emit this emotion when they are in ecstasy. So for my husband, it is a real freedom. He's allowed to let go and communicate: "I'm happy. I'm having a good time. Oh, boy. Wow." These emotions are usually bridled in American males over the age of thirty-five. I think it's the best way he and I communicate. It's an expression of the whole body. (pp. 227–228)

ANAL SEX

Some people take pleasure in anal stimulation. That is, they enjoy having their anus and/or anal area massaged, rubbed, stroked, licked, or penetrated. Contrary to popular stereotypes, anal pleasuring is popular among some heterosexuals, as well as bisexuals and homosexuals (Morin, 1986). Some couples, mostly teens, also see anal sex as a way of avoiding pregnancy and remaining a "virgin."

Medical and sexuality experts currently recommend abstaining from anal-oral and anal-genital sex—"protected" or not—to prevent the transmission of HIV, as well as diseases like hepatitis and intestinal infections. (Many bacteria are normally present in the rectum, that if introduced into the urethra, vagina, or mouth cause serious health problems.) *Anal intercourse is the riskiest behavior connected with contracting and transmitting HIV, the virus that causes AIDS. Knowing this, if you still decide to have anal intercourse, you must use condoms. If you or your partner aren't planning to use condoms, don't even think about anal intercourse.*

ANAL-ORAL SEX

ANILINGUS (AN-I-LIN-GUS)
Sexual activity involving the mouth, lips, and tongue of one partner and the anus of another.

Anilingus ("rimming") is sexual activity involving the mouth, lips, and tongue of one person and the anus of another. During anilingus, one partner kisses, licks, and/or sucks the anal region of his or her partner. Given this activity's potential for spreading disease, strict hygiene is a must. The couple can place a rubber dental dam over the anal region as a barrier against infection. Reactions to this form of sexplay vary considerably.

ANAL-GENITAL SEX

ANAL INTERCOURSE
Sexual activity involving one partner inserting his penis into the other partner's rectum.

During anal-genital sex, or **anal intercourse,** one partner (the "inserter") places his penis into his partner's (the "insertee's") rectum. As with penile-vaginal intercourse, partners engaging in anal intercourse assume any number of positions—variations of the basic *face-to-face* and *rear-entry* positions described earlier (Figure 9.17).

Ordinarily the anal sphincter keeps the anus closed, and tightens even more when stimulated or when the individual is anxious. Because the anus lacks natural lubrication and tissues of the anus and rectum are delicate, the entire region is easily damaged. To minimize the chances of penile infection, as well as the spread of HIV between partners, the inserter must wear one or more condoms properly lubricated (with *nonoxynol-9*). Again, strict hygiene is a must. The inserter must also *never* leave the anus and enter the vagina without first taking off the condom and washing the penis.

FIGURE 9.17 *Face-to-face anal intercourse position.*

INCIDENCE OF ANAL SEX

How many people engage in anal intercourse? In several older, pre-AIDS studies, about 30 percent of heterosexual couples and 90 percent of homosexual male couples reported having experienced anal intercourse at least once. About 10 percent of heterosexuals and 50 percent of homosexuals reported having anal intercourse on a regular basis (Blumstein & Schwartz, 1983; Hunt, 1974; Petersen et al., 1983). In more recent studies, about 10 percent of heterosexual couples in the United States reported "regularly" engaging in anal intercourse (Bolling & Voeller, 1987; Voeller, 1991). In the *Details/Mademoiselle* survey, 34 percent of homosexual men, 2 percent of heterosexual men, and no women reported that anal intercourse was their favorite means to have an orgasm (Rubenstein, 1993).

AFTERPLAY

An often-neglected topic in human sexuality textbooks is **afterplay,** or sexplay that *follows* sexual intercourse. The activities taking place immediately after sexual intercourse influence how a person perceives his or her sexual experience. This may be due in part to the *recency effect,* a psychological phenomenon in which a recent event colors a person's interpretation of previous events. Afterplay activities can include just about anything. Many couples touch, hold, caress, kiss, talk and share, and/or shower together.

Why do people desire afterplay? Probably because afterplay acts as a kind of bridge between the bedroom and other intimate aspects of a relationship. Sexual intercourse is so much more than mechanical copulation consisting of arousal, plateau, and orgasm—it is one of the most powerful ways of expressing love, care, and trust within a relationship. And because sexual expression is perhaps the most rewarding experience that two people can share, why ignore the importance of continuing this intimacy? As one person mentioned, "True lovemaking doesn't end with orgasm; the physical stuff is only the beginning of what really counts in a relationship."

AFTERPLAY

Pleasuring that follows sexual intercourse.

Afterplay activities can be powerful expressions of partners' love, care, and trust for one another.

KEY POINTS

1. Sexual pleasuring normally involves one or more of the following: *sexplay*, *masturbation*, *oral sex*, *sexual intercourse*, *anal sex*, and *afterplay*.

2. *Sexplay* is sexual pleasuring that precedes, continues during, and follows sexual intercourse. Typical sexplay activities involve using the mouth, hands, genitals, and/or sex toys to stimulate one's partner and self. Sexplay activities are complete in and of themselves and do not necessarily have to lead to intercourse.

3. *Masturbation* involves manually self-stimulating the genitals for the purpose of sexual excitement and gratification. Both males and females masturbate, generally to orgasm. A number of masturbatory techniques are possible for each of the sexes.

4. *Oral sex* involves contact between one partner's mouth, lips, and tongue and the other partner's genitals. *Fellatio* is oral contact with the male genitals; *cunnilingus*, with the female genitals. *Sixty-nining* refers to simultaneous oral sex.

5. The most widely accepted and practiced form of sexual activity in our society is *sexual intercourse*. *Coitus* is sexual intercourse involving insertion of a man's penis into a woman's vagina, usually accompanied by pelvic thrusting by one or both partners. Sexual partners have available a variety of intercourse positions to experiment with and enjoy. These generally fall into two categories: (1) *face-to-face* and (2) *rear entry*, each of which divide into a virtually infinite number of variations.

6. Some people take pleasure in anal stimulation. During *anilingus*, one partner kisses, licks, and/or sucks the anal region of his or her partner. During *anal intercourse*, one partner inserts his penis into the anus of his partner.

7. An often-neglected topic in human sexuality textbooks is *afterplay*, sexplay that *follows* sexual intercourse. Afterplay activities can include just about anything, although most couples touch, hold, caress, kiss, talk and share, and/or shower together.

ACTIVITIES AND QUESTIONS

1. Why do you think so many people associate masturbation with sexual immaturity?
2. Research suggests that oral sex is becoming increasingly popular in our society. Why might this be so? Do you think lovers of previous generations avoided fellatio and cunnilingus, or were they perhaps less apt to talk about their oral sex practices?
3. Here is an exercise that frequently prompts a lot of giggles and red faces. With a friend or classmate, list and describe as many different sexual intercourse positions as possible, noting possible advantages and disadvantages of each. How comfortable are you talking about sexual behaviors and positions with this individual?
4. What are some of the reasons our society has traditionally frowned upon (and prohibited) anal sexplay?

RECOMMENDED READINGS

Carter, S., & Sokol, J. (1989). *What really happens in bed: A demystification of sex.* New York: M. Evans and Co. According to the authors, a book about "real" sex, based on interviews with hundreds of people.

Comfort, A. (1991). *The new joy of sex* (rev. ed.). New York: Crown. Perhaps the most famous of today's sex manuals.

Eichel, E., & Nobile, P. (1992). *The perfect fit: How to achieve mutual fulfillment and monogamous passion through the new intercourse.* New York: Signet. This fascinating book introduces the Coital Alignment Technique. Recommended for couples desiring to enhance their sexual pleasure and/or attempting to overcome sexual dysfunctions.

Stubbs, K. R., & Saulnier, L. A. (1989). *Erotic massage: The touch of love.* Larkspur, CA: Secret Garden. Full of illustrations and suggestions for using massage to enhance sexual experiences.

C H A P T E R   1 0

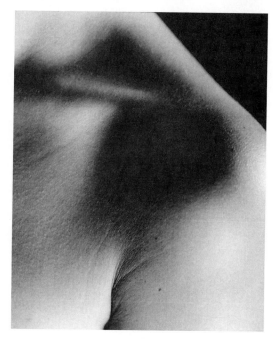

SEXUALITY, HEALTH, AND THE CHALLENGED INDIVIDUAL

O B J E C T I V E S

AFTER READING THIS CHAPTER YOU SHOULD BE
ABLE TO . . .

1. EXPLAIN WHY THE TERM *CHALLENGED* IS
   PREFERABLE TO TERMS LIKE *HANDICAPPED,*
   DISABLED, AND *RETARDED* WHEN REFERRING TO
   SPECIAL INDIVIDUALS OR GROUPS.
2. DESCRIBE SOME OF THE TYPICAL ATTITUDES
   MEMBERS OF OUR SOCIETY HAVE ABOUT
   PHYSICALLY, DEVELOPMENTALLY, AND EMOTION-
   ALLY CHALLENGED INDIVIDUALS.
3. IDENTIFY THE MOST COMMON PHYSICAL,
   DEVELOPMENTAL, AND EMOTIONAL CHALLENGES
   THAT INFLUENCE SEXUAL FUNCTIONING.
4. EXPLAIN HOW IT IS POSSIBLE FOR CHALLENGED
   INDIVIDUALS AND THEIR PARTNERS TO HAVE A
   GRATIFYING SEXUAL RELATIONSHIP.
5. DESCRIBE WHAT SIGNIFICANT OTHERS CAN DO
   TO IMPROVE THEIR INTERACTIONS WITH
   CHALLENGED INDIVIDUALS.

P E R S O N A L   A S S E S S M E N T

WHAT ARE YOUR THOUGHTS AND FEELINGS ON SEX AND THE DISABLED? TO EXPLORE THIS, READ THE FOLLOWING STATEMENTS AND RESPOND USING THIS RATING SCALE: 3 = I *completely agree* WITH THE STATEMENT; 2 = I *mostly agree* WITH THE STATEMENT; 1 = I *mostly disagree* WITH THE STATEMENT; 0 = I *completely disagree* WITH THE STATEMENT. REMEMBER, THERE ARE NO RIGHT OR WRONG ANSWERS HERE; IT'S YOUR OPINION THAT COUNTS.

_____   1. Sexual activity is only for the young, beautiful, and healthy.

_____   2. Labeling someone as *disabled* or *retarded* can have serious emotional and social consequences for that person.

_____   3. People with spinal cord injuries have no sensations in their genitals; therefore, they aren't interested in sexual activity and can't be sexually aroused.

_____   4. It's impolite to stare at someone in a wheelchair.

_____   5. Developmentally and emotionally challenged individuals easily become sexually aggressive.

_____   6. A challenged individual's caretakers or the government should decide if she or he will marry and/or have children.

_____   7. Challenged individuals should be discouraged from sexual self-exploration and gratification.

_____   8. Everyone has a basic right to sexual expression, although with this right comes the responsibility not to act carelessly, hurt, or exploit others.

_____   9. It's possible for many challenged individuals and their partners to have an active and fulfilling sex life.

_____   10. Challenged individuals often suffer from very low self-esteem.

*L*ove does not consist in gazing at each other but in looking outward together in the same direction.

Antoine de Saint Exupéry

Who are the lonely ones? They are those with disabilities of one kind or another: those who are mentally slow, who don't understand why they aren't like everyone else but who keep trying to be; those who are deaf, who have put forth huge efforts day after day just to learn how to communicate; those who have physical disabilities, who have grown up feeling different and ugly, like the teenager with cerebral palsy who wept as he asked, "How can I ever invite a girl to date when I'm always drooling?"; those who are disfigured, like the adolescent girl who was born with a cleft lip and wonders if any boy will ever want to kiss her; those who are blind, who have no visual way to build good self-images as attractive girls or boys or to exchange the meaningful glances that are so often the beginnings of a human relationship. . . .

Among the many things the lonely ones have in common with the rest of the world is their sexuality, at the same ages and stages. This means that they have the same sex-related needs as all of us; they need a loving, caring person to be close to; they need the various forms of expression that relate to being sexual, such as tenderness, touching, kissing, stroking, and caressing; and they need the soft words and the pleasure-giving expressions of sexuality, lovemaking, and sexual intercourse. (Calderone & Johnson, 1989, pp. 144–145)

This excerpt may be a little surprising for many readers. Have you ever thought of the disabled or handicapped as having sexual feelings and needs? Have you ever thought of them as wanting love and intimacy? Sadly, too many people write off the disabled, shunning and avoiding them. Passages such as these should alert you to the fact that everyone is sexual, including those who differ from the norms of mainstream society. Sexuality is an important part of everyone's experience, not just that of healthy young people.

We now turn our attention to the impact that a disability or medical problem can have on sexuality. In this chapter, we'll examine various physical, developmental, and emotional conditions—various *challenges*—that affect a person's sexual well-being. We'll debunk common myths and stereotypes, as well as examine the sources of these attitudes. We'll even have a few words about sexuality-enhancing strategies for these special people.

Finally, you'll note throughout this chapter and others that I generally avoid labels like *handicapped*, *disabled*, and *retarded*, which tend to be needlessly negative and stereotypic. Instead, I prefer the phrases *physically challenged*, *developmentally challenged*, and *emotionally challenged*, which tend to be more positive and liberating. Such language can help an individual to reframe his or her "problem" into a "challenge" that can be dealt with and potentially overcome. A challenge, then, is a *process*, not a label used to define an individual's personality or worth as a human being. I realize that some readers may object to my use of *challenge* over *disability*, given that everybody has assorted challenges in life. But for our challenged friends, everyday problems are much more than nuisances. They are challenges in every sense of the word.

COMMON ATTITUDES ABOUT CHALLENGED INDIVIDUALS

For whatever reasons, Western society has traditionally regarded those who are "different" as somehow being inferior, weird, miserable, unacceptable, unwanted, and/or dangerous. Consider the name-calling that goes on when one group is faced with another, unfamiliar group. In fact, the United States of the 1990s is witnessing a resurgence of racism and hate crimes against minorities, as well as a disinterest in special groups. People tend to fear

Just like anyone else, challenged individuals are sexual beings who need love, attention, and intimacy.

those whom they do not understand, defensively lashing out at others to keep their discomfort at a distance. Society as a whole pays a price for this kind of ignorance.

The notion of needing to be young and beautiful to be sexually happy is especially troublesome. An elderly person might be admonished to "grow old gracefully," "quit acting like a dirty old man," or "be a nice, sweet little old lady." Ignorance about adult sexuality is at the heart of such irrational sexual standards.

Sexual prejudice against individuals with special needs is certainly no less frequent. People equate having a sound mind and body with being sexual, and having a disability with being asexual. That's why most of our society's challenged persons receive little or no information, encouragement, or assistance in fulfilling their sexual needs. Just visit a nursing home or other facility that deals primarily with challenged persons, and ask how the sexual needs of their clients are met. You may be surprised at how little (if any) attention the matter receives.

Challenged individuals may find the sex-negative views of family, friends, and healthcare providers frustrating and defeating. The more severely challenged often encounter even greater obstacles. They may be seen as childlike, scolded for having sexual feelings, or discouraged from acting "shamefully." And in the hope of preventing all sexual activity, many parents and guardians never allow their challenged person any privacy.

Challenged individuals are sexual beings and are entitled to intimacy and love, as well as sexual feelings, expression, and fulfillment. Or as Albert Ellis phrased it in his *Sex Without Guilt* (1966):

> Every human being, just because he exists, should have the right to as much (or as little), as varied (or as monotonous), as intense (or mild), as enduring (or as brief) sex enjoyments as he prefers—as long as, in the process of acquiring these preferred satisfactions, he does not needlessly, forcefully, or unfairly interfere with the sexual (or nonsexual) rights and satisfactions of others. (p. 178)

Many people are also hesitant to interact with challenged persons, sexually or otherwise, often for fear of saying or doing the "wrong thing." Yet people must realize that challenged people need love, attention, and emotional support just like anybody else—qualities that, in a caring person, easily compensate for saying or doing the wrong thing. Listening, validating, problem-solving, reassuring—these are essential to the mental health and well-being of all people. Stereotypes of the challenged as asexual, undesirable, weird, and unapproachable, are just that—stereotypes, which our society would be far better off without.

PHYSICAL CHALLENGES

PHYSICAL CHALLENGE

Any of a number of physical conditions having the potential to disrupt normal functioning.

What is a **physical challenge** (or *physical disability*)? Actually, the phrase is a catch-all for any physical difficulty, change, defect, or condition that is present from birth, results from injury or disease, or develops later, and has the potential to disrupt normal living. A physical challenge, then, can be the absence of a limb from birth, blindness that develops in childhood, a spinal cord injury from an automobile accident, or a chronic illness like diabetes—all of which can directly or indirectly affect daily functioning and sexual behavior.

One myth about the physically challenged is that, in the absence of genital sensation, they have no sexual interests or abilities. This is untrue. Many physically challenged persons enjoy intimate, loving sex with their partners. Even without sexual intercourse *per se*, the challenged are as capable of love, care, and attention as anyone else. This is not to say that sexual activity for the physically challenged is necessarily easy. Dealing with catheters, deafness, or a wheelchair can be quite problematic. But neither is sexual expression impossible for these reasons. A little creativity, imagination, and experimentation can go a long way in enhancing sexual relations (for anybody).

Finally, speaking of the need for love, care, and attention, it is also important to acknowledge the caregiver's sexual needs—a topic that is sometimes neglected. Relationships can change in the face of challenges, whether disabilities, long-term illnesses such as cancer or heart disease, or emotional problems. The lover or partner may become the primary caregiver, which can greatly affect his or her sexual feelings. He or she may find it extremely difficult to feel sexual or romantic when caring for the patient's daily needs, such as diet, hygiene, and pain management; administering medications; and changing colostomy bags (external bags for collecting bodily waste products). The caregiver may find it helpful to call on friends, support networks, or a professional counselor to solve problems and better deal with his or her needs, concerns, and frustrations.

The most frequently encountered physical challenges and their impact on sexuality are discussed in the next several sections. These challenges include *cerebral palsy*, *blindness*, *deafness*, *spinal cord injuries*, and a number of other medical conditions and diseases, such as *reproductive cancer* and *cardiovascular disease*.

CEREBRAL PALSY

Cerebral palsy is a group of disorders characterized by involuntary movements of various muscle groups. A person with cerebral palsy typically experiences limb jerking, trouble walking and speaking, unusual posture, poor balance, frequent falls, tremors of the hands and feet, and facial grimaces. His or her intellect may or may not be affected. Symptoms range from mild to severe. Some individuals have problems in one limb only, others on one or both sides of the body. During times of stress, the neuromuscular spasms can become significantly more severe.

Besides the socialization problems a person might have, like trying to establish an intimate relationship, the individual's inability to control his or her muscles can make sexual activity difficult or impossible. Muscle spasms in the limbs or the vagina can make intercourse painful, although finding a comfortable position sometimes helps. In many cases, sexual activity is possible only with assistance. A significant other might bring the patient to orgasm manually if intercourse is impossible, or position him or her for masturbation, while respecting the individual's need for privacy.

BLINDNESS AND DEAFNESS

Physically speaking, **sensory impairment** of the eyes or ears—the inability to see or hear—does not necessarily restrict a person's capacity to have sex. Psychosocially speaking, though, there can be difficulty, especially when sensory impairment develops early in life. Because so much of our basic sexual learning and initial attraction occurs through our visual and auditory senses, sensory-impaired children often fail to pick up the basics of sexual activity or develop a healthy sexual self-image. Lack of sexual knowledge can cause these individuals to have low self-esteem and later interfere with their ability to form meaningful sexual relationships. As our society becomes more aware of and sensitive to the sexual needs of the visually and hearing impaired, we can develop and make accessible sexual education materials for these populations, such as special tapes, braille books, and anatomically correct dolls, as well as teach partners how to use their own eyes and ears on behalf of the impaired.

SENSORY IMPAIRMENT
Inability to adequately process sensory information.

For Personal Reflection

What kinds of problems might a blind person encounter when trying to date? What about a deaf person?

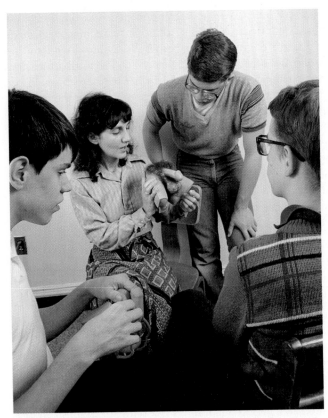

Our society is becoming increasingly aware of the importance of teaching the sensory impaired about sexuality. Here, a sex educator demonstrates the basics of pregnancy using specially designed dolls.

SPINAL CORD INJURIES

Spinal cord injuries (SCIs) involve fracture of the *cervical* (neck), *thoracic* (middle back), or *lumbar* (lower back) regions of the spine and spinal cord. Should the spinal cord be completely severed or compressed, complete paralysis occurs below the site of injury. Consequently, injury higher in the spinal cord results in *quadriplegia*, or paralysis below the neck, while injury lower in the spinal cord results in *paraplegia*, or paralysis below the waist. Because the spinal cord does not normally regenerate itself, the paralysis is almost always permanent.

Whether or not a person with SCI can experience sexual arousal and orgasms depends on the nature of his or her injury, as well as individual differences like sexual attitudes and past sexual experiences. Some partially paralyzed persons have little or no response to genital stimulation while others who are completely paralyzed regularly engage in sexual intercourse.

Men and women with SCIs must sometimes look for new ways to have noncoital sex. Here it usually helps to cast aside traditional notions of coitus as the only way to have good sex. In the absence of genital responsiveness, many people become more sexually sensitive in other areas of the body, developing new erogenous zones. As a result, these individuals can learn to find sexual gratification, even orgasms, through sexual fantasies and/or other types of stimulation, such as a partner kissing the patient's neck, cuddling, and giving sensual massages. A couple's willingness to redefine sexual activity and experiment can make a real difference in terms of the quality of their sexual relationship.

Some male and female SCI patients must also explore new ways of having intercourse. Male patients who are impotent because of a severed spinal cord may choose to "stuff" the

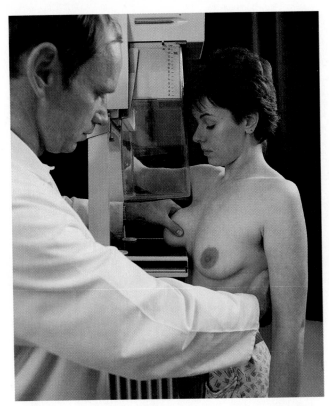

Mammography involves taking two X-rays of each breast. The procedure can help detect breast cancer in its earliest and most curable stages.

or both of their breasts. Cancer treatment is primarily concerned with stopping the spread of disease to prevent the destruction of vital body structures and processes. Female cancer survivors frequently experience sexual concerns and problems following treatment (Andersen & Elliot, 1994).

Ovarian cancer normally involves growth of a malignant tumor on the ovary. The disease is difficult to detect and becomes life-threatening within a few years. Complete recovery is possible when the cancer is identified and treated in its early stages of development. Treatment of ovarian cancer usually involves radiation therapy, *chemotherapy* (drug and hormone therapy), *hysterectomy* (surgical removal of the uterus), *oophorectomy* (removal of the ovaries), and/or *salpingectomy* (removal of the fallopian tubes).

Cervical cancer develops more frequently in women ages 40 and older. Early detection with a Pap smear greatly improves the chances for a complete cure. If untreated, the cancer spreads to the rest of the body via the lymphatic system, eventually causing death. As with ovarian cancer, treatment of cervical cancer involves radiation, chemotherapy, and/or surgery.

Most cases of cancer of the *endometrium* (the lining of the walls of the uterus) occur in women after menopause, generally between ages 50 and 60. Vaginal bleeding is the primary symptom, which should always be checked out by a health-care practitioner. He or she diagnoses the condition based on microscopic examination of a sample of uterine tissue. Treatment is similar to that of the other female cancers. The more localized the cancer and the earlier it is detected, the better the prognosis.

Cancer of the vulva is very rare, mostly striking women ages 60 and older. The primary symptom is itching, and a physician diagnoses the condition based on microscopic examination of a sample of vulval tissue. Surgical removal of the affected tissue is the treatment of choice.

The most common female cancer is breast cancer, which is second only to lung cancer as a cause of death among women (Byer & Shainberg, 1991). If left untreated, this cancer, which affects one or both breasts, spreads throughout the body by means of the lymphatic system and bloodstream, eventually killing its victim. If caught early, the prognosis for complete recovery is very good. Women at increased risk of developing breast cancer include those over age 40, those with a family history of breast cancer, and those who had an early menarche or a late menopause. Women who use oral contraceptives and/or consume excessive amounts of alcohol and/or dietary fat may also be at increased risk (Byer & Shainberg, 1991).

In addition to physical examination, one of the most accurate means of detecting breast lumps and determining if they are *malignant* (cancerous) or *benign* (noncancerous) is a radiographic procedure known as *mammography*. During a mammogram, a technician X-rays the woman's breasts from several directions. A physician then examines and interprets the X-rays, noting abnormalities. With cancer, early detection is essential; the cure rate for breast cancers detected by mammogram ranges from 85 to 95 percent. Once the cancer has spread beyond the breast, however, the survival rate falls to about 10 percent (Byer & Shainberg, 1991).

Besides providing little indication of how far a breast cancer has spread throughout the woman's body, mammography may have potential problems of its own. Critics' primary concerns have to do with accuracy of the equipment, interpretation of test results, and an increased risk of cancer due to the breasts being repeatedly exposed to X-rays. All factors considered, though, the benefits of mammography far outweigh its potential problems. It is generally recommended that women have a baseline mammogram before age 40, yearly or biyearly mammograms during the 40s, and yearly ones during the 50s and beyond. Fortunately, a woman can do much to identify developing lumps and tumors herself by performing monthly *breast self-examinations* (Chapter 4).

Surgery is usually the treatment of choice for breast malignancies, although chemotherapy and radiation therapy may also be necessary. Depending on the nature of the cancer, the surgeon performs either a *lumpectomy* (removal of the tumor only) or *mastectomy* (removal of the entire breast, or varying amounts of breast and surrounding tissues).

Following mastectomy some women choose to undergo *breast reconstruction* surgery. Here, a plastic surgeon forms a new breast from the patient's own skin and inserts an implant into her chest, giving her the look and feel of a real breast. The Food and Drug Administration has recently limited the availability of *silicone* gel-filled breast implants,

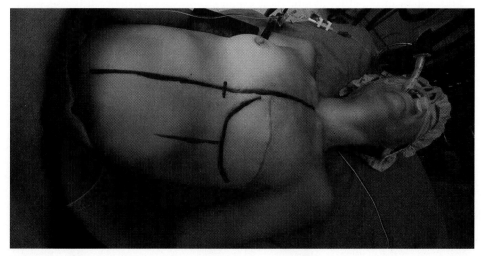

Breast reconstruction surgery.

particularly when used for cosmetic rather than reconstructive reasons. These implants can leak and break, causing serious immune reactions and other health problems.

Psychologically speaking, the removal of one or both breasts is usually an emotionally traumatic experience. Although breast reconstruction may ease the emotional pain, the woman may want to work through a number of issues related to the mastectomy. Questioning her femininity and her worth as a person, depression and low self-esteem are especially common following mastectomy. Many women also find themselves fearful of the breast cancer reoccurring. Besides counseling, a local chapter of the American Cancer Society, Reach for Recovery, United Way, or Department of Human Services can recommend an appropriate cancer support group for the patient and her significant other.

For Personal Reflection

Consider for a moment some of our society's preoccupation with the female breast. What type of psychological impact might these views have on a woman who has lost one or both breasts to cancer?

Male Cancers   Malignancies also strike the organs and structures of the male reproductive system. The three most common male reproductive cancers are *prostatic cancer, testicular cancer,* and *penile cancer.*

Cancer of the prostate is the most common of the male reproductive cancers, with over 100,000 new cases reported in the United States each year (*Statistical Abstracts of the United States,* 1992). The primary symptom of prostatic cancer is difficulty urinating due to enlargement of the gland—the same basic symptom as the less serious condition, *prostatitis,* or infection/inflammation of the prostate. Prostatic cancer rarely spreads to other parts of the body but can be life-threatening if it goes unchecked. Treatments range from shrinking the gland with radiation and chemotherapy, to partially or completely removing the gland—an operation known as *prostatectomy.* Prostatectomy carries with it risks and complications. For example, it can cause erectile dysfunction or *retrograde ejaculation* (ejaculation into the bladder). The American Cancer Society recommends that men over 40 have a yearly rectal exam to screen for prostate cancer (as well as cancer of the colon and rectum). A blood test for *prostate specific antigen* (PSA) and biopsy can confirm the presence of prostate cancer (Thompson, 1989).

Testicular cancer, although rare, most commonly affects men between the ages of 15 and 34 (Tortora & Grabowski, 1993). Scrotal and testicular abnormalities, especially one or more lumps on the testes, warrant immediate medical attention. Treatment generally includes chemotherapy, radiation, and/or surgical excision. Every man should be familiar with his testes and exam them for unusual changes by performing monthly *testicular self-examinations* (Chapter 5).

Nature is kind in that cancers of the penis are very rare. Yet penile cancer can prove fatal if it goes untreated. Symptoms include a wart, sore, or blister on the penis that enlarges and spreads. Surgery is the usual treatment of choice.

Another condition of the penis is *Peyronie's disease,* in which tissue growths and calcium deposits accumulate between its spongy bodies. Besides being a source of pain and discomfort, these growths and deposits cause the penis to become unusually bent or curved when erect, making certain intercourse positions difficult or impossible. Surgery restores penile flexibility.

A narrowing of a portion of the urethra is called a *stricture.* This condition, often due to a noncancerous growth or scar tissue from an infection, obstructs the flow of urine through the urethra, making urination difficult and painful. The stricture is easily removed by surgery.

As with females, male victims of reproductive cancers may have many psychological issues, including fears of being less masculine, no longer having sexual desires, or becoming sexually inactive. In fact, for both men and women, fears about future sexual behavior may be the greatest concern. There may also be new challenges, such as taking longer to obtain an erection, but in many cases the patient can overcome them with patience, ingenuity, and practice (Casey, 1994).

Cardiovascular Diseases   The most common **cardiovascular diseases,** or medical conditions involving the heart and blood vessels, include *angina* (cardiac pain), *arrhythmia* (irregular heartbeat), *atherosclerosis* (fatty deposits in the arteries that block blood flow), *hypertension* (high blood pressure), *hypotension* (low blood pressure), *myocardial infarction* (heart attack), *tachycardia* (rapid heart beat), and *thrombosis* (blood clots). Related to cardiac disease are **cerebrovascular accidents,** or *strokes,* in which damage to the blood vessels supplying the brain destroys brain tissue.

Many people have sexual problems and concerns following a heart attack, other cardiovascular event, or stroke. Recovering from heart surgery can be painful and leave the patient fatigued. Certain cardiac conditions like angina cause excruciating chest pain during physical exertion, including sexual activity. Strokes, depending on their location and severity, may cause physical and mental impairment, including loss of bodily functions, like the ability to walk. Pain, fatigue, physical impairment, and fear of bringing on another attack may limit a person's interest in and ability to have sexual relations.

Other Medical Conditions and Diseases   A multitude of other medical conditions and diseases directly or indirectly affect sexual functioning. Some of the more common ones include *Alzheimer's disease* (progressive deterioration of both short-term and long-term memory), *arthritis* (painful swelling of the joints), *cervicitis* (infection of the cervix), *cystitis* (bladder infection), *diabetes mellitus* (failure of the pancreas to secrete sufficient amounts of insulin to metabolize blood sugar), *endometriosis* (growth of endometrial tissue outside the uterus), *multiple sclerosis* (disease that attacks and destroys the myelin sheath surrounding the nerves of the body), *muscular dystrophy* (wasting away of muscle tissue), *parkinsonism* (tremors of the hands, feet, and head; difficulty walking and speaking), *urethritis* (infection of the urethra), *vaginitis* (infection of the vagina), and *vulvitis* (infection of the vulva), as well as chronic fatigue, genital fungus infections, and influenza. In short, *almost any medical condition—temporary or permanent—can cause sexual problems.*

DEVELOPMENTAL CHALLENGES

Persons who exhibit subnormal intellectual functioning and social maladaptiveness beginning before age 18 are **developmentally challenged** (or *mentally retarded* or *developmentally disabled*). The developmentally challenged have an IQ (intelligence quotient) of 70 or less, and do not evidence age- or culturally appropriate levels of personal independence, communication, living skills, social skills, and responsibility (American Psychiatric Association, 1994).

Sexual stereotypes about the developmentally challenged abound—stereotypes that in no way reflect the wide diversity of personalities found in this population. People mistakenly assume that the developmentally challenged are asexual, sexually aggressive and dangerous, or always sexually inappropriate in public. Some people who are developmentally

CARDIOVASCULAR DISEASE (KAR-DE-O-VAS-KYOO-LAR)
Any of a number of diseases affecting the blood vessels and heart.

CEREBROVASCULAR ACCIDENT (SE-RE-BRO-VAS-KYOO-LAR)
Destruction of brain tissue resulting from damage to the blood vessels supplying the brain.

DEVELOPMENTAL CHALLENGE
Low IQ and absence of age- and culturally appropriate social skills.

challenged have ineffective social and sexual skills, but this is probably due to peculiar socialization patterns and/or inadequate education from parents or caretakers about appropriate sexual behaviors (Bernstein, 1985). Society forgets that these challenged individuals, like all humans, are sexual beings in process.

With patience and repetition, many developmentally challenged individuals can learn social responsibility, the basics of sexuality, and appropriate sexual behaviors (Ragg & Rowe, 1991; Reinisch, 1990). For example, mildly challenged individuals tend to be quite educable. As they acquire more effective verbal and social skills, they can learn to live fairly regular lives. Moderately challenged individuals can learn the basics of reproduction and the importance of using good judgment during sexual interactions. They can also learn that certain sexual behaviors like masturbation, while appropriate in private, are not so in public. The severely and profoundly challenged, on the other hand, do not generally respond well to sex education, and require constant supervision, as in other areas of their lives. Staff can allow institutionalized individuals at least some private time for sexual exploration, as individual circumstances permit. There are now a number of professionals who specialize in providing sex education to the developmentally challenged. Various sexuality organizations and distributors of sex education materials maintain local

The developmentally challenged also have sexual needs, desires, and a basic right to sexual expression.

lists of these professionals, as well as make available videos, tapes, books, and other materials specifically designed for use with challenged populations.

Tragically, because many developmentally challenged individuals have limited comprehension of social forces and interactions, they are more suggestible to others' influence, and therefore more susceptible to sexual exploitation by caretakers, relatives, or anyone else. Any sex education program for the challenged must include information about what is expected from *others* in terms of appropriate sexual behavior, how to say *no*, and how to report sexual harassment and abuse. Good, clear instructions about sexual conduct are imperative (Stavis, 1991).

For Personal Reflection

What are some stereotypes about the developmentally challenged that you've held or known others to hold? Where do you think these stereotypes originated?

EMOTIONAL CHALLENGES

Individuals with an **emotional challenge** (or *mental illness, psychological disturbance,* or *psychiatric disability*) struggle with moderate to severe psychological limitations, problems, or disorders. Even though any emotional condition can conceivably disrupt sexual functioning, two that exert powerful effects on sexuality are the *anxiety disorders* and *affective disorders*.

The **anxiety disorders** are a group of mental disorders having anxiety and/or panic as a characteristic feature. This anxiety typically provokes avoidance of objects, individuals, and/or situations. In many cases, individuals know their anxiety is inappropriate to

EMOTIONAL CHALLENGE
Any of a number of psychological/psychiatric problems having the potential to disrupt normal functioning.

ANXIETY DISORDERS
Group of disorders in which the predominate feature is anxiety.

PERSPECTIVE

Sexual Rights of the Developmentally Challenged

In this day of increased sensitivity to special needs, we must be careful not to downplay or forget *sexual rights* of others. This is especially true of developmentally challenged individuals, whose sexual rights appear below.

1. The right to receive training in social-sexual behavior that will open more doors for social contact with people in the community.
2. The right to all the knowledge about sexuality they can comprehend.
3. The right to enjoy love and be loved by the opposite sex, including sexual fulfillment.
4. The right to the opportunity to express sexual impulses in the same forms that are socially acceptable for others.
5. The right to marry.
6. The right to have a voice in whether or not they should have children.
7. The right for supportive services which involve those rights as they are needed and feasible. (p. 247)

Source: W. Kempton (1977), The mentally retarded person. In H. L. Gochros & J. S. Gochros (Eds.), *The sexually oppressed* (New York: Association Press).

the situation, but do not seem able to control it. Anxiety disorders can severely disrupt daily functioning.

Individuals suffering from chronic anxiety are at risk of eventually developing a sexual dysfunction. Interpreting a particular social stimulus or situation as fear-evoking increases sympathetic nervous system activity, which in turn inhibits their ability to function sexually. In men, this can take the form of erectile and ejaculatory problems; in women, desire and orgasmic problems. As one client described during his first counseling session:

On a Personal Note (Kurt, age 34)

Most of the trouble I have in the bedroom and everywhere else has to do with this persistent fear I have about everything. It all started a long time ago, and affects most everything I do. But now . . . well, the bottom line is I haven't been able to get an erection when I'm with a woman for several years now. Believe me, I've had opportunities, but I just get too anxious about having to perform, doing it wrong, saying something stupid—the list goes on and on. To be honest, this is why I've decided not to get married. I even gave up on dating a couple of years ago. (Author's files)

AFFECTIVE DISORDERS OR MOOD DISORDERS (A-FEK-TIV)

Group of disorders in which the predominate feature is depression and/or mania.

The **affective disorders** (or **mood disorders**) have as a characteristic feature abnormally high and/or low feelings. Although there are a number of mood disorders, the two that most powerfully affect sexuality are *depression*, marked by feelings of sadness, apathy, self-blame, and guilt; and *bipolar disorder* (or *manic-depression*), marked by alternating periods of depression and *mania* (extreme elation and hyperactivity).

The sexual effects of depression and mania vary, although certain behavioral patterns are more common than others. Depressed persons ordinarily experience loss of sexual interest and reduced sexual activity. Manic persons, on the other hand, frequently become impulsive and hypersexual. During a manic episode (which can last for days, weeks, or months), these individuals lose their social inhibitions, and some engage in all sorts of sexual behaviors that they would not normally consider acceptable. They may have sex with numerous partners, visit prostitutes, or expose themselves in public. As one student recalled:

On a Personal Note (Terry, age 21)

Right before finals of my freshman year in college, I got really stressed out, you know, worrying about failing my exams, even though my grades were fine. I was so wound up that I didn't sleep for three days. I just kept studying and wandering around the campus. I know my roommate was getting concerned, but I suppose he didn't want to upset me any further. Then I started getting more and more sexually turned on at the thought of running naked through the campus. When I started obsessing about doing this, and I told my roommate what I was planning to do, he called the school health center. The campus physician checked me into a nearby hospital a couple of hours later. (Author's files)

For Personal Reflection

Which physical, developmental, or emotional challenge(s) would you find to be the most sexually problematic for you or your partner? Why?

SEXUAL ACTIVITY: A FEW WORDS
FOR CHALLENGED INDIVIDUALS

"As a challenged person, is there anything that I can do to resume sex or enhance what I'm already doing?" *Absolutely*. As stated earlier in this chapter, one of the primary sexual obstacles for the challenged person is the *fear of rejection*. And this fear generally takes three forms: (1) avoidance of sexual activity altogether; (2) half-hearted sexual activity, with little or no interest in experimenting; and (3) "overkill," or trying too hard—none of which make for very good sex. For the challenged individual who wants to resume sexual relations but is hesitant, Bernie Zilbergeld offered the following advice (which applies to both men and women) in his book *Male Sexuality* (1978):

So you can sit around for the rest of your life contemplating how wonderful everything would be if only you weren't who you are. A fascinating pastime, perhaps, but always a losing one, for you will never be other than who you are, and you will therefore never get any of the benefits that you think would accrue as the person you wish you were. Sex as you are may well carry risks of disappointment and rejection but, since you'll never be anyone else, it might be in your interest to consider if the risks are worth taking.

. . . You can decide that, whatever the risks, you are interested in a more enjoyable sex life and that you are willing to find out what is possible for you. This may be a difficult decision. No one can guarantee you'll get precisely what you hope for. Even if you put a lot of time and effort into it, you may not end up performing the way you want. And your ideas about what is acceptable sexual expression will probably have to undergo some revision. (p. 353)

This same author also had the following to say in *The New Male Sexuality* (1992):

If the intention is present, if you're willing to expend some time and effort, and if you're willing to experiment with sexual options, it's almost a certainty you can come up with at least several ways of making good love no matter what disabilities you or your partner have and no matter how long you've been together. (p. 389)

In other words, challenged individuals must commit not only to doing things in new and different ways, but also to changing their *perceptions* and *attitudes* about being challenged. Only then can they truly feel at liberty to explore their unique sensual and sexual potentials.

KEY POINTS

1. The phrases *physically challenged*, *developmentally challenged*, and *emotionally challenged* are preferable to labels like *handicapped*, *disabled*, and *retarded*, which tend to be needlessly negative and stereotypic. Such language can help an individual to reframe his or her "problem" into a "challenge" that can be dealt with and potentially overcome.
2. Challenged individuals are sexual beings and are entitled to intimacy and love, as well as sexual feelings, expression, and fulfillment. Unfortunately, most of the challenged individuals in our society receive little or no information, encouragement, or assistance in fulfilling their sexual needs.
3. A *physical challenge* is any physical difficulty, change, defect, or condition that has the potential to disrupt normal living. The most frequently encountered physical challenges affecting sexuality are *cerebral palsy*, *blindness*, *deafness*, *spinal cord*

injuries, and a host of other medical conditions, such as *reproductive cancer* and *cardiovascular disease*.

4. Persons who exhibit subnormal intellectual functioning and social maladaptiveness beginning before age 18 are *developmentally challenged*. The developmentally challenged have an IQ (intelligence quotient) of 70 or less, and do not evidence age- or culturally appropriate levels of personal independence, communication, living skills, social skills, and responsibility.

5. Individuals with an *emotional challenge* struggle with moderate to severe psychological limitations, problems, or disorders. Even though any emotional condition can conceivably disrupt sexual functioning, two that exert powerful effects on sexuality are the *anxiety disorders* and *affective disorders*.

ACTIVITIES AND QUESTIONS

1. What are some of the many common social stereotypes and myths about the challenged? Where do these stereotypes come from, and what can we do to eliminate them? What are some of the advantages and disadvantages of integrating challenged individuals into mainstream society?

2. As a class, discuss the involuntary sterilization of developmentally and emotionally challenged persons.

3. What are some of the problems faced by a quadriplegic who wishes to begin a new sexual relationship?

4. Interview someone from another culture about his or her views on challenged individuals. What cultural norms have influenced their views? How are the challenged treated in that culture? Are they accepted or shunned?

5. Visit a facility that works with challenged populations. Interview staff members regarding the sexual needs of their clients and to what extent these needs are met (if they are met). Also ask how (or if) they make available information about sexuality.

RECOMMENDED READINGS

Schover, L., & Jensen, S. (1988). *Sexuality and chronic illness*. New York: Guilford Press. Thoughtfully addresses sexual issues brought on by chronic illness and other medical conditions, including appropriate treatments and management strategies.

Strong, M. (1988). *Mainstay*. Boston: Little, Brown. Contains particularly valuable information for the spouse of a chronically ill person.

Weitzman, S., Kuter, I., & Pizer, H. F. (1986). *Confronting breast cancer*. New York: Vintage Books. Contains useful information about detecting and treating breast cancer.

Willmuth, M. E. (1987). Sexuality after spinal cord injury: A critical review. *Clinical Psychology Review, 7*, 389–412. A journal article review of some of the many aspects of sexuality that are affected by a spinal cord injury.

C H A P T E R 1 1

SEXUALITY AND THE LIFE CYCLE

O B J E C T I V E S

AFTER READING THIS CHAPTER YOU SHOULD BE
ABLE TO . . .

1. BETTER UNDERSTAND HUMAN SEXUALITY AS A
   DEVELOPMENTAL PROCESS, BEGINNING AT BIRTH
   AND CONTINUING THROUGH THE LIFE CYCLE.
2. DESCRIBE VARIOUS CHILDHOOD AND
   ADOLESCENT SEXUAL BEHAVIORS, INCLUDING
   MASTURBATION, PETTING, AND SEXUAL ACTIVITY
   WITH PEERS.
3. DESCRIBE VARIOUS TYPES OF ADULT SEXUAL
   RELATIONSHIPS, INCLUDING SINGLEHOOD,
   COHABITATION, MARRIAGE, AND EXTRAMARITAL
   RELATIONSHIPS.
4. IDENTIFY SOME OF THE BIOPSYCHOSOCIAL
   FACTORS CONFRONTING THE ELDERLY IN TERMS
   OF SEXUALITY.
5. EXPLAIN THE NECESSITY FOR SEX EDUCATION
   FOR PEOPLE OF ALL AGES.

P E R S O N A L   A S S E S S M E N T

WHAT ARE YOUR THOUGHTS AND FEELINGS ON SEXUALITY AS A LIFE-SPAN, DEVELOP-
MENTAL PROCESS? TO EXPLORE THIS, READ THE FOLLOWING STATEMENTS AND RESPOND
USING THIS RATING SCALE: 3 = I *completely agree* WITH THE STATEMENT;
2 = I *mostly agree* WITH THE STATEMENT; 1 = I *mostly disagree* WITH THE STATEMENT;
0 = I *completely disagree* WITH THE STATEMENT. REMEMBER, THERE ARE NO RIGHT OR
WRONG ANSWERS HERE; IT'S YOUR OPINION THAT COUNTS.

_____   1. Humans are sexual beings from birth until death.
_____   2. Children should be discouraged from playing with their own genitals and masturbating.
_____   3. Children should be discouraged from engaging in sexplay with their peers, as when playing "doctor."
_____   4. Masturbation and petting are expected sexual behaviors for adolescents, allowing them to learn more about themselves and others as sexual beings.
_____   5. It's acceptable for two mature, responsible teenagers to have sexual intercourse if they love each other.
_____   6. Living together before marriage has little or nothing to do with whether a couple will remain together should they eventually decide to marry.
_____   7. For middle and older adults, it becomes harder to find a compatible partner with each advancing year.
_____   8. It's impossible for an elderly person to be "sexy."
_____   9. Sex education belongs in the home, not in the schools: How and what children learn about sexuality is up to the parents or guardians, not teachers or school officials.
_____   10. Sex education is more valuable, and therefore more important, for children and adolescents than for adults.

A s the twig is bent, the tree inclines.

Virgil

The word *sexuality* conjures up many disparate images, although childhood sexuality is rarely among them. When people consider sexuality in youth, it invariably relates to ado-lescents and young adults—and generally in light of negatives and social problems, such as teenage pregnancy and sexually transmitted diseases.

Many people in our society refuse to acknowledge the sexual nature of infants, chil-dren, and older adults. Rather than accepting the very young or the elderly as sexual **ASEXUAL** beings, they prefer to categorize them as **asexual,** as not having sexual interests, desires, *Lacking sexual interest.* needs, or abilities. Our society might as well conjure up images of infants, children, and older adults never needing nutrition.

The images and considerations of the vast majority of people in our culture fail to cre-ate a complete or accurate picture of human sexuality and sexual expression in general. Numerous scientists, philosophers, and other scholars have established that human sexu-ality is a fundamental aspect of human experience and expression at all ages and devel-opmental periods. Thus, according to the *developmental perspective*, sexuality is an aspect of our lifelong process of developing, beginning at birth and ending at death.

In the pages that follow, we'll consider human sexuality from a life span point of view—from infancy to old age. We'll also consider the importance of sex education for people of all ages.

INFANCY

During the first year of life, or *infancy,* children are typically *egocentric,* that is, self-centered. They are primarily concerned with satisfying their physical desires, which Sigmund Freud theorized is a form of self-pleasuring. Infants are particularly interested in activities involving the mouth, such as sucking and biting, and thus Freud labeled the first year of life the *oral stage* of *psychosexual development* (Table 11.1). Given the infant's self-centeredness, Erik Erikson noted that her or his primary *psychosocial task* during this early stage of life is to learn to *trust* the parent or caretaker (Table 11.1).

Parents can help instill trust in their infant in any number of different ways, although eye contact, touching, and timely feedings are perhaps the most important. These, of course, are also expressions of the love and affection parents have for their infant, all of which help him or her eventually grow up to be an emotionally healthy, loving adult.

Physical contact between infant and parent is vital to the emotional health of the infant, and very important to the parents as well (Calderone & Johnson, 1989). But when should this begin? Probably as soon as possible after birth. However, an infant who for whatever reason is separated from the mother at birth is not necessarily doomed to a life of emotional disturbance. Immediate bonding may be optimal, but the infant and parents can later make up for any problems resulting from an initial separation (Goldberg, 1983).

Without a doubt, physical contact between infant and parents is a source of pleasure, which certainly influences the infant's sexuality. But are infants really sexual? *Yes,* at least in the sense of physical responsiveness. Ultrasounds indicate that a developing male fetus is capable of having erections before birth (Calderone, 1983). Male babies also have penile erections, and female babies have vaginal lubrication (Calderone & Johnson, 1989). We need to be clear here that, even though both male and female infants demonstrate sexual responsiveness, they are not aware of their "sexual experiences" as sources and expressions of erotic motivation. In other words, sexual response for infants is not a mature erotic response in the same sense as it is for adolescents and adults.

Infants soon begin to discover their own bodies, including their genitals. As infants acquire *motor skills* (the ability to move with intention), they learn to handle and rub their genitals. This deliberate genital touching quickly becomes associated with pleasant sensations. In fact, researchers have commented on little girls and boys having orgasms through masturbation (Kinsey et al., 1948, 1953). Clearly, these and other observations and studies indicate that sexuality manifests itself very early in life.

TABLE 11.1 Stages of Psychosexual and Psychosocial Development: Freud and Erikson

Period (Age)	Freud's Stage	Erikson's Task or Crisis
Infancy (0–1)	Oral	Trust versus mistrust
Early Childhood (1–3)	Anal	Autonomy versus shame and doubt
Early Childhood (3–6)	Phallic	Initiative versus guilt
Middle (6–7) and late childhood (8–11)	Latency	Industry versus inferiority
Adolescence (12–19)	Genital	Identity versus confusion
Early Adulthood (20–44)		Intimacy versus isolation
Middle Adulthood (45–64)		Generativity versus stagnation
Older Adulthood (65+)		Integrity versus despair

Experiencing their parents' love helps children become loving adults themselves.

For Personal Reflection

Do you think researchers should be allowed to question children about and/or directly observe their sexual behaviors? What are some of the ethical issues and concerns that might arise from such research?

EARLY CHILDHOOD

No longer totally dependent on their parents, preschool children begin the long road of becoming more adept at functioning in the world. In other words, according to Erikson the task of preschoolers is to develop *autonomy*, or self-direction (ages 1 to 3), and *initiative*, or enterprise (3 to 6). During *early childhood*, or the *preschool years*, children gain some sense of being separate and independent from their parents.

According to Freud, once the child enters the *anal stage* (1 to 3), parents face a variety of new challenges as they toilet train him or her. During the *phallic stage* (3 to 6), the child experiences heightened interest in his or her genitals. Although many parents are shocked to discover that their child masturbates, most children engage in this activity at some point during this period. The parents should help the child to learn more about the genitals, rather than scold him or her.

Parents should keep in mind that masturbation is widespread among children. Scientific evidence does not support the position that masturbation is at all harmful, with perhaps the exception of guilt and other negative emotions that may arise in response to others' reactions to the practice.

Curiosity about the genitals is a normal part of growing up.

In addition to a growing interest in their own bodies, preschoolers become deeply curious about the bodies of other children, especially those of the other sex. Why boys have a penis and girls do not is a major concern. Besides seemingly endless questions, this curiosity may lead to any of a number of "peeking" games, or touching and sexual exploration and play with peers, such as playing "doctor" or watching one another urinate. Parents should understand that these activities are normal and to be expected when done *in moderation and with same-age children* (Fishel, 1992). Parents must also remain alert to the potential for older children (even siblings) to sexually exploit younger ones (Finkelhor, 1984; Zgourides et al., 1994).

No evidence suggests that sexplay with same-sex children causes homosexuality, or that sexplay with peers leads to early sexual intercourse (Reinisch, 1990). Nonpunitive and noncritical limit-setting minimizes the possibility that the child will become confused, develop guilt, or later experience sexual problems (Golden, 1989). Parents may opt to open a dialogue with the child about what he or she learned during a particular "game." They should also make themselves available to answer the child's questions about eliminative functions and boy-girl differences.

Around the time they become more conscious of their own bodies, preschoolers also begin to experiment with other aspects of their sexuality. One such activity that elicits a broad range of reactions from adults is the way in which young children use language to refer to bodily functions and the genitals. While young children understand what these terms refer to, they may have little grasp of their true meaning or significance. Thus, parents often do not know how to react to or explain their young child's use of "dirty"

Infants and young children eventually discover their own genitals, as well as the genitals of others.

language. Often, the most advisable route is to make as little fuss as possible while at the same time indicating what language is preferable. Too much attention to such language may reinforce the child's desire to use it. By the same token, parents may wish to correct such language when used in the presence of others.

How do parents' expression of love affect their children's concept of love and sexuality? The ideal role of any parent is to help his or her children become fully functioning, content, and well-balanced adults who are capable of intimacy. Without question, children's primary role models are their parents or guardians. How children conceptualize and express love, happiness, and affection is traceable back to their interactions with and observations of the parents. This is no less the case when it comes to sexuality. Children's views of sexuality and loving relationships—both positive and negative—are generally a reflection of the affection, or lack thereof, that their parents express to each other and their children. Yet parents may be so insecure and uncomfortable with their own sexuality that they go out of their way to keep their children from witnessing any form of loving, sexual expression in the home. No wonder so many of our young people find it hard to accept the fact that their parents have sex—they never see them embracing and kissing, or hear them comforting one another with loving words. Children who never witness affection between their parents may find it difficult or impossible to express it as adults.

How far should parents go in demonstrating sexual feelings in front of their children? First, there appear to be no adverse effects to children seeing their parents nude, as long as such nudity in the home is relaxed and nonseductive (Lewis & Janda, 1988; Smith & Sparks, 1986). Second, while valuable for children to see expression of love between their parents, it is quite another matter for them to witness the parents engaged in coitus. Older children might have some understanding of such a situation, but this is clearly not the case with younger children, who may react to such a scene (sometimes called the "primal scene") with anxiety and fear that the parents are hurting each other. Yet there is little reason to believe that harm is done as long as the channels of honest communication between parents and children remain open. The parents can do much to alleviate their children's fears and concerns by honestly answering their questions about what was accidentally seen, and by not responding to them with anger, criticism, or punishment.

MIDDLE AND LATE CHILDHOOD

The school-age years are frequently divided into *middle childhood* (ages 6 to 7) and *late childhood*, or *preadolescence* (8 to 11). According to Erikson, the primary developmental task of both middle and late childhood is to attain *industry*, or the feeling of social competence. This developmental stage is marked by competition (athletics and daredevil activities) and numerous social adjustments (trying to make and keep friends). Successfully developing industry helps the child build self-esteem, which in turn builds the self-confidence necessary to form rewarding social relationships.

In early childhood, sexual expression is diffuse—an extension of curiosity and pleasurable sensations rather than an outgrowth of eroticism. But by middle and late childhood things begin to change—sexuality and sexual expression become more focused and goal-directed. Although Freud theorized that the years of middle and late childhood are characterized by sexual *latency*, modern researchers do not generally support this view (Reinisch, 1990). Sexual interest, play, and experimentation clearly continue and may even increase in frequency during the grade-school years. Same-sex play and contact are also common during this period.

On a Personal Note (Joey, age 29)

I can't remember the first time I ever masturbated. I just remember masturbating and having orgasms as a little kid, usually alone in the bathroom. My parents used to catch me in the act, and I remember how embarrassed I felt whenever this happened. After several episodes of this, my mother sat me down and told me something, which I've never been able to recall. Whatever she said, though, definitely affected me, because I remember proudly telling people at the time that I didn't play with myself any more. And I did stop for a few years—until I was about 10 or 11. Then I found the urge to masturbate too irresistible. You see, there was then a strong, erotic quality to the whole thing. (Author's files)

Preadolescence, often termed *late childhood* or the *formative years*, is the period of childhood encompassing ages 8 to puberty. During this developmental period, the child's fascination with sexuality is coupled with physical changes taking place in her or his body. Accompanying these changes is a heightened self-consciousness about the body, especially about being seen nude by parents and friends, as at camp or in the school gym showers.

Children ages 8 to 10 generally continue to play and associate with same-sex friends, although they soon begin to develop an interest in members of the other sex. Their growing sexual interests may take the form of "colorful" jokes, notes, and comments. At the same time, they show an increasing interest in their own bodies, asking more specific questions about sexual development and activity, as well as the mechanics of pregnancy and birth. The majority of sexplay for 10- to 12-year-olds is between same-sex friends, even though there now occurs a great deal of talk about the other sex. "Homosexual" sexplay generally takes the form of showing off the genitals, masturbating in front of each other, and fondling each other. For example, some preteen boys enjoy "circle jerking," in which a group of boys masturbate together.

Preadolescence is also a time for youngsters to acquire and practice various social and emotional skills in preparation for the relationships that will arise during adolescence. Groups of preteens frequently go shopping, to the movies, or to school dances or athletic events. Some boys and girls develop "crushes" on each other and may even "date," although there is no suggestion of mature romance at this stage.

Preteens cherish their same-sex friendships, while at the same time developing an interest in the other sex.

ADOLESCENCE

Adolescence is a time of tremendous change and discovery. During these years, physical and emotional changes occur with dizzying speed, challenging the young person to adjust to a new body, social identity, and expanding world view. Indeed, Erikson noted that the chief psychosocial task for the adolescent is to develop *identity*, or individuality. To make matters worse, the curiosity so characteristic of younger children is restrained by societal mores and expectations during adolescence, even though peer pressure to try new things and behave in certain ways is also very powerful. To this must be added the teenager's growing desire for personal responsibility and independence from her or his parents, along with an ever-growing, irresistible interest in sexuality.

PUBERTY

Perhaps no aspect of adolescence is as jarring as the biological changes that occur. In the course of a few short years, a dependent child matures into an independent, fully functioning adult member of society.

PUBERTY

Transitional period between childhood and adulthood marked by rapid physical and sexual maturation.

Puberty is the period of rapid physical development that marks the end of childhood and the beginning of sexual maturity. In other words, puberty is the *transitional* period between childhood and adulthood. Although there is no single, "right" age for puberty to begin, by its completion every normal boy and girl will have undergone the physical and hormonal changes needed for sexual reproduction (Figure 11.1). The onset of puberty also marks the beginning of Freud's final stage of psychosexual development, the *genital stage*, which encompasses all of adolescence and adulthood.

Girls generally reach puberty a few years earlier than boys, somewhere around ages 11 to 12. Increasing levels of estrogen trigger the onset of puberty for girls. They grow taller; their breasts become larger and rounder; the hips widen; hair grows under the arms, on the legs, and in the pubic area; the clitoris elongates; the labia thicken; and the uterus enlarges. Most girls of today begin *menstruating* at about age 12 or 13 (termed *menarche*). At this time, they are capable of becoming pregnant.

Increasing levels of testosterone trigger the onset of puberty for boys around ages 12 to 14. Boys become taller, heavier, and stronger; their shoulders broaden; their voices deepen; hair grows on the face, under the arms, around the genitals, and on other parts of the

Puberty is a period of rapid physical and sexual maturation.

body; the penis and other reproductive organs enlarge; and the testes produce sperm. At this time, boys are capable of impregnating sexually mature females. Teenage boys may also begin to experience *nocturnal emissions* ("wet dreams"), a natural and harmless release of semen during sleep, often accompanied by an erotic dream and orgasm.

In many societies, various *initiation rites, initiation rituals,* or *rites of passage* mark the beginning of puberty, the transition from childhood to adulthood. Depending on cultural norms and practices, these rites and rituals range anywhere from a family celebration to a religious ceremony to a hazardous and torturous ordeal for the youth.

For both teenage girls and boys, skin problems (*acne vulgaris,* or "pimples"), differences in height and weight, and general awkwardness can be sources of great anxiety and frustration. The anxieties associated with self-consciousness about one's appearance are only fueled by our media and advertising industries, which provide our adolescents with unrealistic, unattainable images of physical and sexual "perfection." Consequently, adolescents end up feeling even more inferior and less self-confident than they would have otherwise, and thus feel pressured into purchasing the "right" commercial products.

The hormonal changes of puberty also affect the emotions of adolescents. Up one minute; down the next. Laughing; crying. Best friends; bitter enemies. Teenagers' moods and relationships can seem as changeable as the weather. Added to this is the fact that sexual tension is a daily reality for most adolescents. Just knowing there is the potential for sexual activity in an encounter colors interpersonal interactions. Along with these emotional and sexual fluctuations comes the need for adolescents to question authority and societal values, as well as to test limits within existing relationships. This is nowhere more apparent than within the family system. Here adolescents' needs for independence from the parents can bring about a great deal of conflict and tension at home. Adolescence is definitely a transition time—one of striving, yearning, and bearing the burdens of wanting to be an adult long before becoming one. Yet despite all the changes and crises, most make it through adolescence without serious rifts with parents or other lasting problems.

For Personal Reflection

Think back for a moment on your own puberty and early adolescence. What do you remember the most about this time in your life?

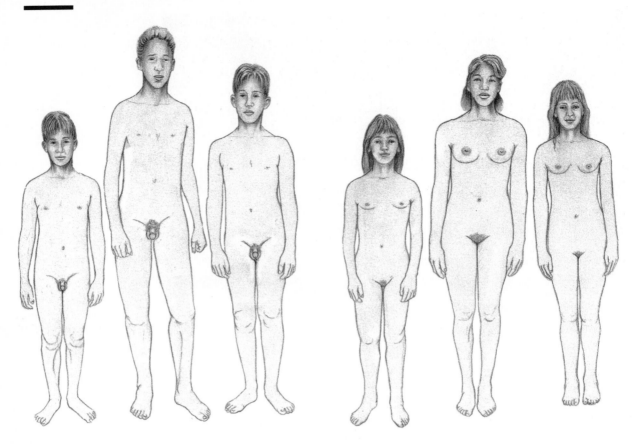

FIGURE 11.1 *Puberty occurs at different rates for different individuals. All of the children in this diagram are 14 years old.*

Virtually all teenagers are overly self-conscious about their appearance and preoccupied with what their peers think.

SEXUAL BEHAVIORS

With sexuality influencing almost every aspect of life, adolescents struggle to find appropriate sexual outlets through which to articulate their needs and desires. Adolescents participate in the same sexual activities as do their adult counterparts—masturbation, oral sex, and intercourse—although usually outside the context of a long-term, committed relationship. Sexually active teenagers may believe they are "in love" and "go steady" for weeks, months or even years, but they generally lack the level of commitment necessary to maintain a mature, intimate, and loving partnership.

Some adolescents (like some adults) have no real interest in long-term, intimate relationships at all. They instead have sexual intercourse indiscriminately, giving little thought to who the next sexual partner will be. Adolescent *promiscuity* may be indicative of larger emotional problems, such as insecurity, low self-esteem, immaturity, deep-seated hostility, or dependence (White & DeBlassie, 1992).

Most teenagers relieve their sexual tensions by masturbating, which by this time in development is certainly an erotically motivated behavior. Some 88 percent of males and 62 percent of females report having first masturbated before age 17 (Janus & Janus, 1993; Table 11.2).

A second form of sexual expression for adolescents is mutual **petting,** or sexual activities other than intercourse. Petting can be either "light" (above the waist) or "heavy" (below the waist), the distinction here being primarily positional. Popular petting activities include kissing and embracing, caressing and massaging, and orally or manually stimulating the breasts or genitals. One or both partners may have an orgasm as a result of petting.

A third sexual outlet for adolescents is sexual intercourse. Like adults, adolescents use a variety of sexual positions and vary in their frequency of intercourse. That is, there is little difference between teenagers and adults in terms of the actual *mechanics* of intercourse. The *passion* of lovemaking may be there, but the *commitment* and *intimacy* of a long-term relationship are frequently missing. However, this may be changing somewhat. More of today's adolescents are reporting a preference for sexual intimacy with a partner they love rather than with a casual acquaintance (Christopher & Cate, 1988).

Although the statistics vary considerably, the average age for Americans' first sexual intercourse is between 16 and 17 (Reinisch, 1990). Twenty-one percent of males and 15 percent of females surveyed (ages 18 to 26) reported having had their first full intercourse by age 14, and 91 percent of males and 83 percent of females by age 19 (Janus & Janus, 1993; Table 11.3). Complicating matters is the fact that these same adolescents either do not use contraception, or use it on an inconsistent basis (Hatcher et al., 1994; Zelnick & Kantner, 1980). Also, they do not consistently take precautions against sexual diseases, even in light of the present HIV/AIDS epidemic (Bigler, 1989; Roscoe & Kruger, 1990).

According to one national survey, about 5 percent of adolescents reported having participated in some form of homosexual activity, usually with same-age partners (Coles & Stokes, 1985). These data, though, do not represent the number of teenagers with a genuine homosexual orientation, as most adolescent homosexual experiences amount to nothing more than sexual play and experimentation.

PETTING

Sexual activity including oral and manual stimulation, but falling short of sexual intercourse.

On a Personal Note (Mark, age 64)

I'm completely straight, but I do remember some homosexual activity when I was an early teen. When we were around 13 or 14, a neighbor friend and I used to exercise—lift weights, that sort of thing—together in the buff. Then we would end our workout by masturbating. Looking back, I can hardly believe I did something like that, although at the time it seemed perfectly okay and normal. (Author's files)

TABLE 11.2 **Age at First Masturbation**

	Male (N = 1,328)	Female (N = 1,390)
a. By age 10	19%	19%
b. 11 to 13	53%	25%
c. 14 to 16	16%	18%
d. 17 to 21	5%	15%
e. 22 to 30	1%	7%
f. 31 and older	1%	5%
g. Never	5%	11%
Before age 17 (lines a + b + c)	88%	62%

Source: S. S. Janus & C. L. Janus (1993), *The Janus report on sexual behavior* (New York: John Wiley). Copyright © 1993. Reprinted by permission of John Wiley & Sons, Inc.

"Making out" is a popular adolescent petting activity.

Some teenagers know all along that they are homosexual. Many of them are hesitant to "come out of the closet" during adolescence, because they are keenly aware of their peers' and society's negative attitudes toward homosexuality (Martin & Hetrick, 1988). These adolescents may shy away from homosexual experiences or, if they have them, suffer anxiety while trying not to acknowledge their significance.

TABLE 11.3 Age at First Full Sexual Relations: Self-Report by 18- to 26-Year-Olds

	Male (N = 254)	**Female** (N = 266)
a. By age 10	3%	2%
b. 11 to 14	18%	13%
c. 15 to 18	70%	68%
d. 19 to 25	9%	16%
e. 26 and older	0%	1%
By age 14 (lines a + b)	21%	15%
By age 18 (lines a + b + c)	91%	83%
After age 18 (lines d + e)	9%	17%

Source: S. S Janus & C. L. Janus (1993), *The Janus report on sexual behavior* (New York: John Wiley). Copyright © 1993. Reprinted by permission of John Wiley & Sons, Inc.

On a Personal Note ("B.K.," age 28)

I've always been sexually attracted to females, as far back as I can remember. But things became a real problem for me in high school. There I was, a lesbian at heart, but unable to say anything to my friends. The other kids and staff at my school were so homophobic, I didn't dare bring it up to anyone, not even the school counselor. (Author's files)

Adolescents may express hatred toward those who are "different," including homosexuals. In some cases, such *homophobia* involves social ostracizing, cutting remarks, and/or threats. In other cases, it involves *gay bashing*, or verbally abusing and/or violently attacking homosexuals. Gay bashing is an all too frequent and tragic occurrence today (Berrill & Herek, 1990). Adolescents who gay bash probably do so for a variety of reasons, including peer pressure, fear of homosexuals, and discomfort with their own emerging sexual identity.

PROBLEMS RESULTING FROM ADOLESCENT SEX

Sexuality can be confusing and overwhelming for adolescents. "Why shouldn't I have sex? I'm physically mature. My body craves it. Everyone else is doing it. I love the other person. What's the harm in doing it?"

Deciding to become sexually active is a complicated matter. In considering whether to have sex, adolescents (or anyone else for that matter) must remember that along with the *right* to have sex comes the *responsibility* of living with any and all consequences, many of which are serious or even life-threatening. Reasons like, "Everyone else is doing it," are weak, and more a sign of immaturity and misunderstanding of what love and sexuality are all about than anything else.

Perhaps the most significant problem sexually active teenagers face is the possibility of pregnancy (Besharov & Gardiner, 1993; Eby & Donovan, 1993). Because so many sexually active teenagers fail to use contraception on a regular basis, teenage pregnancy has reached a critical level in the United States. Each year, about 500,000 babies are born to teenage mothers (*Statistical Abstract of the United States,* 1992). Although some of these mothers make it through without too much trouble, most typically face a great

Few teenage mothers are adequately prepared, emotionally or financially, to provide for their children.

many problems. Medically, pregnancy and childbirth during adolescence are risky to both mother and child. The teenager's body is not yet fully developed, and she may lack proper nutrition and adequate medical care. She therefore stands a greater chance of developing serious complications during pregnancy like toxemia; having a miscarriage; having a premature, low birth-weight baby; or dying during childbirth (Hatcher et al., 1994). Financially, most teenage mothers live in poverty. They usually must drop out of school and thus have limited earning potential. With less money and more expenses, they are likely to have to draw on welfare to support themselves and their children.

Marriage does not solve all of the problems of adolescent pregnancy. Teenage mothers who are married are often no better off than those who are not (Teti & Lamb, 1989). Not surprisingly, teenage marriages are generally plagued by poverty, usually as a result of limited education and earning power. They tend to be unstable, and therefore are highly susceptible to dissolution (Martin & Bumpass, 1989). Teenage pregnancy—coupled with an unsuccessful marriage, financial problems, and lack of education—has multigenerational consequences, negatively affecting the teenagers' families, the teenagers themselves, and their offspring. The number of teenage marriages in the United States appears to be on the decline (*Statistical Abstract of the United States*, 1992).

In spite of the fact that many teenage mothers do not marry, some adolescent fathers are very concerned and eager to help their partners and offspring. But despite a young father's best intentions, he generally does not have the means or ability to help. Like teenage mothers, teenage fathers generally lack the education or training necessary to secure a well-paying job (Robinson, 1988).

For Personal Reflection

How would you respond if your adolescent daughter told you she was pregnant and wanted to marry her boyfriend before finishing high school?

Another serious problem associated with teenage sex is sexually transmitted diseases (STDs). Although I'll have much to say in Chapter 14 about the various STDs, their prevention, and treatment, it bears mentioning here that *anyone—child, adolescent, or adult— who is sexually active with one or more partners is at risk of contracting and spreading STDs.* People of any particular race, creed, sex, sexual orientation, or age group are not immune. The "It'll never happen to me" attitude is best challenged. *It can and does happen every day.* Each year, over 3 million teenagers contract an STD (Besharov & Gardiner, 1993). And this figure is all the more alarming given the current HIV/AIDS epidemic. It quickly becomes clear that people must understand the medical implications of becoming sexually active.

Promiscuity, teenage pregnancies, adolescent marriage, STDs—these are but a few of the problems sexuality presents for adolescents. Obviously, something is wrong when so many young people act in ways that are sexually irresponsible; that disrupt the lives of their families, themselves, and their offspring; and that expose themselves and others to serious and potentially life-threatening sexual diseases. What can be done? How can we teach adolescents and young adults to become sexually responsible and make appropriate decisions? How can we help them avoid the negative consequences of unprotected, premarital sex? How can we help them see that sexual risks are real and not just something "the other person" needs to worry about? I'll answer these and other questions at the end of this chapter in the section entitled, "Sex Education and the Life Cycle."

EARLY ADULTHOOD AND MIDDLE ADULTHOOD

The adult years roughly divide into *early* (ages 20 to 44), *middle* (45 to 64), and *late* (65 and beyond) periods (Levinson, 1978). The ages given here, however, are only guidelines; there are no exact years when these periods of adulthood begin or end. For instance, early adulthood traditionally begins when adolescents become self-reliant and independent from their parents; late adulthood, when individuals retire or reach retirement age.

As mentioned earlier, sexuality takes on various forms of activity and expression during each stage of life. Although during childhood and adolescence sexuality is of a growing, maturing nature, during the adult years it is in full bloom and enjoys a wide range of expression.

A discussion of sexuality in adulthood primarily concerns lifestyles and *relationships*. In other words, except for solitary masturbation, adult sexual activity is realized within the context of one or more relationships—whether long-term or transitory. In our discussion of adolescent sexuality we noted that the primary task of that period is discovering personal identity. Erikson concluded that the primary task of young adulthood is establishing *intimacy* (sharing one's total self with someone else); of middle adulthood, developing *generativity* (expanding one's influence and commitment to family, society, and future generations); and of late adulthood, maintaining *integrity* (holding onto one's sense of wholeness while avoiding despair). In the next few sections, I'll present some of the different types of early- and middle-period adult relationships in which sexual activity occurs.

SINGLEHOOD

One type of adult lifestyle is *singlehood*, or the *single lifestyle*. Interestingly, a great many individuals these days are choosing to remain single and live alone. In recent years the number of singles in the United States has been increasing, with 26.1 percent of men and 19.3 percent of women single in 1991 (*Statistical Abstract of the United States*, 1992). Regardless of their reasons for living alone, many singles clearly lead rewarding and satisfying lives. Many claim that singlehood provides them with maximum independence, freedom from interpersonal obligations, and personal control over the living environment. There is time to read and relax. Things can be tidy or messy. There is the freedom to leave town on the spur of the moment or wash dishes at 2:00 A.M.—no other lifestyle is so unencumbered. But there are also negative aspects to living alone. Not all singles enjoy returning home from work to face an empty apartment or house. The single lifestyle is definitely not for everyone. For those wishing to remain single but not live alone, there are options. One is to share an apartment or house. One or more compatible room- or housemates can support each other, both psychologically and financially. Another option is to seek emotional support from family, friends, co-workers, and so on.

On a Personal Note (Elizabeth, age 33)

People, especially folks who've been married for a while and aren't all that happy, think being single is exciting and glamorous—a life full of adventure, travel, and new people. And for some reason, people don't think you have anything to do with your time—like life's an open schedule or something. Or like you have to have kids to be busy. But to tell you the truth, I want to settle down. I don't mind being single; in many ways it's really great. I've always wanted to get married. I just can't seem to meet the right guy. (Author's files)

Many singles date and are sexually active. Popular sexual activities for singles are the same as those for other adults, although masturbation may play a more central role in the absence of a steady sexual partner. Some singles abstain from sexual relationships altogether (Michael et al., 1994).

COHABITATION AND MARRIAGE

The two primary long-term relationships characteristic of adulthood are *cohabitation* and *marriage*. Cohabitors are unmarried people who live together and are sexually involved. Over 3 million Americans cohabit, the great majority of these (nearly 2 million) being between the ages of 25 and 44 (*Statistical Abstract of the United States*, 1992). Many people state their reason for cohabiting as a "test" for marital compatibility, yet no clear evidence supports the notion that cohabitation increases eventual marital satisfaction. In fact, some studies have shown a relationship between premarital cohabitation and increased divorce rates (Bennett et al., 1988). Others state that they cohabit as an alternative to marriage, rather than as a trial marriage.

By far, the long-term relationship that most Americans choose is *marriage*. Somewhere around 90 or 95 percent of Americans will marry at least once (Allman, 1993; Fitzpatrick, 1988). The average age for first-time marriage is about 26 for males and 24 for females. Interestingly, the number of interracial marriages between blacks and whites has been steadily increasing, accounting for 0.4 percent of all marriages in 1991 (*Statistical Abstract of the United States*, 1992).

Although many singles enjoy the freedom of living alone, others dread the lone-liness that often goes along with singlehood.

The Bizarro cartoon by Dan Piraro is reprinted by permission of Chronicle Features, San Francisco, CA.

Marriage can have many advantages. On average, married people are healthier and happier than their never-married, divorced, and widowed counterparts. Married males also tend to live longer than those of the other groups (Umberson, 1989). People generally affirm that their marriages are happiest during the early years, although marital satisfaction often increases again in the later years once finances have stabilized and parenting responsibilities have ended. On the other hand, marriage can have disadvantages. A variety of difficulties and conflicts are likely to arise within a marriage or other long-term partnership. Unrealistic expectations about marriage, as well as differences over finances, parenting, and household responsibilities are but a few potential problem areas.

EXTRAMARITAL RELATIONSHIPS

American culture is strongly rooted in Judeo-Christian mores and values. That being the case, our society emphasizes *sexual fidelity* (sexual faithfulness, exclusiveness, and monogamy) within marriage. Indeed, *sexual infidelity,* or *extramarital sex* (meaning "sex outside of marriage") is a transgression of religious law, and is thus considered a sin by many. Having an *affair* ("committing adultery") undermines the religious commands that stand at the foundation of our cultural heritage.

Religious dogma aside, *nonconsensual* extramarital sexual activity (not agreed upon in advance by both partners) is a violation of trust and commitment between partners—a fundamental problem for any relationship regardless of religious perspective. Whatever the reasons, nonconsensual affairs can irreparably damage a marriage or other long-term partnership (Pittman, 1993). Marriages in which one or both partners "cheat" frequently end in divorce, although some couples decide to stay married for financial reasons or until children are raised.

Other couples choose—with full knowledge and approval—to have *consensual* affairs as part of their sexual lifestyle. They may engage in a *menage à trois,* or *threesome,*

Some American couples today choose to cohabit rather than marry.

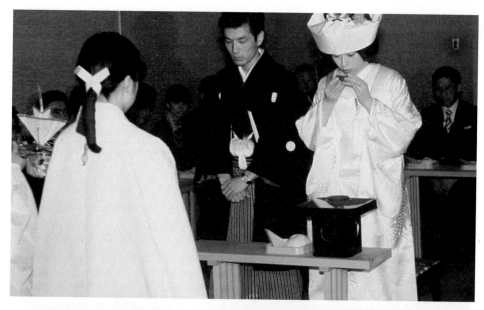

Marriage customs differ considerably around the world.

including a third person into their sexual activities. Or they may have an *open marriage*, in which both partners are free to have sexual relations with others as specified in the couple's "contract." Some couples engage in *swinging*, exchanging partners with another couple or individual. Others may choose sexually *communal living* in which a group of people share food, housing, and sexual relations.

Not surprisingly, the majority of Americans disapprove of affairs, 66.5 percent of males and 78.4 percent of females having reported that they believe extramarital sex is "always wrong" (Klassen et al., 1989). However, what people say they disapprove of and what they actually do are not necessarily the same (Kilmann et al., 1993). In one study, 24.5 percent of married men and 15 percent of married women reported having had at least one affair (Michael et al., 1994). Although surveys indicate that men have affairs more often than women, the incidence of women engaging in affairs may be increasing (Segraves, 1989). The typical affair involves a single woman and a married man (Segraves, 1989).

DIVORCE AND WIDOWHOOD

What about unhappy marriages? What happens when two people discover that they have irreconcilable differences? Some couples choose to stay together, perhaps out of respect for their vows "to honor and uphold" or for fear of being single again. But most others choose divorce, the legal termination of marriage. You'll recall from Chapter 8 that currently about 50 percent of all marriages in the United States end in divorce, the median duration of these marriages being about seven years (*Statistical Abstract of the United States*, 1992).

And what of the effects of divorce on the couple? According to Angus Campbell (1981):

> It is surely a commonplace observation that divorce and the events leading up to it are a damaging experience for the two people involved, sometimes for one more than the other but typically for both. It is no surprise then to discover in the national surveys that separated and divorced people have on the average the most depressed feelings of well-being of any of the major life-cycle groups. They are much more likely than married people to describe their lives as "not too happy," and they are less likely to report positive experiences and much more likely to report negative ones, especially feeling lonely and depressed. These people with failed or failing marriages are also much less willing than married people to call themselves "very satisfied" with life in general and with specific domains of life. They feel more strongly than any of the other life-cycle groups that they have not had their full share of happiness in life. (p. 198)

Indeed, divorce—both the process and the aftermath—is extremely stressful, in most cases negatively affecting both partners. Divorce is frequently associated with increased

"I understand you perfectly, Harold. When you say you want to extend your parameters, it means you want floozies."

Drawing by Handelsman; © 1975 The New Yorker Magazine, Inc.

Divorce takes its toll on all parties involved—the couple, their children, and the couple's extended families.

risk of developing medical conditions like ulcers and/or emotional problems like anxiety and depression, experiencing financial hardship, having a serious accident, committing suicide, or dying prematurely (Kiecolt-Glaser et al., 1987; Spanier & Thompson, 1984; Trovato, 1986). The couple's children and their respective extended families are also likely to suffer as a result of divorce, especially if there are disagreements over custody of the children (Guidubaldi et al., 1983). However, most divorced persons are able to cope, the majority of them eventually remarrying (Spanier & Furstenberg, 1982). Men are more likely to remarry later than women, the median age at remarriage being about 37 for men and 34 for women (*Statistical Abstract of the United States*, 1992). Most children of divorce and other family members also eventually adjust and carry on with life (Wallerstein & Kelly, 1980).

Widowhood, or the disruption of a marriage or other partnership due to the death of the spouse or partner, is another source of emotional pain and stress. *Widows* (females) and *widowers* (males) may grieve and mourn their loss for years in some cases. Nearly 3 percent of men and 12 percent of women in the United States are widowed. In the 75 and older age group, nearly 25 percent of men are widowed, compared to nearly 66 percent of women in the same age group (*Statistical Abstract of the United States*, 1992).

In many ways widowhood is similar to divorce. The significant other is gone. Routines change. Loneliness can at times seem overwhelming. But there are differences, too. Death is often unexpected, whereas divorce is usually the result of a long chain of events. Death is also final, whereas many divorced persons maintain at least a superficial relationship with each other. Although people never really completely "get over" losing a partner or close family member, most are ultimately able to cope.

WIDOWHOOD

Disruption of marriage due to death of the spouse.

How people deal with divorce or widowhood varies, especially by gender. Many attempt to "replace" the lost relationship by seeking out friendships or remarrying. Some become more involved with their work or their children or grandchildren. Others volunteer their time with religious and charitable organizations. Still others seek counseling or find comfort within a local support group. Women may have an easier time emotionally dealing with widowhood than men, but they often have a harder time financially (Wade & Tavris, 1993). They also have to contend with social stigmas associated with widowhood, in particular that widows are asexual and old. Widowers, on the other hand, are more likely to be depressed and attempt suicide than are widows (Riley & Waring, 1976).

LATE ADULTHOOD

Perhaps nothing so astounds the young person as the thought of sexual activity amongst those of advancing years. Indeed, people often react with greater shock to learn of continuing sexuality in the elderly than they do to learn of developing sexuality in the very young. But why? To acknowledge that older people have sex (and all that such activity implies) is to acknowledge that *one's parents and grandparents have sex*. These sorts of images contradict our usual views of middle and older adults as asexual. In fact, researchers have found that young people's attitudes regarding the possibility that their parents have sex are pronouncedly negative (Pocs & Godow, 1976; Zeiss, 1982).

*"Would you excuse me, Miss Arkwright? I just remembered
that I promised to forsake all others."*

Drawing by Handelsman; © 1979 The New Yorker Magazine, Inc.

"Sure you were my sunshine, but you weren't my only sunshine!"

Drawing by Dana Fradon; © 1980 The New Yorker Magazine, Inc.

As with attitudes about sexuality in the very young, *denial* seems to be a key element at work in society's vision of elderly sexuality. Any older person who dares break away from the expected patterns is met with such derisive comments as, "You're a dirty old man!" "Act your age!" "Grow old gracefully!" and "Be a nice little old lady!" Our dominant cultural impression is that older adults have little or no interest in, knowledge of, or experience with sexual activity. For instance, segregating by sex and prohibiting sexual activity are the norm in many retirement and nursing homes, even for married couples (Calderone & Johnson, 1989).

As with so many aspects of human sexuality, society's perceptions of and people's actual sexual practices vary considerably. Even among many people with "liberal" sexual attitudes, the image of grandparents having sex or masturbating can be unthinkable. Sexual desire and activity are *supposed* to wane as people age—an irrational notion that various research studies into the sexual habits of older adults have fortunately refuted. A significant number of men and women over 60 remain sexually active and report high levels of sexual enjoyment and satisfaction into their 80s and beyond (Bretschneider & McCoy, 1988; Cross, 1993; Shaw, 1994).

People never outgrow their need for love, intimacy, physical closeness, and sexual expression. Everyone, regardless of age, needs to feel attractive, loved, and desired. The loving actions that help younger people feel needed and significant—touching, embracing, kissing, and sharing loving words—are just as important to older people, maybe more so.

SEXUALITY AND AGING

The body ages. According to the proverb "The heart is willing but the body falters," age has a real and significant effect on behavior. While studies clearly demonstrate that sexuality is a fundamental part of the lives of elderly adults, an older person's body is no longer the same physical machine it was when he or she was younger. Knowledge of these changes provides additional insights into the nature of sexuality in the older adult population.

Aging inevitably translates into physical decline, some of which is due to lifestyle rather than the aging process *per se*. Muscle mass decreases. Reflexes slow. The immune system is no longer as effective in protecting against disease. Body systems diminish in their efficiency. The litany goes on and, to many, sounds rather bleak. Regardless of our best hopes and efforts, aging is, in fact, a deterioration. However, the speed with which one ages, as well as how it affects one's outlook and various life activities, is highly variable. As many people have pointed out, with age comes wisdom, patience, and experience—three qualities that can improve one's life immeasurably.

Aging also takes a toll on sexual functioning. Older men have more difficulty attaining erection and orgasm than do younger men. This is probably due in part to fewer secretions from the sexual glands and diminished levels of testosterone. Likewise, older men have less urge to ejaculate, and their refractory periods last longer. Older women produce less vaginal lubrication, and the vagina becomes less elastic (Masters & Johnson, 1966). For both sexes, orgasm continues to be as pleasurable an event as it was during early and middle adulthood, although there may be fewer orgasmic contractions. But just as older individuals do not expect to run around the block and choose to walk instead, so might they prefer to engage in slow, sensual sexual behavior. In fact, as older men may "last" longer and women may relax because they do not fear pregnancy, neither person is as insecure, anxious, or in a hurry as they might have been in younger years.

Midlife and the biological and psychological changes accompanying it seem to represent a significant turning point in terms of the age-related declines that eventually

Many older adults continue to be sexually active well into their 70s and 80s.

characterize older adulthood. Yet none of the physiological changes that accompany middle and late adulthood need be an obstacle to sexual enjoyment. Too often, society has erroneously concluded that *menopause* (the cessation of menstruation) inevitably spells the "beginning of the end" of female sexuality. *Not true.* While menopause may give rise to any number of uncomfortable symptoms (migraine headaches, "hot flashes," swelling in various parts of the body, dizziness, and irritability), postmenopausal women frequently report increased sexual desire and enjoyment, in part due to freedom from concerns about menstruation and pregnancy (Reinisch, 1990). For this same reason, women who undergo a *hysterectomy* (surgical removal of the uterus) frequently report improvement in sexual response, rather than decreased desire and enjoyment.

Although men undergo many physiological changes as they age, none is as distinct, sharp, and profound as menopause is for women. Testosterone production diminishes, causing such physical symptoms as poor appetite, weakness, and inability to concentrate for prolonged periods of time. Yet this decline in testosterone does not completely explain the emotional symptoms of anxiety and depression that sometimes accompany middle adulthood. That is, the *male climacteric* ("male menopause") seems to have more to do with psychological events than physical ones. Middle-age men realize that they are no longer 18 or 20 years old, and that they are not going to accomplish everything they originally set out to do. They may also feel less attractive and sexually appealing. Middle-aged men often find themselves balding, developing a "spare tire" around the waist, or just not having as much energy as they used to. As a result of this *male midlife crisis*, men sometimes experience a declining interest in sexual activity during and following their climacteric. Fears of "losing" one's sexuality have prompted many a man to leave his wife for a younger woman, often in the hopes of proving to others (and himself) that he is still sexually desirable and capable. He may also try to reassert his masculinity by engaging in what he believes to be more youthful activities, such as wearing stylish clothes, riding a motorcycle, taking skydiving lessons, or "bungy jumping" off bridges.

The belief that there is a dramatic reduction in the frequency of sexual activity following middle adulthood is unfounded. Actually, the best predictor of future sexual behavior is past and present sexual behavior. The more sexually active a person was and is in her or his earlier years, the more active she or he will probably be in later years (Bretschneider & McCoy, 1988). This is particularly true of activities like touching, caressing, and stimulating oneself and the partner, although not necessarily so of intercourse. There seems, then, to be at least some truth to the old saying, "Use it or lose it" (Cross, 1993)! Barring unrealistic expectations about sexuality and the elderly, a major problem older adults face when it comes to sexual activity is not lack of sexual interest or capability, but absence of a suitable partner (Turner & Adams, 1988). This is a special problem for women, who, having a longer life expectancy than men, find themselves with few or no choices for potential partners. Also, our society generally favors older men marrying younger women, but not the reverse, leaving older women with only one option—celibacy.

Aging rarely means that youthful activities must end, just that they must be approached and enjoyed differently. This is true of tennis (where skill and placement of the ball often replaces sprinting and power), of exercise (where walking briskly might replace jogging), and of sexual activity (where patience and caring often replace sweaty passion). In none of these cases do (or should) the changes that accompany aging in any way detract from the enjoyment of the activity.

This still leaves us with society's negative attitudes about sexuality in the later years. To help put an end to these attitudes, sex researcher Edward Brecher (1984), quoting a 67-year-old consultant, recommended the following: "The common view that the aging and aged are nonsexual, I believe, can only be corrected by a dramatic and courageous process—the *coming-out-of-the-closet* of sexually active older women and men, so that people can see for themselves what the later years are really like" (pp. 20–21).

For Personal Reflection

Identify some of the attitudes you have concerning sexuality and the elderly. Where do you think your attitudes come from? What are some of the things you can to do to help society see that older adults, like all people, are sexual beings?

SEX EDUCATION AND THE LIFE CYCLE

Sex education is just for preteens and teens, right? By now (having read most of this book) you should know the answer to this question. *No,* it's not just for teens and preteens. *Sex education is for everyone—young and old alike.* The most important message of *Human Sexuality: Contemporary Perspectives* is that sex education—at home or elsewhere—is the primary vehicle through which correct sexual information is disseminated to people of all ages. Correct information about sexuality is the foundation upon which people can challenge unrealistic expectations and stereotypes; make good, effective sexual decisions; and overcome and prevent various sexual diseases and problems. Although I described many of the benefits of sex education in Chapter 1, a few more points are in order along these lines.

First, *sex education is a lifelong process that should begin in childhood and continue through the life cycle.* No one can honestly boast of knowing everything about human sexuality, regardless of their age or occupation. A single lifetime is not long enough to grasp the many aspects of human sexuality. Every interaction, every word spoken, every page read carries with it the potential for a new experience and new learning. Therein lies the beauty of human sexuality.

Second, *sex education begins in the home.* Parents or other guardians have a responsibility (and a wonderful opportunity) to teach their children about love, sexuality, and the nature of relationships. The best way to do this is through the parents modeling love while encouraging their children to ask questions and share their feelings. The home should be the first, best, safest place where a child or teenager can learn about sexuality. If they do

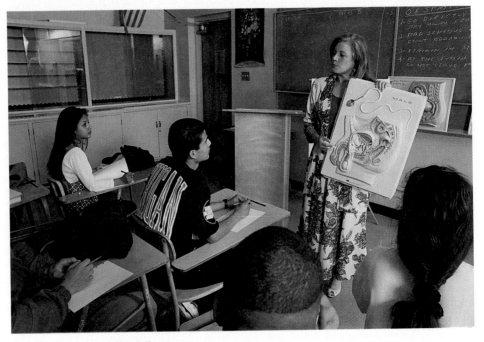

Sex education is for people of all ages.

PERSPECTIVE

Jennifer Fever: Older Men and Younger Women

Bestselling author Barbara Gordon (1988), in her book *Jennifer Fever*, presented the following fascinating insights concerning older men leaving their wives of many years for younger women (popularly called "Jennifers"):

To many observers, both the man and the Jennifer are embarked on a singularly practical arrangement. One hears the criticism that older men and Jennifers are merely expressions of the old power-dominance game, the father-daughter complex, or mentor-student arrangements. As author Joseph Heller quipped, "When I see a couple where one member is much older than the other, I know there's something wrong with *both* of them."

It may be that at times Jennifer Fever, like all relationships, offers secondary gains of psychological satisfactions, satisfactions that may not feed the healthiest part of either the man or the woman....

The conventional wisdom is that a Jennifer is merely an antidote to the all too familiar litany of men's midlife fears and anxieties. Or that one or both of the partners in what sociologists call "age discrepant" relationships is reliving the imprint of an earlier time: a fixation on mother or father which remains unsolved, and is relived in choosing an older or younger partner. But there is one recent explanation that seems remarkably fresh:

Psychologist David Gutmann writes that midlife men and women become involved, quite unconsciously, in a kind of gender swapping, which can have a profound effect on a man's susceptibility to a Jennifer. At midlife, he observes, men begin to feel more tender, more passive, more sensual, qualities they had repressed in their earlier years, when they were focused on building their careers and creating their families....

This sudden burst of passivity can be most disturbing to men and may reach crisis proportions when it is exacerbated by corresponding changes in their aging wives, who, Gutmann says, "generally become managerial, achievement oriented, and relatively tough minded, taking over the 'masculine' qualities that men surrender. In his earlier years, the husband can externalize...the discrepant 'feminine' side of his own nature through indulging and sponsoring his wife's femininity. But as women become more assertive...the aging husband...begins to sense, usually with some discomfort, that so-called feminine traits are a feature of his own internal landscape and not exclusive to his wife...."

His conclusion offers an unusual explanation for Jennifer Fever: "The reason older men leave their wives for younger women is *not*, as is commonly believed, primarily to enhance sexual potency, but rather because the middle-aged wife now refuses to live in her husband's shadow."(pp. 18–21)

Questions for Thought

Have you ever known a "Jennifer Fever" couple? If so, how well do they fit the above description?

Source: B. Gordon (1988), *Jennifer Fever: Older men, younger women* (New York: Harper & Row).

"There are five elements, son— earth, air, fire, water, and women."

Drawing by H. Martin; © 1984 The New Yorker Magazine, Inc.

not learn about the "birds and the bees" from their parents, they *will* learn about it—usually picking up a great deal of *misinformation* along the way—from other sources like friends and popular magazines, most of which are highly suspect as expert sources of sexual knowledge.

Third, *sex education in the home is appropriately supplemented by sex education in the classroom.* In most cases parents, regardless of their good intentions, cannot devote the time necessary to obtaining, researching, and teaching their children the latest information on all sexual topics, as can a qualified sex educator. Further, a great deal of information about sexuality circulates in both professional and lay circles; a trained sex educator is better able to sort through it all and separate out the valuable information. There is much work to be done in developing comprehensive, time-efficient, and gender-unbiased programs for each of the school-age groups.

Finally, *sex education does not end in the classroom or with a particular age group.* Adults of all ages can benefit from sex education offered through community programs and presentations, seminars, church groups, and even in personal and marital counseling. In addition, adults can increase their knowledge of sexuality by taking advantage of the many excellent sex manuals, books, and educational videos available today.

KEY POINTS

1. Many people in our society refuse to acknowledge the sexual nature of infants, children, and older adults, instead believing them to be *asexual*. According to

the *developmental perspective*, human sexuality is a fundamental aspect of human experience and expression at all ages.

2. Childhood roughly divides into *infancy* (birth to 1), *early childhood* (1 to 6), *middle childhood* (6 to 7), *late childhood* or *preadolescence* (8 to 11), and *adolescence* (12 to 19). All of these periods are characterized by age-appropriate sexual behaviors, which become more goal-focused as the child develops.

3. Adulthood roughly divides into *early* (20 to 44), *middle* (45 to 64), and *late* (65 and beyond) periods. A discussion of sexuality in adulthood primarily concerns lifestyles and *relationships*, whether long-term or transitory. The most common of these are *singlehood, cohabitation, marriage,* and *extramarital relationships*. Sexuality also continues following *divorce* and *widowhood*.

4. Many people believe the midlife events of *menopause* in women and the *male climacteric* in men mark the beginning of the physical changes characteristic of late adulthood. Actually, aging is a fairly gradual process that begins in early adulthood. The belief that there is a dramatic reduction in the frequency of sexual activity following middle adulthood is unfounded.

5. *Sex education*—at home or school—is a lifelong process that begins in childhood and continues through the life cycle. Correct information about sexuality is the foundation upon which people can challenge unrealistic expectations and stereotypes, make effective sexual decisions, and overcome and prevent various sexual diseases and problems.

ACTIVITIES AND QUESTIONS

1. How would you respond to the following: "Children don't need to learn about sexuality from parents or teachers; nature will take care of everything when the time is right"?

2. How far should researchers be allowed to go when studying childhood sexuality? Do you think the government should regulate such research to protect child subjects from potential sexual exploitation by unscrupulous or unethical researchers? What limits would you suggest be incorporated into such laws?

3. How does infidelity on the part of one or both partners negatively affect a relationship? What can a couple do to restore their relationship in the aftermath of an extramarital affair?

4. As a class, explore why television and movies so frequently show individuals having extramarital sex. Do these shows and films reflect the way things really are? Do people become more willing to have affairs in response to these materials?

5. As a class, explore how the media perpetuate stereotypes of older adults as asexual beings. Which form of media is the worst offender?

RECOMMENDED READINGS

Betancourt, J. (1983). *Am I normal? An illustrated guide to your changing body.* New York: Avon Books. Deals with boys' sexual development. Written for early teens.

Betancourt, J. (1983). *Dear diary: An illustrated guide to your changing body.* New York: Avon Books. Deals with girls' sexual development. Written for early teens.

Silverstone, B., & Hyman, H. K. (1992). *Growing old together: A couple's guide to understanding and coping with the challenges of later life.* New York: Pantheon. A thorough and sensitive overview of sexuality and aging.

Smith, D. C., & Sparks, W. (1986). *The naked child: Growing up without shame*. Los Angeles: Elysium Growth Press. A fascinating look at family nudity that addresses many of our society's misconceptions about the effects on children of "clothing optional environments."

Somers, L., & Somers, B. C. (1989). *Talking to your children about love and sex*. New York: New American Library. Offers advice for parents seeking to educate their children about sexuality.

Wolf, S. (1994). *Guerilla dating tactics: Strategies, tips, and secrets for finding romance*. New York: Plume. A fun, often humorous, guide to finding romance in the 1990s.

•**P**REPARING FOR CONCEPTION AND PREGNANCY

•STAGES OF PREGNANCY

•PRENATAL CARE

•THE STAGES OF CHILDBIRTH

•COMPLICATIONS DURING PREGNANCY AND
    CHILDBIRTH

•INFERTILITY

C H A P T E R   1 2

CONCEPTION, PREGNANCY, AND BIRTH

O B J E C T I V E S

AFTER READING THIS CHAPTER YOU SHOULD BE
ABLE TO . . .

1. EXPLAIN THE PROCESSES OF CONCEPTION AND
   IMPLANTATION.
2. DESCRIBE THE THE STAGES OF PREGNANCY,
   FETAL DEVELOPMENT, AND BIRTH.
3. DISCUSS THE PROS AND CONS ASSOCIATED WITH
   SELECTING (1) A PHYSICIAN, CERTIFIED NURSE
   MIDWIFE, OR LAY MIDWIFE TO PERFORM A
   DELIVERY; AND (2) A HOSPITAL, BIRTHING
   CENTER, OR HOME AS THE DELIVERY SETTING.
4. DESCRIBE THE EFFECTS THAT EXERCISE,
   NUTRITION, VARIOUS DRUGS, AND SEXUAL
   ACTIVITY HAVE ON THE EXPECTANT MOTHER AND
   HER UNBORN CHILD.
5. LIST AND DESCRIBE SOME OF THE
   COMPLICATIONS THAT CAN OCCUR DURING PREG-
   NANCY AND CHILDBIRTH.

The author wishes to thank Kimberly A. Sarabia, M.S.W., for her input and assistance with this chapter.

P E R S O N A L   A S S E S S M E N T

WHAT ARE YOUR THOUGHTS AND FEELINGS ON HAVING A CHILD AND BEING A PARENT? TO EXPLORE THIS, READ THE FOLLOWING STATEMENTS AND RESPOND USING THIS RATING SCALE: 3 = I *completely agree* WITH THE STATEMENT; 2 = I *mostly agree* WITH THE STATEMENT; 1 = I *mostly disagree* WITH THE STATEMENT; 0 = I *completely disagree* WITH THE STATEMENT. REMEMBER, THERE ARE NO RIGHT OR WRONG ANSWERS HERE; IT'S YOUR OPINION THAT COUNTS.

_____ 1. A good reason to have a child is to please friends and family.

_____ 2. A good reason to have a child is to please your partner.

_____ 3. A good reason to have a child is to help a failing relationship with your partner.

_____ 4. A good reason to have a child is to receive unconditional love from your child.

_____ 5. A good reason to have a child is to avoid loneliness in old age.

_____ 6. A good reason to have a child is to raise someone who will affect society in a positive way.

_____ 7. A good reason to have a child is to relive your childhood through your child.

_____ 8. A good reason to have a child is to prove to your parents that you can do a better job at parenting than they did.

_____ 9. A good reason to have a child is to bring a new life into the world.

_____ 10. There are both good and bad reasons for wanting to have a child; it all depends on an individual's (or couple's) circumstances and preferences.

*E*very baby born into the world is a finer one than the last.

Charles Dickens

Pregnancy provided an in-depth, full force, no screens-up experience of myself. It was ecstatic, primal, scary, rough, revealing. No wonder our Victorian forebears were put off. It was real. More real than anything before it. Everything since happens at a deeper level, and I now know who my husband is: he's my mate. (Marzollo, 1975, p. 17)

I feel terrific, and have since the moment I delivered three weeks ago. Is all this good feeling building up to one terrific case of letdown? (Eisenberg et al., 1991, p. 400)

A healthy pregnancy and birth are so commonplace that most of us take them for granted. Today, the vast majority of mothers-to-be in the United States can expect a normal, routine nine months of pregnancy, followed by uncomplicated labor and delivery of a robust baby. This is not to say that problems cannot and do not arise. They can and do. But carrying a fetus to term is far safer than it used to be, given our tremendous strides in medicine and science. It was not too long ago, around the turn of the century, that many women could expect pregnancy to end in miscarriage, stillbirth, premature delivery, or infant death.

The focus of this chapter is on having a healthy baby—from conception and pregnancy to childbirth and breast-feeding. The decision to conceive and carry a fetus to term is an important one, because pregnancy and birth still carry risks. Yet conception can lead to one of the most rewarding and fulfilling life experiences possible—giving birth to and raising a child.

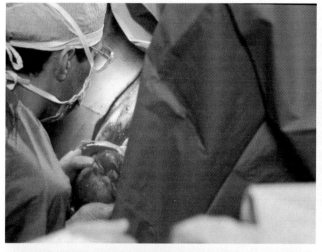
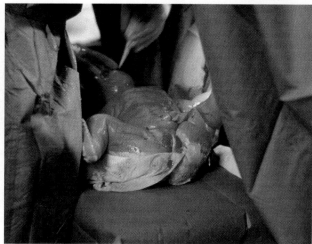
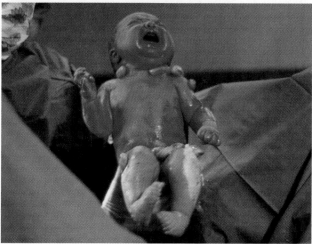

Most American mothers-to-be today can expect uncomplicated labor and delivery of a robust baby.

PREPARING FOR CONCEPTION AND PREGNANCY

Having a healthy baby takes careful planning to ready the woman's body to provide an appropriate environment for **prenatal development,** or development of the embryo and fetus before birth. While not always practical, the best time to start planning for pregnancy is at least several months, even years, prior to conception. A balanced diet, cessation of smoking, abstinence from alcohol and drugs, and routine physical examinations to identify potential complications are all important to the well-being of both the mother-to-be and child. The father-to-be should also monitor his lifestyle practices, especially avoiding drug and alcohol use to prevent damaging his sperm.

To improve the chances of conceiving, intercourse should take place close to the time of *ovulation,* when one of the woman's ovaries releases an ovum. The ovum is generally fertilizable for only 12 to 24 hours following its release from the ovary. Some women determine their time of ovulation by keeping a *basal body temperature chart.* This procedure involves the woman taking an oral temperature every morning immediately upon awakening and graphing the results. Preovulatory temperatures should remain fairly constant, although slightly below normal body temperature (98.6°F). Normally, the woman's temperature drops on the day of ovulation, rises sharply (by about 0.4° to 1.0°F) the following day, and remains at that level until right before menstruation. Keeping a basal

PRENATAL DEVELOPMENT
Fetal development in the uterus.

body temperature chart over a period of a few cycles helps a woman to predict more accurately the day on which she will ovulate.

Conception occurs when a man's sperm unites with a woman's egg, usually after the man ejaculates semen into the woman's vagina during sexual intercourse. The higher a man's sperm count, the better the chances one sperm will reach and penetrate the ovum. To allow the man's sperm count to build, many couples refrain from sexual activity for a few days just before attempting to conceive. The "missionary" (man-on-top) position seems to be best for conceiving, as it allows the man's semen to more easily collect and move through the woman's vagina, uterus, and fallopian tubes. (Other intercourse positions more easily allow sperm to leak out of the vagina.) The woman should avoid douches, lubricants, and vaginal suppositories while the couple is attempting to conceive, as these can destroy sperm. Please note, though, that pregnancy can and does occur with any sexual position and when a woman use douches and so forth. The couple should not rely on sexual positions, douching, lubricants, or vaginal suppositories (except those designed as contraceptives) for birth control.

One question some parents-to-be ask is, "Can we select the sex of our baby?" Actually, the odds can be influenced, at least according to proponents of *sex preselection*. Because sperm bearing the Y chromosome produce males, for those couples wanting a male baby, the idea is to increase the chances of a Y-bearing sperm fusing with the X-ovum. A number of *sperm-separating* procedures supposedly accomplish this. The couple increase their chances of having a male child through artificial insemination of primarily Y-bearing sperm, which have been separated from X-bearing sperm in a test tube. Success rates for sperm-separating techniques are reportedly about 70 to 85 percent, yet there is some question about the accuracy of these figures (Carson, 1988; Glass & Ericsson, 1982; Shapiro, 1993).

STAGES OF PREGNANCY AND FETAL DEVELOPMENT

PREGNANCY
Period of embryonic and fetal gestation.

A full-term **pregnancy,** or the period of *gestation*, in which the woman carries the fetus in the uterus, averages 266 days from conception to birth, or 280 days from the last menstrual period (LMP) until birth. These 280 days divide into 10 four-week *lunar months* of 28 days each, which equal a little over nine calender months. These nine months also divide into three periods of three months or 13 weeks, known as *trimesters* (Figure 12.1).

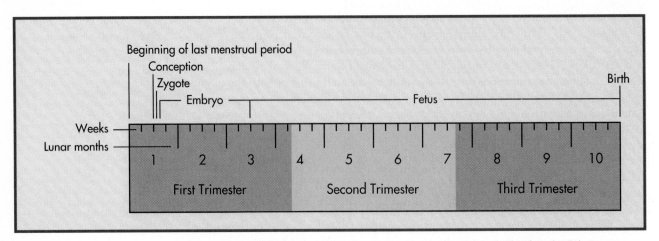

FIGURE 12.1 *The pregnancy timeline. Source: C. O. Byer & L. W. Shainberg (1991), Living well: Health in your hands (New York: HarperCollins). Reprinted by permission.*

To calculate the expected date of delivery, the woman adds 280 days to the beginning date of her LMP. Or she can use *Nagele's rule*, in which she adds seven days to the beginning date of her LMP, then subtracts three months, and then adds one year. Although some babies are born precisely on schedule, most are born within 10 days of their due dates.

CONCEPTION

The average woman ovulates on or about the fourteenth day before beginning her next menstrual cycle. The ovum then enters the nearby fallopian tube. Sperm normally reach the ovum in the portion of the fallopian tube closest to the ovary within 60 to 90 minutes following ejaculation. Mitochondria in the midpiece of sperm cause the tail of the sperm to *flagellate* (lash about). This flagellation propels the sperm through the woman's vagina and into her uterus and tubes. Of the average 200 to 500 million sperm present in each ejaculation, only about 2,000 ever reach the fallopian tube containing the ovum. And perhaps only dozens will actually reach the ovum. The others enter the wrong tube, are killed by the acidic environment of the vagina, or flow out of the vagina as a result of gravity.

As sperm swim through the vagina and fallopian tubes, they undergo changes brought about by various chemicals present in the woman's reproductive organs. This process of *capacitation* enables the sperm to fertilize the woman's ovum. Of all the sperm ejaculated, only one penetrates and fertilizes the egg. The others surround the egg and secrete an enzyme, *hyaluronidase*, which softens the thin, gelatinous covering of the ovum, the *zona pellucida*, and allows one sperm to enter. Once penetrated, the egg's surrounding membrane thickens and toughens, preventing additional sperm from entering (Figure 12.2).

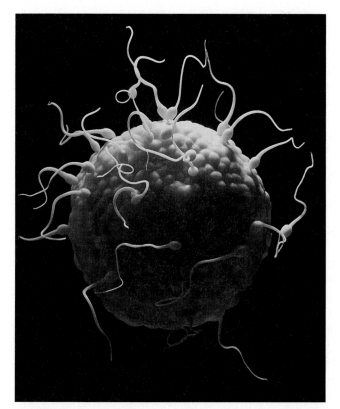

FIGURE 12.2 *An ovum surrounded by sperm. Of the many sperm that reach the ovum, only one penetrates and fertilizes it. © Schuchman/Phototake.*

CONCEPTION

Union of a sperm and ovum.

CONCEPTUS OR ZYGOTE
(KON-CEP-TUS; ZI-GOT)

The product of conception; a fertilized ovum.

Conception—the union of sperm and egg—normally occurs in the fallopian tube. The newly formed **conceptus,** or **zygote,** then proceeds down the fallopian tube and attaches to the uterine wall. If conception does not occur, the ovum dissolves in about 48 hours.

During fertilization, the nucleus of the head of the sperm fuses with the nucleus of the ovum. Even at this early stage, the presence or absence of a Y chromosome determines the sex of the conceptus. The sperm carries either an X or Y chromosome; the egg is always X. After fertilization, the conceptus is then either XX (female) or XY (male).

As mentioned above, the newly fertilized egg is termed a *zygote.* Within 24 to 36 hours, the single-cell zygote begins to divide, even as it travels down the fallopian tube. This cellular division occurs geometrically: One cell becomes two, two become four, four become eight, and so on. A *multiple pregnancy* occurs when two or more ova are fertilized, or a single fertilized ovum divides into two or more zygotes. Two separate ova fertilized by two separate sperm develop into *fraternal twins.* Two zygotes that divide from a single ovum develop into *identical twins;* three zygotes, into *identical triplets.*

IMPLANTATION

IMPLANTATION
(IM-PLAN-TA-SHUN)

Attachment of the blastocyst to the uterine wall.

Within a week after conception, the zygote becomes a *blastocyst,* a hollow sphere of a hundred cells or so. After floating in the uterine cavity for about three days, the blastocyst attaches itself to the inner lining of the uterus, the *endometrium.* This occurs as the outer cells of the blastocyst, called *trophoblasts,* secrete enzymes that break down layers of uterine lining, permitting firm attachment of the blastocyst to the endometrium. This entire process of **implantation** occurs about a week after fertilization (Figure 12.3). Immediately following implantation and for the next eight weeks, the zygote is termed an *embryo.* After that and until birth, it is termed a *fetus.*

As the rate of cell division increases, the first signs of specialized tissues and organs appear. Three weeks after conception, the *neural groove,* a small indentation, forms and later develops into the fetus's nervous system and brain. Trophoblasts and other cells increase in number to form the *placenta, umbilical cord,* and *amniotic sac* (Figure 12.4).

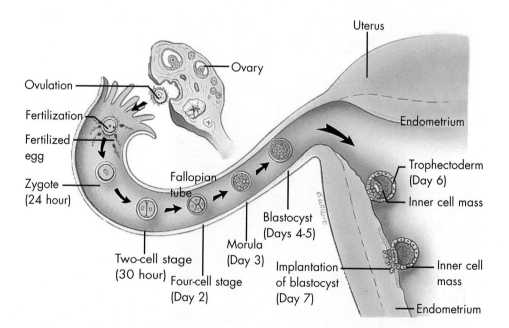

FIGURE 12.3 *Developmental stages of the early embryo. Source: C. E. Rischer & T. A. Easton (1992), Focus on human biology (New York: HarperCollins). Reprinted by permission.*

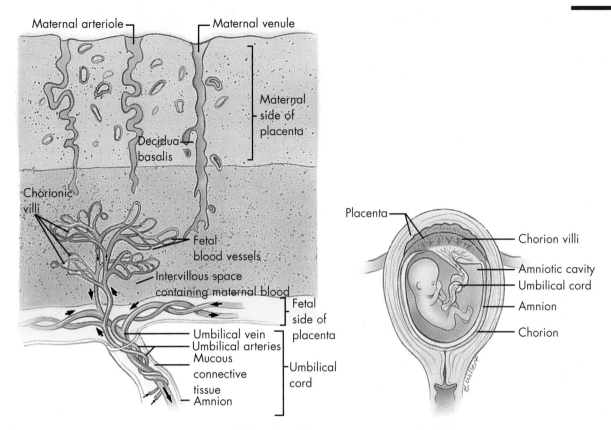

FIGURE 12.4 *The placenta, amniotic sac, umbilical cord, and fetus. Source: C. E. Rischer & T. A. Easton (1992),* Focus on human biology *(New York: HarperCollins). Reprinted by permission.*

The **placenta** (or *afterbirth*) is the structure that passes nourishment, oxygen, and infection-fighting antibodies from the mother's blood to the developing fetus. Waste products are returned to the mother in reverse fashion. The placenta originally surrounds the fetus but eventually moves to its side.

The placenta also secretes the hormone *human chorionic gonadotropin* (HCG). Human chorionic gonadotropin, which stops menstrual periods by maintaining the corpus luteum during the early stages of pregnancy, is present in a woman's urine and blood soon after implantation. The presence or absence of HCG is the basis of most common pregnancy tests: If HCG is present, the test is positive and the woman is pregnant. One type of laboratory blood test, *beta subunit HCG radioimmunoassay,* is about 99 percent accurate when performed as early as five days prior to the woman's next expected period. Home-based HCG pregnancy tests can also be accurate when performed several days after a missed period. However, these tests are more likely than laboratory tests to give *false negative* results, leading the woman to believe she is not pregnant when in fact she is—nearly 25 to 40 percent of the time (Lee & Hart, 1990). The woman may want to repeat the home test later to minimize the chances of false negative results. Pregnancy should always be confirmed by a health-care practitioner.

The **umbilical cord** forms during the fifth week of embryonic development. Its purpose is to carry blood to and from the fetus via two arteries and one vein. The fetal blood circulates through the *chorionic villi,* small projections in the placenta, around which the mother's blood circulates. Even though the mother's and infant's circulatory systems are completely separate, various substances are able to cross the membrane of the chorionic villi, including oxygen, nutrients, carbon dioxide, waste products, certain viruses, and numerous drugs.

PLACENTA (PLA-SEN-TA)

Structure through which nutrients and waste are exchanged between mother and fetus.

UMBILICAL CORD (UM-BIL-I-KAL)

Structure that connects the fetus and its placenta.

The placenta secretes increasing amounts of the hormones estrogen and progesterone. Many of the physical changes experienced during pregnancy are traceable to the actions of these hormones. Estrogen and progesterone prevent ovulation and menstruation, stimulate development of the uterine lining and mammary glands in the breasts, stimulate enlargement of the reproductive organs and relaxation of associated ligaments, and inhibit contractions of the uterus. The placenta also secretes another hormone, *placental lactogen*, which promotes breast development during pregnancy and readies the mammary glands to secrete milk.

The **chorion** and **amnion** are two membranes that surround the developing embryo, the chorion being the outermost. The fetus floats in **amniotic fluid,** a waterlike liquid that fills the **amniochorionic membrane** (or **amniotic sac**), formed from fusion of the amnion with portions of the chorion. Amniotic fluid provides a constant temperature for the developing fetus, as well as cushioning it against shock and injury.

During and after implantation, many women notice some early signs of pregnancy: a light or missed menstrual period, nausea and vomiting, breast and nipple sensitivity, vaginal discharge, urinary frequency, fatigue, rise in basal body temperature, changes in skin color and texture, and minor weight gain. A pregnant woman does not usually experience all of these signs and changes.

CHORION (KO-RE-ON)
Outer membrane surrounding the fetus.

AMNION (AM-NE-ON)
Inner membrane surrounding the fetus.

AMNIOTIC FLUID
Fluid surrounding the fetus.

AMNIOCHORIONIC MEMBRANE OR AMNIOTIC SAC (AM-NE-O-KO-RE-ON-IK)
Fluid-filled sac containing the fetus.

On a Personal Note (Kim, age 26)

My husband Lino and I had been trying to conceive for about five months. I was beginning to think something was wrong. But then I started noticing that I was getting really tired all the time, gaining weight, and getting sick to my stomach almost every morning. I also missed my period. So I bought a couple of home pregnancy tests, just for the heck of it. And guess what? Well, as you might expect, Lino and I are very excited. (Author's files)

If a woman suspects she is pregnant, she should have a pregnancy test as soon as possible. As mentioned earlier, pregnancy is often verified by tests based on the presence of HCG in the woman's urine. Physical examination may also prove useful. *Ballottement,* typically performed between weeks 16 and 20, is a type of pelvic *bimanual examination* that allows a physician or other health-care practitioner to feel for a fetus floating in the uterus. The practitioner may also note a *uterine souffle,* or rushing sound, by listening to the fetus with a stethoscope positioned on the mother's abdomen. In time he or she will listen for a fetal heartbeat (usually evident by weeks 17 to 18) and palpate the mother's abdomen for fetal movement (usually evident by weeks 20 to 24). The fetus's first movement is often referred to as *quickening.* Additional procedures to confirm pregnancy include *ultrasonography* (described later in this chapter) and X-rays, although today's health-care professionals are less apt to use the latter because of the risks of radiation to fetus and mother.

THE FIRST TRIMESTER

During the first 12 weeks of pregnancy, the fetus's major body structures and systems have begun to form. Three layers of cells differentiate to become its various body organs. The *endoderm* forms the glandular, respiratory, and digestive systems; the *mesoderm*, the skeleton, muscles, connective tissues, and reproductive and circulatory systems; and the *ectoderm*, the nervous system, sensory organs, and skin. Fetal development normally occurs in *cephalocaudal* order, beginning with the head and ending with the lower body.

By week 7, the already formed respiratory and digestive organs (lungs, kidneys, liver, pancreas, and intestines) begin limited functioning. Even though the fetus's gender is not clearly visible at this point, the gonads have already begun to develop.

By week 8, the fetus weighs 1/30 of an ounce and is 1¼ inches in length. At this time outlines of the fetus's facial features (lips, tongue, eyes, ears, and nose) are visible. Its head is proportionately larger than the rest of its body due to rapid development of the brain. Arms, hands, legs, feet, and toes are readily apparent by the tenth week. And within another two weeks, the fetus weighs approximately 1 ounce, is 3 to 4 inches in length, and has discernible sex organs.

Most of the mother's physical and emotional experiences during the first trimester are the result of hormonal changes. High levels of estrogen cause stomach irritation, including nausea and vomiting. High levels of progesterone produce drowsiness and fatigue, relax the rectal muscles, and prompt irregular bowel movements and constipation. These hormones also alter the body's water balance, so water retention and swelling are likely. Other physical changes during this trimester include increased breast sensitivity, increased vaginal discharge and a frequent need to urinate and defecate as the uterus expands and presses against the bladder and rectum. As one friend explained:

On a Personal Note (Toni, age 23)

I've been really amazed at how many unusual changes I've noticed since discovering I'm pregnant. The worst is swelling in my feet. I'm usually on my feet quite a bit during the day, but now my shoes feel so tight sometimes that I have to walk around the house bare-foot. I also need to go to the bathroom about every hour, especially at night—not terribly convenient when you're trying to get some sleep. (Author's files)

By weeks 10 to 12, the fetus looks like a miniature human.

All of the physical experiences mentioned above can affect the mother's emotional state during the first trimester. For example, uncomfortable physical experiences, like *morning sickness*, and fear of having a miscarriage may cause the woman to become anxious and/or depressed.

THE SECOND TRIMESTER

The second trimester of pregnancy begins about week 13. By weeks 18 and 20, the mother can usually feel the movements of the 6-inch-long fetus. Between weeks 20 and 25, the fetus may weigh as much as 2 pounds. At this time the eyes are developed enough to open. The fetus also becomes sensitive to light and sounds in the uterus. It sleeps, wakes, and moves its limbs.

A pregnant woman may feel at her emotional best during this trimester, particularly as a number of the discomforts characteristic of the first trimester slowly disappear. Also, feeling the fetus move within her body helps lessen her concerns about possible complications, such as a miscarriage. Some of the discomforts of the first trimester may remain (for example, hemorrhoids, constipation, swollen breasts), others may increase (water retention, leading to swelling of the feet, hands, and face), and new ones may arise (the prescence of *colostrum*, a clear to yellowish fluid that leaks from the nipples). Discomforts aside, many women experience a sense of optimism and good cheer at this time in their pregnancy.

THE THIRD TRIMESTER

The last trimester begins about week 25. As a layer of fat develops beneath its skin, the fetus begins to take on a babylike appearance. It also turns and assumes a head-down position, or *presentation*, in the uterus as it prepares to enter the vagina, or birth canal. Otherwise, a *breech presentation* occurs, in which the baby assumes a hips-first or feet-first position (Figure 12.5).

By the eighth month, the fetus weighs around 5 pounds and begins gaining $1/2$ pound each week. Its wrinkles begin to disappear, and its skin becomes less reddish in color. A waxy material known as *vernix caseosa* forms over the fetus's skin to protect it during delivery.

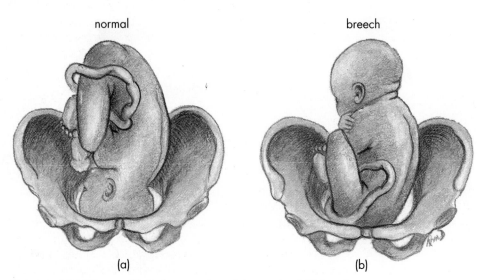

normal   breech

(a)   (b)

FIGURE 12.5 *Two possible fetal presentations: (a) normal and (b) breech.*

During this last trimester, a number of discomforts arise for the mother-to-be. The uterus continues to enlarge and toughen, and it presses even harder against the woman's internal organs. This internal pressure can cause back pain, shortness of breath, stomach problems, fatigue, and urinary urgency. The woman may also experience a number of non-labor, painless *Braxton-Hicks contractions* (sometimes called "false labor contractions"), which are thought to strengthen the uterine muscles in preparation for "real" labor.

Anxiety and depression concerning impending labor, delivery, possible complications, and motherhood are commonly associated with the third trimester. The woman may also become irritable and impatient, especially as she approaches or even passes her expected date of delivery.

PRENATAL CARE

It is never too early for a woman to be concerned about prenatal care. Besides wanting to bring a healthy child into the world, she should be concerned about her own well-being. Maintaining and improving her physical and emotional health through moderate exercise and a wholesome diet, identifying developing problems through regular contact with a health-care practitioner, and making informed choices about her delivery attendant(s) and setting are all important aspects of effective prenatal care (Shapiro, 1993).

EXERCISE DURING PREGNANCY

A health-care practitioner can design a specific prenatal exercise plan for the pregnant woman, given her needs and physical condition. Most authorities recommend an exercise program that incorporates brisk walking, and caution against activities that involve jerky movements, jumping, or switching directions suddenly. The woman who has not been exercising regularly prior to pregnancy must be careful about beginning an intense exercise program during pregnancy (Gillespie, 1992). The already active woman will want to make some changes in her exercise program. According to the American College of Obstetricians and Gynecologists, regular exercise three times a week is the best. The pregnant woman should keep strenuous activities to 15 minutes or less, and her heart rate should not exceed 140 beats per minute. The pregnant women should also be careful to exercise in areas where temperatures are cooler, reducing the risk of neural damage to the

Walking is the exercise of choice for pregnant women.

fetus as a result of increased maternal body temperature. In addition, the pregnant woman should drink plenty of fluids during her workouts. She should immediately stop exercising and contact her health-care practitioner if she experiences unusual symptoms like pain, fatigue, bleeding, shortness of breath, nausea, dizziness, or contractions. Of course, the pregnant woman should first consult with her health-care practitioner before beginning or continuing any exercise program, as exercise during pregnancy is absolutely not recommended for such conditions as cardiac disease and a history of three or more miscarriages (Gillespie, 1992).

NUTRITION DURING PREGNANCY

The fetus depends on its mother for adequate nutrition. A good diet, with plenty of protein, minerals, and vitamins is necessary for normal fetal growth (Gillespie, 1992). Many health-care practitioners suggest supplementing even a good diet with vitamin/mineral tablets, especially those rich in *folic acid* (a type of B vitamin necessary for healthy fetal development). The pregnant woman should consume from 2,300 to 2,500 calories daily. She will want her diet to consist of 50 percent carbohydrates, 25 percent protein, and 25 percent fat (Gillespie, 1992). She will also want to drink plenty of fluids, limit foods containing excessive amounts of animal fats (butter and cheese), and restrict her intake of salt. The mother with poor eating habits is at risk of suffering from anemia, fatigue, muscle pain, and insomnia. Her inadequate diet increases the chances that her child will develop abnormalities, be born below normal weight, or die in infancy (Shapiro, 1993). Women can expect to gain 25–30 pounds during pregnancy, of which up to 5 pounds can be due to breast enlargement.

TABLE 12.1 **Known and Suspected Teratogens and Clastogens**

	Prescription Drugs	Over-the-Counter Drugs	Under-the-Counter Drugs
Teratogens	Thalidomide (a sedative, not available now in the United States) Dilantin (a cerebral relaxant) Warfarin (an anticoagulant) Folic acid antagonist (generally present in anticancer drugs) Androgens and progesterone (hormones) Diethylstilbestrol (DES, a hormone) Mercury (present in some medications) Accutane (used to treat acne)	Ethyl alcohol	
Suspected teratogens	Lithium (a psychiatric drug) Benzodiazepines (tranquilizers) Certain oral contraceptives Amphetamines (stimulants, often taken for weight control) Cortisone (an antiinflammatory) Certain antihistamines	None	
Clastogens	Propranolol (an antihypertensive drug) Thiazides (diuretic drugs) Chloramphenicol (an antibiotic) Tetracyclines (antibiotics) Meprobamate (a tranquilizer) Reserpine (an antihypertensive) Erythromycin (an antibiotic) Streptomycin (an antibiotic)	Aspirin Tobacco Caffeine Certain antihistamines Vitamins A, D, and K in excess	Every one of them, from acid to grass
Common Medications That Are Probably Safe	Penicillin and certain derivatives Mild narcotics, such as codeine taken *occasionally* for pain	Acetominophen	

Source: Gillespie, C. (1992). *Your pregnancy month by month,* 4th ed. New York: HarperPerennial. Copyright © 1978, 1982, 1985, 1992 by Clark Gillespie, M.D. Reprinted by permission of HarperCollins Publishers, Inc.

DRUG USE DURING PREGNANCY

Many drugs and chemicals pass with relative ease from mother to fetus. A **teratogen** is a substance or drug that can cause fetal deformities when ingested by the expectant mother. A **clastogen** is a substance or drug that can damage the fetus, although without necessarily causing visible deformities (Gillespie, 1992). A list of known and suspected teratogens and clastogens appears in Table 12.1.

Even seemingly harmless drugs like caffeine and antihistamines might damage the fetus when taken in sufficient dosages (Shapiro, 1993). Furthermore, what constitutes a normal dosage of any drug for the mother may in fact be a fatal overdose for the fetus. The bot-

TERATOGEN (TER-A-TO-JEN)
Causing defects and deformities.

CLASTOGEN (KLAS-TO-JEN)
Causing damage and impairment.

tom line here is: *If you're pregnant, don't take any drugs (prescription or otherwise) unless specifically told to do so by your health-care practitioner.* Even then, seek a second or third opinion if you have any questions or concerns about the drugs you're taking, or planning to take, while pregnant.

Over-the-Counter and Prescription Drugs A variety of birth defects and deformities (deafness, absence of one or more limbs, mental retardation) are traceable to drug use during pregnancy. A woman should always seek the advice of her health-care practitioner before using drugs or medications during pregnancy. This means she should avoid common over-the-counter medications (cold preparations and aspirin) and prescription medications (antibiotics, steroids, nonsteroid estrogen, oral contraceptives, and opiates), unless directed to take these by her physician.

Alcohol Infants with *fetal alcohol syndrome* (FAS)—the result of the woman's drinking alcohol during pregnancy—have facial defects (slanted eyes, upturned nose, and a thin and flat upper lip), heart defects, and limb deformities. Many FAS infants also suffer from borderline mental retardation. Consuming as little as 2 ounces of alcohol per day during the first three months can be sufficient to cause FAS (Astley et al., 1992). To avoid having a child with FAS, the woman should completely avoid alcohol before (especially during the months when she is not using reliable contraception) and throughout her pregnancy (Brehm, 1993). No safe levels of alcohol use during pregnancy have been established.

Cigarettes Authorities acknowledge the many dangers associated with smoking cigarettes while pregnant. Smoking contributes to vitamin deficiencies, reduced placental blood flow, and oxygen deprivation of the fetus. Some of the poisonous carbon monoxide inhaled by the mother can pass to the fetus. Women who smoke during pregnancy increase their risks of miscarriage or delivering a premature, low-birth-weight baby (Shapiro, 1993).

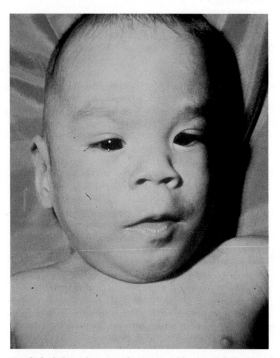

Fetal alcohol syndrome is characterized by facial defects, and in some cases heart defects, limb deformities, and mental retardation.

Illegal Drugs   The pregnant woman must avoid all illegal drugs. It is not yet proven that marijuana, which contains *tetrahydrocannabinol* (THC), affects the fetus. However, THC passes through the placenta, and there are signs of neurological deficits (for example, visual problems) and drug withdrawal (tremors) in newborns exposed to THC in the uterus (Shapiro, 1993).

Cocaine, including "crack," is becoming an increasingly popular recreational drug. Research has shown that pregnant cocaine users increase their risks of having stillbirths, low-birth-weight babies, and/or babies with congenital anomalies (Christmas, 1992). "Crack babies" are those infants born addicted to crack as a result of the mother's use during pregnancy.

Heroin is one of the most frequently abused opiates, or narcotics. Although heroin is illegal, the majority of the opiates (codeine, morphine, dilaudid, and methadone) are legal when prescribed for medical purposes. Opiates pass through the placental barrier, causing fetal drug withdrawal, respiratory problems, and possible brain damage (Shapiro, 1993).

For Personal Reflection

What would you do if you discovered that your pregnant neighbor was eating a lot of "junk food," drinking alcohol, and smoking? How might you inform her of the dangers of these practices during pregnancy? If she in turn became hostile and told you to mind your own business, how would you respond?

SEXUAL ACTIVITY DURING AND FOLLOWING PREGNANCY

Unless a woman is at risk of unusual complications during pregnancy, a couple need not avoid sexual activity at this time. Many women choose to continue having sexual intercourse until the third trimester, and in some cases until the onset of labor. Two common

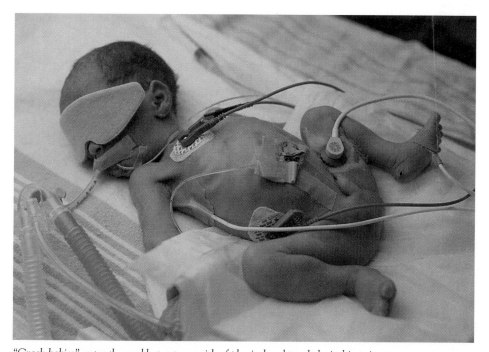

"Crack babies" enter the world at extreme risk of physical and psychological impairment.

concerns about sexual activity during pregnancy have no basis in fact. Orgasmic contractions do not induce labor, and sexual intercourse does not infect or harm the fetus (Colino, 1991; Shapiro, 1993).

A couple's perceptions and feelings about changes in the woman's appearance during pregnancy may inhibit their interest in sexual activity. Honest communication is especially important during pregnancy to maintain closeness and the quality of the couple's relationship. The pregnant woman may also find changes in her size and shape to be somewhat of a challenge during sexual intercourse. For example, she and her partner may need to try different intercourse positions for the sake of ease and comfort. During the middle and late stages of pregnancy, the woman may find the man-on-top position to be uncomfortable. In this case, the couple could try a rear-entry, side-to-side position (Figure 12.6) or a woman-on-top position to avoid pressure on her abdomen, or they could engage in noncoital sexplay and activity. The woman should first check with her health-care practitioner to see if there are any specific reasons to avoid sexual activity during her pregnancy.

What of sex *after* pregnancy and birth? The woman's health-care practitioner is likely to recommend that the couple postpone sexual intercourse for at least one month following delivery to allow tears, vaginal damage, and caesarean and episiotomy incisions to heal. Perhaps most importantly, rather than setting a number of weeks to abstain from intercourse, the couple should gauge when to resume sex based on the woman's physical and psychological readiness. Of course, finding *time* for sexual activity while trying to take care of a newborn is another matter.

BIRTHING ALTERNATIVES

The pregnant woman has several choices when it comes to health care during her pregnancy and delivery. It is never too early for her to begin looking for a practitioner and delivery setting, as well as to begin thinking about whether she wants to attempt a medication-free delivery.

Physician or Midwife? All physicians in the United States receive medical school training in pregnancy and delivery. A specialist in this area is an *obstetrician*. A *gynecologist*, or specialist in female reproductive medicine, is another primary provider of pregnancy care, as is a family practice physician. Some physicians maintain birthing centers (described below); however, most perform hospital deliveries.

FIGURE 12.6 *During pregnancy a couple may try a rear-entry, side-to-side position for sexual intercourse.*

PERSPECTIVE

Sex During Pregnancy

Many people assume that couples automatically lose interest in sexual activity as soon as the woman becomes pregnant. This is not necessarily the case, according to Elisabeth Bing (1988), who holds that pregnancy can be a time of great sexual pleasure:

It is important to bear in mind that the shape of ideal women has changed over the centuries. Fifteen thousand years ago, the voluptuous Venus of Willendorf was viewed as the essence of beauty. The sculpture we have of her portrays a very big woman with enormous breasts. On the other hand, the Venus de Milo represents the ideal image of the ancient Greeks. As all such ideals are relative, it is particularly important that women today not be obsessed by a media version of what they should look like. Indeed, many men find that their wife's new shape excites them and makes them feel protective and loving. Most husbands find the pregnant woman's added roundness and her larger breasts very attractive....

Frequently, pregnant women have an unusually strong desire for sex, especially during the last three months. Many report that they first experienced orgasm at that time. The explanation is that the added blood supply to the pelvic area (indeed to all the body during pregnancy) can make the genitals especially sensitive and enhance the desire for satisfaction compared to the nonpregnant state. The extra blood supply is also why many women discover the resolution period after orgasm lasts longer than usual. Some women may find that masturbation eases some of these strong desires, while for others frequent masturbation does not seem to relieve the tension. Some women may feel reluctant to masturbate because of the age-old belief that masturbation causes madness or is generally undesirable or because masturbation is considered a poor substitute for sexual gratification. Consequently, pregnancy is a good time for couples to learn cuddling, pleasuring, talking to each other, and finding new and comfortable positions for coitus that accommodate the woman's changing shape. (pp. 38–40)

Questions for Thought

How inclined would you be to have sexual intercourse while you or your partner were pregnant? What are some of the factors that might influence your decision?

Source: E. Bing (1988), Yes, yes you can, *Childbirth '88, 5,* 36–38, 40.

Certified nurse midwives (CNMs), who also undergo extensive medical training, are becoming increasingly popular as birth attendants. Their primary goal is to assure that childbirth is a natural process leading to a safe and satisfying birth (Toussie-Weingarten & Jacobwitz, 1987). Certified nurse midwives, who are state licensed to practice, are affiliated with a physician. Whether they deliver in a hospital, birthing center, or home, CNMs should not be confused with the lay midwives who often practice in poor or rural communities. Lay midwives usually lack extensive nursing/medical training and may or may not be affiliated with a physician.

Hospital or Home Birth? Many women prefer to deliver in a hospital, given the ready availability of physicians, nurses, trained technicians, pain medications, and emergency equipment. Most hospitals provide separate delivery and recovery rooms. In addition, many now offer special "birthing rooms," often staffed by CNMs and nurses, for low-risk patients desiring a more homelike atmosphere for delivery.

A home birth usually involves having a midwife (or less commonly a physician) perform delivery in a couple's home, with or without various family members present. Home birthing reportedly encourages a more natural and relaxed delivery, but is recommended only for very healthy women who do not expect complications. Because of the potential for unexpected problems, birthing near a hospital emergency room is wise.

Birthing Centers Birthing centers provide a warm, homelike birth experience through a state-licensed facility, typically staffed by CNMs. These centers, most of which are located near a hospital, offer a variety of benefits, including predelivery education, family involvement during delivery, readily available emergency equipment, and continued care after delivery. Birthing centers are now being built as hospital extensions in some areas.

ANALGESIC (AN-AL-JE-ZIK)
Pain-relieving drug.

**ANESTHETIC
(AN-AS-THE-TIK)**
Sensation-deadening drug.

Anesthesia Besides choosing a practitioner and a birthing site, the pregnant woman must also decide whether she wants to take medications during delivery. Pain relief during delivery is often through use of **analgesics,** or pain killers, and **anesthetics,** or sensation-blocking agents that deaden certain areas of the body. A *pudendal block* deadens the genital area; an *epidural block* deadens the lower abdomen, pelvis, genitals, and legs. These blocking agents decrease a woman's ability to help push the fetus through the birth canal during delivery. These drugs can have a number of side effects, including a sudden drop in blood pressure, headaches, vomiting, nausea, and back pain. Some women also ask for tranquilizers and/or narcotics to relieve their pain during childbirth. In some instances, these drugs can inhibit the functioning of the fetus's nervous system.

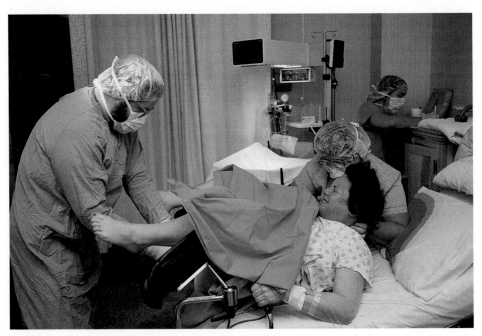

Birthing centers offer a warm, homelike environment for labor and delivery, including family involvement and support.

One of the most popular "prepared childbirth" courses for couples is the Lamaze method.

Prepared Childbirth Many couples choose to prepare for childbirth (including pain control) through education/training classes. Today, many hospitals offer prepared birthing classes, some even free of charge for those who could not otherwise afford them. One of the most popular "prepared childbirth" courses for couples is the *Lamaze method,* developed by Fernand Lamaze in the 1950s. The couple attends weekly Lamaze classes for six to eight weeks. The classes consist of relaxation and controlled breathing training, and education regarding what to expect during labor and birth. The pregnant woman's part- ner also participates in the labor process, serving as a labor coach. He or she assists by helping the woman regulate her breathing, keeping track of contractions, and offering emotional support. A woman who chooses the Lamaze method can still opt for medica- tion if she feels the pain is too uncomfortable.

Two other popular childbirth programs are the *Bradley* and *Leboyer* methods. Developed by Robert Bradley in the 1960s, the *Bradley method* provides education, relax- ation training, and abdominal breathing training—all starting as soon as the woman's pregnancy is confirmed. The program also emphasizes active involvement of the partner during delivery. For example, the "partner-coach" offers words of encouragement to the woman during labor.

Introduced by Frederick Leboyer in the 1970s, the *Leboyer method* emphasizes the importance of an infant entering the world in the least traumatic manner possible. Birth occurs in warm water, accompanied by dim lights and quiet. The method also encourages immediate contact between mother and infant following delivery to facilitate bonding.

The decision to have a medication-free delivery rests with each woman (or couple) as views on the matter vary considerably throughout professional and lay circles. Even though some women desire a completely prepared childbirth, many also recognize their need for pain medication.

THE STAGES OF CHILDBIRTH

Childbirth, or **parturition,** begins with **labor**—contractions of the uterine muscles and opening of the cervix—and concludes with **delivery**—expelling the child and placenta from the vagina (Figure 12.7). Early signs of labor include blood-tainted vaginal discharge as the cervical mucus plug is discharged, the rupturing of the amniotic sac ("broken water"), and short, mild contractions.

**PARTURITION
(PAR-TOO-RISH-UN)**
Another term for childbirth.

LABOR
Contractions of the uterine muscles and opening of the cervix.

DELIVERY
Expulsion of the fetus and placenta from the vagina.

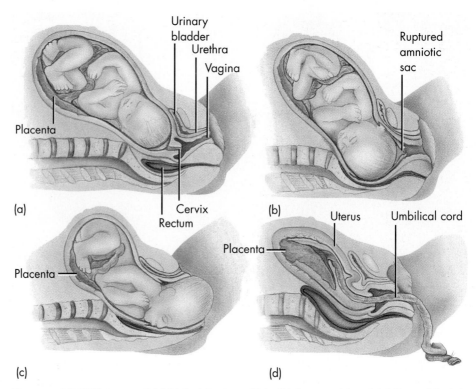

FIGURE 12.7 *The stages of childbirth: (a) prior to birth, (b) first stage labor, (c) delivery of the baby, and (d) delivery of the placenta.*

THE FIRST STAGE OF CHILDBIRTH

The first stage of parturition, or *labor* ("work"), can last anywhere from 2 to more than 24 hours, the duration commonly relating to the number of previous deliveries. In many cases, labor is longer for a first pregnancy (about 12 hours) than for subsequent pregnancies (about 6 to 8 hours) (Gillespie, 1992). Contractions begin to occur regularly and the cervix continues to *dilate*, or open up. Labor further divides into three phases of varying duration: *early*, *middle*, and *late*. During the early phase, there are mild, minute-long contractions every 15 minutes or so. During the middle phase, contractions become stronger and more frequent, and dilation increases. During the late phase, the woman is restless, contractions become very strong, and complete dilation of about 10 centimeters (or 4 inches) occurs.

THE SECOND STAGE OF CHILDBIRTH

As contractions begin to move the fetus through the vagina, the woman is encouraged to bear down, actively push, and help expel the baby. At this point the cervix should be completely dilated. *Crowning* occurs when the baby's head is visible at the vaginal orifice. In some cases, a baby presents with its hips or feet first ("breech presentation"). The attendant may use *forceps* (a grasping instrument similar to tongs) to manually turn a breech baby into a head-first position before its descent into the birth canal (Gillespie, 1992).

Once crowning begins, the woman may undergo an **episiotomy,** a procedure that involves making an incision in the perineum to allow as much space as possible for the baby's delivery (Figure 12.8). Following delivery the attendant repairs the episiotomy with sutures that dissolve and do not need to be removed at a later date. Although some "naturalists" oppose the procedure, advocates believe an episiotomy is better than the risk of

**Episiotomy
(E-PIZ-E-OT-O-ME)**

Incision made in the perineum to prevent tearing during delivery.

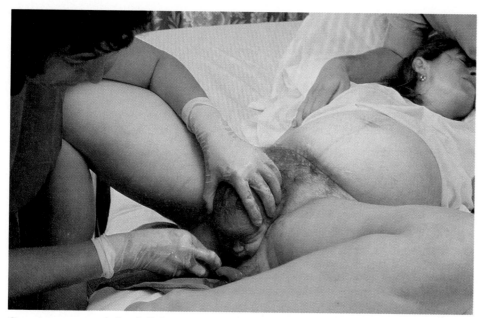

Crowning occurs just before the baby moves out of the birth canal.

perineal tearing during birth (Gillespie, 1992). There will be pain at the incision site once the anesthetic wears off, but it is easier to repair an episiotomy than a random tear.

Upon delivery the attendant suctions the infant's mouth and nose so it can receive oxygen into its lungs, and clamps and severs the umbilical cord. The attendant may then gently pat the baby on the buttocks to initiate a breathing response. Finally, he or she administers drops of silver nitrate to the newborn's eyes to prevent possible infection passed on by the mother during birth.

The physician performs a **caesarean section** (or **C-section**) when normal delivery of the child through the birth canal is inadvisable or impossible. During this procedure an incision is made in the woman's lower abdomen, the uterus is surgically opened, and the baby is removed. Reasons for caesarean delivery include extremely difficult labor, breech presentation, disease (herpes), fetal distress, and/or prior caesarean delivery. (A woman can have a vaginal delivery after a C-section, however). The procedure has saved the lives

CAESAREAN SECTION OR C-SECTION (SE-SAR-E-AN)
Procedure in which an infant is delivered through an incision in the mother's abdomen.

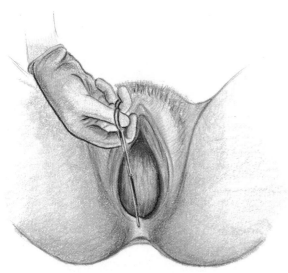

FIGURE 12.8 *Episiotomy.*

of countless infants and mothers, yet the professional community now challenges the routine use of caesareans (Public Citizens Health Research Group, 1992). Furthermore, some authorities have noted an unacceptable increase in the number of C-sections performed today compared to 15 years ago, or compared to other industrialized countries with much lower infant mortality rates (Brody, 1989b). About 25 percent of births today in the United States are C-sections (Taffel et al., 1992).

The birth attendant may choose to evaluate the newborn's physical health (immediately following birth, and again five minutes later) using the *Apgar Scale*. Developed by Virginia Apgar in 1952, this system is an empirical means of identifying neonatal problems and defects. Scores on five criteria—heart rate, respiratory effort, muscle tone, reflex irritability, and color—are summed. While a perfect score is rare, a low score suggests serious trouble.

THE THIRD STAGE OF CHILDBIRTH

During this short, final stage of labor, the placenta separates from the uterine wall and is expelled from the vagina (often with the help of the woman pushing). If the placenta is not intact and pieces of it remain in the uterus, infection and bleeding may occur. That is why the attendant makes sure all of the placenta is removed. It is during this stage that the attendant repairs the episiotomy.

THE POSTPARTUM STAGE OF CHILDBIRTH

POSTPARTUM (POST-PAR-TUM)
After childbirth.

The woman's hormone levels change dramatically during the **postpartum** ("afterbirth") stage of parturition; in particular, the higher-than-normal levels of progesterone and estrogen suddenly decrease. These hormonal changes may be responsible, at least in part, for some women's *postpartum depression*, or "baby blues." Postpartum depression, which is more common for first-time mothers, can last from a few days to months, and ranges in intensity from mild (sad and tearful) to severe (suicidal, requiring professional treatment). In addition to hormones, general letdown and exhaustion from labor probably play a part in the development of milder cases of postpartum blues (Harding, 1989). Women may have other related physical and emotional problems following pregnancy, such as fear of pregnancy and anxiety about resuming sexual activity.

On a Personal Note (Sissy, age 31)

I couldn't believe how depressed I got after the baby arrived. I mean, you're supposed to be elated, right? Lots of hoopla, gifts, cards, visits from friends and family. Well, I cried for about two weeks. The whole thing seemed so anticlimactic. (Author's files)

Interestingly, some *men* seem to suffer from postpartum depression, too (Zaslow et al., 1985). As with women, lack of sleep, generally feeling "let down," being "off schedule," having less time with the partner, and not getting enough sexual attention may play a role in postpartum depression in men.

BREAST-FEEDING

Although not a stage of childbirth *per se*, breast-feeding is for many women an important and desirable postpartum activity. Experts generally agree that breast milk is the most well-balanced source of nutrients for an infant (Stehlin, 1990). Moreover, *colostrum*, a

Experts generally agree that breast milk is the most well-balanced source of nutrients for an infant.

milklike fluid secreted during the first few days of breast feeding, is rich in infection-fighting antibodies. And practically speaking, breast-feeding is inexpensive and readily available. Most cities have local chapters of the *La Leche League*, an organization offering education and support for breast-feeding mothers.

Physical contact between mother and infant during breast-feeding also appears to have important psychological consequences for the infant and perhaps for the mother, as well. Early contact provides a good emotional start for the baby, the closeness between mother and child setting a pattern for later relationships. Many mothers also report sensual arousal when breast-feeding.

What about an infant born to a mother who decides to formula-feed? Will an infant "deprived" of breast-feeding necessarily grow up psychologically impaired? No evidence supports such a notion. The *quality of the relationship* between parents and infant makes the difference, not the *source of nourishment*. Many fathers also share in the responsibilities of formula feeding.

On a Personal Note (Tracy, age 20)

I never really thought anything about it. As far as I know, the women in my family have always breast-fed. I always planned to. I know some women don't like the idea, and I can respect that. But, you know, I really enjoy it. I mean, it feels so good to be so close to my baby. I'm giving her nourishment from my body. And when we look at each other . . . well, I can't describe it. There's just a special connection between us when she nurses. (Author's files)

PERSPECTIVE

Childbearing and the Ashanti

Read what the authors of *African Systems of Kinship and Marriage*, first published in 1950, had to say about the Ashanti's views on motherhood and childbearing:

The Ashanti regard the bond between mother and child as the keystone of all social relations.... Prolific childbearing is honoured. A mother of ten boasts of her achievement and is given a public ceremony of congratulation. As intercourse between husband and wife is prohibited only during the seclusion and convalescent period of eighty days after delivery, children often follow rapidly after one another. By custom, still generally observed outside the big towns, birth must take place in the mother's natal home. This not only ensures that the woman is under the care of her own close maternal kin, in particular her mother, at this time, but it fixes, in a very tangible way, the lineage affiliation and citizenship of the child. This custom greatly strengthens the inclination of women to reside with their mothers or close maternal kin rather than with their husbands during the early years of marriage. Moreover, the care of a young child falls almost wholly on the mother; and as she generally has her own farm to cultivate or other income-earning work to do, it is a great advantage if she can leave her children in her mother's care during her daily absences. Maternal grandmothers (*nana*) play a great part in child-rearing. Indeed they can sometimes be very autocratic in this regard, arguing that a grandchild (*nana*) belongs more to the lineage (*abusua*) than to its parents and therefore comes most appropriately under its grandmother's care. (pp. 262–263)

Questions for Thought

What is your reaction to this feature? Are your values about childbearing and motherhood similar to or different from those of the Ashanti? In what ways?

Source: A. R. Radcliffe-Brown & D. Forde (1987), *African systems of kinship and marriage* (London: KPI Limited). (Original work published 1950)

COMPLICATIONS DURING PREGNANCY AND CHILDBIRTH

A number of serious problems and diseases can arise during pregnancy and childbirth. The most common are *Rh factor incompatibility*, *ectopic pregnancy*, *diabetes mellitus*, *rubella*, *cytomegaloviral infection*, *toxoplasmosis*, *preeclampsia and eclampsia*, *miscarriage*, *stillbirth*, and *prematurity*. A woman typically experiences any of a number of other problems during her pregnancy as well, including *morning sickness*, *chloasma*, and *hemorrhoids*.

RH FACTOR INCOMPATIBILITY

The *Rh factor* is a substance found in the blood of about 85 percent of the population. An individual with the factor is said to be Rh positive (Rh+); an individual without, Rh negative (Rh−).

Problems arise when two partners with different Rh factors conceive a child. Specifically, if an Rh- woman becomes pregnant by a Rh+ man, the child may inherit the Rh+ factor. If so, this poses a serious problem for the mother's *subsequent* pregnancies if

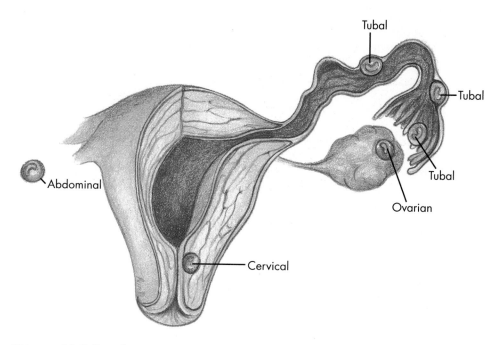

FIGURE 12.9 *Sites where an ectopic pregnancy is most likely to occur.*

her blood happens to become contaminated with the Rh+ factor during her first delivery. Antibodies form and attack the next fetus's red blood cells, leading the mother to develop jaundice or anemia, or to deliver a stillborn or developmentally disabled child.

One technique for dealing with Rh incompatibility involves transfusing Rh- blood to the fetus. After delivery the newborn replaces the transfused Rh- cells with its own Rh+ cells. Another technique involves giving the mother an injection of *RhoGAM*, an Rh-neutralizing substance, to prevent her body from producing antibodies in the first place.

ECTOPIC PREGNANCY

If the fertilized egg implants outside the uterus (in the ovary, cervix, fallopian tube, or abdomen), an **ectopic pregnancy** results (Figure 12.9). The most common type of ectopic pregnancy is a *tubal pregnancy*, in which the zygote attaches to the inside of a blocked or damaged fallopian tube after failing to move through it. Unless detected early and removed, the embryo will grow until the tube ruptures, causing hemorrhaging, excruciating pain, and death in some cases. The woman might mistake an ectopic pregnancy for a normal pregnancy, at least early on, because of similar hormonal changes and experiences like missed menstrual periods and morning sickness. An ectopic pregnancy might spontaneously abort; otherwise, it is surgically removed as soon as it is discovered. Most women are able to conceive and carry subsequent uterine pregnancies to term.

ECTOPIC PREGNANCY (EK-TO-PIK)

A pregnancy occurring outside of the uterus.

DIABETES MELLITUS

Diabetes mellitus, or insulin deficiency with elevated blood sugar, can seriously complicate pregnancy. The effects of diabetes on pregnancy can include miscarriage, stillbirth, prematurity, congenital defects, large infants, and hypertension (Gillespie, 1992). *Gestational diabetes* appears in pregnant women, sometimes for the duration of the pregnancy only, but other times as a precursor to diabetes mellitus. The symptoms, complications, and treatment of gestational diabetes are identical to those of clinical diabetes (Gillespie, 1992). Dietary modifications and daily injections of insulin restore normal blood sugar metabolism.

RUBELLA

Exposure to viral *rubella*, or *German measles*, during pregnancy poses extreme health risks for the developing fetus, especially during the first trimester. Congenital deficiencies associated with rubella include delayed prenatal development, chromosomal abnormalities, blindness, deafness, brain damage, and heart defects. Immunization during early childhood prevents rubella infection, and is usually sufficient to last a lifetime. Any woman who is contemplating pregnancy, but who has not had rubella or been vaccinated against it, should receive immunization prior to conception.

CYTOMEGALOVIRAL INFECTION

Cytomegalovirus primarily affects the fetus rather than the mother. It can be sexually transmitted to adults, and maternally transmitted to children. Adults infected with cytomegalovirus are frequently asymptomatic, while children born to infected mothers are at high risk of having deformities. The child picks up the virus either across the placenta or at birth, potentially leading to severe retardation, seizures, cerebral palsy, blindness, and/or deafness. At present there are no treatments or vaccines for cytomegaloviral infection.

TOXOPLASMOSIS

Toxoplasmosis is a condition arising from the parasite *Toxoplasma gondii*, which is often present in undercooked meat and animal feces. Cats are a major source of toxoplasmosis infections in humans. Infected adults typically evidence minimal symptoms, whereas an infected fetus may succumb to brain damage or death. *Sulfadiazine*, a type of sulfa drug, can be used safely to treat toxoplasmosis prior to the final two months of pregnancy (Gillespie, 1992).

PREECLAMPSIA AND ECLAMPSIA

Women with *preeclampsia*, or *toxemia*, experience high blood pressure, severe fluid retention, and swelling during pregnancy. Symptoms of this disease range from mild (swollen extremities) to severe (seizures and death). Severe toxemia is termed *eclampsia*. The exact causes of toxemia are unknown, although inadequate nutrition may play a part.

OTHER PROBLEMS

Pregnant women also experience a variety of other problems. One of the most common of these is *morning sickness*, a condition characterized by early morning nausea, fatigue, and dizziness. Most authorities believe morning sickness, which typically begins early in the pregnancy but ends by the second trimester, is related to hormonal changes. Eating crackers upon awakening and small meals scattered throughout the day is helpful in many cases.

Chloasma are dark patches on the skin during pregnancy (usually the face, areolas, and abdomen), probably caused by hormonal changes. They tend to disappear early in postpartum. *Stretch marks*, on the other hand, do not completely disappear, but often become lighter with time.

Pregnant women may also suffer from *hemorrhoids*, or stressed veins of the anus. Hemorrhoids often swell, itch, or bleed. Short of surgery, creams or sitz baths are the best treatments.

MISCARRIAGE AND STILLBIRTH

A **miscarriage** is a spontaneous abortion of a *nonviable fetus* (unable to live outside of the uterus) at less than 20 weeks gestation. A **stillbirth** is birth of a *dead fetus* after 20 weeks. Because a woman might mistake a miscarriage for a menstrual period before realizing she is pregnant, it is difficult to determine the number of miscarriages that occur each year. Nevertheless, estimates are that about 20 percent of all pregnancies end in a miscarriage, the majority of these occurring during the first trimester (Friedman & Gath, 1989; Salmon, 1991). Chromosomal abnormalities may be responsible for some miscarriages, as may advancing years. Women over age 35 tend to have a higher incidence of miscarriage.

MISCARRIAGE
Spontaneous abortion early in pregnancy, before viability.

STILLBIRTH
Spontaneous abortion later in pregnancy, after viability.

PREMATURITY

A **premature birth** differs from a miscarriage in that the fetus is born *viable* (able to live outside of the uterus). "Preemies," which account for about 7 to 10 percent of all births in the United States, weigh less than 5.5 pounds and are born at less than 36 weeks gestation. Although the causes of many premature births are unknown, some seem to be related to poor diet and alcohol or drug use during pregnancy, smoking, lack of prenatal care, and a history of premature births. As might be expected, the less the infant weighs, the less chance it has of surviving. Premature infants frequently suffer from hemorrhaging and difficulty breathing, sucking, and digesting. These problems are likely to disappear as the infant gains weight.

PREMATURE BIRTH
Birth at less than 36 weeks' gestation.

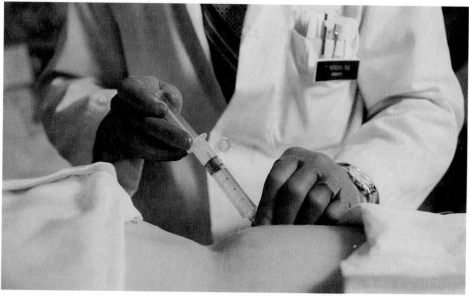

Amniocentesis.

TESTING FOR DISORDERS DURING PREGNANCY

A number of diagnostic procedures are available to test the fetus for potential disorders and defects. Three of the most commonly used are *ultrasonography*, *amniocentesis*, and *chorionic villi sampling*. Experts are divided on the routine use of these procedures, especially for low-risk pregnancies.

An *ultrasound examination*, or *sonogram*, involves taking a moving picture of the fetus. High-frequency sound waves bounce off the fetus, and then become visual images. Ultrasonography is particularly useful for diagnosing prenatal disorders, monitoring fetal heartbeat and development, identifying multiple pregnancies, and determining the sex of the fetus. At present there is no reliable evidence that ultrasounds cause fetal or maternal damage (Gillespie, 1992).

Amniocentesis tests for fetal infections and chromosomal abnormalities. The procedure involves the examination of fluid removed from the amniotic sac using a hollow needle. The physician locates the fetus using ultrasonography to avoid puncturing it with the needle. Amniocentesis is generally performed around week 15, which allows the parent(s) time to make an informed decision about carrying the fetus to full term should a severe abnormality be found. Test results are usually available within three to four weeks. The risk of miscarriage from amniocentesis is less than 1 percent (Gillespie, 1992).

Chorionic villi sampling effectively detects the same abnormalities as amniocentesis, but earlier in the woman's pregnancy, between weeks 9 and 14. The physician inserts a catheter into the uterus through the cervix. Within the placental covering are small *villi* (thin blood-containing extensions). He or she suctions out a small amount of fluid from these villi through the catheter. Test results are often available within a few days. The risk of miscarriage from chorionic villi sampling is about 1 percent (Gillespie, 1992).

INFERTILITY

INFERTILITY
Inability to conceive.

Not every couple wanting to conceive can do so. A couple is usually considered **infertile** if they fail to conceive after one year or more of trying. At any one time, up to 20 percent of couples in the United States may be infertile (Byer & Shainberg, 1991).

Infertility may be caused by male factors, female factors, or a combination of the two. According to Byer and Shainberg (1991), male infertility can result from having too few sperm mature in the testes due to scrotal exposure to high temperatures or postpuberty infectious disease, reduced sperm motility due to abnormal seminal fluids, failure to ejaculate semen into the vagina due to sexual dysfunction or blocked sperm ducts, and/or poor health or diet. Female infertility can result from failure to ovulate regularly, damaged reproductive organs, improperly formed reproductive organs, blocked fallopian tubes, cervical mucus of incorrect consistency or pH that does not permit sperm to enter the uterus, growth of uterine tissue in the pelvic cavity, severe weight gain or loss, and/or poor health or diet. Infertility can also result from combinations of male and female factors, such as reduced sperm motility in the male and irregular ovulation in the female.

According to these same authors, infertility is treatable in many cases. *Fertility drugs* (ovulation-stimulating hormones) are useful when infertility is due to the woman's inability to ovulate. *Artificial insemination* involves collecting and introducing sperm into the vagina using a syringe. This procedure is particularly useful when the man's sperm count is below normal. *In vitro fertilization*, or the "test-tube baby" method, involves fertilizing an egg outside the woman's body and implanting it into the uterus. This procedure is useful when the woman has blocked fallopian tubes. *Gamete intrafallopian transfer* ("GIFT") involves taking eggs from the woman's ovaries, mixing them with the man's sperm, and then inserting them into a fallopian tube. The idea here is for fertilization to take place inside the woman's body rather than outside. To date, over 20,000 babies have been born in the United States by alternatives such as these (Clift, 1993).

Some couples or individuals decide that the best way to deal with infertility is to adopt a child. Others elect to utilize the services of a *surrogate mother*, who contracts with a couple to carry their fetus to full term, deliver it, and adopt it to the couple—usually for a fee of at least $10,000 in addition to medical expenses. A physician may artificially inseminate the surrogate with the man's sperm or implant an *in vitro* fertilized egg into her uterus. Either way, the procedure is certainly controversial, given the many potential ethical, legal, and moral issues it raises.

Similar to surrogate motherhood is *carrier implantation*. The procedure involves implanting a fertilized egg into a relative's uterus. Because a relative carries the fetus to term, the woman or couple avoids the expense and hassle of hiring a surrogate mother. Physicians have now successfully implanted embryos into women in their 50s, following hormone therapy to reverse the effects of menopause (Dowling, 1993; Kolata, 1994).

For Personal Reflection

Wanting to have a baby but not being able to can be a desperate and painful experience.

1. *How would you react if you or your partner were infertile? What treatments would you be willing to try? Which ones would you not try? Why? If you or your partner were unable to conceive, would you consider adopting a child? Why or why not? Would you consider hiring a surrogate mother?*
2. *If you had a baby through "artificial" means, would you tell the child about it later? Why or why not?*

KEY POINTS

1. Having a healthy baby takes careful planning to assure that the woman's body is ready to provide an appropriate environment for *prenatal development*, or development of the fetus before birth. While not always practical, the best time to start planning for pregnancy is at least several months, even years, prior to conception.
2. To improve the chances of conceiving, intercourse should take place close to the time of *ovulation*, when one of the woman's ovaries releases an ovum. The ovum is generally fertilizable for only 12 to 24 hours following its release from the ovary. Some women determine their time of ovulation by keeping a *basal body temperature chart*.
3. A full-term *pregnancy* averages 266 days from conception to birth, or 280 days from the last menstrual period until birth. These 280 days divide into 10 four-week *lunar months* of 28 days each, or three trimesters of three months each.
4. During conception, the man's sperm unites with the woman's ovum, producing a *zygote*, or *conceptus*. Only one sperm *fertilizes* an ovum. The single-cell zygote then begins geometric division as it travels along the fallopian tube. Immediately following implantation and for the next eight weeks of gestation, the zygote is termed an *embryo*. Following this period and until birth, it is termed a *fetus*. After *implanting* into the *endometrium* of the uterus, the embryo continues cellular division.
5. Blood moves in and out of the fetus and its *placenta* via the *umbilical cord*. Even though the mother's and infant's circulatory systems are completely separate, various substances are able to cross the membrane of the *chorionic villi*. The placenta

secretes *estrogen*, *progesterone*, and *placental lactogen*. It also releases *human chorionic gonadotropin*. Detection of human chorionic gonadotropin in the woman's blood and urine is the basis of most common pregnancy tests.

6. The *chorion* and *amnion* are two membranes that surround the developing embryo, the chorion being the outermost. The fetus floats in *amniotic fluid*. This waterlike fluid fills the *amniochorionic membrane*.

7. Late in pregnancy the fetus usually turns and assumes a head-down *presentation* in the uterus as it prepares to enter the birth canal. A hips-first or feet-first positioning is termed a *breech presentation*.

8. Many couples and women choose to prepare for childbirth through education/training classes. The most popular "prepared childbirth" courses for couples are the *Lamaze*, *Bradley*, and *Leboyer* methods.

9. Childbirth, or *parturition*, begins with *labor* and concludes with *delivery*. As *crowning* occurs, the physician may perform an *episiotomy* to make more room for the infant as it emerges from the vagina. Prolonged and difficult labor, breech presentation, and disease often necessitate delivery by *caesarean section*. Following delivery of the baby, the placenta separates from the uterine wall and is expelled from the vagina.

10. Breast-feeding is for many women an important and desirable *postpartum* activity. Breast milk is a readily available, inexpensive, and a well-balanced source of infant nutrition. *Colostrum* is rich in infection-fighting antibodies.

11. A number of serious problems and diseases can arise during pregnancy and birth, including *Rh factor incompatibility*, *ectopic pregnancy*, *diabetes mellitus*, *rubella*, *cytomegaloviral infection*, *toxoplasmosis*, *preeclampsia and eclampsia*, *miscarriage*, *stillbirth*, and *prematurity*. Other problems include *morning sickness*, *chloasma*, and *hemorrhoids*.

12. *Ultrasonography*, *amniocentesis*, and *chorionic villi sampling* are three diagnostic tests available for detecting fetal disorders and defects.

13. A couple is usually considered *infertile* if they fail to conceive after one year or more of trying. Infertility may be caused by male factors, female factors, or a combination of the two. Treatments include use of *fertility drugs*, *artificial insemination*, *in vitro fertilization*, *gamete intrafallopian transfer*, *surrogate motherhood*, and *carrier implantation*.

ACTIVITIES AND QUESTIONS

1. As a class, divide into four groups, each with an equal number of men and women. Describe what you would include in a brochure for pregnant women seeking information about conception, pregnancy, childbirth, and breast-feeding.

2. Identify some of the many factors that go into making the decision to have a child. Under what circumstances should an individual or couple choose to conceive? Under what circumstances should they choose *not* to conceive?

3. How do malnutrition, smoking, and alcohol consumption during pregnancy negatively affect prenatal and child development? What can be done to educate society about the ill effects of these practices?

4. As a class, discuss the ethics of surrogate motherhood. What are possible advantages and disadvantages of this practice? Why do you think certan religious groups might be opposed to the use of surrogates? What should a couple do if their surrogate child is born deformed?

5. Contact a local hospital and ask about their typical fees for a delivery without complications. Contact a local birthing center and ask the same. Are there significant differences in cost? Do any of these facilities offer services for women with little or no money and no insurance? How might such differences affect your choice of a delivery setting? Should potential parents look into the costs of delivery prior to conception? Why or why not?

RECOMMENDED READINGS

Eisenberg, A., Murkoff, H. E., & Hathaway, S. E. (1991). *What to expect when you're expecting* (2nd ed.). New York: Workman. A practical and informative book on pregnancy.

Gillespie, C. (1992). *Your pregnancy month by month* (4th ed.). New York: HarperPerennial. A personal guide and diary to conception and pregnancy.

Nachtigall, R., & Mehren, E. (1991). *Overcoming infertility*. New York: Doubleday. A useful guide for "navigating the emotional, medical, and financial minefields of trying to have a baby."

Shapiro, H. I. (1993). *The pregnancy book for today's woman* (2nd ed.). New York: HarperPerennial. An excellent reference for expectant mothers and their partners.

Worth, C. (1988). *Birth of a father: New fathers talk about pregnancy, childbirth and the first three months*. New York: McGraw-Hill. Examines fathers' experiences, perceptions, and expectations concerning pregnancy and birth.

•**C**ONTRACEPTION

•ABORTION

C H A P T E R   1 3

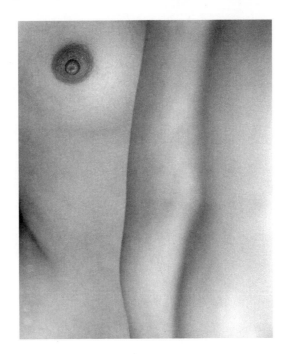

CONTRACEPTION AND ABORTION

O   B   J   E   C   T   I   V   E   S

AFTER READING THIS CHAPTER YOU SHOULD BE
ABLE TO . . .

1. DESCRIBE THE VARIOUS METHODS OF
   CONTRACEPTION, INCLUDING THE ADVANTAGES
   AND DISADVANTAGES OF EACH.

2. DISCUSS SOME OF THE ISSUES SURROUNDING
   CHOOSING A CONTRACEPTIVE.

3. EXPLAIN WHY THERE ARE SO MANY UNWANTED
   PREGNANCIES IN THE UNITED STATES EACH
   YEAR, EVEN THOUGH CONTRACEPTION IS BOTH
   ACCESSIBLE AND AFFORDABLE.

4. DESCRIBE THE VARIOUS METHODS OF ABORTION,
   INCLUDING THE ADVANTAGES AND
   DISADVANTAGES OF EACH.

5. DISCUSS SOME OF THE ISSUES SURROUNDING
   CHOOSING OR NOT CHOOSING TO TERMINATE A
   PREGNANCY.

PERSONAL ASSESSMENT

TEST YOUR GENERAL KNOWLEDGE OF CONTRACEPTION AND ABORTION BY ANSWERING THE FOLLOWING STATEMENTS *true* OR *false*.

_____ 1. All methods of contraception are equally effective.

_____ 2. Withdrawing the penis from the vagina just before ejaculation (*coitus interruptus*) is a 99 percent effective method of contraception.

_____ 3. Contraceptives in pill form are usually more effective than those that block the entrance to the uterus.

_____ 4. Petroleum jelly (*Vaseline*) prevents condom tearing better than a water-based lubricant (*K-Y Jelly*).

_____ 5. *Vasectomy* is the official term for female sterilization.

_____ 6. *Intrauterine devices*, or IUDs, seem to work by preventing sperm from reaching the cervix.

_____ 7. Individuals who hold "prochoice" values believe that having an abortion is a matter of choice for the pregnant woman.

_____ 8. The landmark decision of the United States Supreme Court in *Roe* v. *Wade* (1973) legalized abortions by concluding that a fetus is *potential* life and thus not entitled to any rights in and of itself.

_____ 9. The most common first-trimester abortion procedure performed in the United States is *dilation and curettage*.

_____ 10. A woman who chooses to have an abortion isn't at risk of experiencing guilt or other negative emotions.

ANSWERS
1. F, 2. F, 3. T, 4. F, 5. F, 6. F, 7. T, 8. T, 9. F, 10. F

Contraceptives should be used on all conceivable occasions.

Spike Milligan

Did you know. . . ?

- By chance, 85 percent of fertile couples not using contraception will conceive within one year of beginning sexual activity (Hatcher et al., 1994).
- The pill is the most widely used reversible contraceptive among today's women in the United States (Dawson, 1990).
- The majority of sexually active teenagers do not use reliable contraception on a consistent basis (DiClemente et al., 1992).
- Of the approximately 1 million teenage girls in the United States who become pregnant each year, about 50 percent deliver, 40 percent choose an abortion, and 10 percent miscarry (Trussell, 1988).
- Teenagers account for approximately 25 percent of all legal abortions (Henshaw & Silverman, 1988).

BIRTH CONTROL
Any number of procedures used to prevent conception and birth.

In the last chapter, you learned about pregnancy, birth, and fertility (that is, ways to increase the probability of conceiving). Now let's turn our attention to the other side of the coin—**birth control,** or ways to prevent conception and birth. Although people often use the terms *birth control* and *contraception* interchangeably, the two are not the same. Birth control is the more inclusive term, referring to both preventing conception and terminating a pregnancy that has already occurred. Having an *abortion* is a method of birth control, but not a method of contraception.

In the pages that follow, we'll examine the many different contraceptive methods available today, discussing their use, effectiveness, advantages, and disadvantages. We'll also consider how abortion might be a possible solution to an unwanted pregnancy for some women. All of these topics have to do with **family planning,** or **planned parenthood**—choosing if and when to have children.

CONTRACEPTION

Throughout history men and women have been concerned with **contraception** (meaning "against conception"), or preventing pregnancy by preventing the union of sperm and ovum. From the ancient Egyptian's placing crocodile dung into the vagina to prevent semen from passing through the cervix, to the ancient Jews' use of *coitus interruptus* (withdrawing the penis from the vagina just prior to ejaculation), to modern oral contraceptives and sterilization procedures, humankind has sought ways to avoid conceiving children (Tannahill, 1980). But until fairly recently, the search for effective contraception has for the most part been in vain. Only in the latter part of this century have scientists developed more reliable means of preventing pregnancy. Even so, over 3 million teenage and adult women in the United States will unintentionally become pregnant this year.

A number of contraceptive methods are available, some of which require a health-care practitioner's assistance. Not all contraceptives are equally effective, convenient, or safe; there is considerable variation from method to method. In fact, *with the exception of total abstinence from sexual activity with a partner, no contraceptive is 100 percent effective.* Further, contraceptive failure is usually due to misuse, inconsistent use, or nonuse of the method or device.

Contraceptives fall into the following categories: *hormonal methods, chemical methods, barrier methods, natural family planning methods,* and *sterilization.* Each of these methods has a *typical failure rate* (the percentage of women who experience an unintended pregnancy during the first year of using a method) and an *ideal failure rate* (the percentage of women who experience an unintended pregnancy during the first year of using a method consistently and correctly).

Margaret Sanger led the birth control movement in America during the first half of the twentieth century.

Being prepared is essential to adequate family planning.

HORMONAL METHODS

ORAL CONTRACEPTIVES
Birth control pills.

First available in the United States some thirty years ago, **oral contraceptives,** or "birth control pills," have become the second most widely used method of birth control in the world, following sterilization (Hatcher et al., 1994). Today, estimates are that approximately 60 million women around the world use birth control pills, including 13.8 million in the United States (Hatcher et al., 1994). Not only do women take birth control pills to prevent pregnancy, many take them for the health benefits that they provide (discussed below). "The pill" has a typical failure rate of 3 percent (Hatcher et al., 1994).

Although several forms of birth control pills are available, the three most common are the *minipill* (containing *progestin,* a synthetic form of progesterone), the *combination pill* (containing both progestin and synthetic estrogen, released at constant levels), and the *multiphasic pill* (containing both progestin and synthetic estrogen, released at fluctuating levels). These pills work by altering the levels of a woman's sexual hormones. Specifically, progestin prevents sperm from entering the uterus by thickening cervical mucus and interfering with movement of the ovum through the fallopian tube. Synthetic estrogen primarily inhibits ovulation, disintegration of the corpus luteum, and implantation of the fertilized ovum into the uterine wall. The woman takes the minipill on a daily basis, even during menstruation. Or she takes the combination pill for 21 of the usual 28 days of her cycle. Whichever pill she is on, the woman should take it at about the same time every day. She should also take any missed pill as soon as possible, and then take her next pill at the regularly scheduled time. If she misses more than one pill, she should notify her physician or nurse practitioner for further instructions.

Oral contraceptives are manufactured by different companies and come in a variety of packages.

Another oral contraceptive for women is the *morning-after pill*, which releases large amounts of progestin and synthetic estrogen into the bloodstream over a period of hours or days following coitus. These high levels of hormones can cause potentially severe side effects, including nausea, vomiting, and menstrual cycle disturbances. For this reason, the morning-after pill—usuallly administered once within 72 hours of ovulation—is for emergency situations, such as following rape or when other contraceptive techniques fail.

What about a male birth control pill? The FDA (Food and Drug Administration) is currently testing *gossypol,* derived from the cotton plant, as a possible male oral contraceptive. Chinese men have taken gossypol for over a decade with a reported effectiveness rate of 99 percent. This pill, when taken daily, supposedly reduces a man's sperm count to zero without affecting his testosterone levels. Spermatogenesis does not always resume upon discontinuing the drug, however (Nieschlag et al., 1981). Because gossypol appears to be toxic, causing potassium depletion and cardiac arrhythmias in some men, researchers in the United States have focused on finding a suitable nontoxic version of the drug (Hatcher et al., 1994).

For Personal Reflection

As a man, how would you feel about taking a male birth control pill if one were available? As a woman, how would you feel about your male partner taking a birth control pill?

Advantages of the Pill   The potential health benefits of taking the pill should be weighed against the risk of complications (Hatcher et al., 1994). The most important benefits include protection against ovarian and endometrial cancers, ovarian cysts, benign breast cysts, ectopic pregnancies, and certain forms of pelvic inflammatory disease. Other potential positive effects of the pill include decreased risk of rheumatoid arthritis; elimination of acne; and reduced menstrual flow, PMS-related mood changes, tension, and cramps. As one client noted:

On a Personal Note (Jan, age 23)

> I would have severe PMS—nearly every symptom—for two weeks every month. I tried everything to alleviate the problem—diet control, vitamin therapy, diuretics—everything. And each of those helped a little, but not enough, even when I did them together. Then my doctor tried putting me on the pill, and in one month's time I went from nearly all the symptoms to almost none. Now, after six years, I rarely think about PMS. For me, they aren't birth control pills, they're "happy" pills because they keep me normal and sane. (Author's files)

Pill users also need not fear permanently losing fertility. Most sexually active women will conceive soon after discontinuing the pill. Others can expect a delay of two or three months before becoming pregnant. Only 1 to 2 percent of women will not menstruate for six months after discontinuing the pill (Hatcher et al., 1994).

Disadvantages of the Pill   In some women, the actions of the pill's estrogen and progesterone can lead to a number of complications, including missed periods or very scanty bleeding, breakthrough bleeding between periods, nausea, breast fullness or tenderness, mood changes including depression, weight gain or loss, skin changes including chloasma, decreased sexual drive, inhibited lactation, urinary tract infections, headaches, eye problems, gallbladder disease, and benign liver tumors (Hatcher et al., 1994). These side effects often disappear the longer the woman is on the pill. Should the side effects remain uncomfortable or become problematic, a different dosage or alternative form of contraception may be necessary. Because the pill's hormones are sometimes present in small amounts in breast milk, mothers should probably avoid using the pill while breast-feeding.

Many women express concerns about the risk of breast cancer from taking the pill. To date, the research into this question has yielded inconclusive and often contradictory results (Hatcher et al., 1994). As Sharon Snider (1990), a staff writer for *FDA Consumer* magazine, noted:

> While there are conflicting results among studies on breast cancer and the pill, most investigators have found that women who have taken the pill have no increased risk of developing breast cancer. However, the product labeling on oral contraceptives recommends that women who use the pill and have a strong family history of breast cancer or who have breast lumps or abnormal mammograms be closely monitored by their doctors. (p. 4)

The pill can lead to life-threatening complications in a few women. The risk of *thromboembolism* (formation of blood clots, or *thrombi*) is a serious potential side-effect of using the pill. Severe illness and death can occur if thrombi travel to and become lodged in such vital organs as the lungs, heart, or brain. Fewer than 5 percent of users of the pill develop *hypertension* (high blood pressure), which can cause significant damage to the blood vessels and key organs of the body, especially the brain, heart, and kidneys. In some cases, elevated blood pressure may be responsible for *heart attacks* and *strokes*.

With all these potential complications, a woman might be hesitant to try oral contraceptives. Although research suggests that the pill can be dangerous for high-risk women, such as those who smoke, have blood clotting problems, and are over age 35, for the majority of low-risk women, the pill is one of the safest and most effective contraceptives available (Hatcher et al., 1994). In fact, the chance of death in a year is only 1 in 63,000 for women who take the pill to prevent pregnancy, compared with 1 in 11,000 for women who carry a fetus to full term and deliver (Hatcher et al., 1994).

Other Hormonal Methods Two other hormonal contraceptives are now available in the United States. *Norplant* is a set of six small, long-acting, matchstick-shaped capsules that are surgically implanted beneath the skin on the inside upper arm. The capsules, which are effective within 24 hours after insertion, release progestin and remain implanted until the hormone is completely gone, preventing pregnancy for up to five years (Segal, 1991). The major advantage of Norplant is hassle-free use; the woman need not remember to use it once it is implanted. Norplant is also completely reversible and has a low failure rate of less than 1 percent. Disadvantages include its cost, potential irregular menstrual bleeding, headaches, weight gain, acne, depression, and the continued need to use condoms to prevent STDs (Kantrowitz & Wingert, 1993; Lewin, 1991).

Medroxyprogesterone acetate, or *Depo-Provera,* is a long-acting injectable form of progestin. One injection normally lasts from three to four months. Advantages of Depo-Provera include decreasing premenstrual symptoms, ovulatory pain, menstrual cramps, and blood flow. Depo-Provera also has a low failure rate of less than 1 percent. Disadvantages can include menstrual irregularity, a slow return to fertility (taking perhaps up to one year), decreased libido, headaches, dizziness, depression, and weight gain (Hatcher et al., 1994).

CHEMICAL METHODS

Spermicides are chemical methods of contraception that come in the form of creams, foams, jellies, film, and suppositories. Once the woman introduces a spermicide into the vagina (at least several minutes prior to each ejaculation), it covers the walls of the vagina and opening of the cervix. The spermicide then prevents sperm from reaching the uterus by killing them on contact. Besides the potential to be messy and difficult to apply, spermicides can cause vaginal itching, burning, and urinary tract infection. However popular spermicides might be, none of them used alone are very effective, although they are relatively inexpensive and available without a prescription. The effectiveness of spermicides can be increased by using them along with other methods. Spermicides when used alone have a typical failure rate of 21 percent (Hatcher et al., 1994).

The woman's physician or nurse practitioner inserts the **intrauterine device** (IUD), a small metal or plastic device, through her cervical canal into the uterus. Intrauterine devices come in many shapes and sizes: T-shaped, coils, loops, springs, and rings (Figure 13.1). They also have thin strings or plastic wires that hang down into the vagina so the woman can periodically check to make sure the device is still in place. How these devices work is unclear, but they probably prevent conception by killing the sperm and egg by chemically altering the uterine environment and/or interfering with the egg's implanta-

SPERMICIDE (SPER-mi-sid)
A chemical agent that kills sperm on contact.

INTRAUTERINE DEVICE (in-tra-YOO-ter-in)
Tiny plastic or metal device inserted into the uterus by a physician to prevent pregnancy.

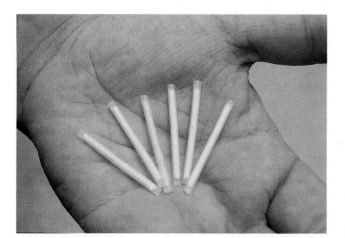 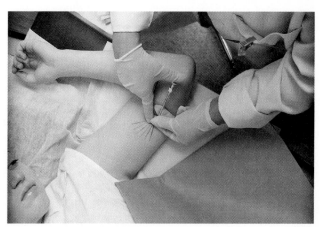

Norplant, a type of hormonal contraceptive, is a set of long-acting capsules surgically implanted beneath the skin on the inside upper arm.

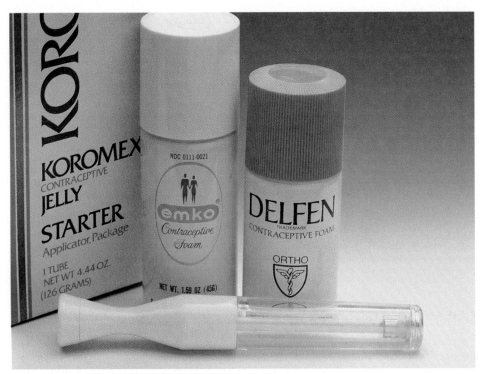

Vaginal spermicides are chemicals that when introduced into the vagina kill sperm.

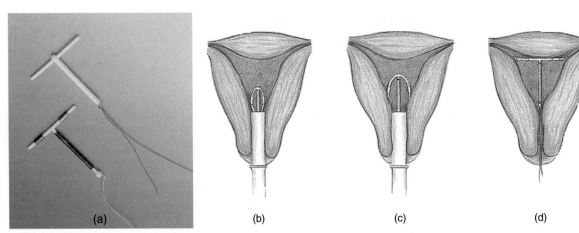

(a)   (b)   (c)   (d)

FIGURE 13.1 *The IUD is a small plastic or metal device that is inserted into the woman's uterus to prevent pregnancy.*

tion. The most common side effect of IUDs is bleeding upon insertion, although a number of other complications can arise, such as spotting, hemorrhaging, cramping, pain, anemia, infection, pelvic inflammatory disease, and perforation of the cervix or uterus. Intrauterine devices tend to be effective contraceptives, with a typical failure rate of no more than 2 percent (Hatcher et al., 1994).

The three IUDs currently available in the United States are *Progestasert, Copper T 380A,* and *LNg 20.* Besides irritating the uterine lining, they probably interfere with implantation, although by different mechanisms. Because other IUDs have been implicated in a number of cases of pelvic inflammatory disease, miscarriages, and deaths, all but the manufacturers of the above IUDs have discontinued production to avoid increasing liability and potential lawsuits. Less than 1 percent of women in the United States using birth control use IUDs (Hatcher et al., 1994).

BARRIER METHODS

Barrier contraceptives prevent conception by blocking sperm before they can reach the egg. The four most common of these are the *diaphragm, cervical cap, contraceptive sponge*, and *condom*.

Many women who use the **diaphragm,** a rubber dome with a flexible metal rim, often do so to avoid the complications of oral and intrauterine contraceptives (Figure 13.2). A physician or other practitioner properly fits the diaphragm to snugly cover the woman's cervix and to assure that it will stay in place comfortably. Because a woman cannot feel a properly fitted and inserted diaphragm, it may require refitting from time to time, particularly after the woman loses or gains 10 or more pounds, or gives birth. The woman inserts the diaphragm each time up to six hours before having sex, and leaves it in place six to eight hours after sex. She also applies a spermicidal agent to the diaphragm for every act of intercourse. The diaphragm can accidentally dislodge during intercourse, due to incorrect fitting and/or insertion. Failure of the diaphragm, however, is more often due to not using it each time than anything else. The typical failure rate for the diaphragm is 18 percent (Hatcher et al., 1994).

The **cervical cap** is a thimble-sized, cuplike device that fits over the cervix (Figure 13.3). It has a higher dome and thicker walls than the diaphragm, and is held in place by

DIAPHRAGM (DI-a-fram)
Rubber dome that covers the cervix to prevent pregnancy.

CERVICAL CAP
Small rubber cuplike device that fits over the cervix to prevent pregnancy.

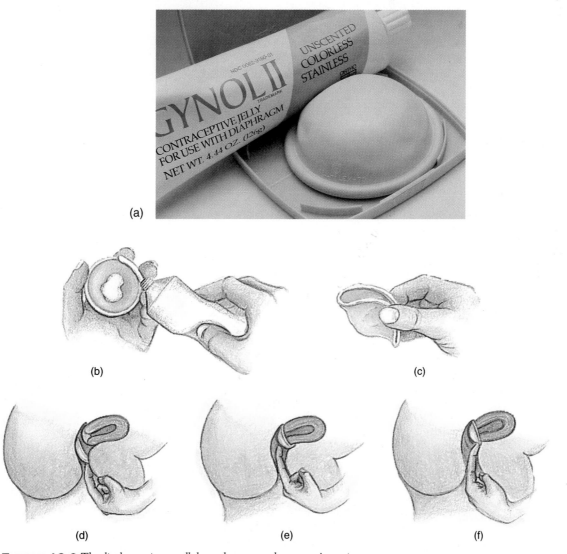

(a)

(b)   (c)

(d)   (e)   (f)

FIGURE 13.2 *The diaphragm is a small dome that covers the woman's cervix.*

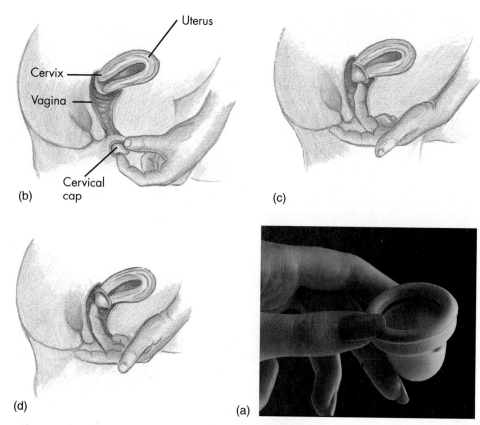

Uterus

Cervix

Vagina

Cervical
cap

(b)

(c)

(d)

(a)

FIGURE 13.3 *The cervical cap is a small cup that covers the woman's cervix.*

suction. As with the diaphragm, the woman inserts the cervical cap each time up to six hours before sex, and leaves it in place six to eight hours after sex. The woman normally fills the cap with a spermicidal agent before placing it into her vagina. The cervical cap is one option for women who have trouble being fitted for a diaphragm. The typical failure rate for the cervical cap for *parous* women (those who have given birth) is 36 percent, for *nulliparous* women (those who have not given birth) 18 percent (Hatcher et al., 1994).

The nonprescription **contraceptive sponge** is a small polyurethane foam pad that is saturated with a spermicide (Figure 13.4). The woman activates the sponge with water before insertion. She then inserts it by hand (or applicator) deep inside the vagina, after which it expands to cover the cervix. The sponge prevents pregnancy by blocking the entrance to the uterus and immobilizing and killing sperm. The woman removes the sponge from the vagina by pulling on its attached strap within 24 hours after insertion. The sponge carries with it a slight risk of causing *toxic shock syndrome* should pieces of it break off in the vagina. This form of contraception has a typical failure rate of 36 percent for parous women and 18 percent for nulliparous women (Hatcher et al., 1994).

The **condom** is a thin latex rubber or membranous sheath that covers the erect penis to prevent sperm from entering the vagina (Figure 13.5). It is the only available form of reversible contraception for men. Condoms come in a variety of colors, sizes, and styles. Some are lubricated, while others have ribs to provide additional penile and vaginal stimulation. If used properly, the condom can be an effective means of preventing pregnancy, with a typical failure rate of 12 percent (Hatcher et al., 1994). The effectiveness of the condom increases when used with a spermicide like *nonoxynol-9* and other methods, such as the woman using a diaphragm. Besides nonuse and misuse, failure can result from minute tears or holes in the condom, or the condom slipping off the penis. Therefore, the man should carefully inspect his condoms for tears prior to use. He should also pinch the tip of the condom, whether possessing a reservoir tip or not, with his thumb and index

CONTRACEPTIVE SPONGE
Polyurethane foam pad or ball saturated with a spermicide and inserted over the cervix to prevent pregnancy.

CONDOM (KON-dom)
Membrane or sheath placed over the erect penis to prevent sperm entering the vagina.

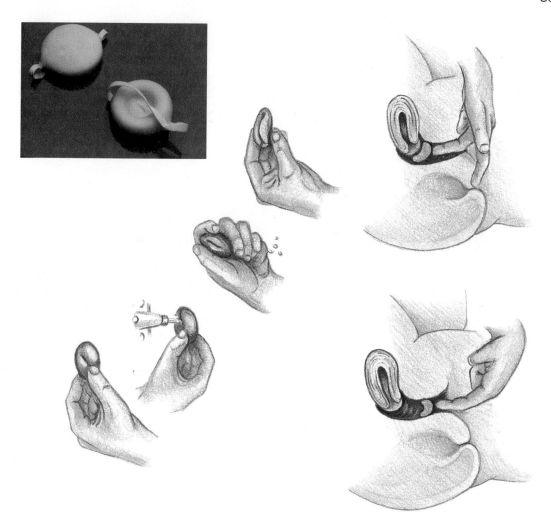

FIGURE 13.4 *The nonprescription contraceptive sponge is a small polyurethane pad saturated with a spermicide.*

finger when placing it on the penis to make sure no air is in the condom. He should *never* use an oil-based lubricant or petroleum jelly (such as *Vaseline*) to lubricate the inside or outside of the condom, as this substance dissolves latex. He should instead use a water-based lubricant (such as *K-Y Jelly*). Today many sexually active women also carry condoms and insist that their partners use them.

The latest in condom technology is the *female condom* to be worn inside the woman's vagina. Made of polyurethane or latex, there are two types. The first type is similar to a "G-string" with a rolled up pouch at the vaginal entrance. As the man inserts his penis into the pouch, the condom unravels in the vagina. The second type of female condom is sheath-shaped with flexible rings on both ends to help keep it in place. Of course, the end of the condom nearest the cervix is closed. The female condom received final approval from the FDA in 1993 (Baker, 1993; Goldberg, 1993).

NATURAL FAMILY PLANNING METHODS

The *rhythm method, symptothermal method, cervical mucus method, coitus interruptus,* and *abstinence* are the most often used non-device, or **natural family planning,** methods of contraception.

NATURAL FAMILY PLANNING
Any of a number of nonhormonal, nonchemical, nondevice methods of contraception.

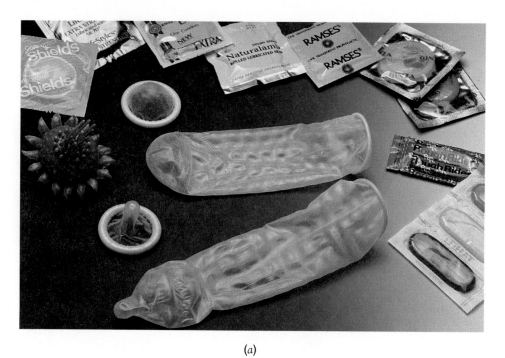

(a)

(b)

FIGURE 13.5 (a) Condoms come in a variety of colors, sizes, and styles. (b) How to pinch the tip of the condom before use.

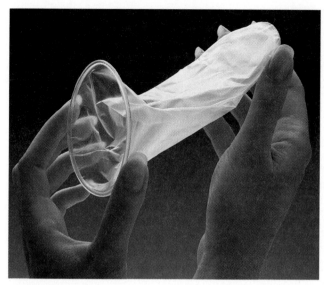

The female condom.

When using the *rhythm method* (or *calendar method*), a couple plans intercourse to coincide with the infertile times of a woman's menstrual cycle. The woman calculates these times by keeping track of the average duration of her cycles for at least eight months. She then subtracts 18 days from the length of the shortest recorded cycle and 11 days from the longest cycle to find the first and last fertile days, between which the couple avoids intercourse. Similarly, the woman may use the *symptothermal* and *cervical mucus methods* to determine infertile times by keeping a basal body temperature chart and monitoring increases in the amount of cervical mucus secreted. Besides having a typical failure rate of 20 percent (Hatcher et al., 1994), these methods are inadvisable for women who have irregular menstrual periods because of the difficulty in calculating fertile times. Furthermore, intercourse can induce ovulation during supposedly infertile times (Clark & Zarrow, 1971). In other words, pregnancy can occur at any time during a woman's cycle, even during menstruation. At no time during the month is pregnancy absolutely 100 percent impossible.

Another technique is *coitus interruptus*, which involves withdrawing the penis from the vagina at some point prior to ejaculation. Even when used in combination with the rhythm method, "withdrawal" has a failure rate of 19 percent (Hatcher et al., 1994), because live sperm frequently seep out of the penis before ejaculation as part of the Cowper's glandular secretions.

On a Personal Note (Carl, age 33)

I'd never use withdrawal as a form of birth control. I'm not sure why, but some of my semen occasionally escapes just before I orgasm and ejaculate. It usually happens after I've been taking allergy medicines, especially decongestants. Just to be on the safe side, I prefer to use a condom. (Author's files)

Abstinence is the voluntary refraining from sexual intercourse, and thus the only 100 percent effective form of contraception. It can be a temporary or permanent means of preventing pregnancy. Difficult or impossible for many couples, abstinence demands cooperation between partners. Yet many enjoy occasionally taking some time off from a sexual relationship to focus on other aspects of life. Other couples choose to practice *outercourse*,

ABSTINENCE
Voluntary avoidance of coitus.

PERSPECTIVE

How Should I Use a Condom?

The following guidelines for using condoms are from the Department of Health and Human Services publication, *Condoms and Sexually Transmitted Diseases . . . Especially AIDS*. These instructions are equally applicable for purposes of contraception and preventing transmission of sexual diseases.

1. Use a new condom for every act of intercourse.
2. If the penis is uncircumcised, pull the foreskin back before putting the condom on.
3. Put the condom on after the penis is erect (hard) and before *any* contact is made between the penis and any part of the partner's body.
4. If using a spermicide, put some inside the condom tip.
5. If the condom does not have a reservoir tip, pinch the tip enough to leave a half-inch space for semen to collect.
6. While pinching the half-inch tip, place the condom against the penis and unroll it all the way to the base. Put more spermicide or lubricant on the outside.
7. If you feel a condom break while you are having sex, stop immediately and pull out. Do not continue until you have put on a new condom and used more spermicide.
8. After ejaculation and before the penis gets soft, grip the rim of the condom and carefully withdraw from your partner.
9. To remove the condom from the penis, pull it off gently, being careful semen doesn't spill out.
10. Wrap the condom in a tissue and throw it in the trash where others won't handle it. Because condoms may cause problems in sewers, don't flush them down the toilet. Afterwards, wash your hands with soap and water.
11. Finally, beware of drugs and alcohol! They can affect your judgment, so you may forget to use a condom. They may even affect your ability to use a condom properly.

Source: Department of Health and Human Services, *Condoms and sexually transmitted diseases... especially AIDS* (Publication FDA 90-4239). Reprinted by permission of the Department of Health and Human Services.

Adam *copyright Universal Press Syndicate. Reprinted with permission. All rights reserved.*

which involves any sexual activity other than intercourse, such as kissing, sensual massage, or mutual masturbation.

Celibacy is the permanent or long-term abstinence from sexual intercourse. Some celibates, such as members of certain religious orders, also avoid autoerotic activities; others find self-stimulation a fulfilling sexual outlet.

STERILIZATION

The most reliable contraceptive available today is **sterilization,** surgical procedures that render individuals incapable of reproducing. Male sterilization, termed *vasectomy,* involves severing a portion of each vas deferens to prevent sperm from moving into the urethra (Figure 13.6). The operation does not really affect the amount of semen ejaculated, as only 1 percent of the total volume of semen is sperm. Female sterilization, termed *tubal ligation* or *salpingectomy,* involves closing the fallopian tubes to prevent ova from entering and being fertilized (Figure 13.6). Specifically, a physician introduces a *laparoscope,* or lighted tube, into a small abdominal incision. Following location of the tubes, each is surgically closed by clipping and then *cauterizing* (searing or burning them shut) or *suturing* (sewing them shut). Possible complications of tubal ligation include injury to the intestines or other abdominal organs, and hemorrhaging. Neither vasectomy nor tubal ligation affect sexual drive or sexual performance.

**STERILIZATION
(STER-I-LI-ZA-SHUN)**
Surgical procedure that renders an individual incapable of reproducing.

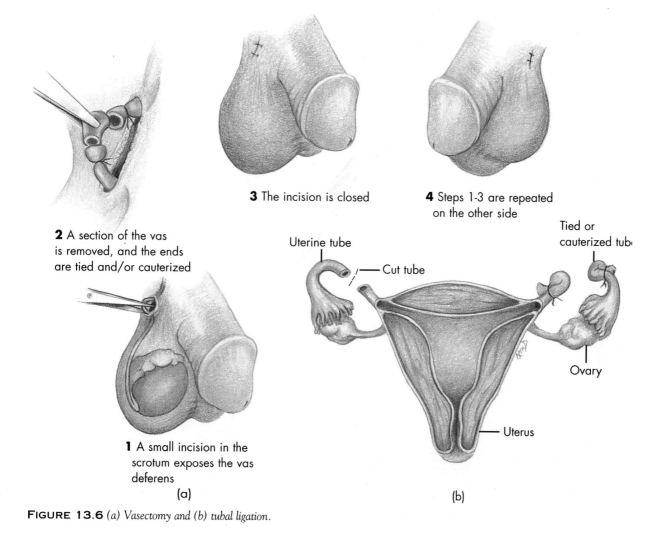

3 The incision is closed

4 Steps 1-3 are repeated on the other side

2 A section of the vas is removed, and the ends are tied and/or cauterized

Uterine tube
Cut tube
Tied or cauterized tube
Ovary
Uterus

1 A small incision in the scrotum exposes the vas deferens

(a)

(b)

FIGURE 13.6 *(a) Vasectomy and (b) tubal ligation.*

Vasectomy has a typical failure rate of 0.15 percent; tubal ligation, a rate of 0.4 percent (Hatcher et al., 1994). Failure in men is normally due to surgical error or having sexual intercourse too soon after the procedure. In fact, a man is advised to practice another method of contraception for at least two months following vasectomy, because it may take a while for his sperm to completely move out of the portions of the vas deferens above the site of surgery. Failure in women is normally due to reopening of the closed tubes. In some cases both male and female sterilization procedures are reversible; however, these procedures are difficult, expensive, and not always successful (Hatcher et al., 1994). For instance, the success rate for male reversal ranges from 16 to 79 percent; for female reversal, from 43 to 88 percent—based on pregnancy rates after surgery (Hatcher et al., 1994).

On a Personal Note (Barry, age 42)

Darla and I originally didn't want to have any kids. We're both pretty socially conscious about world population issues. We've also each been married once before, and had real messy child custody suits—you know how it goes. So after getting married, we both voted for sterilization. Well, believe it or not, after being married for several years, we decided we wanted to have a baby, a product of our love for one another. So we both went in to have our procedures reversed. And it worked for us, much to our mutual astonishment, since our doctors told us that reversal isn't always possible. Well, we are now the proud parents of little Marla. (Author's files)

For Personal Reflection

Under what circumstances would you consider being sterilized? How would you respond if your partner refused to be sterilized but asked you to undergo the procedure?

FUTURE TRENDS IN CONTRACEPTION

Several newly developed contraceptives are now being tested for general use in the United States, even though many companies have discontinued contraceptive research for lack of funds and liability reasons. Here are the most promising methods:

For men
1. *Gossypol* (described earlier).
2. Ultrasound treatment to suppress spermatogenesis.
3. Hormones that suppress spermatogenesis.
4. A polymer injected into the vas deferens that obstructs or closes the tube.

For women
1. A "vaginal ring," worn around the cervix, that releases progestin or a combination of estrogen and progestin. The hormones enter the bloodstream through the vaginal *mucosa*, or membrane.
2. Biodegradable implants placed under the skin, similar to Norplant, that eventually dissolve on their own.
3. Silicone plugs that block the fallopian tubes.
4. A luteinizing-hormone-releasing agonist that prevents ovulation and/or implantation.
5. An antifertility vaccine.

For Personal Reflection

When new drugs are being tested for general use, volunteers are recruited to receive the drug as part of an experimental study. Would you be willing to take an experimental contraceptive drug? If so, under what conditions?

CHOOSING A CONTRACEPTIVE

The "perfect" contraceptive would be 100 percent effective, be comfortable for both partners, function reliably whenever needed, be reversible, have no negative side effects, and require minimal or no attention or hassle. Unfortunately, no such device or method exists, even though researchers continue searching for it.

What is the best contraceptive for an individual or couple? This is not an easy question to answer. Curtis Byer and Louis Shainberg, in their *Living Well: Health in Your Hands* (1991), suggested the following criteria to help people choose the most appropriate method for them:

1. *Safety*—Does the method pose significant health risks to myself or my partner?
2. *Effectiveness*—What is the typical failure rate of this method? Can my partner and I live with the possibility that the method might fail?
3. *Ease of use*—How much trouble is it to use? Can I self-administer or does it require a health practitioner's assistance?
4. *Acceptability*—Do my partner and I have any objections to using the method?
5. *Reversibility*—Can my partner and I expect to become fertile again upon discontinuing the method?
6. *Affordability*—Can my partner and I afford the method?
7. *Availability*—Is the method easy to obtain from my health provider or a pharmacy? (p. 128)

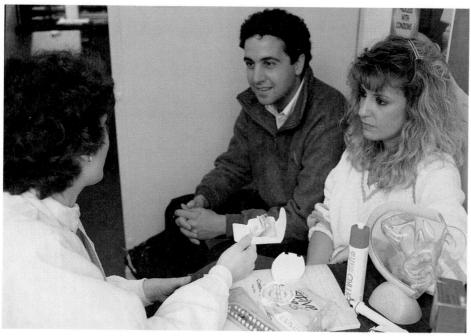

Obtaining information about contraception is the first step to effective decision-making and responsible family planning.

TABLE 13.1 **Lowest Expected and Typical Reported Failure Rates During the First Year of Use of a Contraceptive Method**

Percentage of Women Experiencing an Accidental Pregnancy
Within the First Year of Use

Method	Typical Use	Perfect Use
Chance	85	85
Spermicides	21	6
Periodic Abstinence	20	
Calender		9
Ovulation Method		3
Sympto-Thermal		2
Post-Ovulation		1
Withdrawal	19	4
Cap		
Parous Women	36	26
Nulliparous Women	18	9
Sponge		
Parous Women	36	20
Nulliparous Women	18	9
Diaphragm	18	6
Condom		
Male	12	3
Female (Reality®)	21	5
Pill	3	
Progestin Only		0.5
Combined		0.1
IUD		
Progestasert®	2.0	1.5
Copper T 380A	0.8	0.6
LNg 20	0.1	0.1
Depo-Provera	0.3	0.3
Norplant® (6 Capsules)	0.09	0.09
Female Sterilization	0.4	0.4
Male Sterilization	0.15	0.10

Source: R. A. Hatcher, J. Trussell, F. Stewart, G. K. Stewart, D. Kowal, F. Guest, W. Cates, & M. S. Policar, (1994), *Contraceptive technology (1994–1996)* (New York: Irvington). Reprinted by permission.

Effectiveness and safety are perhaps the two most important considerations when choosing a contraceptive. Hatcher et al. (1994) in *Contraceptive Technologies (1994–1996)*, reviewed expected failure rates in the form of percentages of women who will become pregnant during the first year of using a particular contraceptive. This information appears in Table 13.1.

The question of safety often prompts students to ask about the risks of dying associated with the various contraceptives, as well as with carrying a pregnancy to term. Hatcher et al. (1994) also compared the risks of death from using contraceptives versus engaging in other activities. This information appears in Table 13.2.

TABLE 13.2 Risks of Death Associated with Various Activities

Activity	Chance of Death in a Year
Risks for Men and Women of All Ages Who Participate In:	
Motorcycling	1 in 1,000
Automobile Driving	1 in 6,000
Power Boating	1 in 6,000
Rock Climbing	1 in 7,500
Playing Football	1 in 25,000
Canoeing	1 in 100,000
Risks for Women Aged 15 to 44 Years:	
Using Tampons	1 in 350,000
Having Sexual Intercourse (PID)	1 in 50,000
Preventing Pregnancy:	
Using Birth Control Pills	1 in 63,000
Nonsmoker	1 in 16,000
Smoker	1 in 1000,000
Using IUDs	
Using Diaphragm, Condom, or Spermicide	None
Using Fertility Awareness Methods	None
Undergoing Sterilization:	
Laparoscopic Tubal Ligation	1 in 67,000
Hysterectomy	1 in 1,600
Vasectomy	1 in 300,000
Continuing Pregnancy	1 in 11,000
Terminating Pregnancy:	
Legal Abortion	
Before 9 Weeks	1 in 260,000
Between 9 and 12 Weeks	1 in 100,000
Between 13 and 15 Weeks	1 in 34,000
After 15 Weeks	1 in 10,200

Source: R. A. Hatcher, J. Trussell, F. Stewart, G. K. Stewart, D. Kowal, F. Guest, W. Cates, & M. S. Policar (1994), *Contraceptive technology (1994–1996)* (New York: Irvington). Reprinted by permission.

THE IMPORTANCE OF FAMILY PLANNING

Historically, many groups and societies have discouraged contraception to assure survival of their members and humanity as a whole. Certain religious groups strongly disapprove of "wasting" semen on sexual activity that does not culminate in coitus and the possibility of conception. Others believe the matter to be of little consequence. For example, the Yanomamö of South America have little or no concept of contraception. They instead bear as many children as possible, and then kill off those they view as the "undesirables," such as some females and deformed infants (Chagnon, 1977).

Why then are today's Americans and other people around the world so concerned about birth control? The reasons vary, but an important one is overpopulation of the planet, including dwindling natural resources and the planet's inability to sustain increasing numbers of people. For most of human history, the world's population has remained relatively low as a result of early infant mortality and a limited life span for other age groups, often due to plagues and diseases, poor sanitation, malnutrition, and lack of medical care. But as modern medicine has spread throughout different parts of the world, people of all ages now live longer, literally causing the world's population to "explode." In fact, at about five billion today, the world's population is doubling on average every 35 years, with most of this growth occurring in developing countries. Given this population crisis, certain governments like that of China have decided to regulate the number of births allowed per household.

So why bother with birth control? Besides the issue of overpopulation, there are many good reasons for women and men to practice contraception. First and foremost, a couple who engages in sexual intercourse but does not want to conceive a child as a result should practice contraception. For example, a young couple may want to postpone having children until their finances improve. Or an unmarried, sexually active teenager may wish to finish her education or get married before starting a family, thereby reducing her chances of eventually relying on the government for financial support (Masters et al., 1994).

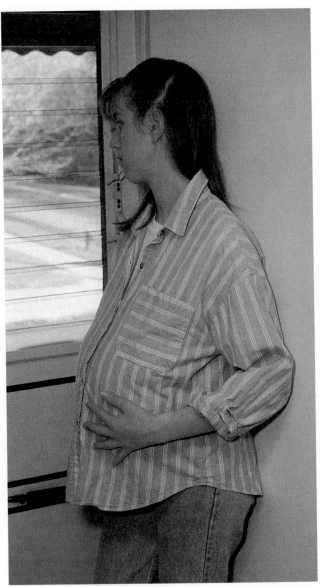

Teenage pregnancy: An unfortunate consequence of unprotected intercourse.

Family planning is also important for protecting the physical health of both mother and child. For most women in their prime reproductive years (about ages 20 to 39), pregnancy and childbirth are relatively safe events. Yet, the older or younger a woman is, and the closer together she bears children (that is, more frequently than every two years), the greater the risk of pregnancy and birth complications, early infant mortality, and maternal death. For example, a child born to a woman over age 40 or under age 19 is at increased risk of low birth weight, and thus a variety of birth defects and even death (Bright, 1987; Reinisch, 1990; Trussell, 1988). Regarding the latter, estimates are that approximately one million teenage women in the United States become pregnant each year (McGrew & Shore, 1991), and that a significant percentage of babies born to these women weigh less than 5 pounds. Not all pregnancies after 40 or before 19 will lead to such problems; the risks, however, do increase.

Family planning can also help preserve the psychological health of the mother and other family members. Giving birth and becoming a parent are both significant and stressful life events. Moreover, parenting is a long-term commitment—emotionally, socially, and financially. Choosing the right time to have a child is one of the most important things a woman or couple can do to lessen the emotional strains of pregnancy and parenthood.

All things considered, why do so many people (but especially teenagers and young adults) avoid, refuse, or forget to use contraception? The reasons vary. Some people feel that obtaining or using contraceptives is simply too much of a bother. Others may wish to get pregnant to receive unconditional love from a baby. Still others may be too embarrassed or have difficulty assertively obtaining and using birth control, or they may have religious objections to its use. Although few adolescents intentionally conceive, many end up doing so as a result of underestimating their chances of getting pregnant (Jones et al.,

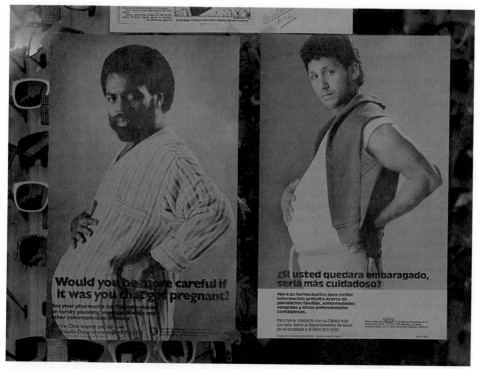

Various organizations have developed educational posters in an attempt to reduce the number of unintended teenage pregnancies that occur yearly.

1988). Because sexually active teenagers either occasionally or never use contraception, many high schools, colleges, universities, and other organizations in this country are providing information about contraception as part of sex education classes, health center services, and community programs in an attempt to limit the number of unwanted adolescent pregnancies that occur each year.

Other sources of information about family planning, conceiving, birth control, and unwanted pregnancy options include the Planned Parenthood Federation of America, National Right to Life Committee, and National Abortion Rights Action League. See the Resources Appendix of this text for the addresses of these organizations.

ABORTION

Abortion: Its mere mention is enough to enrage otherwise calm and sensible people, provoke heated arguments, and turn the best of friends into enemies. Abortion is indeed a hotly debated social and political issue. Try bringing it up at a party, during a family gathering, at a religious meeting, or in class and see what happens.

Realistically speaking, when faced with an unplanned, unwanted pregnancy, a woman and/or couple must decide whether to have the child and raise it, put it up for adoption, or terminate the pregnancy. This last option—an **induced abortion** (or **elective abortion**)—involves any of a number of procedures to intentionally end a pregnancy. Except in extreme circumstances (if it appears the mother will die otherwise), a physician performs an abortion while the embryo or fetus is still *nonviable*, or incapable of living on its own outside of the mother's body. The vast majority of abortions today are performed during the first and early second trimesters of pregnancy.

In some cases, the embryo or fetus aborts naturally due to medical complications, an event known as a *spontaneous abortion* or *miscarriage*. Here, the uterus expels the embryo on its own, usually before week 12. About 20 percent of all pregnancies end in a spontaneous abortion (Friedman & Gath, 1989; Salmon, 1991). Miscarriages seem to be nature's way of preventing the birth of infants with gross abnormalities.

ABORTION METHODS

Even with all of the political, legal, and moral controversy surrounding induced abortion, over 1.5 million women in the United States choose to terminate pregnancy in this way each year (*Statistical Abstract of the United States,* 1992). The five most common methods of accomplishing this are *vacuum aspiration, dilation and curettage* (D and C), *chemical abortion, dilation and evacuation* (D and E), and *hysterotomy*.

Vacuum Aspiration   During *vacuum aspiration,* the physician suctions the embryo or fetus and products of conception out of the uterus with a vacuum tube (Figure 13.7). Following a pelvic exam, the physician anesthetizes and then dilates (opens) the woman's cervix. He or she introduces the vacuum tube into the uterus, and suctions out the fetal material, mucus, and blood—the entire process taking only a few minutes. Complications of the procedure include cramping and vaginal bleeding. Vacuum aspiration is probably the safest method of inducing abortion, and it is usually performed between weeks 6 and 14 of the first trimester of pregnancy.

Dilation and Curettage   Also performed during the first trimester (usually between weeks 6 and 12), *dilation and curettage* (D and C) involves a physician dilating the patient's cervix and scraping the fetus and other tissue from the uterine wall. Scraping ("curettage") is done with a metal, spoonlike instrument, a *curette,* while the woman is

INDUCED ABORTION
(OR ELECTIVE ABORTION)
Intentionally terminating a pregnancy.

PERSPECTIVE

What Type of Contraception Should I Use?

Unless a sexually active couple wants to have a baby in the immediate future, they may want to use some form of contraception. But for birth control to work, the method chosen must be both effective and comfortable for the couple. The *Contraceptive Comfort and Confidence Scale* will help you and your partner determine if a particular contraceptive method is for you. Take this test separately and then compare your answers.

Contraceptive Comfort and Confidence Scale

Method of birth control you are considering using:
Length of time you used this method in the past:
Answer YES or NO to the following questions:

1. Have I had problems using this method before?
2. Have I ever become pregnant while using this method?
3. Am I afraid of using this method?
4. Would I really rather not use this method?
5. Will I have trouble remembering to use this method?
6. Will I have trouble using this method correctly?
7. Do I still have unanswered questions about this method?
8. Does this method make menstrual periods longer or more painful?
9. Does this method cost more than I can afford?
10. Could this method cause me to have serious complications?
11. Am I opposed to this method because of any religious or moral beliefs?
12. Is my partner opposed to this method?
13. Am I using tis method without my partner's knowledge?
14. Will using this method embarrass my partner?
15. Will using this method embarass me?
16. Will I enjoy intercourse less because of this method?
17. If this method interrupts lovemking, will I avoid using it?
18. Has a nurse or doctor ever told me NOT to use this method?
19. Is there anything about my personality that could lead me to use this method incorrectly?
20. Am I at any risk of being exposed to HIV (the AIDS virus) or other sexually transmitted infections if I use this method?

Total Number of YES Answers:

Most individuals will have a few "yes" answers. "Yes" answers mean that potential problems may arise. If you have more than a few "yes" responses, you may want to talk with your physician, counselor, partner or friend to help you decide whether to use this method or how to use it so that it will really be effective for you. In general, the more "yes" answers you have, the less likely you are to use this method consistently and correctly at every act of intercourse.

Source: R. A. Hatcher, J. Trussell, F. Stewart, G. K. Stewart, D. Kowal, F. Guest, W. Cates, & M. S. Policar, (1994), *Contraceptive technology (1994–1996)* (New York: Irvington). Reprinted by permission.

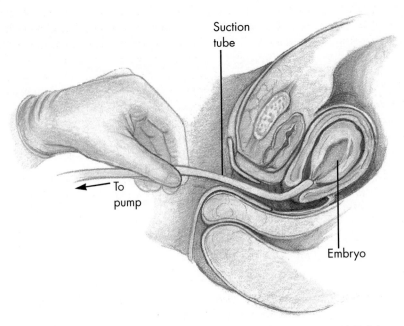

FIGURE 13.7 *Abortion by vacuum aspiration. Source: W. H. Masters, V. E. Johnson, & R. C. Kolodny (1992), Human Sexuality (4th ed.) (New York: HarperCollins). Reprinted by permission.*

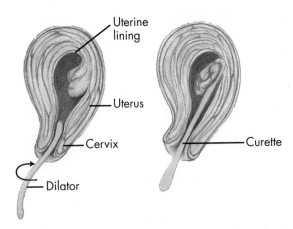

FIGURE 13.8 *Abortion by dilation and curettage (D and C).*

anesthetized (Figure 13.8). Given the risks of infection or other complications, hospitalization is required for this procedure. D and C is also used to scrape the walls of the uterus following a miscarriage or when a sample of uterine tissue is needed for diagnostic testing, as when testing for cancer.

Chemical Abortion By the second trimester, the fetus is too large to abort using vacuum aspiration or D and C. The safest method after week 13 is *chemical abortion*, which involves injecting a *saline solution* (salt solution) or *prostaglandin* (a hormonelike substance) directly into the amnion. As a result, chemical changes in the amniotic fluid surrounding the fetus cause uterine contractions to induce early labor and expel the fetus and placenta.

A number of countries other than the United States—France, Great Britain, West Germany, and China—also permit the use of *RU-486* to induce abortions during the first trimester (Hatcher et al., 1994; Smolowe, 1993). The highly controversial "abortion pill" blocks the action of progesterone, thus preventing implantation and/or causing the fertilized zygote to shed from the uterine wall. Assorted groups have lobbied against its approval in the United States, mainly because of the drug's potential use as a chemical means of inducing abortion. Other groups believe the drug is a safe, effective, noninvasive means of inducing abortion—one that could save many lives each year. With the import ban on RU-486 still under review, the drug's future in this country is uncertain.

Dilation and Evacuation A physician performs *dilation and evacuation* (D and E) during the second trimester when the fetus is too large to be removed by vacuum aspiration or D and C. While the patient is hospitalized and under general anesthesia, a physician dilates the cervical canal and removes the fetus and placenta using vacuum suction and *forceps* (a metal grasping instrument). Afterwards, the physician typically scrapes the walls of the uterus with a curette.

Hysterotomy When a physician performs a *hysterotomy*, he or she surgically removes the fetus through an incision made in the woman's abdomen. Because it is a more serious procedure than the others, hysterotomy is performed only rarely, such as to save the mother's life or when the pregnancy has advanced to the late second trimester. Hysterotomy may also be appropriate for the woman who also desires sterilization, as the fallopian tubes are easily accessible during this surgery. Some professionals think of hysterotomy as comparable to a *caesarean section*.

ATTITUDES, CONSEQUENCES, AND CONTROVERSIES

As mentioned earlier, many people have strong opinions about abortion. Although certain groups vigorously oppose the procedure, legal abortion is one of the most common methods of birth control for people in a number of countries, such as Japan. Legal abortion also tends to be a relatively safe medical procedure, and when performed early should not interfere later with a woman's ability to conceive and have a healthy baby. Yet adequate medical care and follow-up are essential, given possible complications like bleeding and pelvic infection.

The risk of a woman dying after a legal abortion before 9 weeks is 1 in 260,000; between 9 and 12 weeks, 1 in 100,000; between 13 and 15 weeks, 1 in 34,000; and after 15 weeks, 1 in 10,200 (Hatcher et al., 1994). The risk of death following an illegal abortion is 1 in 3,000 (Hatcher et al., 1992). The risk of death in carrying a child to term is 1 in 11,000 (Hatcher et al., 1994). Put simply, if a woman decides not to continue her pregnancy, the risk of death increases the longer the fetus is carried or if she has an illegal abortion (see Table 13.2).

The emotional response experienced before or after an abortion varies (Holden, 1989). One woman might feel depressed, angry, ashamed, or guilty about planning or having an abortion; another might accept the procedure as a matter of fact and have little or no emotional response; and still another might carefully consider her options and decide that she cannot give a child the financial or emotional support it needs. Why these differences? A combination of personal differences, moral/religious views, upbringing, reactions of the health-care practitioner(s), and the presence or absence of emotional support from the partner, family, and friends are factors influencing how a woman will react to having an abortion. Generally, though, the later in pregnancy an abortion is performed, the greater the negative emotional consequences.

Some teenagers choose to become parents rather than have an abortion.

The woman's partner is also likely to have an emotional response to her abortion. Shostak et al. (1984) noted that although many men supported their partner's decision to terminate pregnancy, they also reported underlying resentment and anger about the procedure. This is one reason why counseling for both partners before and after an abortion can be so valuable.

A woman or couple contemplating an abortion may also want to consider other options, including marriage, single parenthood, and adoption. In fact, many pregnant teenagers and their partners decide to marry and start an early family, even though the chances of such a marriage lasting are poor. Other women and men choose single parenthood, relying on the assistance of family and friends. Still others decide to give up their children for adoption immediately after delivery.

Given the strong emotions frequently associated with planning or having an abortion, the decision to terminate a pregnancy can be one of the most difficult a woman or couple will ever face. Of course, opinions on the matter vary widely, particularly across interest groups, such as members of the National Abortion Rights League versus those of the National Right to Life Committee. Numerous ongoing political and moral/religious debates reflect the controversial nature of abortion (Baird & Rosenbaum, 1989). Generally, those who support a woman's right to choose to have an abortion are "prochoice," while those who view abortion as murder of a living being are "prolife." When life actually begins—at conception, birth, or sometime in between—seems to be central to this debate.

In 1973 the United States Supreme Court in *Roe* v. *Wade* ruled that a fetus is *potential* life, and thus not entitled to any legal rights in and of itself. The Court also ruled that (1) prohibiting an abortion during the first trimester of pregnancy infringed on a woman's rights; (2) states could regulate who performed the procedure during the second trimester, although such regulation can only be in the interest of protecting the mother's health; and (3) states could prohibit most abortions during the third trimester, except when the life of the woman is directly threatened. Prior to this ruling, few states allowed abortions.

Abortion is a hotly debated social and political issue, as evidenced by interest groups staging demonstrations around the country.

Although the Supreme Court upheld the *Roe* v. *Wade* decision in 1983 and again in 1986, legislation has threatened to overturn the original 1973 ruling. The *Hyde Amendment* (1977) made it possible for the federal government to refuse to fund abortions for the poor. In 1989 the Supreme Court ruled in *Webster* v. *Reproductive Health Services* that states could also require that health-care practitioners determine a fetus's viability after 20 weeks, restrict use of public facilities for abortions, and prevent public employees from doing abortions not needed to save a woman's life. Furthermore, the Bush administration's *Gag Rule* (1991) prohibited health-care practitioners and personnel from mentioning abortion as an option for patients, and eliminated federal funding for any clinic or hospital that disregarded the regulations. President Clinton eliminated the Gag Rule in January 1993.

Abortion has been a source of moral and religious debate for centuries, even though the arguments for and against the practice have intensified in the United States with the advent of more sophisticated medical procedures. Prolife advocates believe current scientific technology has made it too easy to terminate pregnancy, even in the later stages, resulting in the needless murder of countless unborn children each year—another reflection of our "disposable" society. Prochoice advocates, on the other hand, believe a woman has the right to decide what happens to her body, and that government regulation of abortion destroys this right. If a woman is determined to have an abortion, then she will have one regardless of legal or moral dictates. Both prolife and prochoice advocates hold that a person who chooses to have a child should have adequate financial and social support, and that illegal abortions put a woman at serious risk.

It would seem that the abortion debate is likely to continue for the foreseeable future. As is the case with all ethical dilemmas, there are no easy, clear-cut answers. Although this sensitive issue is a source of contention for many, hopefully those on both sides of the debate (as well as those in between) will better learn to appreciate and respect the political and moral convictions of everyone involved.

KEY POINTS

1. Preventing unwanted pregnancy and birth are central to effective *family planning,* or *planned parenthood*—choosing if and when to have children. The essential purpose of *contraception* is to avert pregnancy by preventing a sperm from uniting with an ovum. Although people often use the terms *birth control* and *contraception* interchangeably, the two are not the same. *Birth control,* or preventing birth, is the more inclusive term, referring to both preventing conception and terminating a pregnancy that has already occurred.

2. Contraceptives fall into the following categories: *hormonal methods, chemical methods, barrier methods, natural family planning methods,* and *sterilization.* Each of these methods has a *typical failure rate* and an *ideal failure rate.*

3. An *induced abortion* involves any of a number of procedures to intentionally terminate a pregnancy. Except under extreme circumstances, a physician performs an abortion while the fetus is still *nonviable.* A *miscarriage,* or *spontaneous abortion,* occurs when a fetus aborts naturally.

4. The five preferred methods of inducing an abortion are *vacuum aspiration, dilation and curettage, chemical abortion, dilation and evacuation,* and *hysterotomy.* A woman or couple contemplating an abortion may also want to consider other options, such as marriage, single parenthood, or adoption.

5. Abortion is a hotly debated social and political issue. Numerous ongoing political and moral/religious debates reflect the controversial nature of abortion. Generally, those who support a woman's right to choose to have an abortion are "prochoice," while those who view abortion as murder of a living being are "prolife." When life actually begins—at conception, birth, or sometime in between—seems to be central to this debate.

ACTIVITIES AND QUESTIONS

1. Why do so many people, especially adolescents, fail to use contraception? What effect do you think education about contraception has on people's willingness to use such methods? At what age should education about contraception begin? Who should provide such education—parents, teachers, friends, or religious leaders?

2. What is the impact on individuals and society when governments regulate the number of children a couple can have?

3. Visit a Planned Parenthood facility and speak with a representative about available services, programs, films, and printed materials. Return to class and describe your experience. Be sure to bring some brochures and pamphlets to show to your classmates.

4. Create a panel to discuss both prochoice and prolife sides of the abortion debate, as well as positions that both sides share. (This activity frequently results in heated arguments, so be sure to have a panel moderator and set up rules in advance.)

5. What are the pros and cons of single parenthood and adoption as alternatives to abortion?

RECOMMENDED READINGS

Baird, R. M., & Rosenbaum, S. E. (Eds.) (1989). *The ethics of abortion.* Buffalo, NY: Prometheus. A collection of 12 essays addressing the complex issues associated with the abortion debate.

Goldstein, R. D. (1988). *Mother-love and abortion: A legal interpretation.* Berkeley: University of California Press. Examines the prochoice and prolife sides of the abortion debate.

Hatcher, R. A., Trussell, J., Stewart, F., Stewart, G. K., Kowal, D., Guest, F., Cates, W., & Policar, M. S. (1994). *Contraceptive technology (1994-1996)*. New York: Irvington. Provides a thorough description of the various contraceptive methods available, including instructions for each. Updated every few years.

Lader, L. (1991). *RU-486: The pill that could end the abortion wars and why American women don't have it*. Reading MA: Addison-Wesley. An interesting look at the pro-choice perspective on RU-486.

Sproul, R. C. (1990). *Abortion: A rational look at an emotional issue*. Colorado Springs, CO: Navpress. An interesting look at the prolife perspective on abortion.

Tribe, L. (1990). *Abortion: The clash of absolutes*. New York: Norton. Another book that examines the prochoice and prolife sides of the abortion debate.

• **B**ACTERIAL INFECTIONS

• VIRAL INFECTIONS

• PARASITIC INFESTATIONS

• OTHER SEXUALLY TRANSMITTED INFECTIONS

• PREVENTING SEXUALLY TRANSMITTED DISEASES

C H A P T E R   1 4

SEXUALLY TRANSMITTED DISEASES

O B J E C T I V E S

AFTER READING THIS CHAPTER YOU SHOULD BE
ABLE TO . . .

1. EXPLAIN THE DIFFERENCES AMONG BACTERIAL,
   VIRAL, AND PARASITIC SEXUALLY TRANSMITTED
   DISEASES (STDs).
2. DESCRIBE THE RESPONSIBLE AGENT(S),
   SYMPTOMS, STAGES, AND COMPLICATIONS OF
   THE MAJOR STDs, AS WELL AS METHODS OF
   DIAGNOSING AND TREATING EACH.
3. EXPLAIN WHY HIV INFECTION IS INCREASING AT
   SUCH AN ALARMING RATE WORLDWIDE.
4. LIST AND DESCRIBE THE VARIOUS "HIGH-RISK"
   SEXUAL ACTIVITIES ASSOCIATED WITH
   TRANSMISSION OF HIV.
5. LIST AND DESCRIBE "SAFER SEX" PRACTICES
   AND BEHAVIORS THAT REDUCE THE RISKS OF
   CONTRACTING AND TRANSMITTING STDs.

P E R S O N A L   A S S E S S M E N T

TEST YOUR GENERAL KNOWLEDGE OF SEXUALLY TRANSMITTED DISEASES BY ANSWERING THE FOLLOWING STATEMENTS *true* OR *false*.

_____ 1. A person can have an STD and not necessarily look sick.
_____ 2. Gonorrhea and syphilis are merely two variations of the same STD.
_____ 3. Currently, chlamydia is incurable.
_____ 4. Currently, genital herpes is incurable.
_____ 5. It's possible to contract genital herpes during sexual activity with an infected partner, even if he or she isn't having an outbreak at the time.
_____ 6. You can become infected with HIV simply by being in the same room with someone who has HIV.
_____ 7. A female can pass along a vaginal yeast infection to her male partner.
_____ 8. Viral STDs respond more quickly to treatment with antibiotic medications than do bacterial ones.
_____ 9. Parasites such as lice and mites can be transmitted sexually.
_____ 10. Using condoms eliminates the risk of contracting STDs.

ANSWERS
1. T, 2. F, 3. F, 4. T, 5. T, 6. F, 7. T, 8. F, 9. T, 10. F

There is a limit to the best of health: disease is always a near neighbor.

Aeschylus

SEXUALLY TRANSMITTED DISEASE

Disease that is spread through sexual contact with an infected partner.

Just a few decades ago, the general population severely underestimated the significance of **sexually transmitted diseases** (STDs), or diseases that pass from person to person through sexual activity. Called "venereal diseases" then—after "Venus," the goddess of love—there was the erroneous belief that all STDs would always be easily treatable with antibiotics, rendering them more like annoyances than real health hazards.

Time and experience have brought home the error of that view. None of us can afford the luxury of ignorance when confronted by the threats posed by such sexually transmitted diseases as HIV, genital herpes, and chlamydia. Indeed, our single most potent weapon to counter the steady rise of these diseases is knowledge.

With many fundamental changes occurring in our society today, we can and must address the issue of ignorance when it comes to sexual health and STDs. To begin, we must challenge societal misconceptions; STDs are not diseases of the poor or uneducated. They instead exist at each level of society, crossing all lines of age, education, income level, and race. Second, the real danger of contracting these diseases comes not from dirty toilet seats or casual contact but from *intimate, sexual contact*—even the "first time." The single greatest risk factor in contracting STDs is having multiple sexual partners, in particular without protection. Third, STDs can pass between sexual partners in the absence of traditional, vaginal-penile sexual intercourse. Further complicating matters, STDs are often **asymptomatic,** or without symptoms, fooling many into complacency about both protection and the need for treatment. If pain and social stigmatization are not enough to take STDs seriously, these diseases frequently impair the sexual organs and can cause sterility or even death.

ASYMPTOMATIC (A-SIMP-TO-MA-TIK)

Producing no symptoms.

Sexually transmitted diseases exist at every level of society, crossing lines of age, race, education, and income.

Although society continues to become better educated about specific STDs, the majority of these diseases remain a mystery to the public. No wonder STDs continue to plague humankind. For this reason, we now examine the *bacterial*, *viral*, and *parasitic* STDs, as well as *trichomonas* and *monilia*.

BACTERIAL INFECTIONS

Some STDs are caused by microscopic single-cell organisms known as **bacteria.** These organisms invade cells of the body, causing infection and disease. The most common bacterial STDs are *gonorrhea, nongonococcal urethritis* and *cervicitis, chlamydia,* and *syphilis.*

BACTERIA
Tiny, single-cell organisms that invade cells of the body and cause disease.

GONORRHEA

One of the most prevalent sexual diseases today is *gonorrhea* ("clap," "drip," or "dose"). In 1993 there were about 600,000 cases of this bacterial STD reported in the United States (Centers for Disease Control, 1994). However, many cases go unreported, and the Centers for Disease Control estimates that as many as 2 to 5 million cases occur each year.

Gonorrhea is caused by the bacterium *Neisseria gonorrhoeae*. Because this bacterium flourishes in the mucous membranes (the moist protective coat that lines all orifices of the body), the genitals provide a fertile haven for these bacteria to proliferate. Most cases of gonorrhea result from genital-genital intercourse. Because of the much larger surface area of the mucous lining of the vagina, women have a much greater chance of contracting gonorrhea than do men. Most women (nearly 80 percent) are asymptomatic and do not realize they have a gonorrheal infection until their infected partner tells them or they happen to have a culture taken during a routine gynecological exam. This alone should encourage sexually active women to seek testing for gonorrhea as part of their regular checkups.

PERSPECTIVE

Facts About Sexually Transmitted Diseases

Did you know...?

- Sexually transmitted diseases (STDs) affect 12 million men and women in the United States each year.
- Anyone can become infected through sexual intercourse with an infected person.
- Many of those infected are teenagers or young adults.
- Changing sexual partners adds to the risk of becoming infected.
- Sometimes, early in infection, there may be no symptoms, or symptoms may be easily confused with other illnesses.

... Sexually transmitted diseases can cause:

- Tubal pregnancies, sometimes fatal to the mother and always fatal to the unborn child.
- Death or severe damage to a baby born to an infected woman.
- Sterility (loss of ability to get pregnant).
- Cancer of the cervix in women.
- Death to infected individuals.

... You should see a doctor if you have any of these symptoms of STDs:

- Discharge from the vagina, penis, and/or rectum.
- Pain or burning during urination and/or intercourse.
- Pain in the abdomen (women), testicles (men), and buttocks and legs (both).
- Blisters, open sores, warts, rash, and/or swelling in the genital area, sex organs, and/or mouth.
- Flu-like symptoms, including fever, headache, aching muscles, and/or swollen glands.

Source: Department of Health and Human Services, *Condoms and sexually transmitted diseases...especially AIDS* (Publication FDA 90-4239). Reprinted by permission of the Department of Health and Human Services.

Although as many as 40 percent of men with gonorrhea are asymptomatic, those who exhibit symptoms do so within two to ten days after contact. In men, the urethra and the rectum are the most likely sites of infection. Generally, symptoms include the sudden onset of frequent, painful urination, as well as a purulent (puslike) discharge from the urethra. In the absence of treatment, the infection will spread into the urinary tract within two to three weeks, affecting the posterior urethra, prostate, seminal vesicles, and epididymis. Infection in the prostate is accompanied by pelvic tenderness and pain, fever, and difficulty urinating. Should the epididymis become inflamed, a feeling of heaviness in the affected testicle and irritation of the scrotal skin can occur. Should the infection spread to the other testicle, infertility may result.

The primary infection site for women is the cervix. Along with this "hidden" infection comes an increased risk of complications, especially *pelvic inflammatory disease*—inflammation/infection of the reproductive and pelvic organs and structures. Within two months, the untreated gonococcal organisms infect the internal reproductive organs and pelvic cavity. During menstruation and immediately following, the organisms travel rapidly, causing painful intercourse, nonmenstrual uterine bleeding, and inflammation of the fallopian tubes. As the body tries to fight off the infection, the tubes can become scarred, in many cases causing infertility.

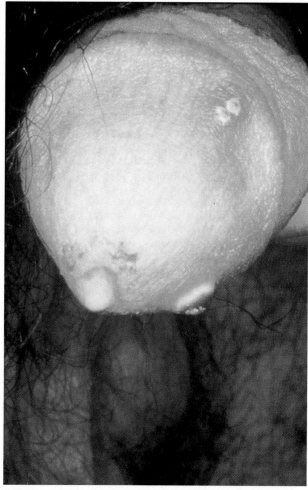

Symptoms of male genital gonorrhea include frequent and burning urination, as well as a puslike discharge from the urethra.

A number of other sites where nongenital infection can occur are possible, including the mouth, throat, anus, rectum, and eyes. The gonococci can also enter the bloodstream and travel to the joints, resulting in *gonococcal arthritis*, or to the heart valves, resulting in *gonococcal endocarditis*.

By contrast with other STDs, gonorrhea has no satisfactory blood test. If one existed, routine screening could help identify the infection in asymptomatic individuals. Diagnosing gonorrhea normally requires taking a culture, in which a sample of discharge is wiped from an affected body site with a cotton-tipped swab. In men, this generally requires a sample taken from the urethra; in women, one taken from the cervix. Samples can be taken from other infected body sites, including the throat, rectum, or vagina itself. Retrieving a sample is sometimes uncomfortable, but rarely painful.

Patients with gonorrhea ordinarily receive injections of an antibiotic medication, such as *penicillin, spectinomycin, ceftriaxone, amoxicillin,* or *ampicillin*. Large doses are sometimes necessary to eliminate the entire infection and prevent resistant strains of the bacteria from developing. Because as many as 50 percent of gonorrhea patients have a coexisting *chlamydial* infection (described below), patients may also receive *tetracycline, erythromycin,* or *doxycycline* over a seven-day period (Moran & Zenilman, 1990). The gonococci can live in the body a number of days after treatment, so patients need retesting after about a week to determine the effectiveness of the treatment, as well as the presence of a penicillin-resistant strain. Patients who mistakenly believe they are free of a resistant strain of the disease may unintentionally transmit it to others.

On a Personal Note (Tim, age 26)

I thought I was through with the big G. My doctor gave me the usual penicillin shot—I've had gonorrhea a couple of times now—and I thought everything was okay. I can't believe it, but my girlfriend caught it from me, *after* I was supposedly cured. I guess I should have gone in for that follow-up appointment. At the time, I didn't want to spend the extra 30 bucks. (Author's files)

NONGONOCOCCAL URETHRITIS AND CERVICITIS

Nongonococcal urethritis (in males) and *nongonococcal cervicitis* (in females) involve infections of the urethra and cervix not due to gonorrhea. Men with nongonococcal urethritis typically experience urethral discharge and pain upon urinating, although perhaps 30 percent of infected men are asymptomatic (Reinisch, 1990). Women with nongonococcal cervicitis typically experience vaginal discharge and irritation, and about 70 percent are asymptomatic. The signs and symptoms of nongonococcal urethritis and cervicitis are similar to those of gonorrhea. Researchers have identified a number of culprit organisms responsible for these infections, including *Ureaplasma urealyticum* and *Chlamydia trachomatis*. Infections due to the latter are usually termed *chlamydia*.

CHLAMYDIA

Genital *chlamydia* has become the most common STD in the United States, with an estimated 3 to 4 million new cases reported annually (Handsfield & Hammerschlag, 1992; Toomey & Barnes, 1990). Chlamydia is caused by the bacterium *Chlamydia trachomatis*.

Because the early symptoms of urinary tract chlamydia are often mild, they regularly go unnoticed. For men who exhibit symptoms, the most common are painful, burning, or difficult urination and a thin, clear urethral discharge. For women, the most common symptoms are painful urination, vaginal discharge, irregular vaginal bleeding, and abdominal pain. Diagnosing chlamydia requires culturing a thin layer of cells scraped from the affected site, smearing the cells onto a microscope slide, and exposing them to a special diagnostic dye.

Chlamydial infections do not respond to treatment with penicillin. In its early stages, the disease is easily treatable with tetracycline, erythromycin, or doxycycline over a seven-day period. Left untreated, chlamydia can cause damage to the urethra and cervix, infection of the epididymis and the fallopian tubes, and pelvic inflammatory disease. For both sexes, sterility is a real and serious complication of long-term, untreated chlamydial infection.

SYPHILIS

Caused by the *Treponema pallidum* (a type of bacterium known as a *spirochete*), *syphilis* presents a major health concern for Americans. In fact, over 50,000 cases of syphilis were reported in the United States in 1990 (Centers for Disease Control, 1994). Although less common than chlamydia and gonorrhea, syphilis is far more dangerous. If left untreated, the infection can seriously damage the vital organs and nervous system, and even kill.

Syphilis is normally transmitted through genital sexual contact, although other types of physical contact can be responsible, such as touching an open lesion. Specifically, the spirochetes pass from the open lesion of an infected person to the mucous membranes or breaks in the skin of another. Only a few hours are required from the time of contact for the spirochetes to enter the bloodstream. Furthermore, after the fourth month of pregnancy, syphilis can cross the placenta to infect the fetus. Consequently, a pregnant woman who is treated prior to the fourth month of pregnancy can protect her fetus from the disease.

Syphilis occurs in four distinct phases or stages: *primary*, *secondary*, *latent*, and *tertiary*.

Primary-Stage Syphilis   Primary syphilis is characterized by the appearance of a *chancre* (a painless, round, ulcerlike lesion with a hard, raised edge). The chancre is first apparent from 10 to 90 days after exposure, although, on average, this symptom appears in 21 days. In most cases a single chancre forms. For males, the glans penis is the likely site for the chancre; for females, the cervix, labia, or walls of the vagina. Because the primary sites for women are not normally visible, this symptom often goes unnoticed. This in itself is a good argument for women to be educated in self-examination with a hand-mirror. Chancres are also known to appear on the mouth, nipples, other parts of the penis or vulva, scrotum, and anus—particularly following oral or anal sex with an infected partner.

Once the chancre disappears (within one to five weeks, with or without treatment), the infected person may mistakenly assume that the disease has healed itself or that she or he never actually contracted it in the first place. A person who suspects exposure to syphilis, no matter how remote the possibility, must have a blood test. Because the test for syphilis can give a negative result during the primary stage, it should be repeated at a later date.

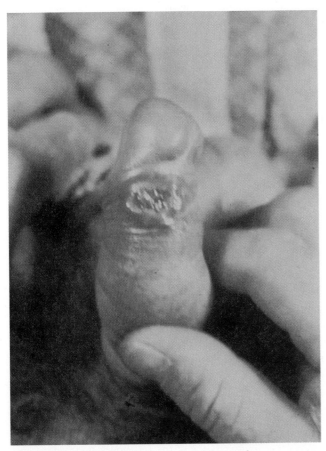

The principal symptom of primary-stage syphilis is a chancre, as shown here on the penis.

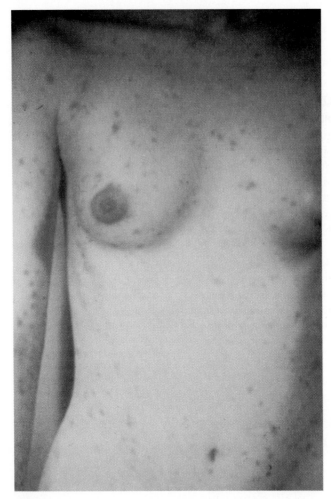

The principal symptom of secondary-stage syphilis is a generalized rash, as shown here on a woman's chest.

Secondary-Stage Syphilis Disappearance of the chancre marks the end of the primary stage, not the end of syphilis. At this point, the disease has "gone underground." The secondary stage is characterized by a body rash that appears one to several months following healing of the chancre. This rash does not itch, and will, like the chancre, vanish without treatment.

In addition to the rash, secondary-stage syphilis can manifest itself by fever, sore throat and mouth, loss of appetite, muscle and joint pain, headaches, hair loss, and depression. Because so many of these symptoms are similar to those of other diseases, the infected individual may not realize that he or she has a serious STD, instead explaining them away as symptoms of allergies, a persistent flu, or stress. Most of the time, however, these symptoms are uncomfortable enough to prompt the individual to seek medical treatment.

Fortunately, the responsible bacteria are easily identifiable by a blood test during this secondary stage. In approximately 25 percent of secondary-stage syphilis cases, the spinal fluid will also test positive for the spirochete. If diagnosed at this stage, the disease can still be cured without permanent damage to the vital organs.

Latent-Stage Syphilis With the disappearance of the secondary-stage symptoms, the disease enters the latent stage, which can last for many years. The disease now presents no external symptoms, and only a blood test can confirm its presence. Yet this does not imply that the *Treponema pallidum* is at rest. Instead, the spirochetes continue to embed themselves into the various tissues and organs of the body (the bones, blood vessels, and brain). Except for a pregnant woman passing the infection on to her baby, the disease may no longer be infectious after several years of latency.

Tertiary-Stage Syphilis Approximately 50 percent of those who enter the *latency* stage experience no additional problems for the remainder of their lives. The other 50 percent, however, move into the *tertiary* (late) stage, in which serious complications develop. The disease then causes permanent damage to one or more of the following: the brain, spinal cord, eyes, lungs, heart, blood vessels, skin, muscles, digestive organs, liver, and endocrine glands. In some cases, depending on the affected site(s), the patient has a good chance of completely recovering with prompt medical treatment. In other cases, though, syphilis that has attacked the heart, brain, or spinal cord ordinarily leads to paralysis, insanity, and even death—sometimes 10 to 40 years after the initial infection.

Because long-term syphilis has such a dire prognosis, early diagnosis and treatment are vital. As noted above, a blood test is effective for this purpose, although it takes time for the antibodies to develop. In fact, the individual may be in the secondary stage before a blood test will accurately detect the infection. If a person suspects exposure to syphilis and has a negative test result close to the time of suspected infection, he or she may want to be retested later when the antibodies are more likely to be present. Microscopically examining the fluid from the chancre or rash for spirochetes is another test for syphilis.

Once diagnosed, syphilis responds to penicillin, doxycycline, and erythromycin (for individuals who are pregnant or allergic to penicillin).

For Personal Reflection

Many STDs have as a principal symptom genital lesions or discharge. How would you feel about asking to inspect your partner's genitals before sexual activity? What would you say and do if your partner refused? How would you feel if your partner asked to inspect your genitals?

VIRAL INFECTIONS

Viruses are noncellular, microscopic particles that replicate themselves within invaded cells. Antibiotic medications are ineffective against them, making viruses very difficult or impossible to eliminate. The most common viral STDs are *genital herpes, human immunodeficiency virus,* and *genital warts*. Other viral diseases that can be sexually transmitted include *cytomegalovirus* and *hepatitis*.

VIRUS

Microscopic particle that reproduces itself within an invaded cell.

GENITAL HERPES

Before AIDS, *genital herpes,* an incurable and sometimes extremely painful infection caused by the virus *herpes simplex,* was the most dreaded STD. Yet society should still be concerned about this disease. Genital herpes is rapidly spreading, with no cure in sight. Estimates are that as many as 500,000 new cases of genital herpes occur annually (Reinisch, 1990), with perhaps as many as 25 million Americans currently infected (Johnson et al., 1989). Efforts to find a cure or vaccine have to date been unsuccessful. Without question, genital herpes has reached epidemic proportions and will likely continue to be a public health problem for many years.

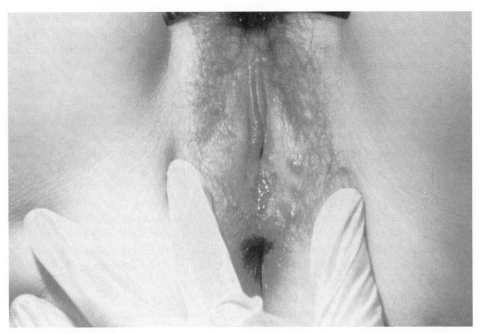

The painful blisters of genital herpes typically cluster, are of varying sizes, and can also involve the perineal area.

The *herpes simplex* virus is of two types: Type I (HSV-I), seen more frequently in the upper body (the mouth and lips); and Type II (HSV-II), seen more frequently in the lower body (the genitals). Either type, however, can infect either area. Type I appears on the genitals about 20 percent of the time; Type II, in the mouth as much as 50 percent of the time (usually from oral-genital sexual activity).

Herpes is caused by direct contact with either HSV-I or HSV-II, usually by touching an affected site. Oral herpes (HSV-I, which causes "cold sores") is spread by such activities as oral sex, kissing, and sharing a drinking glass or moist towel. Genital herpes (HSV-II) is spread through sexual contact, whether it be oral, genital, or anal. It only rarely spreads by direct contact with a toilet seat.

Herpes infections normally follow a course of three stages: *primary, latent,* and *recurrent. Primary herpes* begins at the time of actual infection. Small blisters or bumps soon develop on and around the genitals and anus. After bursting, the blisters form painful lesions, which heal on their own in about three weeks. However, as in the case of the tell-tale chancre of syphilis, the disappearance of the lesions does not mean the disease is cured. The virus continues to live in the body, though remaining inactive—a stage termed *latent herpes.* During this second stage of the disease, antibodies form to combat the virus and, while not protecting against a second outbreak, tend to make future outbreaks less severe. At this time, the virus can reactivate without symptoms, meaning an infected individual can transmit the virus to a noninfected individual without knowing it—a phenomenon termed *asymptomatic viral shedding.* Finally, during the third stage of a herpes infection, termed *recurrent herpes,* the virus can reactivate with symptoms (new blisters and fever).

Although symptoms are usually milder after the primary infection, they can be nevertheless distressing to the infected individual. While the frequency of outbreaks varies—ranging from one or two recurrences in a lifetime to several outbreaks a year—the possibility of recurrence exacts a very real psychological toll on all involved. And because herpes is incurable, sufferers are constantly confronted with very difficult, personal decisions. Should they tell family members or friends they have herpes? Should they tell new partners? Would doing so make them more vulnerable to rejection? Is a life of celibacy the answer? What about joining a herpes support group? Given the many fears and concerns associated with genital herpes, it becomes clear that psychological treatment can be just as important as medical treatment.

Although herpes is incurable, medication is available that minimizes the severity of symptoms and reduces the number of outbreaks. Millions of people in the United States use *acyclovir* (brand name, *Zovirax*) which can be applied topically (as an ointment) or taken orally (in pill form). Females with lesions inside the vagina must take the pill form. Regular use of oral acyclovir is effective in reducing the frequency and severity of outbreaks (Handsfield, 1992).

An outbreak of genital herpes during pregnancy poses problems. If this happens early on, the risk of miscarriage increases significantly. If vaginal lesions leak during delivery, the virus can pass from the mother to the fetus as it moves through the birth canal. Because the virus can severely damage the newborn's brain, some women with herpes choose to have a C-section rather than a vaginal delivery.

Everything considered, the best treatment for herpes is to prevent it from occurring in the first place. To this end, some suggestions follow for preventing transmission of the herpes virus:

1. Avoid sexual contact whenever symptoms are present.
2. Oral lesions are generally no longer infectious several days after their first appearance. To be on the safe side, avoid sexual activities involving the mouth until all oral lesions have healed and disappeared.
3. Because herpes can be transmitted by people who are unaware they are infected, always use condoms and spermicides during sexual intercourse. The same applies to sexual activity with partners who know they are infected but currently do not have any symptoms.
4. Heat, stress, and certain clothing can trigger attacks. Become aware of the conditions that precede symptoms.

On a Personal Note (Mandy, age 27)

My first outbreak of herpes was the worst. In fact, it got so bad my roommate had to take me to the emergency room. I was really sick and in lots of pain. After that, I had a couple of milder outbreaks. Thank goodness I haven't had another one in about three years. My boyfriend didn't even know he was a carrier of the virus. I mean, he's never had an outbreak. He still feels bad about the whole thing. (Author's files)

For Personal Reflection

How would you react if a prospective lover told you he or she has herpes? How would you react if you were told the same by a relative or friend?

HUMAN IMMUNODEFICIENCY VIRUS AND ACQUIRED IMMUNODEFICIENCY SYNDROME

Perhaps no other STD has captured the awareness of the public and elicited such passion and confusion as *human immunodeficiency virus* (HIV), which causes *acquired immunodeficiency syndrome* (AIDS). Unfortunately, much of society's response to the disease is reminiscent of the witch hunts of the Middle Ages—threatening, beating, and even killing identified persons. With such fear and hate running rampant, no wonder myths and stereotypes abound about HIV, AIDS, and its victims. Such is the price of ignorance.

Actually, HIV does not directly cause death; rather it depresses the immune system of its victim to the point that infection and disease overwhelm his or her defenses. The virus accomplishes this by attacking "helper" T-cells (T4 lymphocytes, a type of white blood cell), which signal (1) B-cells to inactivate invading pathogens and (2) "killer" T-cells to destroy the pathogens. Previously, an individual needed to develop at least one serious disease before he or she received a diagnosis of AIDS. In April 1992, the Centers for Disease Control expanded the definition of "full-blown" AIDS to include any HIV-infected individual with a T-cell count of 200 or less, whether or not he or she has symptoms or a serious disease. (A normal T-cell count is 800 to 900.)

In order for HIV to attack a human cell it must first attach itself to a special receptor on the cell's surface. In humans, HIV attaches to T4 lymphocytes. Once it has attached to the T-cell, HIV enters the cell and releases genetic material. Through a series of chemical reactions, the cell itself replicates the HIV. Ultimately, the cells attacked by HIV become "factories" that produce more viruses, which in turn attack more T-cells, which in turn become factories, and so on. So it goes until the immune system is so depressed that various diseases easily overwhelm the victim's immune system.

There is significant cause for alarm regarding the growing numbers of people being diagnosed with HIV and AIDS. It is estimated that there are currently over 1 million cases of HIV infections in North America (Aggleton et al., 1994). By September 1986, over 40,000 cases of AIDS had been reported in the United States; by September 1994, over 350,000 cases had been reported—a frightening increase. Of those diagnosed with AIDS in the United States, about 50 percent are white, 30 percent black, and 17 percent Hispanic (Centers for Disease Control, 1994).

Based on the research, HIV does not appear to be spread by casual contact between individuals, but instead through the exchange of body fluids (blood, semen, and vaginal secretions). *However, this does not mean that transmission of the virus cannot occur in some other way* (Day, 1991). To date, the four most widely accepted, documented ways in which HIV transmission occurs are:

1. By sexual intercourse or other sexual activity with an infected individual, including genital, oral, or anal sex, or some combination of these.
2. By contaminated blood.
3. By contaminated hypodermic needles.
4. From infected mother to child during pregnancy or childbirth, and possibly during breast-feeding.

Also, according to the pamphlet, *An Ounce of Prevention: AIDS Risk Reduction Guidelines for Healthier Sex*, published by the Washington State Department of Social and Health Services (1986):

Extremely high-risk practices include insertion of the penis, fingers, or devices into the rectum, mouth-to-anus contact, and any contact with urine, feces, or blood; these should always be avoided. Condoms do not guarantee safety, but they may reduce the degree of risk associated with vaginal intercourse, anal intercourse, and oral-genital contact. Semen commonly carries the AIDS virus; therefore condoms are desirable for any sexual contact that might result in ejaculation. Since the AIDS virus may be present in saliva, open-mouth kissing—"French" kissing—also may carry some risk.

Currently, heterosexual transmission accounts for 4 percent of the reported AIDS cases in the United States, with HIV more efficiently transmitted from males to females (Padian et al., 1991). Although the primary affected groups in the United States continue to be homosexuals and intravenous drug users, this is not the case in other areas. In Africa, Latin America, and other developing countries, transmission of HIV primarily occurs through heterosexual practices (Aral & Holmes, 1991). The following list summarizes who is at increased risk of HIV infection and AIDS, according to the United States Department of Health and Human Services:

1. Men who have had sex with another man since 1977.
2. People who share needles when they inject drugs.
3. People with symptoms of AIDS or AIDS-related illnesses.
4. Male or female prostitutes and their partners.
5. Sexual partners of people who are infected with the AIDS virus or at increased risk of infection.
6. People with hemophilia who have received clotting factor products.
7. Infants of high-risk or infected mothers.

Once a person is infected with HIV, the disease ordinarily follows a three-phase course. The first is "silent," or asymptomatic, in that the individual is unaware of being infected and so may inadvertently infect others. From the time of contact with an infected person, it may be weeks, months, or years before the antibodies are detectable by blood test (Clerici et al., 1991). Infected individuals may remain asymptomatic for ten or more years.

Individuals eventually progress from being asymptomatic to the second phase of the disease—*symptomatic HIV* (formerly termed *AIDS-related complex*, or ARC). This stage has a number of general symptoms, the most prominent being persistent swelling of the lymph glands (in the neck, armpits, and back of the mouth), fever, fatigue, night sweats, unexplained weight loss, and diarrhea.

Kaposi's sarcoma, with its characteristic skin lesions, is a leading killer of AIDS patients.

As far as researchers know, everyone with HIV goes on to develop AIDS, usually within about ten years. Here, all of the general signs and symptoms of symptomatic HIV continue, although complicated by the presence of dire diseases like *Kaposi's sarcoma* (a type of cancer) or *Pneumocystis carinii* (a type of pneumonia). HIV can also cross the blood-brain barrier, causing deterioration of memory and judgment, personality changes, and brain tumors.

At this time, AIDS is incurable and fatal. Treatments, which begin long before the individual has "full-blown" AIDS, are available that minimize symptoms while slowing the progress of the disease (Haseltine, 1993). In 1987 the FDA approved *zidovudine* (previously called *azidothymidine*, or AZT) as the first drug licensed in the United States for the treatment of AIDS. An antiviral drug, zidovudine delays replication of HIV in human cells. As a result, zidovudine lengthens the survival of HIV patients and lessens the incidence and severity of infections. Other treatments include transfusion of lymphocytes, bone marrow transplants, implants of tissue from the thymus (where the T4 cells are manufactured), and the drug *dideoxyinosine* (DDI). All of these therapies delay destruction of immune system functioning.

No treatment of AIDS can ignore psychological and political considerations. The diagnosis of HIV infection or AIDS, like that of any incurable disease, can be psychologically devastating. Add to this the fact that AIDS carries with it a stigma, and one begins to sense the frightening dimensions of the disease.

Can anything be done, emotionally speaking, to help a friend with AIDS? Yes, according to Walter Batchelor, in his training manual, *AIDS: An Introduction to the Medical, Psychological, and Social Issues* (1988):

> The best way to be friends during these times is to be someone who the person with AIDS can count on. Be someone who calls or writes or visits regularly—but not so much as to invade his or her privacy. Be someone who listens well. Be someone who is not afraid to ask questions or to ask for advice. Be someone who can be called in the middle of the night if it is necessary. Be someone who will remember about compassion and forget about pity. Most importantly, be someone who your friend with AIDS can just sit with, hold hands with, and sometimes cry with. (p. 92)

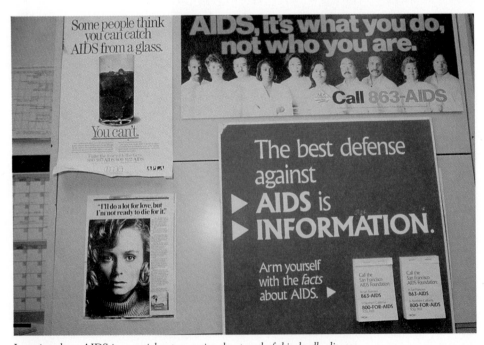

Learning about AIDS is essential to preventing the spread of this deadly disease.

How can AIDS be prevented? When sexual abstinence is not a preferred option, maintaining a monogamous relationship with an uninfected partner is the safest choice. Of course, avoiding direct contact with the mouth, penis, vagina, and/or rectum of a high-risk partner is a must.

GENITAL WARTS

Although the urgency of HIV and AIDS has caught the attention of the media and general public, we must not forget that other viral STDs can have serious physical and emotional consequences for infected individuals and their partners.

Genital warts result from a group of viruses known as the *human papilloma viruses* (HPV). Estimates are that between 12 and 25 million Americans have an HPV infection, and the incidence of this disease appears to be rising (Centers for Disease Control, 1994). Varying in size and appearance, genital warts often resemble cauliflowers and most commonly appear on and around the genitals, perineum, and anus. Transmission occurs through direct physical contact.

Generally, treatment involves burning, freezing, or cutting off the warts from the affected site(s). Topical application of the drug *podophyllin* to the warts causes the outer skin in the area of the virus to shed. Chemical burning with podophyllin is contraindicated in pregnant women, as the drug can cause birth defects. Because of the potential for genital warts to cause cervical cancer, they should be biopsied to determine that they are indeed benign (noncancerous).

OTHER VIRAL INFECTIONS

Two additional viral infections that can be sexually transmitted deserve mention. The common *cytomegalovirus* is found in body fluids, including vaginal secretions and semen. Adults infected with cytomegalovirus are frequently asymptomatic, although children born to infected mothers are at high risk of having deformities.

Hepatitis, of which there are several types, is a viral infection of the liver. *Hepatitis A* (formerly "infectious hepatitis") usually spreads through contact with infected fecal matter, as from contaminated food or during anal sex. *Hepatitis B* (formerly "serum hepatitis") usually spreads by exchange of body fluids, as during sexual activity, through use of contaminated syringes, or through contact with contaminated blood, saliva, or semen. If symptoms of hepatitis are present, they may include yellowing of the eyes and skin ("jaundice"), fever, fatigue, loss of appetite, diarrhea, and abdominal pain. Although there exists a vaccine to protect against hepatitis B, a specific cure (with the exception of bed rest) is not yet available. Some patients are severely affected, yet most recover on their own within several weeks or months.

 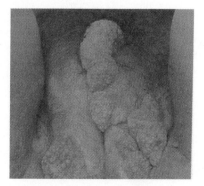

Genital warts in the male and female are caused by the human papilloma virus.

PARASITIC INFESTATIONS

PARASITIC INFESTATION

Invasion of parts of the body by tiny organisms.

In addition to the various diseases and organisms that we have thus far identified, two common STDs involve **parasitic infestation** (tiny organisms that invade and live in or on a host). These parasites are *pubic lice* and *scabies,* both of which are spread by close physical contact (not necessarily sexual) with an infested person, article (clothing and bedding), or toilet seat.

PUBIC LICE AND SCABIES

Lice are of three different breeds, each with a distinct preference for habitat: head louse, body louse, and pubic louse (*Phthirus pubis,* or "crabs"). These parasites, which are visible to the naked eye, dig into the host's skin, suck blood, and lay eggs, causing intense itching. The drugs *pyrethrins* (brand name, *A-200 Pyrinate*) and *gamma benzene hexachloride* (brand name, *Kwell*) both effectively kill lice. A-200 Pyrinate sells over the counter, while Kwell requires a prescription.

Scabies are mites that can live for months under the host's skin where they lay eggs. Scabies also cause intense itching, blisters, and pus. The infestation most commonly occurs on the wrists, in the spaces between the fingers, under the breasts, and on the buttocks. Kwell is the medication of choice for treating scabies. Laundering all clothing, bedding, and towels is necessary to prevent reinfestation of both crabs and scabies. These items should also be reexamined a number of days after the initial treatment to confirm the elimination of all of the parasites.

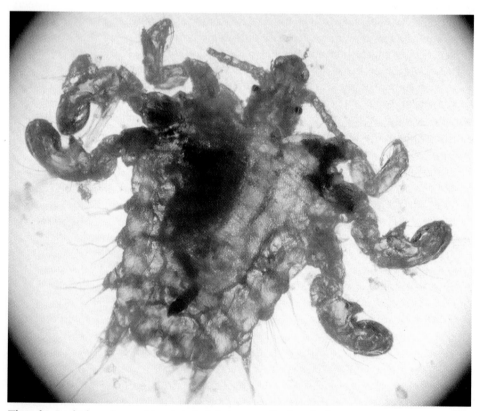

The pubic "crab" louse lives and breeds in body hair, especially the pubic hair.

On a Personal Note (Joel, 38)

> When I was in college, I remember getting crabs from a woman I met at a party. The horrible itching started some hours later. I'll never forget trying not to scratch in class the next day.

OTHER SEXUALLY TRANSMITTED INFECTIONS

A number of other infections can be transmitted sexually. Two of the most common are *trichomonas* and *monilia*.

TRICHOMONAS

Trichomonas vaginalis is a single-celled organism that lives in the vagina, causing *trichomonas*, or "trich." Although the organism can be transmitted by sexual intercourse, it can be contracted following extended exposure to moisture. Women who take oral contraceptives may be more prone to trichomonas due to heightened levels of progesterone, which increases the alkalinity in the vagina, creating a more hospitable environment for the trichomonas organism. Typical symptoms in the female include a vulva-irritating, odorous, white or yellowish vaginal discharge. The male with trichomonas is usually asymptomatic. Since the infection can be passed back and forth between partners, both must be treated should the organism be confirmed in the female partner. The prescription medication *metronidazole* (brand name, *Flagyl*) is the only effective systemic drug used to treat trichomonas.

MONILIA

Some women suffer from *monilia* (or *candidiasis*), a vaginal yeast infection caused by *Candida albicans*. Like "trich," yeast infections grow well in alkaline environments and therefore proliferate under similar circumstances. Symptoms of monilia in women include vaginal itching, irritation, and discharge; in men, penile itching, redness, and a burning sensation. For women with diagnosed yeast infections, *clotrimazole* (brand name, *Lotrimin*) and *miconazole* (brand name, *Monistat*) can be helpful.

PREVENTING SEXUALLY TRANSMITTED DISEASES

Education is the single most important weapon in fighting STDs. Teaching individuals and groups about safer sex practices and communication is vital to halting the pandemic of STDs (Keeling, 1993; Willis, 1993).

To this end, individuals should be aware of a number of precautions and **prophylactic,** or preventive, measures. The following guidelines for individuals choosing to be sexually active are from the brochure *What Are Sexually Transmitted Diseases?*, published by the American College Health Association (1989):

1. Form a monogamous relationship in which you and your partner make an agreement to be faithful sexually and stick to it. Avoid sexual intimacy until you and your partner have been tested for preexisting STDs.
2. Use condoms. While condoms do not provide 100 percent protection, they do provide the best protection now available. . . . If possible, also use a vaginal spermicide to create an additional barrier against some STDs. Women who feel hesitant about providing condoms and insisting on their use need to remember that

PROPHYLACTIC (PRO-FIL-AK-TIK)

A preventive measure or device.

Education is the single most important weapon in fighting STDs.

many STDs are more dangerous for them—females have fewer obvious symptoms and a higher risk of serious health consequences.

3. Include STD testing as part of your regular medical check-up, especially if you have changed partners or have more than one partner. Do not wait for symptoms to appear.

4. Learn the common symptoms of STDs. Seek medical help if any suspicious symptoms develop, even mild ones.

5. Do not use drugs, including alcohol, in potentially intimate situations. Drugs lower your ability to make sensible, self-protecting decisions.

Or as Hatcher et al. (1992) had to say about preventing transmission of STDs:

> Risk-free options include completely abstaining from sexual activities that transmit semen, blood, or other body fluids, or that allow for skin-to-skin contact. Alternatively, having a mutually faithful relationship with an uninfected partner eliminates any STD risk. Examining a partner for lesions, discussing each new partner's previous sexual history, reducing the number of sexual partners, and avoiding partners who have had many previous sexual partners can all augment other measures to prevent the transmission of STDs. (p. 94)

In short, you can minimize your risk of contracting an STD by practicing abstinence or maintaining a long-term monogamous relationship with an uninfected partner; regularly checking your (and your partner's) genitals for any unusual sores, lesions, or discharges; using condoms with all partners; and openly discussing your (and your partner's) sexual history. Knowledge of protection *and* action are your best guarantees against STDs.

If you suspect you've contracted an STD, see a health-care provider. Self-diagnosis can be confusing and dangerous. If you're diagnosed with an STD, follow your provider's instructions carefully. Take all medications as prescribed, and return for follow-up visits as requested. Refrain from sex with your partner until your provider gives you permission to proceed.

Last but not least, if you have an STD, you must inform your partner(s), who will need testing and possibly treatment, too. Treating your STD does little good if your partner isn't also treated. All sorts of excuses for not talking about STDs exist; however, they all pale in light of the possibility of spreading disease to others.

Knowledge about STDs is a call to action—in terms of both personal sexual activity and public health policy. We must all work to defeat STDs. Only by becoming a genuine community dedicated to the well-being of all its members can we effectively abolish ignorance and disease.

KEY POINTS

1. An all-too-frequent result of sexual relations is contraction of an infectious disease—in particular, a *sexually transmitted disease* (STD). Further complicating matters is the fact that STDs are often *asymptomatic*, fooling many into complacency about both protection and the need for treatment.

2. The majority of STDs are *bacterial*, *viral*, or *parasitic*. The most common bacterial STDs are *gonorrhea*, *nongonococcal urethritis*, *nongonococcal cervicitis*, *chlamydia*, and *syphilis*. The most common viral STDs are *genital herpes*, *human immunodeficiency virus*, and *genital warts*. Two STDs that involve parasitic infestations are *pubic lice* and *scabies*.

3. Education is the single most important weapon in fighting STDs. Teaching individuals and groups about safer sex practices and communication is vital in halting the pandemic of STDs.

4. An individual can minimize his or her risk of contracting an STD by practicing abstinence or maintaining a long-term monogamous relationship with an uninfected partner; regularly checking the genitals for any unusual sores, lesions, or discharges; using condoms with all partners; and openly discussing sexual histories with all partners.

5. Anyone diagnosed with an STD must follow the provider's instructions to the letter, take all medications as prescribed, return for a follow-up visit if requested to do so, inform all partners of the diagnosis, and refrain from sex with all partners until the provider gives permission to proceed.

ACTIVITIES AND QUESTIONS

1. In this class exercise, generate a list of excuses that people commonly use for not practicing safer sex. Write these on one side of a chalkboard. On the other side, create a list of "Pro–Safer Sex" responses to challenge these excuses. For example, you might confront the excuse, "I'll lose my erection if I have to put on a condom" with, "You'll stay hard the way I'll put the condom on you." After creating the two lists, break into pairs to role-play both parts and practice responding to a partner who pressures you against safer sex.

2. For two weeks, make note of all magazine features, newspaper articles, and television programs dealing with STDs. Return to class and describe the various ways these diseases are presented by the media.

3. What are the pros and cons associated with mandatory HIV testing? Should such testing be done? If so, on whom? Everyone? Health-care workers? Restaurant employees? Prison inmates? Why or why not? What effect might mandatory testing have on those individuals found to be HIV-positive?

4. Identify some of the myths and stereotypes about HIV—who contracts it and how, how you can tell if your partner is HIV-positive, and so on. Where do you think these stereotypes come from? What role do the popular media play in perpetuating myths about HIV and AIDS? What about family, friends, the government, religious institutions, special interest groups, and other organizations? What can you do to help eliminate these myths and stereotypes?

5. Visit an AIDS counseling center, agency, or crisis hotline. Interview a staff member about available services and programs, such as diagnostic testing, medical treatment, emotional support/counseling, financial resources for the poor, and community outreach and educational programs. Report your findings in class. Be sure to pick up some written materials to show your classmates.

6. Given their typical failure rate of 12 percent for preventing conception (and unknown failure rate for preventing the transmission of STDs), do you think condoms should be distributed at public colleges and universities? High schools? Junior high schools? With or without instructions? For free? Defend your position.

RECOMMENDED READINGS

Ankerberg, J., & Weldon, J. (1993). *The myth of safe sex: The tragic consequences of violating God's plan*. Chicago: Moody Press. The authors of this thoroughly documented Christian book promote abstinence and take a strong stand against relying on condoms for "safe sex."

Davis, M., & Scott, R. S (1988). *Lovers, doctors, and the law*. New York: Harper & Row. Presents the legal implications of "harming" another, intentionally or not, by transmitting an STD. The authors discuss the importance of sharing sexual histories between partners and legal safeguarding, and include a state-by-state guide to the legality of various sexual practices.

Turner, C. E., Miller, H. G., & Moses, L. E. (Eds.) (1989). *AIDS: Sexual behavior and intravenous drug use*. Washington, DC: National Academy Press. Presents a great deal of information on IV drug use and sexual practices relating to HIV infection and AIDS.

Westheimer, R. (1992). *Dr. Ruth's guide to safer sex: Exciting, sensible, sexual directions for the 90s*. New York: Warner Books. An easy-to-read guide to safer sex.

•**S**EXUAL DYSFUNCTIONS

•SEXUAL THERAPIES

•PREVENTING SEXUAL DYSFUNCTIONS

C H A P T E R   1 5

SEXUAL DYSFUNCTIONS AND THERAPIES

O B J E C T I V E S

AFTER READING THIS CHAPTER YOU SHOULD BE
ABLE TO . . .

1. DESCRIBE THE VARIOUS SEXUAL DYSFUNCTIONS
   MEN AND WOMEN EXPERIENCE, AS WELL AS
   WAYS TO PREVENT DYSFUNCTIONS FROM
   OCCURRING IN THE FIRST PLACE.
2. IDENTIFY SOME OF THE MOST COMMON CAUSES
   OF SEXUAL DYSFUNCTIONS.
3. DESCRIBE MASTERS AND JOHNSON'S (1970)
   AND KAPLAN'S (1974) RESPECTIVE MODELS
   OF SEX THERAPY, INCLUDING THE BASIC
   TECHNIQUES COMMON TO THESE AND OTHER
   APPROACHES.
4. EXPLAIN HOW TO FIND A REPUTABLE SEX
   THERAPIST.
5. BETTER UNDERSTAND YOUR OWN SEXUAL
   FUNCTIONING.

You mustn't force sex to do the work of love, or love to do the work of sex.

Mary McCarthy

Have you ever experienced a sexual difficulty? If so, don't feel alone. At one time or another, almost everyone has. It's normal. Maybe you weren't in the mood and lacked interest in your partner. Perhaps you felt pressured and couldn't become aroused. Maybe intercourse or masturbation was painful. Whatever the difficulty, it was probably temporary or appears only intermittently.

But what about those sexual problems that recur on a frequent, even daily basis? What causes such problems? What are some of the more typical and atypical problems experienced? What is sex therapy, and how effective is it? To answer these questions, we turn our attention in this chapter to the first category of sexual disorders—chronic problems of the sexual response cycle, termed *sexual dysfunctions*.

SEXUAL DYSFUNCTIONS

SEXUAL DYSFUNCTION (DIS-FUNK-SHUN)

Persistent and recurrent problems in sexual response.

A sexual disorder is likely when a given sexual stimulus (for example, seeing the partner nude) consistently fails to prompt the expected response (penile erection or vaginal lubrication). Specifically, **sexual dysfunctions** involve a chronic malfunction in the individual's capacity to respond effectively to sexual stimulation. These disorders are chronic in that the individual is unable to have satisfying sexual relations after repeated attempts with a desirable, willing partner over extended periods of time. Clinicians diagnosing and treating these disorders also specify whether a particular client's dysfunction is biological and/or psychosocial in origin, or a combination of the two. The categories of sexual dysfunctions are *sexual desire disorders, sexual arousal disorders, orgasm disorders, sexual pain disorders, and sexual dysfunction "not otherwise specified."*

SEXUAL DESIRE DISORDERS

The **sexual desire disorders** are disorders of the appetitive phase of the sexual response system. That is, they have to do with whether or not, or with what frequency, an individual desires sexual activity. Of course, levels of sexual interest, or *libido*, vary a great deal across individuals, couples, and circumstances. This is why it is difficult or impossible to determine exactly what a "normal" level of sexual interest is, as well as what is too high or low. Clinicians, then, diagnose low sexual desire by taking into account factors such as age and context, and by asking the individual if she or he feels capable of sexual satisfaction. The diagnostic process can be tricky, though, as a number of people carry irrational expectations about what is normal or how they *should* function (Pietropinto & Simenauer, 1990).

The sexual desire disorders are *hypoactive sexual desire disorder* (lack of desire) and *sexual aversion disorder* (fear of sexual activity).

Hypoactive Sexual Desire Disorder Hypoactive **sexual desire disorder** (often termed *low sexual desire* or *inhibited sexual desire*) involves chronically deficient or absent sexual fantasies and desire for sexual activity (American Psychiatric Association, 1994). The man or woman with hypoactive sexual desire disorder has little or no interest in sexual activity, and normally does not initiate sexual activity or respond to the partner's advances. Because one partner desires sexual activity and the other does not, hypoactive sexual desire disorder can cause the one to end up feeling pressured and the other deprived. Treatment involves helping the client identify and work through her or his sexual and relationship conflicts, anxiety, and anger.

SEXUAL DESIRE DISORDERS
Disorders of the desire phase of sexual response.

HYPOACTIVE SEXUAL DESIRE DISORDER (HI-PO-AK-TIV)
Lack of sexual desire.

Most sexual dysfunctions result from a combination of psychological and social factors, such as frequent conflicts within a long-term relationship.

SEXUAL AVERSION DISORDER
Fear of sexual activity.

Sexual Aversion Disorder

Sexual aversion disorder involves extreme aversion to and avoidance of genital contact and sexual activity (American Psychiatric Association, 1994). In other words, the individual with sexual aversion disorder is overwhelmingly fearful, even phobic, of sexual situations and activity. Like the individual with hypoactive sexual desire disorder, he or she does not initiate sexual activity or respond to a partner's advances, and is likely to avoid all sex-related situations. The disorder is more common in women than men. Treatment normally involves helping the client eliminate her or his sexual anxieties by identifying and working through the underlying sexual conflicts.

SEXUAL AROUSAL DISORDERS

SEXUAL AROUSAL DISORDERS
Disorders of the excitement phase of sexual response.

The **sexual arousal disorders** reflect problems in the excitement phase of sexual response (American Psychiatric Association, 1994). In other words, they have to do with an individual's ability to become aroused and to ready herself or himself for sexual activity. The arousal disorders are *female sexual arousal disorder*, and *male erectile disorder*.

FEMALE SEXUAL AROUSAL DISORDER
Inability to gain and sustain clitoral erection and vaginal lubrication sufficient to initiate and complete sexual activity.

Female Sexual Arousal Disorder

The woman with **female sexual arousal disorder** desires sexual activity, but is unable to experience the physical changes necessary for sexual pleasuring (American Psychiatric Association, 1994). Normally, when a woman becomes sexually aroused, drops of lubrication form on the walls of her vagina to facilitate penile penetration. In the absence of this vaginal lubrication, sexual intercourse is painful, difficult, or even impossible. Absence of sexual excitement due to ineffective sexual stimulation, such as bypassing sexplay activities, is unrelated to female sexual arousal disorder.

Treatment of female sexual arousal disorder is directed at helping the woman overcome her sexual inhibitions, negative perceptions, guilt, shame, anxiety, performance fears, and anger toward the partner. The therapist may also recommend that the woman learn how to arouse and stimulate herself (termed *masturbation training*, described later in this chapter), and that she and her partner practice various nondemand pleasuring exercises (termed *sensate focus*, also described later) before attempting sexual intercourse.

MALE ERECTILE DISORDER
Inability to gain and sustain penile erection sufficient to initiate and complete sexual activity.

Male Erectile Disorder

Male erectile disorder (commonly termed *impotence*, meaning "without power") refers to a chronic inability to attain and/or maintain penile erection sufficient to initiate and complete sexual activity (American Psychiatric Association, 1994). The man with this disorder desires sexual activity but cannot become or keep erect long enough to begin or finish sexual intercourse. If he has never had an erection, he has *lifelong* erectile disorder. Otherwise, he has *acquired* erectile disorder (American Psychiatric Association, 1994). The latter disorder differs from both temporary and normal age-related decline in erectile ability. By far, most cases of male erectile disorder are of the acquired type.

Erection is not an all-or-nothing phenomenon, nor is it always necessary for lovemaking. Some men can have sexual intercourse with only a partial erection. Others attain full erections at certain times but not others, or with a specific partner. Many men with erectile disorder are otherwise good lovers; they may become particularly skilled at stimulating the partner with the flaccid penis, manually stimulating their partner's genitals, or performing oral sex to compensate for lack of erectile ability.

When male erectile disorder is of biological origin, treatment involves medications and/or *prosthesis* (described later). When the disorder is of psychological origin, treatment in the form of psychotherapy involves helping the client feel less pressured and anxious about his sexual abilities and performances (Reinisch, 1990). Sensate focus exercises are especially useful for this purpose (Masters & Johnson, 1970).

ORGASM DISORDERS

The **orgasm disorders** have as their primary characteristic a malfunction in the orgasm phase of sexual response. Orgasm may occur too quickly, occur only occasionally, lack intensity, or be delayed or entirely prevented—the common feature here being an inability to control the orgasmic reflex. The orgasm disorders are *female orgasmic disorder, male orgasmic disorder,* and *premature ejaculation.*

Female Orgasmic Disorder Female orgasmic disorder (or *anorgasmia*) is defined as a delay in, or absence of, orgasm following adequate levels of sexual stimulation (American Psychiatric Association, 1994). The anorgasmic woman desires sexual activity and becomes aroused, but she cannot climax. Her sexual response does not progress beyond the plateau phase.

As with female sexual arousal disorder, treatment of female orgasmic disorder involves helping the woman overcome her negative, self-defeating attitudes and feelings about sexual activity. As the woman's awareness of her body and feelings increases, and as she overcomes her fears of "letting go," her sexual inhibitions lift. In addition to sensate focus and masturbation training, the therapist may recommend that the woman and her partner employ a special reconditioning technique, the *bridge maneuver.* Here, the woman progresses through a series of graduated sexual "steps"—from climaxing via masturbation to climaxing via the partner's manual stimulation to climaxing via intercourse (Kaplan, 1987).

A fairly common phenomenon among many women (nearly 60 percent) is to pretend to have an orgasm (Darling & Davidson, 1986). When asked why she would do this, one client responded:

On a Personal Note (Jeannie, age 26)

I have a really difficult time coming during intercourse. I don't have too much problem with it when Joel uses his hands to stimulate me, but during sex it just doesn't happen. Anyway, he's *super sensitive* about satisfying me. And rather than hurt his feelings, I go ahead and let on like I'm coming. It makes him happy, and I don't really mind too much. I mean if that's the worst problem I've got to deal with, I'm really pretty lucky. (Author's files)

Faking orgasms is a conscious decision not to communicate needs. People fake orgasms for many reasons, but they usually do it to avoid hurting the partner's feelings or to maintain a certain "performance" standard during sex. Deceiving the partner in this way can have serious consequences. Without knowing that the one partner has faked an orgasm, the other partner continues to do whatever it was that prompted the one to fake in the first place. With time, this cycle of deception becomes harder to interrupt.

Male Orgasmic Disorder Male orgasmic disorder (or *retarded ejaculation*) refers to a man's inability to have an orgasm and ejaculate following adequate sexual stimulation (American Psychiatric Association, 1994). That is, the man with inhibited orgasm finds it difficult or impossible to climax, even though he has an erection and may masturbate or coitally thrust for an hour or more (Zgourides & Warren, 1989). Male orgasmic disorder differs from a condition known as *retrograde ejaculation,* in which semen is expelled into the bladder instead of from the body through the penis.

ORGASM DISORDERS
Disorders of the orgasm phase of sexual response.

FEMALE ORGASMIC DISORDER
A woman's inability to attain orgasm following sexual stimulation.

MALE ORGASMIC DISORDER
A man's inability to attain orgasm following sexual stimulation.

The treatment of choice for male orgasmic disorder involves reconditioning the client's orgasmic reflex and helping him work through his sexual conflicts about "letting go." One useful technique for accomplishing this is the *bridge maneuver*. The man gradually learns to ejaculate alone, then in front of a partner, next with the partner, and finally into the vagina. In most cases, the man's inhibitions disappear as soon as he ejaculates a few times inside his partner (Kaplan, 1987).

It may surprise some readers to learn that some men with male orgasmic disorder fake orgasms to hide the problem or maintain a reputation as a "sexual workhorse." As one client mentioned:

On a Personal Note (Jeff, age 30)

I've never been able to come inside a woman's vagina. I mean, *never*—no matter how hard I try or how long I work at it! There have been plenty of times when Kirsten and I have gone after it pretty fiercely for over an hour, and then off and on for another couple of hours. In the beginning, I was so embarrassed about it that I'd fake an orgasm when I couldn't go any longer. I had to look like a man, right? One of the problems with this disorder is that a lot of women love a guy who can last really long. Who wants to ruin a sexual reputation like that? (Author's files)

PREMATURE EJACULATION
A man's inability to delay ejaculation.

Premature Ejaculation   In the case of **premature ejaculation,** the individual ejaculates before he and his partner have had a satisfying sexual encounter. There is a recurrent and persistent inability to exert "reasonable" voluntary control over the ejaculatory reflex during sexual activity (American Psychiatric Association, 1994). In defining "reasonable" control, the clinician must take into account such variables as the individual's age, usual frequency of intercourse, and novelty of the partner and situation. The key point here has to do with the man's ability to *control* his ejaculation, not so much with the amount of *time* that passes before he climaxes (Kaplan, 1974).

On a Personal Note (Hank, age 19)

It's really embarrassing when I'm kissing a woman and I come in my pants—long before anything really goes down. You know, this happens just about every time when all I'm doing is making out in the car or something. And I might come a couple of times this way in an hour or two. It's all very frustrating. (Author's files)

Treatment of premature ejaculation involves assisting the man in working through his sexual issues, learning to anticipate climax, and reconditioning his ejaculatory reflex (McCarthy, 1994). With respect to the latter, two popular methods for learning ejaculatory control are the *stop-start* and *squeeze* techniques (both described later in this chapter).

SEXUAL PAIN DISORDERS

SEXUAL PAIN DISORDERS
Disorders involving genital pain.

Pain associated with sexual activity is the principle characteristic of the **sexual pain disorders,** in particular, *dyspareunia* and *vaginismus*.

**DYSPAREUNIA
(DIS-PA-ROO-NE-A)**
Genital pain before, during, or after sex.

Dyspareunia   Recurrent and persistent genital pain before, during, or after sexual intercourse is termed **dyspareunia.** The condition occurs in both males and females, and can happen at any point in the sexual response cycle (American Psychiatric Association,

1994). A male might experience a painful erection upon penetration; a female might experience vaginal burning or pelvic cramping during thrusting. The disorder, however, is more common among women than men. Treatment of dyspareunia is directed at correcting or eliminating the underlying causes of the disorder, whether they be medical or psychological. There is no single, standard therapy for dyspareunia.

Vaginismus   Sometimes considered a specific type of female dyspareunia, **vaginismus** involves powerful, involuntary contractions and spasms of the muscles of the outer third of the vagina (American Psychiatric Association, 1994). These spasms may or may not be painful, but generally interfere with coitus by preventing entry of the penis into the vagina. In many cases, the woman with vaginismus is 100 percent sexually responsive, except during sexual intercourse. She and her partner may enjoy other forms of sexual pleasuring as long as they do not lead to intercourse.

The usual treatment strategy for vaginismus is to help the woman overcome her sexual conflicts and recondition the muscles surrounding her vaginal orifice to accept objects of increasing size. In most cases, penile insertion is possible once the woman comes to feel more at ease with her sexuality, and her vagina becomes accustomed to penetration.

VAGINISMUS (VA-JI-NIS-MUS)

Painful spasms of the muscles of the outer third of the vagina.

SEXUAL DYSFUNCTION NOT OTHERWISE SPECIFIED

Sexual dysfunctions, or any other disorders for that matter, do not always fall into neat, "black-or-white" diagnostic categories. To be sure, many possible problems are associated with human sexual response. Clinicians reserve the *sexual dysfunction "NOS"* (not otherwise specified) diagnostic category for those sexual dysfunctions that do not meet the criteria of any other sexual dysfunction. An example of a sexual dysfunction NOS is total lack of erotic sensation despite the presence of normal physiological components of orgasm (American Psychiatric Association, 1994).

Worth mentioning here are two additional sexual dysfunctions. *Hypersexuality* (also called "nymphomania" in females and "satyriasis" in males) involves *excessive* sexual desire and interest. A specific diagnostic category does not exist for hypersexuality. Why? First, defining "high," or even "normal," libido is virtually impossible. One person may desire sexual activity twice daily while another desires it only once a month. Second, level of sexual interest reflects different things for different people at different times. Increased sexual interest may be the result of improved health for one person, or a way of dealing with severe stress for another.

Some people, however, engage in what might be seen as compulsive sexual behavior that interferes with one or more life areas, such as school performance. An example of this might be missing classes due to masturbating daily for several hours. This phenomenon has prompted a number of authors and therapists to propose the idea of *sexual addiction*, similar in many respects to an alcohol or other drug addiction (Carnes, 1983; Trachtenberg, 1988). According to Stephen Arterburn (1991) in his book *Addicted to Love*:

> For thousands—perhaps millions—of people, sex has become a drug. Like any drug, it is used in an attempt to deaden pain: the pain of rejection, loneliness, fear, anxiety, childhood abuse, or any of a dozen other hurts.
>
> But it doesn't work. Sex masks the pain for a moment, providing a brief mood change. The short-lived relief comes not just from the orgasm, but also the ritual leading up to it—the seeking of which becomes the central organizing factor of daily life. But in the long run, instead of making the pain better, it ends up making it worse as the person experiences deepening humiliation and loss of control over his or her life. (pp. 104–105)

The proposal that sexual addiction is a psychiatric disorder is controversial. Who can say for sure what "compulsive" or "addictive" sex is? And is excessive, compulsive sex (or compulsive religion, exercise, and so on) really an "addiction"? There does seem to be at least some anecdotal evidence to support the notion of sexual addiction (Carnes, 1983). Organizations like *Sex Addicts Anonymous* and *Sexaholics Anonymous*, which use a modified "12-step" program based on that of *Alcoholics Anonymous*, are becoming increasingly popular resources for people seeking to overcome compulsive sexual thoughts and behaviors.

HOW PREVALENT ARE SEXUAL DYSFUNCTIONS?

How many people have a sexual dysfunction? This a difficult question to answer, as we don't have available a current, large-scale survey study of the prevalence and frequency of sexual dysfunctions in our society. We must rely on information gleaned from smaller studies to make conclusions about the general population. Data from a recent review of community samples provide us with some insights into the prevalence and frequency of sexual dysfunctions in nonclinical samples (Spector & Carey, 1990). These data appear in Table 15.1.

CAUSES OF SEXUAL DYSFUNCTIONS

The causes of sexual dysfunctions are many and complex. Given so many variables to consider—the nature and severity of the problem(s), the individual's unique background and circumstances, the meaning that a particular symptom holds for the individual or couple—generalizations are difficult. But because some patterns are discernible, we now briefly consider a few of the many causes of sexual dysfunctions as a diagnostic group.

Biologically speaking, any condition, disorder, disease, or drug that alters nervous system functioning has the potential to disrupt sexual functioning (Olivera, 1994; Reinisch, 1990). At one time, experts believed that biology was responsible for only 10 to 20 percent of cases of sexual dysfunctions (Masters & Johnson, 1970; Kaplan, 1974; Kolodny et al., 1979). More recent research, however, has challenged this view, suggesting a widespread influence of biology on sexual functioning (Masters et al., 1994; Reinisch, 1990). Kaplan (1974, 1979, 1987) grouped the various physiological/medical sources of sexual dysfunctions as follows:

1. *Medical Conditions and Disorders.* This category includes a variety of diseases and infections that interfere with sexual functioning, such as general ill health, chronic infections, cardiac disease, diabetes mellitus, and multiple sclerosis.
2. *Neurological Disorders and Trauma.* Damage or trauma to the brain, nervous system, and genitals belong to this category.
3. *Medications and Drugs.* This category includes chemicals that disrupt sexual functioning by depressing the nervous system and/or altering mood, such as antihypertensives, antidepressants, tranquilizers, narcotics, nicotine, and alcohol.

Therapists normally pay a great deal of attention to the *psychological* processes that shape an individual's sexuality. A vast majority of sexual dysfunctions result from *intrapsychic conflicts*, *learning* and *conditioning*, and *cognitive distortions*.

TABLE 15.1 Prevalence of Sexual Dysfunctions in Nonclinical Samples

Dysfunction or Problem	Men	Women
Delayed or inhibited orgasm	4–10%	5–10%
Premature ejaculation	36–38%	—
Erection difficulties	4–9%	—

Source: Adapted from I. P. Spector & M. P. Carey (1990), Incidence and prevalence of the sexual dysfunctions: A critical review of the empirical literature, *Archives of Sexual Behavior, 19,* 389–408.

PERSPECTIVE

Casanovas and Compulsive Love

Peter Trachtenberg (1988) had the following to say about "Casanovas" (men with a long history of transitory love affairs) in his popular book, *The Casanova Complex:*

> For the men [described] in this book, the primary object of compulsion is women. To Casanovas, women are at different times objects of maddening desire, sources of sexual pleasure and self-validation, and focuses of overwhelming dread. For all their outward insouciance—their air of men surveying the canapé tray at a cocktail party—they pursue women with an urgency and single-mindedness that makes ordinary courtship seem casual and desultory and with a recklessness that often jeopardizes their marriages, careers, and health. With the advent of AIDS, some of them are undoubtedly risking their lives. Some of these men are indiscriminate womanizers; others have rigid criteria of attractiveness. But all of them to some extent seem powerless in their frenzied pursuit of sexual opportunity.
>
> Powerlessness is not the same thing as helplessness. Many addicts and alcoholics are at least superficially successful and effective individuals. One need only point to the examples of Hermann Goering, F. Scott Fitzgerald, or Judy Garland to realize that such people may radiate charisma and authority while remaining in thrall to their disease....
>
> Paradoxically, their compulsion and its psychic concomitants give Casanovas a great deal of power over women—a persistence, an urgency, a persuasiveness and sexual authority that many women find overwhelming. These men are as adept at finding sexual partners as alcoholics are at finding a drink when the bars are closed, as skillful at seduction as drug addicts are at getting money for their next fix. Unconsciously viewing women as objects whose sole purpose is to satiate and adore them, Casanovas often have the unhappy facility of making women briefly conform to their inner scenarios—and of choosing the women who are most likely to comply. If they are victims of their compulsion they are also victimizers, whose exploitation of women is no less pernicious because it goes by the name of love.
>
> By calling their condition a compulsion, I have implied that Casanovas are sick people. In our time sickness has become the fashionable explanation for what used to be called wickedness; sometimes it has been used to excuse it. I offer no excuses for these men, and my explanations of why they act the way they do are basically informed hypotheses, the kind that any student of human nature is forced to make do with for lack of a surer blueprint. The condition that I call the Casanova complex—the compulsive pursuit and abandonment of women—encompasses a number of psychiatric disorders, much as addiction does. (pp. 28–30)

Questions for Thought

Do you know, or have you ever known, someone—male or female—with a Casanova complex? If so, do they fit the above description? In what way(s)?

Source: P. Trachtenberg (1988), *The Casanova complex* (New York: Poseidon Press).

In terms of intrapsychic ("internal" versus "interpersonal") factors, Freud and other psychoanalytically and psychodynamically oriented therapists have traditionally held that various sexual conflicts arise during specific childhood developmental periods in response to deprivation or overgratification of assorted primary needs. For example, a girl whose parents discourage her from masturbating might *fixate* (become "stuck" and conflicted) at an early stage of psychosexual development. As an adult, she may develop such internal conflicts about relations that she becomes sexually unresponsive.

Here we see the influence of learning on sexuality. Most of us learn to think of certain sexual stimuli and activities as appealing and arousing. Such sexual conditioning has a positive effect when the person's social environment has fostered healthy attitudes about sexuality, loving relationships, open communication, and freedom of choice. Unfortunately, this is not always the case. Many people receive negative, defeating childhood injunctions about sexuality, which in turn lead to negative, defeating adult attitudes and feelings. These early messages might go something like this:

- Sex is wrong.
- Don't touch your genitals.
- Never touch anyone else's genitals.
- Sexual thoughts are wrong.

These injunctions can affect sexual functioning by interfering with the person's thinking processes and reinforcing undesirable sexual behaviors. For example, the man who learns during childhood that sexual activity is sinful may feel pressured as an adult to climax as quickly as possible, in this way satisfying his sexual needs while reducing his guilt about having sex ("The faster I go, the less time I'll spend sinning"). As these negative thoughts and patterns continue, the man learns premature ejaculation, reinforcing dysfunctional behaviors with each hasty sexual encounter.

Children learn a great deal—both good and bad—about love and sexuality from their parents and other primary caregivers.

Many sexually disordered individuals also engage in *spectatoring*, or sexual self-monitoring (Masters & Johnson, 1970). Rather than giving themselves over to the erotic sensations of lovemaking, they "step outside of themselves" and focus on and monitor the sexual process and their performance. Spectatoring can give rise to *orgasm focus* (preoccupation with having an orgasm during sex) and/or *sexual performance anxiety* (excessive fear of not measuring up, not being able to satisfy one's partner or self, or being ridiculed by the partner). The nervous system mediates these kinds of anxiety, fear, guilt, and obsession reactions, all of which can block sexual desire, arousal, and orgasm (Kaplan, 1974).

Of course, relationship issues also affect sexual functioning. Anger, outrage, hostility, and disapproval—like anxiety, fear, and guilt—interfere with sexual activity by inhibiting the nervous system reactions necessary for sexual arousal and response. Sexual boredom, conflicting sexual expectations, unwelcomed criticism, power struggles, financial worries, and fears of pregnancy can also manifest themselves as sexual problems.

Social influences contribute to the development of sexual dysfunctions. Some of the more common of these are a sexually repressive upbringing, parents' negative views of sexuality and the genitals, sexual myths perpetuated by the media, childhood sexual abuse, incest, and rape. Some of the strongest social determinants of sexual disorders, however, have to do with societal and cultural attitudes and prohibitions. The way we feel about and choose to express our sexuality exists within a particular cultural context. Our parents, extended family, teachers, and religious leaders all help shape our sexual attitudes and chosen avenues of sexual expression.

Cultural norms and mores are not always realistic or even desirable. Take, for example, our society's traditional ideas about proper female and male sexual roles—the belief that women are less sexual than men, or that men are always ready for sex. These sorts of irrational demands can plant seeds of doubt and bring about sexual dysfunctions.

SEXUAL THERAPIES

Only decades ago, people had to endure sexual problems in silence. Today, as society has become better informed about the nature of sexual dysfunctions and available treatments, more and more people are reading self-help sexual manuals and/or seeking out the assistance of professional sex therapists. In fact, developments in the field of sexology over the last 25 years or so have made available a variety of treatments for couples seeking to overcome their sexual problems.

The discipline of sexology (including sex therapy) is relatively young and without its own distinctive theoretical base. Professionals from a variety of backgrounds and theoretical perspectives practice sex therapy without a single, preferred treatment approach. Moreover, the phrase *sex therapy* is vague, having different meanings for different therapists. In its loosest sense, the phrase refers to any method that is used to treat sexual problems. In its strictest sense, the phrase refers to specific, research-validated programs for eliminating specific sexual dysfunctions. Our concern here is with this latter category.

Most sex therapies have as their basic format what has come to be termed PLISSIT— an acronym for *permission, limited information, specific suggestions,* and *intensive therapy* (Annon, 1974). First, the therapist gives clients *permission* to have, or not have, intercourse when they feel ready. Next, the therapist provides clients with *limited information* of a factual nature concerning sexual functioning, followed by *specific suggestions* concerning activities that the therapist believes will be helpful. During *intensive therapy*, the therapist assists clients in uncovering and dealing with intrapsychic conflicts, cognitive distortions, and assorted relationship issues. Of course, not everyone needs all four steps of PLISSIT.

MASTERS AND JOHNSON'S MODEL

The first model of sex therapy to be widely accepted and used is that of Masters and Johnson (1970)—a comprehensive approach based in part on the principles of behavioral psychology. Masters and Johnson follow an intensive two-week program for couples. They believe sexual problems are relationship problems, and must be treated within this context. The program begins with each partner undergoing a complete physical and psychological examination. Next, both partners meet on a daily basis with a male-female therapist team. Masters and Johnson believe each partner best identifies with and feels appreciated by a same-sex therapist. The cotherapists help the couple define and update treatment goals while guiding them through the various phases of therapy.

Masters and Johnson's "here-and-now" approach mostly focuses on eliminating sexual symptoms—not delving into and trying to correct deep-seated emotional conflicts. Although critics hold that the underlying problems of the sexual symptoms must be removed to effect a "cure," Masters and Johnson argue that relieving symptoms with specific techniques is just as viable, especially for those couples who do not want or cannot afford several months or years of intensive psychotherapy.

Other principles important to Masters and Johnson's method include:

1. Therapy is individualized to meet the specific needs of each couple.
2. Sex is assumed to be a natural function, controlled largely by reflex responses of the body.
3. Because fears of performance and "spectatoring" are often central to cases of sexual dysfunction, therapy is approached at several levels, such as relabeling expectations and increasing communication.
4. Determining who is to blame for a sexual problem is discouraged as counterproductive.
5. Helping couples see that sex is just one component of their relationship is stressed. (Masters et al., 1992, p. 555)

KAPLAN'S MODEL

Built on her *triphasic model* of human sexual response, Helen Singer Kaplan (1974, 1979, 1987) created the *New Sex Therapy* to treat dysfunctions occurring at any of the three levels of response—desire, arousal, and orgasm. Like Masters and Johnson, Kaplan (1974) believes sexual problems result from multiple causes. However, she also believes some sexual problems are due to "immediate" and more accessible causes (which are easier to treat), and others to "unconscious" and less accessible causes (which are harder to treat). To this end, she developed a therapy model that integrates many of the techniques of Masters and Johnson with various principles of Freudian therapy, such as acknowledging the role of unconscious processes in sexual functioning.

Kaplan's method differs from that of Masters and Johnson in other respects. Kaplan does not limit her work with clients to two weeks. Although she stresses short-term behavioral therapy in many cases, she also recommends long-term intensive therapy for those clients who evidence deep-seated sexual conflicts. Further, Kaplan treats premature ejaculation with the *stop-start technique* (Semans, 1956), rather than the *squeeze technique* (Masters & Johnson, 1970). Both of these techniques are described later.

THE BASIC TECHNIQUES OF SEX THERAPY

Sex therapists have available a number of techniques, some of which are common to Masters and Johnson's model, Kaplan's model, and other approaches. These are *sensate focus, masturbation training,* the *stop-start technique,* the *squeeze technique, cognitive therapy, surgery, medications, prosthesis,* and on rare occasions the use of *sexual surrogates.*

Sex therapy at the Masters and Johnson Institute involves a male-female cotherapist team counseling both partners.

Sensate Focus Because so many sexual dysfunctions are the result of spectatoring, performance anxiety, performance demands, guilt, and ineffective communication, Masters and Johnson recommend that patients master a variety of nondemand, giving and receiving exercises very early in therapy. Termed *sensate focus*, these exercises begin with touch-focused awareness activities (body massages) and gradually progress to more direct sexual activities (genital fondling) (Figure 15.1).

Throughout sensate focus, the partners take turns touching and being touched, as well as sharing their thoughts and feelings with one another. The idea here is for both partners to learn to give and receive goal-free, nondemand pleasuring.

Masturbation Training   Many people who have trouble experiencing orgasm during sexual intercourse do not have the same trouble during masturbation. Hence, *masturbation training*—with or without a vibrator, alone or with a partner—can be an invaluable therapy for orgasm problems. In the case of lifelong inhibited orgasm, the sex therapist might recommend that the client first learn to masturbate to orgasm before attempting to reach orgasm during sexual intercourse. In the case of acquired inhibited orgasm, the therapist might recommend a series of sensate-focus and arousal-enhancing exercises to help the client "loosen up." In most cases, acquired inhibited orgasm is easier to treat than its lifelong counterpart.

After masturbating to orgasm, then what? The individual must generalize her or his sexual responses from manual to coital stimulation. Concerning women learning to find what feels good during intercourse, Shere Hite, the author of the *Hite Report* (1976), had this to say:

> Orgasms during intercourse in this study usually seemed to result from a conscious attempt by the woman to center some kind of clitoral area contact for herself during intercourse, usually involving contact with the man's pubic area. This clitoral stimulation during intercourse could be thought of, then, as basically stimulating yourself while intercourse is in progress. Of course the other person must cooperate. This is essentially the way men get stimulation during intercourse: they rub their penises against our vaginal walls so that the same area they stimulate during masturbation is being stimulated during intercourse. In other words, *you* have to get the stimulation centered where it feels good. (p. 276)

Some women also become orgasmic after learning to *Kegel*, that is, learning to contract and relax their pubococcygeal ("PC") pelvic floor muscles (Chapter 4). The woman first identifies these muscles by stopping and starting her urine flow. She then continues to practice contracting and relaxing her pelvic muscles when not urinating, perhaps while standing, sitting, or even talking on the telephone. Based on the sexuality-enhancing techniques of the ancient Tantric religion, Arnold Kegel originally developed the Kegel exercises in the late 1940s as a treatment for urinary incontinence. Western therapists and researchers have since rediscovered, however, that control over the pelvic floor muscles is also associated with enhanced orgasm in both men and women (Brauer & Brauer, 1990).

For Personal Reflection

What do you think of the therapeutic technique of learning to masturbate to overcome a sexual dysfunction?

The Stop-Start Technique   Developed by James Semans (1956), the *stop-start technique* is used to treat premature ejaculation. Here, the partner stimulates the man's penis almost to the point of ejaculation, but then pauses until the urge to climax has passed. The process is repeated many times, each successive episode generally prolonging the amount of time needed between pauses to inhibit ejaculation. The man eventually develops the capacity to control his ejaculatory reflex in the presence of intense, prolonged stimulation.

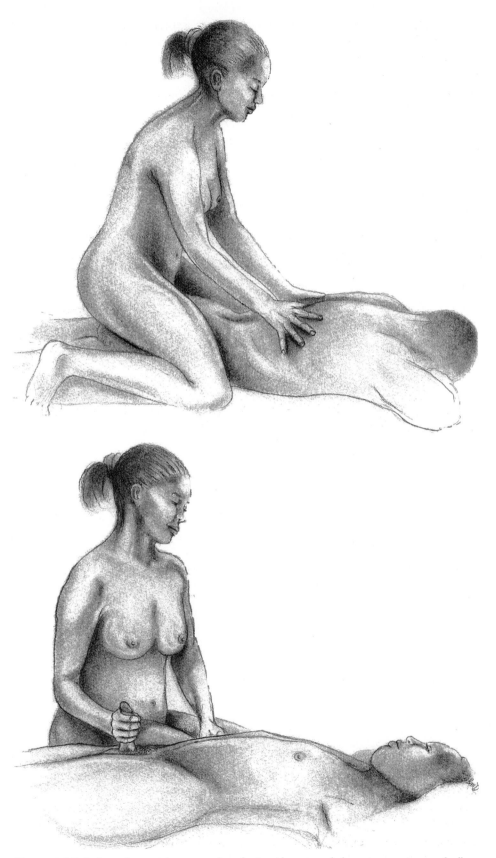

FIGURE 15.1 *A couple practicing sensate focus begin with nonsexual pleasuring exercises, gradually moving to more direct sexual contact.*

The Squeeze Technique Masters and Johnson's (1970) *squeeze technique*, like the stop-start technique, is also used to treat premature ejaculation. The procedure involves the man's partner gently squeezing his erect penis at the head or the base. The partner performs the "squeeze" as soon as the man indicates an urge to ejaculate and until this urge has passed (usually about four seconds). Sexual activity resumes, and the process is repeated (usually three to four times in any given sexual encounter) until the man learns ejaculatory control (Figures 15.2 and 15.3).

Cognitive Therapy Many professionals (Barlow, 1988; Beck, 1988; Ellis, 1976; Firestone, 1990) believe effective treatment of sexual dysfunctions must also include techniques directed at the problematic thinking patterns described earlier. The sex therapist

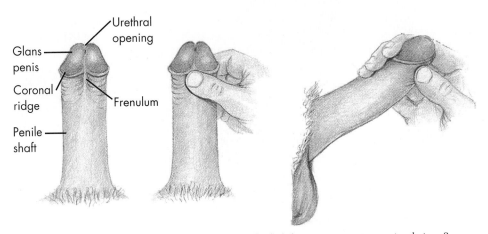

FIGURE 15.2 *The squeeze technique (at the coronal ridge) for treating premature ejaculation. Source: W. H. Masters, V. E. Johnson, & R. C. Kolodny (1992), Human sexuality (4th ed.) (New York: HarperCollins). Reprinted by permission.*

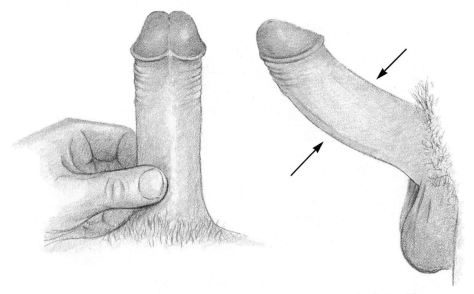

FIGURE 15.3 *The squeeze technique (at the base) for treating premature ejaculation. The arrows show the direction for applying pressure to the penis—always from front to back, never side to side. Source: W. H. Masters, V. E. Johnson, & R. C. Kolodny (1992), Human sexuality (4th ed.) (New York: HarperCollins). Reprinted by permission.*

should show clients how their thoughts, feelings, and behaviors interact to create sexual problems, as well as how to eliminate faulty patterns. Cognitive therapy is appropriate for individuals, couples, and groups. Keep in mind that cognitive therapy is an excellent, and in this author's opinion, necessary *adjunct* to behavioral therapy, but not a *substitute* for it.

Surgery, Medications, and Prosthesis   The sexual dysfunctions that result from organic factors usually require some type of medical intervention. Physicians may use surgery to correct structural abnormalities of the reproductive organs, or they may use one or more medications to improve sexual functioning.

Some health-care providers choose to deal with certain sexual dysfunctions mechanically with a *prosthesis* (an artificial device that replaces a missing body part). For instance, one possible treatment for chronic, irreversible impotence involves surgical implantation of a *penile prosthesis* to bring about erections. The surgeon inserts one or two slender, hollow cylinders into the penile shaft, and a fluid-filled pump into the scrotal sac (Figure 15.4). When the man wants his penis to become erect, he merely squeezes the pump, which moves fluid into the cylinders. When he wants his penis to become flaccid again, he releases a small valve, which returns the fluid to the scrotal pump. Many men with a penile prosthesis report satisfactory results when using the device during sexual activity (Collins & Kinder, 1984; McCarthy & McMillan, 1990).

For Personal Reflection

If you were a man with irreversible erectile disorder due to a medical condition, would you consider a penile prosthesis? Why or why not?

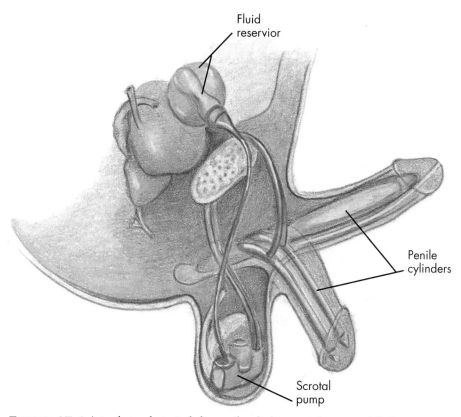

FIGURE 15.4 *A penile prosthesis, including penile cylinders, scrotal pump, and fluid reservoir.*

Sexual Surrogates The great majority of sex therapists ask both partners to participate in therapy, as most of the sexual techniques described in this section require two people to be effective. But what if a sex therapy client is single, or if his or her partner refuses to participate?

In most instances, therapists do their best to work with the client given his or her circumstances. A few therapists, however, assign the client a *sexual surrogate*, who performs the sex therapy functions of the absent spouse or sexual partner. The components of sex therapy in this case remain the same, except the client schedules joint counseling sessions with both the therapist and the surrogate, and individual practice sessions with the surrogate only. The typical surrogate participates in a full range of sexual activities—from sensate focus exercises to sexual intercourse—depending on the client's specific sexual needs and the therapist's recommendations.

Sexual surrogation remains highly controversial in the field of sexology, even more so now in the age of HIV and AIDS. Many health-care professionals and members of the general public criticize the practice as nothing more than glorified, rationalized prostitution. Nonetheless, proponents claim that surrogation is unavoidable in some clinical instances and is even associated with significantly higher success rates when compared with traditional methods—of course, when the surrogates are properly trained and closely supervised (Bancroft, 1989; Dauw, 1988). The vast majority of sex therapists do not employ the services of sexual surrogates.

FINDING THE RIGHT SEX THERAPIST

Generally speaking, sexual dysfunctions respond well to treatment when therapy is directed at specific symptoms or causes of a particular problem. *Intentionality* (Ivey, 1993), or choosing the right therapy for a specific client's problem, is not always easy, but it is the most efficient way of going about therapy. Gone are the days when clinicians recommended that *all* patients with sexual problems undergo years of strict Freudian psychoanalysis to uncover and overcome deep-seated sexual conflicts.

The first step to finding the right therapy for a sexual problem is finding the right therapist. Following are some suggestions to help you locate a *reputable* sex therapist who is right for you:

1. If at all possible, first seek therapy from a practitioner whose clinic is affiliated with a medical school, university, college, or hospital. Obtain a list of professional therapists in your area from a local medical/nursing, psychological, counseling, or social work association, or obtain a referral from your health-care provider. *Never* simply look up a name under "Sex Therapists" in the phone book and make an appointment. Remember, most states do not regulate or license sex therapists. It's conceivable, then, for a person without any training whatsoever to hang a shingle on an office door and open a sex therapy clinic and practice . . . *Caveat emptor!*— *Let the buyer beware!*

2. Though not "sex therapists," *per se*, many state licensed and certified psychiatrists, psychologists, counselors, and social workers treat sexual dysfunctions as part of a larger range of professional activities. One of these providers may be an option for you.

3. You should preferably see a therapist who is nationally certified by the *American Association of Sex Educators, Counselors, and Therapists* (AASECT) and/or a member of one of the national sexuality organizations, like the *Society for Sex Therapy and Research* (SSTAR) and the *Society for the Scientific Study of Sex* (SSSS).

4. During your initial appointment, be sure to ask your therapist about her or his professional qualifications, education, training, years in practice, treatment per-

spective, and professional associations. She or he should have a graduate degree from an accredited institution, as well as substantial postgraduate training in sex therapy, including direct, personal supervision. Also discuss issues of cost, insurance, projected length of therapy, confidentiality, where to have a complete medical exam performed, and what you should do in an emergency or crisis. You should feel comfortable with all aspects of the therapist's approach, etc., including her or his personal style of interacting with you. Leave no stone unturned—always be an *informed consumer!* Whether you're buying a refrigerator or seeking a therapist, get all the facts—up front!

5. Be sure to question any therapeutic recommendations that sound inappropriate or make you feel uncomfortable. *Under no circumstances should a reputable therapist ever advise you to disrobe (partially or fully) or engage in any sexual activity with her- or himself for any reason, including therapeutic purposes!* Immediately report any such request to the nearest professional licensing board or the police. (Zgourides, 1993, pp. 195–196)

For Personal Reflection

What professional and personal qualities would you look for in a sex therapist?

HOW EFFECTIVE IS SEX THERAPY?

With the publication of their book *Human Sexual Inadequacy*, William Masters and Virginia Johnson (1970) made the assertion that sex therapy is not only effective, but *very* effective—reporting an overall failure rate of only 20 percent in their original sample of 790 patients. Sounds pretty clear-cut, right? Well, maybe not. A decade after the publication of Masters and Johnson's pioneering work, psychologists Bernie Zilbergeld and Michael Evans published an article ironically entitled "The Inadequacy of Masters and Johnson" (1980). Questioning Masters and Johnson's astoundingly low failure rates, Zilbergeld and Evans claimed it was impossible to evaluate their methods or determine their true success rate based on vague and misleading reports of their procedures and results (among other things). For instance, Masters and Johnson failed to explain their screening procedures and report how many potential subjects were excluded from their study, which according to Zilbergeld and Evans are fundamental research flaws by any scientific standards.

In another critique, *Sex by Prescription* (1990), psychiatrist Thomas Szasz—outspoken critic of the psychiatric/medical model, and a controversial figure in his own right—maintained that Masters and Johnson's early work had more to do with moral, value, and political judgments than with sound medical/scientific research. Commenting on the professional sex therapy community at large, Szasz pointed out:

Today, it is dogmatically asserted—by the medical profession and the official opinion-makers of our society—that it is healthy or normal for people to enjoy sex, that the lack of such enjoyment is the symptom of a sexual disorder, that such disorders can be relieved by appropriate medical (sex-therapeutic) interventions, and that they ought, whenever possible, to be so treated. This view, though it pretends to be scientific, is, in fact, moral or religious: it is an expression of the medical ideology we have substituted for traditional religious creeds. (pp. 164–165)

None of this means that sex therapy is ineffective. Criticisms notwithstanding, research on the whole indicates that sex therapy can help couples overcome specific sexual problems, and may be beneficial in other ways as well. In fact, more recent research out of the Masters and Johnson Institute has confirmed the positive benefits of sex therapy (Masters et al., 1992). Their data appear in Table 15.2.

PREVENTING SEXUAL DYSFUNCTIONS

Preventing sexual problems entails avoiding as many of the sources of sexual dysfunctions as possible, as well as following the principles of effective communication presented in Chapter 8. Here are a few additional suggestions that you should find helpful:

1. Keep the lines of communication open between you and your partner. Practice expressing your feelings, preferences, likes, and dislikes to one another.
2. Challenge your personal irrational attitudes and beliefs about sexuality. Remember that your sexual values and preferences come from a variety of sources, many of them dating back to early childhood. Knowing where you're coming from can help you figure out where you're going.
3. Avoid setting sexual performance goals. Don't make unrealistic performance demands of yourself, such as *having* to engage in rigorous coitus every night. And don't fall into the trap of making orgasm (the "Big O") the all-important goal of sex.
4. Avoid *spectatoring*. Instead, enjoy the erotic sensations of lovemaking, in whatever form. Keep in mind that there's no right or wrong way to have sex—it's up to you and your partner to decide what you both find appealing and comfortable.

TABLE 15.2 **Results of Sex Therapy at the Masters and Johnson Institute**

	N[a]	Failures	Successes[b]	Success Rate(%)
Primary impotence	65	21	44	67.7
Secondary impotence	674	134	540	80.1
Premature ejaculation	543	35	508	93.6
Ejaculatory incompetence	113	27	86	76.1
Male totals	1395	217	1178	84.4
Anorgasmia	811	207	604	74.5
Vaginismus	130	2	128	98.5
Female totals	941	209	732	77.8
Combined totals	2336	426	1910	81.8

[a]Cases seen between 1959 and 1985.
[b]A case was categorized as successful only if the change in sexual function was unequivocal and lasting. For all patients seen before 1973, follow-up lasted five years. From 1973, the follow-up period was reduced to two years. If a patient were successful during the two-week sex therapy program but then slipped back into dysfunction, the case was listed as a failure.

Source: W. H. Masters, V. E. Johnson, & R. C. Kolodny (1992), *Human sexuality* (4th ed.) (New York: HarperCollins). Copyright © 1991 William H. Masters, Virginia E. Johnson, and Robert C. Kolodny. Reprinted by permission of HarperCollins Publishers, Inc.

5. Avoid comparing yourself to others or sex statistics. "Locker-room" talk is usually just that—*talk!*

6. Take time out for sex. There's no need to rush (unless you and your partner want to). Relax and enjoy!

7. Never hesitate to seek out professional help for a sexual problem. And usually the earlier this is done, the better. A false sense of modesty or embarrassment about sexual matters is no reason to suffer in silence. Keep in mind the old saying, "In our secrets lie our sickness." Don't be afraid to talk things out, both with your partner and a professional therapist. (Zgourides, 1993, p. 134)

For Personal Reflection

What are some things that you would find helpful for avoiding sexual dysfunctions?

Last but not least, a key element in preventing sexual problems is having correct information about sexuality. By taking a human sexuality class and reading this textbook, you've taken that first important step. Congratulations! But it doesn't stop here. Read everything you can on the topic. Keep up-to-date on STDs. Talk with friends and loved ones. Take sexuality-related classes and seminars. Ask questions.

As for the role of sexologists in preventing sexual problems, Sandra Leiblum and Raymond Rosen concluded in the second edition of their *Principles and Practice of Sex Therapy* (1989):

Sex therapists and educators must embrace a philosophy of prevention rather than providing treatment alone in the next decade. We can no longer afford to see the victims of sexual ignorance or misinformation only after the fact, since for some it will be too late. We must become better facilitators of behavior change and more adept at integrating a variety of approaches to our clinical armamentarium. We must become more knowledgeable about the impact of disease and drugs on sexual functioning. We must teach some individuals how to eroticize safe sex, how to say "no" when they are sexually disinterested, and how to make virginity and abstinence acceptable choices for more individuals. We must also find effective sexual and nonsexual ways to encourage and sustain intimacy over a lifetime and to overcome sexual boredom. While preaching caution, we must avoid fear mongering, since sexuality will always be a positive and life-affirming force that warrants celebration. We have our work cut out for us! (p. 14)

KEY POINTS

1. At one time or another, almost everyone experiences at least some difficulty in their sexual functioning. Many individuals, however, experience a chronic malfunction in their sexual response cycle—a *sexual dysfunction*. They are unable to have satisfying sexual relations even after repeated attempts with an interested partner.

2. The *sexual desire disorders* are disorders of the appetitive phase of the sexual response system. These disorders are *hypoactive sexual desire disorder* and *sexual aversion disorder*.

3. The *sexual arousal disorders* reflect problems in the excitement phase of sexual response. These disorders are *female sexual arousal disorder* and *male erectile disorder*.

4. The *orgasm disorders* have as their primary characteristic a malfunction in the orgasm phase of sexual response. These disorders are *female orgasmic disorder, male orgasmic disorder,* and *premature ejaculation.*

5. The *sexual pain disorders* involve genital pain associated with sexual activity. These disorders are *dyspareunia* and *vaginismus.*

6. Biological sources of sexual dysfunction include *medical conditions and disorders, neurological disorders and trauma,* and *medications and drugs. Psychological* sources of sexual dysfunctions include *intrapsychic conflicts, learning* and *conditioning,* and *cognitive distortions. Social* sources of sexual dysfunctions include a sexually repressive upbringing, parents' negative views of sexuality and the genitals, sexual myths perpetuated by the media, childhood sexual abuse, incest, and rape. *Cultural attitudes* and *prohibitions* also play a major role in shaping our sexual values and mores.

7. Professionals from a variety of backgrounds and theoretical perspectives practice sex therapy. Most sex therapies have as their basic format PLISSIT—an acronym for *permission, limited information, specific suggestions,* and *intensive therapy.*

8. Two of the most widely accepted and used models of sex therapy are those of Masters and Johnson (1970) and Kaplan (1974). A few of the basic techniques common to these and other approaches are *sensate focus, masturbation training, stop-start technique, squeeze technique, cognitive therapy, surgery, medications, prosthesis,* and on rare occasions the use of *sexual surrogates.*

9. This chapter also includes suggestions for locating a reputable sex therapist and preventing sexual dysfunctions from occurring in the first place.

ACTIVITIES AND QUESTIONS

1. Do traditional sexual roles affect sexual functioning? How? What can a couple do to minimize or eliminate the negative influences of these roles on their relationship?

2. Find a friend or classmate for this role-playing activity. Take turns telling each other (pretending to be prospective sexual partners) about your sexual dysfunctions. How does it feel to tell someone this? How does it feel to hear the same from your partner? What have you learned about yourself from this activity?

3. Plenty of self-help manuals, books, newspaper advice columns, and television shows are available for people seeking relief from sexual problems. What are some of the potential positives and negatives of following the advice offered by these sources?

4. Identify some of the reasons individuals and couples might be hesitant to seek the services of a professional sex therapist. What can society do to raise people's awareness of the importance and effectiveness of sex therapy?

5. Create a panel discussion on the pros and cons of sexual surrogation. What of the charge that sexual surrogates are nothing but prostitutes pretending to be "clinicians"? When might sexual surrogation be a valuable addition to a sex therapy program? Should state governments regulate the practice of sexual surrogation? What kind of training should surrogates undergo before seeing clients? Should they receive ongoing supervision from a licensed therapist, such as a clinical psychologist?

RECOMMENDED READINGS

Beck, A. T. (1988). *Love is never enough.* New York: Harper & Row. Cognitive expert Aaron Beck explains how many married couples engage in the same sorts of distorted thinking patterns as anxious and depressed people. Contains actual conversations of distressed couples, as well as useful self-assessment instruments.

Kaplan, H. S. (1987). *The illustrated manual of sex therapy* (2nd ed.). New York: Brunner/Mazel. A practical guide to overcoming sexual dysfunctions. Includes information on the nature of sexual problems and a variety of useful sexual exercises ("erotic techniques") for dealing with specific dysfunctions.

Levine, S. B. (1989). *Sex is not simple*. Columbus, OH: Ohio Psychology Publishing. Another practical guide to sexual dysfunctions, written for the general public.

Pietropinto, A., & Simenauer, J. (1990). *Not tonight dear: How to reawaken your sexual desire*. New York: Doubleday. Practical suggestions for overcoming low sexual desire.

Pope, K., & Bouhoutsos, J. (1986). *Sexual intimacy between therapists and patients*. New York: Praeger. A book dealing with various aspects of this important topic.

Wincze, J. P., & Carey, M. P. (1992). *Sexual dysfunctions: A guide for assessment and treatment*. New York: Guilford. A brief, straightforward text on sexual problems and therapies, written for students and practitioners alike.

•**S**EXUAL PARAPHILIAS

•CAUSES AND TREATMENT

C H A P T E R   1 6

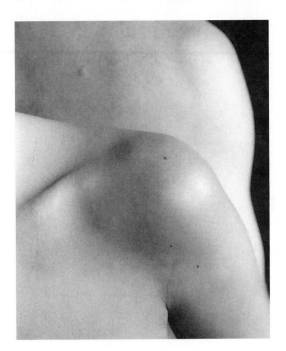

S E X U A L   P A R A P H I L I A S

<u>O B J</u> E C T I V E S

AFTER READING THIS CHAPTER YOU SHOULD BE
ABLE TO . . .

1. LIST AND DESCRIBE SOME OF THE MORE
   COMMON PARAPHILIAS.

2. LIST AND DESCRIBE SOME OF THE LESS COMMON
   PARAPHILIAS.

3. DISCUSS HOW BIOLOGICAL, PSYCHOLOGICAL,
   AND SOCIAL PROCESSES CAN INTERACT TO
   CREATE AND MAINTAIN PARAPHILIAS.

4. EXPLAIN WHY THE PARAPHILIAS ARE SO HARD TO
   TREAT SUCCESSFULLY.

5. BETTER UNDERSTAND YOUR OWN POSITION ON
   ATYPICAL SEXUAL BEHAVIOR.

PERSONAL ASSESSMENT

WHAT ARE YOUR THOUGHTS AND FEELINGS ON SEXUAL VARIATIONS? TO EXPLORE THIS, READ THE FOLLOWING STATEMENTS AND RESPOND USING THIS RATING SCALE: *3* = I *completely agree* WITH THE STATEMENT; *2* = I *mostly agree* WITH THE STATEMENT; *1* = I *mostly disagree* WITH THE STATEMENT; *0* = I *completely disagree* WITH THE STATEMENT. REMEMBER, THERE ARE NO RIGHT OR WRONG ANSWERS HERE; IT'S YOUR OPINION THAT COUNTS.

_____ 1. I have a clear sense of what normal sexual activity is.
_____ 2. I have trouble accepting those whose views of sexuality differ from mine.
_____ 3. I have trouble accepting those who aren't as masculine (or feminine) as I.
_____ 4. Society must maintain strict standards regarding what is acceptable sexual behavior.
_____ 5. Society has the right to decide what individuals are allowed to do in the privacy of their bedrooms.
_____ 6. People who engage in unusual sexual practices do so because they are morally weak.
_____ 7. People who engage in unusual sexual practices do so because they have a mental disorder.
_____ 8. I experience shame and guilt over my sexual feelings.
_____ 9. I find it hard to talk about sexual preferences or variations.
_____ 10. I am open to trying out new and different sexual behaviors.

The only abnormality is the incapacity to love.

Anaïs Nin

What is "normal" sexual behavior? This question has stirred the curiosity of individuals and societies for countless generations. Even though most people believe they have a good idea about what constitutes normal sexual expression, many forget that society and culture help shape and define our sexual "norms." They forget that what is considered acceptable to one group is not necessarily so to another. They forget that what is considered "normal" is relative and not absolute for everyone.

In this chapter, we turn our attention to the second major category of sexual disorders—unusual sexual desires and activities, termed *sexual paraphilias*.

SEXUAL PARAPHILIAS

**PARAPHILIA
(PAR-A-FI-LE-A)**

Unusual sexual practice or fantasy.

Some adults find sexual satisfaction through "variations" that depart from what society considers traditional and acceptable sexual outlets (Simon, 1994). **Paraphilias** (meaning "love beyond the usual") are unusual—sometimes bizarre and dangerous—sexual fantasies and/or practices that an individual finds necessary for sexual excitement and release. That is, the individual *requires* the unusual fantasy and/or practice to find sexual satisfaction. Some paraphilias, like cross-dressing, are victimless and harmless. Others, like exposing oneself and molesting children, are not. Paraphilias appear to occur only rarely in the United States, although no one knows for certain how prevalent they are given people's general hesitancy to report unusual sexual practices. Overall, far more men than women have paraphilias (American Psychiatric Association, 1994; Money, 1986).

Distress is a common feature of mental disorders, including the paraphilias.

Paraphiles often describe their sexual urges as "overpowering" and "irresistible." Paraphilic urges range in severity from *mild* (being distressed by the urges) to *severe* (repeatedly acting on the urges). Ordinarily, the more severe the paraphilic urge, the more the individual experiences distress.

Many of the paraphilias also have counterparts within the normal range of sexual expression. It is perfectly normal for a husband to enjoy seeing his wife wear sexy shoes and outfits. It is abnormal for him to *need* to have his wife's shoes present to become sexually excited, or become solely interested in shoes to the exclusion of his wife. Only when sexual patterns become chronic and distressing, or interfere significantly with a relationship, does the individual necessarily have a sexual disorder.

Let's now examine the eight most common types of paraphilias—*exhibitionism, voyeurism, fetishism, transvestism, frotteurism, sexual sadism, sexual masochism,* and *pedophilia*—as well as several less common types. I limit the following discussion to paraphilias in the United States and other Western countries, given inherent difficulties in trying to define normal and abnormal sexual practices and variations across cultures.

EXHIBITIONISM

Many people want to be admired for their attractiveness, so they enjoy showing off their bodies in socially acceptable ways. Some people, on the other hand, feel compelled to expose themselves to nonconsenting and unsuspecting persons. Such acts of **exhibitionism** ("indecent exposure" or "flashing") can involve the genitals, buttocks, or breasts, and can occur just about anywhere in public. The typical exhibitionist is a younger male in his late teens to early 30s who may have an erection, masturbate, and ejaculate during the

EXHIBITIONISM (EKS-I-BI-SHUN-IZ-UM)
Sexual arousal from exposing the genitals to an unsuspecting person.

exposure, or masturbate to ejaculation a short time later (American Psychiatric Association, 1994). Female exhibitionism, on the other hand, is apparently rare (Freund & Blanchard, 1986).

Exhibitionists are rarely dangerous and therefore are unlikely to commit other crimes, although some go on to engage in more sexually aggressive behaviors (Maletzky, 1991). Exhibitionism can have an emotionally traumatizing effect on the victim, leaving him or her feeling sexually exploited and violated (Cox, 1988).

While many adults do not take exhibitionism seriously, indecent exposure in front of a child can be quite emotionally damaging. He or she may pick up on messages that it is acceptable to use one's body to shock others, or that personal power is best asserted at the expense of another, especially someone who is vulnerable. Most exhibitionists are not child molesters, although molesters sometimes begin sexually offending as exhibitionists (Bradford et al., 1992).

What should you do if you're "flashed"? Because the typical exhibitionist relies on the victim's reaction of shock, surprise, or fear for sexual arousal, the best course of action is to ignore him or her. Asking the offender to cover his or her genitals or making a similarly neutral response is another appropriate tactic. A report to local authorities following the incident is also advisable, as the prospect of arrest may help persuade the exhibitionist to seek professional help.

VOYEURISM

Viewing nude or partially nude bodies is acceptable entertainment for many Americans, given the popularity of magazines like *Playboy* and *Playgirl*, topless bars, "ladies-only" nights at local clubs featuring male "G-string" dancers and strippers, and X-rated videos. Many people in our society value opportunities to look at sexy bodies. But what about someone who does so without the other person's knowledge or permission? What if he or she watches while the person undresses, showers, or has sex? What if this is the only way he or she can become sexually aroused?

VOYEURISM
(VOI-YUR-IZ-UM)
Sexual arousal from watching an unsuspecting person.

Voyeurism involves sexual arousal and satisfaction associated with observing an unsuspecting person who is disrobing, naked, or engaging in sexual activity (American Psychiatric Association, 1994). The voyeur (or "peeping tom") ordinarily masturbates during the act or shortly thereafter, and frequently prefers this activity to intercourse.

The typical voyeur is a lonely, insecure, and timid male, usually in his 20's. He often has only a limited amount of heterosexual experience, as well as a history of difficulty forming sexual relationships. He typically has low self-esteem and therefore feels very threatened by mature loving relationships. To him, voyeurism is a viable method of avoiding social interactions and sexual relationships while still having a sexual outlet (American Psychiatric Association, 1994).

Most voyeurs find pleasure in secretly watching others in potentially humiliating situations and imagining their embarrassment if they were to realize what was happening. This gives the voyeur a false sense of power over the victim. Moreover, voyeurs (unlike exhibitionists) normally prefer to remain at a distance to avoid being caught. Yet "peeping" can be especially exciting if it occurs in a setting where the risks of detection are great, which explains why voyeurs are not usually interested in peeping in places where nudity is the norm, like nudist beaches or camps (American Psychiatric Association, 1994).

On a Personal Note (Jose, age 19)

I live in a coed dorm, and watching women shower is my way of getting a little action. Like once, I just "accidentally" walked into the women's restroom when a bunch of them were in the showers. None of them saw me. That was great, but that kind of stunt only works once or twice. I wouldn't want anybody to get suspicious. (Author's files)

FETISHISM

Fetishism involves sexual attraction to one or more inanimate objects, usually nonsexual in nature but somehow related to the human body (American Psychiatric Association, 1994). Clothing (brassieres, panties) and related accessories (shoes, gloves) are the most popular, even though just about any object can become a fetish.

In milder cases, the fetishist, who is almost always male, may use the fetish object to become aroused before and during intercourse, or masturbate to fantasies about scenarios involving the object. Although sexual activity without the fetish is possible, it is generally not as exciting or satisfying. In more severe cases, the fetishist can achieve sexual arousal and gratification only when the fetish object is present. The fetishist has to hold, fondle, and kiss the object to become aroused or orgasm, sometimes to the exclusion of the partner. Naturally, severe fetishism can be problematic for an ongoing sexual relationship (American Psychiatric Association, 1994).

TRANSVESTIC FETISHISM

Transvestism occurs when an individual receives sexual gratification from dressing up in clothing customarily reserved for members of the other sex (American Psychiatric Association, 1994). Many people confuse transvestism with *transsexualism*, which is the belief that one is literally "trapped" in the wrong anatomical body, or *homosexuality*, which is sexual attraction to members of the same sex.

There exist a few reports of female transvestites, but the great majority are heterosexual males, who appear unmistakably masculine when not cross-dressed (Stoller, 1982). They typically hold traditionally masculine jobs, are married with children, and have otherwise rewarding heterosexual relationships. At the same time, these men are able to escape, at least temporarily, from their demanding male roles by cross-dressing, which is usually done in private or in small groups. Transvestic behaviors include secretly wearing other-sex undergarments to the office to completely dressing up as a member of the other sex. Most transvestites prefer to hide their alternative practices from friends and loved ones, although spouses are usually aware of the cross-dressing behavior, some

**FETISHISM
(FET-ISH-IZ-UM)**
Sexual attraction to objects.

**TRANSVESTISM
(TRANZ-VEST-IZ-UM)**
Sexual arousal from wearing opposite-sex clothing.

Any of a number of everyday objects can become fetishes.

Is this man secretly wearing pink panties?

even helping their mates select appropriate makeup and attractive clothing (Brown, 1994). Nevertheless, a few choose to "come out of the closet." They may even go to bars, restaurants, and shopping malls. Public cross-dressing does not typically occur until early or middle adulthood.

On a Personal Note (Peter, age 61)

I couldn't believe it! I've known J.J. for the last 4 years, ever since we became neighbors when I moved in next door. Early one morning, earlier than usual actually, I was out getting the newspaper. So was J.J., except I had to look twice. He came out in drag. I'm talking pumps, stockings, a mini slip, and a pink fluffy robe. He didn't act like anything was wrong. Well . . . I sure didn't want to say anything to him about it. He's a big guy, probably about 225 lbs. (Author's files)

FROTTEURISM

**FROTTEURISM
(FROT-ur-iz-um)**

Sexual arousal from rubbing up against a nonconsenting person.

The risk of being caught or exposed during illicit activities is for some individuals a source of sexual arousal. This sort of arousal, characteristic of many of the paraphilias, is certainly true of **frotteurism.** This paraphilia usually involves a clothed male rubbing his genitals up against the body of a clothed female, especially her legs or buttocks, in a crowded setting, such as in an elevator or subway, for the purpose of sexual excitement (American Psychiatric Association, 1994). He may have an orgasm during the act, or later masturbate to mental images of the act. The typical offender is careful to make his "bumping up" against someone look like an accident. As a result, many victims do not even notice or realize what has happened.

Most, but not all, transvestites prefer to cross-dress in private.

The personality profile of the frotteurist is much like that of the exhibitionist. Sexual insecurity and feelings of personal inadequacy are common. Given a fear of sexual relationships, the frotteurist's method of finding sexual satisfaction includes others in the least threatening manner possible. Frotteurism, then, serves as a substitute for a consenting, mature sexual relationship.

SEXUAL SADISM AND MASOCHISM

Most people in our society would condemn the intentional infliction of pain on an unwilling, undeserving person. Crimes often involve at least some degree of this, leading victims to feel abused and exploited. Basic to these victims' distress is the sense that their personal control has been taken away.

Given issues of control and consent between offender and victim, what about a sexual partner who willingly inflicts pain on a consenting "victim" who seems to enjoy being hurt in this way? **Sexual sadism** involves sexual arousal and gratification associated with humiliating, restraining, beating, or torturing others (American Psychiatric Association, 1994). **Sexual masochism,** on the other hand, involves sexual arousal and gratification associated with being on the receiving end of such activities (American Psychiatric Association, 1994). Although separate categories, these two paraphilias frequently occur together, hence the term *sadomasochism* ("S/M"), or sexual expression involving domi-

**SEXUAL SADISM
(SA-DIZ-UM)**

Sexual arousal from inflicting pain on others.

**SEXUAL MASOCHISM
(MA-SO-KIZ-UM)**

Sexual arousal from receiving pain from others.

Think twice the next time someone bumps up against you in a crowd!

nance, submission, and pain. The remainder of this discussion will treat sexual sadism and masochism as a single phenomenon.

As mentioned above, many of the paraphilias have counterparts within the normal range of sexual expression. This is certainly true of sadomasochism. Many couples like to add a little spice to their sex life by incorporating some playful sadomasochism into their usual sexual routines. Some couples tie each other up. Others tickle one another. Some give spankings or "love pats." True sadomasochism, however, is not a kind of sexual play. Pain, suffering, and humiliation—voluntary or not—are necessary to find sexual fulfillment.

Sadomasochism takes many forms. Some S/M partners act out fantasies of submission and dominance ("S & D"), while others act out fantasies of bondage and discipline ("B & D"). Submission and dominance activities involve both partners having scripts and acting out roles as in a play, such as police warden and inmate, or king and slave. Many sadomasochists enjoy alternating their roles, although one role may be generally favored over the other (Moser & Levitt, 1987; Reinisch, 1990). In S & D, the dominant partner requires the submissive partner to obey. If he or she does not, the dominant partner may punish the other with physical pain or humiliation. Punishment usually lasts only as long as the submissive partner wants.

In B & D, one partner is bound, while the other provides discipline in the form of whippings, spankings, beatings, bitings, and verbal abuse. Whips, chains, shackles, gags, orifice plugs, and various torture devices are typical accessories for B & D, all of which are commercially available from mail order catalogs and S/M shops. Partners may also

Some of the traditional garb and accessories of S/M enthusiasts.

incorporate other paraphilic behaviors into their B & D rituals. For instance, one partner may urinate or defecate on the other as a means of degrading and humiliating the other partner.

Most S/M practitioners maintain reasonable personal boundaries. In some cases, though, criminal sadism occurs. Here, a submissive partner decides to completely relinquish control, submitting to a variety of painful activities. There have been reports of masochists who, while initially trusting a partner, have ended up being held hostage for extended periods of time, have been treated in the most nightmarish ways imaginable, and only then have barely managed to escape before being mutilated or killed.

S/M enthusiasts may have difficulty locating a suitable, willing partner. Many join S/M clubs to meet eligible partners, while others seek out prostitutes to act out their fantasies. Still others take out classified advertisements in the "personals" sections of magazines and newspapers that cater to S/M practitioners. Some of these magazines also publish detailed S/M "how-to" articles and photos. Following are two typical S/M "personals" from one underground Oregon newspaper:

> Attractive, spontaneous, professional MWM; 35, fit and generous, seeking two ladies for weekend fun. Pleasures include love bites, pinches, spanking, Greek and French, and water sports. Answer Box _____.

> Enema specialist looking for customers. Hospital or dungeon environments available. House calls. Reasonable hourly rates. Answer Box _____.

PEDOPHILIA

Few disorders so enrage people as does **pedophilia** (meaning "love of children"), which refers to sexual attraction to and sexual activity with prepubescent children (American Psychiatric Association, 1994). Although some pedophiles never act on their urges, many others ("child molesters") unfortunately do.

The typical pedophile is a male under age 40, who is probably married with children and prone to marital, sexual, and emotional problems (Crewdson, 1988), although the professional literature also carries reports of female pedophiles (Elliott, 1992; Rowan et

**PEDOPHILIA
(PED-O-FI-LE-A)**
Sexual attraction to children.

Child sexual abuse is one of the most serious social problems of our time.

al., 1990). Alcohol abuse plays a significant role in many cases of molestation (Finkelhor, 1984). For these molesters, alcohol seems to allow them to act on their urges or fantasies.

Our society and media have traditionally portrayed child molesters as strangers lurking in dark alleys who seduce unsuspecting children by offering them candy or gifts. Actually, only a small number of perpetrators are strangers to their victims. Most often the perpetrator is a relative, caretaker, babysitter, or friend of the family.

Heterosexual male pedophiles tend to victimize young girls, ages 8 to 10, while homosexual male pedophiles tend to victimize slightly older boys. This latter form of pedophilia—*pederasty*—usually involves anal intercourse with a prepubescent boy. About twice as many molesters prefer other-sex children as same-sex children. Some pedophiles have no preference for either girls or boys, tending to prefer younger children of either sex. The vast majority of pedophiles, though, are men who sexually abuse young girls (American Psychiatric Association, 1994).

No single sexual behavior is universally characteristic of pedophilia. According to Erickson et al. (1988), child molesters initiate any of a number of activities, including vaginal or penile contact, anal contact, oral-genital contact (giving or receiving), and fondling (giving or receiving). The majority of pedophiles (an estimated 89 percent) also use some degree of physical force against their victims, in many cases causing injury (Stermac et al., 1989). Until recently, experts generally accepted that most sexual contact between adults and children did not include physical violence, although the Stermac et al. (1989) findings have challenged this position.

The harmful effects of pedophilia on the victim are many. Besides obvious physical harm, the child victim experiences major emotional trauma. Fear, disgust, and feelings of helplessness and responsibility for the abuse are common, and in many cases discourage the child from ever reporting the incident. The child may also pick up on the message that sexual activity between child and adult is acceptable behavior. Or she or he may come to believe that weak and vulnerable individuals are supposed to be at the mercy of more powerful individuals. If the attack is violent, the child may see molestation as a viable means of dealing with aggression. Consequently, these children may develop severe behavioral problems, and as adults later become sexually nonresponsive or dysfunctional with their partners (Elliott & Briere, 1992; Feinauer, 1989; Jones & Emerson, 1994). Another negative effect of pedophilia—a potential intergenerational, familial pattern— is worth noting (Freund & Kuban, 1994; Gaffney et al., 1984; Zgourides et al., 1994).

What should you do if you discover that your child has been a victim of sexual abuse? First, be careful not to overreact, but don't ignore what has happened, hoping everything will be okay once things settle down. The child is probably dealing with an assortment of confused feelings, and surely needs your help sorting through these. Make sure the child knows that the sexual abuse wasn't his or her fault. Next, take steps to ensure that the child is never alone again with the molester. Reassure the child that you'll protect him or her. Third, have the child examined by a physician to assess for physical harm or disease. In most cases, professional counseling is also recommended. Finally, be sure to report the molester to the proper authorities.

What should you do if *you* were abused but never talked about it, or are being abused now? *Talk to a qualified professional,* be it a physician, counselor, pastor, rabbi, or teacher. He or she can help you sort through your feelings and generate options for dealing with your particular situation. You're not alone. Plenty of people out there are willing to help you overcome this emotional trauma.

OTHER PARAPHILIAS

Several paraphilias do not fit into any of the categories already mentioned. The following occur even less frequently in the general population than do the above paraphilias.

Telephone Scatologia   Often called "obscene phone calling," *telephone scatologia* is a specific form of *coprolalia* (meaning "filthy babbling"), which is sexual arousal from writing or talking in a lewd or obscene manner. Coprolalia does not refer to sexual partners who "talk dirty" to one another, unless the lewd talk is necessary for arousal. The counterpart to coprolalia is *narratophilia*, which is sexual arousal from listening to lewd stories.

The obscene phone caller is frequently a male who becomes sexually excited by using obscene language in phone conversations with unsuspecting females (Matek, 1988). The

---

PERSPECTIVE

University Males and Sexual Interest in Children

Briere and Runtz (1989) surveyed 193 male undergraduates to collect data on university males' sexual interest in children. In this sample, the authors found child-focused sexual thoughts to be surprisingly common, summarized here:

- 21 percent reported sexual attraction to children.
- 9 percent reported sexual fantasies about children.
- 5 percent reported having masturbated to fantasies about children.
- 7 percent reported a willingness to engage in sexual activity with a child if able to avoid being caught and punished.

Question for Thought

How do you feel about the finding that seven percent of the males in this study expressed a willingness to have sex with a child, especially if they could avoid detection and punishment?

Source: J. Briere & M. Runtz (1989), University males' sexual interest in children: Predicting potential indices of "pedophilia" in a nonforensic sample, *Child Abuse & Neglect, 13,* 65–75.

perpetrator typically masturbates during the call or shortly thereafter. Calls vary, but often include lewd requests, graphic descriptions of masturbation, probing questions about the victim's sex life, or physical threats. Subsequent physical or sexual assaults on the victim are rare.

Like other paraphilias, much of the excitement of telephone scatologia has to do with its "shock value." Although similar to exhibitionists in many ways, obscene callers are perhaps more anxious about confronting their victims directly, so they make a call instead of a "personal visit" (Money, 1986). Otherwise, obscene callers generally exhibit personality traits similar to those of other paraphiles, including feelings of inadequacy, sexual insecurity, and timidity.

As expected, victims of obscene telephone calls often feel harassed and exploited. Some may blame themselves for somehow not handling the situation correctly. Other victims do not pay much attention to the obscene calls, or inadvertently encourage obscene callers by staying on the line or overreacting.

To coax victims into disclosing personal sexual information, more sophisticated obscene callers try to appear legitimate at first by pretending to be a "sex researcher" or "interviewer" for a university or clinic, or a "marketing representative" for a store or mail order catalog. Once convinced of the caller's sincerity, the victim speaks at some length about his or her sexual preferences, types of undergarments worn, or methods of contraception. The caller eventually makes an obscene remark, and the person realizes that he or she has been victimized.

If you receive an obscene phone call, try not to act disgusted, troubled, or shocked. The caller is relying on your horrified reaction for arousal. Because he or she has probably picked your number at random from the phone book, don't make more of the call than what it actually is. Gently hanging up and ignoring the phone if it rings again immediately are good ways to prevent rewarding the caller. Obscene callers can be persistent, however. A reminder that the call is being recorded and traced, and that an officer is listening in is often sufficient to stop the repeat offender. In some cases, it might be necessary to change your phone number. Should you decide to have a number listed in the phone book, use only your last name and first initial to avoid identifying yourself as a female or male. If calls persist or the caller threatens you with violence, contact your local telephone company and the appropriate authorities. Both are good sources of information on how to handle harassing or threatening phone calls.

Necrophilia A bizarre and quite rare disorder, *necrophilia* refers to sexual attraction to, fantasies about, or intercourse with corpses (Tollison & Adams, 1979). Occurring almost exclusively among males, necrophilia includes a range of behaviors, from being turned on by thinking about or viewing corpses to fondling or having intercourse with them. Perpetrators are likely to work at jobs where they can be around new corpses, such as funeral homes or morgues. Others may steal corpses from gravesites. Because access to corpses is limited, some necrophiles purchase inflatable dolls or hire prostitutes to wear white makeup and various accessories like shrouds to appear dead.

Partialism A type of fetishism, *partialism* refers to exclusive focus on a particular part of the body for sexual excitement. Similar to the object fetishist, the partialist must see and/or fondle a certain part of the exposed body to be aroused and attain orgasm (Wise, 1985). A example of partialism is the man who focuses his erotic energy solely on his partner's breasts.

Zoophilia *Zoophilia,* or *bestiality,* refers to sexual attraction to or contact with animals, most commonly those found on farms or at home, such as sheep, calves, dogs, and cats. The zoophile fantasizes about having sex with animals, and may act on his or her urges.

The chosen animal may be trained to rub, lick, or mount the person, or be forced to submit to intercourse. The animal is usually of a type the person frequently encountered during childhood (American Psychiatric Association, 1994).

The reasons for zoophilia vary, but some of the more common explanations include fear of adult relationships, need to exert power, hatred of other-sex partners, and an unconscious equation of human intercourse with incest. In addition, sexual activity with animals sometimes occurs as a form of sexual experimentation, as a result of curiosity, or when a human partner is unavailable (American Psychiatic Association, 1994).

Coprophilia *Coprophilia* refers to sexual excitement from viewing, smelling, or handling feces, as well as fantasizing about these activities. A coprophile may be aroused by watching his partner defecate, for example. Related to coprophilia are *klismaphilia*, which is sexual excitement from giving or receiving enemas, and *urophilia*, which is sexual excitement from urinating on others or being urinated upon. Urophilic activities are sometimes called "golden showers" or "water sports." As a whole, this group of paraphilias appears to be rare.

Table 16.1 lists some even rarer paraphilias.

For Personal Reflection

Do you think the following behaviors are indicative of a sexual paraphilia? Why or why not?

1. *A woman who enjoys going topless at a nearby nude beach on weekends.*
2. *A middle-aged man who refuses to date women because he is sexually attracted to teenage boys, although he never acts on these urges.*
3. *A woman who occasionally enjoys having her husband tie her to the bed before sexual intercourse.*
4. *A young man who can't attain an erection or have sex with his girlfriend unless he first looks at a Playboy magazine. This upsets both him and his partner.*
5. *A woman who likes having her husband urinate on her before intercourse. This doesn't seem to bother either of them.*

CAUSES AND TREATMENT

Researchers are uncertain about the exact causes of the paraphilias, although they probably develop from a combination of factors that come into play in particular ways for particular individuals. The various combinations, some more predominant at times than others, lead to the different avenues of sexual expression described throughout this chapter.

One biological explanation holds that some people are simply "wired" to have paraphilias (Moser, 1992). Another holds that some men have stronger and more pervasive sex drives, possibly due to increased amounts of or sensitivity to the male sexual hormone testosterone. Consequently, these men are more likely to look for other sexual outlets, especially if more "traditional" outlets are not readily available. Their increased sexual reactivity may also facilitate the learning of paraphilias (Lang et al., 1989).

Psychologically, the typical paraphile is confused, repressed, fearful of adult intimate relationships, and often angry. Hostility may actually play a greater part in motivating paraphilic behavior than does sexual interest, explaining why much paraphilic behavior is *forced* sexual behavior—involving a perpetrator and an unwilling victim. In some cases,

TABLE 16.1 Other Paraphiles

Acrotomophilia	Sexual attraction to amputees
Apotemnophilia	Sexual arousal at the thought of being an amputee
Asphyxiophilia	Sexual arousal from attaining partial asphyxiation (by hanging) to enhance orgasm
Autagonistophilia	Sexual arousal from being observed on camera or stage
Autassasinophilia	Sexual arousal at the thought of being murdered
Biastophilia	Sexual arousal from violently attacking and assaulting a surprised stranger
Formicophilia	Sexual attraction to small creatures, such as frogs and ants
Hyphephilia	Sexual arousal from touching hair, skin, fabric, or fur
Mysophilia	Sexual arousal from viewing or handling unclean or filthy items, such as soiled underwear
Pictophilia	Sexual arousal from viewing sexy pictures, implying dependency on such materials
Somnophilia	Sexual arousal from viewing or touching someone who is sleeping
Statuophilia or *pygmalionism*	Sexual attraction to mannequins and statues
Stigmatophilia	Sexual attraction to a partner who has been scarred, tattooed, or pierced for wearing jewelry

The following two compulsive behaviors, although not paraphilias *per se*, have sexual significance for some offenders:

Kleptomania	Compulsive desire to steal
Pyromania	Compulsive desire to start fires

Sources: J. Money (1986), *Lovemaps.* (New York: Prometheus).
B. Love (1992), *Encyclopedia of unusual sex practices.* (Fort Lee, NJ: Barricade Books).

the individual symbolically or literally acts out feelings of hostility and aggression in the form of a paraphilia. Conditioning also plays a major role in an individual's learning paraphilic behavior. Repeatedly masturbating to orgasm in association with the paraphilic behavior reinforces the individual's atypical sexual desires and behaviors, making it harder to break the patterns as time passes (Money, 1986; Levine et al., 1990).

An example of a multidimensional approach to understanding paraphilias is John Money's (1986) theory of "lovemaps." Money stressed that sexual variations develop as a result of early childhood sources of erotic arousal that are later activated by particular combinations of psychosocial factors. Sexual variations can occur at any point along the developmental path or remain latent indefinitely. Individuals from similar backgrounds need not necessarily develop similar sexual patterns. The question of who develops what depends largely on the unique combinations of events that are present in a given situation for a given person.

Because paraphilias appear to be powerfully and deeply embedded in the personality, treatment is difficult at best. The most usual approach is to try to break the undesirable behavioral patterns and replace them with desirable patterns, all the while exploring the patient's thoughts, emotions, reasons for engaging in paraphilic behavior, and social history. There are so many individual variables to consider—the exact nature and severity of the problem(s), causes, patient's background and personality, family system, the therapist's method of conceptualizing and treating paraphilias—that a meaningful discussion of all of the possible treatments for paraphilias is beyond the scope of this book.

An example of one fairly standard therapy for these disorders, however, is *orgasmic reconditioning*, the idea being to substitute a nonparaphilic object, urge, or practice for the paraphilic one. This technique involves having the patient (let's say a male in this case) masturbate to his usual paraphilic fantasies. Then during masturbation, at the point when orgasm is inevitable, the patient switches his focus to a nonparaphilic object or fantasy (let's say a photo of a nude woman). Orgasm occurs while the patient is looking at or thinking about the nonparaphilic object, which reinforces appropriate sexual expression. The patient repeats this procedure each time that he masturbates, except that he switches his focus to the nonparaphilic object earlier and earlier. If all goes according to plan, he eventually finds the nonparaphilic object more arousing than the paraphilic one. He soon loses interest in and abandons his paraphilia in favor of appropriate sexual expression.

KEY POINTS

1. *Paraphilias* are unusual—sometimes bizarre and dangerous—sexual fantasies and/or practices that an individual finds necessary for sexual excitement and release. The most common paraphilias are *exhibitionism* (sexual arousal from exposing one's genitals to an unsuspecting person), *voyeurism* (sexual arousal from watching an unsuspecting person), *fetishism* (sexual attraction to objects), *transvestism* (sexual arousal from wearing other-sex clothing), *frotteurism* (sexual arousal from rubbing up against a nonconsenting person), *sadomasochism* (sexual arousal from giving and/or receiving pain), and *pedophilia* (sexual attraction to children).

2. Other less common paraphilias include *telephone scatologia* (sexual arousal from making obscene phone calls), *coprolalia* (sexual arousal from speaking or writing in a lewd manner), *narratophilia* (sexual arousal from listening to lewd stories), *necrophilia* (sexual attraction to corpses), *partialism* (sexual attraction to a specific part of the body), *zoophilia* or *bestiality* (sexual attraction to animals), *coprophilia* (sexual attraction to feces), *klismaphilia* (sexual arousal from giving or receiving enemas), and *urophilia* (sexual arousal from urinating on others or being urinated upon).

3. Researchers are uncertain about the exact causes of the paraphilias, although they probably develop from a combination of factors that come into play in particular ways for particular individuals. The various combinations, some more predominant at times than others, lead to different avenues of sexual expression for different individuals.

4. Because paraphilias appear to be powerfully and deeply embedded in the personality, treatment is difficult at best. An example of one fairly standard therapy for these disorders is *orgasmic reconditioning*, the idea being to substitute a nonparaphilic object, urge, or practice for the paraphilic one.

ACTIVITIES AND QUESTIONS

1. Of all the paraphilias described in this chapter, which ones do you find the least acceptable? Why?

2. How would you react if someone close to you told you that he or she enjoys engaging in an unusual sexual practice?

3. For one month, make note of the different television shows or movies that you watch and see if any make reference (even casually) to unusual sexual practices or paraphilias. Bring your notes to class at the end of the month. Break up into small groups and discuss your findings.

4. How can we as a society prevent child sexual abuse? How can you as an individual do the same? What might be some effective methods of educating the general public about the consequences of sexual abuse?

RECOMMENDED READINGS

Docter, R. E. (1988). *Transvestites and transsexuals: Toward a theory of cross-gender behavior*. New York: Plenum. A fascinating overview of transsexualism, written from the perspective of a psychologist.

Garber, M. (1992). *Vested interests: Cross-dressing and cultural anxiety*. New York: HarperPerennial. A critical look at cross-dressing from a sociocultural perspective.

Laws, D. R. (Ed.) (1989). *Relapse prevention with sex offenders*. New York: Guilford. Examines current methods of treating sex offenders.

Love, B. (1992). *Encyclopedia of unusual sex practices*. Fort Lee, NJ: Barricade Books. A fascinating, albeit sometimes shocking, look at literally hundreds of unusual sexual behaviors, from paraphilias to genital piercing.

Scott, G. G. (1992). *Erotic power: An exploration of dominance and submission*. New York: Citadel Press. The author's account of two years of witnessing and participating in the "sexual underworld" of sadomasochism.

•**E**ROTIC, PORNOGRAPHIC, OR OBSCENE?

•SEX IN ADVERTISING

•SEXUAL PRODUCTS

•SEXUAL SERVICES

C H A P T E R   1 7

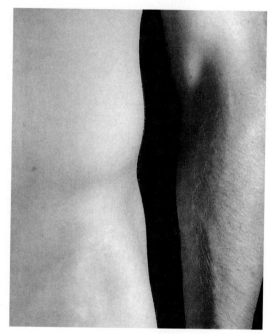

T H E   S E X U A L   M A R K E T P L A C E

O B J E C T I V E S

AFTER READING THIS CHAPTER YOU SHOULD BE
ABLE TO . . .

1. DEFINE THE TERMS *EROTIC, PORNOGRAPHIC,* AND
   OBSCENE.
2. IDENTIFY THE PROS AND CONS OF SEXUAL
   EXPLICITNESS IN VARIOUS MEDIA, SUCH AS
   TELEVISION.
3. CITE SOME OF THE NEGATIVE EFFECTS
   ASSOCIATED WITH VIEWING VIOLENT FORMS OF
   PORNOGRAPHY.
4. DESCRIBE THE NUMEROUS SEXUAL PRODUCTS
   AND SERVICES AVAILABLE TO CONSUMERS.
5. DESCRIBE THE SEVEN CATEGORIES OF
   PROSTITUTES AND THEIR TYPICAL CLIENTELE.

WHAT ARE YOUR THOUGHTS AND FEELINGS ON SEXUAL CONSUMERISM? TO EXPLORE THIS, READ THE FOLLOWING STATEMENTS AND RESPOND USING THIS RATING SCALE: 3 = I *completely agree* WITH THE STATEMENT; 2 = I *mostly agree* WITH THE STATEMENT; 1 = I *mostly disagree* WITH THE STATEMENT; 0 = I *completely disagree* WITH THE STATEMENT. REMEMBER, THERE ARE NO RIGHT OR WRONG ANSWERS HERE; IT'S YOUR OPINION THAT COUNTS.

_____ 1. The idea that "beauty lies in the eyes of the beholder" should be what determines whether something is erotic, pornographic, or obscene.

_____ 2. The community has a responsibility to decide what is erotic, pornographic, or obscene, as well as set standards regarding the availability of certain sexual products and services.

_____ 3. Hard-core and violent forms of pornography degrade women (and in some cases men) and desensitize viewers to the seriousness of sexual violence; therefore, these materials should be banned.

_____ 4. Advertisers who use sex to sell products contribute to the social myths that you have to be young and beautiful to be sexy.

_____ 5. It's nobody's business what people choose to read, do, or watch in the privacy of their own homes, as long as laws are upheld and no one is harmed.

_____ 6. Prostitution is a legitimate profession.

_____ 7. "Live-sex" stage shows should be banned.

_____ 8. Most consumers of "1-900" telephone sexual services probably have sexual or relationship problems.

_____ 9. There is nothing wrong with showing sexually explicit materials on cable television. People who don't want to watch such materials can change the channel.

_____ 10. Censorship of sexual materials in any form is a violation of citizens' rights.

If it is not erotic, it is not interesting.

Fernando Arrabal

Professionals tell us that sexual release as a physical need of a healthy human body is just as compelling as the need for food and water. Sadly, entrepreneurs have often sought to capitalize on the needs of fellow humans. Sexual needs are no exception. Supplying means for sexual pleasure and release has become a multimillion dollar industry, involving a wide range of ways and means, most classified as legitimate business ventures.

We now turn our attention to the business of selling sex. In the next pages, I'll describe many sexual products and services available to today's consumers—from erotic literature to prostitution. But first, we need to take a few moments to define some important terms.

EROTIC, PORNOGRAPHIC, OR OBSCENE?

Labeling sexually oriented materials can be slippery business. Like the word *beauty*, the words *erotic*, *pornographic*, and *obscene* escape exact definition because such definitions are

"Turgid. I love it."

Drawing by Donald Reilly; © 1982 The New Yorker Magazine, Inc.

subjective. One person's "obscenity" may be another's "literary classic." For our purposes, **erotica** (from the Greek *eros,* meaning "sexual love") refers to sexual materials that are artistically motivated, created, and presented; **pornography** (from the Greek *porneia,* meaning "prostitution") to sexual materials that are intended to arouse sexual excitement; and **obscenity** to sexual materials that are lewd, disgusting, and offensive to accepted standards of decency. I'll speak more to the issue of *obscenity,* which is actually a legal term, shortly. What this means, of course, is that each individual viewer's standards are just as sincere as the next viewer's. Common definitions of erotica, pornography, and obscenity certainly reflect this variance in standards. Some feminists vehemently oppose pornography, which they believe depicts women in degrading, demeaning, subordinate, submissive ways, and as victims of violence and aggression (Cowan & Dunn, 1994; Dworkin et al., 1994). On the other hand, some feminists approve of erotica, which they believe celebrates sexuality as part of larger human expressions of love, respect, equality, mutuality, consent, and pleasure (Saunders & Naus, 1993).

Many experts add two gradations when using the terms *erotica* and *pornography. Hard-core* materials are explicit in their portrayal of the genitals and various sexual activities, such as close-ups of the penis thrusting in and out of the vagina. *Soft-core* materials are merely suggestive in their portrayal of these activities. Thus, hard-core pornography or erotica is explicit in its portrayal of sexual anatomy and activity, whereas soft-core pornography or erotica is only suggestive in its portrayal. Typically, adult bookstores, theaters, video rental stores, and mail order catalogs are the primary sources of hard-core materials like XXX-rated videos, while newsstands and convenience stores are sources of soft-core materials like *Penthouse* and *Playboy* magazines, if they carry sexual materials at all.

American law complicates the issue further by introducing another term—*obscenity.* It refers to sexual materials that are lewd, disgusting, and offensive to accepted standards of decency. Historically, obscenity meant anything that should remain out of view or be kept from sight. The term did not apply exclusively to sexual matters, but did include any object or event that involved extremely personal matters. Of course, this traditional definition of obscenity is no longer applicable, at least not in a legal sense.

In *Roth* v. *United States* (1957) and *Miller* v. *State of California* (1973), the Supreme Court established the following three basic criteria for classifying material as obscene. It

EROTICA

Sexual materials that are artistically motivated, created, and presented.

PORNOGRAPHY

Sexual materials that are intended to arouse sexual excitement.

OBSCENITY

Sexual materials that are lewd, disgusting, and offensive to accepted standards of decency.

Madonna's book Sex (1992): Erotica or pornography?

Sexual representations have found their way into various art forms throughout history.

must be (1) lacking in serious artistic, literary, scientific, or social value; (2) appealing to *prurient interests*; and (3) considered offensive by contemporary community standards. The term **prurient interests** (from the Latin *prurire*, meaning "to itch, crave, or be wanton") refers to interests of a lustful sort, implying sexual immorality and, in some cases, debauchery. Legal definitions of prurient interests usually go something like this: "Shameful and morbid interests in nudity, sexual activity, or excretion, which goes beyond customary limits of candor." Legal definitions of obscenity often contain the phrase "appealing to the prurient interest," and/or the words *lascivious* and *indecent*.

Although many people equate obscenity with pornography, under the law obscenity is illegal, whereas pornography (unless obscene) is not. Again, definitions ultimately rest upon the individual observer's viewpoint. So to rule on obscenity cases, courts have resorted to basing judgments on what are believed to be "contemporary community standards." Needless to say, community standards are not uniform or easily established, given the wide variety of individuals and groups composing most American communities. At present no generally accepted legal definitions of erotica, pornography, and obscenity exist, given Americans' frequently changing attitudes and preferences (Chew, 1994; Winick & Evans, 1994). The courts continue to wrestle with this issue.

> ### For Personal Reflection
> *When presented with sexual explicitness in any media, how do you determine what is erotic, pornographic, or obscene?*

THE EFFECTS OF VIOLENT PORNOGRAPHY

Researchers have conducted numerous studies to determine the effects of sexual materials on viewers and readers. To date, at least when it comes to mutually consensual, soft-core, nonviolent erotica and pornography, there is little evidence to prove either negative or positive effects. However, violent pornography that depicts women in degrading, humiliating, and demeaning ways may be another story. The topic of the effects of pornography is controversial and hotly debated, and more research is definitely needed in this area (Fisher & Grenier, 1994).

In the late 1960s, Congress and President Lyndon B. Johnson formed the Commission on Obscenity and Pornography. Their 1970 report concluded that pornography was basically harmless. Although the commission confirmed that both men and women are sexually aroused by erotica and pornography, they also noted that their general behavior was not affected, particularly in negative ways. Moreover, the report referenced a study in Denmark showing that an increase in the availability of pornographic materials did not result in an increase in the number of reported sexual crimes. Critics of the Johnson Commission report pointed out that the types of violent pornography so common today were rather uncommon when the commission gathered their information, and that it is difficult, if not impossible, to draw cause-and-effect conclusions from the Denmark study.

Studies conducted in Canada and England either supported the commission's 1970 findings or produced primarily inconclusive results. Not until the early to mid-1980s did evidence begin to mount suggesting that, in fact, some men are negatively affected by pornography. For instance, researchers have found that certain men are likely to exhibit aggressive behaviors and attitudes toward women after viewing violent pornography (Malamuth et al.,1986). This is especially true of materials that picture women enjoying being raped, even though they might have resisted initially (Donnerstein et al., 1987). (It must be noted here that the "aggressive behaviors and attitudes" in these types of studies usually consist of researchers measuring subjects' responses to written questionnaires and/or artifi-

PRURIENT INTERESTS
Sexual interests that are lustful, immoral, and given to debauchery.

cial situations with women "targets" in laboratories immediately following exposure to the pornography. Also, most subjects are male college undergraduates. Therefore, it is difficult to make generalizations about the effects of pornography on the general public based on the findings from these artificial scenarios with such limited samples.)

During the Reagan administration, the United States Attorney General's Commission on Pornography, more commonly remembered as the Meese Commission (named after Edwin Meese, Attorney General at the time), arrived at conclusions surprisingly different from the 1970 governmental study. The Meese Commission claimed a causal link between violent pornography and sexual violence toward women. They based their report on a review of a large collection of pornography in various forms and listening to the views of numerous experts, victims, and judges. Based on this assertion, they made almost 100 recommendations designed to curb the dissemination of pornographic materials.

In response to the commission's conclusions, social scientists pointed out that what the research showed was not that exposure to aggressive/violent pornography affects sexual behavior *per se*, but that it affects aggressive behavior, a theory borne out by other studies involving nonsexual aggressive behavior (Linz et al., 1987, 1988). It may be that pornography simply reinforces already present attitudes about sexual violence, such as rape (Linz et al., 1987, 1988). Or it may be that pornography serves a *cathartic* purpose, helping some readers vent sexual energy that might otherwise lead to sexual crimes (Goldstein & Kant, 1973).

More recent research has much to say concerning what happens when adults watch or read violent pornographic materials—mainly, that sex and violence are a particularly harmful mix. Viewing such materials can increase males' acceptance of sexual and other types of aggression toward females (Donnerstein et al., 1987). Males who have viewed violent pornography are also more likely to believe such myths as women like to be sexually overpowered or raped, "no" really means "yes," rape victims' injuries are not severe, or that wife-battering is acceptable (Donnerstein et al., 1987; Linz, 1989). Further, pornographers rarely depict sexual aggressors and perpetrators negatively, or show them being punished for their sexual aggression (Palys, 1986). Of course, there is always the possibility that viewing violent pornography, with its subsequent emotional numbing regarding the seriousness of sexual assault, actually causes violent acting out against women (Malamuth et al., 1986). This notion, however, has not yet found empirical support.

Edward Donnerstein and colleagues (1987), based on a review of the professional literature and their own research, concluded that:

> some forms of pornography, under some conditions, promote certain antisocial attitudes and behavior. Specifically, we should be most concerned about the detrimental effects of exposure to violent images in pornography and elsewhere, particularly material that portrays the myth that women enjoy or in some way benefit from rape, torture, or other forms of sexual violence. It is important to remember, however, that the portrayal of this theme is not limited to pornography. Many mass media depictions that either contain little explicit sex or are only mildly sexually explicit portray the same myth.
>
> To date, the evidence supporting the contention that so-called degrading pornographic materials, as long as they are not violent, are harmful is sparse and inconsistent. The few studies that have been done on these materials, including our own, have yielded contradictory findings, and the question of the effects of these materials awaits further research. Brief exposure to less degrading materials or simple nudity appears to result in few, if any, antisocial effects. (p. 171)

The issue of the effects of pornography remains murky. The only conclusion that the research clearly substantiates is that violent pornography can have the negative effect of making violence toward women seem more acceptable to some men. This is especially true of pornography depicting women as welcoming and even liking abusive sexual treat-

Opponents frequently protest and picket stores that sell pornography.

ment from men. *Women Against Violence Against Women* (WAVAW) is one of several groups dedicated to protesting the demeaning of women in the media, including pornographic films.

THE PROBLEM OF CHILD PORNOGRAPHY

"Kiddie porn," as child pornography is often called, is probably the most destructive pornography on the market. Authorities estimate that many thousands of children under the age of 18, mostly runaways, become involved in child pornography each year. Many of these children also steal and become prostitutes to survive.

Children who get pulled into this sadly profitable business suffer extreme emotional and physical harm (Silbert, 1989). Psychologists report that children involved in such acts, which range from nude modeling to erotic posing to intercourse with other children or adults, often become withdrawn, anxious, depressed, guilty, paranoid, and/or distrustful of adults in general. As adults they may find themselves incapable of intimate relationships, and they may carry a massive burden of guilt, shame, and anger. Because many of these children are victims of multiple negative circumstances, such as physical abuse, neglect, poverty, and drug and alcohol abuse, it is difficult to determine to what degree their emotional problems stem from their involvement in pornography.

Lawmakers have criminalized child pornography, drafting stringent laws against all forms of it. The Child Protection and Obscenity Act of 1988 provides stiff penalties for those who produce, distribute, and/or sell child pornography. Furthermore, because children are incapable of giving informed consent when it comes to sexual activity, perpetrators can also be charged under child abuse laws. Some believe this latter charge is more appropriate, claiming that depictions of children, whether nude or clothed, are not necessarily obscene, but that forcing children to participate in pornography is.

For Personal Reflection

How would you feel if you discovered a friend of yours had been arrested for purchasing, possessing, or even filming "kiddie porn"?

Mark Wahlberg

Advertisers frequently use "sex appeal" to sell their products.

SEX IN ADVERTISING

Sex seems to be everywhere in the media. It is almost impossible to read a popular magazine or watch an evening of television without confronting an advertisement using sex to sell a product or service. Over the years advertisers have increasingly relied upon nudity and the suggestion of intercourse to appeal to consumers. Beautiful, sexy, slender, and decidedly young men and women suggestively pose in various states of undress to sell everything from spark plugs to cologne. In American culture, sexuality symbolizes beauty, attractiveness, companionship, power, and wealth. Advertisers hope that consumers will identify with the sexy people in their ads and, in turn, believe using the advertised product will make them just as attractive, desirable, or powerful.

Although this message of sex in ads may be overt, advertisers often employ "subliminal" or "embedded" advertising strategies, meaning sexual words or images are hidden in the ad in such a way that the sexuality is supposedly picked up only by the subconscious mind (Key, 1980). For example, the crotch of a tree branching in two directions might represent the spread legs of a woman, or the shape and size of women's toiletry articles, such as deodorant and cologne containers, might represent the male sexual organ. The idea here is that because the subliminal message is supposedly out of the censoring capabilities of conscious awareness, the consumer will respond to the ad with high suggestibility, finding the product irresistible. Although the research on the true effectiveness of subliminal advertising is shaky at best, advertisers continue to use such strategies (Balay & Shevrin, 1988).

Ironically, those who have studied the effects of sexual ads report that, unless the product itself is directly related to sexuality, the consumer is not likely to remember either the ad's principle message or the product's brand name (Severn et al., 1990). Although an ad with "sex appeal" may draw immediate attention, an ad without it may sell more products.

SEXUAL PRODUCTS

A variety of sexual products are available to today's consumers. The most common are sexual literature; adult magazines, newspapers, and tabloids; adult computer software and services; cable television; adult movies, films, and videotapes; and erotic aids and sex toys.

LITERATURE

Sexuality has had a longstanding place in literature. For example, the ancient Greeks described Dionysian fertility rites in explicit terms, while the Romans viewed sex as wildly pleasurable and spiced their stories with ribald tales of sexual adventures. Much later during the nineteenth century, prudery reached new heights, especially evident in the literature of the period. Victorian social forces worked to squelch erotic writing, at least on the surface. They were not completely successful, as erotica and pornography were readily available, for example, on the streets of London. Victorian sexual prudery eventually made its way to the United States, where even today it remains the sexual norm for many communities.

Although never repressed completely, eroticism in literature did not fully emerge in American society until the twentieth century. Novels such as D. H. Lawrence's *Lady Chatterley's Lover* and James Joyce's *Ulysses* were highly controversial in this country. These works were explicit in their treatment of sexual themes, at least by standards of that day. Because *Ulysses* contains passages dealing with masturbation and adultery, it was banned for years until 1933, when U.S. District Judge John M. Woolsey deemed it acceptable due to its "sincere and serious attempt to devise a new literary method for the observation and description of mankind." Interestingly, both Lawrence and Joyce are considered literary giants today.

Contemporary America has made little or no effort to censor erotic literature, and as a result authors are relatively free to deal with almost any subject in any way they choose—be it subtly suggestive or overtly graphic. Contemporary literary works deal with a multitude of sexual themes, such as bisexuality, homosexuality, prostitution, masturbation, sadomasochism, and "safer sex," to name just a few.

Drawing by Roz Chast; © 1982 The New Yorker Magazine, Inc.

Adult books, magazines, and videotapes are as popular as ever in America today.

MAGAZINES, NEWSPAPERS, AND TABLOIDS

In the early 1930s, *Esquire, The Magazine for Men* was the first magazine to focus on sexuality in such a way as to make the topic presentable enough to be displayed openly. *Playboy* entered the market in the early 1950s, and, with the exception of *National Geographic* and its naked villagers, was the first widely distributed and "acceptable" magazine to show photographs of bare breasts and buttocks. Balancing illustrations with articles on men's issues and quality fiction, *Playboy* is certainly the most well known, if not the most widely distributed, soft-core magazine today.

Adapting *Playboy*'s formula, *Playgirl* and *Cosmopolitan* appeared on the scene as erotica for female readers. Many others followed for both men and women, but especially for men. Some, like *Hustler* and *Oui* moved to the hard-core side of sex to attract readers. In the 1970s, both *Playboy* and *Penthouse* became the first widely distributed magazines to show models' pubic hair, yet this—and showing much, much more—is now standard practice.

Sexuality remains a common theme in popular magazines for both men and women. For evidence, one need only glance at the article titles prominently displayed on magazines in the supermarket racks. *Time, Newsweek, Rolling Stone, People, U.S. News and World Report, Omni, Sports Illustrated*—none is immune. Even the conservative *Reader's Digest* regularly features sexually oriented articles.

Sex tabloids, with such illustrative titles as *Screw, Stud,* and *Smut,* also began to flourish in the 1960s and 1970s, many continuing to do so today. Exhibiting photos of male and female nudes participating in various sexual escapades, these tabloids are especially popu-

TABLE 17.1 **An Analysis of the Pictorial Content of 430 Sexually Explicit Magazines**

Content Categories	Incidence
Women in various degrees of undress	27.8%
Male-female sexual activity (simulated)	15.5%
Male-female sexual activity (actual)	8.4%
Bondage and discipline	4.9%
Heterosexual oral-genital sex	2.9%
Special sexual activity, like use of dildos	2.8%
Female body-parts other than genitals	2.7%
Lesbian sex	2.6%
Swingers	1.9%
Young women	1.9%
Women with special characteristics, like shaved genitals	1.4%
Interracial heterosexual sexual activity	1.4%
Gay sex	1.3%
Sadomasochism	1.2%
Asian, black, or other ethnic woman	1.2%
Fetishistic sexual activity	1.1%
Group sex	1.1%
Nudism	1%
Heterosexual anal intercourse	1%
Women wrestling	1%
Mixed (involving one or more of the above)	14.4%
Other (not fitting any of the above)	2.5%

Source: C. Winick (1985), A content analysis of sexually explicit magazines sold in an adult bookstore, *Journal of Sex Research, 21,* 206–210. Reprinted by permission of the Society for the Scientific Study of Sex; P.O. Box 208; Mount Vernon, IA 52314 USA.

lar because of their "personal classifieds," where customers place and respond to "want ads" for sexual partners. Moving away from the tabloid format in an effort to increase their market share and acceptability, some gay magazines like *The Advocate* have begun to offer subscribers the option of purchasing a separate "personals" section. Adult book stores are the primary distribution centers for sex tabloids, magazines, and newspapers.

What kinds of explicit sexual acts do adult magazines typically depict? Data on the pictorial content of 430 sexually explicit magazines appears in Table 17.1.

For Personal Reflection

How would you feel if your partner enjoyed reading pornographic magazines and watching pornographic videos?

COMPUTERS

As with every other form of the media, sexuality has managed to find its way into the high-tech world of computers (Walsh, 1993). Users can trade sexual messages on computer bulletin boards, play erotic games, have overtly sexual conversations with a distant playmate, purchase tickets for a cruise, or access the latest sex education information. Some computer networks cater to heterosexuals, some to homosexuals, others to both.

Perhaps the most valuable computer services, though, are those offering customers access to sex education and therapy-oriented information. Networks focusing exclusively on sexual topics often provide subscribers with access to all kinds of sexual information, usually for an annual fee and hourly charge. Parents can access it for their children, as computer sex education might be the most comfortable way for them to educate their children about sexuality. Because of the popularity of sexual information services, it is not surprising that a number of computer networks are now joining the "sex info" business.

Is having instant access to all kinds of sexual information through computer necessarily problem-free? As is the case with cable television, accessing sexual networks presents Americans—parents in particular—with a number of questions and potential problems. From where does the sexual information come? How is it presented? Who decides if the information provided is accurate or inaccurate? Perhaps most importantly, how can parents keep their children from accessing sexual information on the computer if they do not want their children to learn about sexuality in this way? This is not to imply that accessing sexual information on the home computer is necessarily bad. Sexual information networks have much to offer. But with constant advances in technology, we must acknowledge the potential problems that these services might bring to our families.

TELEVISION

The rating system for theatrical films reassures parents that, theoretically, their young children will not be admitted to R, NC-17, or adult-only movies; however, television is another matter. Because parents feel—and with good reason—that they do not always have control over what their children watch on television, networks have come under considerable scrutiny concerning the sexual content of their programing.

Some controls have been arranged. The larger networks may allow local station managers the opportunity to preview controversial programing and decide whether to air the piece. Warning messages for parents often precede programs having sexual content. Films made for theaters are edited for television; nudity, sexual scenes, and explicit language are usually cut.

But despite these controls, sexuality is part of prime-time television. Daytime soap operas have recurring themes of premarital and adulterous sex, homosexuality, prostitution, and rape. Weekend music video shows, which cater to teenagers, run music videos loaded with sexual material. Evening television has become increasingly daring in its depictions of men and women wearing provocative outfits and even "G-strings."

Critics object not so much to sexual themes on television, but to the manner of their portrayal. Television depicts sex as glamorous, carefree, and only for the young and beautiful. And with the exception of public television like that of PBS, it rarely addresses the real-life problems of unplanned pregnancy and sexually transmitted diseases, especially HIV and AIDS, or the realities of sexual activity among older adults.

MOVIES, FILMS, AND VIDEOTAPES

In the early days of the cinema, censorship was substantial and severe, keeping sexual and other controversial issues out of films shown in public theaters. Standards set by the Legion of Decency (established by the Roman Catholic Church) and other institutions in the 1930s helped to produce the "Hays Code," which prohibited nudity, adultery, illicit sexual behavior, long sessions of kissing and embracing, and suggestive poses in motion pictures. Protestant groups tightened control even further by protesting depictions of prostitution, alcohol and drug use, and assorted other "unmentionables." This stringent censorship consequently generated a market for adult films, the earliest dating back to the first quarter of this century. Called "blue movies" in Great Britain and "stag films" in the United States, they were typically shown at men-only gatherings and were extremely expensive considering their poor quality (Smith, 1990).

In the late 1960s, the Swedish film *I am Curious (Yellow)*, debuted in the United States. It was the first X-rated film to show in regular theaters and was definitely soft-core compared with what is available today. As social attitudes have become more liberated, Hollywood films have become increasingly sexual and violent. The movie rating system, however poorly enforced, was originally designed to alert audiences to graphic and explicit material. Yet now this appears to be true only for sexuality in movies. Contrary to what common sense might dictate, rape scenes are far more common in films rated R (restricted) and PG (parental guidance) than in X-rated ones. In fact, the great majority of mainstream X-rated films depict mutually consensual sexual behavior, rather than forced sexual behavior, sexual assault, or other forms of sexual violence. Violence is now so commonplace in most R- and PG-rated films (and even in some children's films) that "slasher" films like *Friday the 13th* and *A Nightmare on Elm Street* hardly shock or offend the general public anymore.

With the advent and proliferation of home videocassette recorders, many hard-core viewers who wish to abandon the public movie theater can now watch adult films in the privacy of their own homes. Hard-core videos, like their theatrical counterparts, are quick to show close-ups of both male and female sexual organs joined in a variety of positions. Generally aimed at the heterosexual Western male (and perhaps his partner, too), they fulfill male fantasies through stories of sex-hungry females unable to resist any male who comes along. Plots are shallow, acting is poor, but sexual arousal is the usual result. Although these films are often the object of public protest, the depiction of violent sexual behavior and victimized women is rare. Many adult films also portray lesbian sexual activity, although these films are usually marketed to heterosexual males rather than lesbians. Some adult videos are specifically produced for gays and lesbians.

EROTIC AIDS AND SEX TOYS

Erotic aids and sex toys are sexual products and devices that people use to enhance masturbation or sexual activity with a partner. Why are these products so popular? Surely for many reasons. Manufacturers and entrepreneurs claim that these products increase sexual pleasure and satisfaction, with or without a partner. Many people would rather self-

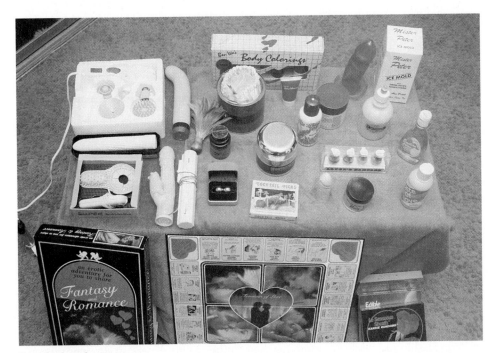

Sexual aids and erotic toys.

pleasure than deal with relationship issues or risk having sex with a stranger who might be HIV-positive or have another STD. An array of companies claim that sexual products can revitalize any stale monogamous relationship. Therapists often advise clients to use them to overcome sexual dysfunctions. The list goes on and on.

The variety of erotic aids and sex toys available in the 1990s could stock a large store. Life-size dolls with lifelike orifices and humanlike skin. Vibrators. G-spot stimulators. Prostate stimulators. Dildos. Penile attachments. Anal plugs. A vast selection of lotions, lubricants, and oils—some candy-flavored to enhance fellatio; others designed to warm and stimulate the clitoris. Potions, designed to increase male "staying power," that work by numbing the penis and lengthening erection time. All of these are readily available by mail order. Some customers are opting instead to purchase sex toys at "home parties" where they can see and sometimes operate the items beforehand.

On a Personal Note (Natalie, age 31)

My husband and I decided to order a bottle of one of those "Workhorse x10" kind of lotions. Jesse comes a little too fast sometimes, so we thought, "What the hey?" Anyway, we get this stuff in the mail, which wasn't cheap, and Jesse puts some on one night. Does it turn him into a "workhorse"? No. What does it do? It burns his penis. He still complains about it. (Author's files)

Most of these products appear to be harmless, generally performing at least somewhat as promised. There is one major exception, though. Consumers should avoid erotic aids, "magic sex pills," and lotions that are advertised as cures for every sexual ailment, from female unresponsiveness to male premature ejaculation. Besides being an expensive hoax, sex pills and other such aids bought through the mail can be dangerous.

For Personal Reflection

Are there any erotic aids that you would consider purchasing and using? If so, which ones and why? Are there any you would find offensive or objectionable? If so, which ones and why?

SEXUAL SERVICES

In addition to sexual products, consumers can purchase a variety of sexual services. Some of the more popular of these are strippers, telephone sex, and prostitutes.

STRIPPERS

The first "striptease" reportedly took place in Paris on February 9, 1893, when an artist's model by the name of Mona undressed for students present at the Moulin Rouge. For her services, Mona received 100 francs. Although a riot soon followed in the Latin Quarter when protesters overran the local police station, this form of entertainment quickly caught on in Europe and later in America (Smith, 1990).

Today, primarily a female occupation, *stripping* is for many a legal way to make a living. (Given the negative social perceptions of this particular occupation, some strippers prefer to refer to themselves as "dancers" and their movements as "art.") Strippers usually dance on a stage or in "boxes" surrounded by seats, moving erotically to music in a bump-and-grind fashion while slowly removing their clothes. Many American communities prohibit the complete removal of clothing, so strippers undress down to a skimpy "G-string"

Male strippers—and their enthusiastic female audiences.

or "thong." Some women wear "pasties" over their nipples. Many strippers also earn extra pay when members of their audience seek sex with them after the show.

In recent years men have entered the striptease profession, performing on stage and on tables in front of enthusiastic crowds. Like their female counterparts, most male strippers undress down to a G-string, exposing their buttocks but rarely their genitals. Spectators earn kisses and caresses by tucking bills under performers' G-strings.

TELEPHONE SEX

Telephone sex, or "1-900" and "1-800" "Dial-a-Porn" services, is an extremely profitable form of sexual service that has steadily grown in popularity since the 1980s. For a fee (which is discreetly added to the customer's telephone and credit card bills), customers can listen to live or recorded male or female sexy voices describe sexual acts as they are performed, complete with moans, groans, and screams of ecstasy. Many of these services cater to customers who fantasize and masturbate during the call. As one man described his telephone encounter with "Mistress Olga":

On a Personal Note (Carl, age 24)

I'd always wanted to call up one of those "1-900" sex lines, so I got up my nerve and phoned in one evening. The first woman I talked to was very professional, took down my credit card number, and then asked me what kind of fantasy I was interested in. When she mentioned "Mistress Olga" and her leather and whips, I couldn't resist. A few moments later, a woman with a fake-sounding Eastern European accent came on the line, and began to direct my "phone fantasy." She led me through this bizarre sadomasochistic fantasy, you know, the good Mistress talking dirty to me, tying me up, spanking me without mercy, biting my butt, and even threatening to pee on me. And the more I played it up, the more she provoked me in return. After several minutes, I faked an orgasm, and then hung up. The whole thing was pretty funny, that is until I got the credit card bill the following month. (Author's files)

The issue of sending obscenities over the phone and across state lines has generated debate. The potential for minors to access telephone sex services has been of special concern. Granted, ads state that the individual must be 18 or older to call, and the "1-800" services require a credit card, but neither of these inevitably deter ingenious youth. Phone companies offer consumers the option of "blocking" access to "1-900" numbers from their home phone lines, but minors can still reach any "1-800" telephone sex services.

PROSTITUTION

PROSTITUTION
Selling and buying sex.

Prostitution (from the Latin *prostituere*, meaning "to expose"), or the selling and buying of sex, is a widespread practice. It is also a timeless practice, commonly known as the "world's oldest profession." Prostitution is illegal in all parts of the United States, save for a handful of counties in Nevada.

Whenever and wherever there has been poverty in the world, there has also been prostitution. This practice has always served as a way for desperately poor and homeless women, youths, and men to earn a living and survive (Jolin, 1994). Prostitution flourished in ancient Rome and Greece, as it did in Europe during the Middle Ages and beyond. During the Reformation, both Roman Catholics and Protestants condemned prostitution, their objections stemming from a sense of righteousness and fear of the syphilis epidemic of the 1500s. The Victorian Age, famous for stifling sexual passion, nevertheless tolerated prostitution as a way for good husbands to release their evil urges (Tannahill, 1980).

In early twentieth-century Europe and America, "houses of ill repute" were common. The women prostitutes lived and worked together in a large home, or *brothel* ("whorehouse" or "cathouse") run by a "madam." The madam's duties included providing room and board, supervising the women, managing finances, and arranging for and greeting customers, among other things. A red light marked the outside of the brothel, explaining the derivation of the phrase *red light district*. For the most part, brothels went underground after World War II and are rarely heard of today, except for the state-licensed brothels in Nevada.

Today's prostitutes ("hookers" or "whores") generally fall into seven categories: (1) call girls, (2) escort service and convention prostitutes, (3) massage parlor prostitutes, (4) bar and hotel prostitutes, (5) streetwalkers, (6) male prostitutes, and (7) juvenile prostitutes. Many service both heterosexual and homosexual customers. Most female prostitutes come from troubled backgrounds characterized by physical and sexual abuse, drug and alcohol addiction, family problems, low-paying menial jobs, and academic failure (Bagley & Young, 1987; Jolin, 1994; Rio, 1991; Simmons & Whitbeck, 1991). Several studies have found that from 10 to 85 percent of the female and male prostitutes surveyed had been victims of childhood sexual abuse (Seng, 1989).

At the top of the ladder is the *call girl*, who charges a high price and works out of her own, sometimes luxurious, apartment. Very attractive and intelligent, she carefully screens her clients by phone. Besides providing sexual services, she may also hire out as a highly presentable date for public appearances. The call girl's prices are normally the highest in the business.

Bogus escort services also provide sexual favors. *Escort prostitutes* may be students, housewives, or professional women who prefer to earn extra money by moonlighting in this way. *Convention prostitutes* work large conventions, selling sexual services and stripping for groups of convention participants. *Massage parlor prostitutes*, working under the guise of a legitimate business, massage customers and then offer them manual (massage and masturbation, or "M & M") and/or oral sexual stimulation for an "under-the-table" bonus.

Hotel and bar prostitutes are likely to strike a deal with hotel and bar owners whereby they receive a certain percentage of the business they bring in to the particular establishment. Hotel owners look the other way, rent rooms by the hour, and then give the pros-

On the bottom of the pay scale is the streetwalker.

titutes a small kickback. Bar owners encourage the prostitutes to mingle with and tease customers into buying more drinks, and then give them a kickback on the number of drinks sold.

Streetwalkers make the least money and work under the worst possible conditions. They are usually managed by "pimps," males who pretend to protect and take care of them, but who, in fact, are often abusive and take most of their earnings. Many of these women work to maintain drug habits, frequently recruiting their clients from adult theaters and stage shows. Streetwalkers, who are typically minorities with little or no education and from poverty-stricken backgrounds, are the most frequently arrested. They are also the most at risk of contracting sexual diseases from customers and transmitting them back, and the most at risk of being severely abused by customers and their pimps.

Men have also found a place in the profession selling themselves to women and men, often older and well-to-do, as escorts and providers of sex. *Male prostitutes* who cater to females are "gigolos"; males who cater to other males are "hustlers." Adolescent boys who prostitute themselves to older males are "chickens." Hustlers and chickens are far more common than gigolos. The typical hustler is between the ages of 17 and 18, and began prostituting around the age of 14 (Coleman, 1989). Most often his sexual encounters involve masturbation and fellatio and least often involve being the recipient of anal intercourse (Pleak & Meyer-Bahlburg, 1990). Males are drawn into prostitution for the same reasons as females, primarily financial ones.

Like adults, adolescents—male and female—become prostitutes in order to support themselves while on the streets. Most *juvenile prostitutes* are runaways or throwaways, some of whom are as young as 12. They come from a variety of impoverished backgrounds; sexual and physical abuse, poverty, school failure, and parental abandonment are typical

Many homeless youths are forced into prostitution to survive on the streets. Frequently runaways from troubled homes, some are as young as 12 or 13.

(Rio, 1991; Seng, 1989). Many juvenile prostitutes must also participate in child pornography, some out of financial desperation, others out of fear of being attacked or killed if they do not cooperate with the pornographers.

Prostitutes do not always match common stereotypes. Most describe themselves as heterosexual or bisexual, not lesbian or gay (Carmen & Moody, 1985; Savitz & Rosen, 1988). Furthermore, a good percentage of them (about 70 percent) claim to enjoy their work all or part of the time (Savitz & Rosen, 1988). "Johns" (another name for the male customers of female prostitutes) do not always match common stereotypes either (Adams, 1987). Rather than being ugly, brutish derelicts, most are upper- and middle-class business or professional men who are pleasant, polite, and of average to above-average attractiveness and intelligence. Before an encounter, they tend to bathe, use cologne and deodorant, and dress neatly.

The streetwalker's income generally depends on bringing to climax as many customers as possible. Most average 4 to 12 johns a day. Because it is faster and less trouble, most streetwalkers—and their johns—prefer oral sex over full intercourse (Reinisch, 1990). Many, but by no means all, prostitutes now require that their johns wear condoms (Freund et al., 1989). Johns who consistently use condoms with prostitutes tend to have a higher level of education and more carefully weigh the risks of contracting STDs than do inconsistent users or nonusers (Vanwesenbeeck et al., 1993). Licensed brothels in Nevada now require that prostitutes have monthly HIV tests.

Why do people hire prostitutes in the first place? Certainly the reasons vary with customers. Individuals may look to prostitutes for sexual novelty, for a technique or position that the regular partner is unwilling to try. Others who are away from their regular partner—on a business trip or serving in the military—may seek temporary liaisons with prostitutes. Still others who do not have a partner may turn to prostitutes to relieve their sexual tensions without the complications of dating or committing to others.

PERSPECTIVE

Working Women

Are women typically forced into prostitution by a pimp? Contrary to popular misconceptions, the answer is *no* in most cases, at least according to Arlene Carmen's observations of New York prostitutes over a period of eight years. Here's how a number of "working women" answered the question, "Were you forced into the life by a pimp?"

Shannon:

Many people say every woman, or most, are forced to become a prostitute. Most girls do it for love. Most girls were young when they started, and the idea of money and living good was a thrill. No one that I know has ever told me they were forced to start. They mostly all met the guy, liked him, and then started. No one, in my opinion, can really be forced to do anything; if they are, there is always a way out.

Vickie:

I was all by myself, had nowhere to go. I was hungry, couldn't go home, and I had no money to eat or live. So I came on the streets and started working to make some money, and now I'm not hungry and have a place to live. No one had to put me on the streets. The money is cool, but at least I don't have to be hungry or sleep on the streets, or worry about where my next meal is coming from, or where I'm going to sleep.

Nikki Mae:

No, it was by choice. The fascination of having money. Then I fell in love. I'm still in love. It's not all that bad. And people not in this life cannot conceive it. All they believe is their fairy tale ideas of it, with unhappy endings.

Blanche:

No. The reason why I became a prostitute is because of the money. I could not find a job and I needed money. And my man, he doesn't force me to come out on the streets—it's because I want to. I find it's an easier way to make a living and to have more things out of life. I was never forced into prostitution. If I don't want to come out, he doesn't make me. I'd rather work the streets and get all the things I want. (pp. 101–104)

Source: A. Carmen & H. Moody (1985), *Working women: The subterranean world of street prostitution* (New York: Harper & Row).

Prosecution of prostitutes has been inconsistent, primarily because society has trouble making up its mind about prostitution. The vast majority of Americans disapprove of prostitution, 61 percent of males and 83 percent of females believing the practice to be "always wrong" or "almost always wrong" (Klassen et al., 1989). Yet as one prostitute pointed out, a married woman who sleeps with an abusive husband night after night is selling her body for the support of herself and her children. And how many people expect a date to "put out" after an evening of expensive wining and dining? Yes, sex can be bought and sold in a number of ways. The key word here, and in most legal definitions, is *indiscriminate*. Put another way, a prostitute is a person who has sex indiscriminately for pay.

One major problem in trying to arrest and prosecute prostitutes is the sheer number of sellers and buyers. A conservative estimate is that, at any one time, 5 million American females have been engaged in some form of prostitution, and that 18 million American males have been involved in some form of commercial sex with prostitutes (Janus & Janus, 1993). Another is the bias in the criminal justice system toward arresting prostitutes more often than their johns. Still another is the bureaucratic nature of the criminal justice system, which is excessively time-consuming and expensive. Even if arrested, most prostitutes are poor and cannot afford legal representation, so the system has to cover the costs. The entire ordeal is frustrating for all involved. Rather than attempting to arrest and prosecute prostitutes, some communities prefer to focus their efforts on ridding themselves of *overt* prostitution, usually by preventing prostitutes from loitering and soliciting johns in public.

Some prostitutes have organized into active unions: the *National Task Force on Prostitution* (formerly COYOTE, or "Call Off Your Old Tired Ethics"), *PONY* ("Prostitutes of New York"), and *Scapegoat*. Their purpose is to promote prostitutes' civil rights by legalizing or decriminalizing their profession. Some proponents argue that *legalization* (governmental condoning and regulation) of prostitution would save enforcement dollars, eliminate the need for pimps, bring in license fees and taxes, and keep prostitutes disease-free through regular medical examinations. Others argue that *decriminalization* (lifting criminal penalties without governmental condoning and regulation) of prostitution would allow people to have control over their work and what they do with their own bodies, and protect the privacy of prostitutes and their customers. Opponents of both legalization and decriminalization generally hold that prostitution is immoral, a source of STDs, and a catalyst for other types of criminal activity. They argue that for the good of all of its members, society must work to eliminate prostitution—not encourage, condone, regulate, or ignore it (Calderone & Johnson, 1989; Rio, 1991).

For Personal Reflection

1. *Do you believe prostitution is a "victimless" crime, as some advocates maintain? Why or why not?*
2. *In states where prostitution is illegal, do you think johns should be prosecuted more severely, less severely, or as severely as the prostitutes themselves?*

KEY POINTS

1. Defining and labeling sexually oriented materials is a difficult task, because the words *erotic, pornographic,* and *obscene* escape exact definition. *Erotica* refers to sexual materials that are artistically motivated, created, and presented; *pornography,* to sexual materials that are intended to arouse sexual excitement; *obscenity,* a legal term, to sexual materials that are lewd, disgusting, and offensive to accepted standards of decency. *Prurient interests* refer to interests of a lustful sort, implying sexual immorality and, in some cases, debauchery.
2. *Hard-core* erotica and pornography are described as sexual materials that are explicit in their portrayal of the genitals and various sexual activities, whereas *soft-core* erotica and pornography are merely suggestive of these activities. Adult bookstores, theaters, video rental stores, and mail order catalogs are the primary sources of hard-core materials.
3. Researchers have conducted numerous studies to determine the effects of sexual materials on viewers and readers. To date, at least when it comes to mutually consensual, soft-core, nonviolent erotica and pornography, there is little evidence to prove either negative or positive effects. However, violent pornography that depicts

women in degrading, humiliating, and demeaning ways may be another story. Recent research has much to say concerning what happens when adults watch or read violent pornographic materials—mainly, that sex and violence are a particularly harmful mix. Viewing such materials can increase males' acceptance of sexual and other types of aggression toward females.

4. Over the years advertisers have increasingly relied upon nudity and the suggestion of intercourse to appeal to consumers. In many ads, this message of sexuality is overt. In others, advertisers employ "subliminal" or "embedded" advertising strategies.

5. A variety of sexual products are available to today's consumers. The most common are sexual literature; adult magazines, newspapers, and tabloids; adult computer software and services; network and cable television; adult movies, films, and videotapes; and erotic aids and sex toys.

6. In addition to sexual products, consumers can purchase a variety of sexual services. Some popular services include strippers, telephone sex, and prostitutes.

7. Today's prostitutes, many of whom cater to both heterosexual and homosexual customers, generally fall into seven categories: (1) call girls, (2) escort service and convention prostitutes, (3) massage parlor prostitutes, (4) bar and hotel prostitutes, (5) streetwalkers, (6) male prostitutes, and (7) juvenile prostitutes.

ACTIVITIES AND QUESTIONS

1. What are some of the pros and cons for models posing nude for soft-core porn magazines? Hard-core magazines? What about participating in sexual activities for these magazines? What about doing the same on videotapes?

2. What are some of the pros and cons of always using sexy young, beautiful, tanned, and emaciated models in advertisements? What are some of the messages manufacturers and advertisers are inadvertently sending when they rely solely on such models? Do you think these messages have any effect on viewers' sexual functioning? Why or why not? And if so, in what way(s)?

3. Why do more men attend female strip shows than the other way around? Do men and women have different motives for attending such shows? Explain.

4. If you would feel comfortable doing this, locate and interview a professional "call-girl" about the services she offers (and renders), her hourly rates, typical clientele, and if, how, and when she practices "safer sex."

5. If you would feel comfortable doing this, visit an "Adult Book, Mag, and Video Store," making note of the various products for sale. Share the results of your investigation with the rest of your class.

6. First, imagine a society in which there is total censorship and banning of all sexual materials and services, where, for example, no one could purchase an erotic magazine. What do you think such a society would be like? Describe some of the advantages and disadvantages of this society.

   Now, imagine a society in which there is absolutely no censorship or banning of any sexual materials and services, where for example, anyone could watch XXX-rated movies on publicly broadcast stations at any time of the day. Describe some of the advantages and disadvantages of this society.

   What did you learn from this exercise?

RECOMMENDED READINGS

Bullough, V., & Bullough, B. (1987). *Women and prostitution: A social history.* Buffalo, NY: Prometheus Books. Explores the history of prostitution, from ancient times to the present.

Carmen, A., & Moody, H. (1985). *Working women: The subterranean world of street prostitution*. New York: Harper & Row. A fascinating look into the lives of New York City prostitutes. The authors challenge a number of myths and stereotypes in an attempt to present prostitutes as human beings.

Delacoste, F., & Alexander, P. (1987). *Sex work: Writings by women in the sex industry*. Pittsburgh, PA: Cleis Press. Personal and professional accounts by women who sell sex, including porn stars, strippers, and prostitutes.

Donnerstein, E., Linz, D., & Penrod, S. (1987). *The question of pornography: Research findings and policy implications*. New York: Free Press. Presents current research findings on pornography, in addition to legal and policymaking issues.

Kimmel, M. S. (Ed.). (1990). *Men confront pornography*. New York: Crown. A collection of 35 essays by male authors candidly exploring the role of pornography in their lives. Topics include the issue of censorship, feminism and pornography, fantasy and pornography, the Meese Commission, and pornography and violence toward women.

Opposing Viewpoints Pamphlets (1995). *Is pornography harmful?* San Diego, CA: Greenhaven Press. This excellent pamphlet presents both sides of the pornography issue.

•**S**EXUAL LAWS

•SEXUAL MORALS AND ETHICS

•SEXUAL COERCION AND THE LAW: RAPE, INCEST,

AND SEXUAL HARASSMENT

•FUTURE TRENDS IN SEXUAL LAWS

C H A P T E R 1 8

S E X U A L I T Y A N D T H E L A W

O B J E C T I V E S

AFTER READING THIS CHAPTER YOU SHOULD BE
ABLE TO . . .

1. DISTINGUISH AMONG THE TERMS *SEXUAL LAWS*,
   MORALS, AND *ETHICS*.
2. DESCRIBE THE RELIGIOUS ORIGINS AND
   PURPOSES OF SEXUAL LAWS IN THE UNITED
   STATES.
3. CITE SOME PROBLEMS ASSOCIATED WITH
   DEVISING LAWS TO REGULATE SEX EDUCATION IN
   THE PUBLIC SCHOOLS AND THE USE OF NEW
   REPRODUCTIVE PROCEDURES.
4. DEFINE AND GIVE SPECIFIC EXAMPLES OF THE
   FOLLOWING FORMS OF SEXUAL COERCION: *RAPE*,
   INCEST, AND *SEXUAL HARASSMENT*.
5. DESCRIBE SOME OF THE SOCIETAL MYTHS THAT
   PROMOTE SEXUAL COERCION.

P E R S O N A L   A S S E S S M E N T

WHAT ARE YOUR THOUGHTS AND FEELINGS ON SEXUAL LAWS, MORALS, ETHICS, AND SEXUAL COERCION? TO EXPLORE THIS, READ THE FOLLOWING STATEMENTS AND RESPOND USING THIS RATING SCALE: 3 = I *completely agree* WITH THE STATEMENT; 2 = I *mostly agree* WITH THE STATEMENT; 1 = I *mostly disagree* WITH THE STATEMENT; 0 = I *completely disagree* WITH THE STATEMENT. REMEMBER, THERE ARE NO RIGHT OR WRONG ANSWERS HERE; IT'S YOUR OPINION THAT COUNTS.

_____ 1. Morals are relative; there are no absolute values of right and wrong.

_____ 2. It doesn't matter what people do in the privacy of their own homes or bedrooms, as long as no one is hurt or coerced into doing something they wouldn't normally do.

_____ 3. The fabric of our society is based on and held together by morals; therefore, society must regulate those aspects of sexuality that the majority of its members find unacceptable and undesirable.

_____ 4. Legislators should repeal any sexual laws that prohibit sexual activities between consenting adult partners.

_____ 5. Sexual laws should become increasingly restrictive.

_____ 6. Some women who are raped actually "ask for it" by the way they dress and behave in public.

_____ 7. Male victims of rape are just as traumatized as female victims, if not more so.

_____ 8. If things continue the way they are going, our society will soon face the lifting of "age of consent" restrictions for sexual relationships between adults and youths.

_____ 9. Sexual harassment is little more than harmless "flirting"; people shouldn't get so uptight about it.

_____ 10. Men who experience sexual harassment on the job secretly enjoy the attention.

*I*f there is a man who commits adultery with another man's wife, one who commits adultery with his friend's wife, the adulterer and adulteress shall surely be put to death. If there is a man who lies with his father's wife, he has uncovered his father's nakedness; both of them shall surely be put to death. . . . If there is a man who lies with his daughter-in-law, both of them shall surely be put to death; they have committed incest. . . . If there is a male who lies with a male as those who lie with a woman, both of them have committed a detestable act; they shall surely be put to death. . . . If there is a man who marries a woman and her mother, it is immorality; both he and they shall be burned with fire, that there may be no immorality in your midst. If there is a man who lies with an animal, he shall surely be put to death; you shall also kill the animal. If there is a woman who approaches any animal to mate with it, you shall kill the woman and the animal; they shall surely be put to death. . . . If there is a man who takes his sister, his father's daughter or his mother's daughter, so that he sees her nakedness and she sees his nakedness, it is a disgrace; and they shall be cut off in the sight of the sons of their people. . . . If there is a man who lies with a menstruous woman and uncovers her nakedness, he has laid bare her flow, and she has exposed the flow of her blood; thus both of them shall be cut off from among their people.

Leviticus 20:10–18

SEXUAL LAWS

How many times have educators, newspaper editors, and even politicians proclaimed, "You can't legislate morality!"? These words have become a banner for any of a number of groups and individuals seeking greater freedom of sexual expression. Yet if our inability to legislate morality is a truism, why do we have so many laws that govern "moral conduct," as some might define it?

In this country, legislators continue to pass (and *attempt* to pass) assorted **sexual laws,** or laws designed to regulate and protect individuals from unwelcomed sexual attention, remarks, gestures, and behaviors. The number of sexual laws enacted and enforced today is significantly reduced compared with past generations, yet many states and municipalities have sexual laws that, if enforced, would incriminate large numbers of otherwise healthy and law-abiding citizens—without their even knowing it. For example, a number of states in this country have *sodomy laws* forbidding "crimes against nature," which are loosely (and specifically, in some instances) interpreted to include, among other behaviors, oral-genital and anal-genital sex—two popular sexual behaviors these days. Technically, in such states and communities the police could arrest scores of married couples for engaging in mutually consensual oral sex. *Selective* enforcement of sodomy laws, which is more often the case today, serves as a mechanism to control individuals whom society considers immoral and undesirable.

Certainly, questioning the purpose and "rightness" of sexual laws is in itself a rather recent phenomenon. It was not so long ago that sexual laws were simply accepted as a matter of fact. So rather than ask why certain sexual laws (including those some might view as "archaic") remain on the books, let's instead consider the origins and purposes of sexual laws in general.

THE ORIGIN OF SEXUAL LAWS

Although the ultimate beginnings of sexual laws may not be traceable, our examination of the history of sexual laws in Western society begins with the Jewish and Christian scriptures. The laws governing behavior as outlined in these texts became the foundation for the moral standards of countries and cultures influenced by Judeo-Christian values and traditions (Nelson, 1978). For example, the *Pentateuch* (the first five books of the Bible) contains such sexual laws as these:

- For this cause a man shall leave his father and mother, and shall cleave to his wife; and they shall become one flesh. (Genesis 2:24)
- You shall not lie with a male as one lies with a female; it is an abomination. (Leviticus 18:22)
- You shall not commit adultery. (Deuteronomy 5:18)

In the New Testament, St. Paul of Tarsus went on to say:

- Do you not know that your bodies are members of Christ? Shall I then take away the members of Christ and make them members of a harlot? May it never be! (1 Corinthians 6:15)
- Flee immorality. (1 Corinthians 6:18)
- For this is the will of God, your sanctification; that is, that you abstain from sexual immorality. (1 Thessalonians 4:3)

Although the ultimate interpretation of these and other biblical sexual standards has stimulated a great deal of controversy in scholarly circles, such have clearly played a pivotal role in shaping what Western Judeo-Christian cultures consider to be "normal" and "acceptable" modes of sexual expression. Whereas some individuals might now argue that sex—and all matters considered private and intimate—should rightly be considered the

SEXUAL LAWS

Laws designed to regulate and protect individuals from unwanted sexual attention and behavior.

Beginning with Adam and Eve in the Garden of Eden, Judeo-Christian religious principles and traditions are at the heart of our society's sex laws.

domain only of those mutually consenting persons involved, the traditional Judeo-Christian view holds that moral matters do, in fact, affect society and culture. In short, our sexual laws are based on our Judeo-Christian heritage, with its strong emphasis on societal values and laws.

THE PURPOSE OF SEXUAL LAWS

Even if we were to argue that "matters of the bedroom" belong in the bedroom and, therefore, should fall outside the scope of the law, most of us believe that at least some sexual laws are desirable, and even necessary. For example, our society is in general agreement that we must enact and support laws against forced, or coerced, sexual acts. Few would argue against laws prohibiting sexual assault (rape); sexual abuse of minors (child molestation), one's own children or other relative (incest), and individuals who are too immature or incapable of being responsible for their own sexuality (rape of developmentally challenged persons); and sexual exploitation in the workplace or classroom (sexual harassment). Even though it may be difficult to reach a consensus on this point, many proponents of sexual laws also believe that lawmakers should take local community values and concerns into account, prohibiting sexual behaviors that members of a particular community might find repulsive and fear will somehow lead to sexual assault or offense.

Historically, sexual laws have served the political and social function of maintaining the status quo: male headship and the integrity of the family unit—husband, wife, and children. However, as society has become more flexible in describing what makes a "family," it has become more outspoken in scrutinizing strict governmental definitions. Many people argue that sexual behavior legislation must be changed to address the various needs of assorted combinations of single and divorced partners and parents representing supportive and protective family environments.

Examining the purpose of sexual laws brings us back to our initial concern—regulating sexuality. Ultimately, laws that prohibit sexual behaviors forced on others are very different than those that prohibit "nonprocreative" and extramarital sexual acts between mutually consenting adults. Whereas the former help guard against demonstrable trespass, the latter hinge on the assumption that the behaviors in question are morally wrong, and that such moral trespass is damaging to the fabric of society. Such sexual laws based on moral judgments involve an attempt to impose the majority's set of beliefs on all members of society. Of course, this was much easier in the days when the largest proportion of American citizens were of a similar Judeo-Christian perspective. With so many diverse groups in America—diversity in terms of religion, race, income, and gender—identifying, not to mention imposing, a dominant morality is a concept largely rejected today. Sexual laws based on moral judgments tend to come under critic's fire much more often than those based on "protection."

Nowhere is this issue of sexual laws more apparent than with *sex education* in public schools and *new reproductive techniques* that allow conception to occur in a nontraditional manner. The issue of making sex education available in public schools is especially

Today's homosexuals believe the traditional sodomy laws discriminate against them.

complex for many parents' and citizens' groups. Since the 1960s, when sex education programs were first being developed and used in secondary schools and colleges, numerous individuals and groups (primarily concerned parents, many with religious affiliations) have attacked laws that permit sex education in the schools. These opponents often fight public sex education on moral grounds, believing in some cases that teaching morals and sexuality is the responsibility of the parents, and in other cases that teaching sex education without values promotes sexual promiscuity. While court decisions have upheld schools' right to teach sex education, opponents continue to denounce these classes, lobbying, picketing, and persuading local school boards and officials to alter or remove sex education from their school programs. Proponents believe that the large numbers of new cases of sexually transmitted diseases and unplanned teenage pregnancies each year make the need for sex education in the schools both pertinent and urgent. They continue to forge ahead with new sex education curricula designed to meet what they believe are the needs of today's students. In any event, the 1990s are witnessing a move toward developing school programs that promote decision-making about sexuality, from the benefits of abstinence to instructions on how to use contraception and practice safer sex.

Laws aimed at both preventing and ending pregnancy have been quite popular in America. In the 1870s, the *Comstock Laws* prohibited people from mailing information about contraception or contraceptive devices. As recently as the 1960s, both Massachusetts and Connecticut had laws making it illegal to practice contraception during coitus, although the Supreme Court eventually banned these laws as unconstitutional. More recent court battles have raised the issue of whether states can or should steril-

The issue of sex education in the public schools is a source of continued (and heated!) debate for parents, citizen groups, religious groups, and school boards.

ize developmentally challenged individuals against their will. Court battles have also raged over legislation specifying the age at which a young woman can purchase contraception and have an abortion without parental knowledge or consent. Although the Supreme Court ruled in 1973 that abortion is legal, lawmakers continue to introduce legislation aimed at limiting this availability.

But what about new reproductive procedures? What sorts of legal issues arise, for example, in response to *surrogate motherhood* and *in vitro fertilization*? Many, with more on the way, to be sure.

Perhaps what complicates these issues the most is the fact that almost all of the new technologies introduce into the equation an "extra party" in addition to the couple who want to have a child. This extra person may donate the sperm or the egg, or may provide the uterus for gestation. Consequently, there arises the issue of blood relationships and legal responsibilities. For the baby conceived and born through some combination of advanced procedures, who is the father? The mother? The parents? Theoretically, there may be as many as five individual parents—sperm donor, egg donor, surrogate mother, and the couple who raise the child; or three sets of parents—the *genetic parents, gestational parents,* and *social parents* (Andrews, 1989; Chavkin et al., 1989; Shapiro, 1986).

Other important questions arise, too. What happens to the extra embryos once one of them is successfully implanted? Which parent receives custody of frozen embryos during a divorce proceeding? What are the rights of the adoptive versus the biological parents? Will any of these parents have visiting rights? Who will have custody of the child if the adoptive parents divorce or die prematurely? Will the child eventually be told how he or she was conceived? If so, by whom and when? If not, who will assure confidentiality, and how? Who of the several potential parents will take care of the child if he or she is born impaired? Add to all of this the extended families and stepfamilies of all of the "parents," and it quickly becomes evident that legally unraveling this maze of potential relationships, not to mention their rights and responsibilities, may be nothing short of miraculous.

In the end, and perhaps of the most significance, is the question, "Who is going to decide all of this?" Lawyers? Doctors? Educators? Scientists? Rabbis? Priests? There is no easy answer. The law must, by definition, determine the parental outcomes of children born through new reproductive procedures. Yet to date, lawmakers have been reluctant to take on such complex matters.

The case of "Baby Jessica" is an example of how complicated sorting out biological, adoptive, and legal rights and responsibilities can be.

SEXUAL MORALS AND ETHICS

Thus far in this chapter, we've been referring to morality without defining the terms *morals* and *ethics*. With all this talk of reproductive rights and technologies, of victim and victimizer, of regulating sexual behavior, let's back up for a moment and examine the nature of morals and ethics in a little more detail.

MORALS
Standards of right and wrong.

Morals, or personal standards of right and wrong, are central to dealing with sexual matters. Our morals ultimately determine our sexual attitudes and influence our sexual decision-making and eventual choice of sexual behavior. At a larger level, this translates into assorted sexual laws that we as a society decide are desirable and necessary.

Morals are often rooted in either the *humanistic* or *religious* world views. The humanistic begins with the premise that human principles are the primary consideration in human affairs; the religious, with the premise that obeying God's will is the primary consideration. In the former, the Golden Rule (or some variation thereof)—"Do unto others as you would have them do unto you"—determines our attitudes and behaviors. In the latter, God's revealed word determines these.

Humanistic moralists seek to define sexual laws in terms of practical application rather than religious ideals. For example, if it could be shown without a doubt that premarital sex is detrimental to later marital happiness, then the humanistic moralists would decry such activity based on its negative consequences. Religious moralists, on the other hand, while not necessarily disagreeing with the humanists' point of view, would condemn premarital sex based primarily on its violating God's word. Of course, few people come wholly from one perspective or the other.

Where do our sexual morals originate? For the humanistic and religious individual alike, the answer to this question is the same. We learn our morals and values—sexual or otherwise—from those closest to us and from the world around us. Family, friends, teachers, pastors, books, television, movies, music, magazines—anyone and anything to which we are exposed contributes to our sexual morals. This is clearly the case as suggested by the relationship between the popular media's presentation of sexuality and corresponding increases in sexual activity. "Chicken" or "egg"—who knows? What is clear is that, while being quick to promote very liberal, carefree views of sexuality, the entertainment media are equally quick to avoid dealing with the implications of unbridled sex. Rarely do they portray the negative consequences of promiscuous sexual behavior, such as acquiring gonorrhea. Sexuality has everything to do with love and romance, but it also has a great deal to do with maturity and responsibility.

The biology of sexuality is straightforward enough. But how one chooses to behave in a given situation is ultimately a moral question—one that brings us into a potential conflict between the religious and humanistic. Yet this need not be the case; the two can agree and work together. For example, a humanistic moralist, alarmed at the rate of sexual diseases and unwanted teenage pregnancies along with the negative implications such pregnancies carry for the mothers, their babies, and society, might well agree with the religious moralist to argue for sexual abstinence among the young.

ETHICS
Self-regulatory guidelines that people use to make decisions about their behavior.

Ethics are self-regulatory guidelines that people use to make decisions about their behavior. For our purposes there are two basic categories of ethics: *professional* and *personal*. Although laws allow society as a whole to regulate the behavior of its members, *professional ethics* are self-regulatory guidelines that define a profession, as well as the expected conduct of its members. Various professional organizations like the American Psychological Association and the American Association of Sex Educators, Counselors, and Therapists have developed *ethical principles,* with the intention of assuring the proper use of skills and techniques by their members. *Personal ethics* are also self-regulatory guidelines, but ones that people use to make decisions in everyday life.

Although our moral values are at the heart of our ethics, ethics may or may not also take into consideration the social context in which behavior occurs. Individual decision-

PERSPECTIVE

Dr. Ruth Speaks Out on the Need for Sexual Morals

Dr. Ruth Westheimer—perhaps the best-known and most popular sex therapist today—and colleague Louis Lieberman shared their views on sexuality and morals in *Sex and Morality: Who Is Teaching Our Sex Standards?* (1988). Consider the following:

It was and still is our view, undoubtedly reinforced by our backgrounds, that moral choices should not be made *ad hominem;* that is, depending on the person or emotions. Moral and ethical choices depend on some kind of system or moral code to provide the guidelines for people to use in these new situations. Do these young people really have a moral code that they understand and accept to help them make correct decisions, or is that code merely in the minds, prayers and hopes of their parents? How can people learn to make these choices as unique, individual personalities, particularly as young persons without sufficient experience to reflect on previous choices? We cannot be born with the wisdom of Solomon. Young or old, we cannot spend our lives in the analytic study of ethical and moral systems and logic and the probability of outcomes. We need a clear voice in the back of our minds reminding us that there is a sound basis for the correct decisions we must make—not one based on impulse, passion, drink, fear of rejection or whatever....

...It is true that people are different when it comes to various aspects of moral decision making, but they are alike in the sense that all humans need guidelines, particularly in the years during which we develop what we end up believing is our own *personal* value system. Without values consistent with our accepted moral beliefs, our choices may be confused and our responsibility for the consequences questionable.

We believe that a firm sense of traditional concepts of right and wrong, the difference between moral and immoral behavior and a responsibility for the consequences of choices is fundamental to a civilized society. (pp. 4–5)

Question for Thought

Where do you stand on the issue of having "a firm sense of traditional concepts of right and wrong"?

Source: R. Westheimer & L. Lieberman (1988), *Sex and morality: Who is teaching our sex standards?* (Boston: Harcourt Brace Jovanovich).

making based on social context is known as *contextual ethics,* or *situation ethics* (Fletcher, 1967). An example of this is the individual who determines if a sexual behavior is right or wrong based on his or her circumstances, such as being on a vacation. In contrast, individual decision-making based on adherence to a fixed set of guidelines is *deontological ethics.* An example is the individual who determines if a sexual behavior is right or wrong based on religious scripture and beliefs. Of course, contextual and deontological ethics are but two ends on the continuum, with many other individual decision-making ethics in between. And what people believe or say is the right thing to do and what they actually do are often very different.

SEXUAL COERCION AND THE LAW: RAPE, INCEST, AND SEXUAL HARASSMENT

SEXUAL COERCION

Sexual remarks, pressure, or behavior forced on one person by another.

Having briefly discussed sexual laws, morals, and ethics, let's now turn our attention to a particularly important area of legal concern, that of **sexual coercion**, or the forcing of sexual remarks, pressure, or behavior on another person. In the following pages, we'll examine three particularly troublesome manifestations of forced sexual behavior: *rape, incest,* and *sexual harassment.*

RAPE

RAPE

Forced sexual violation of one person by another.

As we noted earlier in this chapter, laws that protect people from unwanted sexual behaviors are appropriate and necessary. This is certainly the case with **rape** (from the Latin *rapere,* meaning "to steal"), the forced sexual violation of one person (usually female) by another (usually male). To some, rape is a crime of violence and aggression, not one of sex. To others, it is a crime of both violence and sex (Paglia, 1993).

Rape is hardly a phenomenon of recent origin. Because men have traditionally treated women more like "property" than individuals, society has seen abuses against women less as crimes against them than as crimes against their fathers, husbands, or owners (Brownmiller, 1975). This has begun to change in recent decades. For instance, some state courts have finally ruled that a woman can charge her husband with *marital rape* if he forces her to have sexual relations (Estrich, 1987).

The situation is not yet where it should be, though. It may now be easier for rape victims to bring charges against their attackers, but winning a conviction in court is still difficult. To make matters worse, the legal system has too often turned the tables on rape victims, suggesting that they actually "invited" the attack and putting on trial their past behavior rather than the act perpetrated against them.

These women are marching in protest to bring attention to the seriousness of sexual assault and rape.

As mentioned above, rape is the coercion of another person to engage in sex. In some states the term exclusively refers to the penetration of the vagina by the penis, but in most states it refers to any penetrative coercion by members of the same or other sex to perform any kind of sexual act. Although rape crosses all lines—racial, socioeconomic, age, and marital status—single, white women in their teens and 20s are at the greatest risk of being victims. Most rapists are males between the ages of 18 and 44 (*Statistical Abstract of the United States*, 1992).

In recent years, the incidence of rape has increased, but authorities believe this is due to more women today reporting the crime than to the actual number of rapes increasing. Still, many never report the assault or file charges. Why? They may fear being victimized again, this time in the courts. They may dread the social stigma of being a rape victim, or the publicity that accompanies a rape report. They may realize that the chances of winning a conviction are small. They may feel emotionally traumatized and drained. Or they may feel dirty, guilty, and demoralized, coming to the erroneous conclusion that their behavior or dress somehow inadvertently indicated a desire to be forced into sex.

Because of this ambivalence over reporting rape (not to mention false rape allegations and inherent problems defining "rape"), the exact number of rapes in the United States may never be known (Gilbert, 1992; Kanin, 1994; Koss, 1992). In 1990, 102,560 forced and attempted rapes were reported. The incidence of rape was 96.6 per 100,000 females 12 years old and over (*Statistical Abstract of the United States*, 1992). One estimate is that between about 15 and 25 percent of women in the United States have been or will be victims of rape during their lifetimes (Calhoun & Atkeson, 1991). These figures may or may not be representative of the actual number of rapes taking place in this country (Muehlenhard et al., 1994). They are nonetheless alarming.

There are six basic types of rape: *outsider rape, gang rape, acquaintance rape, date rape, marital rape,* and *statutory rape*. Many people mistakenly believe *outsider rape* (or *stranger rape*), an attack from someone entirely unknown to the victim, is the most common type of rape, probably because it is the one victims usually bring to the attention of authorities. Outsider rape is frequently the most violent rape of all. Victims frequently suffer severe and even fatal injury, often through the use of knives, guns, and other weapons. In many cases, perpetrators of outsider rape pick their victims carefully, and plan the best times and places for the assault. *Gang rape* occurs when two or more perpetrators—either strangers or acquaintances—commit rape.

The perpetrator of *acquaintance rape* is someone the victim knows—a co-worker, a neighbor, or anyone else with whom she or he has come in contact. Studies have found acquaintance rape to occur more frequently than any other kind (Koss, 1992). Copenhaver and Grauerholz (1991) found that 95 percent of college female victims knew their attackers. Perpetrators of acquaintance rape are more likely to use methods of coercion like intimidation, threat, lies, ignoring protests, and intoxicating the victim, rather than a knife or gun.

A specific type of acquaintance rape is *date rape*, in which the perpetrator is a dating partner. Date rape can occur at any time during courtship, from the first date to long after a stable relationship has formed. It often happens when one or both individuals have been drinking alcohol or taking drugs, and when one individual takes "no" to sexual pressure from the other to mean "yes" or "maybe."

Some states still do not recognize *marital rape* (or *mate rape*) unless it occurs between separated marital partners or results in serious injury. The frequency of marital rape may be as high as 2 million cases per year (Groth & Gary, 1981). Another estimate is that about one in seven wives will be a victim of marital rape (Gibbs, 1991). Although abuse and cruelty are frequent during marital rape, prosecutions are rare.

Marital rape is one aspect of a larger problem, that of *spouse abuse*. One estimate is that nearly one million women in the United States each year seek medical treatment for injuries sustained during beatings by their husbands, and nearly one thousand women are

---

PERSPECTIVE

Avoiding Date Rape

The Association of American Colleges provides the following suggestions for avoiding date rape:

1. *Set sexual limits.* It is your body, and no one has the right to force you to do anything you don't want to do.
2. *Decide early if you would like to have sex.* The sooner you communicate firmly and clearly your sexual intentions, the easier it will be for your partner to hear and accept your decision.
3. *Do not give mixed messages; be clear.* Say "yes" when you mean "yes" and say "no" when you mean "no."
4. *Be forceful and firm.* Do not worry about not being polite.
5. *Do not do anything you do not want to do just to avoid a scene or unpleasantness.* Do not be raped because you were too polite to get out of a dangerous situation.
6. *If things start to get out of hand, be loud in protesting, leave, go for help.*
7. *Trust your gut-level feelings.* If you feel you are being pressured, you probably are, and you need to respond. If a situation feels bad, or you start to get nervous about the way your date is acting, confront the person immediately or leave the situation as quickly as possible.
8. *Be aware that alcohol and drugs are often related to date rape.* They compromise your ability (and that of your date) to make responsible decisions. If you choose to drink alcohol, drink responsibly. Be able to get yourself home and do not rely on others to "take care" of you.
9. *Avoid falling for such lines as "You would if you loved me."*
10. *If you are unsure of a new acquaintance, go on a group or double date.*
11. *Have your own transportation, if possible, or taxi fare.*
12. *Avoid secluded places where you are in a vulnerable position.* This is especially critical at the beginning of a relationship. Establish a pattern of going where there are other people, where you feel comfortable and safe.
13. *Be careful when you invite someone to your home or you are invited to your date's home.* These are the most likely places for acquaintance rapes to occur.
14. *Socialize with people who share your values.* If you go out with people who are more sexually permissive than you are, you may be perceived as sharing those same values. (p. 3)

Source: J. O. Hughes & B. R. Sandler (1987), *"Friends" raping friends: Could it happen to you?* (Washington, DC: Association of American Colleges).

---

murdered each year by their husbands (Perrotto & Culkin, 1993). Research has demonstrated a relationship between marital rape and violence against the spouse. Husbands who batter their wives are also likely to rape them. In one study, over one third of 137 battered women reported having been raped by their husbands (Frieze, 1983).

Many wives respond to their battering, raping husbands with anger, but others respond with self-blame (Frieze, 1983). Sarason and Sarason (1993) recommended that abused spouses develop better feelings about themselves by practicing the following self-statements, which are also applicable to victims of marital rape:

- I am not to blame for being beaten or abused.
- I am not the cause of another person's violent behavior.
- I do not have to take it.
- I deserve to be treated with respect.
- I do have power over my own life.
- I can use my power to take good care of myself.
- I can make changes in my life if I want to.
- I am not alone. I can ask others to help me.
- I deserve to make my own life safe and happy. (p. 560)

Sexual activity between an adult and minor, even if consensual, is *statutory rape,* or *child molestation.* In other words, statutory rape occurs when sexual intercourse involves a person under the legal "age of consent," 16 to 18 in most states. Why "rape," especially if both parties agree to have sex? Authorities believe minors have only a limited understanding of sexuality, so they cannot possibly make informed, valid decisions regarding sexual interactions. The issue of what can be considered statutory rape is clear when a 46-year-old man has sex with a 14-year-old girl, but is not so clear when an 18-year-old woman has sex with her 17-year-old boyfriend of two years. Whether the action was coerced or voluntary is irrelevant. The main issue is the violation of a person too young to understand the physical and emotional complications of a sexual relationship.

We should also note that rape is not exclusively a crime committed against women. Men, too, are raped, generally by heterosexual men through anal penetration, but also occasionally by women (Calderwood, 1987; Sarrel & Masters, 1982). Extremely common in prison settings, *male rape* by other males is rarely reported or prosecuted in regular society. Male rape by males is not homosexuality *per se,* nor is it necessarily an outlet for frustrated sexual needs. Instead, it is usually a display of power and dominance over others, such as occurs among prison inmates (Lockwood, 1980). As A. Nicholas Groth and Ann Wolbert Burgess (1980) reported, quoting one male rapist:

On a Personal Note

I cornered him in the shower and said, "You think I'm a punk? I'm going to prove you are what you called me." He was real scared and said, "Forget what I said," and then he asked me if I wanted a hand-job. I said, "What do you think I am, a homo?" Then I told him, "You're going to give me some ass," and I fucked him. It wasn't for sex. I was mad and I wanted to prove who I was and what he was. (p. 808)

Do women ever rape men? *Yes,* but not typically. In one study of 204 college students, 22 percent of the males reported having been the victims of coercive sexual intercourse on at least one occasion (Struckman-Johnson & Struckman-Johnson, 1994). Because females are not anatomically equipped for "forceful" rape in the traditional sense, female rapists may use psychological pressure to push men into undesired sexual activity (Muehlenhard & Cook, 1988).

In some cases, women have been known to use weapons to tie up their male victims, and then threaten them with injury, castration, or death if they do not "perform." A common myth is that men are unable to attain and maintain an erection and engage in sex when threatened with harm or death during a rape. They can, in fact, have erections and ejaculate under force (Sarrel & Masters, 1982). In other cases, women function as accomplices to male rapists.

For Personal Reflection

Why do you think male victims of male rape are more likely to suffer severe injury than female victims? Why do you think male victims are less likely to report being sexually assaulted than female victims?

Pychologists have studied convicted rapists to determine whether a "rapist personality profile" exists. Are there certain characteristics that typify the average rapist? Appearance, race, and income are irrelevant. Even though young men in their late teens and early 20s are more likely to be involved, men of all ages commit rape (*Statistical Abstract of the United States*, 1992). Unlike the good-looking hero of popular romance novels who ravishes his victims in exotic settings, or the unattractive, sex-starved sociopath who attacks his victims in dark alleys, the "real" rapist looks like an ordinary man. Some are handsome, some are not. Many have on-going, long-term relationships with a wife or girlfriend (Groth, 1979).

Despite research showing rapists to have had unhappy and dysfunctional childhoods, other studies have found little support for a rapist personality profile. Substantiating the notion of the rapist as an "ordinary guy," is the research of Malamuth (1981), who in studying American and Canadian male college students found that almost one-third of the men in his study admitted that they might force sex on a woman against her protests if there were little chance of getting caught. In other words, large numbers of otherwise normal young men admitted freely to entertaining the possibility of participating in rape.

Nevertheless, rapists tend to fall into four broad categories—*anger rapists, power rapists, sadistic rapists,* and *sexual rapists* (Groth, 1979; Groth et al., 1977). These rapists may see women as "the enemy" who cannot be trusted or who will "do them in" at work or school should the opportunity arise. Or they may have a poor self-concept, high level of anxiety, bitterness, and anger. For these men, rape becomes a way of putting women in their place, compensating for feelings of inferiority, and expressing deep-seated anger.

Anger Rapists Rape is sometimes a release of anger. Men who have felt belittled or humiliated by females in life experiences take out their rage on other women through the act of rape. For example, by forcing their victims to engage in oral or anal sex, they degrade their victims, taking revenge for past injuries, imagined or real.

Power Rapists Another kind of rapist uses rape as a means of gaining power. It becomes the only way for him to feel dominant and in control in a life where he feels emasculated, anxious, and powerless. By subjecting another person to his will, he boosts his ego. His rapes are frequent and well planned. As one woman victim described:

On a Personal Note

He seemed as if he needed to be reassured and so I tried to reassure him. I was lying on my back in the gravel . . . he was odd saying those things . . . then I had to bargain with him to get my clothes back. He also wanted my address and to know if he could come and do it again. I felt if I could convince him I was being honest, he would let me go. He had my pocketbook and would know who I was so I told him where I lived but not the right apartment. (Groth et al., 1977, p. 1241)

Sadistic Rapists Unable to enjoy a normal sex life, some rapists can receive sexual satisfaction only through the sadistic torture of their sexual partner. The victim is often bound and then mercilessly subjected to verbal and physical abuses, including threatening, slapping, biting, burning, and mutilating. Confusing sexuality with brutality, the sadistic rapist finds rape to be his only sexual outlet.

Sexual Rapists These rapists are interested in attaining sexual gratification, whatever the costs. They are willing to use manipulation, humiliation, intimidation, and verbal threats, and they may intoxicate their victims to achieve their ends. The vast majority of acquaintance and date rapists probably fall into this category.

So what causes men (and women) to rape? Is it psychological, social, or cultural influences, or a combination of all three? As with most human behavior, the motivation behind the act of rape varies depending on the life experiences of the individual. Rape is seldom simply sexual fervor out of control.

Perhaps one reason "normal" men rape has something to do with our rape-tolerant society. Authorities suggest that various sociocultural influences may make rape seem acceptable to certain individuals under certain circumstances. Numerous surveys taken among diverse groups reveal that many Americans, regardless of age, race, or economic status, feel that a man has a right to force sex on a woman if (1) he has known her for some time and spent considerable time and money on her, or (2) he feels aroused and "led on" by the woman's dress and manner. Social scientists point to movies, films, books, and song lyrics that deliver the message that forced sex is acceptable and even expected. Court decisions reinforce these same ideas when rapists are acquitted because the court decides the victim "asked for it" through her suggestive dress and behavior, or because she failed to put forth enough resistance to counter the rapist's advances. Feminists note that the victim of a robbery is never blamed for leading a criminal on by carrying a fat wallet, nor is a robbery victim ever questioned on whether he or she exerted sufficient resistance. In the case of rape, though, society turns the blame on the victim—a sad result of societal misconceptions about this issue.

Susan Estrich (1987) commented on these last couple of points in her book *Real Rape: How the Legal System Victimizes Women Who Say No*:

I would not be surprised if, someday, some study or studies definitively prove that there are substantial differences, more subtle than the categorization of factors or review of overall statistics suggest, in the way prosecutors treat rape cases. But we need not await that day to argue for change in the system. Sometimes the failure to discriminate is discriminatory; where there are real differences, failure to recognize and take account of them is the proof of unfairness. If the defenders of the system are right in saying rape cases are treated just like assault, and just like robbery and burglary, they are surely wrong in taking this as evidence of a fair and just system. The weight given to prior relationship, force and resistance, and corroboration effectively allows prosecutors to define real rape so as to exclude the simple case, and then to justify that decision as neutral, indeed inevitable, when it is neither. (p. 25)

Effects of Rape Victims of rape often suffer battered faces with cut lips and broken noses, bruises, abrasions, broken ribs, bites, and internal damage and bleeding. These immediate effects can bring on emotional symptoms characteristic of a severe anxiety reaction, a condition termed *rape trauma syndrome* (Burgess & Holmstrom, 1988; Rynd, 1988). Some women react with uncontrolled crying, anxiety, restlessness, depression, and feelings of self-blame. In addition to the pain and discomfort from the physical abuse suffered during the rape, they may have other physical complaints, including gastrointestinal upsets, headaches, insomnia, and loss of appetite. Other women encase themselves behind a smiling, cool, and relaxed exterior, masking the trauma and emotional turmoil held inside.

Without therapy or support, these and other effects may last a lifetime. Fears of being alone at home or walking outside, sexual dysfunctions, psychosomatic illnesses, and nightmares of the event may plague a rape victim for years. Given all of this, some form of psychological counseling is usually necessary to facilitate a return to normalcy. Rape trauma syndrome is much easier to treat in the early stages of development. Many local police departments hire rape advocates to support victims throughout the medical and legal processes. Both individual counseling sessions and rape victim support groups provide safe environments where victims can discuss their emotional issues (Burgess & Holmstrom, 1988).

Preventing Rape Because the causes of rape often stem from sociocultural attitudes rather than from biological impulses, successful prevention efforts would seem to lie in educational programs and changes in the messages propagated by the popular media. There seems to be a much lower incidence of rape in those societies that value care-giving and nonviolence, and where women and men have equal power. In contrast, rape seems to run rampant in those societies that glorify and emulate violence and machismo attitudes, where women must struggle for political and economic equality (Mosher & Tomkins, 1988; Sanday, 1981).

In terms of strategies to combat prevailing lax attitudes and societal misconceptions, our society should continue to challenge the myth that women secretly enjoy being raped. Neither a skimpy outfit nor a woman out alone after dark are invitations for sex. Contrary to popular stereotype, most men can control their sexual behavior, even at the height of arousal. Individuals have a choice. Violence is never necessary.

Women, too, need to learn about rape and how to prevent it. Lessons in how to assertively say "no" to a would-be rapist can be helpful. Too many women rely on a "no" that, in fact, comes across as a "maybe." A clear "yes" or "no" is imperative for effective communication. Understanding that the best sexual experience involves mutual consent

Most rape victims require psychological counseling and support to deal with the emotional aftereffects of their assault.

and not the "carrying away" or "overpowering" of someone else so commonly romanticized in the media, no one need place the decision to have sex in someone else's hands.

To prepare for those cases of outsider attack, as well as those times when a firm "no" fails to dissuade, many women benefit from self-defense training. Authorities disagree on which method is the most effective, but a combination of tactics—ranging from talking it out to physical retaliation to feigning sickness and disease—seems to work in some cases. Although physical resistance can incite some rapists to become even more violent, women who actively resist their attackers *probably* have a better chance of avoiding a potential rape than those who do not (Copenhaver & Grauerholz, 1991; Powell, 1991).

Rape education—be it informational or self-defensive—must extend to all men and women, from those in high schools and colleges to those behind prison walls. But it does not stop there. Popular films, music lyrics, and TV shows that portray sexual violence and demean women promote culturally incorrect stereotypes and attitudes. The mass media must change their message of accepting violent coercion to one of promoting mutual consent and respect. Only then, when cultural attitudes change, will rape-tolerant laws, lax enforcement, and light punishments become realities of the past.

For Personal Reflection

If your date spent money on you, and later that evening began pressuring you to have sex, how would you respond and why? What would you do if you clearly said "no" but your date continued to pressure you? What can you do to prevent this kind of misunderstanding from ever occurring in the first place?

INCEST AND CHILD SEXUAL ABUSE

Child sexual abuse, or *child molestation*, occurs when an adult or teenager entices or forces a child to participate in sexual activity (American Psychiatric Association, 1994). Ranging from simple touching to vaginal, oral, or anal penetration, child sexual abuse is culturally forbidden in most parts of the world, and is illegal in every state of this country. Experts estimate that probably 25 percent of girls and 10–15 percent of boys in the United States have been sexually abused (Finkelhor et al., 1990; Perrotto & Culkin, 1993). Additional data on the percentage of adults who report having experienced this type of early trauma appear in Table 18.1.

Every state in our country has laws against a specific type of child abuse known as **incest** (from the Latin *incestus*, meaning "impure"), which is sexual activity between closely related persons of any age. The primary intent of these laws is to protect children against forced sexual acts, abuse, and exploitation by immediate and extended family members. Child sexual abuse is incest when the abuser is a relative, although not necessarily blood-related, explaining why stepfathers are sometimes cited for molesting stepchildren (Sagarin, 1977). The perpetrators of incest are usually men; their victims, usually young girls (Finkelhor et al., 1990).

INCEST
Sexual activity between closely related persons of any age.

Sadly, most children willingly submit to their abuser. Because they may admire or love the adult and cannot grasp what is happening, they do as they are told. If they begin to understand or if they protest, intimidation and threats of violence keep them quiet and submissive.

Most Americans think of father-daughter abuse as the most common form of incest, while in fact cousin, sibling, or uncle abuse may be just as frequent or more so, depending on the study and author cited (Canavan et al., 1992; Finkelhor, 1980, 1984, 1990; Hunt, 1974; Macallair, 1994). Mother-son, father-son, and mother-daughter forms of incest are probably not as common as other forms, but details are sketchy, as some experts believe these forms of abuse may be less likely to be reported.

On a Personal Note (Wyona, age 42)

I still can't remember all of the details, but I distinctively remember my 17-year-old brother sneaking into my room at night and fondling my breasts while I was in bed. I always just pretended to be asleep, because I knew he'd leave after a few minutes. I didn't know what to do; you know, I was only 14 at the time. I never told my parents, because I didn't think they'd believe me. And to this day my brother has never mentioned anything about it to me. (Author's files)

For Personal Reflection

What would you do if you learned a friend was involved in an incestuous relationship with his or her child, nephew, or niece?

Effects of Incest and Child Sexual Abuse Most authorities today believe child sexual abuse is harmful to the emotional development of children (Finkelhor, 1990; Haugaard & Reppucci, 1989; Kendall-Tackett et al., 1993). Adults who were sexually abused as children frequently suffer from deep feelings of shame, guilt, and betrayal. If the experience was traumatic or painful emotionally or physically, victims may repress memories of the experience and suffer deep, unexplainable depression. They may also experience sexual dysfunctions as adults. Researchers have noted a wide range of emotional problems both during, soon after, and long after the experience: anxiety attacks, suicidal tendencies, angry outbursts, eating disorders, withdrawal, fear, depression, substance abuse, age-inappropriate sexual behavior, and sexual promiscuity, to name but a few (Browne & Finkelhor, 1986; Elliott & Briere, 1992; Everstine & Everstine, 1989; Feinauer, 1989; Jones & Emerson, 1994). One especially negative effect of incest and child sexual abuse is a potential intergenerational, familial pattern (Freund & Kuban, 1994; Gaffney et al., 1984; Zgourides et al., 1994). In spite of the range and intensity of the after-effects of child sexual abuse, many victims are able to accept the experience as a regrettable and unfortunate part of their lives, but one that they can leave behind (Finkelhor, 1984).

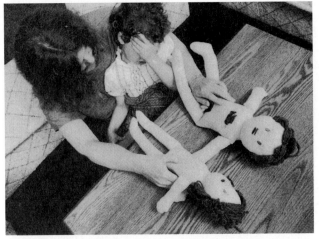

Counselors use a variety of methods and aids to assist victims of child sexual abuse and incest, including anatomically correct dolls.

TABLE 18.1 **Incidence of Child Sexual Abuse**

	Men	Women
N =	1,318	1,371
Yes	11%	23%
No	89	77
Yes Responses: *N* =	142	318
a. *Who was the molester?*		
Adult stranger	33%	21%
Relative	44	62
Person in authority position	23	17
b. *How often?*		
Once	42%	41%
Often	44	39
Ongoing	14	20
c. *Was the incident(s) reported to authorities?*		
Yes	12%	12%
No	88	88
d. *Any arrest?*		
Yes	12%	5%
No	88	95
e. *Any convictions?*		
Yes	9%	3%
No	91	97

Source: S. S. Janus & C. L. Janus (1993), *The Janus Report on Sexual Behavior* (New York: John Wiley & Sons). Copyright © 1993. Reprinted by permission of John Wiley & Sons, Inc.

Preventing Incest and Child Sexual Abuse Education is one of the best preventive measures for child sexual abuse. Within the context of comprehensive sexuality education, parents and teachers can teach children the difference between appropriate and inappropriate touching. They can explain how to avoid being touched inappropriately, and what to do if touched in that way. Along these lines, Jeffrey Haugaard and N. Dickon Reppucci (1989) noted in their book *The Sexual Abuse of Children:*

> Although this effort to learn about child sexual abuse continues, its urgency seems to have abated somewhat in the public mind, perhaps because the impression exists that we are now taking meaningful action. We believe, however, that the problem of child sexual abuse has not diminished and that our knowledge about child sexual abuse is still at a rudimentary level. The development of this knowledge is at an important turning point. Either we can continue to provide legal and therapeutic services to victims, families, and perpetrators based on what we think we know—which is sufficient to have gotten us started—or we can review what we actually know about child sexual abuse, look for gaps in our knowledge or the places where our assumptions and prejudices have been inserted to fill these gaps, and then begin a new effort to learn more. We clearly believe that the second alternative is preferable, even though it is more difficult to pursue. Discovering what one does not know is immeasurably harder than espousing what one does know. Recognizing and dealing with the nuances of a problem are more difficult than the initial plunge into its solution. (p. 5)

For Personal Reflection

Certain fringe groups like NAMBLA (North American Man Boy Love Association) maintain that sexual relations between adults and minors are desirable and can even be a positive growth experience for youngsters. Others believe that breaking this taboo against sexual activity between adults and minors is nothing short of an abomination—one that seriously jeopardizes the emotional and physical health of our children. What are your views on the matter? Should society lift "age of consent" restrictions so that "consenting" minors and adults can have sexual relations?

SEXUAL HARASSMENT

SEXUAL HARASSMENT
Unwanted sexual advances, suggestions, comments, or gestures.

Especially prominent in news headlines of the 1990s, sexual harassment is reported more frequently today than ever before. **Sexual harassment** is legally defined as unwanted sexual advances, suggestions, comments, or gestures—usually ongoing in nature. Additionally, lawyer Catharine MacKinnon (1979) defined it as "the unwanted imposition of sexual requirements in the context of a relationship of unequal power" (p. 1). Sexual harassment takes many forms, a few of which are listed here (Powell, 1991):

- Verbal harassment or abuse
- Subtle pressure for sexual activity
- Sexist remarks about a person's clothing, body, or sexual activities
- Leering or ogling at a person's body
- Unnecessary touching, patting, or pinching
- Constant brushing against a person's body
- Demanding sexual favors accompanied by implied or overt threats concerning one's job or student status
- Physical assault (p. 110)

Women are most often the object of sexual harassment, especially in the workplace. One review of the literature found that 42 percent of women reported having experienced some form of sexual harassment at work, compared to 15 percent of men (Charney & Russell, 1994). The practice is so pervasive in worksites in the United States that many

The issue of sexual harassment in the workplace received national attention during the 1991 Anita Hill/Clarence Thomas hearings.

Work and school are the most common settings in which sexual harassment occurs.

women have come to expect it and the vast majority (over 95 percent) never file a formal complaint (Goleman, 1991). Others simply find another job.

Sexual harassment is not confined to the workplace. College students may come under sexual pressure from their instructors, with grades, graduation, and letters of recommendation used as threats or bribes. One survey of university undergraduates found that 29 percent of women and 20 percent of men reported having experienced some form of sexual harassment from instructors (Mazer & Percival, 1989). Patients of physicians and psychologists may also become the object of unwanted sexual attention from their providers. Lawyers may coerce clients into sex in exchange for legal services. Even pastors may convince parishioners that sex with the clergy is a viable road to finding spirituality and true peace of mind. It would seem that no profession, institution, or individual is immune from sexual harassment, as situations of unequal power can exist anywhere (Branan, 1994; Fitzgerald, 1986; Hughes & Sandler, 1987; Pope & Bouhoutsos, 1986; Powell, 1991). Fortunately, most companies and universities now have policies and reporting structures in place to deal with complaints of sexual harassment, and some states have passed laws prohibiting sexual activity, for example, between therapists and their clients.

On a Personal Note (Betty, age 32)

I'd seen this psychologist a couple of times, then after one session he hugged me. I didn't think too much of it at the time, but he started hugging me after each session. I started feeling pretty uncomfortable. I hated to stop the therapy, though, because we'd been making some real headway. But then—oh, I think it was during our ninth or tenth session—he actually made a pass at me. He told me that most of my problems had to do with sexual frustration, and that I needed to have sex with him to overcome my inhibitions. I can't describe the awful feeling I had. I mean, I'd been sharing my life history with this creep, and what does he do? He uses it all against me. And for what? Sex! Did I feel violated! (Author's files)

Effects of Sexual Harassment The effects of sexual harassment can be numerous and long-lasting (MacKinnon, 1979; Powell, 1991). With good jobs at a premium, the possible financial effects of resisting sexual harassment on the job—demotions, pay reductions, and even termination—can be devastating. The psychological effects of sexual pressure on the job, at school, in the doctor's office, or wherever—anxiety, fear, depression, repressed anger, and humiliation—can be equally devastating. Guilt and shame are also common because victims of sexual harassment, similar to victims of rape, may somehow feel responsible. They fear that their dress and/or mannerisms may be bringing on the unwelcome sexual attention.

Preventing Sexual Harassment From victims' perspectives, dealing with and preventing sexual harassment might at first seem impossible. The following suggestions are for dealing with and preventing this form of abuse, wherever it occurs:

1. Immediately inform the offender that his or her remarks or advances are unwelcome. If need be, send a registered letter to the offender. If the harassment continues, the letter can be evidence for court.
2. Document in writing all incidents, noting the time, place, and other details of the offense, including the offender's response to the victim's resistance.
3. Describe the harassment to and enlist the support of trusted co-workers, fellow students, or helping professionals.
4. If the behavior persists, report it to the offender's immediate boss, supervisor, manager, dean, or state licensing board.
5. File a complaint with the Equal Employment Opportunity Commission, Civil Rights Commission, the American Civil Liberties Union, or other appropriate city, state, or national organization.
6. As a last resort, take legal action.

For Personal Reflection

1. Have you ever been the victim of sexual harassment on the job or at school? If so, how did you deal with the situation? How do you distinguish between sexual harassment and harmless "flirting"?

2. What would you do if your teacher suggested you both "get together" for dinner soon, with the implication that your class grade might be in jeopardy if you don't comply?

TREATING SEXUAL OFFENDERS

Psychologists, psychiatrists, and other professionals have available a number of techniques for treating rapists, child molesters, and other sexual offenders. Generally, the long-term prognosis for these individuals' recovery is poor, regardless of the methods used (Berlin & Meinecke, 1981; Maletzky, 1991; Quinsey, 1977). Here are three of the most common.

Incarceration With or Without Treatment The most commonly used technique for dealing with sex offenders is incarceration, which involves serving a jail sentence. In some cases, but not all, the convicted perpetrator is also required to participate in either individual or group psychotherapy.

Psychotherapy Psychological methods range from counseling to "aversion" therapies. During *psychodynamic* therapy, a therapist reviews the client's early childhood experiences and identifies developmental impasses, whereas during *cognitive-behavioral* therapy, he or she helps the client challenge irrational beliefs and devise strategies for handling unwanted sexual desires and impulses. *Aversion therapy* involves presenting the client with highly unpleasant visual, olfactory, or tactile stimuli during sexual arousal in response to inappropriate stimuli, such as pedophilic fantasies. An example of aversion therapy is electrically shocking the client (usually on the hand or arm) whenever he or she becomes sexually excited while looking at slides of nude children. The therapist may also introduce—without aversion—slides depicting consensual adult sexual activity in an effort to recondition the client to appropriate sexual stimuli.

Castration Probably the least common method of treating sex offenders is castration, which involves surgically removing (surgical castration) or chemically destroying the testes (chemical castration), or using drugs and hormones to suppress sexual desire. Castration, however, is no guarantee that a sex offender will not strike again.

FUTURE TRENDS IN SEXUAL LAWS

Regardless of the issue—sex education, new reproductive procedures, or sexual coercion—we are left with the question, "Where's it all going?" As we've seen in a somewhat cursory manner, our society's laws have changed dramatically over time, and continue to do so in response to changing social norms, mores, and values. For this reason, speculating about what laws might exist in the future is, at best, difficult business.

As I've mentioned throughout *Human Sexuality: Contemporary Perspectives,* sexuality, in all of its forms, is both complex and subtle. Yet society clearly has a very real stake in considering the "rightness" or "wrongness" of some sexual activities. Coercing an individual into a behavior—sexual or otherwise—that he or she does not want to engage in or cannot make an informed decision about because of age or incapacity is without a doubt a crime against that individual—a closed case. But when it comes to those many "gray" areas of sexuality, the appropriateness of sexual laws is less clear—a not-so-closed case.

Society obviously wants sexual laws. There have always been sexual laws, even if these have not been satisfactory to all members of a society. Most people seem to want some degree of authoritative guidance when it comes to sexual matters. In today's society, that authoritative guidance translates into sexual laws, the issue of privacy versus the common good determining the details of these laws. Depending on society's interpretation of these issues, its sexual laws will be more or less prohibitive.

KEY POINTS

1. Legislators pass assorted *sexual laws* to regulate and protect individuals from unwelcomed sexual attention, remarks, gestures, and behaviors. For example, a number of states in this country have *sodomy laws* forbidding "crimes against nature."
2. The laws governing behavior as outlined in the Jewish and Christian texts became the foundation for the moral standards of countries and cultures influenced by Judeo-Christian values and traditions. The traditional Judeo-Christian view holds that moral matters do, in fact, affect society and culture. This being the case, our sexual conduct falls within the appropriate domain of the law.
3. Most people would argue that at least some sexual laws are desirable, and even necessary. For example, our society is in general agreement that we must enact and support laws against forced, or coerced, sexual acts. Sexual laws have historically

served the political and social function of maintaining the status quo: male headship and the integrity of the traditional family unit.

4. *Morals* are personal standards of right and wrong. Our morals, which are usually rooted in either the *humanistic* or *religious* world views, ultimately determine our sexual attitudes and influence our sexual decision-making and eventual choice of sexual behavior. At a larger level, this translates into assorted sexual laws that society deems as desirable and necessary.

5. *Ethics* are self-regulatory guidelines that people use to make decisions about their behavior. *Professional ethics* are self-regulatory guidelines that define a profession, as well as the expected conduct of its members. *Personal ethics* are also self-regulatory guidelines, but ones that people use to make decisions in everyday life.

6. A particularly important area of legal concern is that of *sexual coercion*. *Rape* is the forced sexual violation of one person by another. There are six basic types of rape: *outsider rape, gang rape, acquaintance rape, date rape, marital rape,* and *statutory rape*. Rapists tend to fall into four broad categories: *anger rapists, power rapists, sadistic rapists,* and *sexual rapists*.

7. *Child sexual abuse* occurs when an adult or teenager entices or forces a child to participate in sexual activity. *Incest* is defined as sexual activity between closely related persons of any age. The perpetrators of incest are almost always men; their victims, almost always young girls.

8. *Sexual harassment*, "the unwanted imposition of sexual requirements in the context of a relationship of unequal power," is reported more frequently today than ever before. Women are most often the object of sexual harassment. Sexual harassment is not confined to the workplace. College students, patients of physicians and psychologists, legal clients, and parishioners are vulnerable. No profession, institution, or individual is immune from sexual harassment, as situations of unequal power can exist anywhere.

9. Psychologists, psychiatrists, and other professionals have available a number of techniques for treating rapists, child molesters, and other sexual offenders. The most common are *incarceration with or without treatment, psychodynamic therapy, cognitive-behavioral therapy, aversion therapy,* and *castration*. The long-term prognosis for sexual offenders' recovery is poor, regardless of the methods used.

ACTIVITIES AND QUESTIONS

1. As a class, discuss whether sexual laws prohibiting "crimes against nature," such as sodomy, should remain on the books or be abolished.

2. Interview a local priest, pastor, minister, rabbi, or other religious official about his or her views on morality and sexuality. Sample topics for discussion might include masturbation, premarital and extramarital sex, oral and anal sex, contraception, abortion, and homosexuality. If you interview two or more individuals, compare their responses.

3. Which societal myths contribute to the false beliefs that (1) rape victims are responsible for their attack by the way they converse, dress, and act; and that (2) they secretly enjoy being coerced into sex? How might these societal myths influence lawmakers as they devise and pass rape legislation? How might these myths affect the way the judicial system treats rape victims?

4. What can parents do to protect their children from being victimized by sexual offenders? What can teachers, religious officials, and community leaders do?

5. Sexual harassment between instructors and students on campuses around the country is common. Interview fellow students about their experiences with sexual

harassment at your college. What similarities are there between the people you interviewed? Differences? Is sexual harassment of female students more common than that of male students? Are the perpetrators typically junior or tenured faculty? Male or female faculty? What can you do to help fight sexual harassment at your campus? What can the administration do?

RECOMMENDED READINGS

Bass, E., & Davis, L. (1988). *The courage to heal: A guide for women survivors of sexual abuse*. New York: Harper & Row. Provides excellent information for sexual abuse and incest survivors.

Estrich, S. (1987). *Real rape: How the legal system victimizes women who say no*. Cambridge: Harvard University Press. The author argues for widespread reform in our legal system, which in her opinion deals only casually with rape cases.

Haugaard, J. J., & Reppucci, N. D. (1989). *The sexual abuse of children: A comprehensive guide to current knowledge and intervention strategies*. San Francisco, CA: Jossey-Bass. As its title states, this book is about child sexual abuse. Major topic sections include "Understanding Child Sexual Abuse," "Identifying Victims of Child Sexual Abuse," "Helping Victims and Families," and "Legal Issues."

Parrot, A. (1988). *Coping with date rape and acquaintance rape*. New York: Rosen Publishing Group. Offers sound suggestions for dealing with and preventing these very common, but often dismissed, types of rape.

Powell, E. (1991). *Talking back to sexual pressure*. Minneapolis, MN: CompCare Publishers. Offers practical advice on resisting persuasion, avoiding sexual diseases, stopping harassment, and avoiding acquaintance rape.

Westheimer, R., & Lieberman, L. (1988). *Sex and morality: Who is teaching our sex standards?* Boston: Harcourt Brace Jovanovich. A book primarily concerned with issues of sexual morality from a social perspective. Incorporating interviews with assorted religious leaders, scholars, and lay people, the authors explain the need for moral literacy when it comes to sexual issues like masturbation, nudity, nonmarital sex, adultery, contraception and abortion, oral and anal sex, and homosexuality.

APPENDIX

RESOURCES

SEXUALITY ORGANIZATIONS AND INSTITUTES

Alan Guttmacher Institute
111 5th Avenue
New York, NY 10003
212-254-5656

American Association of Sex Educators, Counselors,
  and Therapists
435 North Michigan Avenue, Suite 1717
Chicago, IL 60611
312-644-0828

Kinsey Institute
Indiana University
416 Morrison Hall
Bloomington, IN 47405
812-855-7686

Masters and Johnson Institute
24 South Kingshighway
St. Louis, MO 63108
314-361-2377

Sex Information and Education Council of the United
  States
130 West 42nd Street, Suite 2500
New York, NY 10036
212-819-9770

Society for the Scientific Study of Sex
P.O. Box 208
Mount Vernon, IA 52314
319-895-8407

GENDER ISSUES

National Organization for Changing Men
794 Penn Avenue
Pittsburgh, PA 15221
412-432-3010

National Organization for Women
1000 16th Street NW, Suite 700
Washington, DC 20036
202-331-0066

HOMOSEXUALITY

Lambda Legal Defense and Education Fund
666 Broadway
New York, NY 10012
212-995-8585

National Gay and Lesbian Task Force
1734 14th Street NW
Washington, DC 20009
202-332-6483

FAMILY PLANNING

Committee on Population
National Research Council
2101 Constitution Avenue
Washington, DC 20418
202-334-3167

Family Service Association of America
11700 West Lake Park Place
Milwaukee, WI 53224
414-359-2111

National Abortion Rights Action League
1101 14th Street NW
Washington, DC 20005
202-408-4600

National Clearinghouse for Family Planning
  Information
P.O. Box 10716
Rockville, MD 20850
301-558-4990

National Family Planning and Reproductive Health
  Association
122 C Street NW, Suite 380
Washington, DC 20001
202-628-3535

National Right to Life Committee
419 7th Street NW, Suite 500
Washington, DC 20004
202-626-8800

Parents Without Partners
8807 Colesville Road
Silver Spring, MD 20910
301-588-9354

Planned Parenthood Federation of America
810 7th Avenue
New York, NY 10019
212-541-7800

PREGNANCY, CHILDBIRTH, AND PARENTING

American College of Nurses and Midwives
1522 K Street NW, Suite 1120
Washington, DC 20005
212-347-5445

American College of Obstetricians and
  Gynecologists
409 12th Street SW
Washington, DC 20024
202-638-5577

LaLeche League International
9616 Minneapolis Avenue
P.O. Box 1209
Franklin Park, IL 60131
708-455-7730

March of Dimes Birth Defects Foundation
1275 Mamaroneck Avenue
White Plains, NY 10605
914-428-7100

Parents of Prematures
2990 Richmond, Suite 240
Houston, TX 77098
713-524-3089

HEALTH AND DISEASES

American Cancer Society
1599 Clifton Road NE
Atlanta, GA 30329
800-227-2345

American College Health Association
1300 Piccard Drive, Suite 200
Rockville, MD 20850
301-963-1100

American Foundation for the Prevention of Venereal
  Disease
799 Broadway, Suite 638
New York, NY 10003
212-759-2069

Coalition on Sexuality and Disability
380 2nd Avenue, Floor #4
New York, NY 10010
212-242-3900

Division of Sexually Transmitted Diseases
Centers for Disease Control
1600 Clifton Road NE
Atlanta, GA 30333
404-639-2564

Impotence Information Center
P.O. Box 9
Minneapolis, MN 55440
800-843-4315

National AIDS Information Clearinghouse
P.O. Box 6003
Rockville, MD 20849
800-458-5231

National AIDS Network
729 8th Street SE, Suite 300
Washington, DC 20003
202-546-2424

National Association of People with AIDS
P.O. Box 65472
Washington, DC 20335
202-483-7979

National Resource Center on Women and AIDS
2000 P Street NW, Suite 508
Washington, DC 20036
202-872-1770

PMS Access
P.O. Box 9326
Madison, WI 53715
800-222-4PMS

Premenstrual Syndrome Action
P.O. Box 16292
Irvine, CA 92713
714-854-4407

Society for the Second Self
P.O. Box 194
Tulare, CA 93275
209-688-6386

SEXUAL ADDICTIONS AND COMPULSIVITY

Sex Addicts Anonymous
P.O. Box 3038
Minneapolis, MN 55403
612-339-0217

Sexaholics Anonymous
P.O. Box 300
Simi Valley, CA 93062
805-581-3343

SEXUAL VICTIMIZATION

Antisocial and Violent Behavior Branch
National Institutes of Mental Health
5600 Fishers Lane
Rockville, MD 20857
301-443-3728

National Center for Missing and Exploited Children
1835 K Street NW, Suite 600
Washington, DC 20006
800-843-5678

National Center for the Prevention and Control of Rape
National Institutes of Mental Health
5600 Fishers Lane,
Rockville, MD 20857
301-433-3728

National Center on Child Abuse and Neglect
U.S. Department of Health and Human Services
P.O. Box 1182
Washington, DC 20013
202-245-2858

National Child Safety Council
4065 Page Avenue
Jackson, MI 49204
800-222-1464

National Clearinghouse on Marital and Date Rape
2325 Oak Street
Berkeley, CA 94708
415-548-1770

PUBLISHERS AND SUPPLIERS OF SEX EDUCATION MATERIALS

CompCare Publishers
2415 Annapolis Lane
Minneapolis, MN 55441
800-328-3330

Films for the Humanities and Sciences
P.O. Box 2053
Princeton, NJ 08543
800-257-5126

Focus International
14 Oregon Drive
Huntington Station, NY 11746
800-843-0305

Hazelden Foundation
P.O. Box 176
Center City, MN 55012
800-328-9000

Institute for Advanced Study of Human Sexuality
1523 Franklin Street
San Francisco, CA 94109
415-928-1133

Multi-Focus
1525 Franklin Street
San Francisco, CA 94109
800-821-0514

Open Enterprises
1210 Valencia Street
San Francisco, CA 94110
415-550-7399

The Sinclair Institute
P.O. Box 8865
Chapel Hill, NC 27515
800-955-0888

GLOSSARY

ABSTINENCE Voluntary avoidance of coitus.

AFFECTIVE DISORDERS OR MOOD DISORDERS (A-FEK-TIV) Group of disorders in which the predominate feature is depression and/or mania.

AFTERPLAY Pleasuring that follows sexual intercourse.

AMBISEXUALITY OR BISEXUALITY Sexual attraction to people of both sexes.

AMNIOCHORIONIC MEMBRANE OR AMNIOTIC SAC (AM-NE-O-KO-RE-ON-IK) Fluid-filled sac containing the fetus.

AMNION (AM-NE-ON) Inner membrane surrounding the fetus.

AMNIOTIC FLUID Fluid surrounding the fetus.

ANALGESIC (AN-AL-JE-ZIK) Pain-relieving drug.

ANAL INTERCOURSE Sexual activity involving one partner inserting his penis into the other partner's rectum.

ANAPHRODISIAC (AN-AF-RO-DIZ-I-AK) Chemical sexual inhibitor.

ANDROGYNY (AN-DRAH-GI-NE) Blending of feminine and masculine attributes within an individual.

ANESTHETIC (AN-AS-THE-TIK) Sensation-deadening drug.

ANILINGUS (AN-I-LIN-GUS) Sexual activity involving the mouth, lips, and tongue of one partner and the anus of another.

ANORGASMIA OR INHIBITED FEMALE ORGASM (AN-OR-GAZ-ME-A) A woman's inability to attain orgasm following sexual stimulation.

ANXIETY DISORDERS Group of disorders in which the predominate feature is anxiety.

APHRODISIAC (AF-RO-DIZ-I-AK) Chemical sexual stimulant.

AREOLA (A-RE-O-LA) Area immediately surrounding the nipple.

ASEXUAL Lacking sexual interest.

ASYMPTOMATIC (A-SIMP-TO-MA-TIK) Producing no symptoms.

BACTERIA Tiny, single-cell organisms that invade cells of the body and cause disease.

BARTHOLIN'S GLANDS (BAR-TO-LINZ) Small glands that open into the vestibule.

BIOCHEMICAL PERSPECTIVE View that sexual functioning reflects biological and chemical processes.

BIOLOGICAL PERSPECTIVES Views concerned with the effects of biological and physical processes on sexuality.

BIOPSYCHOSOCIAL PERSPECTIVE View that attributes complex sexual phenomena or events to interacting biological, psychological, and social causes.

BIRTH CONTROL Any number of procedures used to prevent conception and birth.

BISEXUALITY OR AMBISEXUALITY Sexual attraction to people of both sexes.

CAESAREAN SECTION OR C-SECTION (SE-SAR-E-AN) Procedure in which an infant is delivered through an incision in the mother's abdomen.

CANCER A malignant tumor that invades bodily structures.

CARDIOVASCULAR DISEASE (KAR-DE-O-VAS-KYOO-LAR) Any of a number of diseases affecting the blood vessels and heart.

CASE STUDY RESEARCH In-depth study of an individual or small group.

CAVERNOUS BODIES (KA-VER-NUS) Two columns of erectile tissue in the penis.

CEREBROVASCULAR ACCIDENT (SE-RE-BRO-VAS-KYOO-LAR) Destruction of brain tissue resulting from damage to the blood vessels supplying the brain.

CERVICAL CAP Small rubber cuplike device that fits over the cervix to prevent pregnancy.

CERVIX (SER-VIKS) Neck of the uterus that opens into the vagina.

CHORION (KO-RE-ON) Outer membrane surrounding the fetus.

CIRCUMCISION (SER-KUM-SIZH-UN) Surgical removal of the penile foreskin.

CLASTOGEN (KLAS-TO-JEN) Causing damage and impairment.

CLITORIS (KLI-TO-RIS) Organ composed of erectile tissue; homologous (corresponding) to the penis.

COGNITIVE-BEHAVIORAL PERSPECTIVE View that learning, behavior, and thinking processes each play a role in determining how an individual interacts in the world.

COGNITIVE LABELS An individual's interpretations and evaluations of events.

COMPANIONATE LOVE Warm, affectionate, and committed love.

CONCEPTION Union of a sperm and ovum.

CONCEPTUS or ZYGOTE (KON-CEP-TUS; ZI-GOT) The product of conception; a fertilized ovum.

CONDOM (KON-DOM) Membrane or sheath placed over the erect penis to prevent sperm entering the vagina.

CONTRACEPTION (KON-TRA-SEP-SHUN) Preventing pregnancy.

CONTRACEPTIVE SPONGE Polyurethane foam pad or ball saturated with a spermicide and inserted over the cervix to prevent pregnancy.

CORONAL RIDGE or CORONA (KO-RO-NAL; KO-RO-NA) Sensitive area where the glans joins the shaft of the penis.

CORPUS LUTEUM (KOR-PUS LYOO-TE-UM) Hormone-secreting, empty Graafian follicle.

CORRELATIONAL RESEARCH Identifying the nature of the relationship between two variables.

COWPER'S GLANDS (KOW-PERZ) Accessory sexual glands that secrete a urine-neutralizing fluid into the urethra.

CREMASTER MUSCLES (KRE-MA-STER) Scrotal muscles that raise and lower the testes within the scrotum.

CROSS-CULTURAL PERSPECTIVE View that variations in customs, norms, and standards exist across cultures.

CROSS-CULTURAL RESEARCH Studying the variations that exist across cultures.

CROSS-SPECIES PERSPECTIVE View that similarities and differences exist across species.

CUNNILINGUS (KUN-I-LIN-GUS) Performing oral sex on the female genitals.

DECISION/COMMITMENT Decision to maintain a loving relationship.

DELIVERY Expulsion of the fetus and placenta from the vagina.

DEVELOPMENTAL CHALLENGE Low IQ and absence of age- and culturally-appropriate social skills.

DEVELOPMENTAL PERSPECTIVE View concerned with how changes occur throughout the life span.

DIAPHRAGM (DI-A-FRAM) Rubber dome that covers the cervix to prevent pregnancy.

DRIVE State of tension that motivates the individual to reduce a need.

DYSPAREUNIA (DIS-PA-ROO-NE-A) Genital pain before, during, or after sex.

ECTOPIC PREGNANCY (EK-TO-PIK) A pregnancy occurring outside of the uterus.

EJACULATION (E-JAK-YOO-LA-SHUN) Process in which semen is expelled from the penis.

EJACULATORY DUCT Sperm-carrying tube joining the vas deferens and the urethra.

EMOTIONAL CHALLENGE Any of a number of psychological/psychiatric problems having the potential to disrupt normal functioning.

EPIDIDYMIS (EP-I-DID-I-MIS) Coiled structure in which sperm mature and are stored.

EPISIOTOMY (E-PIZ-E-OT-O-ME) Incision made in the perineum to prevent tearing during delivery.

ERECTION (E-REK-SHUN) Process in which the penis engorges with blood, lengthens, and stiffens.

EROGENOUS ZONES (E-ROJ-E-NUS) Erotically sensitive areas of the body.

EROTICA Sexual materials that are artistically motivated, created, and presented.

ETHICS Self-regulatory guidelines that people use to make decisions about their behavior.

EXHIBITIONISM (EKS-I-BI-SHUN-IZ-UM) Sexual arousal from exposing the genitals to an unsuspecting person.

EXISTENTIAL-HUMANISTIC PERSPECTIVE View that stresses the importance of immediate experience, self-acceptance, and self-actualization.

EXPERIMENTAL RESEARCH Identifying cause-and-effect relationships.

FALLOPIAN TUBES (FAL-LO-PE-AN) Pair of tubes connecting the ovaries and the uterus.

FAMILY PLANNING or **PLANNED PARENTHOOD** Choosing the best time to have children.

FELLATIO (FEL-LA-SHE-O) Performing oral sex on the male genitals.

FEMALE ORGASMIC DISORDER A woman's inability to attain orgasm following sexual stimulation.

FEMALE SEXUAL AROUSAL DISORDER Inability to gain and sustain clitoral erection and vaginal lubrication sufficient to initiate and complete sexual activity.

FETISHISM (FET-ISH-IZ-UM) Sexual attraction to objects.

FLACCID (FLAK-SID) Nonerect state of the penis.

FOLLICLES (FOL-I-KULZ) Thin sacs containing unreleased ova.

FORESKIN or **PREPUCE (PRE-PYOOS)** Thin sheath of skin covering the glans.

FRENULUM (FREN-YOO-LUM) Sensitive area lying on the underside of the corona.

FROTTEURISM (FROT-UR-IZ-UM) Sexual arousal from rubbing up against a nonconsenting person.

GENDER An individual's anatomical and psychological makeup as male or female.

GENDER DYSPHORIA (DIS-FO-RE-A) Distress and confusion over one's gender identity.

GENDER IDENTITY An individual's personal sense of being male or female.

GENDER ROLE Outward expression of an individual's gender according to cultural expectations.

GENDER STEREOTYPES Generalizations about the gender attributes, differences, and roles of others.

GLAND Organ that secretes one or more substances.

GLANS (GLANZ) Head of the penis.

GRAAFIAN FOLLICLE (GRAF-E-AN) Follicle that releases the matured ovum.

GYNECOLOGICAL EXAMINATIONS (GI-NE-KO-LO-JI-CUL) Medical exams pertaining to women's reproductive disorders.

HETEROSEXUALITY Sexual attraction to people of the other sex.

HISTORICAL PERSPECTIVE View that variations in customs, norms, and standards exist across time and influence the future.

HOMOPHOBIA Both irrational fear of being perceived as homosexual and contempt for gays and lesbians.

HOMOSEXUALITY Sexual attraction to people of the same sex.

HORMONE Secretion affecting chemical processes elsewhere in the body.

HYMEN (HI-MEN) Membrane that covers, or partially covers, the vaginal orifice.

HYPOACTIVE SEXUAL DESIRE DISORDER (HI-PO-AK-TIV) Lack of sexual desire.

IMPLANTATION (IM-PLAN-TA-SHUN) Attachment of the blastocyst to the uterine wall.

INCEST Sexual activity between closely related persons of any age.

INDUCED ABORTION or **ELECTIVE ABORTION** Intentionally terminating a pregnancy.

INFERTILITY Inability to conceive.

INTERACTION FACTORS Factors existing between two people that influence their relationship, such as proximity and familiarity.

INTERACTIONAL THEORY Theory that sexual orientation is the result of complex interactions of biological, psychological, and social factors.

INTERPERSONAL ATTRACTION Feelings of attraction that develop between two people.

INTERSTITIAL CELLS OF LEYDIG (LI-dig) Cells that produce testosterone.

INTIMACY Sense of closeness, warmth, and self-disclosure within a loving relationship.

INTRAUTERINE DEVICE (IN-TRA-YOO-ter-in) Tiny plastic or metal device inserted into the uterus by a physician to prevent pregnancy.

LABIA MAJORA (LA-BE-A ma-JO-ra) Outer folds or "lips" of the vulva.

LABIA MINORA (LA-BE-A MIN-OR-A) Inner folds or "lips" of the vulva.

LABOR Contractions of the uterine muscles and opening of the cervix.

LACTATION (LAK-TA-SHUN) Production of milk by the mammary glands.

LEGAL AND ETHICAL PERSPECTIVE View that legal and ethical standards affect an individual's choice of behavior.

LOVE Intense feelings of joy within a relationship.

MALE ERECTILE DISORDER Inability to gain and sustain penile erection sufficient to initiate and complete sexual activity.

MALE ORGASMIC DISORDER A man's inability to attain orgasm following sexual stimulation.

MASTURBATION (MAS-TUR-BA-SHUN) Genital self-stimulation for the purpose of sexual gratification.

MENSTRUAL CYCLE (MEN-STROO-AL) Woman's 28-day reproductive cycle.

MENSTRUAL PROBLEMS Pain, discomfort, or other problems associated with a woman's monthly cycle.

MENSTRUATION (MEN-STROO-A-SHUN) Monthly menstrual bleeding.

MISCARRIAGE Spontaneous abortion early in pregnancy, before viability.

MONS VENERIS (MONZ VEN-er-is) Hair-covered fat pad over the pubic bone.

MOOD DISORDERS or **AFFECTIVE DISORDERS (A-FEK-TIV)** Group of disorders in which the predominate feature is depression and/or mania.

MORALS Standards of right and wrong.

MULTIPLE ORGASMS Experiencing more than one orgasm during any single episode of sexual activity.

NATURAL FAMILY PLANNING Any of a number of nonhormonal, nonchemical, nondevice methods of contraception.

NIPPLE Center structure of the breast through which milk passes.

OBSCENITY Sexual materials that are lewd, disgusting, and offensive to accepted standards of decency.

OBSERVATIONAL RESEARCH Monitoring subjects visually and/or physiologically.

OOGENESIS (O-O-JEN-E-SIS) Maturation of the ovum.

ORAL CONTRACEPTIVES Birth control pills.

ORAL-GENITAL SEX or **ORAL SEX** Sexual activity involving the mouth, lips, and tongue of one partner and the genitals of another.

ORGASM DISORDERS Disorders of the orgasm phase of sexual response.

OVARIES (O-VAR-EZ) Female reproductive organs that produce and release ova.

OVULATION (O-VYOO-LA-SHUN) Monthly process whereby ova are released from the ovaries.

PARAPHILIA (PAR-A-FI-LE-A) Unusual sexual practice or fantasy.

PARASITIC INFESTATION Invasion of parts of the body by tiny organisms.

PARTICIPANT OBSERVATION RESEARCH Studying subjects from within their community or social system.

PARTURITION (PAR-TOO-RISH-UN) Another term for childbirth.

PASSION Feelings of arousal, especially sexual.

PASSIONATE LOVE Intense, obsessive love.

PEDOPHILIA (PED-O-FI-LE-A) Sexual attraction to children.

PENIS (PE-NIS) Male organ of urination and sexual response.

PERINEUM (PER-I-NE-UM) Sensitive area of skin between the vaginal orifice and anus.

PETTING Sexual activity including oral and manual stimulation, but falling short of sexual intercourse.

PHYSICAL CHALLENGE Any of a number of physical conditions having the potential to disrupt normal functioning.

PLACENTA (PLA-SEN-TA) Structure through which nutrients and waste are exchanged between mother and fetus.

PLANNED PARENTHOOD or **FAMILY PLANNING** Choosing the best time to have children.

PORNOGRAPHY Sexual materials that are intended to arouse sexual excitement.

POSTPARTUM (POST-PAR-TUM) After childbirth.

PREGNANCY Period of embryonic and fetal gestation.

PREMATURE BIRTH Birth at less than 36 weeks' gestation.

PREMATURE EJACULATION A man's inability to delay ejaculation.

PRENATAL DEVELOPMENT Fetal development in the uterus.

PREPUCE or **CLITORAL HOOD (PRE-PYOOS; KLI-TO-RAL)** Covering over the clitoris.

PREPUCE or **FORESKIN** Thin sheath of skin covering the glans.

PROPHYLACTIC (PRO-FIL-AK-TIK) A preventive measure or device.

PROSTATE GLAND (PROS-TAT) Accessory sexual gland that secretes an acid-neutralizing fluid that improves sperm motility.

PROSTITUTION Selling and buying sex.

PRURIENT INTERESTS Sexual interests that are lustful, immoral, and given to debauchery.

PSYCHIATRIC PERSPECTIVE View that both biological and psychological processes are responsible for sexual functioning.

PSYCHODYNAMIC PERSPECTIVE View that an individual's unconscious motivations determine her or his patterns of interacting in the world.

PSYCHOLOGICAL PERSPECTIVES Views concerned with the effects of thoughts, attitudes, emotions, and behaviors on sexuality.

PUBERTY Transitional period between childhood and adulthood marked by rapid physical and sexual maturation.

RAPE Forced sexual violation of one person by another.

RELIGIOUS PERSPECTIVE View that religious doctrine and scriptures affect an individual's choice of behavior.

ROOT Base of the penis.

SCIENTIFIC METHOD Systematic approach to research involving specific methods and values.

SCROTUM (SKRO-TUM) Sac behind the penis containing two testes.

SEMEN or SEMINAL FLUID (SE-MEN; SEM-I-NAL) Collective term for sperm and various fluids ejaculated from the penis.

SEMINAL DUCT or VAS DEFERENS (VAZ DEH-FER-ENZ) Sperm-carrying tube joining the testis and the body cavity.

SEMINAL VESICLES (VES-I-KULZ) Accessory sexual glands that secrete an acid-neutralizing fluid that provides nourishment for sperm.

SEMINIFEROUS TUBULES (SEM-I-NI-FER-US TOO-BYOOLZ) Stuctures that produce sperm.

SENSORY IMPAIRMENT Inability to adequately process sensory information.

SERTOLI CELLS (SER-TO-LE) Provide secretions that nourish the developing sperm.

SEXOLOGY Scientific discipline devoted to the study of human sexuality.

SEXPLAY Non intercourse sexual activities.

SEX ROLE A gender role that is anatomically limited to one sex or the other.

SEXUAL AROUSAL Excitation of a person's libido.

SEXUAL AROUSAL DISORDERS Disorders of the excitement phase of sexual response.

SEXUAL ASSIGNMENT An individual's biological makeup as male or female.

SEXUAL AVERSION DISORDER Fear of sexual activity.

SEXUAL COERCION Sexual remarks, pressure, or behavior forced on one person by another.

SEXUAL DESIRE DISORDERS Disorders of the desire phase of sexual response.

SEXUAL DIFFERENCES Biological and psychological male-female differences.

SEXUAL DIFFERENTIATION (DIF-E-REN-SHE-A-SHUN) Processes that determine sexual assignment.

SEXUAL DYSFUNCTION (DIS-FUNK-SHUN) Persistent and recurrent problems in sexual response.

SEXUAL FANTASIES Self-generated sexual images.

SEXUAL HARASSMENT Unwanted sexual advances, suggestions, comments, or gestures.

SEXUAL IDENTITY An individual's sexual assignment, gender, gender identity, gender role, sex role, and sexual orientation.

SEXUAL INTERCOURSE Genital-genital sex.

SEXUAL LAWS Laws designed to regulate and protect individuals from unwanted sexual attention and behavior.

SEXUAL MASOCHISM (MA-SO-KIZ-UM) Sexual arousal from receiving pain from others.

SEXUAL ORIENTATION An individual's sexual, emotional, romantic, and affectionate attraction to members of the same, opposite, or both sexes.

SEXUAL PAIN DISORDERS Disorders involving genital pain.

SEXUAL RESEARCH Scientific means of gathering information and drawing conclusions about sexuality.

SEXUAL RESPONSE The body's reaction to sexual stimulation.

SEXUALLY TRANSMITTED DISEASE Disease that is spread through sexual contact with an infected partner.

SEXUAL SADISM (SA-DIZ-UM) Sexual arousal from inflicting pain on others.

SHAFT Body of the penis.

SIXTY-NINING Simultaneous oral sex.

SOCIAL PENETRATION THEORY Theory that self-disclosure increases as a relationship develops.

SOCIAL PERSPECTIVES Views concerned with the effects of society and culture on sexuality.

SPERM or **SPERMATOZOA (SPER-MA-TO-ZO-A)** Male sexual cells.

SPERMATIC CORDS (SPER-MAT-IK) Supporting stuctures that contain nerves, blood vessels, tissue, and a sperm-carrying duct.

SPERMATOGENESIS (SPER-MA-TO-JEN-E-SIS) Production of sperm.

SPERMICIDE (SPER-MI-SID) A chemical agent that kills sperm on contact.

SPONGY BODY Smaller column of erectile tissue, the tip of which forms the glans penis.

STATISTICAL PERSPECTIVE View that group norms are defined by the frequency of occurrence of an attitude or behavior within a society.

STERILIZATION (STER-I-LI-ZA-SHUN) Surgical procedure that renders an individual incapable of reproducing.

STILLBIRTH Spontaneous abortion later in pregnancy, after viability.

SURVEY RESEARCH Use of questionnaires, self-report measures, or interviews with large numbers of people.

SYSTEMS PERSPECTIVE View concerned with how different social systems interact and influence individuals, couples, and families.

TERATOGEN (TER-A-TO-JEN) Causing defects and deformities.

TESTICLES or **TESTES (TES-TI-KULZ; TES-TEZ)** Male gonads that produce sperm and testosterone.

TRANSVESTISM (TRANZ-VEST-IZ-UM) Sexual arousal from wearing opposite-sex clothing.

TRIANGULAR THEORY OF LOVE Theory that the basic components of love are passion, commitment, and intimacy.

UMBILICAL CORD (UM-BIL-I-KAL) Structure that connects the fetus and its placenta.

URETHRAL ORIFICE (YOO-RE-THRAL) Opening of the urethra.

UTERUS (YOO-TE-RUS) Female reproductive organ that receives and nurtures the zygote.

VAGINA (VA-JI-NA) Female reproductive structure connecting the uterus and vaginal orifice.

VAGINAL ORIFICE (VA-JI-NAL) Opening of the vagina.

VAGINISMUS (VA-JI-NIS-MUS) Painful spasms of the muscles of the outer third of the vagina.

VASCULAR SPACES (VAS-KYOO-LAR) Small cavities within erectile tissue that fill with blood.

VAS DEFERENS or **SEMINAL DUCT (VAZ DEH-FER-ENZ)** Sperm-carrying tube joining the testis and the urethra.

VESTIBULE (VES-TI-BYOOL) Area between the labia minora.

VIRUS Microscopic particle that reproduces itself within an invaded cell.

VOYEURISM (VOI-YUR-IZ-UM) Sexual arousal from watching an unsuspecting person.

VULVA (VUL-VA) External genitals of the female.

WHEEL OF LOVE Theory that love increases as rapport, self-revelation, and mutual dependency develop and personal needs are met.

WIDOWHOOD Disruption of marriage due to death of the spouse.

ZYGOTE or **CONCEPTUS (ZI-GOT; KON-CEP-TUS)** The product of conception; a fertilized ovum.

REFERENCES

Adams, G., Adams-Taylor, S., & Pittman, K. (1989). Adolescent pregnancy and parenthood: A review of the problem, solutions, and resources. *Family Relations, 38,* 223–229.

Adams, R. (1987). The role of prostitution in AIDS and other STDs. *Medical Aspects of Human Sexuality, 21,* 27–33.

Adler, J. (1993). Sex in the snoring '90s. *Newsweek,* April 26, 55–57.

Aggleton, P., O'Reilly, K., Slutkin, G., & Davies, P. (1994). Risking everything? Risk behavior, behavior change, and AIDS. *Science, 265,* 341–345.

Akerley, B. E. (1989). *The X-rated Bible.* Austin, TX: American Atheist Press.

Allman, W. F. (1993). The mating game. *U.S. News & World Report, July 19,* 82–85.

Altman, I., & Taylor, D. A. (1973). *Social penetration: The development of interpersonal relationships.* New York: Holt, Rinehart & Winston.

American College Health Association. (1989). *What are sexually transmitted diseases?* Rockville, MD: Author.

American Psychiatric Association. (1987). *Diagnostic and statistical manual of mental disorders* (3rd ed., rev.). Washington, DC: Author.

American Psychiatric Association. (1994). *Diagnostic and statistical manual of mental disorders* (4th ed.). Washington, DC: Author.

Andersen, B. L., & Elliot, M. L. (1994). Female cancer survivors: Appreciating their sexual concerns. *Canadian Journal of Human Sexuality, 3,* 107–122.

Andrews, L. B. (1989). Position paper: Alternative modes of reproduction. In S. Cohen & N. Taub (Eds.), *Reproductive laws for the 1990s.* Clifton, NJ: Humana Press.

Ankerberg, J., & Weldon, J. (1993). *The myth of safe sex: The tragic consequences of violating God's plan.* Chicago: Moody Press.

Annon, J. S. (1974). *The behavioral treatment of sexual problems (Vol. I: Brief therapy).* Honolulu, HI: Enabling Systems.

Aral, S. O., & Holmes, K. K. (1991). Sexually transmitted diseases in the AIDS era. *Scientific American, 264,* 62–69.

Arndt, W. B., Foehl, J. C., & Good, F. E. (1985). Specific sexual fantasy themes: A multidimensional study. *Journal of Personality and Social Psychology, 48,* 472–480.

Arterburn, S. (1991). *Addicted to "love": Recovering from unhealthy dependencies in romance, relationships, and sex.* Ann Arbor, MI: Servant Publications.

Assalian, P. (1994). Premature ejaculation: Is it really psychogenic? *Journal of Sex Education and Therapy, 20,* 1–4.

Astley, S. J., Clarren, S. K., Little, R. E., Sampson, P. D., & Daling, J. R. (1992). Analysis of facial shape in children gestationally exposed to marijuana, alcohol, and/or cocaine. *Pediatrics, 89,* 67–77.

Athanasiou, R., Shaver, P., & Tavris, C. (1970). Sex. *Psychology Today, July,* 39–52.

Atwood, J. D., & Gagnon, J. (1987). Masturbatory behavior in college youth. *Journal of Sex Education and Therapy, 13,* 35–42.

Bagley, C., & Young, L. (1987). Juvenile prostitution and child sex abuse: A controlled study. *Canadian Journal of Community Mental Health, 6,* 5–26.

Bailey, J. M., & Pillard, R. C. (1991). A genetic study of male sexual orientation. *Archives of General Psychiatry, 48,* 1089–1096.

Baird, R. M., & Rosenbaum, S. E. (Eds.). (1989). *The ethics of abortion.* Buffalo, NY: Prometheus Books.

Baker, B. (1993). The female condom. *Ms., March/April,* 80–81.

Balay, J., & Shevrin, H. (1988). The subliminal psychodynamic activation method: A critical review. *American Psychologist, 43,* 161–174.

Baldwin, D. (1993). *Understanding male sexual health: A handbook for adult males, partners, and parents.* New York: Hippocrene Books.

Bancroft, J. (1989). *Human sexuality and its problems* (2nd ed.). New York: Churchill Livingstone.

Bancroft, J. (1990). Commentary: Biological contributions to sexual orientation. In D. P. McWhirter, S. A. Sanders, & J. M. Reinisch (Eds.), *Homosexuality/heterosexuality: Concepts of sexual orientation.* New York: Oxford University Press.

Barlow, D. H. (1986). Causes of sexual dysfunction: The role of anxiety and cognitive interference. *Journal of Consulting and Clinical Psychology, 54,* 140–148.

Barlow, D. H. (1988). *Anxiety and its disorders.* New York: Guilford.

Basow, S. A. (1992). *Gender: Stereotypes and roles* (3rd ed.). Belmont, CA: Brooks/Cole.

Bass, E., & Davis, L. (1988). *The courage to heal: A guide for women survivors of sexual abuse.* New York: Harper & Row.

Batchelor, W. F. (1988). *AIDS: An introduction to the medical, psychological, and social issues.* Training manual.

Baumrind, D. (1985). Research using intentional deception: Ethical issues revisited. *American Psychologist, 40,* 165–174.

Beck, A. T. (1988). *Love is never enough.* New York: Harper & Row.

Bell, A. P., & Weinberg, M. S. (1978). *Homosexualities.* New York: Simon & Schuster.

Bem, S. L. (1974). The measurement of psychological androgyny. *Journal of Consulting and Clinical Psychology, 42,* 155–162.

Bem, S. L. (1984). Androgyny and gender schema theory: A conceptual and empirical integration. *Nebraska Symposium on Motivation, 32,* 179-226.

Bem, S. L., & Lenney, E. (1976). Sex typing and the avoidance of cross-sex behavior. *Journal of Personality and Social Psychology, 33,* 48–54.

Bem, S. L., Martyna, W., & Watson, C. (1976). Sex typing and androgyny: Further explorations of the expressive domain. *Journal of Personality and Social Psychology, 34,* 1016–1023.

Bennett, N. G., Blanc, A. K., & Bloom, D. E. (1988). Commitment and the modern union: Assessing the link between premarital cohabitation and subsequent marital stability. *American Sociological Review, 53,* 127–138.

Berlin, F. S., & Meinecke, C. F. (1981). Treatment of sex offenders with antiandrogenic medicine. *American Journal of Psychiatry, 138,* 601–607.

Bernard, M. E., & DiGiuseppe, R. (Eds.). (1989). *Inside rational-emotive therapy: A critical appraisal of the theory and therapy of Albert Ellis.* San Diego, CA: Academic Press.

Bernstein, N. R. (1985). Sexuality in mentally retarded adolescents. *Medical Aspects of Human Sexuality, November,* 50–61.

Berrill, K. T., & Herek, G. M. (1990). Violence against lesbians and gay men: An introduction. *Journal of Interpersonal Violence, 5,* 269–273.

Besharov, D. J., & Gardiner, K. N. (1993). Truth and consequences: Teen sex. *The American Enterprise, January/February,* 52–59.

Betancourt, J. (1983a). *Am I normal? An illustrated guide to your changing body.* New York: Avon Books.

Betancourt, J. (1983b). *Dear diary: An illustrated guide to your changing body.* New York: Avon Books.

Bieber, I., et al. (1962). *Homosexuality: A psychoanalytic study.* Northvale, NJ: Jason Aronson.

Bigler, M. O. (1989). Adolescent sexual behavior in the eighties. *SIECUS Report, October/November,* 6–9.

Bing, E. (1988). Yes, you can. *Childbirth '88, 5,* 36–38, 40.

Blumenfeld, W. J., & Raymond, D. (1993). *Looking at gay and lesbian life.* Boston: Beacon Press.

Blumstein, P., & Schwartz, P. (1983). *American couples.* New York: William Morrow.

Blumstein, P., & Schwartz, P. (1990). Intimate relationships and the creation of sexuality. In D. P. McWhirter, S. A. Sanders, & J. M. Reinisch (Eds.), *Homosexuality/ Heterosexuality: Concepts of sexual orientation.* New York: Oxford University Press.

Bockting, W. O., & Coleman, E. (1992). A comprehensive approach to the treatment of gender dysphoria. *Journal of Psychology & Human Sexuality, 5,* 131–155.

Boles, J., & Elifson, K. W. (1994). Sexual identity and HIV: The male prostitute. *Journal of Sex Research, 31,* 39–46.

Bolling, D. R., & Voeller, B. (1987). AIDS and hetero-sexual anal intercourse. *Journal of the American Medical Association, 258,* 474.

Boston Women's Health Book Collective (1992). *The new our bodies, ourselves.* New York: Simon & Schuster.

Boswell, J. (1994). *Same-sex unions in premodern Europe.* New York: Villard.

Bowe, C. (1992). Everything we think, feel, and do about divorce. *Cosmopolitan, February,* 199–203.

Boyd, B. R. (1990). *Circumcision: What it does.* San Francisco: Taterhill Press.

Bradford, J., Boulet, J., & Pawlak, A. (1992). The para-philias: A multiplicity of deviant behaviours. *Canadian Journal of Psychiatry, 37,* 104–108.

Branan, K. (1994). Out for blood: The right's vendetta against Anita Hill's supporters. *Ms., January/February,* 82–87.

Brauer, A. P., & Brauer, D. J. (1990). *The ESO ecstasy program: Better, safer sexual intimacy and extended orgas-mic response.* New York: Warner.

Brecher, E. M. (1979). *The sex researchers.* San Francisco: Specific Press.

Brecher, R., & Brecher, E. (1966). *An analysis of human sexual response.* New York: New American Library.

Brecher, E. M., & the Editors of Consumer Reports Books. (1984). *Love, sex, and aging.* Boston: Little, Brown.

Brehm, B. A. (1993). *Essays on wellness.* New York: HarperCollins.

Brehm, S. S. (1992). *Intimate relationships* (2nd ed.). New York: McGraw-Hill.

Brehm, S. S., & Kassin, S. M. (1990). *Social psychology.* Boston: Houghton Mifflin.

Bretschneider, J. G., & McCoy, N. L. (1988). Sexual interest and behavior in healthy 80-to-102-year-olds. *Archives of Sexual Behavior, 17,* 109–129.

Briere, J., & Runtz, M. (1989). University males' sexual interest in children: Predicting potential indices of "pedophilia" in a nonforensic sample. *Child Abuse & Neglect, 13,* 65–75.

Bright, P. D. (1987). Adolescent pregnancy and loss. *Maternal-Child Nursing Journal, 16,* 1–12.

Brody, J. E. (1989a). How women can begin to cope with premenstrual syndrome, a biological mystery. *The New York Times, January 5,* B12.

Brody, J. E. (1989b). Research casts doubt on need for many Caesarean births as their rate soars. *The New York Times, July 27,* B5.

Brown, G. R. (1994). Women in relationships with cross-dressing men: A descriptive study from a non-clinical setting. *Archives of Sexual Behavior, 23,* 515–530.

Brown, W. (1987). Hormones and sexual aggression in the male: Commentary. *Integrative Psychiatry, 5,* 91–93.

Browne, A., & Finkelhor, D. (1986). Impact of child sexual abuse: A review of the research. *Psychological Bulletin, 99,* 66–77.

Brownmiller, S. (1975). *Against our will: Men, women and rape.* New York: Simon & Schuster.

Buffum, J. (1985). Pharmacosexology update: Yohimbine and sexual function. *Journal of Psychoactive Drugs, 17,* 131–132.

Bullough, V., & Bullough, B. (1987). *Women and prosti-tution: A social history.* Buffalo, NY: Prometheus.

Bullough, V. L., & Weinberg, T. S. (1989). Women married to transvestites: Problems and adjustments. *Journal of Psychology & Human Sexuality, 1,* 83–104.

Burgess, A. W., Dietz, P. E., & Hazelwood, R. R. (1983). Study design and characteristics. In R. R. Hazelwood, P. E. Dietz, & A. W. Burgess (Eds.), *Autoerotic fatalities.* Lexington, MA: Lexington Books.

Burgess, A. W., Hartman, C. R., MacCausland, M. P., & Powers, P. (1984). Response patterns in children and adolescents exploited through sex rings and pornography. *American Journal of Psychiatry, 141,* 656–662.

Burgess, A. W., & Holmstrom, L. L. (1988). Treating the adult rape victim. *Medical Aspects of Human Sexuality, January,* 36–43.

Burr, C. (1993). Homosexuality and biology. *The Atlantic, March,* 47–52, 55, 58–62, 64–65.

Buss, D. M. (1985). Human mate selection. *American Scientist, 73,* 47–51.

Byer, C. O., & Shainberg, L. W. (1991). *Living well: Health in your hands.* New York: HarperCollins.

Byrne, D., Clore, G. L., & Smeaton, G. (1986). The

attraction hypothesis: Do similar attitudes affect anything? *Journal of Personality and Social Psychology, 51,* 1167–1170.

Byrne, D., & Kelley, K. (Eds.). (1986). *Alternative approaches to the study of sexual behavior.* Hillsdale, NJ: Erlbaum.

Calderone, M. S. (1983). Fetal erection and its message to us. *SIECUS Report,* May–July, 9–10.

Calderone, M. S., & Johnson, E. W. (1989). *The family book about sexuality* (rev. ed.). New York: Harper & Row.

Calderwood, D. (1987). The male rape victim. *Medical Aspects of Human Sexuality,* May, 53–55.

Calhoun, K. S., & Atkeson, B. M. (1991). *Treatment of rape victims: Facilitating psychosocial adjustment.* New York: Pergamon Press.

Campbell, A. (1981). *The sense of well-being in America.* New York: McGraw-Hill.

Canavan, M. M., Meyer, W. J., & Higgs, D. C. (1992). The female experience of sibling incest. *Journal of Marital and Family Therapy, 18,* 129–142.

Carey, P. O. , Howards, S. S., & Vance, M. L. (1988). Transdermal testosterone treatment of hypogonadal men. *Journal of Urology, 140,* 76–79.

Carmen, A., & Moody, H. (1985). *Working women: The subterranean world of street prostitution.* New York: Harper & Row.

Carnes, P. (1983). *Out of the shadows: Understanding sexual addiction.* Minneapolis, MN: CompCare.

Carpenter, C. R. (1942). Sexual behavior of free-ranging rhesus monkeys (Macaca Mulatta). *Journal of Comparative and Physiological Psychology, 33,* 113–162.

Carson, R. C., & Butcher, J. N. (1992). *Abnormal psychology and modern life* (9th ed.). New York: HarperCollins.

Carson, S. A. (1988). Sex selection: The ultimate in family planning. *Fertility and Sterility, 50,* 16–19.

Carter, S., & Sokol, J. (1987). *Men who can't love.* New York: Berkley.

Carter, S., & Sokol, J. (1989). *What really happens in bed: A demystification of sex.* New York: M. Evans and Co.

Casey, R. W. (1994). Sexual function and urologic cancers in men. *Canadian Journal of Human Sexuality, 3,* 171–176.

Centers for Disease Control and Prevention. (1994). *CDC Fax information service disease directory.*

Chagnon, N. A. (1977). *Yąnomamö: The fierce people* (2nd ed.). New York: Holt, Rinehart and Winston.

Charney, D. A., & Russell, R. C. (1994). An overview of sexual harassment. *American Journal of Psychiatry, 151,* 10–17.

Chartham, R. (1971). *The sensuous couple.* New York: Ballantine Books.

Chavkin, W., Rothman, B. K., & Rapp, R. (1989). Position paper: Alternative modes of reproduction: Other views and questions. In S. Cohen & N. Taub (Eds.), *Reproductive laws for the 1990s.* Clifton, NJ: Humana Press.

Chew, S. (1994). Pornography: Does women's equality depend on what we do about it? *Ms.,* January/February, 42–45.

Christmas, J. (1992). The risks of cocaine use in pregnancy. *Medical Aspects of Human Sexuality, 26,* 36–43.

Christopher, F. S., & Cate, R. M. (1988). Premarital sexual involvement: A developmental investigation of relational correlates. *Adolescence, 23,* 793–803.

Clark, J. H., & Zarrow, M. X. (1971). Influence of copulation on time of ovulation in women. *American Journal of Obstetrics and Gynecology, 109,* 1083–1085.

Clark, M., & Carroll, G. (1986). Conquering endometriosis. *Newsweek,* October 13, 95.

Clerici, M., Berzofsky, J. A., Shearer. G. M., & Tacket, C. O. (1991). Exposure to human immunodeficiency virus type 1—specific T helper cell responses before detection of infection by polymerase chain reaction and serum antibodies. *The Journal of Infectious Diseases, 164,* 178–182.

Clift, E. (1993). Making babies: Miracle or marketing hype? *On the Issues: The Progressive Woman's Quarterly,* Spring, 38, 40, 56.

Clunis, D. M., & Green, G. D. (1988). *Lesbian couples.* Seattle, WA: Seal Press.

Cobb, M., & Jallon, J. M. (1990). Pheromones, mate recognition and courtship stimulation in the Drosophila melanogaster species subgroup. *Animal Behaviour, 39,* 1058–1067.

Cohen, S. S. (1987). The power of touch. *New Woman,* April, 41–43.

Cohen-Kettenis, P. T., & Gooren, L. J. G. (1992). The influence of hormone treatment on psychological functioning of transsexuals. *Journal of Psychology & Human Sexuality, 5,* 55–67.

Coleman, E. (1989). The development of male prostitution activity among gay and bisexual adolescents. *Journal of Homosexuality, 17,* 131–149.

Coles, R., & Stokes, G. (1985). *Sex and the American teenager.* New York: Harper & Row.

Colino, S. (1991). Sex and the expectant mother. *Parenting, February,* 111.

Collins, G., & Kinder, B. (1984). Adjustment following surgical implantation of a penile prosthesis: A critical overview. *Journal of Sex & Marital Therapy, 10,* 225–271.

Comfort, A. (1991). *The new joy of sex* (rev. ed.). New York: Crown.

Copenhaver, S., & Grauerholz, E. (1991). Sexual victimization among sorority women: Exploring the link between sexual violence and institutional practices. *Sex Roles, 24,* 31–41.

Cowan, G., & Dunn, K. F.(1994) What themes in pornography lead to perceptions of the degradation of women? *Journal of Sex Research, 31,* 11–21.

Cox, D. J. (1988). Incidence and nature of male genital exposure behavior as reported by college women. *Journal of Sex Research, 24,* 227–234.

Crenshaw, T. L., Goldberg, J. P., & Stern, W. C. (1987). Pharmacologic modification of psychosexual dysfunction. *Journal of Sex & Marital Therapy, 13,* 239–250.

Crewdson, J. (1988). *By silence betrayed: Sexual abuse of children in America.* Boston: Little, Brown.

Crispell, D. (1992). The brave new world of men. *American Demographics, January,* 38–43.

Cross, R. J. (1993). What doctors and others need to know: Six facts on human sexuality and aging. *SIECUS Report, June/July,* 7–9.

Crowe, L. C., & George, W. H. (1989). Alcohol and human sexuality: Review and integration. *Psychological Bulletin, 105,* 374–386.

Darling, C. A., & Davidson, J. K. (1986). Enhancing relationships: Understanding the feminine mystique of pretending orgasm. *Journal of Sex & Marital Therapy, 12,* 182–196.

Dauw, D. C. (1988). Evaluating the effectiveness of the SECS' surrogate-assisted sex therapy model. *Journal of Sex Research, 24,* 269–275.

Davis, M. & Scott, R. S (1988). *Lovers, doctors, and the law.* New York: Harper & Row.

Davison, G. C. (1978). Not can but ought: The treatment of homosexuality. *Journal of Consulting and Clinical Psychology, 46,* 170–172.

Dawson, D. A. (1990). Trends in use of oral contraceptives: Data from the 1987 National Health Interview Survey. *Family Planning Perspectives, 22,* 169–172.

Day, L. (1991). *AIDS: What the government isn't telling you.* Palm Desert, CA: Rockford Press.

Delacoste, F., & Alexander, P. (1987). *Sex work: Writings by women in the sex industry.* Pittsburgh, PA: Cleis Press.

Department of Health and Human Services. *Condoms and sexually transmitted diseases . . . especially AIDS.* Publication FDA 90–4239.

Department of Health and Human Services. *Tips on Preventing AIDS.* Publication FDA 88–1145.

Diagram Group (1976). *Man's body: An owner's manual.* New York: Bantam.

DiClemente, R. J., Durbin, M., Siegel, D., Krasnovsky, F., Lazarus, N., & Comacho, T. (1992). Determinants of condom use among junior high school students in a minority, inner-city school district. *Pediatrics, 89,* 197–202.

Diokno, A. C., Brown, M. B., & Herzog, A. R. (1990). Sexual function in the elderly. *Archives of Internal Medicine, 150,* 197–200.

Docter, R. F. (1988). *Transvestites and transsexuals: Toward a theory of cross-gender behavior.* New York: Plenum.

Dodson, B. (1987). *Sex for one: The joy of selfloving.* New York: Crown.

Donnerstein, E., Linz, D., & Penrod, S. (1987). *The question of pornography: Research findings and policy implications.* New York: Free Press.

Dowling, C. G. (1993). Miraculous babies. *Life, December,* 75–84.

Downing, C. (1989). *Myths and mysteries of same-sex love.* New York: Continuum.

Dunn, M. E., & Trost, J. E. (1989). Male multiple orgasms: A descriptive study. *Archives of Sexual Behavior, 18,* 377–387.

Durden-Smith, J. (1980). How to win the mating game by a nose. *Next, November/December,* 85–89.

Dworkin, A., French, M., Ramos, N., & Shange, N. (1994). Where do we stand on pornography? *Ms.*, January/February, 32–41.

Dym, B., & Glenn, M. (1993). Forecast for couples. *Psychology Today*, July/August, 54–57, 78–79, 81–83, 86.

Eby, L., & Donovan, C. A. (1993). Single parents and damaged children: The fruits of the sexual revolution. *The World & I*, July, 405–419.

Eichel, E., & Nobile, P. (1992) *The perfect fit: How to achieve mutual fulfillment and monogamous passion through the new intercourse.* New York: Signet.

Eisenberg, A., Murkoff, H. E., & Hathaway, S. E. (1991). *What to expect when you're expecting* (2nd ed.). New York: Workman.

Elliott, D. M., & Briere, J. (1992). The sexually abused boy: Problems in manhood. *Medical Aspects of Human Sexuality*, February, 68–71.

Elliott, M. (1992). Tip of the iceberg? *Social Work Today*, March, 12–13.

Ellis, A. (1962). *Reason and emotion in psychotherapy.* New York: Lyle Stuart.

Ellis, A. (1966). *Sex without guilt.* North Hollywood, CA: Wilshire.

Ellis, A. (1976). *Sex and the liberated man.* Secaucus, NJ: Lyle Stuart.

Ellis, A. (1988). *How to stubbornly refuse to make yourself miserable about anything—yes, anything!* New York: Lyle Stuart.

Ellis, A., & Harper, R. A. (1975). *A new guide to rational living.* North Hollywood, CA: Wilshire.

Ellis, H. H. (1933). *Psychology of sex: A manual for students.* New York: Long & Smith.

Ellis, H. H. (1936). *Studies in the psychology of sex.* New York: Random House. (Original work published 1896–1928)

Ellis, L., & Ames, M. (1987). Neurohormonal functioning and sexual orientation: A theory of homosexuality-heterosexuality. *Psychological Bulletin, 101,* 233–258.

Erickson, W. D., Walbek, N. H., & Seely, R. K. (1988). Behavior patterns of child molesters. *Archives of Sexual Behavior, 17,* 77–86.

Erwin, J., & Maple, T. (1976). Ambisexual behavior with male-male anal penetration in male rhesus monkeys. *Archives of Sexual Behavior, 5,* 9–14.

Estrich, S. (1987). *Real rape: How the legal system victimizes women who say no.* Cambridge: Harvard University Press.

Everstine, D. S., & Everstine, L. (1989). *Sexual trauma in children and adolescents.* New York: Brunner/Mazel.

Fay, R. E., Turner, C. F., Klassen, A. D., & Gagnon, J. H. (1989). Prevalence and patterns of same-gender sexual contact among men. *Science, 243,* 338–348.

Feinauer, L. L. (1989). Sexual dysfunction in women sexually abused as children. *Contemporary Family Therapy, 11,* 299–309.

Feingold, A. (1990). Gender differences in effects of physical attractiveness on romantic attraction: A comparison across five research paradigms. *Journal of Personality and Social Psychology, 5,* 981–993.

Feminist Review (Eds.). (1987). *Sexuality: A reader.* London: Virago Press.

Fielstein, E. M., Fielstein, L. L., & Hazlewood, M. G. (1992). AIDS knowledge among college freshmen students: Need for education? *Journal of Sex Education and Therapy, 18,* 45–54.

Finkelhor, D. (1980). Sex among siblings: A survey on prevalence, variety, and effects. *Archives of Sexual Behavior, 9,* 171–194.

Finkelhor, D. (1984). *Child sexual abuse: New theory and research.* New York: Free Press.

Finkelhor, D. (1990). Early and long-term effects of child sexual abuse: An update. *Professional Psychology: Research and Practice, 21,* 325–330.

Finkelhor, D., Hotaling, G., Lewis, I. A., & Smith, C. (1990). Sexual abuse in a national survey of adult men and women: Prevalence, characteristics, and risk factors. *Child Abuse and Neglect, 14,* 19–28.

Firestone, R. W. (1990). Voices during sex: Application of voice therapy to sexuality. *Journal of Sex & Marital Therapy, 16,* 258–277.

Fishel, E. (1992). Raising sexually healthy kids. *Parents,* September, 110-116.

Fisher, W. A., & Grenier, G. (1994). Violent pornography, antiwomen thoughts, and antiwomen acts: In search of reliable effects. *Journal of Sex Research. 31,* 23–38.

Fitzgerald, K. (1986). Sexual blackmail: Schools get serious about harassment. *Ms.*, October, 24–26.

Fitzpatrick, M. A. (1988). *Between husbands and wives: Communication in marriage.* Newbury Park, CA: Sage.

Flaherty, J. F., & Dusek, J. B. (1980). An investigation of the relationship between psychological androgyny and components of self-concept. *Journal of Personality and Social Psychology, 38,* 984–992.

Fletcher, J. (1967). *Moral responsibility: Situation ethics at work.* Philadelphia: Westminster.

Ford, C. S., & Beach, F. A. (1951). *Patterns of sexual behavior.* New York: Harper & Brothers.

Freeman, E. W., Rickels, K., & Sondheimer, S. J. (1992). Course of premenstrual syndrome symptom severity after treatment. *American Journal of Psychiatry, 149,* 531–533.

Freud, S. (1905). Three essays on the theory of sexuality. In the *Standard edition of the psychological works of Sigmund Freud, Vol. 7.* London: Hogarth Press.

Freud, S. (1966). Symbolism in dreams. In J. Strachey (Ed.), *Introductory lectures on psychoanalysis.* New York: Norton. (Original work published 1917)

Freund, K., & Blanchard, R. (1986). The concept of courtship disorder. *Journal of Sex & Marriage Therapy, 12,* 79–92.

Freund, K., & Kuban, M. (1994). The basis of the abused abuser theory of pedophilia: A further elaboration on an earlier study. *Archives of Sexual Behavior, 23,* 553–563.

Freund, M., Leonard, T. L., & Lee, N. (1989). Sexual behavior of resident street prostitutes with their clients in Camden, New Jersey. *Journal of Sex Research, 26,* 460–478.

Friedman, J. (1989). The impact of homophobia on male sexual development. *SIECUS Report, May–July,* 8–9.

Friedman, T., & Gath, D. (1989). The psychiatric consequences of spontaneous abortion. *British Journal of Psychiatry, 155,* 810–813.

Frieze, I. H. (1983). Investigating the causes and consequences of marital rape. *Signs, 8,* 532–553.

Fromm, E. (1956). *The art of loving.* New York: Harper & Row.

Gaffney, G. R., Luries, S. F., & Berlin, F. S. (1984). Is there familial transmission of pedophilia? *Journal of Nervous and Mental Disease, 172,* 546–548.

Garber, M. (1992). *Vested interests: Cross-dressing and cultural anxiety.* New York: HarperPerennial.

Garcia, L. T. (1982). Sex-role orientation and stereo-types about male-female sexuality. *Sex Roles, 8,* 863–876.

Gerow, J. R. (1992) *Psychology: An introduction* (3rd ed.). New York: HarperCollins.

Geschwind, N., & Behan, P. (1982). Left-handedness: Association with immune disease, migraine, and developmental learning disorder. *Proceedings of the National Academy of Science USA, 79,* 5097–5100.

Gibbs, N. (1991). When is it rape? *Time, June 3,* 48–54.

Gilbert, N. (1992). Realities and mythologies of rape. *Society, May/June,* 4-10.

Gilder, G. (1986). *Men and marriage.* New York: Pelican.

Gillespie, C. (1992). *Your pregnancy month by month* (4th ed.). New York: HarperPerennial.

Gittelson, N. (1980). Marriage: What women expect and what they get. *McCall's, January,* 87–89, 150–151.

Glass, R. H., & Ericsson, R. J. (1982). *Getting pregnant in the 1980s.* Berkeley: University of California Press.

Gold, S. R., Balzano, B. F., & Stamey, R. (1991). Two studies of females' sexual force fantasies. *Journal of Sex Education and Therapy, 17,* 15–26.

Goldberg, M. S. (1993). Choosing a contraceptive. *FDA Consumer, September,* 18–25.

Goldberg, S. (1983). Parent-infant bonding: Another look. *Child Development, 54,* 1355–1382.

Golden, G. (1989). Parental attitudes to infant's sex play determine child's later attitudes to sex. *Medical Aspects of Human Sexuality, May, 73,* 82.

Goldstein, M. J., & Kant, H. S. (1973). *Pornography and sexual deviance.* Berkeley: University of California Press.

Goldstein, R. D. (1988). *Mother-love and abortion: A legal interpretation.* Berkeley: University of California Press.

Goleman, D. (1991). Sexual harassment: It's about power, not lust. *The New York Times, October 22,* C1, C12.

Goodpasture, H. C. (1991). Antiviral drug therapy. *American Family Physician, 43,* 197–204.

Gooren, L. (1991). Body politics: The physical side of gender identity. *Journal of Psychology & Human Sexuality, 4,* 9–17.

Gordon, B. (1988). *Jennifer fever: Older men, younger women*. New York: Harper & Row.

Gordon, S., & Snyder, C. (1989). *Personal issues in human sexuality* (2nd ed.). Needham Heights, MA: Allyn & Bacon.

Gray, P. (1993). What is love? *Time, February 15,* 47–49.

Gregersen, E. (1983). *Sexual practices: The story of human sexuality*. New York: Franklin Watts.

Groth, A. N. (1979). *Men who rape*. New York: Plenum.

Groth, A. N., & Burgess, A. W. (1980). Male rape: Offenders and victims. *American Journal of Psychiatry, 137,* 806–810.

Groth, A. N., Burgess, A. W., & Holmstrom, L. L. (1977). Rape: Power, anger, and sexuality. *American Journal of Psychiatry, 134,* 1239–1243.

Groth, A. N., & Gary, T. S. (1981). Marital rape. *Medical Aspects of Human Sexuality, 15,* 122–127, 131–132.

Guidubaldi, J., Cleminshaw, H. K., Perry, J. D., & McLoughlin, C. S. (1983). The impact of parental divorce on children: Report of the nationwide NASP study. *School Psychology Review, 12,* 300–323.

Halpern, C. T., Udry, J. R., & Suchindran, C. (1994). Effects of repeated questionnaire administration in longitudinal studies of adolescent males' sexual behavior. *Archives of Sexual Behavior, 23,* 41–57.

Handsfield, H. (1992). Recent developments in STDs: II. Viral and other syndromes. *Hospital Practice, January 15,* 175–200.

Handsfield, H. H., & Hammerschlag, M. R. (1992). Chlamydia: The challenge is diagnosis. *Patient Care, February 15,* 69–84.

Harding, J. J. (1989). Postpartum psychiatric disorders: A review. *Comprehensive Psychiatry, 30,* 109–112.

Harrison, M. (1985). *Self-help for premenstrual syndrome*. New York: Random House.

Haseltine, W. A. (1993). The future of AIDS. *Priorities, Winter,* 30–32.

Hassett, J. (1978). Sex and smell. *Psychology Today, March,* 40–42, 45.

Hatcher, R. A., Stewart, F., Trussell, J., Kowal, D., Guest, F., Stewart, G. K., & Cates, W. (1992). *Contraceptive technology (1990–1992)*. New York: Irvington.

Hatcher, R. A., Trussell, J., Stewart, F., Stewart, G. K., Kowal, D., Guest, F., Cates, W., & Policar, M. S. (1994). *Contraceptive technology (1994–1996)*. New York: Irvington.

Hatfield, E., & Rapson, R. L. (1993). *Love, sex, & intimacy: Their psychology, biology, and history*. New York: HarperCollins.

Haugaard, J. J., & Reppucci, N. D. (1989). *The sexual abuse of children: A comprehensive guide to current knowledge and intervention strategies*. San Francisco: Jossey–Bass.

Hazan, C., & Shaver, P. (1987). Romantic love conceptualized as an attachment process. *Journal of Personality and Social Psychology, 52,* 511–524.

Heath, D. (1984). An investigation into the origins of a copious vaginal discharge during intercourse: "Enough to wet the bed"—that "is not urine." *Journal of Sex Research, 20,* 194–215.

Henshaw, S. K., & Silverman, J. (1988). The characteristics and prior contraceptive use of U.S. abortion patients. *Family Planning Perspectives, 20,* 158–168.

Herek, G. M. (1989). Hate crimes against lesbians and gay men. *American Psychologist, 44,* 948–955

Herek, G. M. (1991). Myths about sexual orientation: A lawyer's guide to social science research. *Law & Sexuality, 1,* 133–172.

Herek, G. M., & Berrill, K. T. (1992). *Hate crimes: Confronting violence against lesbians and gay men*. Newbury Park, CA: Sage.

Hersch, P. (1988). Coming of age on city streets. *Psychology Today, January,* 28–37.

Hite, S. (1976). *The Hite report*. New York: Dell.

Hite, S. (1981). *The Hite report on male sexuality*. New York: Knopf.

Hite, S. (1987). *Women and love: A cultural revolution in progress*. New York: Knopf.

Holden, C. (1989). Koop finds abortion evidence "inconclusive." *Science, 243,* 730–731.

Howard, J. A., Blumstein, P., & Schwartz, P. (1987). Social or evolutionary theories: Some observations on preferences in mate selection. *Journal of Personality and Social Psychology, 53,* 194–200.

Hughes, J. O., & Sandler, B. R. (1987). *"Friends" raping friends: Could it happen to you?* Washington, DC: Association of American Colleges.

Hunt, M. (1974). *Sexual behavior in the 1970s*. Chicago: Playboy Press.

Hurlbert, D. F., & Whittaker, K. E. (1991). The role of masturbation in marital and sexual satisfaction: A comparative study of female masturbators and non-masturbators. *Journal of Sex Education and Therapy, 17*, 272–282.

Hurt, S. W., Schnurr, P. P., Severino, S. K., Freeman, E. W., Gise, L. H., Rivera-Tovar, A., & Steege, J. F. (1992). Late luteal phase dysphoric disorder in 670 women evaluated for premenstrual complaints. *American Journal of Psychiatry, 149*, 525–530.

Hyde, J. S. (1991). *Half the human experience: The psychology of women* (4th ed.). Lexington, MA: D. C. Heath.

Ivey, A. E. (1993). *Intentional interviewing and counseling* (3rd ed.). Pacific Grove, CA: Brooks/Cole.

Janus, S. S., & Janus, C. L. (1993). *The Janus report on sexual behavior*. New York: Wiley.

Jay, K., & Young, A. (1979). *The gay report*. New York: Summit Books.

Johnson, R. E., Nahmias, A. J., Magder, L. S., Lee, F. K., Brooks, C. A., & Snowden, C. B. (1989). A sero-epidemiologic survey of the prevalence of herpes simplex virus type 2 infection in the United States. *New England Journal of Medicine, 321*, 7–12.

Jolin, A. (1994). On the backs of working prostitutes: Feminist theory and prostitution policy. *Crime & Delinquency, 40*, 69–83.

Jones, E. F., Forrest, J. D., Henshaw, S. K., Silverman, J., & Torres, A. (1988). Unintended pregnancy, contraceptive practice and family planning services in developed countries. *Family Planning Perspectives, 20*, 53–67.

Jones, W. P., & Emerson, S. (1994) Sexual abuse and binge eating in a nonclinical population. *Journal of Sex Education and Therapy, 20*, 47–55

Kanin, E. J. (1994). False rape allegations. *Archives of Sexual Behavior, 23*, 81–92.

Kantrowitz, B., & Wingert, P. (1993). *Newsweek, February 15*, 37–41.

Kaplan, H. S. (1974). *The new sex therapy: Active treatment of sexual dysfunction*. New York: Brunner/Mazel.

Kaplan, H. S. (1979). *Disorders of sexual desire*. New York: Brunner/Mazel.

Kaplan, H. S. (1987). *The illustrated manual of sex therapy* (2nd ed.). New York: Brunner/Mazel.

Keeling, R. P. (1993). Campuses confront AIDS: Tapping the vitality of caring and community. *Educational Record, Winter*, 30–36.

Kelly, D. D. (1985). Sexual differentiation of the nervous system. In E. R. Kandel & Schwartz, J. H. (Eds.), *Principles of neural science* (2nd ed.). New York: Elsevier.

Kempton, W. (1977). The mentally retarded person. In H. L. Gochros & J. S. Gochros (Eds.), *The sexually oppressed*. New York: Association Press.

Kendall-Tackett, K. A., Williams, L. M., & Finkelhor, D. (1993). Impact of sexual abuse on children: A review and synthesis of recent empirical studies. *Psychological Bulletin, 113*, 164–180.

Key, W. B. (1980). *The clam plate orgy*. Englewood Cliffs, NJ: Prentice Hall.

Kiecolt-Glaser, J. K., Fisher, L. D., Ogrocki, P., Stout, J. C., Speicher, C. E., & Glaser, R. (1987). Marital quality, marital disruption, and immune function. *Psychosomatic Medicine, 49*, 13–34.

Kiefer, O. (1993). *Sexual life in ancient Rome*. New York: Dorset.

Kilmann, P. R., Boland, J. P., West, M. O., Jonet, C. J., & Ramsey, R. E. (1993). Sexual arousal of college students in relation to sex experiences. *Journal of Sex Education and Therapy, 19*, 157–164.

Kimmel, M. S. (Ed.). (1990). *Men confront pornography*. New York: Crown.

Kinsey, A. C., Pomeroy, W. B., & Martin, C. E. (1948). *Sexual behavior in the human male*. Philadelphia: Saunders.

Kinsey, A. C., Pomeroy, W. B., Martin, C. E., & Gebhard, P. H. (1953). *Sexual behavior in the human female*. Philadelphia: Saunders.

Kipnis, A. R., & Herron, E. (1993). Ending the battle between the sexes. *Utne Reader, January/February*, 69–76.

Klassen, A. D., Williams, C. J., & Levitt, E. E. (1989). *Sex and morality in the U.S.* Middletown, CT: Wesleyan University Press.

Klein, M. (1992). *Ask me anything*. New York: Fireside/Simon & Schuster.

Kolata, G. (1994). Reproductive revolution is jolting old views. *New York Times, January 11*, A1, C12.

Kolodny, R. C., Masters, W. H., & Johnson, V. E. (1979). *Textbook of sexual medicine*. Boston: Little, Brown.

Koss, M. P. (1992). The underdetection of rape: Methodological choices influence incidence estimates. *Journal of Social Issues, 48,* 61–75.

Kraft-Ebing, R. V. (1978). *Psychopathia sexualis*. New York: Stein & Day. (Original work published 1886)

Kursh, E. D., & Resnick, M. I. (Eds.). (1987). *Urology*. Oradell, NJ: Medical Economics Books.

Labbock, M. H. (1989). Breastfeeding and fertility. *Medical Aspects of Human Sexuality, March, 43,* 56.

Ladas, A. K., Whipple, B., & Perry, J. D. (1982). *The G spot and other recent discoveries about human sexuality*. New York: Dell.

Lader, L. (1991). *RU-486: The pill that could end the abortion wars and why American women don't have it*. Reading, MA: Addison-Wesley.

Lake, M. (1991). *Scents and sexuality: The essence of excitement*. London: John Murray.

Lang, R. A., Langevin, R., Bain, J., Frenzel, R., & Wright, P. (1989). Sex hormone profiles in genital exhibitionists. *Annals of Sex Research, 2,* 67–75.

Laws, D. R. (Ed.). (1989). *Relapse prevention with sex offenders*. New York: Guilford.

Lee, C., & Hart, L. L. (1990). Accuracy of home pregnancy tests. *Annals of Pharmacotherapy, 24,* 712–713.

Leiblum, S. R., & Rosen, R. (Eds.). (1989). *Principles and practice of sex therapy* (2nd ed.). New York: Guilford.

Leiser, B. M. (1989). Is homosexuality unnatural? In J. Rachels (Ed.), *The right thing to do: Basic readings in moral philosophy*. New York: Random House.

Leshner, A. I. (1978). *An introduction to behavioral endocrinology*. New York: Oxford University Press.

LeVay, S. (1991). A difference in hypothalamic structure between heterosexual and homosexual men. *Science, 253,* 1034–1037.

Levin, M. (1993). Why homosexuality is abnormal. In S. J. Gold (Ed.), *Moral controversies: Race, class, and gender in applied ethics*. Belmont, CA: Wadsworth.

Levin, R. J., & Levin, A. (1975). Sexual pleasure: The surprising preferences of 100,000 women. *Redbook, September,* 51–58.

Levine, S. B. (1989). *Sex is not simple*. Columbus, OH: Ohio Psychology Publishing.

Levine, S. B., Risen, C. B., & Althof, S. E. (1990). Essay on the diagnosis and nature of paraphilia. *Journal of Sex & Marital Therapy, 16,* 89–102.

Levinson, D. J. (1978). *The seasons of a man's life*. New York: Knopf.

Lewin, T. (1991). 5-year contraceptive implant seems headed for wide use. *The New York Times, November 29,* A1, A26.

Lewis, R. J., & Janda, L. H. (1988). The relationship between adult sexual adjustment and childhood experiences regarding exposure to nudity, sleeping in the parental bed, and parental attitudes toward sexuality. *Archives of Sexual Behavior, 17,* 349–362.

Licht, H. (1993). *Sexual life in ancient Greece*. New York: Dorset.

Linn, M. C., & Hyde, J. S. (1989). Gender, mathematics, and science. *Educational Researcher, 18,* 17–19, 22–27.

Linz, D. (1989). Exposure to sexually explicit materials and attitudes toward rape: A comparison of study results. *Journal of Sex Research, 26,* 50–84.

Linz, D., Donnerstein, E., & Penrod, S. (1987). The findings and recommendations of the Attorney General's Commission on pornography. *American Psychologist, 42,* 946–953.

Linz, D. G., Donnerstein, E., & Penrod, S. (1988). Effects of long-term exposure to violent and sexually degrading depictions of women. *Journal of Personality and Social Psychology, 55,* 758–768.

Livermore, B. (1993). The lessons of love. *Psychology Today, March/April,* 30–34, 36–39, 80.

Lockwood, D. (1980). *Prison sexual violence*. New York: Elsevier.

Love, B. (1992). *Encyclopedia of unusual sex practices*. Fort Lee, NJ: Barricade Books.

Lundgren, J. D., Phillips, A. N., Pedersen, C., Clumeck, N., Gatell, J. M., Johnson, A. M., Ledergerber, B., Vella, S., & Nielsen, J. O. (1994). Comparison of long-tem prognosis of patients with AIDS treated and not treated with zidovudine. *Journal of the American Medical Association, 271,* 1088–1092.

Macallair, D. (1994). Disposition case advocacy in San Francisco's juvenile justice system: A new approach to deinstitutionalization. *Crime & Delinquincy, 40*, 84–95.

MacKinnon, C. (1979). *Sexual harassment of working women*. New Haven: Yale University Press.

Malamuth, N. M. (1981). Rape proclivity among males. *Journal of Social Issues, 37*, 138–157.

Malamuth, N. M., Check, J. V., & Briere, J. (1986). Sexual arousal in response to aggression: Ideological, aggressive, and sexual correlates. *Journal of Personality and Social Psychology, 50*, 330–340.

Maletzky, B. M. (1991). *Treating the sexual offender*. Newbury Park, CA: Sage.

Marcus, E. (1993). *Is it a choice? Answers to 300 of the most frequently asked questions about gays and lesbians*. New York: HarperCollins.

Marshall, D. (1971). Sexual behavior on Mangaia. In D. Marshall & R. Suggs (Eds.), *Human sexual behavior: Variations in the ethnographic spectrum*. New York: Basic Books.

Marshall, D., & Suggs, R. (Eds.). (1971). *Human sexual behavior: Variations in the ethnographic spectrum*. New York: Basic Books.

Martin, A. D., & Hetrick, E. S. (1988). The stigmatization of gay and lesbian youth. *Journal of Homosexuality, 15*, 163–183.

Martin, T. C., & Bumpass, L. L. (1989). Recent trends in marital disruption. *Demography, 26*, 37–51.

Marzollo, J. (1975). *9 months 1 day 1 year: A guide to pregnancy, birth, and babycare*. New York: Harper & Row.

Masters, W. H., & Johnson, V. E. (1966). *Human sexual response*. Boston: Little, Brown.

Masters, W. H., & Johnson, V. E. (1970). *Human sexual inadequacy*. Boston: Little, Brown.

Masters, W. H., & Johnson, V. E. (1979). *Homosexuality in perspective*. Boston: Little, Brown.

Masters, W. H., Johnson, V. E., & Kolodny, R. C. (1992). *Human sexuality* (4th ed.). New York: HarperCollins.

Masters, W. H., Johnson, V. E., & Kolodny, R. C. (1993). *Biological foundations of human sexuality*. New York: HarperCollins.

Masters, W. H., Johnson, V. E., & Kolodny, R. C. (1994). *Heterosexuality*. New York: HarperCollins.

Matek, O. (1988). Obscene phone callers. *Journal of Social Work and Human Sexuality, 7*, 113–130.

Matthews, G. (1987). *"Just a housewife": The rise and fall of domesticity in America*. New York: Oxford University Press.

Mazer, D. B., & Percival, E. F. (1989). Students' experiences of sexual harassment at a small university. *Sex Roles, 20*, 1–22.

McCarthy, B. W. (1989). Cognitive-behavioral strategies and techniques in the early treatment of early ejaculation. In S. R. Leiblum & R. C. Rosen (Eds.), *Principles and practice of sex therapy: Update for the 1990s* (2nd ed.). New York: Guilford.

McCarthy, B. W. (1994). Etiology and treatment of early ejaculation. *Journal of Sex Education and Therapy, 20*, 5–6.

McCarthy, J., & McMillan, S. (1990). Patient/partner satisfaction with penile implant surgery. *Journal of Sex Education and Therapy, 16*, 25–37.

McGrew, M. C., & Shore, W. B. (1991). The problem of teenage pregnancy. *The Journal of Family Pregnancy, 32*, 17–25.

Mead, M. (1963). *Sex and temperament in three primitive societies*. New York: Morrow.

Michael, R. P., Bonsall, R. W., & Warner, P. (1974). Human vaginal secretions: Volatile fatty acid content. *Science, 186*, 1217–1219.

Michael, R. T., Gagnon, J. H., Laumann, E. O., & Kolata, G. (1994). *Sex in America: A definitive survey*. Boston: Little, Brown.

Mix, M. C., Farber, P., & King, K. I. (1992). *Biology: The network of life*. New York: HarperCollins.

Money, J. (1986). *Lovemaps*. Buffalo, NY: Prometheus.

Money, J. (1987). Sin, sickness, or status? Homosexual gender identity and psychoneuroendocrinology. *American Psychologist, 42*, 384–399.

Money, J. (1988). *Gay, straight, and in-between*. New York: Oxford University Press.

Money, J., & Lamacz, M. (1989). *Vandalized lovemaps*. New York: Prometheus.

Moran, J. S., & Zenilman, J. M. (1990). Therapy for gonococcal infections: Options in 1989. *Reviews of Infectious Diseases, 12*, S633–S644.

Moreno, F. J. (1977). *Between faith and reason*. New York: New York University Press.

Morin, J. (1986). *Anal pleasure and health: A guide for men and women*. Burlingame, CA: Yes Press.

Morris, N. M., & Udry, J. R. (1978). Pheromonal influences on human sexual behaviour: An experimental search. *Journal of Biosocial Science, 10,* 147–157.

Moser, C. (1992). Lust, lack of desire, and paraphilias: Some thoughts and possible connections. *Journal of Sex & Marital Therapy, 18,* 65–69.

Moser, C., & Levitt, E. E. (1987). An exploratory-descriptive study of a sadomasochistically oriented sample. *Journal of Sex Research, 23,* 322–337.

Mosher, D. L., & Tomkins, S. S. (1988). Scripting the macho man: Hypermasculine socialization and enculturation. *Journal of Sex Research, 25,* 60–84.

Mosher, D. L., & MacIan, P. (1994). College men and women respond to X-rated videos intended for male or female audiences: Gender and sexual scripts. *Journal of Sex Research, 31* 99–113.

Muehlenhard, C. L., & Cook, S. W. (1988). Men's self-reports of unwanted sexual activity. *Journal of Sex Research, 24,* 58–72.

Muehlenhard, C. L., Sympson, S. C., Phelps, J. L., & Highby, B. J. (1994). Are rape statistics exaggerated? A response to criticism of contemporary rape research. *Journal of Sex Research, 31,* 144–156.

Murstein, B. I. (1974). *Love, sex, & marriage through the ages*. New York: Springer.

Myers, L. S., Dixen, J., Morrissette, D., Carmichael, M., & Davidson, J. M. (1990). Effects of estrogen, androgen, and progestin on sexual psychophysiology and behavior in postmenopausal women. *Journal of Clinical Endocrinology and Metabolism, 70,* 1124–1131.

Nachtigall, R., & Mehren, E. (1991). *Overcoming infertility*. New york: Doubleday.

Nelson, J. B. (1978). *Embodiment: An approach to sexuality and Christian theology*. Minneapolis, MN: Augsburg.

Nieschlag, E., Wickings, E. J., & Breuer, H. (1981). Chemical methods for male fertility control. *Contraception, 23,* 1–10.

O'Donohue, W., & Plaud, J. J. (1994). The conditioning of human sexual arousal. *Archives of Sexual Behavior, 23,* 321–344.

Olivera, A. A. (1994). Sexual dysfunction due to clomipramine and sertraline: Nonpharmacological resolution. *Journal of Sex Education and Therapy, 20,* 119–122.

Opposing Viewpoints Pamphlets. (1993). *Can homosexuals change their sexual orientation?* San Diego, CA: Greenhaven Press.

Opposing Viewpoints Pamphlets. (1993). *Should society encourage increased acceptance of homosexuality?* San Diego, CA: Greenhaven Press.

Opposing Viewpoints Pamphlets. (1993). *Should society legally sanction gay relationships?* San Diego, CA: Greenhaven Press.

Opposing Viewpoints Pamphlets. (1995). *Is pornography harmful?* San Diego, CA: Greenhaven Press.

Padian, N. S., Shiboski, S. C., & Jewell, N. P. (1991). Female-to-male transmission of human immunodeficiency virus. *Journal of the American Medical Association, 266,* 1664–1667.

Paglia, C. (1993). It's a jungle out there, so get used to it. *Utne Reader, January/February,* 61–65.

Palys, T. S. (1986). Testing the common wisdom: The social content of video pornography. *Canadian Psychology, 27,* 22–35.

Parrinder, G. (1980). *Sex in the world's religions*. New York: Oxford.

Parrot, A. (1988). *Coping with date rape and acquaintance rape*. New York: Rosen Publishing Group.

Peplau, L. A., & Cochran, S. D. (1990). A relationship perspective on homosexuality. In D. P. McWhirter, S. A. Sanders, & J. M. Reinisch (Eds.), *Homosexuality/heterosexuality: Concepts of sexual orientation*. New York: Oxford University Press.

Perrotto, R. S., & Culkin, J. (1993). *Exploring abnormal psychology*. New York: HarperCollins.

Petersen, J. R., Kretchmer, A., Nellis, B., Lever, J., & Hertz, R. (1983). The Playboy readers' sex survey, part two. *Playboy, March,* 90–92, 178–182.

Pietropinto, A., & Simenauer, J. (1990). *Not tonight dear: How to reawaken your sexual desire*. New York: Doubleday.

Pittman, F. (1993). Beyond betrayal: Life after infidelity. *Psychology Today, May/June,* 32–38, 78, 80, 82.

Pleak, R. R., & Meyer-Bahlburg, H. F. L. (1990). Sexual behavior and AIDS knowledge of young male prostitutes in Manhattan. *Journal of Sex Research, 27,* 557–587.

Pocs, O., & Godow, A. (1976). Can students view parents as sexual beings? *Family Coordinator, 26,* 31–36.

Pool, R. (1993). Evidence for homosexuality gene. *Science, July 16 (261),* 291–292.

Pope, K. S., & Bouhoutsos, J. C. (1986). *Sexual intimacy between therapists and patients.* New York: Praeger.

Powell, E. (1991). *Talking back to sexual pressure.* Minneapolis, MN: CompCare Publishers.

Prager, D. (1993). Homosexuality, the Bible, and us—a Jewish perspective. *The Public Interest, Summer,* 60–83.

Public Citizens Health Research Group. (1992). Unnecessary cesarean sections: Halting a national epidemic. *Health Letter, June,* 1–6.

Quinsey, V. L. (1977). The assessment and treatment of child molesters: A review. *Canadian Psychological Review, 18,* 204–220.

Radcliffe-Brown, A. R., & Forde, D. (1987). *African systems of kinship and marriage.* London: KPI Limited. (Original work published 1950)

Radakovich, A. (1994). Love rules: The 1994 *Details* survey on romance and the state of our unions. *Details, May,* 108–113.

Ragg, D. M., & Rowe, W. (1991). The effective use of group in sex education with people diagnosed as mildly developmentally disabled. *Sexuality and Disability, 9,* 337–352.

Reinisch, J. M. (1990). *The Kinsey Institute new report on sex: What you must know to be sexually literate.* New York: St. Martin's Press.

Reinisch, J. M., Rosenbaum, L. A., Rubin, D. B., & Schulsinger, M. F. (1991). Sex differences in developmental milestones during the first year of life. *Journal of Psychology & Human Sexuality, 4,* 19–36.

Reisman, J. A., & Eichel, E. W. (1990). *Kinsey, sex and fraud: The indoctrination of a people.* Lafayette, LA: Lochinvar-Huntington House.

Reiss, I. L. (1960). Toward a sociology of the heterosexual love relationship. *Marriage and Family Living, May,* 139–145.

Reiss, I. L. (1993). The future of sex research and the meaning of science. *Journal of Sex Research, 30,* 3–11.

Reuben, D. (1969). *Everything you always wanted to know about sex but were afraid to ask.* New York: Bantam.

Riley, M. W., & Waring, J. (1976). Age and aging. In R. K. Merton & R. Nisbet (Eds.), *Contemporary social problems* (4th ed.). New York: Harcourt Brace Jovanovich.

Rio, L. M. (1991). Psychological and sociological research and the decriminalization or legalization of prostitution. *Archives of Sexual Behavior, 20,* 205–218.

Rischer, C. E., & Easton, T. A. (1992). *Focus on human biology.* New York: HarperCollins.

Robbins, M. B., & Jensen, G. G. (1978). Multiple orgasm in males. *Journal of Sex Research, 13,* 21–26.

Robinson, B. E. (1988). *Teenage fathers.* Lexington, MA: D. C. Heath.

Roscoe, B., & Kruger, T. L. (1990). AIDS: Late adolescents' knowledge and its influence on sexual behavior. *Adolescence, 25,* 39–48.

Rosen, R. (1991). Alcohol and drug effects on sexual response: Human experimental and clinical studies. *Annual Review of Sex Research, 2,* 119–179.

Rosen, R. C., & Beck, J. G. (1988). *Patterns of sexual arousal.* New York: Guilford.

Rousseau, L., Couture, M., Dupont, A., Labrie, F., & Couture, N. (1990). Effect of combined androgen blockade with LHRH agonist and flutamide in one severe case of male exhibitionism. *Canadian Journal of Psychiatry, 35,* 338–341.

Rowan, E. L., Rowan, J. B., & Langelier, P. (1990). Women who molest children. *Bulletin of the American Academy of Psychiatry and the Law, 18,* 79–83.

Rubenstein, C. (1983). The modern art of courtly love. *Psychology Today, July,* 43–49.

Rubenstein, C. (1993). Generation sex: The Details/Mademoiselle report. *Details, June,* 82–89.

Rubin, L. B. (1990). *Erotic wars: What happened to the sexual revolution?* New York: Farrar, Straus, & Giroux.

Ruffin, M. T., & Van Noord, G. R. (1991). Improving the yield of endocervical elements in a Pap smear with the use of the cytology brush. *Family Medicine, 23,* 365–369.

Rynd, N. (1988). Incidence of psychosomatic symptoms in rape victims. *Journal of Sex Research, 24,* 155–161.

Ryrie, C. C. (1978). *The Ryrie Study Bible.* Chicago: Moody Press.

Sagarin, E. (1977). Incest: Problems of definition and frequency. *Journal of Sex Research, 13*, 126–135.

Salmon, D. K. (1991). Coping with miscarriage. *Parents, May*, 106–108, 110.

Sanday, P. R. (1981). The socio-cultural context of rape: A cross-cultural study. *Journal of Social Issues, 37*, 5–27.

Sarason, I. G., & Sarason, B. R. (1993). *Abnormal psychology: The problem of maladaptive behavior* (7th ed.). Englewood Cliffs, NJ: Prentice-Hall.

Sarrel, P. M., & Masters, W. H. (1982). Sexual molestation of men by women. *Archives of Sexual Behavior, 11*, 117–131.

Saunders, E. J. (1989). Life-threatening autoerotic behavior: A challenge for sex educators and therapists. *Journal of Sex Education and Therapy, 15*, 82–91.

Saunders, R. M., & Naus, P. J. (1993). The impact of social content and audience factors on responses to sexually explicit videos. *Journal of Sex Education and Therapy, 19*, 117–130.

Savitz, L., & Rosen, L. (1988). The sexuality of prostitutes: Sexual enjoyment reported by "streetwalkers." *Journal of Sex Research, 24*, 200–208.

Schoen, E. J., Anderson, G., Bohon, C., Hinman, F., Poland, R. L., & Wakeman, E. M. (1989). Report of the Task Force on circumcision. *Pediatrics, 84*, 388–391.

Schover, L. R., & Jensen, S. B. (1988). *Sexuality and chronic illness*. New York: Guilford.

Schultz, T. (1980). Does marriage give today's women what they really want? *Ladies' Home Journal, June*, 89–91, 146–155.

Schwartz, B. (1992). *The one hour orgasm*. Houston, TX: Breakthru Publishing.

Schwartz, P., & Jackson, D. (1989). How to have a model marriage. *New Woman, February*, 66–74.

Scott, G. G. (1992). *Erotic power: An exploration of dominance and submission*. New York: Citadel Press.

Segal, M. (1991). *Norplant: Birth control at arm's reach*. Rockville, MD: Department of Health and Human Services.

Segraves, K. B. (1989). Extramarital affairs. *Medical Aspects of Human Sexuality, 23*, 99–105.

Semans, J. (1956). Premature ejaculation: A new approach. *Southern Medical Journal, 49*, 353–358.

Seng, M. J. (1989). Child sexual abuse and adolescent prostitution: A comparative analysis. *Adolescence, 24*, 665–675.

Severn, J., Belch, G. E., & Belch, M. A. (1990). The effects of sexual and nonsexual advertising appeals and information level on cognitive processing and communication effectiveness. *Journal of Advertising, 19*, 14–22.

Shapiro, E. D. (1986). New innovations in conception and their effects upon our law and morality. *New York Law Review, 31*, 37–59.

Shapiro, H. I. (1993). *The pregnancy book for today's woman* (2nd ed.). New York: HarperPerennial.

Shaw, J. (1994). Aging and sexual potential. *Journal of Sex Education and Therapy, 20*, 134–139.

Shostak, A. B., McLouth, G., & Seng, L. (1984). *Men and abortion: Losses, lessons, and love*. New York: Praeger.

Sidorowicz, L. S., & Lunney, G. S. (1980). Baby X revisited. *Sex Roles, 6*, 67–73.

Signorielli, N. (1990). Children, television, and gender roles: Messages and impact. *Journal of Adolescent Health Care, 11*, 50–58.

Silbert, M. H. (1989). The effects on juveniles of being used for pornography and prostitution. In D. Zillmann & J. Bryant (Eds.), *Pornography: Research advances and policy considerations*. Hillsdale, NJ: Erlbaum.

Silverstone, B., & Hyman, H. K. (1992). *Growing old together: A couple's guide to understanding and coping with the challenges of later life*. New York: Pantheon.

Simmons, R. L., & Whitbeck, L. B. (1991). Sexual abuse as a precursor to prostitution and victimization among adolescents and adult homeless women. *Journal of Family Issues, 12*, 361–379.

Simon, W. (1994). Deviance as history: The future of perversion. *Archives of Sexual Behavior, 23*, 1–20.

Simon, W., & Gagnon, J. H. (1986). Sexual scripts: Permanence and change. *Archives of Sexual Behavior, 15*, 97–120.

Small, M. F. (1993). The gay debate: Is homosexuality a matter of choice or chance? *American Health, March*, 70–76.

Smeaton, G., Byrne, D., & Murnen, S. K. (1989). The repulsion hypothesis revisited: Similarity irrelevance or dissimilarity bias? *Journal of Personality and Social Psychology, 56*, 54–59.

Smith, D. C., & Sparks, W. (1986). *The naked child growing up without shame—Social nudity: Its effect on children*. Los Angeles: ELYSIUM Growth Press.

Smith, R. (1990). *The encyclopedia of sexual trivia: A collection of anecdotes, facts, and trivia about the world's oldest diversion*. New York: St. Martin's Press.

Smolowe, J. (1993). New, improved and ready for battle. *Time*, June 14, 48–51.

Snider, S. (1990). *The Pill: 30 years of safety concerns*. Rockville, MD: Department of Health and Human Services.

Snyder, H. M. (1991). To circumcise or not. *Hospital Practice*, January 15, 201–207.

Somers, L., & Somers, B. C. (1989). *Talking to your children about love and sex*. New York: New American Library.

Sorensen, R. C. (1973). *Adolescent sexuality in contemporary America*. New York: Times Mirror/World Publishing.

Spanier, G. B., & Furstenberg, F. F. (1982). Remarriage after divorce: A longitudinal analysis of well-being. *Journal of Marriage and the Family*, August, 709–720.

Spanier, G. B., & Thompson, L. (1984). *Parting: The aftermath of separation and divorce*. Beverly Hills, CA: Sage.

Spector, I. P., & Carey, M. P. (1990). Incidence and prevalence of the sexual dysfunctions: A critical review of the empirical literature. *Archives of Sexual Behavior*, 19, 389–408.

Sproul, R. C. (1990). *Abortion: A rational look at an emotional issue*. Colorado Springs, CO: Navpress.

Statistical Abstracts of the United States (112th ed.). (1992). Washington, DC: Reference Press.

Stavis, P. F. (1991). Harmonizing the right to sexual expression and the right to protection from harm for persons with mental disability. *Sexuality and Disability*, 9, 131–141.

Stehlin, D. (1990). *Feeding baby: Nature and nurture*. Rockville, MD: Department of Health and Human Services.

Stermac, L., Hall, K., & Henskens, M. (1989). Violence among child molesters. *Journal of Sex Research*, 26, 450–459.

Sternberg, R. J. (1986). A triangular theory of love. *Psychological Review*, 93, 119–135.

Sternberg, R. J. (1988). Triangulating love. In R. J. Sternberg & M. L. Barnes (Eds.), *The psychology of love*. New Haven: Yale University Press.

Stewart, F., Guest, F., Stewart, G., & Hatcher, R. (1987). *Understanding your body*. New York: Bantam.

Stewart, J. (1990). *The complete manual of sexual positions*. Chatsworth, CA: Media Press.

Stoller, R. J. (1982). Transvestism in women. *Archives of Sexual Behavior*, 11, 99–115.

Storms, M. D. (1981). A theory of erotic orientation development. *Psychological Review*, 88, 340–353.

Strong, M. (1988). *Mainstay*. Boston: Little, Brown.

Struckman-Johnson, C., & Struckman-Johnson, D. (1994). Men pressured and forced into sexual experience. *Archives of Sexual Behavior*, 23, 93–114.

Stubbs, K. R., & Saulnier, L. A. (1989). *Erotic massage: The touch of love*. Larkspur, CA: Secret Garden.

Sturgis, E. T., & Adams, H. E. (1978). The right to treatment: Issues in the treatment of homosexuality. *Journal of Consulting and Clinical Psychology*, 46, 165–169.

Suggs, D. N., & Miracle, A. W. (1993). *Culture and human sexuality*. Pacific Grove, CA: Brooks/Cole.

Szasz, T. (1990). *Sex by prescription: The startling truth about today's sex therapy*. New York: Syracuse University Press.

Taffel, S. M., Placek, P. J., & Kosary, C. L. (1992). U.S. cesarean section rates 1990: An update. *Birth*, 19, 21–22.

Tannahill, R. (1980). *Sex in history*. New York: Scarborough House/Stein and Day.

Tannen, D. (1990). *You just don't understand: Women and men in conversation*. New York: Ballantine Books.

Tavris, C., & Sadd, S. (1977). *The Redbook report on female sexuality*. New York: Delacorte Press.

Teti, D. M., & Lamb, M. E. (1989). Socioeconomic and marital outcomes of adolescent marriage, adolescent childbirth, and their co-occurence. *Journal of Marriage and the Family*, 51, 203–212.

Thompson, I. M. (1989). Carcinoma of the prostate: Changing incidence associated with annual urologic screening *Southern Medical Journal*, 82, 335–337.

Tiefer, L. (1994). Three crises facing sexology. *Archives of Sexual Behavior*, 23, 361–374.

Tollison, C. D., & Adams, H. E. (1979). *Sexual disorders: Treatment, theory, and research*. New York: Gardner Press.

Toomey, K. E., & Barnes, R. C. (1990). Treatment of chlamydia trachomatis genital infection. *Reviews of Infectious Diseases, 12*, S645–S655.

Tortora, G. J. (1992). *Principles of human anatomy* (6th ed.). New York: HarperCollins.

Tortora, G. J., & Grabowski, S. R. (1993). *Principles of anatomy and physiology* (7th ed.). New York: HarperCollins.

Toussie-Weingarten, C., & Jacobwitz, J. (1987). Alternatives in childbearing: Choices and challenges. In L. Sherwen (Ed.), *Psychosocial dimensions of the pregnant family*. New York: Springer.

Trachtenberg, P. (1988). *The Casanova complex*. New York: Poseidon Press.

Tribe, L. (1990). *Abortion: The clash of absolutes*. New York: Norton.

Trovato, F. (1986). The relationship between marital dissolution and suicide: The Canadian case. *Journal of Marriage and the Family, 48*, 341–348.

Trussell, J. (1988). Teenage pregnancy in the United States. *Family Planning Perspectives, 20*, 262–272.

Turner, B. F., & Adams, C. G. (1988). Reported change in preferred sexual activity over the adult years. *Journal of Sex Research, 25*, 289–303.

Turner, C. F., Miller, H. G., & Moses, L. E. (Eds.). (1989). *AIDS: Sexual behavior and intravenous drug use*. Washington, DC: National Academy Press.

Turner, W. J. (1994). Comments on discordant monozygotic twinning in homosexuality. *Archives of Sexual Behavior, 23*, 115–119.

Udry, J. R. (1993). The politics of sex research. *Journal of Sex Research, 30*, 103–110.

Umberson, D. (1989). Marital benefits for men vs. women. *Medical Aspects of Human Sexuality*, May, 56.

U.S. Attorney General's Commission on Pornography (1986). *Final report of the Attorney General's Commission on Pornography*. Washington, DC: U.S. Justice Department.

Van de Ven, P. (1994). Comparisons among homophobic reactions of undergraduates, high school students, and young offenders. *Journal of Sex Research, 31*, 117–124.

Vance, E. B., & Wagner, N. N. (1976). Written descriptions of orgasm: A study of sex differences. *Archives of Sexual Behavior, 5*, 87–98.

Vanwesenbeeck, I., de Graf, R., van Zessen, G., Straver, C. J., & Visser, J. H. (1993). Protection styles of prostitutes' clients: Intentions, behavior, and considerations in relation to AIDS. *Journal of Sex Education and Therapy, 19*, 79–92.

Vella, S., et al. (1992). Survival of zidovudine-treated patients with AIDS compared with that of contemporary untreated patients. *Journal of the American Medical Association, 267*, 1232–1236.

Voeller, B. (1991). AIDS and heterosexual anal intercourse. *Archives of Sexual Behavior, 20*, 233–276.

Wade, C., & Tavris, C. (1993). *Psychology* (3rd ed.). New York: HarperCollins.

Walen, S. R. (1985). Rational sexuality: Some new perspectives. In A. Ellis & M. E. Bernard (Eds.), *Clinical applications of rational-emotive therapy*. New York: Plenum.

Walen, S. R., & Roth, D. (1987). A cognitive approach. In J. H. Greer & W. T. O'Donohue (Eds.), *Theories of human sexuality*. New York: Plenum.

Wallerstein, J. S., & Kelly, J. B. (1980). *Surviving the breakup*. New York: Basic Books.

Walsh, F. M., Stahl, C. J., Unger, H. T., Lilienstern, O. C., & Stephens, R. G. (1977). Autoerotic asphyxial deaths: A medicolegal analysis of forty-three cases. In C. H. Wecht (Ed.), *Legal medicine annual: 1977*. New York: Appleton-Century-Crofts.

Walsh, J. (1993). The new sexual revolution: Liberation at last? Or the same old mess? *Utne Reader*, July/August, 59–65.

Warren, R., & Zgourides, G. D. (1991). *Anxiety disorders: A rational-emotive perspective*. Needham Heights, MA: Pergamon Press/Allyn & Bacon.

Washington State Department of Social and Health Services. (1986). *An ounce of prevention: AIDS risk reduction guidelines for healthier sex*. Olympia, WA: Author.

Weitzman, S., Kuter, I., & Pizer, H. F. (1986). *Confronting breast cancer*. New York: Vintage Books.

Welch, B. (1990). *Press statement on reparative therapy*. Washington, DC: American Psychological Association.

Westheimer, R. (1992). *Dr. Ruth's guide to safer sex: Exciting, sensible, sexual directions for the 90s*. New York: Warner Books.

Westheimer, R., & Lieberman, L. (1988). *Sex and morality: Who is teaching our sex standards?* Boston: Harcourt Brace Jovanovich.

White, S. D., & DeBlassie, R. R. (1992). Adolescent sexual behavior. *Adolescence, 27,* 183–191.

Whitley, B. E. (1987). The relationship of sex-role orientation to heterosexuals' attitudes toward homosexuals. *Sex Roles, 17,* 103–113.

Whitley, B. E. (1989). Correlates of oral-genital experience among college students. *Journal of Psychology & Human Sexuality, 2,* 151–163.

Wilkes, M. S., & Blum, S. (1990). Current trends in routine newborn male circumcision in New York State. *New York State Journal of Medicine, 90,* 243–246.

Willis, J. L. (1993). Preventing STDs. *FDA Consumer,* June, 33–35.

Willmuth, M. E. (1987). Sexuality after spinal cord injury: A critical review. *Clinical Psychology Review, 7,* 389–412.

Wincze, J. P., & Carey, M. P. (1992). *Sexual dysfunctions: A guide for assessment and treatment.* New York: Guilford.

Winick, C. (1985). A content analysis of sexually explicit magazines sold in an adult bookstore. *Journal of Sex Research, 21,* 206–210.

Winick, C., & Evans, J. T. (1994). Is there a national standard with respect to attitudes toward sexually explicit media material? *Archives of Sexual Behavior, 23,* 405–419.

Wise, T. (1985). Fetishism—etiology and treatment: A review from multiple perspectives. *Comprehensive Psychiatry, 26,* 249–257.

Wolf, J. G. (1989). *Gay priests.* New York: Harper & Row.

Wolf, S. (1994). *Guerrilla dating tactics: Strategies, tips, and secrets for finding romance.* New York: Plume.

Wolfe, L. (1981). *The Cosmo report.* New York: Arbor House.

Wolff, C. (1971). *Love between women.* New York: Harper & Row.

Worth, C. (1988). *Birth of a father: New fathers talk about pregnancy, childbirth and the first three months.* New York: McGraw-Hill.

Zaslow, M. J., Pedersen, F. A., Cain, R. L., & Suwalsky, J. T. D. (1985). Depressed mood in new fathers: Associations with parent-infant interaction. *Genetic,*

Social, and General Psychology Monographs, 111, 133–150.

Zaviacic, M., Dolezalova, S., Holoman, I. K., Zaviacicova, A., Mikulecky, M., & Brazdil, V. (1988). Concentrations of fructose in female ejaculate and urine: A comparative biochemical study. *Journal of Sex Research, 24,* 319–325.

Zaviacic, M., & Whipple, B. (1993). Update on the female prostate and the phenomenon of female ejaculation. *Journal of Sex Research, 30,* 148–151.

Zeiss, A. M. (1982). Expectations for the effects of aging on sexuality in parents and average married couples. *Journal of Sex Research, 18,* 47–57.

Zelnik, M., & Kantner, J. F. (1980). Sexual activity, contraceptive use, and pregnancy among metropolitan-area teenagers: 1971–1979. *Family Planning Perspectives, 12,* 230–237.

Zgourides, G. (1993). *Don't let them psych you out!* Port Townsend, WA: Loompanics Unlimited.

Zgourides, G., Monto, M., & Harris, R. (1994). Prevalence of prior adult sexual contact in a sample of adolescent male sex offenders. *Psychological Reports, 75,* 1042.

Zgourides, G. D., & Warren, R. (1989). Retarded ejaculation: Overview and treatment implications. *Journal of Psychology & Human Sexuality, 2,* 139–150.

Zilbergeld, B. (1978). *Male sexuality: A guide to sexual fulfillment.* New York: Bantam Books.

Zilbergeld, B. (1992). *The new male sexuality: The truth about men, sex, and pleasure.* New York: Bantam Books.

Zilbergeld, B., & Ellison, C. (1980). Desire discrepancies and arousal problems in sex therapy. In S. R. Leiblum & L. A. Pervin (Eds.), *Principles and practices of sex therapy.* New York: Guilford.

Zilbergeld, B., & Evans, M. (1980). The inadequacy of Masters and Johnson. *Psychology Today,* August, 29–43.

Zuger, B. (1988). Is early effeminate behavior in boys early homosexuality? *Comparative Psychiatry, 29,* 509–519.

Zuger, B. (1989). Homosexuality in families of boys with early effeminate behavior: An epidemiological study. *Archives of Sexual Behavior, 18,* 155–166.

CREDITS

AUTHOR INDEX

SUBJECT INDEX